RADCLYFFE HALL

RADCLYFFE HALL
A WOMAN CALLED JOHN

SALLY CLINE

THE OVERLOOK PRESS
WOODSTOCK & NEW YORK

First published in the United States in 1998 by
The Overlook Press, Peter Mayer Publishers, Inc.
Lewis Hollow Road
Woodstock, New York 12498

Library of Congress Cataloging-in-Publications Data

Cline, Sally.
Radclyffe Hall : a woman called John / Sally Cline.
p. cm.
Includes bibliographical references and index.
1. Hall, Radclyffe—Biography. 2. Women authors, English—20th century—
Biography. 3. Lesbians—Great Britain—Biography. I. Title.
PR6015.A33Z62 1998 823'.912—dc21 [B] 97-24200

Originally published in Great Britain by
John Murray (Publishers) Ltd

Manufactured in the United States of America
ISBN 0-87951-831-6
First Edition
1 3 5 7 9 8 6 4 2

This book is dedicated to
EM MARION CALLEN *and*
MARMOSET ADLER

This book is also for
BA SHEPPARD *and* VIC SMITH
with love

CONTENTS

Illustrations   ix
Acknowledgements   xi

Introduction   1

PART 1: WHAT'S IN A NAME? 1880–1906
 1. Early Naming   11
 2. In the Name of the Fathers   23
 3. Renaming Love   37

PART 2: POETRY AND PASSION 1907–1916
 4. The Sweetest Violet   51
 5. The April Grandmother   59
 6. Sapphists, Suffrage and Catholic Conversion   73
 7. First Fictions, First Infidelities   91
 8. From a Lapse to a Life: Una Troubridge   107

PART 3: SPIRITUALIST TO SPIRITUAL NOVELIST
1916–1927
 9. The Penitential Period   129
10. Striking Out   148
11. Finding Her Voice   158
12. The Twenties   169
13. Forging Ahead   186
14. Critical Acclaim   204

PART 4: CRUSADE AND MARTYRDOM 1928–1933
15. Boldness   225
16. *The Well*   245

17. The Trolley Years   268
18. The Rye Relationship   286

PART 5: THE BOOK OF LETTERS 1934–1943
19. Souline   311
20. Same Heart and Severe Differences   329
21. Sickness, Death and Beyond   348
22. After Words   371

    Notes   379
    Bibliography   408
    Index   416

ILLUSTRATIONS

(*between pages 210 and 211*)

1. Family group: great-grandmother Jane Jones, Marguerite Radclyffe-Hall, grandmother Sarah Diehl and mother Marie Diehl Radclyffe-Hall
2. Marguerite and her cousins: Marie Diehl Visetti, Marguerite Radclyffe-Hall, Jane Randolph, her sons Thomas and Decan, Aunt Emma Jones Reade and Aunt Lode Diehl
3. Marie Diehl Visetti
4. Marguerite with curls: portrait of Marguerite Radclyffe-Hall by Katinka Amyat
5. Radclyffe Hall as a young woman
6. Mabel Batten and her grandchildren Peter and Honey, Christmas 1900
7. Mabel Batten and Radclyffe Hill, *c*. 1910–14
8. May Sinclair, 1910
9. Violet Hunt, *c*. 1907–16
10. Clemence Dane, 1923
11. Toupie Lowther and her all-women ambulance unit, *c*. 1917–19
12. Gladys Leonard
13. Una Troubridge, 1915
14. Ernest, Una and Cubby Troubridge, 1914
15. Una, John and dachshunds
16. Romaine Brooks, *c*. 1925
17. Colette Willy, *Fantasio*, 15 April 1909
18. Djuna Barnes and Natalie Barney, *c*. 1928–30, Nice, France
19. Havelock Ellis, 1931, by Sir William Rothenstein
20. Audrey Heath
21. Edy Craig, Christopher St John, Clare 'Tony' Atwood and Vera 'Jack' Holme, *c*. 1921

22. Naomi 'Mickie' Jacob, from a greetings card made by Naomi Jacob and
    sent to Audrie Atcheson
23. Vita Sackville-West, 1928
24. Vera Brittain, 1936
25. Compton Mackenzie with Yeats and friends, 1924
26. Virginia Woolf and Ethel Smyth
27. Radclyffe Hall, 1936
28. Evguenia Souline
29. Radclyffe Hall and her poodle Fido
30. Radclyffe Hall's inscription on the back of a snapshot of Fido

The author and publishers would like to thank the following for their kind
permission to reproduce illustrations: 1 (photograph by Gilbert & Bacon,
Philadelphia), 2, 3 (photograph by Ray Vaughn, London), 27, 29 and 30,
Photography Collection, Harry Ransom Humanities Research Center,
University of Texas at Austin; 4 (photograph by Sally Cline), 13 (photograph
by Lafayette) and 15, Dr A. Rossi-Lemini; 5, A.M. Heath & Co.; 6 and 7,
Cara Lancaster; 8, Mary Evans Library/Fawcett Library; 10 (photograph by
Graphic) and 17, Mary Evans Picture Library; 11, The Trustees of the
Imperial War Museum, London; 12, University Library, University of
Bristol; 14 (photograph by A.C. Cooper, London), Sir Thomas and Lady
Troubridge; 16 (photograph by Maître Léon-Marie Emmanuel), © 1997
Meryle Secrest; 18, Papers of Djuna Barnes, Special Collections, University
of Maryland at College Park Libraries; 19 and 24 (photograph by Howard
Coster), National Portrait Gallery; 21 (photograph by Alice Carr), The
National Trust, Ellen Terry Memorial Museum, Smallhythe Place; 22,
Audrie Atcheson; 23, Nigel Nicolson; 26, Estate of the late Professor
Quentin Bell; 28, Monica Still and Joan Slater. The drawing of 'St Stephen'
by Beresford Egan lampooning *The Well of Loneliness* on p. 279 is reproduced
courtesy of Maxine Hunt and Oriol Bath.

ACKNOWLEDGEMENTS

My principal acknowledgement must be to Rosemary Smith, my exceptionally talented research assistant, who transcribed hundreds of tapes, devised research systems, organized photographs, compiled the bibliography, co-indexed, edited and proofread drafts, and helped cut and structure the final version. Her scholarly attention to detail was balanced by an imaginative resourcefulness (and a limitless kindness) without which I might not have reached the final page.

I am grateful to the British Academy for awarding me a small personal research grant in 1995 which enabled me to carry out archive research in Italy, Canada and the United States.

I owe a particular debt of gratitude to the Harry Ransom Humanities Research Center at the University of Texas for awarding me an Andrew W. Mellon Foundation Fellowship (1995–6) to work on Radclyffe Hall's writings, and special thanks for his kind interest to the Director, Dr Thomas F. Staley, and to Dr Elizabeth Dunn for her help and support both during my stay and thereafter. I am further indebted to the research librarian, Cathy Henderson, to Barbara LaBorde, Diane Goldenberg-Hart, Pat Fox, Ken Craven and Jake Baxter for their valuable assistance with and knowledge of manuscripts, and to Ann Paterra for her endless patience in the matter of photographs. In Texas I must thank Martha Campbell too for her wonderful hospitality and generosity.

I am grateful to Radclyffe Hall's literary executor Jonathan Lovat Dickson in Toronto for his unstinting support and for facilitating my research at the National Archives of Canada where Anne Goddard (manuscript division) and Janet Murray (reading room) aided and encouraged my work. I thank Kathy Mullen and Robert Hess for accommodation in Montreal; Cheryl Lean and Graham Metson in Ottawa for accommodation, cordon bleu meals and advice on Hall's court cases; Peggy Harris at the Ottawa Women's Bookstore.

In Rome Dr Alessandro Rossi-Lemeni Makedon showed me kindness and gave me full access to Una Troubridge's Day Books and Hall's unpublished writings. I thank Rosy Howden for providing Italian translations, as well as encouragement in many forms.

Cara Lancaster put all Mabel Batten's diaries and letters at my disposal and put up with me for a week; her aid and friendship throughout this research has been invaluable.

Monica Still and Joan Slater, who had spent two decades researching Radclyffe Hall, gave me access to unpublished photographs and writings of Evguenia Souline and the inestimable benefit of their knowledge of Hall's life. Joan Slater generously showed me parts of her own unpublished biography; Monica Still showed me great hospitality. My good fortune in acquiring further information on Souline and more of her unpublished writings was brought about by Ariadne Nicolaeff and Iris Furlong.

I thank Sir Thomas and Lady Troubridge for discussions about and photographs of Una, Ernest and Andrea Troubridge. I thank Hall's former secretary Winifred Reed for an enlightening and enjoyable visit, and Audrie Atcheson for providing written materials on Naomi Jacob. Hall's previous biographer Michael Baker offered me contacts, advice and literary support, as did Michael Thomas of A.M. Heath.

I am indebted to the following individuals for advice, writing space, inspiration, financial understanding, and encouragement of many kinds: Jean Adams, Dr Sue Benson, Inge Blackman, Kathy Bowles, Bunny Catterall, Anne Christie, Dr Georgette Donchin, Dr Jeanne Druce, Kay Dunbar, Olga Foottit, Professor Anthony Giddens, Alison Hennegan, Patricia Hubbard, Jane Jaffey, Joel Jaffey, Lilian Kahale, Sam Kahale, Josie McConnell, Linnie Price, Nick Price, Cynthia Reavell, Fiona Rose, Anthony Rota, Michael Rubinstein, Vera Segal, Aliye Seif, Dr Chris Singer, Professor Robert Smith, Dale Spender (inspired suggestions for Part 5), Professor Michelle Stanworth, Christine Toothill, Peter Toothill, Maggie Ward, Ralph Ward, and Esther Whitby. Literary guidance came from the Cambridge Women Writers (Em Marion Callen, Chris Carling, Joy Magezis, Geraldine Ryan) and Wendy Mulford. Crucial personal help in the last months came from Carol Jones, and throughout the project Angie North fortified me at home and cared for my house and cat during research trips abroad.

Librarians, curators and archivists who have given me help include: David Doughan (Fawcett Library), Deborah Edel (Lesbian Herstory Archives), Ms G. Revell (Cambridge University Library), Stephanie Macek (Social and Political Sciences Library, Cambridge University), Mrs M.W. Poynton (Society for Psychical Research), Ellen M. Shea (Radcliffe College, Cambridge, Mass.), Jeff Walden and Neil Somerville (BBC Written Archives), and most particularly Chris Avery and her team at Arbury Court Library, Cambridge.

Assistance with illustrations came from Beth Alvarez (University of Maryland), Audrie Atcheson, the late Professor Quentin Bell, Meryle Secrest Beveridge, John Delaney and Paul Kemp (Imperial War Museum), Maxine Hunt and Oriol Bath, Professor François Lafitte, Andro Linklater, David McLoughlin (National Library of Ireland), Tim Moreton and Paul Cox (National Portrait Gallery), Christina Morgan (Mary Evans Picture Library), Ann Paterra (University of Texas), Omar S. Pound, Roderick Taylor (National Museum of Photography, Film and Television, Bradford), Monika Tews (Bristol University Library), Michael Thomas, Margaret Weare (National Trust Ellen Terry Memorial Museum), Joanna Weinberg.

My literary agent Barbara Levy's rigorous analysis of every chapter and her escalating enthusiasm could not be bettered. Her assistant Emma Lynch bolstered my spirits with her cheery staunchness.

At my publishers John Murray, who are remarkable for caring about authors as well as books, Grant McIntyre has been supportive throughout; Howard Davies a meticulous and patient copy-editor. As for my editor-friend Caroline Knox, it is hard to find fresh adjectives to describe her consideration, courtesy, patience, perception and buoyant reassurance. She shared my vision and was on my side throughout every crisis.

My family and extended family have again been a source of strength. For their many and varied contributions I thank Elsie Sheppard, Manda Callen, Aaron Callen, Helen Bamford, Jane Shackman (especially for her attentive draft readings), Joan Harris (for readerly understanding) and Jonathan Harris (for literary and gastronomic sustenance). I am grateful for Beth Callen's professional tape transcriptions and draft bibliography and was challenged by her stern views of Hall's character. Vic Smith's unfailing optimism and Aunt Het (Harriet) Shackman's photocopies, cuttings and daily encouragement kept me afloat. I thank Ba Sheppard for providing the seventeenth, eighteenth and nineteenth years of faith in the writer and a healthy and useful scepticism for the project. The biography is dedicated to Marmoset Adler and Em Marion Callen whose importance in my life is matched by their commitment to my writing. I thank my daughter Marmoset Adler especially for her diplomatic media and editorial advice at the book's most critical stage. Em Callen has read and commented on key drafts, her editorial flair has helped shape chapters, she has suffered every year of Hall's life and sustained my own. Deepest thanks to the writer's closest conspirator.

The author and publisher would like to thank the following for permission to reproduce quotations: the Estate of the late Radclyffe Hall and the copyright holder, Jonathan Lovat Dickson, for Radclyffe Hall's published and unpublished fiction, poetry and other writings; Dr Alessandro Rossi-Lemeni for Una Troubridge's diaries and letters; 'Little Gidding' from *Four Quartets*, © 1943 by T.S. Eliot and renewed 1971 by Valerie Eliot, reprinted by permission of Harcourt Brace and Company and Faber and Faber Limited; excerpt from *A Room of One's Own* by Virginia Woolf, © 1929 by Harcourt Brace and Company and renewed 1957 by Leonard Woolf, reprinted by permission of the publisher, and by permission of the Society of Authors as the literary representative of the Estate of Virginia Woolf; the Estate of the late Violet Hunt and André Deutsch Limited for Violet Hunt's diaries; the Society for Psychical Research for extracts from the Archives of the Society; Lillian Faderman, *Odd Girls and Twilight Lovers: A History of Lesbian Life in Twentieth-century America*, © Lillian Faderman 1991, first published Columbia University Press 1991, Penguin 1992, reprinted with permission of Columbia University Press and Penguin Books Ltd.

Every effort has been made to contact copyright-holders, but if any have inadvertently been overlooked the author would be glad to hear from them.

INTRODUCTION

Radclyffe Hall was a legend in her own time and in the years up to and including ours. She was also a lesbian: a fact which became part of that legend. As a writer and a woman, Radclyffe Hall lived on the margins but then entered the mainstream, only to find that after several years of critical success the mainstream rejected her.

In 1928, when she was forty-eight, Radclyffe Hall created a sensation with her fifth novel, *The Well of Loneliness*. After a notorious and dramatic trial – perhaps the most famous in the history of British censorship law – attended by Virginia and Leonard Woolf, E.M. Forster, Vita Sackville-West, Rose Macaulay and many other eminent writers prepared to speak in its defence, the British courts banned the book for obscenity. It was taken to trial in America where the New York police arrested the publisher and seized over 800 copies of the book, again on charges of obscenity. The impressive list of writers who came to the book's defence in America included Theodore Dreiser, Upton Sinclair, Scott Fitzgerald, Sherwood Anderson, Ernest Hemingway and Edna Ferber. Although the Manhattan Magistrates also judged the book obscene, the Appeal Court later overturned the verdict in Hall's favour.

Ironically the court cases turned the book into a best-seller both at the time and thereafter and turned Radclyffe Hall and her writings into a critical part of literary history and censorship politics.

In her early career she was certainly not a polemical writer who set out to wave a banner or preach a gospel. She made her début as a lyric poet with five volumes of pastoral poetry – many of the poems set to music by well-known composers. 'The Blind Ploughman' became a national favourite and was sung before an audience of thousands in the Usher Hall. Though her poems were less interesting in form and content than her novels, they share many of the same preoccupations – a sense of kinship with nature, concern with love, longing for permanence, fear of loss, and the need to find personal and spiritual meaning within a mysterious universe.

Her career as a poet was followed by several intensive years as a serious researcher into psychical and spiritualist phenomena. As a novelist she was, at forty-four, a late starter. Surprisingly she achieved public recognition first as a comic novelist. However, within two years her most serious novel, *Adam's Breed*, was received with acclaim. An instant sales success, it was translated into several languages, then won both the Prix Femina Vie Heureuse and the James Tait Black Prize in a single year – an honour shared only with E.M. Forster.

This acclaim encouraged her to take the daring step of writing a novel about the hitherto taboo subject of lesbianism. A major writer who is prepared to become a martyr to her cause, to invite the opprobrium of a sensational court case, to suffer the literary consequences of having her suddenly 'infamous' book overshadow her other critically more interesting novels and short stories, is an artist worth investigating. The fact that Radclyffe Hall's writings have affected sexual politics and influenced lesbian literary images for more than fifty years invites a biographer to explore those images.

However in this literary biography I have tried to concern myself as much with the rest of her books and the rest of her life as with that particular aspect which brought her prominently to public attention.

As a woman Radclyffe Hall was complex, conscientious and highly contradictory. Shy, awkward and introverted she nevertheless became a bold spokeswoman for a challenging cause. She flamboyantly cross-dressed, sported the male name of John, yet expected to be ignored. She was a rebel and a misfit yet also politically conservative, staunchly religious, with a substantial private income. She was a devout convert to Catholicism yet at the same time a lifelong spiritualist. She did not like conflict but she was high-handed and litigious, entering three law suits in two countries in a comparatively short life.

Dedicated to sexual fidelity she nevertheless had blazing love affairs outside of and affecting two of her serious sexual partnerships. Though her most famous lesbian character, Stephen Gordon, is presented as a freak and a misfit, Hall's own life as a lesbian was that of a passionate, sexually fulfilled independent woman. Though she promoted the view of the born-lesbian in *The Well of Loneliness* Hall was also familiar with the proposition that homosexuality can be environmentally induced or self-chosen, an alternative viewpoint offered in the same book as well as in *The Unlit Lamp* and her other novels. These ideas, more in tune with our notions today, sprang from her friendship with the American writer Natalie Barney, who profoundly influenced Radclyffe Hall, and from Hall's involvement with Natalie Barney's Modernist circle in Paris who included Djuna Barnes, Romaine Brooks, Janet Flanner and Colette.

Though Hall had many male friends and worked well with male publishers, it was women who were central to each phase of her life and work. From her childhood until she was twenty-seven the main protagonist – and most controversial figure – was her mother, Marie Diehl Visetti. During this period Hall had several same-sex affairs and produced her first book of poetry and first short fiction.

Between the ages of twenty-seven and thirty-six the pivotal personage was her partner Mabel 'Ladye' Batten, a popular amateur lieder singer and noted beauty. During this period Hall produced some fine short stories, four more volumes of poetry and absolute havoc in her personal life. Affairs and quarrels ended in the violent and shocking death of Ladye.

Between the ages of thirty-six and forty-eight the central figure was Hall's new lover, the artist Una Troubridge, a young married woman with a small daughter. After an initial guilt-ridden period of psychical research, Hall soon embarked on her serious career as a writer of fiction. She produced four highly successful novels: *The Forge*, *The Unlit Lamp*, *A Saturday Life* and *Adam's Breed*.

Between the ages of forty-eight and fifty-four it was Radclyffe Hall herself who played the cardinal role. It was the era of Hall the crusader, Hall the martyr. She wrote *The Well of Loneliness*, fought two trials in defence of its reputation and her own, and faced financial success but a bitter aftermath. As her relationship with Una waned, and her subsequent novels were belittled, she became isolated and reclusive.

Between the ages of fifty-four and sixty-three a young Russian woman, Evguenia Souline, became integral to her life and work. This was the period of her last most intense love affair. Out of ecstasy and torment she produced one volume of short stories: *Miss Ogilvy Finds Herself*, one novel, *The Sixth Beatitude*, and an extraordinary Book of Letters.

As her biographer I have looked at this period as one in which she found a new voice, significantly through the more than 600 letters she wrote daily or twice daily for nine years to Evguenia Souline. The phase marks her squabbles with yet support from Una, the gradual disintegration of her relationship with Souline, her long illness, her near blindness, and her gruelling death.

Two related areas of Radclyffe Hall's life are of special interest but have been under-documented. One is her involvement in women's politics; the other her strong friendships with women, many of whom were writers, several of whom were suffragettes. Radclyffe Hall, consistently described as a loner, has been depicted as a woman whose sole emotional sustenance came from her sexual partnerships: I have not found this to be the case. She had strong supportive and continuous friendships with women, several of whom, including Violet Hunt, Ida Wylie, May Sinclair and Ethel Smyth, encouraged her early recognition of feminist ideals, though they cannot be held responsible for her later ambivalence. Her foray into feminism is an interesting example of the contradictory patterns in her life.

The main problem encountered by any biographer of Radclyffe Hall is the small amount of personal material written by the novelist herself. She kept no diaries or journals and wrote surprisingly few letters until the final period of her life. During their twenty-eight years together her second partner Una Troubridge kept a daily diary and later also a day book. After Hall's death Una also wrote a hagiographic biography in which she tried to describe what she believed were Hall's feelings as well as her own. Where Una Troubridge is useful is on the minute transactions of each novel's progress; publishers' reports, manipulations, critical reviews, sales; books Hall read, jewels she bought, functions she attended. Where her documentation is less helpful is in the way it can blind the reader to an alternative view of Radclyffe Hall. 'John' became the principal character in a novel created for others' benefit by Una Troubridge, the person with inside knowledge. In previous biographies Radclyffe Hall has been presented as an artist defined not only by others, but by others dependent upon Una's version.

Where events involved Hall's lovers, however, Una Troubridge's accounts must be accepted with great caution. I have therefore attempted wherever possible to rely on Radclyffe Hall's own words and writings, and to supplement Una's account from other sources. I have been exceptionally fortunate in finding new material, both literary and personal, for the periods with Mabel Batten and Evguenia Souline, though it is important to recognize that Souline's autobiographical writings, like Una's memoirs, are likely to have been written some years after the events they describe (probably, according to sources obtained from her friends, between 1942 and 1950). Several key people talked to me and offered me photos, diaries, letters and documents not available to previous biographers. I also had the good fortune to discover in an old trunk in Rome manuscripts of unpublished short stories, novellas, early drafts of published fictions, several versions of the novels *Michael West*, *The World*, *Emblem Hurlstone* and others, as well as autobiographical essays which had mercifully escaped Una Troubridge's ritual burning of 'everything left unpublished' after Hall's death.

Although Hall never saw herself as part of a literary coterie she nevertheless had strong links with and drew on the same tradition of psychological fiction as May Sinclair, Dorothy Richardson, Storm Jameson, Sheila Kaye-Smith, Violet Hunt, Ida Wylie, Vere Hutchinson and Rebecca West. Though Hall had a wide literary canvas, she, like other women novelists of the period, illustrated women's feelings of frustration in their emotional relationships with men.

Radclyffe Hall admired two kinds of people: people who wrote books and wrote them well; and people who 'did things' but stayed true to themselves. She herself wrote books and wrote them well. She 'did things', outrageous, complex, challenging and contradictory things, yet she stayed true to herself. She was also prepared to stand up and be counted for what she believed in. That too must provoke admiration.

One of her most contradictory acts was to name, misname and rename herself and her characters. The process weaves itself in and out of her life and her texts. She called herself by three names: Marguerite, John and Radclyffe Hall. I devote substantial space in the book to a discussion of the meanings behind this process as it brings to light central issues in her life and her art.

In the biography I follow her own usage. For the period of her childhood, adolescence, and her life as a young woman she called herself Marguerite, the name by which she was christened at birth in 1880. For the years 1906 to 1915 – the period of her autobiographical essays, poetry and early unpublished fiction – I use Marguerite Radclyffe-Hall, the name under which she wrote her five volumes of poetry. In discussing her personal relationships from 1912 onwards I have referred to her as John, as did her lovers, friends and intimates. In analysing her seven published novels, her published volume of short stories and the remainder of her mature unpublished work at my disposal, I use the name Radclyffe Hall, her chosen professional name as a fiction writer.

Radclyffe Hall had claimed publicly that *The Well of Loneliness*, her one novel which associated social change with art, would survive her times. She has been proved right. At Hall's death, though the novel was selling an extraordinary 100,000 copies per year world-wide, it remained unpublished in Great Britain. However in 1949, though the law had not been changed, Una Troubridge discovered a publisher brave enough to retest it. When the Falcon Press (subsequently Hammond, Hammond) published it in Hall's own country without any official obstruction, Radclyffe Hall's unrealized ambition was achieved.

Since then *The Well of Loneliness* has had several successful reprints and has been translated into dozens of languages. The most recent English language version was published by Virago in 1982. Between 1982 and 1996 it sold 71,421 copies in Great Britain alone.[1] Part of its sales appeal over the years was implicit in one of Hall's aims, which was to explain lesbianism to heterosexual readers. As the book has sold millions of copies it is reasonable to suppose that a large proportion of its readership was and is drawn from this group. Hall's second avowed aim was to make lesbianism visible to homosexuals and heterosexuals alike. This the trial did for her, by putting the banned book on the cultural map. It remains today the one lesbian novel everyone has heard of. It has even been broadcast as the BBC's Book at Bedtime.[2]

Such publicity however has meant that if Radclyffe Hall has not been neglected as a writer she has largely been remembered as a one-book author. Her place in the literary canon has been diminished by the dramatic effect of a single novel that made censorship headlines.

During more recent decades she has been viewed as the proponent of an essentialist image of homosexuality based on a dubious medical model which focused on heterosexual masculinity as a desirable norm. Such a stance appeared more useful to a traditional homophobic society than to contemporary women in search of a lesbian identity within a feminist context.

Since the 1980s in the USA and Great Britain, where Feminist Studies and Lesbian Studies have developed as two distinct areas of sociological inquiry and literary criticism, there has been a substantial revival of interest in Radclyffe Hall as a writer. Again, however, it has been largely in terms of a reappraisal of her most notorious book.

The new criticism[3] acknowledges the problems contemporary readers have had with *The Well of Loneliness*. Simultaneously it places *The Well* in its historical context to show the limited choices that were available to Radclyffe Hall in the 1920s within the competing ideologies of traditional femininity, new suffragette feminism and the pervasive medical sexology of Ulrichs, Krafft-Ebing, Carpenter, Hirschfeld and Ellis. Today, when many women grow up knowing they can *choose* to be lesbian as an extension of their feminism, Hall's ideas can seem desperately outdated, and gloomy to boot.

In this biography I have tried to open up the question of whether we should consider Radclyffe Hall predominantly as a boundary-breaking lesbian writer or as an important novelist whose concern with oppressive lesbian labelling was but one part of her interest in the position and function of the multiple exile.

If lesbian writing is writing which displays within the limits of the text itself that which is distinctive of lesbian experience or that which is descriptive of lesbian feeling, then Hall's importance in lesbian cultural history cannot be overestimated. In an era of shadows, mystification and mists, she let in more light. Several poems and most profoundly *The Well of Loneliness* remain for all time 'a testament to the invisibility of lesbians and the unthinkable nature of lesbianism'.[4] Though Stephen Gordon and Mary Llewellyn are more famous, the secondary lesbian couple Jamie and Barbara illustrate a similar same-sex commitment as they act out parallel butch and femme roles unto and after death.

In the other six novels and the short stories, several major and minor characters are either presented as inverts or illuminate the passion of homoerotic bonds. The most forceful female examples are Joan Ogden, Elizabeth Rodney, Venetia Ford, Frances Reide and, strongest of all, Wilhelmina Ogilvy, the trenchant independent invert fulfilled during wartime, as Hall fervently believed she could have been.

But Radclyffe Hall's fictional interests are considerably wider than a concern with sexual difference. Looking at the whole body of her work, it is clear that what interested her were the emotions and position of the stranger in society. In her fiction she focuses on the ways in which society, through its terrors of the 'abnormal', punishes those who stand outside it. From this perspective *The Well of Loneliness* is not the only one of her books to deal with inversion. Though Stephen Gordon enacts the life of a man within the body of a woman, in *The Master of the House*, as Margaret Lawrence and Claudia Stillman Franks point out, Christophe Bénédit re-enacts the life of Christ within the body of a man.

Nor, viewed from this wider perspective, does the rest of her work stand in contradiction to the theme of *The Well*. Although Radclyffe Hall herself pointed out that Miss Ogilvy foreshadows Stephen Gordon, Miss Ogilvy also stands for any person out of tune with their time.[5] It is Miss Ogilvy the Outsider rather than Miss Ogilvy the Invert who is linked to Hall's other exile-protagonists, Henry Dobbs, Fräulein Schwartz,[6] and Charles Duffell in 'The Rest Cure'. Duffell, who stands so outside his own life that he attempts to throw off the connection between label and existence by being reincarnated as a stone, becomes a particularly profound portrait[7] within Radclyffe Hall's gallery of characters who inhabit an introspective, isolated world alienated from love, cut off from friendship.

It is possible to read into the complexity of Radclyffe Hall's 'outsider texts' the emotions of the lesbian woman in the early twentieth century standing outside both family and society. It is equally possible, however, to see the homosexual portrayals in her individual novels as part of her encompassing vision of the alienated individual confronted with the mystery of the universe.

I have tried to show that it is more productive to see each perspective as informing the other. For Radclyffe Hall sexual identity is part of the search for transcendence and spiritual wholeness. Hall was a writer passionately committed to her cause, though the cause (and the passion) grew in direct proportion to the mounting hostility towards it. The woman called John was perilously at odds with a society not yet ready for her, a writer who occupied a symbolic position in relation to her time. Her literary range included the unseen as well as the seen world, she made visible the invisible, she spoke for her time but was ahead of it. As our times have changed, Radclyffe Hall has not lost her relevance; her novels are both timely and timeless.

PART 1

WHAT'S IN A NAME? 1880–1906

1

EARLY NAMING

In the life and art of Radclyffe Hall names had a special significance. Born on 12 August 1880, as a child at home she was Marguerite – a detested name bestowed by the mother she detested.

As a published poet from 1906 to 1915 she was Marguerite Radclyffe-Hall: one French appellation, one hyphen. With this came five volumes of poetry, some credentials, some discomfort.

As a novelist from 1924 to 1943 she was Radclyffe Hall – no hyphen. Seven novels. One book of short stories. Two outrageous court cases. The name of the legend.

To her friends, lovers and intimates from 1912 she was a woman called John – a name she loved bestowed by a woman she loved: her first important partner, Mabel Batten, nicknamed Ladye.

Names and nicknames, naming and renaming, haunted her childhood and haunt her fiction. The issue of identity fascinates and preoccupies her. In her novels she uses names as markers, as badges, as symbols of sameness and difference. Miss Wilhelmina Ogilvy in her short story 'Miss Ogilvy Finds Herself', like Marguerite 'a queer little girl, aggressive and awkward', insisted with 'tears and some temper that her real name was William and not Wilhelmina', just as Marguerite would later insist her name was John.[1]

In her novel *The Well of Loneliness* her most famous heroine is named Stephen Gordon by her father Sir Philip, who longed for a son. The boyish name and the child's likeness to her father struck her mother as an outrage, just as Marguerite's own likeness to her father and her tomboyish habits would similarly disturb her mother.

In her childhood Marguerite had feelings about herself she could not name. Later she would tell Ladye, Una and Souline, her three important lovers, that from her earliest years she had felt odd and different. The documented difference was one of loneliness. Perhaps there were other emotions involved that the adult John would later categorize as sexual. Perhaps there were not. At the very least Marguerite had wanted to do what young girls were not allowed to do – ride bareback, climb trees, have sporting adventures, wear trousers. Her father, named Radclyffe Radclyffe-Hall by his father, the eminent and snobbish physician Dr Charles Radclyffe-Hall, had had stable-boys as companions who had nicknamed him Rat. Marguerite had no companions and her nicknames were cuddly and girlish. Her loving grandmother Sarah Diehl called her Suggie Plum. The composer Sir Arthur Sullivan, a colleague of her despised stepfather Albert Visetti, called her Toddles, so at four years old the child signed her verses Marguerite Toddles before presenting them to the great musician.

On a rare visit to his small daughter, Rat the Romantic rode on a horse up to her door, spotted the child as pretty as a flower, nicknamed her Daisy, promised her for her birthday a cream and white pony. The father departed, the birthday arrived, a doll was sent. Daisy got dolls. John would ride horses.

This problem of naming is highlighted in her story 'The Rest Cure – 1932' which focuses on the collapse and mental fragmentation of failed businessman Charles Duffell. Charles begins his breakdown by talking to a blowfly: 'What is Charles Duffell? The purest illusion . . . A name is a frightful thing to possess, from the first it imposes an intolerable bondage, the bondage of traditions attached to that name.'[2]

The two traditions into which Marguerite Radclyffe-Hall was born and bondaged were those of a Victorian patriarchal culture which carefully defined the role of women as passive and feminine, and of upper middle class England where hansom bells jingled and lamps were discreetly shaded in elegant drawing-rooms. Marguerite's own connections were highly reputable. Her family line which included a knighthood given to her grandfather Charles was set firmly within medicine, law and the clergy, and could trace links to Charles II and even Shakespeare.

The unpretentious Halls had their roots in Lancashire. From her Mancunian great-great-grandfather the Reverend Samuel Hall (1748–1813), 'a pugnacious fighter'[3] and tutor to the writer Thomas de Quincey, she inherited her stubbornness and the fact that she was 'blessed or cursed with an inability to be anything but thorough'.[4] From Sam Hall's son, her great-grandfather John, of Congleton, Cheshire (1785–1861), she inherited what she believed was his 'very hot temper and an abrupt and overbearing manner'. Her likeness to his portrait is astonishing. There lurk his blue eyes, fair skin, aquiline features, and a nose that was 'big, high-bridged and arrogant'.[5] That she felt an affectionate kinship with great-grandfather John was shown when she let her lover Ladye call her 'John', then informally adopted his name socially.

The Radcliffes (spelt with an 'i') first appeared in the Hall history in 1776 when Sam Hall married Elizabeth Russell (1751–1815), daughter of the Reverend Radcliffe Russell, Vicar of Easingwold, Yorkshire. Radclyffe Hall called them the 'luckless Radcliffes' or 'feckless Radcliffes'[6] but was beguiled by their romantic origins.

Edward Radcliffe, 2nd Earl of Derwentwater, had married Charles II's illegitimate daughter, Lady Mary Tudor. Two of Edward and Mary's sons were beheaded on Tower Hill. Stuart sacrifices, lost causes: this was the heady stuff which fed Marguerite's imagination, and later reinforced her desire to champion the hapless, the star-crossed and the indigent. The Stuart cause early kindled her creative spirit. In her volume of poetry *Rhymes and Rhythms*, the Stuart Songs glorify 'brave deeds and battles won' and 'wild words and follies done'.[7]

The romantic Radcliffe name was added to that of the sturdy Halls by the truculent John, an eminent surgeon. He established the family estates in Congleton, Cheshire, where he became a magistrate and an alderman, and encouraged Marguerite's grandfather Charles to follow him into medicine. Marguerite, fascinated by her grandfather's interest in the new phenomenon of Mesmerism on which he wrote a series of articles for the *Lancet* in 1845, later developed his theories when she began her psychical research in 1916. Charles shifted his professional attention from hypnosis to tuberculosis when he contracted the disease. For the sake of his health he moved first to Bristol,[8] then to the milder climate of Torquay where in 1851 he opened a sanatorium for chest diseases. Its success brought him fame and earned him a knighthood. Having made a name for himself, Charles hyphenated his father's name, spelt Radcliffe with a 'y', and took out armorial bearings, which traced his descent back to William Shakespeare through the marriage of Dr John Hall of Stratford-upon-Avon to Shakespeare's daughter Susannah.[9]*

Although she expressed scorn for her grandfather's status-seeking, John later admitted: 'There are times when I am glad that he had the foresight to entail our handful of family portraits. For I feel that ancestral matters are now too much ignored, that the world cannot go on existing without roots and above all perhaps without traditions. Am I perhaps also a snob?'[10] In her novel *The Forge*, Hilary Brent, a sciolistic writer like the early Hall, says to his wife Susan, a painter like Una Troubridge: 'Tradition is a terrible but rather fine thing . . . It always thrills me when I meet it.'[11]

Hall's ambivalence about tradition as bondage and as roots was to be mirrored throughout her life by related contradictions. Respectability remained

---

* As Una Troubridge records (*The Life and Death of Radclyffe Hall*, p. 7), the Radclyffe Hall family crest's 'Talbot's head makes its first appearance . . . in the churchyard at Stratford-upon-Avon on the tomb of Dr John Hall who lived . . . in that town and married Susanna, daughter of William Shakespeare. They had, however, no male issue, and the descent is not in the direct line.'

her roots; her sexual identity became her bondage. But the reverse is also true. In 1926, having firmly established a respectable name for herself in literary terms with her traditional award-winning novel *Adam's Breed*, she deliberately espoused the outrageously unpopular lesbian cause only two years later. Thereafter her self-chosen sexuality was embedded within her roots. Though she lived a radical lifestyle in the face of personal notoriety and punishing reviews for her post-*Well* literature, she stood firm as a Catholic convert, consistently voted Conservative, and in contemporary terminology would be considered classist.

Indeed she had much in common with her grandfather Charles, who beneath his worldly exterior was sensitive and subtle. Charles, who on 1 October 1847 had married Esther Westhead, a mother of three children – two daughters and a son by a previous marriage – became unhealthily obsessed with his youngest stepdaughter. When she died shortly after Charles and Esther's marriage, his coercive grief sank his household into unremitting gloom: gloomy households feature in many of Hall's novels.

In *The Forge*, despite its light-hearted resiliency, Radclyffe Hall depicts the effects of a forbidding environment on her characters' attempts to find freedom. Hilary Brent

> had been an only child living in large, melancholy houses. It seemed to him now that the houses he had lived in had always been darker than any of their neighbours . . . Looking back upon his earliest youth, he found it full of shadows, somewhat dispelled later on at Eton, it is true, but the life of every man was coloured by his nursery, and his nurseries had always been drab.[12]

Although Marguerite's father Rat later dispelled the despondency of Dr Charles Radclyffe-Hall's stately house by means of hunting and horses, mandolin playing and music, verse-making and wildly amorous adventures, those shadows remained. Rat felt as rejected by his father as Marguerite was to feel by the shadows in her nursery and her own father's absences.

The Hall tradition of hard work and persistence, which Marguerite would inherit, halted with Rat. His father suggested he become a barrister. Rat refused. He loved dogs and horses, as Marguerite would, and an easy life, which initially she too selected.

Like Hilary Brent, Rat went to Eton. Like Hilary Brent, Rat became a literary dabbler. Becoming a dilettante was a fate Hall feared for herself. Though Rat matriculated at St John's College, Oxford, in 1869, there is no record extant of his having taken a degree. At Oxford he was much given to diamonds, an expensive taste Marguerite inherited. Diamonds on his fingers, diamonds scattered over smart suits, Rat sported stylish sideburns and showed a talent for conjuring. Did the singular lack of magic in his home life turn him into the devilish magician Radclyffe Hall later romanticizes?

In receipt of generous family finances Rat had little incentive to earn a living. His sole recorded occupation in the 1870s, when gentlemen did not enter the theatre, was that of an actor. Intent on renaming himself, he took Hubert Vane as his theatrical alias. Dr Charles Radclyffe-Hall cut off his allowance. In retaliation, Rat joined a touring company. In respectable Torquay he appeared as Charles Surface in *The School for Scandal*. A scandal with a fisherman's daughter led Charles to drive him from the family home.

Rat the restless gave up the theatre and took up yachting. He also took up with a woman in London, probably Mary Ratcliffe Farmer of Paddington. When he died, Rat left an annuity to the fisherman's daughter and ample provision for the London woman and her child which may well have been his. The adult John felt that 'women swarmed like locusts around him . . . [I]f I had known him longer could I have put up with my father's affairs?'[13] No, she decided. Yet she shared that trait. In her late teens and throughout her twenties young women swarmed around her. When the affairs were over, or converted into companionable friendships, like Rat she continued to offer them financial support.

Rat's canny pragmatism which Radclyffe Hall was too honest or stubborn ever to share, led him to a partial reconciliation with his father. Certainly Charles's will written in 1872 left Rat as the main heir to the substantial family fortune when Charles died in 1879.

In the year before his father's death, through his Cheshire cousins* Rat met and married Mary Jane (the young widow of an American, Wallace Sager [or Sanger]), daughter of Philadelphia businessman Edwin Diehl and Sarah Bishop,† who was to play a vital role in young Marguerite's life. Mary Jane had been married at seventeen and widowed by twenty-three. Her father came of Dutch emigrant stock, hence the name Diehl. A self-made American, he died during her childhood. Perhaps it was from him that she inherited her grasping streak. Mary Jane, always prone to self-aggrandizement and with a taste for the fanciful, often repeated the family claim that the Diehls' veins streamed with the blood of the American Indian Pocahontas. Whatever the truth of the legend, it coloured the imagination of young Marguerite. Curiously, despite her blue eyes and fair hair, her features and facial construction were so reminiscent of a North American Indian that at fancy dress balls she would dress up as one.[14]

The wedding between Mary Jane and Rat took place in Southport,

---

* Cousins of Marguerite's great-grandfather John. In 1878 James Reade, a Cheshire cousin, brought over to England his American wife Emma together with Emma's niece, the pretty young widow Mary Jane Sager (on records also spelt Sanger) (1851–1945). James met his cousin Rat in Southport and introduced him to Mary Jane. The couple married there later that year.
† Sarah Bishop was born in Penn in 1831, the second of five children of Jane and Elijah Jones of Huntingdon, New Jersey.

Lancashire. It was conducted by Rat's lifelong – perhaps his only real – friend, the Reverend Walter Begley, later Marguerite's confidant, who as Rat's tutor at Oxford had encouraged his passion for the mandolin.

Mary Jane's family were Quakers and believed in a simple standard of living. However, the class-conscious Halls were not impressed with Rat's bride, and considered her American relations vulgar. Hall's relatives isolated Mary and Rat when they first took rooms in Piccadilly, London, and Diehl relatives ignored them when they visited Philadelphia. Adherents of low-key manners and appearance, the Diehls were outraged by Rat's barbed wit, offhand ways, vulgar check trousers, emerald velvet jacket. His flashing diamonds and shoulder-length hair led his new mother-in-law to remark: 'Poor Mary has married a side-walk artist!'[15]

Poor Mary and her side-walk artist, who saw himself rather as a 'poet-fellow',[16] set up a tempestuous ménage in a gloomy Bournemouth house inappropriately called Sunny Lawn.

> Violent quarrels turned Sunny Lawn into a hell . . . My father is reported to have said to my mother: 'It is hell with you and hell without you' . . . They quarrelled in private, they quarrelled in public, they quarrelled before friends and acquaintances. They quarrelled before the negro servants. Temper crashed on temper. Tinder and flint kindled the brushwood of pettyness into a blaze that all but consumed them . . . She was jealous and watchful. He was undisciplined, restless, intolerant of all opposition. They were both so utterly spoiled, so violent, so self-centred that disaster was bound to ensue.[17]

The disaster for the child, and later for the writer, was not merely the presence of the terrible marital tension which she painfully evokes in her fictional world but also the wretchedness of the home which 'had neither dignity nor repose and moreover was deplorably lacking in beauty. There are spiritual values in bricks and mortar. In my home there were none.'[18]

It was in Sunny Lawn where no sunny spirits prevailed that Marguerite was born in 1880. Marguerite's 'advent was far from being free from alarms and even further from being placid'.[19]

A writer's life can become her guiding narrative structure. Although Radclyffe Hall denied that her prose work was autobiographical she constantly projects upon significant life experiences a structure of meaning that forms many of her fictional and autobiographical themes (and where her birth appears as a dominant metaphor in her symbolic landscape). She plays with the facts in a number of ways.

She creates three conflicting versions of the alarms surrounding her birth. In the first version her father is living at home but is absent from the birth: 'I rushed headlong into the world several hours before my advent was expected. The nurse had gone out for something from the chemist – my father was out and so was the doctor. Fortunately the nurse returned just in time to sever the navel cord.'[20]

In the second version her father is present, though more intent on marital disruption than on paying attention to his daughter's arrival: 'At the time of my birth a most deadly quarrel was reigning between my father and mother. I rushed impetuously into life and even the nurse and doctor were not present.'[21]

Parts of the third version, in which her father has finally left the marital home before her birth, are scrawled through, with the same lines written and rewritten:

> I awaited my birth in an atmosphere of tears and threats and increasing recriminations. She accused him of chasing her round the house with a pistol. She accused him of boxing her ears then rushing from her blind with anger. She accused him of throwing a joint at the cook because he disliked cold leg of mutton. He accused her of just being herself. This it seemed was sufficient. Then he went the whole hog and was blatantly unfaithful. Blatantly crudely unfaithful. When I was born he was far away. Far away. I was born like a bird with a broken wing. A rabbit in a trap with a splintered bone. I was born where the sound of the waves is the sound of tears . . . If one could only learn not to care . . .[22]

West Cliff, Holdenhurst, Bournemouth, the place of her birth, would indeed have been within the sound of waves. But it is the sound of those words that she carries forward into her poetry and fiction. In her first published volume of poetry, *'Twixt Earth and Stars* (1906), in a poem called 'To . . .', the first verse recalls her birth: 'The sound of the waves is the sound of tears . . .'[23] In the same volume she describes her love as 'a bird with a broken wing' and 'the soul of a burning past'.[24]

The burning past, herself at birth seen as a rabbit in a trap with a splintered bone, is evoked fifty-four years later, in her unpublished novel *Emblem Hurlstone* (1934), about a man unable to deal with pain. She recalls Emblem as a boy of twelve listening to the sound of the waves:

> He fancied he could still see the pale washed blue of the sky, the pale foam-flecked blue of the rising tide . . . these things had filled him with joy . . . then he had seen a rabbit in a trap, had seen its terrified glistening eyes, the gasping mouth and its futile struggles. The creature had got itself caught by the leg, and a splinter of bone had struck out through the skin . . . he should have released it but instead he turned and fled from the pain.[25]

Emblem Hurlstone in her novel cannot face the pain. Radclyffe Hall in her life cannot forget the pain. Whether it is the grief at being born unwanted – in several essays she records her mother's attempts at abortion – whether it is the malaise of continuous parental conflict or the sorrow at her father's absences, it is desolation that dominates her childhood memories.

Whether her father was present or absent at her birth remains unclear. What we can deduce is that as a child Marguerite missed him so keenly that every absence was seen almost as a presence, and his occasional presence was too wavering, too unpredictable, to offer her security. Against the rhythmic sound of the waves, the domestic sound of tears, her father's absences became a current in her life and writing. Lonely creatures, growing up without fathers, many with abusive mothers, became Hall's fictional protagonists.[26]

The lonely Marguerite was in fact a second child, but her sister Florence Maude (born 16 July 1879) had died on 5 September 1880 – only a few weeks after Marguerite's birth – from dentition, eight days of diarrhoea and eight hours of mysterious convulsions, leaving Marguerite to lament the loss of a sister as she was always to lament the loss of relatives.

A few weeks after Marguerite's birth, her playboy father, living up to his nickname, ratted on the family, deserted home, wife and his remaining daughter in order to philander more freely in less restricted arenas. Marguerite's mother thereafter refused to see the absentee Rat's English relations.

She christened their second daughter Marguerite for reasons of breeding and femininity. For the same reasons the biblically named Mary relabelled herself the more fanciful Marie. In several versions of an unfinished autobiographical essay, Radclyffe Hall constantly redrafts the same few sentences about the irony of her mother's naming, just as she reworked her father's role at her birth. Crossed out, scrawled over, and rewritten again are these lines:

> When I began my career as an author I kept the Radclyffe but dropped the hyphen. Radclyffe Hall was a good writing name I felt. And now I am going to reveal a dark secret . . . my mother had a passion for fancy names thus I was christened *Marguerete* . . . not plain Margaret which I could have endured, no *Margerite*, she having just seen Faust or was it 'La dame aux caméllias'? What's in a name? A most foolish question – why everything for the one who must bear it, who must live with it, morning noon and night, who must hear it on nearly every occasion. Had I remained *Marguerite* Radclyffe-Hall I am sure I should now never have written a word. I might have developed a complex. Marguerite is no more. She has passed away to a better land . . .[27]

Radclyffe Hall's linguistic cross, and indeed her shame, was her atrocious spelling. Her former secretary Winifred Hales, now Reed, to whom she dictated *The Master of the House*, recalled that 'she liked to hear her words read aloud and she did not spell at all well.'[28] Nevertheless it is more than a little curious that she should have misspelt her own Christian name twice within one sentence.

Equally curious is the bitter echo which came from her mother in 1943. When a newspaper report of her daughter Marguerite's death was shown to her, still resentful of her daughter's fame and of the stigma attached to Hall's name after *The Well*, Marie wrote to her niece Jane Caruth: 'You will see by the enclosed [newspaper cutting] that Margarite is dead. I can't even spell her name!'[29] Marie's final linguistic and maternal rejection of her daughter was the last act in a lifetime of rejection and abuse. The former biblical Mary inexorably became the unChristian mother whose vicious temper left marks on her child's body and bruised Marguerite's spirit.

Radclyffe Hall in her correspondence rarely names the sordid sense of shame engendered by her mother's maleficent battering. Jerkily, reluctantly, her unswerving sense of loyalty in conflict with her need to express the pain, she writes in an essay: 'My mother was a fool but a terribly cruel fool . . . a terribly crafty and cruel fool for whom life early had become a mirror in which she saw only her reflection . . . Her cruel influence so potent that it held my grand-mother perpetually in chains.'[30]

Those chains leave their impress on another autobiographical essay: 'My grandmother who so firmly believed in God and in prayer and in me her beloved grandchild could never free herself from those chains . . . I watched her poor ineffectual struggles while the chains tightened with the years – and the chains were in truth forged by fear.'[31]

Bonds and chains form her earliest imagery. In recollections of restless travel with the mother who scorned her, she wrote: 'I was taken to America by my mother when I was only a few months old . . . [and] on several subsequent occasions. As an only child of seven I remember I envied American children . . . they seemed free and independent. I never felt free, I never felt independent. I felt chained.'[32]

Memories of herself as a child, fettered and chained, are evident in her first completed novel *The Unlit Lamp*,[33] where the predominant cluster of images are fetters and where the theme of helplessness pervades the book with a sense of doom. Although the fetters symbolism in her light-hearted work *The Forge* is a positive illustration of the empowering influence of commitments, nevertheless Hilary and Susan Brent often feel emotionally chained.

Earlier, in 1915, that deluge of helpless feelings poured through her first autobiographical novel *Michael West*. It remained unpublished and would appear to have been unread by previous biographers, but it deserves attention for it illustrates the young Marguerite's feelings better than any of her other writings.

Five-year-old Michael, 'a thin little boy in a tight sailor suit trimmed with white braid, all arms and black-stockinged legs', feels 'steeped with grief and wonders why they did not drown him in a bucket as he had seen Mrs Billings drown some kittens in the scullery'. His mother, Sarah West, like Marguerite's mother Marie, throws 'uncontrollable fits of passion that made Michael slink away in despondent nervous misery'. Between Michael and his mother there was antagonism sharp as a sword in their eyes, the antagonism of two strong wills in collision . . . Then Michael set his lips. He drew them into a pale line and as Mrs West saw it her heart hardened. For at that moment Michael had all unconsciously assumed the look of his father, the cold look of active dislike that Mrs West knew so well. She sprang to her feet, caught him by the shoulder, then pushing him into the bed she whipped him. It was the first of many whippings . . . Mrs West whipped him while her strength lasted.[34]

The boy is fettered by the repetitious use of the word 'antagonism'. Though the hostility cuts like steel between mother and son, though the boy is strong-willed, he has no power. Michael is as helpless as Marguerite faced with her mother Marie's intransigence. When the young girl's features began to resemble Rat's, Marie would shout scornfully, as she pounded her: 'Your hands are just like Radclyffe's!' When Michael sets his lips, unknowingly reflecting his father's expression, it drives Mrs West into instant sadistic action. As she rises in fury so does the prose. The energy of the passage is released through the whippings.

'Surely youth is the most helpless thing in the world. For at least sixteen years it is constantly subject to circumstances it cannot control,' Radclyffe Hall wrote later.[35] Her mother's baiting and battering were one of those circumstances which would shape her life and her fiction.

Early lack of control and a devouring need for control are evident in the adult John's incessant list-making, her repeated instructions to others, her grasping for order within a desperately disordered world, her belts-and-braces attitude to survival – traits psychologically characteristic of an abused child. Home, Hall wrote, should be 'something safe and kind in a world of peril, cruelty and change'.[36] Una Troubridge's description of young Marguerite's mother shows how far theirs fell short: 'There was a violence of temper equal to that of the father, but unaccompanied by intellect or talent of any description'. In Una's view, Marie 'had from the hour of birth . . . disliked her second daughter'.[37]

This second child was sickly: double pneumonia as an infant was followed by scarlet fever, which led to an adolescence plagued by asthma and bronchitis, then to a maturity gripped by hypochondria. Small wonder that Una Troubridge remarked:

It is not pleasant to think of her [Marie] as the guardian of an ailing and intensely sensitive child, whose only protection was an ageing grandmother who loved her but was too weak and too much intimidated by bullying and by actual violence to protect her. An early champion, her nurse, known and beloved as 'M'Nana' was very soon dealt with by Mrs Radclyffe-Hall. This nurse, finding on the child's body the marks of cruel beatings, protested that it was one thing to punish a child but a scandal to reduce it to such a condition.[38]

We often exhibit towards others what we most lack or need ourselves. Thus it is no surprise that, in terrible need of protection, the young Marguerite embarked on a lifetime of protectiveness towards animals and humans weakened by personal circumstances or character flaws. Just as Sarah Diehl, her grandmother, imported from America to look after her, vainly attempted to save her from Marie's harsh beatings, in later years Marguerite would try and save Sarah from Marie's punishing wrath. Even as a small child, when walking with her elderly grandmother, she said: 'Hold on to me, granny, and I'll take you across [the road]. Don't be afraid.'[39]

Many of the children in Hall's later novels and stories are shown living under the threat of brutal slaps and beatings. In 'The Lover of Things', young Henry Dobbs, beaten regularly by his mother, felt an 'alien' and 'went his own way'.[40] The girl Marguerite, also beaten regularly, felt an alien and went her own way. In a childhood world chaotic and painful, she turned to servants and animals for consolation, then portrayed them in fiction with enduring affection.

Though childhood regimes of melancholy shape her narratives, an affinity to the harmony of nature, a sense of spiritual quest, and a stubborn determination to affirm her experience and not be beaten by it, wrest her writing and her life from despair. It is courage, not defeat, that becomes her trademark.

Early on, however, part of her defence against a childhood disruptive, discontinuous and violent was an aloofness of spirit like that of Henry Dobbs. One consequence was an alienation from her body. Though she admired women's physical beauty she equated it with weakness.

Beautiful as a child, handsome as a young woman, her relationship with her appearance was convoluted. Her piercing blue eyes, masses of ringlets, matched the floral delicacy of her name. By the age of five her curls were shoulder-length and thickly clustered. She was the pride of her adoring grandmother, who in 1885 decided it was time for the child to be painted.

She commissioned a portrait in oils from society artist Katinka Amyat. It is a period piece of great conventionality. The little girl clutches at a bouquet of marguerites with white and yellow rays billowing from the central golden disc. A gold haze tinges the child's cheeks as she sits in her white muslin dress with frilly puffed sleeves and a ruffled collar. The later John had a great affection for the portrait. She was not unhappy with her curls. Una Troubridge, partner of the lesbian icon, did not approve at all. Curls were not in keeping with congenital inversion. She waited till John's death, then commissioned their painter friend Clare (Tony) Atwood to paint out the curls.

Until now the only photographs published have been of the revamped painting with the shorn head. For more than seventy years no one has seen the original. Dr Rossi-Lemeni, Una's godson, who owns the portrait, showed it to me at his house in Rome. He had carefully scraped away all the paint to reveal the unemancipated child.

The childhood portrait was placed only a few feet away from a more famous painting of Radclyffe Hall, in which she sits cross-dressed in bow tie, starched white shirt, masculine velvet smoking jacket, cropped head bent over her papers, pen in hand at her large oak desk.

The contradictions evident in the two visual images were threaded through her fiction and her life. Her attitude to her hair is but one thread. In her middle years her masculine haircut was to become a fashionable part of her public cross-dressing style, yet John did not in fact cut her own waist-length hair, which she wore braided or chignoned on top of her head, until 17 December 1920.

Hall in later years, looking over her shoulder in amazement at the girlish Marguerite, draws her major heroines decisively as boyish. In several novels her heroines, already out of step with society, cut their hair as a gesture of revolt. Miss Wilhelmina Ogilvy, who feels defrauded that she cannot be sent to the front line during the war, cuts off her hair to outrage her sisters.[41] In *The Unlit Lamp*, Joan Ogden, 'lanky as a boy', shy and awkward like Marguerite, enrages her mother by 'hacking at her hair with a pen-knife'.[42] Joan is seen as odd, unsuitable, though frankly very clever, while her entirely suitable sister, long-haired Milly, is warmly known as 'the pretty one'.[43]

As a child Marguerite encountered the worst of both worlds: patently 'a pretty one', she was yet at odds with her beauty, invoking as it did her mother's conventional expectations. Did her beauty violate the tomboy code? Certainly from her youth she rebelled against the age's repressive strictures on women, as did her most famous heroine Stephen Gordon. At seven, Stephen slinks off to her nursery, stops in front of the nursery looking-glass, cannot deal with her feminine image: 'Her heart felt very empty and tearful . . . having looked at herself in the glass, she had decided that she loathed her abundant long hair.' She would threaten the nursery staff or even her parents. '"I shall cut all my hair off, you see if I don't!" or, "I hate this white dress and I'm going to burn it . . ."'[44]

New evidence on her life suggests that Radclyffe Hall's early ambivalence about her appearance might be linked to sexual abuse in her childhood – abuse that took place after her father's death and her mother's remarriage.

A father, a mother, regretted absences, untenable presences – these lay behind her. Guidance from governesses, the lure of mentors, the love of women, poetry and passion, these were her ways forward.

2

IN THE NAME OF THE FATHERS

The father, the grandfather, the stepfather, each in turn bequeathed her a legacy which exerted a potent influence on Radclyffe Hall's life and writing as each took up space in her gawky world.

Rat bequeathed her an idealized version of himself. Fathers in her childhood dreams, when not absent, frequently appeared as noble or romanticized. Fathers in her adult fiction, when not absent, frequently appear the same. Very occasionally a note of realism is struck. Here is Rat in a working-class setting: 'Mr Dobbs had possessed a versatile mind, a liking for liquor, and an amorous nature. Jack of all trades and master of none, he had drifted from badly paid job to job until double pneumonia had closed his career when Henry was just eleven.'[1]

It is a portrait close to the emotional if not the social truth. It was 1898. Marguerite was eighteen. Rat, who had seen her less than a dozen times during her life, summoned her to the Paddington Hotel, London, for what was to be his deathbed scene. There was a bitterly cold wind that October day when nervously she went upstairs to her father's rooms. She saw Radclyffe Radclyffe-Hall, the formerly elegant Rat, lying emaciated, his Eton and Oxford élan dashed by haunted breathing, a racking cough and bladder trouble. He had an unkempt, bushy moustache and grey shadows on his face. Marguerite, concerned and tearful, questioned him about his illness. In a gallant attempt at summoning up his characteristic insouciance he told her it was merely asthma which would improve when he reached the Riviera. He was marking time before taking the train to Dover, there to board his yacht for Cannes. Affectionately he commented on her wistful beauty, asked her to send him a photograph. Then he gave her his first and last piece of fatherly advice: 'Be warned by me; decide what you want to do and stick to it. Never be a Jack-of-all-trades as I have been.'[2]

He assured her that he would make a new will. Instead of sharing his wealth between his daughter and his Cheshire cousins, she would become his sole heiress. Rat did indeed attempt for once to implement his resolution. He asked his friend Walter Begley to put the arrangement in train, but Rat did not live long enough to see it through. He was too sick to sail from Dover so he and his party attempted an overland journey through France. In Paris it was obvious that Rat the remorseful was dying. He was brought back to the Leas Hotel, Folkestone, where he sank into a coma from which he did not recover. For a time, young Marguerite, poignantly aware when she left him in his Paddington hotel room that she would be unlikely to see him again, thought that her father had died of pneumonia. Rat however, who was only fifty-two, after a short and rakish life died on 29 October 1898 of pulmonary tuberculosis.

A memorial to Rat in his father's town of Torquay records his age incorrectly: 'In memory of Radclyffe Radclyffe-Hall only son of Dr Charles Radclyffe-Hall, who died 29 October 1898 aged 49. After life's fitful fever he sleeps well.' In truth, it is not under that headstone that the restless Rat sleeps. He was buried miles away in Highgate Cemetery – where his daughter Marguerite would one day lie – probably because his friend and executor Walter Begley held a living in Hampstead.

The fantasy scene of Rat's death, together with the reckless romance of his life, which would be worked and reworked in her fiction, held two bitter ironies for Marguerite. The first was that she herself developed a mild form of tuberculosis. The Italian doctors who discovered severe scarring on her lungs in 1939 thought she might have caught the infection during that last visit.

The second more predictable irony was that despite his good intentions Rat's personal fortune of almost £52,000 went not to her but to her Cheshire cousins.

Fortunately for Marguerite, her grandfather Charles had sagely stipulated that Rat was not permitted to touch his father's capital. Under Charles's will, at the age of twenty-one Marguerite as Rat's only legitimate child would inherit Charles's vast estate (the bulk of which was held in trust) – an inheritance which in 1901 gave her her first freedom but which trapped her into the belief that money means control.

If her father and grandfather had led Marguerite to see felicity in terms of fantasy or finance, it was her mother who instilled in her the notion that happiness is always somewhere else, always round the corner. This dislocation, this discontent, would become the restless river that meandered like a displaced person through her prose.

Bored with the quiet New Forest, Marie escaped to London. Photographs show Marguerite thin, bony, anxious and self-absorbed, wheezing with asthma, silently watching her mother change moods, messuages and men. Marie roamed relentlessly from England to America, then wove her way to Europe, child in tow, an unimportant piece of baggage.

Since Marie had begun petitioning for divorce in 1882,[3] her resentment of Marguerite had markedly increased. She had petitioned on grounds of cruelty, alleging Rat's repeated assaults. Rat counter-claimed that he had merely tried to restrain his wife, albeit forcibly. The lawyers argued, but not as hysterically as the claimants. The court awarded custody of two-year-old Marguerite to Marie together with a settlement of £2,000. Rat refused to pay. Whimsical and irresponsible, he elected to settle £200 on his baby daughter and a further £200 on the child of Marie's housemaid. Was this yet another of his illegitimate children?

Marie never received her £2,000 settlement, but had no qualms over misspending her daughter's funds. Decades later Marie still claimed that Radclyffe Hall, the successful writer who for years had been the Visettis' financial support, owed her the £2,000.

Marie's outrage at her reduced circumstances, vented in virulent outbursts against Marguerite, left their mark in Radclyffe Hall's first, unpublished novel *Michael West*.[4] Michael's divorced mother Sarah rages constantly against the absence of money and the presence of her 'tiresome child'. This word becomes a sad refrain in Radclyffe Hall's early fictional vocabulary. Several of her autobiographical essays have references to herself as 'a tiresome baby', 'that tiresome child', 'such a tiresome girl'.[5]

Michael grows 'to associate all that was worst in man' with his father. Though Marie, like Sarah West, attempts to inculcate in Marguerite the belief that Rat was 'all that was worst in man' she fails. Marguerite's fiction offers fathers who, if present, can seem to be all that is best in man. Here is Rat, at his best, in an upper-class setting: 'Sir Philip was . . . exceedingly well-favoured, but his charm lay less in feature than in a certain wide expression . . . that might almost be called noble.'[6] Stephen Gordon's father, like Rat, 'had sown no few wild oats'. When Sir Philip asks Stephen: '"What is honour, my daughter?" [s]he looked into his anxious, questioning eyes: "You are honour," she said quite simply.'[7]

Forlorn and dejected Marguerite became, but unlike Michael she was financially cocooned. Lawyers finally persuaded Rat to put aside £10,000 in a trust fund for her welfare and education to be administered during her minority by his lawyers Hastie & Company.

It was Mr Hastie, rather than her father, whom she saw at regular three-monthly intervals. Hastie dealt with all her practical arrangements before he passed on progress reports to Rat reclining in foreign hotels or on his yacht. It was Mr Hastie, rather than her father, who impressed upon the shy young girl that becoming an heiress was an awesome responsibility. The girl learnt her lesson well. Throughout her life Radclyffe Hall was highly responsible in her handling of money, but also saw it as a means of acquiring love or running relationships.

In her first two partnerships, with Mabel Batten (Ladye) and Una Troubridge, where each had independent funds, this control was subsumed under John's 'quasi-masculine' role. Generally, like a Victorian husband, she became the house purchaser. But the underlying reasons were, firstly, that in her childhood it was *her* trust fund which kept her mother's residence going whilst inside it everything else fell apart; secondly, it was *her* inheritance which finally enabled her to leave home and buy one of her own.

In her third relationship, with Evguenia Souline, a penniless Russian refugee, there was no subtlety about the issue of money and control. Her protection of Evguenia, which began with gifts, extended to a regular allowance, cut off if Evguenia 'disobeyed' John. Though in no way commendable, her behaviour needs to be seen in the context of a joyless shifting childhood where money alone offered her a small measure of stability.

During Mr Hastie's regime, while still in London, Marie was courted by her singing master, a stout excitable Italian in his early forties, Alberto Visetti. Visetti had been born in Salone, Dalmatia, in May 1846, the son of a village organist and his English wife – though later he would claim to be the son of a wealthy Italian landowner. He studied at the Milan Conservatoire, and before meeting Marie in the mid-1880s had adopted British nationality. At the time of their meeting he was a professor of singing at the Royal College of Music, whose pupils later included Sir Keith Faulkner, the future principal of the Royal College of Music. Awarded the Order of the Corona d'Italia by the King of Italy, when he arrived in England in 1871 he was already well known as a musician.

Marriage to her somewhat hesitant suitor was Marie's aim, so in 1889 she left Visetti behind in London and headed for Belgium where she camped in a series of hotels in Bruges, trailed by the loyal Sarah Diehl, Miss Knott (Nottie), a favoured governess, and the unwilling eight-year-old Marguerite, who was breathing now with difficulty as bronchial ailments superseded her already acute asthma. Marguerite's constitution was less of a consideration to Marie than the success of her plan.

Marie's plan paid off. Alberto Visetti followed them and proposed in Belgium. As no record of their marriage exists in England, and evidence shows that Marie was still in Belgium in February 1890 we may reasonably speculate that they married abroad between late autumn 1889 and February 1890.

In Belgium, Marguerite, lacking friends, acquired a canary.

In *The Unlit Lamp* Joan Ogden's heart warms to a canary. Like Joan Ogden, Marguerite trained her canary Pippin to put his beak between her lips and kiss her. To Visetti's annoyance, Pippin accompanied her everywhere. In one hotel, Alberto Visetti cruelly decreed that Pippin and his cage were an encumbrance and must be handed over to a hotel waiter. The child pleaded, the child entreated, there is every likelihood the child screamed. Visetti was implacable.

Marie was too indifferent to her daughter's welfare to oppose her new husband. The group moved out of the hotel minus Pippin.

Radclyffe Hall never forgot the misery of leaving her canary unprotected amongst strangers. Her fiction becomes a home for defenceless canaries, and powerless children attached to canaries. The story resurfaces first and most forcibly in *Michael West*. The child Michael is forced by his father to leave his first love, an older woman, Auntinot, who as a parting present gives him a canary. The car comes to fetch Michael and his mother. The mother is silent. The son clutches the canary.

> He must leave Auntinot because he was such a little boy too weak to protest. Why didn't Auntinot protest? He bumped the cage against the door. The bird fluttered in terror. In the midst of his misery he stooped to rescue it . . . he sat huddled up in his corner, the cage balanced perilously on his thin little knees.[8]

Auntinot and Michael are too weak to protest against his father's unjust action just as Nottie, Marie and Marguerite were powerless to protest against Visetti's ruthless behaviour. The Michael/Marguerite figure, frail and forlorn, cannot stand up to the hostile male forces ranged against them.

When the Visettis returned to London they set up at 14 Addison Road, Earl's Court, then a relatively salubrious area. They had a carriage and servants, paid for by Visetti, without scruple, from Marguerite's trust fund.

In the walled garden Alberto Visetti built a music studio, where he tutored singing pupils, most of them girls, all young, all attractive, several of whom lodged in the house. Marie Visetti, her jealousy constantly aroused, seethed at Marguerite as well as at Alberto. He too had an explosive temper. The discordance and detonation at Sunny Lawn were repeated at Addison Road. Hysterical scenes from a bad opera were transformed into savage brutalities. Marie hurled objects. Visetti beat her up. What started as local brawls erupted into warfare. Granny Diehl, older now, worn by the storms, was unable to protect the thin-legged asthmatic girl with shoulder-length blonde hair. Marguerite retreated with her scribbling book to the walled garden where she slunk in fear listening to their quarrels.

She had no friends. Desolate, she may have made some up. Certainly her early fiction suggests this strategy.

Like Marguerite, Michael West is 'strictly forbidden to make friends with other children'. He invents a chum called Daisy, the name Rat called Marguerite. On a walk with his nurse, Michael plays with Daisy. The nurse calls him a liar. The Michael/Marguerite figure 'ducked his head and bit his nurses hand . . . He yelled with . . . thwarted love. "Daisy, Daisy, I want Daisy, I do see Daisy."' His mother, like Marie Visetti, whips him to make him admit that Daisy doesn't exist. Stubborn like Marguerite, he says: 'I won't say there is no Daisy, because there is one. She's a little girl that wears a blue hair ribbon. She's pretty and . . .' Later when his special friend Auntinot says consolingly that she knows Daisy exists, he whispers tragically: 'She's not real. I just made her up because I was lonely. She's all a make-believe little girl. Auntinot, there is no Daisy.'

For the real Daisy there was no Michael. No friends at all. Instead, she turned to dogs for companionship. In later years, first with Ladye, then with Una, dogs symbolized home. Her first dog she immortalized in a childhood poem.

Marguerite wrote turbulently as a defence against the tensions. Like Sidonia in *A Saturday Life* and Millie Ogden in *The Unlit Lamp*, her talent manifested itself early: 'I must have been a tiresome baby and a disconcerting one, for one day when I was only three years old, I suddenly spurted a poem.'[9] Later, Radclyffe Hall recalled: 'Who can hope to explain an impulse that occurred at three years old except by saying whatever its origin it must have been fairly strong?'[10] Her poetic strength grew as she fought through the flurried years.

Although her social world was not especially literary it was musical. She was, she said, 'never able to write verse except at the piano, improvising a musical setting to my words'. Well-known composers told her later 'that they found my work unusually easy to set, owing to its musical rhythm'.[11] As she recalled: 'I could perhaps have made a musical career for myself as I was said to have a certain talent for composition. A very well known German conductor who heard some of my compositions urged me to go out to Germany to study with him. But at that time I was exceedingly lazy . . . unwilling to face the necessary grind.'[12]

The conductor was Arthur Nikisch who stayed with the Visettis. Despite Nikisch's enthusiastic approval, Albert Visetti, who as a professional music teacher might have encouraged his stepdaughter to take up the proffered musical training, chose to ignore any talent evinced by the young girl.

Religion as well as music consoled Marguerite. Marguerite's family – the Hall side – conservative and patriarchal, accepted without question the place of Anglicanism within their middle-class world. This formal commitment to religion with its possibility of heaven contrasted strangely with the hell on earth that was her home. She turned to her grandmother Sarah Diehl: 'To her I owe an early religious training of the kind that could only envisage God as love.'[13]

At Addison Road, however, love was largely absent. Living in frightening chaos, Marguerite hung on to the hope that inside some religion she might find routine and order. It was to Roman Catholicism with its ritual and mystery that she turned, being received into the Church ultimately in February 1912. It offered her a belief she never lost in a spiritual world that could give some meaning to the sufferings of the temporal one.

Her patchy education she received for the most part at the hands of indifferent governesses. A discontinuous home-based education was usual among middle-class young women of the period. Victorian convention allotted rational and analytic modes to men. Intuitive and sympathetic sensitivities were perforce adopted by women. If there was a life of the mind, generally that mind was male. It was young men who went off to prestigious schools and universities. When they returned, if they courted the few girls who had also gone to university, as Radclyffe Hall shows in her fiction, the men were often sardonic. As Lawrence Benson, who woos the Ogdens' governess, Cambridge graduate Elizabeth Rodney, says in *The Unlit Lamp*: 'Surely a woman doesn't need to go to Cambridge to be charming? Personally I think it's a great mistake this education craze.'[14]

In later years when her literary mentor-friends included the writers Violet Hunt, Ida Wylie, May Sinclair and Rebecca West, Hall became increasingly conscious that her education had been merely that of a well-bred lady within a restricted social world where intellectual freedom was reserved for men.

Nevertheless she draws affectionate and positive images of governesses, less for their intellectual capacities than for the comfort they offer her heroines. In *The Well of Loneliness* Stephen Gordon's first tutor, Mademoiselle Duphot, 'a youthful French governess with a long, pleasant face that reminded Stephen of a horse', is as academically inept as Nottie, 'so foolishly loving, so easily coerced'.[15]

Not so Stephen's second tutor, Miss Puddleton, known as Puddle, who used her eclectic array of knowledge to order Stephen's dishevelled, disorganized mind: 'Stephen found herself put into harness for the first time in her life, and she loathed the sensation'; but before long Stephen had the 'uncomfortable conviction that this queer little woman was going to mean something, was going to become a fixture'.[16]

Indeed she did. Radclyffe Hall modelled Puddle on her grandmother. Photographs of Sarah Diehl show her like Puddle as a little grey figure, 'square all over – square shoulders, square hips, a flat, square line of bosom; square tips to the fingers, square toes to the shoes, and all tiny; it suggested a miniature box that was neatly spliced at the corners.'[17] That box becomes Stephen's lifelong friend. Stephen felt what Marguerite felt: 'I can always be comfortable with you, Puddle . . . you're like a nice chair; though you are so tiny yet one's got room to stretch.'[18]

When Marguerite reached her teens, the ill-equipped tutors were superseded by attendance at several day schools, of which the best was Miss Coles' fashionable Kensington establishment. This school had numbered amongst its earliest pupils the Vanbrugh sisters Violet and Irene and Ellen Terry's daughter Edy Craig, who in the late thirties was to become one of John's closest friends. The school was attended also by Leonard Woolf's eldest sister Bella who recalled Marguerite visiting the Woolfs' house. There is a photograph of Marguerite taken at this time which shows her looking, as Bella Woolf remarked, like 'a regular society girl'.[19] This was Marie Visetti's aim as she forced her adolescent daughter into ruffles, soft draperies and plumed hats in the hope that she would resemble a Gainsborough lady.

After the nominal experience of school Marguerite went for a brief period to King's College, London, and then for a year to Dresden to study literature. Neither governesses, tutors, schools nor college made much impression on her early grasp of literature.

Nor was her atrocious spelling ever remedied. Internal evidence from *Michael West* intriguingly suggests that there may have been a psychological as well as a linguistic origin to her difficulties. Sarah West and Auntinot discuss the legal case against Richard, the Rat figure. Each time Michael tries to listen,

> the discussion . . . would be carried on in undertones, many of the words would be spelt out. How he hated this trick of spelling out words. It made him feel very small, very stupid and in the way. He could not spell most of the words. He felt very stupid, very small, not being able to spell the words that mattered.[20]

It is possible to see the effects of her hit-and-miss education on the style of her novels. Though they contain incisive psychological analysis, her style remains traditional. She adopts the Victorian and Edwardian novel formula not unlike her contemporaries John Galsworthy, Arnold Bennett or H.G. Wells. Previous literary critics[21] have pointed out that in a golden age of literary experimentation, Radclyffe Hall's prose is rarely given to metaphorical fireworks. Her style is nearer to Vita Sackville-West's (whose background was not dissimilar) than to Virginia Woolf's. That she substituted sturdy narrative structure and omniscient narrators for insurrectionary intellect was a choice not only related to the social values she inherited but one rooted in her early experience of exclusion from intellectual habits of mind. As a result Hall leant more heavily on solid classical structures.

Her need for solidity, for structure, is evident in every area of her life. This need was exacerbated when relations between Marie and Marguerite, already strained to breaking point, were 'intensified by the mother's suspicions that her daughter was not what she considered "normal"'.[22] Marie believed that Marguerite 'fell in love in turn with several of Visetti's pupils who were lodging in the house'.[23] She may have done so or she may have looked to them for the kindness and affection she did not receive from her mother. Whatever the case, Marie translated Marguerite's behaviour into suspected sexual 'deviance'. Her daughter did not behave like other daughters. Marie's 'initial dislike' was fanned by these suspicions to a 'blind fury' and Marie 'flew at her and tore her hat (and some of her hair with it) from her head'.[24]

Marie's qualms began during Marguerite's tomboy years, when Marguerite was ten or eleven. She may have confided her disquieting notions about her daughter's 'abnormal' attitudes to the man Radclyffe Hall later calls 'my disgusting old stepfather'.[25] If this were so, it may have had some bearing on Visetti's desire to 'normalize' his pretty young stepdaughter by making unwanted sexual advances to the child. It is also possible that the 'lecherous' Visetti, as Una describes him,[26] who regularly indulged in irresponsible affairs with the female students who lodged with them, merely transferred his advances to the young girl in his charge who was nearest to hand.

Exactly what these sexual advances were remains unclear. It is probable that they occurred first when she was about eleven, the time of the canary incident. In Una Troubridge's unpublished 'Letters to John' she records that her initial draft of her biography of Radclyffe Hall included a long description of the disturbing 'sexual incident' in young Marguerite's life at the hands of 'the disgusting old man' Alberto Visetti.[27] In later drafts and the published biography Una removed these passages. In letters to her dead partner written at the same time as the draft of her biography around 1947, she explained why:

> I have to rewrite and revise nearly forty pages of my book. I have deleted the sexual incident with the egregious Visetti lest we have psycho-analytic know-alls saying you [John] would have been a wife and mother but for the experience.[28]

Although Una decided to exclude the question of sexual abuse from her biography, in the Day Book and Journal she kept during Radclyffe Hall's life, she is unrestrained in her vituperations against Visetti. In 1936, when John and Una are still together, during John's affair with Souline, Una receives a letter from a potential biographer employed by Marie Visetti to help write a life of Alberto Visetti. Marie has suggested that John owed her career to the 'valuable early influence exercised by her distinguished stepfather'. Visetti's biographer is trying to elicit suitable anecdotes from Radclyffe Hall to confirm this influence. Una becomes apoplectic:

> The only suitable reply is to get Harold Rubinstein [their solicitor] to write an answer that John forbids any mention of her name in the proposed memoir . . . We cannot allow her to be made ridiculous in connection with *that dreadful cretinous lecherous old man*, or any lies to be published concerning his fictitious influence.[29]

In Una's 'Letters to John' she talks of the sexual incident as violent and frightening. Radclyffe Hall's own confidences reveal that her stepfather's swings from icy psychological indifference (as in the matter of her music) to heated physical approaches left her in a state of constant dread.

There are several photos of Marguerite taken with her stepfather during this period which illustrate what Una Troubridge calls 'the ill-treatment she suffered'.[30] There is 'a faded shiny carte-de-visite obviously taken to exploit the "paternal affection" of Alberto Visetti'. Una describes Marguerite as 'a very thin, bony little girl of about ten . . . with all the appearance of an unloved child, standing awkwardly beside the seated Visetti . . . the epitome of smug self-satisfaction and conceit'.[31] A slightly later photograph shows Marguerite 'shy and unhappy-looking at about eleven years of age standing beside her step-father'.[32]

It is possible to speculate at length about the type of abuse suffered by Marguerite which imprinted that melancholy upon her later years. There are clues enough in her essays and fiction themselves which can be supplemented in the light of what we know today about the psychopathology of child sexual abuse. But whatever Visetti did, Radclyffe Hall's writings suggest that it was his hands that stamped fear upon her mind. For the young Marguerite whose 'hands are just like Radclyffe's', hands began early to take on a sinister meaning. In her biography of Radclyffe Hall, Una Troubridge tells us that John always noticed hands. In every one of her novels there is some reference to a character's hands. It is probable that the observation and categorization of hands into 'beautiful' or 'disgusting' began when she felt Visetti's hands upon her.

In her early stories 'The Career of Mark Anthony Brakes' and 'The Woman in a Crêpe Bonnet' as well as in *Michael West* (early drafts of all three stories written between 1912 and 1915) there are repeated references to abusive male hands and coarse lips. The victims of the hands and lips are all powerless to help themselves. In one draft the lines run: 'He was disgusting. The blunt-fingered hands were disgusting. There were big red muscles on the hands that made one afraid.'[33] These lines resurface in several ways. Billings, a lodging-house keeper in *Michael West*, who becomes Mrs Billings the landlady in a later version, possesses 'one solitary yellow tooth and hands with big red muscles'. Young Michael is afraid of Billings and thinks 'Billings ought to be dead'. When Billings changes sex into Mrs Billings the narration moderates to 'Mrs Billings was so old she ought to be dead.'[34]

The same phrases reappear in the story 'The Woman in a Crêpe Bonnet'. The protagonist, a young man in his twenties, on trial for his life, has 'coarse lips' and 'one blunt-fingered hand' which has beaten a pregnant woman to death with a chair. Like Marguerite, 'she had been attacked when her physical condition precluded all possibility of self-defence'.

The red-muscled hands appear again in a much later novel, the unfinished *Emblem Hurlstone*. Here the young male narrator 'has always found something obscene in pain', especially his dying mother's pain. Emblem, who 'knows with a sense of shame' that he 'has wanted no other woman', fastens on his mother's once 'elegant perfectly modelled hands' now 'shrunken and pitifully ugly'. Hands for Emblem have always meant fear and death. Thus as the nurse comes to warn him that his mother's death is imminent 'he instinctively glanced at her hands. "I don't like those big red muscles of yours."' After his mother's death he becomes involved with Felia, an ugly young Polish woman. Something about her hands disturbs him. '"Why are you afraid of me?" Felia asks. "Is it because of my hands?" . . . "Is it because of my hands?" she repeats. He knows . . . the hands made him afraid.'[35]

In early notebooks there are further lines featuring struggles with hands that are as strong as steel girders: 'He caught the girl with hands that grew strong as steel girders and their strength was a terrible strength . . . She struggled wildly but he held on to her in an iron grip.' The comparisons are repeated in the early 'The Career of Mark Anthony Brakes' and the later 'Malise'.[36]

Mark Anthony Brakes is an ambitious American Negro lawyer who takes on the case of a poor white actress and then becomes besotted with her. He wins her case, proposes, and she repulses him for being 'a black nigger'. He uses his hands:

> With his hands outstretched, he found her, caught her to him, kissing her brutally on eyes, neck and lips. He gloated over her like a beast over its prey, grotesque and at the same time terrible, with a strength that was a terrible strength, forcing her roughly back on to the divan . . . She tried to scream, but he choked back her cries. She struggled fighting wildly, but he held her in an iron grip.[37]

In 'Malise', written around the time of *The Well of Loneliness*, the sexual encounter has changed from a heterosexual to a lesbian one: 'She caught the girl to her crushing her roughly in strong peremptory arms so that Pamela had some ado not to wince because of the pain of that crushing . . . The arms that held her grew strong as steel girders and their strength was that terrible strength . . .'[38]

Later in the story Malise describes that love as lust, as 'their grosser passion'. In this story we are offered evidence that her physical and spiritual violation by her stepfather, together with the deep-rooted effects of her parents' violent marriage, gave her an adolescent picture of heterosexual sex as little more than animal lust.

It is the view she projects back in time when she rewrites her conception as 'rather dreadful, a night of physical passion and then me created solely of bodily desire, of an animal impulse and nothing more'.[39] This is the view she projects forward into her early story, 'The Lover of Things' (written in 1924 but not published until 1934), in which Mrs Dobbs reflects on the late Mr Dobbs: 'Don't talk to me about men, dirty, stinkin' 'ounds, we all knows what they wants when they comes round a woman . . . it's always the same.'[40] The view reappears in *The Unlit Lamp*, written in 1922 and published in 1924, as Mrs Ogden recalls her wedding night: 'She shuddered . . . It had not been her night, but all James's, a blurred and horrible experience filled with astonished repugnance.'[41]

What is missing from all these early accounts of 'love' between men and women is the spiritual dimension. Imagining her parents' sexual intimacies, she pronounces: 'I cannot believe that those parents of mine can ever have known the love of the spirit.'[42]

After her first few casual love affairs in her twenties, Marguerite's own physical passions for women surged and intensified, often so fiercely that she later described her 'poor exasperated physical body' as 'too tormented'.[43] Yet alongside this erotic intensity grew an increasing need to establish a spiritual dimension to sex. Even in her most tumultuous love affair, with Evguenia Souline in the last nine years of her life, John insists, in letter after letter, that her love 'goes far beyond the body'.[44]

The evidence we have of Marguerite's early environment gives us an alarming picture of a violently disturbed family where the child experiences several kinds of trauma and is at inordinate risk. Lifelong suffering can occur when the trauma is inflicted by those on whom the child is dependent and from whom the child cannot escape.[45] Some children, like Marguerite, blaming themselves, make excuses for those who have abused them; some even protect them, as she was to continue to protect both her mother and stepfather till late in her life. Like many incest survivors,[46] Radclyffe Hall in adulthood felt more sympathy for her father than for her mother.

The psychological effects of abuse on her were typical: extreme nervousness, outbursts of wild temper, feelings of restriction, fears of being out of control, a sense of dread, usually a fear or belief that the self has been lost, and often the need to recapture an authentic identity by an ambitious drive to greater and greater efforts accompanied by a feeling of wonder or disbelief at the achievement attained.

Lost innocence, the search for a lost self, the need for an authentic identity are recurring motifs in Radclyffe Hall's fiction. In her novel-writing period from 1924 onwards she drove herself relentlessly, often writing for long periods throughout the night. She frequently expressed amazement at her literary success to her cousins Jane Caruth and Winifred Macey and even to her partner Una. Her attempts to control a shaky world can be seen in her compulsive drawing up of lists, itineraries, schedules all with carefully wrought back-up clauses; her repeated instructions to others, her peremptory letters to agents and publishers with detailed warnings and advice; her fear, at all times, of letting the reins out of her hands.

Abuse and beatings similar to those experienced by young Marguerite were of course not uncommon in the early twentieth century[47] any more than they are today. The important difference however was that a greater wall of silence surrounded the subject. This was possibly one reason why Una Troubridge elected to delete forty pages dealing with it from her biography that today stands at a mere 190 pages.

Una gives readers a second reason. She explains the deletion by saying that she did not want readers to think that John's inversion – the term used for male and female homosexuality at this period – was a consequence of those dreadful acts in her childhood. In her Foreword she pronounces: 'I have decided . . . to tell the truth, the whole truth and nothing but the truth.' However when she reaches the point, 'His [Visetti's] marriage to her mother, even apart from such incidents as I have already mentioned, was a disastrous affair for John,'[48] she breaks off and gives us less than the whole truth, deciding that such an admission might be dangerous to Radclyffe Hall's stance on the genesis of inversion. Una Troubridge took great pains to promote the ideology of the born lesbian which Radclyffe Hall had made her *cause célèbre*.

Today in an era of gay liberation and lesbian and feminist studies one viewpoint is that all human beings are potentially bisexual, that homosexuality is not an aberration, and that cultural or religious strictures and taboos against different forms of sexual expression at different times shape the subjectivity and complexity of sexuality. Today for instance one can ask whether there is such a thing as gay sensibility, or in what way literature such as Hall's signifies sexual difference. Though some scholars suggest that some 'choices' such as heterosexuality are no more natural than homosexuality but have merely been given a desirable, normative status – an interpretation which allows us to believe that lesbianism can be 'chosen' and is not deviant – the 'causes' of sexual identity are still debated.

Radclyffe Hall herself thought that most people were at least potentially bisexual (at one point she suggests to Souline that Souline may be so). As Joanne Glasgow confirms in her Introduction to *Your John*, Radclyffe Hall believed that the congenital invert was defined not by mannish dress styles or behaviour but by the object of her desire. Thus Radclyffe Hall who had always been attracted to women, and professed erotic feelings for them, defined herself as an invert. Even though Una had been married and had a child, because she told John she had never felt sexual desire for men, in John's view Una also was a congenital invert.[49]

Hall was however fully aware of alternative views held by some of her lesbian friends, and incorporated these into her books. Her writing is both a reflection and an expression of social attitudes about inversion as well as about individual sensibilities. A literary study of a writer who was an invert will both invite such questions of definition and identity as well as throwing up the issue of the extent to which sexuality is the product of social forces.

In Radclyffe Hall's own era, two sets of theories were running in parallel, both of which Radclyffe Hall was aware of. The sexologists' viewpoint, enunciated by Havelock Ellis and Richard von Krafft-Ebing (Radclyffe Hall's 'experts'), that sexual inversion was innate and congenitally tainted, was counterbalanced by the idea held by several of Hall's friends, including the

Australian writer Ida Wylie, the American writer Natalie Barney and the painter Romaine Brooks, that lesbianism might entail problems but could be a guilt-free choice.

Radclyffe Hall came increasingly to believe in the idea of the born lesbian who bears the mark of Cain,[50] but it is arguable that she promoted this view as a more expedient method of winning sympathy for her cause. Given this, it becomes easier to understand why Una decided to tamper with the truth.

Obviously lesbianism is not rooted in a single cause. It is a complex phenomenon made up of environmental, physiological, psychological, volitional and emotional elements. What can be said is that sexual abuse from her stepfather and physical violence both from her mother and between her parents would have been unlikely to persuade young Marguerite that heterosexual sex was warm, loving and spiritual. Such a home life might well have encouraged her to seek the affectionate attentions of older, motherly women, attentions she never received from her own mother.

Marguerite's grandfather's legacy confirmed her sense that affection came in funds. Her father's legacy was the notion of parental love as remote, romanticized or in abeyance. Alberto Visetti, her repulsive stepfather, bequeathed her a legacy of pain. In the broadest sense, the Fathers (absent, dead or all too present) influenced her formative years in ways that brought disruption, disgust and disarray. That Radclyffe Hall uses those legacies in her fiction with courage and compassion indicates her remarkable strength of will.

Male hands had harmed her. It was not surprising that when she first fell in love it was with a voice – a woman's voice. The voice of Agnes Nicholls.

3

RENAMING LOVE

In a world threatened by physical touch, a voice could feel safe. Curiously, Marguerite heard the beautiful abandoned notes of the Voice before she met its owner. Agnes Nicholls was an exceptional singing student to whom Alberto Visetti had awarded a scholarship to enter the Royal College of Music in 1894; there she had won the prestigious Dove Prize. She practised in Visetti's garden studio.

Marguerite began to idolize the unknown soprano, listened for her step down the garden, read her reviews in the *Musical Times* which quickly established Agnes as a young woman with rare musical expression and amazing promise.[1] It was a promise fulfilled when in 1900, her final year, Agnes, 'the most generally deserving pupil', was given the Gold Medal. The magazine *Opera* recalled her Royal College professors describing her fine musicianship, vivid imagination and great industry.[2]

Only a year after leaving college Agnes made her début at Covent Garden. '[Her voice] was unique, and once heard quite unforgettable; a strange blend of woman, choirboy and angel.' When years later Una Troubridge heard her she said: 'I cannot wonder that John, adolescent, intensely musical and emotional, listening day by day in her own home to the gradual evolution of this exquisite thing fell deeply in love with the voice and the singer.'[3]

Marguerite hankered for this 'exquisite thing' to be her friend. When the Visettis took Agnes on holidays, her hopes increased. Swiftly Marguerite became an ardent votary to a more than willing musical saint.

Agnes, though only three years older than Marguerite (who at the height of her passion was seventeen), was infinitely more confident and self-possessed, thoroughly aware of her talent and her emotional power. Her driving ambition ensured an immediate success on the concert circuit; but it was a detailed regime and it was Marguerite who saw to its details: she was always good at these. If the singer's career demanded soft scarves for the throat to block out the wind, inhalers for the larynx at the slightest whiff of soreness, empathy for a difficult musical score, enthusiasm when she brilliantly overcame it, above all consistent support, Marguerite could provide it. The future prima donna insisted attention must be paid. Marguerite paid it. She became for a time less an equal companion than handmaiden to Agnes's gracious goddess.

Their combined efforts paid off. Agnes, with Marguerite's support, attracted public notice and prestigious reviews.[4] Marguerite's love was both self-sacrificial and romantic. Idolization of Agnes acted like a light breaking through her childhood melancholy. Suddenly sunshine filtered through the shadows of sombre Addison Road.

For several years Marguerite, taken out of herself for the first time to a new enchanted place, 'worshipped and served and followed that voice to and fro on the initial stages of a big career. Wherever engagements in opera, concerts or oratorio took the young singer, there also went John, listening, encouraging, sympathizing and adoring. Holding cloaks, mufflers, bouquets, gargles and inhalers; in hotels, lodgings, trains and dressing-rooms, her existence entirely regulated by the imperious demands of that wonderful voice.'[5]

In her first novel *The Unlit Lamp*, there is a wicked portrait of Agnes Nicholls in the character of Harriet Nelson, 'plump and pretty, with her red hair and blue eyes'.[6] Joan Ogden, the book's heroine, meets Harriet, an ambitious singing student at the Royal College of Music, who has a 'pure, sexless voice, the voice of an undreamt-of choir-boy or an angel'.[7] Joan Ogden watches the way Harriet is attended by the infatuated and nervous art student Rosie Wilmot who rushes around the star with inhalers and flowers just as Marguerite raced around Agnes.

Suddenly Rosie rebels and hurls a handkerchief at Harriet. The soprano loses her control, her temper and her unforgettable voice: '"Where's my inhaler?" she demanded.'[8]

Though Hall's portrait of Harriet sardonically captures Agnes's most irritating characteristics, it does not show us the depth of feeling Marguerite cherished for the older woman, nor the affectionate companionship that existed between them. In a sense they grew up together. Marguerite began to laugh where formerly she had moped. Under Agnes's tutelage she took an interest in composition and harmony, although she never learnt to transcribe music. When she composed verses to her own tunes, she still improvised at the piano. She began to write more poems in this haphazard fashion, many of which were later set to music by popular composers. But she never applied herself to the task in a way that would prevent her from attending to Agnes's career.

Marguerite's awareness of her forthcoming legacy left her free to write poetry for pleasure and to offer her precious friend her commitment. Though not a sexual attachment, sensual it certainly was. Marguerite, slowly recovering from her harsh physical experiences, needed a relationship of high romance. She found solace and sensuality in ministering to Agnes's needs.

To understand Marguerite's intense first love for Agnes, we must turn to *The Well of Loneliness* where we find feelings of infatuation, yet more than that, feelings of joy. Here Stephen Gordon is only seven when she is swept away by an inexplicable emotion for Collins, the pert and rounded housemaid. Pink and plump, rosy and rounded female figures appear many times in Hall's fiction. Such was the Collins/Agnes type that regularly attracted Marguerite: broad face, sensual mouth, body ranging from statuesque to plump and comely. The hands would be exquisite, the touch gentle. These would be energetic, adventurous women who laughed a lot.

Collins was chubby, Agnes statuesque and ample; Collins a servant, Agnes a singer. Yet the two, in their physical effect on Marguerite and her heroine Stephen, were remarkably similar. In the novel Stephen, a sturdily honest child, rebukes Collins for telling a lie:

> Collins suddenly stooped and kissed her. Stephen stood speechless from a sheer sense of joy . . . At that moment she knew nothing but beauty and Collins, and the two were as one, and the one was Stephen – yet not Stephen either, but something more vast, that the mind of seven years found no name for.[9]

It is the lack of names that interests Radclyffe Hall, as it had been the wordlessness that had confirmed Marguerite's passion for Agnes. When Stephen Gordon thinks about Collins, 'she could never quite put [it] into words'.[10]

At this point in Marguerite's life she was desperate for comfort, for excitement, for a spiritual love, and what she sought in Agnes Nicholls was a mentor, as she had sought it in vain when younger from her governesses. It was that disciple–leader aspect of her relationship with Agnes that gave rise to the many mentor characters in her early fiction.

In her novel *A Saturday Life* young Sidonia, the fatherless child with Marguerite's artistic precociousness, searches for help in dealing with her strange problem of being both victim as well as creator of her wild impulses towards singing, dancing, sculpting. In adolescence Sidonia receives sage advice from her mother's lesbian companion, the remarkable Frances Reide. Frances nurtures Sidonia's talent, keeps her sane and briefly opens up Sidonia's inclinations towards same-sex affections. Later Sidonia turns for guidance instead to the hunchbacked Elinar Jensen, sculpting teacher at the Royal College of Art. Jensen is not merely the male mentor Marguerite did not have, he is both Rat in gnome's clothing and Agnes in male attire.

The feelings engendered by the frightening absence in her childhood of a wise mentor-mother did not disappear but sent her in wild search of mothering from most of her intimates and lovers. At seventeen, in love with love as well as with Agnes, like Sidonia Marguerite was desperate to find an earth mother figure. Sidonia successfully locates one in Liza Ferrari, her singing teacher and mother of nine happy children.

Agnes however was no Liza. Agnes was too young, too intent on making her own way in the world, to fulfil the complicated needs of her myrmidon Marguerite. What she did offer was something which in later years Radclyffe Hall would consistently seek: a companionship that was never tedious.

Una Troubridge wrote of John that life with her was never dull. The singer Parry Jones later wrote of Agnes: 'She . . . never committed the unpardonable sin of being dull . . . There was no moping in her company.'[11] For young Marguerite who had moped more than was bearable for seventeen years this was a revelation.

During the next few years Marguerite rode horses, drove a car, began to drink (though only for excitement; it never became a habit). She thought of putting her poems into a collection. Below the surface, nameless emotions gathered. In a poem written during this period, 'From My Soul' (published in her first volume *'Twixt Earth and Stars* in 1906), she attempts to describe these as yet unnamed desires.

> O! But to have the gift to put in words
> That potent passion, that divine desire,
> That thrills the aching spirit with unrest
> And sets the brain on fire . . .

Although technically of little interest, the poem sums up unnamed passions which Marguerite was to feel for several women (perhaps more than the countable number on record) in the next few years. It also adumbrates two other significant themes which continue to dominate her work: the struggle to 'rise above the flesh' during moments of passion, and the necessity to 'realize ourselves', to act in harmony with our underlying nature.

Agnes was either indifferent or too self-protective to view Marguerite's hidden feelings closely. She had left the Visettis, was a public performer, she was on her way. That way was to include men and marriage. It was not to be Marguerite's way. The two grew apart; they parted; the romantic fever was over. A few years later Agnes married the conductor-composer Hamilton Harty.

Though Marguerite's first love did not last more than a few years, for 'the Lord had not designed [her] to be a satellite',[12] Marguerite and Agnes never entirely lost touch. Agnes 'always remembered John with affection' and remained 'a great admirer of her work'.[13] As an established writer, Hall attended Agnes's concerts at regular intervals. When Hall died, Una Troubridge invited Agnes to sing the solo at her Requiem Mass. Agnes agreed but suddenly became ill. She was able neither to perform at nor attend an occasion which for her would have held mixed emotions. Regret, even guilt, it appears, were amongst those feelings.

Agnes, by then Lady Harty, wrote to Una and 'waxed eloquent on her brutal treatment' of Visetti's stepdaughter during her stay in their household,[14] yet brutality was not the impression Marguerite was left with. Agnes had been her first friend, as well as her first love. For Radclyffe Hall, friendship like love was 'no ordinary thing'. In *The Unlit Lamp*, Joan Ogden thinking about her tutor Elizabeth Rodney knows that friendship like love can give two people a 'new-found intimacy' in which 'something was lost and something gained'.[15] In Hall's determination to stay friends with her former lovers she has much in common with contemporary lesbians, who often integrate ex-lovers into a new extended family.

Half-consciously Marguerite and Agnes had modelled their relationship on the acceptable romantic friendships between women common in the second half of the nineteenth century and the start of the twentieth. These relationships were loving, devoted and generally not viewed as genital or deviant. In an intriguing essay which appeared in a Vermont newspaper in 1843, American author William Cullen Bryant described in glowing terms a 'female friendship' between two maiden ladies who when young had probably felt the same romantic passion as Agnes and Marguerite but who had let it strengthen into a daily commitment.

> In their youthful days, they took each other as companions for life, and this union, no less sacred to them than the tie of marriage, has subsisted . . . for 40 years, during which they have shared each other's occupations and pleasures and works of charity while in health, and watched over each other tenderly in sickness . . . They slept on the same pillow and had a common purse, and adopted each other's relations, and . . . I would tell you of their dwelling encircled with roses . . . and I would speak of the friendly attentions which their neighbors, people of kind hearts and simple manners, seem to take pleasure in bestowing upon them.[16]

What is apparent from this example and hundreds of others now documented by social historians is that women's intimate relationships, when similar to Agnes and Marguerite's, were positively encouraged in centuries previous to our own, most assuredly during Radclyffe Hall's childhood and adolescence. Certain restrictions, however, were placed on these friendships. Should two women who felt like Marguerite and Agnes wish to pursue their attachment by forming an established ménage, they had to remember three caveats: first, that if an eligible male appeared he must not be discouraged but must be integrated alongside the women's friendship; secondly, that two women in love were not expected to try and find employment to support their relationship; thirdly, that as such a relationship was not perceived by the outside world as erotic, the two women concerned must take great care not to indicate that it was. Given these restrictions, intimate, exclusive, discreetly erotic relations between white middle and upper class women were perceived as 'normal' and compatible with heterosexuality in Anglo-European culture.

If such a description of love between two women (sleeping on the same pillow, no less!) had been published in an American or English newspaper during or after Radclyffe Hall's late twenties, the Editor's desk would have overflowed with correspondence about immorality. As Lillian Faderman points out, the two women would probably have had to sue Bryant for defamation to clear their good names.

Marguerite's relationship with Agnes was socially acceptable according to the conventions of romantic friendship current at the time, no matter what sensual or sexual activities took place, but by the time of her relationship with Ladye important changes had occurred in the depiction and classification of same-sex friendships between women. Their relations were now open to the charge of physical eroticism and hence 'abnormality'.

Whether romantic friendships such as Agnes and Marguerite's in the early 1900s were 'sexual' has recently been a matter of much debate. Although Lillian Faderman initially suggested that women probably did not have sex with each other before this century,[17] the publication in the late 1980s of the journals of Yorkshire estate owner Anne Lister (1791–1840) showed that this belief was unfounded. Anne Lister was clearly having full physical relations with women in the eighteenth and early nineteenth century; her diaries of her romantic and sexual relationships with other women (once decoded and published) offer unmistakable accounts of physical expressions of passion.

Though Agnes and Marguerite kept no diaries, and may not have named the erotic undercurrents which gathered between them, in the outside world their kind of love was being renamed. The medical theories of five key sexologists[18] who attempted to map human sexuality profoundly influenced Radclyffe Hall's literary portrayals, though she was not as uncritical of such theories as has been suggested. Radclyffe Hall drew on the first volume of Havelock Ellis's *Studies in the Psychology of Sex*, published in 1897 (at the time of her passionate attachment to Agnes), for her portrait of Stephen Gordon. This medical colonization of sexuality, in which new terms were coined classifying people as 'normal' or 'abnormal' according to their sexual inclinations, was a move towards the pathologization of same-sex desire. She used Krafft-Ebing and Ellis's belief that homosexuality was inborn, together with Hirschfeld and Carpenter's notion of a Third Sex, because it suited her literary purposes. The consequence of the sexologists' work was that people began to see homosexuality and lesbianism as diseased. Same-sex relationships like that between Agnes and Marguerite, hitherto labelled romantic friendship, were renamed 'inversion' and viewed as perverse. Though lesbianism had suddenly become more visible it could now be castigated, as Radclyffe Hall would dramatically discover.

While the renaming of friendships between women was going on in the world outside, in Marguerite's own emotional life from 1901 similar changes were occurring. With the departure of Agnes romantic friendship had run its course. From her early poems and later letters it seems that her next two relationships with her cousins Jane and Dolly focused on physical passion.

Again the power that came to Marguerite with money gave her the confidence to act on those desires. At her coming-of-age on 12 August 1901 she inherited her grandfather's fortune. Quarrels with her mother and stepfather had escalated. The final row before Marguerite's departure came when Mr Hastie, her solicitor, told her to her horror that the Visettis had illegally overspent her maintenance allowance by a gigantic £12,000. Marie Visetti's substitute for an explanation was another towering rage.

With an eye to sanity and self-preservation, Marguerite moved out of Addison Road and took a lease on a house in Campden Hill Terrace in Kensington. Aware that she needed a chaperone, and fearing for her beloved Granny Diehl's safety in the Visetti household, she invited her grandmother to live with her. In the same period she used her new funds to purchase the lease on Highfield, a grandly gabled country house in the Worcestershire village of Malvern Wells.

A new pleasure-loving stage of her life opened out, though one only sketchily documented. Radclyffe Hall never kept a journal and if during this time she wrote personal letters, few have survived. Given the life she had been forced to lead at Addison Road, her need now for privacy is easily understood. Marguerite spent her days

> as soon as she became mistress of her own time, in pleasure; in hunting, travelling, writing an occasional poem, in entertaining and being entertained. And periodically from the age of seventeen and onwards, falling in and out of love. She was exceedingly handsome, had plenty of charm, plenty of intelligence, plenty of money, no education to speak of and was out exclusively to enjoy herself and give others a good time. She systematically over-smoked, anything and everything, including green cigars.[19]

Cigarettes and horses became her addictions. Smoking she never gave up. The addiction grew stronger when she began to write novels. In later years she would sit at her American roll-top desk smoking her words out, far into the night.

From 1900 to 1907 hunting was a major preoccupation. Before she purchased Highfield with its spacious stables, she would hunt near Ledbury and need looseboxes. One night, staying at the Feathers, she asked where they could be obtained. She was directed to Colonel Llewellyn who not only provided looseboxes but also companionship in the form of his two daughters Margaret, known as Peggy, and Maud. From 1905 Peggy Llewellyn (who five years later married Harold Austin), initially a nurse, later an inspector of governesses, became Marguerite's close friend. Radclyffe Hall used Peggy's maiden name for her heroine Mary Llewellyn, the lover of Stephen Gordon in *The Well of Loneliness*. Peggy came frequently to Highfield and helped with Marguerite's five horses.

Rafferty, Stephen's beloved horse in *The Well of Loneliness*, was modelled on Joseph, Marguerite's favourite hunter, whom she nursed through injuries until old age, when he had to be shot in her presence. In the novel where she describes how Rafferty is shot, Marguerite's fervent attachment to Joseph is illustrated with exquisite compassion.

Though established in Malvern Wells and in London, Marguerite was suddenly seized with a surge of Rat's restlessness. She felt driven to go abroad, to visit her unknown Diehl relatives in the United States. This was a pattern she would repeat endlessly and reflect on in her fiction. Hilary and Susan Brent in *The Forge* constantly move between city and country, England and Europe. Once established in a new home, they would renovate it, furnish it, love it, then leave it. During John's long partnership with Una, they would fix on an uninspiring country house, transform it to idyllic proportions, become disenchanted, then move to town. Two years later the town house would be sold, cities deemed polluted, a return to nature re-envisaged. 'Something in the climate, or something in a book . . . awakens the wanderlust . . . things not yet known, even further afield' beckoned and tormented Marguerite.[20]

At this first beckoning, still tormented in her twenties, Marguerite visited America and stayed for a year, mainly in Washington, where she was captivated by her Diehl cousin Jane Randolph, a widow ten years older than herself. Jane, who had Agnes's laughter and zest for life, with the sexual sophistication of an older woman, was a descendant of their great-grandmother Jane Jones, Elijah's wife, and the daughter of Albert Diehl, Sarah's brother. She had two small sons Thomas and Decan and a young daughter Winifred. Marguerite saw Jane as 'a plain young woman with projecting teeth but with a perfect figure, lovely hands and feet and masses of long and beautiful auburn hair'.[21]

Marguerite's own hair at the time was ash-blonde, fine as silk, down to her knees but worn in a coil on the top of her head twisted under a jaunty male hat. She was a gallant, ready for adventures in a foreign country. Jane, who was not short of admirers of both sexes, was delighted to provide them. She encouraged Marguerite to smoke small green cigars and to drink, often to excess. On one memorable bender, the cousins spilled out from a Christmas feast drunk on champagne and collapsed giggling into the frosty night air. Jane shrieked: 'I want to schlide!' Helpless with laughter she slid with such catastrophic results that Marguerite, whose 'head of iron' survived the champagne somewhat better, had to carry her home, tiptoeing with her silently past the bedroom door of her cousin's prim mother.[22]

Those were wild and wonderful days. She loved a woman more daring than herself, eager to love and dare in return. The two women left Jane's unruly children with the prim mother in Washington while they embarked on an escapade in an antediluvian jalopy for a tour of the Southern states. Marguerite drove furiously, her eyes not always on the road ahead. Much of the time she watched Jane's exquisite hands. One clutched a revolver, the other held tight to Charlie, the fierce bull-terrier, in case they met 'obstreperous negroes'. Those 'lovely hands', erotically outstretched towards her, remained in Marguerite's memory. Una described Jane as a 'hard-going, reckless and somewhat fickle but loyal-hearted seductress'.[23] Seduction is Una's interpretation. Evidence suggests that the sexual sprees of their salad days were mutually entered into and mutually enjoyed.

Una acknowledges that though Marguerite embarked on several sexual escapades, Jane's loyal heart captured Marguerite's 'at that time rather volatile fancy' and held it 'through various vicissitudes for several years'.[24] Her loyalty was displayed when she accompanied Marguerite into hospital for the removal of an impacted wisdom tooth. She occupied an emergency cot in her cousin's room 'with a devotion undeterred by the acute sickness' that was always Marguerite's reaction to anaesthetics.[25]

After a year in the States, Marguerite became homesick for England and returned to London bringing Jane and the boisterous trio to live with her grandmother at Campden Hill Terrace. Characteristically protective, she paid all the Randolphs' bills, as Rat had done for his mistress in London.

> It never seems to have struck John that she took over a heavy burden in assuming complete financial responsibility for an impecunious young widow and three children . . . the story of her friendship with Jane Randolph-Caruth shows that this was an early and fundamental characteristic . . . responsibility once assumed, it was never in any circumstances repudiated.[26]

That responsibility only ended when Jane returned to America for a visit, met a wealthy Texan called Harry Caruth and remarried. It is likely that her relationship with Marguerite cooled before her departure abroad. Their needs were conflicting. Marguerite, independent, rich, erotically charged, too head-strong and mercurial to care about her 'reputation', was enchanted by desire and diversion. Jane as a mother with no independent means was looking for a secure and respectable future.

As with Agnes, however, so with Jane. The loving was over but solid bonds of affection remained. For many years she corresponded intimately with Jane, and later with Jane's daughter Winifred and her elder son Decan who visited John at Cadogan Court during the First World War. John was supportive when Jane's younger son Thomas died in childhood, and when Jane became widowed for the second time. During this period Jane visited John and Una at their first home, Chip Chase in Hadley Wood. Una's statement that John 'was quite unable to like her' has to be viewed with caution since she also admits that Jane 'definitely disliked me [Una] and, incredible as it seemed after so many years, resented my existence'.[27]

It seems less incredible if we begin to glimpse the fascination and fireworks sparked off by this heady, handsome, wealthy young woman. Marguerite's pyrotechnical presence attracted other women towards her. Sometimes years after the original romance had broken up or had been transformed, they were still bewitched, often devoted, occasionally jealous. Marguerite in return, having forged a sensual or sexual bond, would commit herself to a passionate attachment which she saw as lasting throughout this life and into the hereafter. As a result she found herself not infrequently in complex triangular situations where boundary lines became blurred and she became unsure exactly where her love and loyalty lay.

This blurring of lines showed itself in her next affair, with her cousin Dorothy (Dolly) Diehl. Marguerite met Dolly during her second visit to America. She was the only daughter born to Marie Visetti's brother William in 1887. This American cousin, unlike Jane and Agnes, was seven years younger than Marguerite. This allowed Marguerite to protect as well as desire her.

Like Agnes, Dolly was 'plump and very pretty in a blue-eyed, golden-haired, pink and white style suggestive of the Dutch maiden of the musical comedies of our youth. She certainly had a charming mouth with deeply indented up-turned corners and an infectious smile.'[28] When she finally met her, Una admitted: 'I thought her very amusing; but her wit had a cutting edge to it and her nature a crudity that was revealed in the coarsest hands I ever remember seeing on any woman.'[29]

Ambivalent feelings about Dolly doubtless underlay Una's cutting remark about the hands. Marguerite herself seems to have taken those hands in hers and for the first time seized the initiative in a love affair. She led Dolly in crazy capers across the States for several months, then suggested that her cousin accompany her back to England. Did Dolly settle down too quickly, too comfortably, with Marguerite and her grandmother initially at Campden Hill Terrace then at Albert Gate, Kensington, when they moved? Did Dolly acquiesce too easily in Marguerite's decision to become financially responsible for all her outgoings? It is hard to escape Una Troubridge's peevish depiction of Dolly as a manipulative, mercenary young woman to whom Marguerite gave 'a good deal, both morally and financially, and received in return not even elementary gratitude or loyalty'.[30] But this may well not have been the whole story. Una's habit when describing other women who were important in John's life was to cast them in the role of mercenary ingrates. We must not forget Marguerite's domineering ways with money and her insistence on acting the protector. In Dolly's case her youth and Marguerite's high-handed nature would be enough to account for the resettling of Dolly in the London home.

After the affair had run its course and Dolly, like Jane and Agnes, had married, she became in effect Marguerite's closest friend. At the start their relationship seems to have been sexually exciting, though perhaps not as stable as Marguerite needed, for her energetic young cousin kept her eyes open for other possibly more lasting partners. It did however allow Marguerite during this period to write a considerable number of love lyrics, many of them entitled simply: 'To . . .' – the discreet titles indicating that they were written for one (or more) special lovers whose names go unacknowledged and whose sex remains invisible. One love lyric, not published until her second volume *A Sheaf of Verses*[31] but written at this time, is entitled 'To My Little Cousin'. Several early poems devised while Marguerite and Dolly were in the throes of their unclouded love affair describe a fulfilled lesbian passion, in which two people are a 'complete glorious living whole'.[32] This theme was a constant poetic and later fictional strain of Radclyffe Hall's, but if it voiced Marguerite's hope for her relationship with Dolly, it failed. The younger cousin met and became attracted to Robert Coningsby Clarke, a talented composer in his twenties, who was later to set many of Marguerite's poems to music and help her establish herself as a lyricist.

Clarke, who had studied law at Trinity College, Oxford, where he had been chapel organist, and who started his musical career as an articled student to Sir Frank Bridge at Westminster Abbey, was to become one of the best known composers of light music of his day. His music and his personality excited Dolly. She shifted her erotic attention from the wealthy young woman to the impoverished young man. Marguerite's lyrics begin to speak of unrequited love. A poem called 'Dissatisfaction' suggests:

> Our love is near akin unto regret,
> We love, and are beloved again, and yet
> There oft is something that we lack.[33]

The shadow of sadness tinges many of the love poems. Human love is seen as less substantial than the beauty of landscape or nature.

In the summer of 1906 Radclyffe Hall's first volume of poems *'Twixt Earth and Stars* was published by John & Edward Bumpus. A few months later in 1907 Dolly, now twenty, told Marguerite of her passion for Bobby. As Dolly and Bobby were young and impecunious John 'helped the course of what she was assured was true love to run more smoothly by supplying an allowance which was continued for many years'.[34] When years later Dolly and Marguerite's friendship came to grief, that allowance was curtailed. Once again the characteristic manner in which Marguerite deployed her funds shows both her enormous protective generosity and her tendency to use money as a means of control. Heart strings and purse strings were umbilically linked.

Initially her own wealth financed her writing. She paid for the publication of *'Twixt Earth and Stars* herself. This first volume is dedicated to 'My Inspiration', a self-revealing phrase for the poems had indeed been written only when the mood took her. She was not yet a dedicated professional. Nor at this time did she document her literary development as did many of her contemporaries including Violet Hunt, May Sinclair and, later, Virginia Woolf. For a self-appraisal of this first publication we have to turn to her fiction.

> He supposed that had he not come into so generous an income when he was twenty-one, he might have made more of his talent for writing. As it was he had done very little. A few slight books of his poetry had been published and well received, presumably on their merits, since he knew no literary critics. Still, he had never been recognised as a poet of any importance, perhaps he wasn't worth it!

The self-deprecatory words are Hilary Brent's, the writer hero of *The Forge*.[35] The analysis of her art is Radclyffe Hall's. She is correct that the poems (some pastoral lyrics which echo A.E. Housman; some, the more successful, ballads easily set to music) were slight. However it was also true that the reviews were highly favourable, a first indication that Marguerite Radclyffe-Hall might be able to make her way in literary society.

According to the *Publisher and Bookseller* the volume had 'considerable merit'.[36] *The Lady* informed readers that Marguerite Radclyffe-Hall had 'real talent',[37] while *Queen* magazine singled out her felicitous gift for phrasing and her exceptional feel for rhythm.[38] Her rhythmic sense brought further rewards. The popular song market suddenly took notice of her. Several poems from *'Twixt Earth and Stars* were set to music by well-known composers.[39] Marguerite and Bobby began a successful musical collaboration. It was Bobby's way of acknowledging the usefulness of the allowance Marguerite afforded them.

In 1909, Bobby Clarke married Dolly at St Paul's Church, Knightsbridge, with Marguerite as witness. Dolly, like Jane and Agnes, entered the fashionable conformist world of matrimony with its inevitable dependence on men.

It was time for Marguerite to meet independent women like herself. Women interested in art, music, writing and personal freedom. Freethinkers who knew that women needed marriage for the societal status it gave them, for the financial protection it offered them, but who were prepared to live outside that norm. Women who were bold enough to attempt socially unacceptable relationships and to write about them.

The first of these remarkable women was an immodest Violet.

PART 2

POETRY AND PASSION

1907–1916

4

THE SWEETEST VIOLET

The socially unacceptable interested Violet Hunt. She shared with Radclyffe Hall an understanding of the role of the outsider. Like Radclyffe Hall, Violet Hunt has always been seen as scandalous. Both were outrageous and outspoken in their own time and are remembered for it in ours. Violet's attitude towards sex and marriage was seen as shocking, as she wickedly flouted the codes of her class with a series of risqué affairs and 'improper' novels, which Marguerite had read before she met her.

Born in Durham on 28 September 1862, daughter of the painter Alfred Hunt, Violet was eighteen years older than Marguerite. In the year of Marguerite's birth she had been proposed to by the 26-year-old Oscar Wilde, who would later be Hall's hero. Wilde, who kept his preferred sexual passions discreetly concealed, called her 'the sweetest Violet in England', then dropped her when she returned his interest. On Wilde's defection, Violet abandoned her role as the 'sweetest Violet', launched herself into a series of discreditable liaisons, and earned herself the nickname of Violent Hunt.[1]

The elderly John Ruskin, who doted on schoolgirls,[2] became her literary mentor, as she was to become Marguerite's. The elderly Henry James rejected Violet's sexual overtures but became her friend. The 50-year-old landscape painter George Boughton, her father's friend, used Violet as a scantily clothed model when she was only twenty. Two years later, to her family's horror, they became lovers. When Boughton married, Violet, then twenty-eight, hastily consoled herself with another elderly suitor: the 56-year-old British consul at Oporto, Oswald Crawfurd, with whom she had à perilous affair and who infected her with syphilis. Violet's relationship with Crawfurd spanned the period of Marguerite's romance with Agnes. Violet's recovery took place during Marguerite's affairs with Jane and Dolly. When Marguerite returned to

London with Dolly, controversial and contradictory rumours about Violet reached her ears.

Those who were charmed by Violet told Marguerite she was the wittiest woman in London or that she was 'fashionable, brilliant, daring; a leading spirit . . . glamour personified'. Those who were not charmed told Marguerite she was a 'thin viperish looking woman with a long pointed chin'. Others in Marguerite's circle said Violet was 'coarse and plain with a skin like leather'. As Bobby Clarke began to court Dolly, Marguerite and Violet met. Marguerite *was* charmed. Indeed she was instantly attracted by this New Woman's badinage, bad behaviour and lovely appearance.[3]

Brigit Patmore drew a sympathetic portrait of Violet, who began to replace Dolly in Marguerite's affections: '[M]uch has been made of her [Violet's] malice, wit and cleverness, but very little of her good looks and strange pathos.'[4] It was the pathos and vulnerability beneath Violet's brittle veneer that had an impact on Marguerite, as such qualities always did.

As a girl Violet had consciously tried to model herself on Burne-Jones's paintings. It was a look Marguerite found erotically disarming. Violet's mouth had the fullness and fine moulding Marguerite celebrated in her fiction. Violet's auburn hair was fluffy, styled not unlike Dolly's, pulled back behind her ears but low on the forehead. Though her nose was pronounced, her eyes were beautiful and deeply challenging, 'a curious green colour' with perfect leaf-shaped lids.[5] From photographs I suspect Violet's hands would have endeared her to Marguerite.[6]

Their upbringing had certain similarities. But whereas Marguerite's background was musical, her new friend had been born into an artistic family with close connections among the Pre-Raphaelites – Holman Hunt, John Ruskin, Dante Gabriel Rossetti and Edward Burne-Jones.

Marguerite discovered that their mothers had certain traits in common. Violet's mother, the novelist Margaret Hunt, put her self-effacing husband Alfred Hunt and his landscape painting before the needs of her three daughters, just as Marie Visetti had put Alberto Visetti's needs before those of Marguerite. Like Marie Visetti, Violet's mother was a prudish parent who never talked of sexual matters. Like Marie Visetti, Margaret Hunt reared her daughter to think of sex with men as dirty. Both Marguerite and Violet recreated this notion in their fictions.

The young women's childhoods were both London-based, middle-class, somewhat haphazard, and attended by governesses and servants. Governesses feature as heroines in Violet's books as they do in Radclyffe Hall's. Though Violet spent longer at school than did Marguerite, she too learnt very little there. The education of both young women came largely from their extensive reading, but the books in Violet's home were of a high literary calibre and the company in which her family mixed was intellectual as well as artistic. Violet was a late starter like her friend. She too began as a precocious poet and turned herself into a novelist of note.

By the time of their meeting, when Marguerite was nearly twenty-six, Violet had already published a collection of short stories,[7] a translation and seven witty dramatic novels which focused on the conflict between women's desire for the status of marriage and their need for the independence achieved by men. Her shocking behaviour helped these stylish autobiographical novels to become best-sellers, just as Radclyffe Hall's outré appearance and habits were to help her own novels to success.

When Violet dissected the sexual politics behind her rackety relationship with Crawfurd in her daring novel *Sooner or Later: The Story of an Ingenious Ingenue*,[8] Somerset Maugham's review pointed out that Violet had 'explored undiscovered country'. As Violet Hunt explored the taboo area of a mistress's relationship with her male lover, so Radclyffe Hall would explore the taboo area of a woman's relationship with her female lover.

Violet and Marguerite had much in common in their contempt for established norms and their breathless excitement for life. When they met in 1906 Violet was still looking for a grand passion but was taking her writing very seriously. Marguerite's grand passion had not materialized, and she was still too hesitant (and still too rich) to dedicate herself to more than her second book of poems. She was ripe for a friend (or a partner) who shared her enthusiasms and could undertake her re-education.

Their friendship began through their shared interest in literature. Through Violet Marguerite met an increasing number of writers, editors and publishers. A particular friend of Violet's had been the poet Robert Browning whom she had met through her father, and to whose work she now introduced Marguerite. His poetry was to have a lasting effect on Radclyffe Hall. In 1910 Marguerite's *Poems of the Past and Present* reflected that interest. In 1914 she visited Florence where the Brownings had lived. In 1943 when she was dying she asked for the poems of Robert Browning and Elizabeth Barrett Browning to be read to her. In a semi-conscious moment she murmured that when she recovered she would like to write in Florence where her favourite poets had been so happy.

Marguerite and Violet discussed Violet's novels and Marguerite's poetry and early short stories. It is probable that Marguerite showed Violet some first drafts of her novel *The Cunninghams*, and there is evidence that they discussed the initial draft of her story 'The Woman in a Crêpe Bonnet'. Violet was Radclyffe Hall's first critical reader, and the first of her literary mentors to read that story in its final form some years later.

Both Radclyffe Hall's earliest stories and Violet Hunt's abrasive novel *The Workaday Woman*[9] illustrate the two women's preoccupation with the changing roles of women and men. Both of them despised the conventional depiction of 'feminine' women in literature. Violet's heroine Jehane Bruce in *The Workaday Woman* could almost have served as a model for Radclyffe Hall's Miss Ogilvy, Malise or Stephen Gordon, for Jehane is 'one of those women who ought to have been a man – a well known and puzzling breed'.[10] Both of them criticized the sexual mores of the period, which were becoming the focus of women's campaigns for reform prior to the First World War.[11]

In Hall's first draft of 'The Woman in a Crêpe Bonnet', her early suffering from male sex aggression is creatively wound into this story of a court case. A man with blunt-fingered hands stands trial for his life for attacking and murdering a woman pregnant with his child. Radclyffe Hall's description of the dying woman's defence of her attacker is a moving delineation of women's painful loyalty to their male abusers, a topic in the forefront of women's minds at the time.

The last years of the nineteenth and the first decades of the twentieth centuries 'witnessed a massive campaign by women to transform male sexual behaviour and protect women from the effects of the exercise of a form of male sexuality damaging to their interests'.[12] Key campaigners included suffragists and some lesbians such as Christopher St John, Naomi (Mickie) Jacob, Rachel Barrett and Mary Allen, who later became Radclyffe Hall's close friends. They were concerned with issues of child abuse and prostitution in which men were cast as sexual aggressors and women as their victims. Later, when Radclyffe Hall lived with Ladye, she too was to become involved with these issues.

At the time of her meeting with the more politically-conscious Violet, Marguerite was still filled with romantic notions, periodically falling in and out of love; but curiously, she appears to have given no hint of this to others. Violet's diary for 1906 records: 'Marguerite is a poet but she hasn't a bit of romantic feeling about her. Her heart only goes out to physical geography sort of things like sunsets and autumn tints.'[13]

Marguerite's heart however, unbeknown to Violet, was going out to her writer-friend. To Violet's surprise, romance swiftly superseded literary conversations. With characteristic determination Marguerite decided she wanted a more intimate relationship with Violet. While they were spending a weekend with mutual friends, Marguerite declared her love.[14] Violet was intrigued. Marguerite was passionate. Violet had spent many years in sexual experimentation, but it was a new experience to find herself desired by another equally audacious woman. She was flattered but initially hesitant: 'I lunched with Marguerite Hall and there is a coolness only because she loved me so hotly, poor darling. She was good to me.'[15]

Marguerite's goodness included extravagant protestations, letters of entreaty, expensive gifts. Violet thrived on Marguerite's attention just as Agnes had done. But although Violet saw herself as an emancipated woman who found marriageable men dull and stifling, nevertheless when her two younger sisters both married she suddenly felt overlooked rather than free. Despite her sharp feminist politics, Violet was beginning to contemplate the advantages of marriage. An affair with Marguerite would hardly aid that goal. She rebuffed her initial overtures: 'She [Marguerite] is so strong and has put it behind her and now like Rossetti's girl "Her eyes looked on me from an emptied heart" because my heart has never been full of her! She used to write and say that I erected a brick wall between her and me. "Why brick?" I would ask nervously.'[16]

Marguerite in fact had not put the idea of a love affair behind her. She invited Violet to Malvern. Violet accepted and the flirtation continued.

In 1906, in Malvern with Violet, Radclyffe Hall wrote a first draft of her series of Malvern poems which would be published in *A Sheaf of Verses*.[17] As she smoked and the two writers talked, the 'sweetest Violet' inspired Marguerite's muse:

> . . . And from my cigarette a little wreath
> Of memories to meet their fragrance went.
> It was an evening full of bygone things,
> That mingled with emotions newly born
> As night will ever clasp and kiss the dawn,
> And leave those kisses on her ardent wings.[18]

The ardent wings of newly born emotions both irritated and pleasured Violet. She recorded in her journal:

To Malvern with Marguerite Hall to her new house. I was tetchy about the food and gave myself airs of sultana. It is her fault for being so at my feet poor dear. She is a stately intent sort of body . . . I behave like a minx; shows how easily one is corrupted by adoration . . . I had the room next to Marguerite and she used to come and sit on my bed in the clearest and coldest Japanese kimono from Liberty's with a streak of blue on the collar and her fine sandy auburn hair in a plait. Marguerite *avant la faute* as I called her . . . she knew about OC [Oswald Crawfurd] for she told me once with an effect of temerity . . . something Mrs Call had said . . . 'What did Mrs Call actually say?' I pressed her. 'She said . . . she said that once . . . you made a great mistake!' That was all I could get out of Marguerite and I marvelled at the hypocritical English way of alluding to seduction.[19]

Marguerite had in fact been less allusive, and not a whit hypocritical, about her own proposed seduction of her friend. Among the precious gifts she gave Violet was a string of pearls. Initially Violet accepted the gift but resisted its erotic implications. In her diary she wrote: 'I wear a pearl necklace she gave me and [a friend] twits me and says I am wearing goods unpaid for [,] not the wages of sin.'[20]

Marguerite recorded the occasion in a poem called 'A Pearl Necklace':

Go, cold white pearls, with the luring eyes.
The woman is waiting who longs to win
But the rainbow light that within you lies,
But the soft cool touch of your satin skin.
You are undefiled, and the price of sin
Has passed you by . . .[21]

It seems highly likely that sometime later the pearls *were* paid for – at least once, and possibly twice on two separate trips, one to Grasmere and one to Edinburgh, where according to Violet's 1906 diaries they shared a bed as well as a bedroom. Marguerite felt a great need to express her affection physically. Violet was fascinated by sex and many of her relationships with men had been in the nature of sexual experiments. They were by then intimate with and fond of each other.

What they did or did not do in their shared bed and bedroom is of course of far less significance than the quality of their enduring friendship. In considering the nature of their relationship, and that role model within lesbian history which Radclyffe Hall has become, it is important to bear in mind the varying definitions of 'lesbian' love that have arisen over time.

Today, erotic relationships between women may contain many elements (such as romance, woman-to-woman affection, social and political interests directed away from men) only one of which may involve full sexual contact. Sometimes sexual activity may be seen as less important than hugging, kissing and emotional intimacy. Sometimes it may be entirely absent but the two women may nevertheless consider themselves 'lesbians'.

Historically in a society where 'real sex' generally required a penis and penile penetration, where cultural beliefs suggested that anything women did together without a man could not be 'sexual', the variety and forms of women's burning passions for each other were often overlooked, disregarded, or renamed – even by the women themselves.

Whether as a result of the restrictive typology newly created by the sexologists, or whether, known for her furious frankness, Violet for once decided to keep an affair of the heart to herself, the version she offered her next lover, the writer Ford Madox Ford, was discreetly tailored. According to Ford's diaries Violet reassured him that Marguerite's lavish gifts were not 'the wages of sin'.[22] As Violet Hunt's biographer Joan Hardwick emphasizes, after these passionate beginnings, before long 'they entered into a less fevered and intimate relationship which was to prove long-lasting'.[23]

Though Violet and Marguerite had visited Pitlochrie alone, on several occasions during the autumn Marguerite began to include Dolly on their trips. The two cousins twice visited Violet at her sister's house in Bredburn, the kind of outdoor, hunting and shooting trips Marguerite most enjoyed. Violet recorded in her diary: 'Marguerite takes her gun as she is going to shoot rabbits with

Walton.'[24] Later that weekend she noted: 'Marguerite is a rather tough proposition, cold and manly, and Dolly . . . is American born and bred and *noli me tangere* written on every line of her.'[25]

Later in September the three women visited a ruined chapel adjacent to a Jacobean house in Swaledale. Violet Hunt, inspired by the atmosphere, devised a story whose style had certain elements of Radclyffe Hall's. Dolly's bubbly presence on these weekends allowed the two older women to make the shift from their short erotic encounter to a more enduring literary friendship.

Looking at their reputations today, what we see is the whiff of scandal constantly attached to their names. For Violet Hunt and Radclyffe Hall's reputations have rumbled down the decades without growing a whit more respectable. Radclyffe Hall is still known less for her award-winning novel *Adam's Breed* than for her infamous lesbian book. Violet Hunt has fared little better. In 1990 John Sutherland, reviewing a biography of Ford Madox Ford, wrote of her: 'After a dozen years, two daughters and several nervous breakdowns, Ford transferred his affections to Violet Hunt, a literary groupie whose ambition seems to have been to sleep with every male novelist of the period. Hunt was pretty, brilliant and infected with incurable syphilis.'[26]

Overlooked in this review is the fact that the 'literary groupie' was not only a noted writer but also an enduring supporter of other major twentieth-century literary talents including Radclyffe Hall. From the turn of the century Violet nurtured these talents by running a fashionable literary salon at South Lodge, her home in 80 Campden Hill Road, which became the centre for two generations of artists, writers and poets. Violet brought Marguerite into the heart of this meeting place where experienced authors such as Henry James, Thomas Hardy, May Sinclair, Ford Madox Ford, Arnold Bennett and H.G. Wells could meet younger artists ('*les jeunes*' as Violet Hunt and Ford Madox Ford called them) such as Ezra Pound, H.D. (Hilda Doolittle), Richard Aldington, Wyndham Lewis, D.H. Lawrence, T.S. Eliot, Rebecca West. Many of these writers helped Radclyffe Hall establish herself in literary circles.

The misnaming of Radclyffe Hall as a one-book lesbian thesis writer, flashy with diamonds, and of Violet Hunt as a sexual coquette overlooks both women's uncompromising psychological realism as novelists and their courage in dealing with harsh areas of their lives. For many years Violet dealt as bravely with the shame of syphilis, which at the time was incurable and devastating to a woman of her background and upbringing, as Marguerite dealt with the stigma of lesbianism. And among women of their time Marguerite Radclyffe-Hall and Rebecca West, along with others of Violet's friends, were unusually enlightened in both sympathizing with sufferers from syphilis and seeing the victims as unfortunate rather than guilty.

The defining of Violet Hunt and Radclyffe Hall by their sexual natures and the 'confessional' strands in their novels has meant that the worth of their writing has been disregarded. Nor has their loyalty to each other and to their women friends been emphasized in writings about them. Marguerite's dedication to the concept of loyalty meant that she never let her friends down. Violet who empowered both male and female writers strove particularly to ensure that the women were given the critical respect they deserved. At every stage in Radclyffe Hall's literary career we find that Violet Hunt supported her in public and in private encouraged her.

Late in September 1906 the two writers shared a room in the North British Hotel in Edinburgh. It was a very special occasion for both of them. Marguerite said later that she would always remember the place, the month and the change in their relationship. It was easy to remember. For not only had Violet marked the occasion by giving her a book on the flyleaf of which she wrote the date and place but, that same weekend, Marguerite's attention had been caught and captivated by a stranger sitting in the hotel dining-room.

The woman was considerably older than either of the young writers. She had beautiful hands that were less accustomed to rough work than to playing the piano and plucking the guitar. Marguerite watched and listened from across the room. The unknown woman had an enchanting speaking voice, an ample and gracious figure, and a sensual warmth that demanded notice. She was accustomed to recognition. Marguerite and Violet recognized her.

The stranger was Mabel Veronica Batten, a noted amateur lieder singer, another beautiful woman with a beautiful voice. In deference to the homage Mabel Batten was accustomed to receive, society had nicknamed her Ladye. She was to be Radclyffe Hall's first significant partner.

In Violet Hunt, Marguerite had been looking for someone to satisfy what her lover the poet Wilfred Blunt called in Mabel Batten 'nameless cravings'.[27] Blunt had not been able to satisfy them for Mabel Batten. Violet had not been able to satisfy them for Marguerite.

At this first sighting – they did not meet again for another year – did Marguerite suspect that with the remarkable Ladye she might find the satisfaction she had long been craving?

5

THE APRIL GRANDMOTHER

It was an eccentric occasion, that second sighting: the first significant encounter between Radclyffe Hall and Mabel Batten on 22 August 1907.

They were sipping spring water in the fashionable German spa of Homburg, where the elderly and other sufferers from rheumatism or arthritis came for dips in the saline baths. Many who had lived in India or who had tropical ailments also found the baths useful. Mabel Batten had lived in India. She was not young – at fifty-one – and she took care of her limbs. That was why she was there.

Marguerite was not elderly – she was just twenty-seven – and she did not have rheumatism. Indeed, previous biographers have found no reason at all for Radclyffe Hall to turn up in Homburg. Michael Baker says her visit was shrouded in mystery. Una Troubridge, who aspired to an intimate knowledge of all her partner John's comings and goings, confessed herself baffled. She must have gone there 'for some frivolous purpose',[1] she says lamely. But the adult John did not tell Una everything.

Marguerite, though persistent, had not found it easy to make contact with the fashionable woman in the hotel lounge; they moved in very different circles. For nearly a year Marguerite had sought the singer she had sighted; we may surmise that her unexpected appearance at what was a regular haunt of Mabel Batten's was part of that search. Romantic? Of course it was romantic. Every quest on which Radclyffe Hall engaged in her later years was dedicated, serious, often ruthless, but also rhapsodic, quixotic, soulful, even sentimental. At twenty-seven she was high on her hunting achievements, autocratic and plumped with pride at her poetic prowess, but still young, still nervous and romantically inclined. In this guise she presented herself to the worldly woman who had enjoyed an affair with Edward VII before he became king, the man who had subsequently become godfather to her eldest grandchild.

Had Marguerite planned what she would say when she finally engaged the sophisticated stranger in conversation? Did she realize that to a clever cultured singer now in her middle years her own achievements might seem insignificant, her lack of education glaring? In Mabel Batten's eyes Marguerite was 'a half-educated young cub who ignored all the important aspects of a civilised existence and preferred hunting to literature, music or the arts'.[2] Although Marguerite had embarked in the previous year, under Violet's influence, on a programme of self-improvement, there was truth enough in the statement.

Mabel Batten, however, was intrigued by the coltish creature wearing severe diamond studs and a tailor-made jacket who nervously presented her with a signed copy of *'Twixt Earth and Stars*. King Edward VII himself had presented her with a signed photo. Mabel Batten, lionized for years, took veneration for granted.

The two women looked each other over. What did they see? If you look at the period photographs of young ladies of Marguerite's age, you can almost nestle in the fabric of their long flowing Greek-inspired dresses. The softness of the pose is not only a trick of the photographers. Turn to a photograph of Marguerite herself and you see a physical jauntiness, hard edges, a striking form still held in by stays, but offset by masculine stiff collars. But look at her eyes, as Mabel did. The eyes are not jaunty: Marguerite had sad eyes.

There is a strange association between Radclyffe Hall and her fictional characters. Many possess her own self-contained sorrowfulness. If you saw that, if you were a woman with a kind spirit, as Mabel was, you might be drawn, might want to transform that brooding melancholy into ease.

What did the young poet see as she looked up at this fashionable singer? We know her preoccupation with hands. A swift glance at Mabel Batten's fourth finger of the left hand showed the statutory ring. She saw another married lady. Her life had been haunted by women lovers who became married ladies. This one was married with a daughter Cara five years older than Marguerite herself; she was a devoted grandmother with at that point two grandchildren, Peter aged eleven, and Pamela, nine, known as Honey. That was part of what Marguerite saw.

She saw also a woman accustomed to be gazed upon. Beauty does that to you.

Mabel Batten and her sister Emmie, Lady Clarendon, a woman with aristocratic pretensions, were two 'striking Irish beauties',[3] but it was Mabel not Emmie who was constantly photographed and painted. The strong painting of her by Sir Edward Poynter* is owned today by Mabel's great-granddaughter and hangs in her London house. There is another portrait by Koopman in which the sitter has an air of detached amusement – is she smiling to herself? Better known is the 1895 portrait (now in the Tate Gallery, London) where

---

* President of the Royal Academy, he also encouraged Una Troubridge's art.

John Singer Sargent captures Mabel Batten mid-song. She might have been well advised to have been painted first and sung afterwards as the picture with its touch of a double chin is less flattering than the others. Mabel Batten's self-assurance however is barely ruffled.[4]*

Mabel Batten and Emmie Clarendon, though a generation older, were cousins of Una Troubridge through her mother. Una's side of the family were artistic, Mabel's musical and linguistic. As a young girl she studied harmony and composition in Dresden and Bruges, where Radclyffe Hall also lived as a child. With Genoese great-grandparents and French and Irish ancestors, Mabel Batten studied Italian in Florence, spoke French and Italian fluently, and read widely in both languages.

By 1890 she had become a leading mezzo-soprano, an exceptional pianist and guitarist, who composed her own songs and set others to music. At Homburg in 1902, the April Grandmother, as she was known to the press, had sung her most famous composition 'The Queen's Last Ride', to lyrics by Ella Wheeler Wilcox, before the King, to whom she dedicated it.

Mabel Batten's wealth allowed her to give practical patronage to promising musicians such as Gabriel Fauré, Reynaldo Hahn, Mischa Elman and the young Percy Grainger. She was more than a patron, she was a friend to those whose art she respected.[5]

Where did Mabel Batten's wealth come from? Partly it was family money, used with a generous spirit. Partly it came from her marriage in India in 1875 at the age of nineteen (she had been born at Barrackpore on 27 October 1856) to the 43-year-old widower George Batten, the brother of Lady Strachey. Within a year of the marriage they had their only daughter Cara and until 1882 when George retired they stayed in Simla. On leaving India, they had resettled in London at 3 Ralston Street, where the Battens lived in 1907, the year of the two women's momentous meeting.

Mabel Batten, daughter of Mary Cecilia Hatch and General George Cliffe Hatch, Judge-Advocate General of India, had returned to India after her education abroad. She was familiar with Simla society which Elizabeth Longford described as 'either dowdy or fast'. Entering the fast set with no trouble at all, Mabel Batten found it easy to flout the conventions in this 'very immoral Anglo-Indian world'.[6]

Her own 'immoralities' included a well-documented flirtation with the British Viceroy Robert, Earl of Lytton, to whom her husband George was Private Secretary, and a brief affair with Lytton's close friend, the poet Wilfred Blunt.

---

* At the time of their meeting the portrait was in the Battens' Ralston Street drawing-room where it stayed until 6 October 1911 when Mabel Batten proudly moved it into the first home she shared with Marguerite at 59 Cadogan Square.

The poet, who acknowledged he had 'never seen the point of the so called New Woman',[7] totally ignored Mabel Batten's intellect and wit. He saw her as a pretty woman who complained of a husband much older than herself whom she did not love, who was 'gay, fond of pleasure, quite depraved'.[8]

Later evidence from her own diaries, letters and family records suggests that, on the contrary, Mabel was exceptionally fond of George, her elderly husband. The charge of depravity may have had something to do with the less well documented but heavily rumoured liaisons with persons of her own sex. Radclyffe Hall was later accused of being 'immoral' partly because she had previously lived with that 'most objectionable person' Mabel Batten, herself an immoral and notorious woman.*

This then was the woman, with an intriguing past and respectable present, whom Marguerite came face to face with on 22 August 1907.

Marguerite 'fell head and heart and soul in love with her',[9] not least because Ladye, as she asked Marguerite to call her, though her golden times on the concert platform had passed, was still, at fifty-one, a powerful and 'a very lovely woman'.[10]

Una Troubridge, Mabel's young cousin, remembered her cousin's mouth as 'one of the loveliest mouths I ever saw'. She recalled too her cousin's eyes: 'she kept the charm of her perfectly set eyes, chiselled and slightly uptilted nose . . . until her death eight years later.' Of her cousin's figure, she records with only modest irony:

> If she was no longer slim, she was no more than graciously ample and she had great dignity and length of line. She had that characteristically Irish colouring of a pale complexion, dark blue eyes and dark hair and not only her beautifully produced singing voice, but also her speaking voice, were quite enchanting.[11]

We must not be surprised that Una had such a good memory of this 'very lovely woman'. During the last two years of Ladye's life, Una had spent many hours with her cousin and her cousin's partner John Radclyffe Hall – plenty of time in which to dwell on Ladye's kindness to her, the young cousin who ruthlessly seduced John's kisses away from the 'loveliest mouth' she had ever seen. Hers after all was a younger mouth.

On several occasions in later years, Marguerite was to find the youthfulness of younger women's mouths a spur to sexual adventures outside her permanent partnership. But in 1907 Marguerite was entranced by the first older woman to reciprocate her passion without restraint. Ladye led her lovingly into what

---

* This was among the charges levelled against Radclyffe Hall in 1920 by George Lane Fox-Pitt, council member of the Society for Psychical Research, who had been urged on by Ernest Troubridge (Una's estranged and jealous husband) to denounce Hall as 'immoral' by virtue of her association with Ladye – so persistent even after her death were the rumours of Ladye's scandalous same-sex sorties.

Marguerite had formerly regarded as impossible desires. Although they did not immediately become lovers, Ladye slowly but surely made everything possible for Marguerite.

Back in England Ladye expected Radclyffe Hall to apply herself to her writing. When she did so, Ladye introduced her new friend to eminent composers who turned her poems into songs. By 1910 Ladye herself was composing music for Marguerite's verses, at the same time revising and classifying them. Ladye became Marguerite's unofficial editor and publicist. Marguerite's writing thrived on the attention.

Ladye found great satisfaction in leading her 'young cub' to waters from which she had never drunk, in opening doors for her which had hitherto been closed. Learn French, Ladye said, you'll like it. Marguerite learnt French. She may have hated it, at least at the beginning, but she liked being approved of, she liked acquiring a new skill.

Try Spanish culture, Ladye said, it will be useful. Marguerite immersed herself in Spanish culture. It was useful. They took rapturous holidays in Tenerife. Marguerite spoke a little Spanish, understood a good deal. Later it was very useful. In *The Well of Loneliness* she immortalized Orotava, on the slopes of the Teide volcano, as the backdrop to Stephen Gordon's love affair with Mary Llewellyn.

Art was invigorating, Ladye thought. Go to a gallery, she told the young woman. Books were a tonic, Ladye believed. Read more, Marguerite. Try this one. What about that? There's a new one out. Let's meet the author. There's a fine play being produced. Book us some tickets. Try for the First Night. Ask the cast back for food and wine.

There are no extant diary entries for their first three years of cultural explorations, but January to June 1910 offers a breathtaking regime. On 10 January a spree: the pantomime *Aladdin*. On 5 February they saw Lady Constance Stewart Richardson dance and Vesta Tilley sing at the Palace. On 8 February they viewed 'Modern Painters' at the Prince's. On 29 April came a private view at the Royal Academy; later *Orpheus* with Marie Bremer and Viola Tree as Eurydice. On 24 May they attended 'a clever play called *Chains*' at the Repertory Theatre; four days later the Japanese Exhibition. On 1 June together with Cara Harris and Toupie Lowther, who was to become one of Radclyffe Hall's closest lesbian friends (and the model for Miss Ogilvy), they enjoyed *Trelawny of the Wells*. The next day it was art again: 'Pictures of Fair Women' at the Grafton Gallery. On 8 June they heard Melba sing. On the 22nd with Cara and Ladye's lesbian friend Gabrielle Enthoven they heard *Lakmé* at the Opera. With only a break for sleep, Cara, Marguerite and Ladye rallied themselves to take Toupie Lowther to see Pavlova dance at the Palace Theatre. It must have been a relief to find on 30 June that a song recital by Gervase Elwes was 'a dull concert'. At least during dullness one could doze.

Marguerite was intoxicated, awe-struck, baffled. Ladye's zest galvanized her, her excitement electrified her. It was like the thrill of the hunt, entering this new world. There was the chase; there was colour, speed, the same surge of feeling. Later, the glow of achievement.

Ladye has been presented as a martinet who would not tolerate a lover who did not make her mark.[12] Rather, she seems to have been a woman eager to share exuberant passions, striving to get the best from the young woman in her arms and under her wing. She began the custom of reading aloud to Marguerite, initially from French and English novels. In 1910 Violet Fane and Arnold Bennett became their English favourites. The following year, Ladye introduced Marguerite to nineteenth- and early twentieth-century French literature with its focus on same-sex erotic novels.

Marguerite read Guy de Maupassant and Emile Zola, whose lascivious depictions of lesbian love were largely intended to titillate male audiences. Influenced by her lesbian friends the composer and suffragette Ethel Smyth and Winaretta Singer, the widowed Princesse de Polignac, Ladye moved Marguerite on to George Sand and Sappho, a decided influence on Radclyffe Hall's series of Greek poems. Later Hall became a devotee of the writer Renée Vivien's Sapphic poetry.

Ladye introduced Marguerite to novels by the lesbian writer Vernon Lee, the nom de plume of French-born Violet Paget (1856–1935). Marguerite was struck by several coincidences: Paget used a male name for writing to lend greater credence to her work, adopted male attire and featured cross-dressing heroines. Paget's first passionate attachment, to Mary Robinson, ended in Mary's marriage, just as Marguerite's first romantic friendship with Agnes had ended in the latter's marriage.* The two writers probably met sometime between 1910 and 1916 through Ethel Smyth.† Following this introduction to same-sex literature, Radclyffe Hall maintained her interest in it. When Clemence Dane published *A Regiment of Women* in 1917 and Rosamond Lehmann produced *Dusty Answer* in 1927 she read them quickly. In 1928 she maintained that her own novel *The Well of Loneliness* was bolder than either.[13]

Ladye was as skilled a tutor in vacations as she was in literature. For her, time away from England in what they called 'dear abroad' was time away from propriety. In the summer of 1908 they went to Bruges, to rediscover together the

---

* Paget's passion, like Marguerite's, was finally requited by a Ladye-like figure called Kit Anstruther-Thompson who was also 'a woman of beauty, a friend and a spiritual lover'. (Claude J. Summers (ed.), *The Gay and Lesbian Literary Heritage*, p. 444.)

† Lee/Paget, a feminist who was one of the signatories to the Women's International Congress at The Hague in 1915, was loosely tied into London lesbian circles. Ladye's diaries mention their enjoyment of Lee's novel *Amor Dura*, but their attention was probably drawn earlier to her *Studies of the Eighteenth Century in Italy* which describes the lives of musicians and singers and had attracted the notice of London's artistic circles in which both Vernon Lee and Mabel Batten moved. (Ibid.)

place of their separate childhoods. They went as friends but returned as lovers. Thereafter they celebrated 12 August, the day they crossed the Channel to Ostend, as the anniversary of their relationship as well as Marguerite's birthday.*

The following Christmas Eve, 1908, Marguerite, hunting near Malvern, was thrown by her horse Xenophon, suffered concussion and almost broke her neck. She was left with a badly bruised spine and constant headaches for which the doctor recommended prolonged rest and sea air. This led to the first of their several cruises to Tenerife. It also offered Ladye a justification for asking Marguerite to devote less time to horses and more to intellectual pursuits. Marguerite hated to give up riding but she was under a spell – and blossoming. 'There is no joy to equal that of loving, / Even Immortals find no deeper pleasure,' she wrote.[14]

Pleasures deepened and accumulated in the course of these years. They breakfasted, lunched and dined together. They continued the round of opera, theatre, pantomime, concerts and galleries. They dined with Emmie Clarendon to please Ladye; visited Highfield House in Malvern to satisfy Marguerite; played bridge with 'the Dollies' (Ladye's label for the Clarkes when she wasn't calling them 'the Bobbies'), and endless poker, which pleased them both.

Ladye introduced Marguerite to the risks of roulette, first in London's West End, then abroad: in Santa Cruz and Monte Carlo. Marguerite was a fast learner and in later years she and Austin Harris, Ladye's son-in-law, devised a 'system' at which not infrequently she won.

Ladye encouraged Marguerite's almost daily visits to Ralston Street to which Marguerite took Grandma Diehl and the Visettis. Suddenly Albert Gate, Marguerite's flat, did not seem near enough to her beloved, so she and Granny Diehl moved to a flat in Shelley Court, Tite Street, a mere hair's-breadth away from Ladye.

Dolly and her new husband Bobby Clarke (who had been introduced to her by Ladye) lived a few minutes from Tite Street at 1 Swan Walk, Chelsea. The two couples (sometimes with Cara who became close to Dolly) saw each other regularly for tea or lunch at the Bath Club where Ladye swam, her sole form of exercise.

Marguerite knew that if she were to have an enduring relationship with Ladye, the approval of both Cara and George Batten was imperative. There was no question of Ladye leaving George. They cared for each other and had interests and tastes in common. As George aged and his health declined, Ladye knew that by the terms of their marriage, their class and their society, loyalty

---

* See Michael Baker, *Our Three Selves*, p. 36. However Ladye in her diaries for 1913 and 1914 gives 22 August as the date of their fifth and sixth anniversaries.

meant remaining his wife and acting publicly with discretion. Perhaps George as well as Ladye saw the vigorous young Marguerite as an insurance for Ladye's future.

According to his great-granddaughter, George had 'not been a popular person in business circles outside the family' but inside it he was 'enormously affectionate and that affection was reciprocated by all of them'.[15] He spent much time at his club, and seemed undisturbed when Ladye took holidays with Marguerite.

In letters to Cara written in 1909, while Ladye and Marguerite (whom initially he called Margaret) were on a cruise, George tells his daughter that though 'your mother and Margaret . . . want me to travel by sea . . . to Genoa [to join them] I do not like the idea'.[16] He really must join them, wrote Ladye, they were not content without him. George, amused but firm, wrote again to Cara enclosing Ladye's enthusiastic letters:

> Darling Cara, You will see that she [Mother] arrives at Molino di Sopra, Alassio, Italy, tomorrow . . . I have made up my mind not to go there and have written to the proprietor of the Pwllycrochan Hotel, Colwyn Bay preparatory to suggesting rooms there for myself.[17]

Safely ensconced at Colwyn Bay, while Ladye and her young lover were beset by mosquitoes abroad, George wrote again to 'Darling Cara' enclosing Mabel's account of her 'sufferings from 'skitoes': 'Poor darling,' he added, 'I hope she has got over the effects. It must have been really annoying to Johnnie who is the most unselfish of creatures.'[18]

As we see from his affectionate rendering of Radclyffe Hall's new name, his wife had renamed Marguerite. She was to be Johnnie to the family and intimates and John to outsiders, Ladye reserving to herself the name Jonathan as a reminder of the biblical bond between David and Jonathan who 'in their death . . . were not divided'[19] – an association which makes more poignant that most famous line in *The Well of Loneliness*, when Radclyffe Hall's heroine Stephen finally makes love to young Mary Llewellyn: 'Stephen bent down and kissed Mary's hands very humbly, for now she could find no words any more . . . and that night they were not divided.'[20]

Ladye's addiction to nicknames for everything from people to pendants included 'Jones' and 'Charlie' for her two hot water bottles, 'poon' for decent behaviour, 'sneevish' for tiresome peevish behaviour, and 'pogging' for making eyes at people. Cara Lancaster remembers her Aunt Honey (Ladye's granddaughter) still using Ladye's whimsical expressions – 'sporks' for bad people and 'poons' for good ones.[21]

In later letters there is a sense that George is 'handing over' his wife to a 'younger man'. At seventy-six George was more than old enough to be Marguerite's father. In his jokey, paternalistic but patently affectionate attitude towards her, he often behaved like one. Sometimes he treated his wife's lover as his son-in-law. They discussed business and speculations, hunting and country matters. There seems little doubt that George was aware of the nature of their relationship. His family are sure he was fully cognisant but that, loving his wife as he did, he benevolently accepted it. In this respect Radclyffe Hall's wealth and cultural standing allowed George to make his own adjustments to their domestic situation. This became evident when Johnnie, the 'poon', helped him out when he lost money in a poor speculation.

George, faced with a woman who both resembled yet did not resemble the society women he knew, never placed John in the same category as Mabel, that most feminine of creatures who organized his household. Expectations of male and female roles were so rigid that those who did not fit the feminine must perforce be in some sense masculine.

When Radclyffe Hall finally conceived the character Stephen Gordon, she offered us the first portrait in English literature of a butch woman who is not a man, who does not ape men, but who adopts roles traditionally associated with men, thus assuming on the surface a masculine identity whilst being fully aware that she is a lesbian woman. In the 1920s, when a heterogenderal pattern for relationships seemed the only conceivable model for homosexuals, John and Una both saw themselves as *women* (one more masculine than the other) who used a butch-femme relationship as a way to configure their lives.

But in 1909 John, then twenty-nine, who never fitted the feminine stereotype, was ready enough to be considered a 'male' rather than a 'lesbian female' if that meant that George and Austin Harris, the men who mattered to Ladye, accepted her as Ladye's lover.

There were times when Radclyffe Hall herself was confused about what role to play. Even as late as 1925 the publisher Rupert Hart-Davis recalls that 'It was always said at a dinner party, when the women left the table, Johnny Hall . . . found it hard to make up her mind whether to go with the women or remain with the men.'[22]

To be approved of by Cara was a trickier matter. She and her banker husband Austin lived at Thurloe Square, South Kensington, but spent weekends at Aspenden Hall, their country house at Buntingford, Essex, where John would go for long country walks with Austin, Peter and Honey, while Ladye spent time with Cara.

Ladye's devotion to Cara is well attested within her family. 'She wrote to her almost every day throughout her life, and saw her constantly, more than she saw anyone else . . . She and Cara, my grandmother, were real friends as well as mother and daughter.'[23] The hundreds of letters addressed to 'my darling child' from 'your loving Mummie' bear out this testimony. Letters until 1915 between John and Cara, the young woman only slightly her senior, provide evidence of a fondness that settled into friendship. Cara however had a jealous streak while the adult John was never less than competitive; there was thus an undercurrent which was later to result in a damaging breach between them.

Cara's discomfort had less to do with her mother's sexuality, which she appeared to accept, than with her rivalry with Johnny for attention as Ladye's beloved 'daughter'. John did indeed yearn for a mother as well as a lover. Her relationship with Marie Visetti, rooted in fear, shame and constant rejection, had left her with a hopeless longing, and a strange terrible loyalty. After so much pain, she hungered now for a safe haven. This was what Ladye offered, but John's brooding restlessness, her self-destructive discontent, ultimately would not allow her to rest.

After the slow evolution of their love during the first three years, crucial events in 1910 quickened the pace. From this point until her death in 1916, Ladye kept a daily diary of events and emotions, but her record of painful episodes must be viewed with caution.

John's Malvern friend Peggy Llewellyn, who, after her father's death in 1907, had been cheerfully incorporated into life with Ladye, married Harold Austin in 1910. She spent the next three years with him in Chile and made only one return visit to England to see John in August 1912. The departure of the friend who shared her love of horses and the countryside led John to rely for the first time on the support of urban artistic friends.

On 22 January 1910 George celebrated his seventy-eighth birthday. His health, as well as her own, had begun to cause Ladye anxiety. From February 1910 Ladye's diary begins a persistent record of coughs, asthma, breathlessness, shingles and what she calls 'heart pains' which continued during the February trip with John to Tenerife, their April jaunt to Paris, and most months thereafter. Constant entries of 'seediness' suddenly pinpointed to John the gap in their ages, and her lover's increasing frailty.[24]

Three critical deaths followed. On 6 May Ladye records: 'King Edward VIIth (God rest his soul) died at midnight.' The following day, proof of her affection for her former lover, Ladye embarked on a month of mourning. Her staunch patriotism* – she put John also into mourning clothes – and monarchist beliefs had a decided influence on John's own conservative tendencies.

Nine days later George Batten became seriously ill. By August he was too weak to walk so when he joined John and Ladye in Sidmouth he took a pony chair. Though the lovers marked John's birthday with Ladye's gift of a diamond neck slide and their anniversary on 22 August with John's gift of a 'darling malachite old round brooch' George's illness clouded celebrations.

By 11 October when his chest infection necessitated a swift operation, Granny Diehl had also fallen ill. George, only intermittently conscious, weak-

---

* On 20 May she took John, Cara and Honey to see the royal funeral procession, arriving at Piccadilly at 6.50 a.m.

ened. John was in turmoil. Her grandmother needed her; her lover needed her.[25] Time was on nobody's side. On 18 October Granny Diehl, John's most steadfast support, died. Four days later John took Marie Visetti and her grandmother's coffin to Southampton. On her return the following day, 23 October, she prayed in Westminster Cathedral with Ladye and Cara for George's recovery. It was too late for prayers to prevail. On 24 October 'George died peacefully whilst I held his head in my arms,' wrote Ladye.[26]

John slept at Ralston Street that night. A new era had begun for the two women. Their shared grief was deep and genuine, but with their grieving came an awareness that with the deaths of the two people closest to them there was now no obstacle to a permanent partnership. The lovers had been living in separate residences. John had no further need of a chaperone nor a life alone in Shelley Court. Ladye, who had inherited Ralston Street and more than £8,000, was a wealthy widow.

Convention required at least a month's solitary mourning, but on 27 November Ladye and John crossed the sea first to Paris and Monte Carlo, then journeying on to Alassio and Molino di Sopra, the house where they had spent idyllic summer weeks in 1909. There they had their first quiet Christmas together, saw in the New Year, and invited Dolly and Bobby to join them in February 1911. That their intimates could now spend time with them as a couple was a turning point. They slowly recovered their spirits in the sunshine. In Monte Carlo they lunched with Vita Sackville-West, who in 1928 became Radclyffe Hall's firm supporter throughout the *Well of Loneliness* court case. In Alassio Ladye succumbed to a Florentine brocade evening cloak with crimson lining and hood.[27] John bought herself a mandolin – was it in memory of her father the 'poet-fellow'? In Nice in March, she bought Ladye a diamond safety pin – diamonds would always remind her of the roguish Rat.

By 25 April 1911 they had returned to London. Ladye wrote to Cara: 'My darling child . . . It seems queer to be home again without dear old Father's welcoming voice from the smoking room . . . It is so strange ordering everything myself. There seems no end to bills etc. I'll get in the way of it very soon.'[28]

John and Ladye fell to flat hunting in London. Within the week they had found an ideal first home at 59 Cadogan Square. At the same time, coincidentally, John, now thirty-one, was forced to watch her old horse Joseph destroyed before her eyes. The demise of Joseph marked the end of John's life as a huntswoman, and as a solitary single woman. The decision on 16 May that Ladye would let Ralston Street and John would buy the lease of Cadogan Square (which would become vacant in the autumn) symbolized John's entry into an openly lesbian domestic ménage, and also, as the house-purchaser, her role within that partnership.

In celebration, on 27 April, John bought Ladye a Yorkshire terrier – they called him Claude – and four days later a French bulldog called Otero. Homes for John always meant dogs. In return on 12 May Ladye bought John 'a platinum and gold heavy curb chain bracelet'.[29] For the apartment they ordered an Italian bed, gilt chairs and an Italian table, put up blue Italian twisted pillars in Ladye's bedroom. In September 1911 Ladye redrafted her will to make provision for John.

On 2 October the two women were ready to move in to 59 Cadogan Square. As they paused for a moment outside the door of their apartment, did they acknowledge to each other what great daring it took to establish themselves as wife-and-wife? We know they were happy but were they also nervous? Ladye had carried off several sexual adventures with panache, but she, as Vita Sackville-West and Virginia Woolf were to do later, had undertaken her exploits beneath the sheltering sky of a husband and family. John had no family to speak of, only an obstinate courage, a bulldog honesty. Would that be enough for open exposure?

They lived in a place and a period when homosexuality was suddenly under severe scrutiny. The Victorian moral code that decreed discretion for 'deviance', or powerful penalties for publicly proclaimed proclivities, had been shocked and shaken when the silence around same-sex love had been broken by Oscar Wilde in 1895, when Radclyffe Hall was fifteen and already falling in love with women. Imprisoned for two years, before dying in exile in Paris in 1900, Oscar Wilde was victimized by the bigotry and pretence of the society he had exposed but had never entirely rejected. It was the same society, the same milieu, to which Mabel Batten belonged, and to which Radclyffe Hall had been given an entrée.

Like Wilde, Radclyffe Hall stood outside that society, with its heterosexual imperative conventionally rooted in children and family. Like Wilde, in her bones she wanted to belong to it. Wilde had become the scapegoat for that society's moral and sexual insecurities, just as Radclyffe Hall would become seventeen years hence.

We cannot look into the future. John could not rationally 'know' that the path she took up to the front door of Cadogan Square, that led her into the house with her woman lover, would also lead her inexorably into the blaze and shame of a courtroom trial. Yet there are many and varied kinds of 'knowing'. When Oscar Wilde left Oxford two years before Radclyffe Hall's birth, he declared prophetically: 'Somehow or other, I'll be famous, and if not famous, I'll be notorious.'[30]

Somehow or other John, on the brink of her new life, may have sensed that her chosen way forward would not bring safety, might bring notoriety. In his defence of 'the Love that dare not speak its name', Wilde talked of the 'great affection of an elder for a younger man as there was between David and Jonathan . . . that deep spiritual affection which is as pure as it is perfect'.[31]

This Jonathan and her David felt their love as 'that deep spiritual affection' but they knew also that those who watched them did not always see it as pure.

For two women to take that step, to name that love aloud in 1911 and to feel they could achieve some degree of success, some protection from social disgrace, they needed several sources of support and a lot of luck. With no man for financial protection, they needed to be sure they had independent funds to sustain them; in this respect they were fortunate. In addition, if they were to avoid ostracism, they needed the backing of their families. John's mother and stepfather, dependent financially upon her, would be unlikely to be publicly hostile. Through George Batten's benevolence and Cara's acquiescence Ladye had achieved familial support, and that umbrella would shield them both, at least as long as Ladye lived.

A further aid to immunity from public disapproval, which would also serve to strengthen their self-esteem as an openly inverted couple, could come from belonging to a lesbian community. Reliance on the company of like-minded women would reinforce same-sex values and save them from possible isolation. Ladye already belonged to a group of wealthy well-educated homosexual women. John's shyness and awkward individualism had never allowed her more than one friend at a time, one lover after another.

The final – and most problematic – element in trying to ensure the permanency of a lesbian union within a hostile world is that leap of faith that we have to make if our partnership is to last a lifetime; the faith that we will keep our side of the emotional contract. If devotion is needed, devoted we shall be. If flexibility is needed, compromises we shall make. If fidelity is part of the lifetime plan – ah fidelity . . .

As far as Ladye was concerned fidelity *was* part of their plan. By redrafting her will, by publicly acknowledging that the widow who had lost her much loved husband was now embarking on a union with a boyish young wife, she was prepared – as she had not been prepared with George – to put her heart, and the chastity of her body, where her money was. For Ladye it was her final love match. She determined on fidelity unto death.

For John too it was a love match. She was very sure about her feelings for Ladye. She was less sure – she would always be less sure – about fidelity, though her intentions then as later would be honourable.

She was uncertain too about her feelings for Ladye's friends, or theirs for her. How would she fit into Ladye's circle? How would they react to her unsettling mixture of explosive confidence and spiky insecurity? Some of the women were suffragettes: radical, rebellious, concerned with injustice. She too was a rebel, but she had never run with the crowd. She was also conservative, a creature of her class rather than a woman who identified with women. The loose ends would not tie up.

Many of Ladye's friends were established writers, sure of the medium, sure of themselves. Radclyffe Hall had published three slim volumes of poetry, a slim hold indeed on the literary ladder. She was becoming less convinced that poetry was the medium through which she would find her authentic voice.

Poetry or prose? Women's interests or men's? Where do I belong? Can I be faithful? Can I write fiction?

As she stood on the steps of 59 Cadogan Square in 1911 those were the questions she might have asked herself. Those were the questions she raised in her poems. Those were the issues that preoccupied her for the next five years.

6

SAPPHISTS, SUFFRAGE AND CATHOLIC CONVERSION

When Ladye led John into the world of women-friends, in 1911, it was gaucherie not reluctance that made the younger woman hesitate. For John had always valued friendship – often in vain. As a child, she had ached for friends. When they did not appear, defiantly she had made them up. Now in Cadogan Square there was a ready-made circle, though not of her making. These women, creative, clever and largely lesbian, were not her invention, not under her control.

Gabrielle Enthoven was a playwright. Winaretta Singer was a writer and like Ladye a wealthy patron of the arts. Ethel Smyth and Adela Maddison were composers, and Violet Gordon Woodhouse was a talented harpsichordist and a woman later to become – for a brief spell of time – important to John. Adela, a former pupil of Fauré's, who lived in France but visited Ladye at intervals, had composed 'Hätt' ich Geld' which was sung at the Bechstein Hall on 27 October 1911 with Ladye and Cara in the audience. On first meeting Adela, John considered her eccentric. The rhyme Ladye invented: 'Adela Maddison, Mad as a Hattison', appears to bear out this view.

Their first visitor to Cadogan Square, on 5 October 1911, after of course Dolly and Cara, was the highly theatrical Gabrielle Enthoven. She was an imposing broad-faced woman, Slavic in appearance, who had met Gordon in the Egyptian desert, chatted behind the scenes with Queen Victoria, introduced Sarah Bernhardt to Mrs Patrick Campbell as a result of which they starred together in *Pelléas et Mélisande*: 'a perfect performance', according to Ladye.[1]

Born on 12 January 1868, Gabrielle Enthoven, like Ladye, had spent much of her youth in India where her father, William Govett Romaine CB, held official posts. In England she lived with him at Windsor until his death in1892, after which she married Major Charles Enthoven, who died the same year as George Batten (1910), when she was forty-two. Whether she, like Ladye, had undertaken discreet lesbian involvements before his death is not clear, but from the start of her widowhood she pursued open homosexual relationships. Every story Gabrielle told was 'tall' and Hall later fictionalized some of the tallest.[2]

As a widow Gabrielle's theatrical enthusiasms expanded. In 1912 John and Ladye saw her play *Montmartre* at the Alhambra. In 1915 she adapted D'Annunzio's poetic drama *The Honeysuckle* which was later produced at New York's Lyceum Theatre. In 1916 John, Ladye and Una Troubridge attended her play *Ellen Young* at the Savoy.

Gabrielle was president and founder, in 1911, with Christopher St John and Edy Craig (later John's friends), of the Pioneer Players: an important theatre club specializing in new, foreign and feminist plays, several seen later by John. She also collected rare theatrical posters dating as far back as 1755. In an obituary following her death at the age of eighty-two, James Laver described her as 'a great woman of the theatre' whose fame rested on this unique collection of more than 100,000 playbills.[3] They became part of the national treasure.

Though Gabrielle opened a new theatrical world for John, it was her war work which John respected. Between 1914 and 1918 Gabrielle worked first with the War Refugee Committee, then with the Red Cross on the welfare of British prisoners-of-war in Germany, Turkey and Russia. It came as no surprise to her friends when Gabrielle was awarded the OBE.

John, who felt forced to stay sedately at Ladye's side when war broke out, was frankly envious. Her own modest efforts – attending Red Cross lectures, learning first aid, ferrying wounded Tommies between hospitals and transporting library books to casualty wards – were hardly the stuff of heroism.

Barbara 'Toupie' Lowther, another friend of Ladye's, eldest daughter of the 6th Earl of Lonsdale, provoked a similar response in John on the matter of war work. Toupie, who had married Lieutenant-Colonel James Innes in 1914 and become the mother of two small babies, did not allow marriage or motherhood to restrict her activities. Even before she divorced James in 1921 she and Norah Desmond Hackett had formed a spectacular, women-only ambulance unit which despite opposition from the authorities eventually drove alongside the French army on the Compiègne battlefront.[4]

Several of Hall's forceful heroines are modelled on Toupie. In 'Malise', the Toupie-figure, Hilary Gordon, is a novelist in peacetime but during the war heads a 'splendidly valiant' women's unit 'of gallant and much battered cars . . . for ever rescuing victims from hell'.[5]

Splendidly valiant units occur again in 'Miss Ogilvy Finds Herself' and in *The Well of Loneliness*. Despite her disclaimer at the start of *The Well* – 'although the unit mentioned in this book, of which Stephen Gordon becomes a member, operates in much the same area [of the Allied Front as the British women's ambulance unit], it never had any existence save in the author's imagination'[6] – Hall's imagination was well supplied by Toupie's war efforts. An apocryphal story has it that Toupie was once arrested at the Franco-Italian frontier for masquerading as a man; on the return journey, wearing skirts, she was arrested for masquerading as a woman.[7]

Toupie, a Sorbonne science graduate, a cousin of Ladye's friend Claude Lowther MP who owned Hurstmonceux Castle, though well-connected socially, was an accomplished sportswoman rather than one of the artists who prevailed in Ladye's set. This appealed to John. One of the first women in Britain to own and ride a motorcycle, Toupie introduced John and Una to the joys of motoring.[8] Male-oriented in her interests like John, Toupie 'paid court' to Ladye but 'pokered' with John.

John had less ambivalent feelings towards another close friend of Ladye's, Winaretta Singer,[9] daughter of Isaac Merrit Singer, the American sewing machine tycoon, and widow of Prince Edmond de Polignac. From her fashionable home in King's Road she paid frequent visits to Cadogan Square during 1912 and 1913, when the women would discuss the works of George Sand and Sappho before Winaretta read aloud to John and Ladye from her new travel book on Greece, while John in return read her poems to Winaretta.

Through Winaretta, an ex-lover of Ethel Smyth's, in 1911 John met the composer herself. Ethel was twenty-two years older than John though they died within a year of each other. Ethel's family, steeped in army and navy traditions, rigorously opposed her career in music. Ethel took no notice, and studied first at Leipzig and later in Berlin where she was encouraged by Clara Schumann, Joachim and Brahms.

Ethel Smyth's Mass in D, performed at the Albert Hall, led to her recognition as England's first significant woman composer. Despite this success it was still hard for her as a woman to gain recognition for her work. Her involvement in the suffrage movement and her friendship with the musician Violet Gordon Woodhouse, who had already attracted John's notice, increased Ladye and John's interest in the movement. In 1910 Ladye and John had attended a meeting at Park Place organized by Christopher St John and Violet Gordon Woodhouse (whom Ethel Smyth called 'that supreme harpsichordist') in order to hear Mrs Pankhurst speak to a group of feminist sympathizers including Winaretta de Polignac and Edy Craig.[9] The following year on 29 June 1911 they went to Ethel's suffragette concert in London.

John's interest was aroused more by Ethel's literary output than her musical prestige. As well as her two-volume autobiography Ethel's eight largely autobiographical books reflected her twin passions for sport and friendship which created another bond between them.

Una described Ladye's literary and musical circle as 'people who "did things" and who counted for something in the world'.[10] In the wings of Ladye's world, John's idleness snailed into ambition. People who 'did things' occupied centre stage. Maybe centre stage would be an interesting place to be.

'People who did things': that concept whirled in John's mind as she and Ladye attended concerts, masked balls and literary luncheons. She wove the idea into early drafts of *The Forge*. Susan Brent, the failed artist, meets the established painter Venetia Ford for the first time at a masked ball.

> Venetia said suddenly: 'You look as though you did something interesting. What work do you do?'
> Susan was conscious of a sharp little pang.
> 'I don't do anything,' she said uncertainly.
> Venetia's face fell, she looked ludicrously disappointed.
> 'Nothing at all?' she asked incredulously.
> 'No, nothing at all.'[11]

John was not quite in Susan's position. Even as early as 1911, when she mixed with Ladye's clever companions, she *had* done things. She had already published three volumes of poetry, was secretly engaged on several stories. Yet intuitively she sensed she had not tapped more than the tip of her creative powers. She did not yet believe that the things she did would count for anything with Ladye's friends.

For five years until 1913 John had lived with Ladye and had seemed content with her subordinate position. Ladye's great-granddaughter Cara Lancaster suggested that thereafter 'Johnnie began to feel her own power' and when she began 'to exercise that power, she became unkind, and unfair to Ladye'.[12]

Her image changed as that power grew. She began to dress like some of Ladye's circle. Though many wore exquisite gowns, others emulated by John bought their shirts from Jermyn Street, wore manly belts, sported a tailored style, and pulled the wine corks when they 'pokered'. A few even had their hair bobbed at gentlemen's hairdressers. John tried out this idea on Ladye. Mabel Batten was aghast. Racy masculine clothes? Yes. Shorn hair? Absolutely not. So John pinned up her waist-length hair and turned androgyny into haute couture.

Her outré masculine outfits stylistically signified her sense of social dislocation. It allowed her to distance herself from women who desired men, whilst signalling her own desire for other women.

Underneath her dramatic outfits John's nervousness showed in her interactions with Ladye's 'poonery'. Until she grew to know the women, she was gruff when they were poised, overbearing when they were satirical. They had style. She had brashness. They had their place in the circle. She was not quite sure where her place was.

To start with she stayed close to Dolly Clarke, watching her new friends from a distance. Dolly, being family, was important to John; with her grandmother dead, only a thin veneer of loyalty held her to Marie Visetti. She saw Dolly several times a week, though the addition of Bobby changed the nature of their friendship.

John also relied heavily on the fact that Ladye was her 'best friend' as well as her lover. What John learnt over the years about attachment was formulated in Cadogan Square from 1911 where the word 'friendship', already well established in the adult John's vocabulary, became its most significant term. When sexual desire waned, as with Jane and Dolly, John offered friendship. If her erotic overtures were rebuffed, as they were initially by Violet Hunt, she offered friendship. When later she herself rebuffed Romaine Brooks' sexual overtures, again she offered friendship. The result? 'For love she [Romaine] has very courteously accepted my friendship,' she wrote.[13]

When Una Troubridge died at the age of seventy-six, twenty years after John's death, she left instructions for the coffin to bear as part of its inscription the words:

Una Vincenzo Troubridge
The friend of Radclyffe Hall.

One possible reading is that the word 'friend' is a discreet lesbian alternative for 'lover'. But Una had no need to be discreet in death for she had not been so in life. After Ladye's death in 1916, she and John had courageously lived together for twenty-eight years in the full glare of bad publicity. More plausibly, the word 'friend' on Una's coffin signifies the essential component that permitted her relationship with John to endure. For Una 'friend' meant comrade, wife, consort, secretary, editor, hostess, organizer, and in John's last years nurse. To become John's 'friend' she relinquished husband, mother, family and social approval.

For John too the concept of passionate friendship was basic to her interpretation of lesbian love. Love without friendship was emotion without honour. It was 'a tarnished shield and a blunt sword and would be entirely unworthy of you'.[14] In her romance with Agnes, her affairs with Jane and Dolly, her intimacy with Violet, she sought the enduring quality of comradeship.

John's view of friendship hinged on protection, aid for the underdog, and a keen sense of justice. Those same beliefs initially drew her towards the suffrage movement, which was supported by Violet Hunt and many of Ladye's friends. John's interest in enfranchisement was based on the importance she attached to individual rights, whereas other suffragists argued on the basis of the special contribution women could make in the public sphere. There is no evidence that John thought women had a special or useful contribution to make (indeed, rather the reverse), but she believed strongly that women, like homosexuals, were unfairly discriminated against.

In the early 1900s the existing suffrage campaigns were organized by ladylike law-abiding 'suffragists' (a term John used for herself), who included men as well as women. Their work was co-ordinated by the National Union of

Women's Suffrage Societies (NUWSS) led by Mrs Millicent Garrett Fawcett. Their genteel low-level campaign, supported for a time by John and Ladye, had achieved no progress in winning the vote for women.

In October 1903 Mrs Emmeline Pankhurst and her three daughters, Sylvia, Christabel and Adele, determined on a new approach. They founded the Women's Social and Political Union (WSPU) to supplement the forty-year-old British women's suffrage movement. It was high profile, dangerous, civilly disobedient. In spring 1906 the WSPU's militant tactics, about which John had severe reservations, earned them the patronizing label (coined by the *Daily Mail*) 'Suffragettes'.

Suffragette activities, passionately espoused by many of John's friends, challenged notions of male authority and asserted that women's social duties outside the household were as great as men's.[15] Violet Hunt and May Sinclair incorporated these theories in their novels, which focused on women's independence and profoundly influenced John's fiction.

Although several male writers described Violet Hunt as 'preferring personal politics to public questions'[16] this is neither fair nor accurate. Between 1907 and 1909, the start of John's affair with Ladye and her own burgeoning romance with Ford Madox Ford, Violet dedicated herself to the women's movement with such vigour that for two years Ford found himself neglected in favour of women's politics.

May Sinclair co-opted Violet to the movement by introducing her to the militant Women's Freedom League and the Women's Suffrage League. They took part in the self-denial week organized to raise funds for the WSPU. Later they held collecting boxes for three days near Kensington High Street, close to their own homes. It was public, it was provocative. It was not easy for two middle-class Edwardian women to support suffrage in this manner. Violet said she felt 'suddenly stripped naked'.[17] They became involved in violent confrontations with the police and witnessed terrible brutality from those whom up to then Violet, like John, had respected as symbols of law and order.

John's interest and sympathy were aroused. Although the WSPU's revolutionary tactics somewhat shocked her, she admired their courage. The language and visual imagery, peppered with militaristic and religious references, had a decided appeal. Suffragettes were warriors waging a crusade for women's freedom, and for John, like her heroine Joan Ogden in *The Unlit Lamp*, 'It was what she considered injustice that roused the devil in [her].'[18] In the same novel, on a related issue, the heroine's cousin leaves her fortune to found Recreation Homes for Prostitutes, whilst Hall's awareness of the challenge presented by women's struggle for independence is recalled in the governess Elizabeth Rodney's resolve to show young Joan Ogden the myriad ways in which women are held back or 'bottled'.[19]

Predictably, when Ethel Smyth's strong political commitment reinforced

Violet Hunt's and May Sinclair's, Ladye and John readily backed the Votes for Women campaign.

Ethel was the most famous lesbian involved in the pre-war suffrage campaign. Her own letters suggest that she had had an affair both with novelist Edith Somerville (1858–1949) and with Emmeline Pankhurst. If the latter were the case, it would put lesbianism at the heart of the suffrage movement. Smyth's most significant gift to the movement was 'The March of the Women', a suffrage anthem which she conducted with a toothbrush from a window of her Holloway prison cell.

During the period of John's support, the suffragettes stepped up their tactics. In 1908 two suffragettes chained themselves to the railings of the prime minister's residence, No. 10 Downing Street, whereupon five women were arrested. In the 'Trojan Horse' incident a band of suffragettes tried to gain entrance to the House of Commons hidden in a furniture van. They began harassing politicians and attacking private and commercial property. Aiming to coerce the Government into action they adopted a nation-wide campaign of window smashing and arson attacks which were not at all to John's liking. Her sympathies began to waver.

By 1913 Emmeline Pankhurst had suffered four prison sentences on charges ranging from breaking a window at No. 10 to conspiracy to incite riot. By then John's support for the cause had undergone a change. She was disturbed when the miners' strike threatened to shut down the industry on 29 February 1912. A suffragette demonstration planned for 4 March in Parliament Square was banned by the police. As a consequence hundreds of women fought their way through London streets smashing windows. Ninety-six arrests were made as windows were broken in fashionable stores in Knightsbridge and Kensington. *The Times* weighed in against 'turbulence and hysteria'.

Radclyffe Hall took up her pen, albeit anonymously. In the *Pall Mall Gazette* on 4 March 1912 appeared this letter:

Sir – Have the Suffragettes no spark of patriotism left, that they can spread revolt and hamper the government in this moment of grave national danger? According to Mrs Pankhurst, they are resorting to the methods of the miners! Since when have English ladies regulated their conduct by that of the working classes? But, indeed, up to the present, the miners have set an example of orderly behaviour which the Suffragettes might do well to follow!

I was formerly a sympathiser with the cause of female suffrage, as also were many women who, like myself, are unrepresented, although taxpayers. Women who are capable of setting a revolutionary example at such a time as this could only bring disgrace and destruction on any Constitution in which they played an active part.

Yours etc.,
A FORMER SUFFRAGIST.[20]

John's political instincts were neither sophisticated nor radical. It was not that she saw femininity and militancy as necessarily incompatible. She could be intensely moved by social injustice but her conservative leanings led her to abhor any attack on the Establishment or on the class to which she belonged.

Despite this change from active participation to passive intermittent sympathy, John and Ladye still followed suffrage activities and attended certain events, while Ladye recorded key moments in her diary. On Sunday 16 June 1912 Ladye went with Gabrielle Enthoven and other suffragette friends to a special performance by the Pioneer Players of Bernard Shaw's play *Mrs Warren's Profession*, then banned from public staging for its discussion of prostitution. On 14 June 1913 Ladye records: 'Emily Davison suffragette brought down the King's horse and injured a jockey.' A year later, on 21 May Ladye noted the daring adventure of the suffragette who tried to climb into Buckingham Palace, and on 4 June with wry admiration she recorded how 'a Miss Blomfield attempted at the Court to speak on Women's Suffrage to the King'.

Despite John and Ladye's interest in politics and the vigorous social life they enjoyed during their first years together, family still came first. They spent Christmas 1911 with Cara and Austin at Aspenden. The Austins were welcome visitors at Highfield in Malvern Wells. The Visettis, who were less welcome though dutifully invited, gave John renewed cause for concern in 1912 when Alberto left bills unpaid and massive debts piled up.

Ladye became as enamoured of the landscape around Malvern as John could have wished. After the romance of seeing Tintern Abbey by moonlight, they decided that John should sell Highfield so that together they could choose a smaller property in the area. The summer of 1911 was spent joyously scouting for houses. On 30 August they spied a former inn and cider house, now joined into a low gabled villa called the White Cottage, with a glorious view over the Severn Valley to the distant Bredon Hills.

That year saw a further deterioration in Ladye's health. Throughout the spring she was breathless and asthmatic. However the excitement of preparing for their presentation at court and the business of superintending the removal of furniture from Highfield to the White Cottage kept her from succumbing to illness.

They moved into the White Cottage on 4 August 1912. On 6 August they drove to the station to meet their 'beloved parrot Cocky'. On 'my J's birthday' Ladye wrote: 'We hung pictures nearly all day and bought two bedroom chairs at Worcester.' In her bedroom she had installed the Italian bed and hung the newly framed oval portrait of George.

They invited the family to view their first country home: Cara and Austin were followed on 28 August by the Visettis, then Dolly and Bobby on 7 September.[21] With joint abodes in town and country John felt a stronger measure of security.

Seven days after the move Ladye wrote to Cara: 'The lease [on 3 Ralston Street] is signed at last so the house won't bother me for three years and I hope for longer . . . I am so glad to think, darling, that when I "pass on" I may have close on £400 a year to leave you, though I hope I shall live to be seventy and not get boring and tiresome as old people do.'[22]

At the start of 1912, in her thirty-second year, John had taken another significant step. She converted to Roman Catholicism. The move was to influence the rest of her life and would permeate her fiction with its most characteristic feature: spiritual speculation.

Radclyffe Hall had always been interested in a world beyond appearances. Her spiritual sense allowed her to create landscapes discerned fleetingly by the inner eye. Margaret Lawrence in a critique of Hall's literature writes: 'She is preoccupied with the mysteries, as the priestesses were, and she pities the human race as it passes them by for things that can be added up and multiplied and subtracted and divided.'[23] It may seem paradoxical to use the term 'priestess' for a writer whose most notorious novel was banned for 'obscene libel', yet every major protagonist in Hall's literary canon strives for a vision of unity between the mundane and the eternal.

Granny Diehl's benign Anglicanism had started young Marguerite's spiritual search. She needed to find 'all perfect growing harmonies',[24] for harmony there had not been in her childhood. Her struggle for faith – one in which she was obliged to contend fiercely with devils within as well as without – led her to write in 1908:

> Ah! Faith I'd barter all I own to know
> But one brief moment of your magic charm . . .
> My mind is weary, and would seek release
> From thoughts terrestrial.[25]

It was this same weariness, this same struggle for faith, that allowed her to feel, finally, at ease within the rituals of the Roman Catholic Church to which she was introduced by Ladye, herself a convert. John's early religious instruction had emphasized a God of judgement: stern and unyielding. The God she was shown by Ladye seemed somewhat more relaxed.

Ladye had encouraged John to attend services with her at Brompton Oratory. In their continental travels, she had introduced John to the music, art and literature of Catholicism with its rich repertoire of sensory expression. John's predilection for mystery fed on these experiences. Her need for connection and order opened up her heart.

On 3 January 1912 John accompanied Ladye to Max Reinhardt's production of *The Miracle* at Olympia. A mimed miracle play, with music by Humperdinck, it told the story of a nun seduced from her vows by a trickster. Savaged by guilt, the nun finally repents and recovers her faith through the miraculous intervention of a statue of the Madonna. The piece was stickily religious and undeniably sentimental. But its theme of suffering and salvation brought sobs from the audience, and provoked an immediate response from John, as suffering and salvation always would.

There was also a more pragmatic consideration for a newly-fledged lover who had noble intentions but an uncertain practice in the matter of *sexual* faith. A union embraced by Catholicism would offer the couple hope of an after-life together no matter what might or might not happen in this.

On 4 January Ladye happily recorded: 'Took John to Father Bowden at the Oratory.'[26] Sebastien Bowden, then in his late seventies, was, according to Richard Ellmann, one of the most fashionable Brompton Oratorians, to whom many of the famous, talented or wealthy turned for spiritual guidance and instruction.[27] He is said to have been the priest to whom Oscar Wilde went after his release from Reading Gaol. Curiously Bowden, who refused to receive Wilde into the Church, appeared to be perfectly sanguine about putting Radclyffe Hall under instruction. Bowden was aware that the young woman seeking guidance was living with Mabel Batten. John made no secret of it. Her behaviour was open and her appearance conspicuous. Her stetson hat, bow tie, tailored suit – already the talk of London's literary circles – were not likely to be the garb of many of Bowden's would-be converts. Yet, without a quibble, he acquiesced.

Doubtless the priest saw what he wanted to see: a genuinely religious woman seeking guidance. With her Anglican upbringing John was already familiar with the moral codes and doctrines of Christianity: all she needed was instruction in the differences between the two churches. In Father Bowden's eyes, Ladye already represented high social standing as well as impeccable piety. Joanne Glasgow argues from the evidence of church documents, catechisms, conduct manuals, and the writings of Catholic women that lesbian sexuality was seen as innocent by the Church. Indeed according to Glasgow, 'lesbianism did not exist as a Catholic reality.'[28] That John's conversion went forward without impediments tends to confirm this.

On 21 January John and Ladye heard Mass in Westminster Cathedral. On 5 February Bowden solemnized her conversion at the Oratory. St Anthony, patron saint of lost things, became her name-saint. Ladye was her sponsor. She was left only to choose a baptismal name. Having adopted John and Jonathan as her secular names, she might have been expected to take the name of a male saint. However, she confounded expectations. As Ladye reported: 'She took the name of Antonia. Bitterly cold day.'[29] On 20 October, John was confirmed at Westminster Cathedral by Bishop Butt.

In view of their new religious undertaking Ladye decided they should spend their winter holiday in Rome, and seek a private audience for John with the Pope. Despite Ladye's worsening health, indicated by constant diary entries such as: 'Heart bothered me all night',[30] they left England for Rome on 17 November accompanied by two maids, Cocky their grey parrot in his cage, and enough luggage for a year.

Staying in Rome until 26 February 1913, the travellers were grateful for Cardinal Gasquet's guidance through religious observances and functions. It was the Cardinal who obtained for them an audience with the Pope. Ladye's diary records:

> *Wednesday December 4*: J and I were received in a semi-private audience at the Vatican by His Holiness Pius Xth.

> *December 10*: We heard early Mass in St Peter's Crypt said by Bishop Brindle and were received by Pope Pius Xth at the Bishop's private audience. He gave me a signed picture.

That was not the whole story. Una Troubridge has a more amusing version:

> The saintly peasant-Pope abhorred ceremony and his humility deprecated homage . . . the Cardinal warned them to omit the customary three genuflexions . . . in her shyness and reverence she [John] forgot and fell on her knees, the Cardinal clutched her by the scruff of the neck and hauled her to her feet, hissing 'Get up! What did I tell you!'
>
> In any case it was Ladye who was the success of that audience . . . Ladye was self-possessed and said and did the right thing, putting the Pope at his ease, while John hovered in the background tongue-tied. The result was that when the Cardinal presented two photographs for signature, Ladye's bore a lengthy inscription: '*Alla diletta figlia Veronica* . . .' while John's received only an unadorned autograph.[31]

Today in Anglo–American society the Catholic Church is seen as a prime enemy of homosexuality among both women and men. Official voices imply that this has always been Catholicism's position. Yet as Radclyffe Hall's conversion shows, for women at least this was not always the case. Her conversion was but one amongst many undertaken by lesbian writers, several of them John's friends, in the early years of this century.

In 1901 Violet Shiletto, childhood friend of poet Renée Vivien and a major inspiration for her poetry, converted on her deathbed, attended only by a priest. At the time of Violet's death, Renée Vivien was in the arms of her new lover Natalie Clifford Barney, Radclyffe Hall's Paris friend who was the model for Valérie Seymour in *The Well of Loneliness*. Renée, guilty and grief-stricken, became obsessed with the idea of converting to Catholicism in order to retrieve her 'chaste love' for her friend,[32] and in 1909, on her own deathbed, she did indeed convert. As Joanne Glasgow points out, like John Renée Vivien not only felt no conflict between faith and sexual morality but also through Catholicism she rediscovered 'purity'.[33]

In 1907 in Florence, Una Troubridge, then twenty, became a Catholic five years before John converted. Her childhood faith was Anglican, but on a visit to her Catholic cousins she found, as John did, that the rituals and routines which made up the everyday fabric of Catholic lives gave her a joyous sense of belonging. She also discovered that her family thought she was in danger of damnation. Shortly afterwards she was received into the Roman Catholic Church.[34]

Even after Una and John began their affair, Una never at any time, in her more than two hundred diaries, recorded any emotional or intellectual struggle between her religion and her inversion. In 1963, the year before her death, she was asked by Ethel Mannin how she and John had squared their relationship with their Catholicism. What did they do about Confession? Una replied: 'There was nothing to confess.'[35]

How was it that John and other lesbian converts to Catholicism suffered no self-doubt, no crisis of conscience, and felt able to reconcile their 'alternative sexuality' with the teachings of their Church? Although priests may not have been fully aware of what these women did in private, the women themselves were perfectly aware of what they were doing, indeed they were highly self-conscious and articulate. Moreover their understanding of their sexuality had by this point been permanently altered by the works of Havelock Ellis and other sexologists.

It has been suggested by Joanne Glasgow that at this stage the Catholic Church had virtually eradicated lesbianism through 'the agency of language'.[36] Popular church teaching stated that sexual acts by definition required ejaculation by a penis. Other sexual acts, as Joanne Glasgow points out, were discouraged and labelled 'occasions of sin', but since the term 'sex' denoted solely penile penetration, the acts performed by lesbians were therefore not 'sex'.[37]

If John's lesbianism was not problematic in religious terms, nor it seemed were aspects of her early feminism. For under Ethel Smyth's influence both John and Ladye advocated divorce law reform, a stance at the time unusual for Catholics.

During this period of Ladye's religious influence, Marguerite Radclyffe-Hall (her professional name) produced three more volumes of poetry which reflected critical changes in her life and thinking, specifically her conversion to Catholicism and her self-assurance as a lover of women.

In the autumn of 1908 her second volume, *A Sheaf of Verses*, was published by Bumpus. Dedicated to 'Sad Days and Glad Days', most poems reflected her new-found gladness. Two poems, 'On the Road to Tennalley Town Maryland, USA' and 'To My Little Cousin', looked back jauntily to her roistering days with Jane and Dolly. Several intense lyrics recaptured her relationship with Violet.

There is an interesting progression from the silence and hesitation of 'One Night' (was it with Violet?) with the lines:

> The stillness made me dumb, those words
> I dared not utter choked my breath,
> Each crushing each, as mad with life
> They rose, to die a silent death[38]

to new, open, confident love lyrics with Ladye as their wellspring. In 'Ardour' she records, 'the thought of you has filled the night with wonder . . . till all my senses thrill'.[39]

'House Hunting' extols the safety of a loving partnership:

> *Suppose we fetter our lives with love . . .*
> More fair than ocean, or skies above,
> And learn to dwell in each other's hearts,
> Safely where no harm parts.[40]

It is significant that even in that contented verse Radclyffe Hall cannot entirely escape the notion of love as fetters. Love's bonds are chains. They incur penalties. Her kind of loving is a passion where

> The dark was breathless, and the skies
> Filled with a thousand prying eyes.[41]

John's consolation came from feeling that love has more than an earthly endurance. Listen to 'Re-Incarnation' where she speaks directly to her lover:

> Meeting you I felt a thrill,
> Strangely sad, and strangely sweet!
> Some compelling force of will,
> Sprung from sympathies complete,
> Sympathies, that rose again
> After death's ennobling pain.[42]

In an essay written after Ladye's death, Radclyffe Hall emphasizes that Ladye's sympathies with her work included a vigorous 'blue pencil' used with 'a kind but unsparing hand' on her poetry as well as 'on my character . . . enlarging my character by teaching me charity in which she herself abounded'.[43]

The poems which survived the blue pencil show a growing compassion, discipline and maturity. Swinburne and Bridges influenced her, but paramount was her affection for Robert Browning, inspired by Violet and encouraged by Ladye on their Italian trips. There is Browning in the rhythm of 'My Castle'; in the tension between monastic strength and earthly lust in 'Brother Filippo'; his love of Italy in:

> And then drink in my love; the whole of me,
> In one deep breath, one vast impassioned kiss,
> That come what may thou canst remember this:
> That thou has lived and loved in Italy.[44]

But the collection's most significant feature is her first overt espousal of the love of women. Her 'Ode to Sappho' boldly begins:

> Immortal Lesbian! Canst thou still behold
> From some far sphere wherein thy soul doth sing
> This earth, that once was thine . . .

Her readings of Sappho and her preoccupation with the namelessness of lesbian desire inspire the lines:

> Passion-wan Lesbian, in that awful place
> Where spirits wander lost *without a name*
> Thou still art Sappho, and thine ardent face
> Lights up the gloom with love's enduring flame.[45]

The gloom is dispelled as in 'The Scar' her love is worn with pride:

> Upon my life I bear one precious scar:
> Each night I kiss it, till anew it bleeds . . .
> To me it seems to beautify not mar
> My inner self, for from that deep wound leads
> *A path to gained respect . . .*[46]

In 1910 Chapman & Hall published her third volume: *Poems of the Past and Present.*[47] The style has a marked assurance, an exhilarating variety of metre; the images are no longer conventional. Detached irony replaces sentiment.

This volume was the first to be dedicated to Mrs George Batten. 'A Song of Youth', 'To a Child' and 'Fruit of the Nispero No. XVI' (one of a series celebrating the Nispero tree's golden fruit as a symbol of lesbian love) were set to music by Ladye. Ladye also introduced Marguerite to Liza Lehmann who, like Bobby Clarke who composed settings for eight of these poems, was to become a keen collaborator. Another well-known composer, Coleridge Taylor, set a further three to music.

Marguerite's admiration for the Brownings continued with a poem of homage to Elizabeth Barrett Browning:

> I leave my paper still its virgin white.
> Beside those mighty truths that thou did'st write,
> My thoughts are dust upon a desert land.[48]

Radclyffe Hall, like Virginia Woolf after her, was impressed by 'the vigour with which she [Elizabeth Barrett Browning] threw herself into the only life that was free to her and lived so steadily and strongly in her books that her days were full of purpose and character'.[49] When Hall herself wrote novels it was a purpose she imitated.

In this collection most poems are unusually optimistic. 'Nought shall harm us, my dearest dear: / Be of good cheer', suggests one.[50] The challenge of living with a lover is positively portrayed in 'On Entering into a Closer Friendship':

> Give me your hand, that I may find my way
> About the garden of your mind, *and see*
> *With inward eyes* all that was hid from me
> Before I knew you as I do today.[51]

Seeing with inward eyes is a recurring theme in Radclyffe Hall's work. Ordinary eyesight can deceive; only the inner eye can stave off spiritual blindness. Sight, sustenance and service become key motifs in Hall's work.[52] They chart her fictional protagonists' journeys from sensual mundane experience to those spiritual truths which transcend mere mortal cravings. In *Adam's Breed* the hero Gian-Luca, a successful waiter, moves from self-deception in the rich world of restaurants to a vision of truth that all is not as it seems. The soul needs more food than cordon bleu cuisine. In *The Sixth Beatitude* her heroine Hannah Bullen, a cleaning woman, sees life clearly with her inner eye, and 'seeing life neither feared nor despised it'.[53]

But given her characteristic fatalism not even this third volume of poems can escape one anxious note. In 'Non Omnes Moriar' she imagines herself and Ladye dead and mourns the fact that though her lover will 'live in memory as a rose', she, the poet, will be forgotten.

> Perhaps some day when men shall speak of fame
> And then remember you, a man will say,
> 'She had yet one more lover in her day,
> A poet fellow; I forget his name.'[54]

Contemplating failure in both love and art Hall cannot help resorting to the term 'poet fellow', the name Rat the poet-father and failure used for himself.

Reviewers however were delighted with the general mood of optimism of the poems. The *Daily Telegraph* extolled her 'wistfulness that is of beauty rather than of sadness'. *The Times* commented on her 'exceptional gift for enshrining a single thought' in a lyric which 'makes the reader pause and meditate'. Not to be outdone, the *Pall Mall Gazette* described her work as 'facile, flowing, and often really musical'. The *Sussex Daily News*, however, pleased her most: 'Her volume is full of pearls; they are to be gathered from every page, and sometimes they are very brilliant.'[55]

Marguerite Radclyffe-Hall garnered the reviewers' symbolic pearls as eagerly as Violet had garnered the material ones. Ladye, brilliant at public relations, gathered the reviews together and ensured they were seen in the right places. Another collection was called for.

Her fourth volume, *Songs of Three Counties and Other Poems*, published in 1913 by Chapman & Hall, was more experimental. Its tone drew on A.E. Housman's melancholic and nostalgic rural poetry and celebrated her love of nature. The three counties around Malvern, Worcestershire, Herefordshire and Gloucestershire, whose landscapes were endearingly familiar, provided the setting. Hall's conversion to Catholicism accounted for an even stronger religious tone.

Most of the poems were songs which had already been set to music by Bobby Clarke and Liza Lehmann prior to the book's publication, and were being reprinted highly profitably as sheet music. One of them, 'The Blind Ploughman' – in which a ploughman's loss of sight is shown to intensify his appreciation of nature, allowing him to see with his soul – became one of the most famous ballads of the day. Set to music by Bobby Clarke, it acquired national celebrity during the First World War, and was still sung during the Second World War and long afterwards. Dame Clara Butt, Chaliapin, Powell Edwards, Paul Robeson and Nicola Rossi-Lemeni all used the song as a powerful appeal for those who had lost their sight in the war. In the ballad's final verse, Marguerite repeats the theme of a few years earlier:

> God has made his sun to shine
> On both you and me;
> God, who took away my eyes,
> That my *soul* might see.

On 23 November 1913 John, thrilled but slightly puzzled at her own success, took Ladye, with Dolly and her friend Phoebe Hoare (who was to play a significant part in all their lives), to hear 'The Blind Ploughman' performed by Charles Tree at the Queen's Hall evening concert.[56]

By the end of the war the poet Marguerite Radclyffe-Hall was a public figure. Her former secretary Winifred Reed described to me the scene in the Usher

Hall, Edinburgh, in 1918 when a blinded officer Captain McRobert sang the ballad before an audience of three thousand. He received a standing ovation. A description of that momentous occasion was sent to Radclyffe Hall by the singer Mignon Nevada who had been in the audience:

> What a tremendous impression 'The Blind Ploughman' made . . . I quote from his [the singer's] letter . . . 'I felt I was just an instrument for the three thousand odd people, through those wonderful words, that no matter what trials we have to go through, even our blindness, it is that our souls, our inner self might see the Divine Wisdom in all things.'[57]

Hall's view of herself as a gifted amateur was now transformed by the succession of established composers who queued to collaborate with her. On 27 June 1913 Ladye proudly recorded in her diary: 'John received a very eulogistic letter re her poems from Sir Arthur Quiller-Couch.'

Sir Arthur was not her only literary fan. The poet and traveller J.B. Cunninghame Graham wrote a flattering preface to this collection. He praised her for 'not striving to be modern or filled with strange conceits; but with a love and trust of the brown earth . . .' The 'only true modernity,' Graham suggests, 'is talent'; it is talent which Marguerite Radclyffe-Hall possessed. The reviewers agreed.

The *Lady* magazine likened her 'deft workmanship' to the 'chiselled setting of a precious stone'; the *Daily Telegraph* considered her work as stimulating to read as to hear; other reviewers praised her economical and skilled technique. *Songs of Three Counties* marked the peak of her poetic reputation,[58] but though she was preparing a fifth volume of poems, she was beginning to recognize that this was not to be her literary medium.

With Violet's encouragement she had begun work on some prose fragments. Now with Ladye's support she began a professional attempt at writing short stories.

But with the first fictions came the first infidelities. By 1913 John's relationship with Ladye had become quarrelsome. Ladye's physical debility had increased. She was ill, and growing older: worry made it show. John became by turns irritated and guilt-ridden. There were tensions, half-truths. Sadnesses seeped in. The tone of the collection mirrored this: the poetic mood is one of regret. The shadows brooding over Radclyffe Hall's personal life increased the note of anxiety hinted at in earlier volumes.

John had called Mabel Batten 'the ladye of my heart'. But that position was slowly being eroded. When on 31 December Ladye told her diary: '1912 was a very happy year,' she was not to know it would be the last time she would write that in her journals.

From 12 October 1911 the name Phoebe Hoare appears in Ladye's records.

Phoebe was married to a banker Oliver Hoare, a colleague of Ladye's son-in-law Austin Harris. On 12 October Dolly brought Phoebe to see her cousin and Ladye in their new flat at Cadogan Square. Fourteen days later John went into a nursing home at 45 Devonshire Street for a slight operation. On 1 November Phoebe turned up with flowers. During 1912 Ladye and John occasionally called on the Oliver Hoares but John's interest was not in Oliver. By 1913 Phoebe, who had once come to the flat to see both of them, was returning again and again to see John.

In May 1912 Ladye's pretty young cousin Una Troubridge, wife of Ernest Troubridge and mother of two-year-old Andrea, also paid several visits to her cousin. John, away in Malvern, missed these initial visits, though Ladye's diary for 21 June 1912, following John's return to town, records that they met Una 'at Mrs Trevor Bigham's tea party'. This appears to have been the first time John met Una, who afterwards was frequently out of England with her husband. Once they met again in August 1915 John would never again miss a visit from Una.*

As Ladye with her characteristic graciousness poured the tea and passed the cakes at different times to these two young women, did she suspect, could she guess, in what tragic ways her hospitality would be repaid?

---

* There is conflict in the sources on the date of John and Una's first meeting. Ladye's diary for 21 June 1912 records them all as taking tea at Mrs Trevor Bigham's, as outlined above. However, earlier biographers give the date of their first meeting as September 1913, when Ladye and John attended a reception at Cheyne Walk, where they sat and talked in the garden, and afterwards drove Una home. Since it appears from Ladye's diary that she and John were in Malvern at this time, it seems unlikely that they met Una then. Whatever the date – and whether these occasions are one and the same – neither John nor Una had any recollection of their first meeting, and as Richard Ormrod, Una's biographer says, 'It had no sequel' (*Una Troubridge*, p. 55).

7

FIRST FICTIONS, FIRST INFIDELITIES

When the person we love suddenly takes another lover what is it we notice about the person who has replaced us? Is it their face? Their figure? Do we care about their intellect, their job, their social connections?

In Ladye's case it seemed she noticed none of these features. What she noticed, and recorded unremittingly day after day, was Phoebe Hoare's persistence.

Phoebe Hoare was everywhere – everywhere, that is, that John went. Ladye left no record of what Phoebe looked like, or how she dressed, of her background or the company she kept. She did not measure Phoebe's intellect or her waistline. She simply measured and calculated the number of times John saw her – whether outside, at home (*their* home) or at the home of their friends. In her neat black script in her red and blue journals, she catalogued not only the meetings but, as far as she could ascertain it, exactly what they saw at art gallery, theatre or concert; who went with them; what they talked about, what they ate, whom they visited.

One matter is always recorded: the time John came home, and whether she and John still ate together, or whether John ate with Phoebe, while Ladye dined alone or with friends.

Phoebe buzzes around Mabel Batten's diaries for 1913 and 1914 like a fly she cannot swat but can only trail after miserably, tracing its flight, estimating its progress. Faithfully she records her misery, her depressions; John's moods, John's tempers, John's growing nervousness and increasing loss of weight as the affair took hold. The diary entries say it all.

On 21 May 1913 John and Ladye took Mrs Oliver Hoare and her husband to see *Tosca*. Six days later, John took Phoebe to lunch at the Berkeley. Then John and Ladye invited the Hoares to Ascot. For the next few days John, fearful of transgressing too many boundaries, spent time with family and friends.

Peggy Austin and her husband lunched with them and the Harrises. They went to *La Bohème* with Gabrielle Enthoven. On 21 June John accompanied Ladye to Hurstmonceux Castle to spend a weekend with Toupie and Claude Lowther. But back at Cadogan Square family and friends began to take second place to engaging trysts with Phoebe. On 30 June John dined at Dolly's house in Swan Walk specifically to meet Phoebe. From this point onwards John saw the new woman every few days, often using Dolly's home as their meeting place.

Dolly Clarke's regular intervention as go-between is curious considering her position both as John's cousin and former lover and as a close friend of Ladye and Cara. Later events indicate that Dolly's interest in John remained erotic, albeit unconsciously. During the first years of her marriage to Bobby Clarke such an interest was either submerged in Dolly's marital excitements or was repressed. It is possible however that John's affair with Phoebe, who never it seems evinced any desire to leave her husband, offered Dolly a new entrée into John's love life.

Ladye had begun a second journal in which she wrote fuller accounts of their daily lives. But under her entry for 23 May, the day John went to Malvern, someone else has written: 'She [Ladye] burnt her diaries then I think to prevent M.H. [Marguerite Hall] getting them.' Relatives of Mabel Batten suggested that the handwriting may have been that of Cara or Honey Harris. That scribbled note suggests that a possibly more bitter record of John's involvement was being kept.

During July, while John rode with Phoebe on a merry-go-round of pleasure, Ladye spent her time with Adela Maddison and Marta Mundt at Markham Square or lunched with Lady Elgar and Liza Lehmann at the Berkeley. On 15 July Winaretta Singer spent the evening with Ladye and John discussing poetry and relationships. John, disloyal and disconsolate, rushed out into the pelting rain with Rufus their dog. The following day Ladye admitted sadly: 'Felt upset and depressed as my heart bothered me greatly.'[1] Four days later Ladye reported: 'J. very upset afterwards with "*remords de conscience*". I got no sleep at all.'[2]

Conscience however did not stop John's erotic activities. While Ladye chose a diamond safety pin for John's birthday, her lover took off in pursuit of Phoebe. When Winaretta asked them both to listen to her new book on 27 July, only Ladye was available. A lengthy visit to the White Cottage gave Ladye a brief reprieve but little hope.[3] They celebrated John's thirty-second birthday by inviting Adela and Marta to Malvern but John's attention was patently elsewhere. Ladye's 'seediness' and 'heart-bothers' escalated as did their quarrels. The diamond pin, kept back during a bitter birthday, was handed over on 22 August to commemorate their fifth year together. Ladye hesitantly recorded: 'J seemed alright again and was very loving and made me feel happy.'[4]

Her hesitation was confirmed when John left her on 25 August to spend five days with Dolly and Phoebe at Southbourne. John's prodigal impudence threatened Ladye's stronghold. On her return they talked 'far into the night' after which Ladye 'got no sleep . . . felt depressed and breathless'.[5]

In September, when Otero their dog had to be destroyed, John became 'tired and not the thing' and 'depressed and fighty'. Cara's hopes of a May baby were confirmed, but Ladye despite her pleasure developed shingles. When Ladye, in malaise, elected to visit Cara, John retaliated by going off to Brighton, ostensibly to see Dolly although both partners were now clear that John and Phoebe were lovers and would meet at the seaside.[6]

In the autumn Adela Maddison, Ethel Smyth and Gabrielle Enthoven supported Ladye, took her Christmas shopping, sympathized with her breathlessness and pain, and, as friends will do, speculated on the outcome. They made sceptical pronouncements as Ladye corrected Radclyffe Hall's poems and stories. John, tango dancing with Phoebe, cared little for their speculations.

Occasionally she would accompany Ladye to visit the musical Mrs Woodhouse who was as opposed to convention as John herself.[7] Violet Gordon Woodhouse, whose musical salon had become a cult, currently shared her intimate life with one husband and three male lovers in a scandalous *ménage à cinq*, but it is possible that what intrigued John even in the midst of her affair with Phoebe was the passionate devotion Violet attracted from women including Ethel Smyth.[8]

Christmas 1913 was spent at Aspenden. Parochial pursuits legitimated their presence. John took her mare Judy and began riding again. Ladye rested, constantly bothered by her heart. While John and young Honey made toffee, Ladye wrote sadly in her diary: 'Felt very pleased that this horrid year has finished.'[9]

Several years after Ladye's death, John wrote that Ladye, 'one of the most generous minded and brilliant women', had taught her 'charity' and encouraged her to 'look for the good' in other people.[10] During the latter years of Ladye's life, John did not return that charity. It was left to Ladye to look for the good in John.

In Ladye John had what she thought she had wanted: a loyal and loving partner, an artistic adviser, a best friend. She ought to have felt safe. Possibly she did feel safe: that may have been part of the problem. From her childhood onwards safety was not a familiar notion; the unsafe was all too familiar. Recent research on the sexual abuse of girls suggests two patterns of response: first, that in adult life the young woman may exhibit marked seductive behaviour, and secondly that she may abandon her belief in the possibility of her own personal safety and re-create dangerous situations for herself and her intimates.[11] John's behaviour then and at later moments of crisis was a cogent illustration of the impact of violent and incestuous child rearing on the development of a personality.

In this first infidelity with Phoebe other factors may have played a part.

There was the attraction of taking up a position centre stage. No longer content to be the satellite, John had begun to feel her own sexual power. Guilt-ridden but triumphant, she occupied the central place in the affections of two puissant women.

Ladye's increasing frailty, her real or imagined ailments, meant that boredom crept stealthily into John's view of her partner. Ladye coughed her way into 1914, a year she spent in depression and illness. On 27 January John was momentarily distracted from Phoebe by the news that her friend Peggy Austin was in hospital. She hurried there with Dolly and waited until the news was better. When Cara almost had a miscarriage on 1 February John, chastened, returned her attentions temporarily to her family. She agreed to go with Ladye to Tamaris near Toulon in the South of France on 9 February. Without Phoebe in tow, they managed a reasonable vacation until 30 March. The diary is a dull chronicle, a testament to enervation on the one part, agitation on the other.[12]

For the last two weeks of the holiday Dolly came out to join them, bringing John news of Phoebe. John skirted penitence and desired release. It came in April when joylessly they dawdled home, stopping first in Monte Carlo, then at Ethel Harter's villa in Florence, the city beloved of the Brownings. Florence, the home of art, once home-abroad to both of them, vibrant and vivid, now seemed pale and grey. Though John purchased another mandolin, she did not play it. This time the trip lacked melody.

Back at Cadogan Square they visited Peter, Honey and Cara in their new home at 10 Catherine Street where John and Ladye attempted to play the part of beguiled *boulevardiers*, but their false enthusiasm fooled no one.

Reassuring platitudes, tired certainties were shot through with apprehension. During April and May John, 'in bad spirits', began riding in the Park with Phoebe. Ladye, 'cold and depressed', stayed in the warm. Most nights they quarrelled till two in the morning. Cara's troubled pregnancy produced several further alarms but on 12 May her baby was born safely. Ladye rushed to be with her. John had told Cara she would like to be the child's 'godfather' especially if it was a boy.[13] The baby was a girl, called Karen. John was noticeably absent. She was taking tea with Phoebe.

During May and June John also went out of her way to see more of the fascinating Violet Gordon Woodhouse, whom she and Ladye called Morena. John and Ladye spent a weekend at Violet's house in Stratford, and John visited her alone in London in June.[14]

Relations between John and Ladye had deteriorated to such an extent that during Whitsun they separated. Ladye went alone to the South Eastern Hotel in Deal leaving John to escort Phoebe on a romantic weekend to Felixstowe.

Oliver Hoare, blind and cuckold to the situation, decided to open his eyes. In June he intervened. From then onwards John was frequently forced to see Phoebe under her husband's watchful gaze or, further to allay suspicion, to suggest that the Hoares accompany her and Ladye to the theatre.[15] Occasionally the lovers slipped off, or Ladye would tolerantly drive John to Swan Walk to see Phoebe discreetly.

Should we marvel at Ladye's acquiescence, or see in it her stricken desire to spend time with John under any circumstances? Once John contracted mumps on 26 June some of the romance was tarnished. Her ensuing thinness and nerves became of primary concern to Ladye as well as to Phoebe.

It was a triangle in which everyone's loyalty was strained beyond recognition. John valued loyalty, as she always would. Yet she jumped headlong into a situation in which she was openly, flagrantly, disloyal. The openness was Ladye's idea, her one vestige of control in a situation that grew daily more dangerous. She insisted on honesty even though it brought her incalculable distress.

This triangle in which everyone suffered would not be the last triangle or the last bout of suffering. The themes John lived out with Ladye, of commitment versus bondage, loyalty versus infidelity, she wove into her first completed novel *The Unlit Lamp*. Hall reinvents the triangle in the guise of the mother Mrs Ogden and the beloved governess Elizabeth Rodney, who fight each other for love and possession of the triangle's third member, young Joan Ogden.

Images of suffering were the hieroglyphs of John's childhood, imprinted for life. When Una was the 'other woman' in the triangle with John and Ladye, and years later in the bitter triangle with John and Souline, when Una symbolically took Ladye's place as the cast-off old coat, she tells us that John's addiction was suffering.

John and Ladye's growing estrangement can be seen in a letter Ladye wrote to her daughter Cara about their need to occupy separate bedrooms if they were to accept the Harrises' invitation to join them in July at Horsey Hall, their rented summer place in Norfolk. The letter, which also illustrates John's insistence on her 'husbandly rights' of a separate dressing-room, is curious.

> My dear child, about the double bedded room, certainly if there is a dressing room for John we shouldn't mind at all, but I don't see how we *could* both dress in one room without any privacy! . . . I don't think it would work . . . Perhaps you will find you can put her up in a small bedroom not next mine. She says she'd far rather do that . . . We don't at all mind sleeping in a two bedded room . . . Perhaps you would rather not have us at all?[16]

Hints of war began to infiltrate domestic life. On 28 July Ladye reported: 'War threatening with Germany.' However as bedrooms at Horsey had been sorted out, it was in Norfolk that they heard the first news. After tea in the cottage, Ladye wrote: '*Sat. Aug 1st*: City news very depressing and Germany declared war on France and invaded Luxemburg. Austin and J both very depressed – the others didn't seem to mind.' As they bathed from the cottage the next day, Germany declared war on Russia. 'Everyone – especially Johnny depressed. Heard that the Banks were refusing to pay out gold.' On 4 August, England was mobilizing and on the brink of war. Ladye and John returned to London on 6 August. The following day they got gold from their banks, the servants left for Malvern, and they both called on Phoebe. With separation inevitable, were there suddenly momentous matters which all three needed to talk about? Ladye's openness fails us.

On 8 August they went to Confession at the Cathedral, then John had tea alone with Phoebe. In the evening Ladye and John with Phoebe and Oliver made up a tortured foursome for dinner at Lucca's restaurant. The next day John and Ladye left for the White Cottage.

John would not see Phoebe again for a year.

During August the war news got worse. Adela Maddison wrote to Ladye from France with her worries about her partner Marta Mundt, who was German. Ladye wrote to Cara: 'The prejudice against Germans is terrible. Marta is very cultivated and clever and with a tremendous sense of humour, but this won't keep her alive I'm afraid.'[17] Adela wrote to John and Ladye: 'I am so sick of life in general and so tired of "ideals" that only lead to the utmost abyss of sordid realities, but one can't be untrue to one's nature.'[18] It was a sentiment John agreed with. Finally to their relief Adela and Marta managed to escape from France as the Germans entered Brussels, and the British forces suffered huge losses at Mons.[19]

Domestic privations as well as public pronouncements bespoke the times. Harrods ran out of sugar. In an attempt to economize, Ladye and John sent their parlourmaid Packer packing, then attended their first nursing lectures.

Dolly and Bobby wrote to say they were penniless and would be forced to let Swan Walk. Ladye wrote to Cara: 'I suppose it will end in her [John] supporting them more or less till the war is over.'[20] John went to London and brought Dolly back to Malvern, together with the Clarkes' dogs Toto and Clayton as 'animal refugees'. On 4 September Bobby Clarke wrote to say he had enlisted and that his brother had been killed at the front. The war had reached their intimate circle.[21]

John and Ladye decided to let Cadogan Square and stay in Malvern. By 9 September when they went to London to sign over a six-month lease of the flat, Oliver and Phoebe Hoare had left the city. The affair with Phoebe was effectively over.

Malvern became a centre for the war wounded. The Red Cross and the Order of St John set up between them five hospitals. Three battalions of soldiers were stationed in the area, and Belgian refugees began to arrive. John and Ladye attended ambulance lectures, bandaging classes, and home nursing tutorials. They made two rooms of the White Cottage available for wounded soldiers, even Germans. John said frequently that had she been a man she would have enlisted at once. Had she been a woman without a partner she might well have enrolled in the all-women ambulance units which patrolled the French and German fronts. Ladye's frail health meant that the younger woman could not envisage leaving her, though she did not always stay with good grace.

John's frustration at not being able to join the main war effort told on her nerves and became the impetus for her fictional portrayals of women who had found satisfaction in work at the front. Malise (Pamela Gordon), the forerunner of Stephen Gordon and Miss Ogilvy, all the fictional New Women 'released by the war', watched in old age by Joan Ogden the 'pioneer who had got left behind',[22] managed to achieve what John felt she had not. As she wrote of Stephen in *The Well*: 'Every instinct handed down by the men of her race, every decent instinct of courage, now rose to mock her so that all that was male in her make-up seemed to grow more aggressive, perhaps as never before, because of this new frustration.'[23]

To make up for it, she occupied herself by writing recruiting leaflets, running enlistment campaigns, and giving speeches on the importance of joining up. In an impromptu speech at a meeting in Castlemorton she urged the all-women audience to insist their menfolk enlisted. On 19 September John and Ladye joined Bobby Clarke, resplendent 'in his new khaki', for a farewell lunch in London[24] before they prepared Cadogan Square for the tenants, then on 21 September, exhausted by packing, they slept at Cara's in Catherine Street.

The following day had tragic implications. On 22 September, *en route* back to Malvern, their hired 22-hp limousine, driven by their usual chauffeur Serpell, was suddenly struck broadside by a small open top car at the Burford crossroads. John's angry description of the crash was repeated to Una Troubridge: 'The violence of the first impact was such that it flung the heavy car over against a stone wall which it demolished, while the aggressor proceeded to pound it repeatedly before her engine stalled. The big car ended up on its side, terribly shattered (the body-makers subsequently expressed surprise that anyone had come out of it alive).'[25]

John, Serpell and the maid Garry were only marginally hurt, but Ladye's injuries were extensive. She lay unconscious at the bottom of the car, with several broken ribs, blood dripping from severe cuts on her face, a neck vertebra injured, and as they later discovered serious damage to her lower spine.

John would always show a cool head, quick thinking and courage in emergencies. She had Ladye carried into a house nearby owned by a Mrs Pigott. A Dr Cheadle was sent for at once. Then John rounded on the driver of the other car, Mrs Lakin, and accused her of trying to kill them. The woman was forced to admit that Serpell had the right of way, though she refused to accept John's view that she was travelling fast, did not sound her horn, did not brake. Subsequent court proceedings between the insurance companies proved John to have been correct and Mrs Lakin to have lied in her own defence.

At Dr Cheadle's insistence Ladye remained at Mrs Pigott's for eleven days, at the end of which he considered that she was still too ill to be moved. But when Frank Romer, the Harrises' doctor, arrived he decided – in John's retrospective view, erroneously – that it was safe to move her to Malvern. Once there she was virtually an invalid. The Burford crash reversed their roles at home. John took over the housekeeping and saw to the maids; Ladye remained in bed or on the sofa, with John in constant attendance.

Ladye's incapacity at home and John's frustration at being unable to make a useful contribution to the war forced them apart, and drove John deeper into her writing. There is some evidence to suggest that at this point John turned to Violet Gordon Woodhouse certainly for sympathy and understanding and according to Violet's biographer Jessica Douglas-Home possibly for an erotic adventure. Jessica Douglas-Home believes that in the absence of three of Violet's four male consorts John 'fell under Violet's spell'.[26] Certainly in 1915 John visited Violet regularly at her house in Ovington Square and took her for lunch at the Berkeley.[27] She even dedicated her next volume of poetry, *The Forgotten Island*, to Violet or Morena as she called her. Printed at the beginning of the book is the inscription:

> Dedicated to Mrs Gordon Woodhouse. My dear Friend, Please accept these few poems, which I dedicate to you. I have written them down just as they came to me, and such as they are I now offer them. Perhaps they may find favour with you, perhaps no. In any case they must plead their own cause. M.

During the first tempestuous triangle with Phoebe and Ladye, John had nevertheless managed to write with vigour and lyricism. Sexual excitement, possibly increased by her infatuation with Violet Gordon Woodhouse, heightened her emotions as she prepared her fifth volume of poems, *The Forgotten Island*.

The success of *Songs of Three Counties* had encouraged Radclyffe Hall to experiment with blank verse, and to use a unified theme for the new collection. Neither approach had she tried before. Arranged around the memory of a previous incarnation on a mythical Greek island, probably Lesbos, the lyrics – forty-three in all – dwell reflectively upon a love affair, constituting together a passionate love song addressed to a young girl. So movingly is the affair recalled there can be little doubt that it reflected an event that had occurred.

The affair starts at the height of passion, then slips into dull routine when the poet longs for a new and more exciting love. In the old love she beholds '. . . the oil and the wick for the burning, / Yet the light of the lamp is absent.'[28] A recurring image in the collection is that of a ship sailing towards new shores. Are we to see in this John's growing dissatisfaction with Ladye and her torn feelings for Phoebe? Are we to see in it a newer attachment to her second Violet? It is hard to tell – just as it is hard to tell exactly how far the romantic experiment with Violet went. Violet's propensity for encouraging violent emotions and then withdrawing would suggest that no deep physical involvement took place.[29] However John's characteristic insistence on maintaining close friendships with women ensured that she and her second Violet stayed good friends for some years.

Radclyffe Hall sent the proofs of *The Forgotten Island* to Sir Arthur Quiller-Couch at Cambridge. John paraphrased Quiller-Couch's 'wonderful' reply in her own letter to the writer Douglas Sladen: 'With me [Quiller-Couch] thinks that there is a great future for this style in English lyrical poetry.'[30] However, on its publication, although the *Pall Mall Gazette* thought highly of it, not all the reviewers agreed.[31] The tone of the poems seemed out of key with the current wartime mood of patriotic enthusiasm.

Hall's response to poor reviews was professional and pragmatic: 'I myself have always been inspired to write well after a good review . . . This cannot always happen however and meanwhile one must keep a good heart knowing that one has done one's best.'[32]

In this case a 'good heart' was more easily kept now that her literary interests were engaged in her first fictions. Early in 1914 she had begun a story entitled 'Bonaparte'.[33] She finished the manuscript by 27 December, then began at once on 'Out of the Night', a story completed in seven days. With amazing speed, by 10 January 1915 she polished off another story, 'The Recording Angel', which loyal Ladye, in severe muscular pain, copied, between neck massages, before it was read aloud together with 'The Career of Mark Anthony Brakes', which John had been redrafting for some months.[34]

Radclyffe Hall had already discovered that a critical audience was the best means of assessing the worth of her fiction. Four days later, on 21 January, she wrote a draft of 'Modern Miss Thompson' which was finalized the following day. By 10 February she had decided that the stories were worth taking to an agency to be typed. Nervous but triumphant, she went to tea with Adela Maddison and Marta Mundt. On 13 February John read Cara the typescript of 'Two Poets and a Pretty Woman'. The following day Adela came to dinner to listen to all the fiction now in typed form. While John talked about her fiction, Ladye diligently re-corrected it.

For Ladye at this point John's writing was the only part of their relationship that was conducted without tension. It says a good deal for her tolerance that, during a period fraught with emotional scenes and physical pain following the Burford accident, she was prepared to occupy herself in this way on John's behalf. 'Through all the month of March – neck bad and teeth troublesome, perpetual sore gums or lips – and shingles . . . I did an immense amount of copying her MSS for her.'[35]

On 13 April the actor Ernest Thesiger, nicknamed by Ladye the 'Ace of Diamonds', walked to Little Malvern with John, stayed for dinner, and afterwards heard a rendering of 'Out of the Night'. He praised it. She listened. But her mind was now on her new novel.

On 26 March Ladye's journal tells us: 'John overdoing herself by writing for hours at a stretch both morning and evening . . . in fact [she] wrote nearly all day at her new book *Michael West*.'[36] As Una Troubridge said later, 'reluctantly, intermittently, inexpertly, she was awakening to self-criticism, she was beginning to try to work.'[37] And work she did, assiduously blocking out personal problems: writing as a defence against the present, as a foundation for her future. Her output was prolific, her speed extraordinary.

Though the narratives are exquisite bric-à-bracs, innocent of intellectual architecture, devoid of structural rigour, they are irreproachably assured, speaking of larger expectations. Hall's poetic skill prompts some perfect cadences, some Swinburnian touches of languor and voluptuousness, some profound moments of high drama.

Earlier biographers suggested that these stories were destroyed by Una Troubridge after John's death, but among Hall's unpublished papers in Rome I found drafts of several stories, scribbled, corrected, scored out, redrafted, badly spelt, hardly legible, strikingly similar to her subsequent manuscripts. Her dissatisfaction with draft after draft, her determination to create something better can be seen in the meticulous changes she made from version to version. Some years later, writing about her methods of constructing a novel, Radclyffe Hall said:

> The principal characters first come into my mind together with the circumstances surrounding them. I build up the skeleton of a story. My next concern is always with the psychology of my characters as it would be affected by their circumstances and surroundings . . . I begin to live the life of my principal characters and all the minor characters fit in just as they would in my own everyday life.[38]

An interesting feature of these early stories is that they carry precisely this trademark. They are cleverly wrought, well-sustained psychological portraits, which may have been influenced by Hall's reading during this period of Somerset Maugham, John Galsworthy and May Sinclair. From Galsworthy's *The Dark Flower* and Somerset Maugham's *Of Human Bondage* she learnt the value of a dramatic construction that offered also a social and moral critique. In the fiction of May Sinclair, seventeen years her senior, Hall heard a melody whose strains echo resonantly throughout her early narratives. When May Sinclair died, found amongst her papers, in Richard Garnett's handwriting, were two lines of Henry Thoreau: 'If I do not keep step with others, it is because I hear a different drummer. Let a man step to the music which he hears, however measured and however far away.'[39]

By the time she wrote *The Well of Loneliness* Radclyffe Hall had the confidence to remain out of step, to ensure that what was singular did not have to become standardized. In the early years the drumming in the distance heard by both women writers was a growing awareness of the effects of unconscious impulses upon the everyday music.

John may have been casually introduced to May Sinclair by Violet Hunt during their suffragette days, but it was not until the 1920s that their friendship flowered. During the years 1910 to 1920, before the emergence of Virginia Woolf as a major writer, May Sinclair was considered England's foremost woman novelist.

Her literary importance rests on her power of psychological analysis and dramatic portrayal in novels which often deal with religious as well as ethical questions. Interested in Idealism – the belief that thought is the only reality and that the external world is fundamentally immaterial and a dimension of the mind – her influence on Hall was less by way of these ideas than through her interest in psychology. She was amongst the first writers to explore and develop the 'stream of consciousness technique' – she coined the phrase, appropriating the psychological term 'stream of consciousness' to describe the representational literary technique of Dorothy Richardson in a review of the latter's *Pilgrimage* in 1918. Sinclair utilizes this stream of consciousness in both *Mary Olivier: A Life* (1919) and *The Life and Death of Harriett Frean* (1920).

Like Radclyffe Hall (although for somewhat different reasons), May Sinclair was fascinated by the 'new psychology', as the literature of psychoanalysis was then called. Radclyffe Hall was to follow Sinclair in seeing psychoanalysis as a means for people to further their self-development and to cast off that Victorian puritanism which Hall, Sinclair and Hunt found so constricting. Sinclair was a staunch supporter of women's rights and many of her novels show this and explore the destructive influence of the Victorian view of marriage. Novels like *The Three Sisters* (1914), *Mary Olivier* and *Harriett Frean* all dealt with the psychological struggle of women whose conflict is between sexual or social repression and desire.

Radclyffe Hall's curiosity was initially roused by Sinclair's *The Three Sisters*, which Ladye read aloud to her in 1914. Set near Swaledale in Yorkshire, the novel's characters and landscape were undoubtedly influenced by Sinclair's earlier study of the Brontës. Critics have detected this influence, not only in the nature of the story itself, but in Sinclair's ability – much like that of Charlotte Brontë herself – to unpick the seams between her characters' conscious acts and subconscious motives. This interest in psychological delineation, especially in the context of a spiritual quest, was to make a special appeal to Hall, who was to exploit it in her own first completed novel, *The Unlit Lamp*.

The power of landscape to influence and shape characters, which Sinclair uses powerfully in *The Three Sisters*, also becomes a motif and reference point for Hall's own writing. Radclyffe Hall uses the town of Seabourne in *The Unlit Lamp* to suggest the suburban stuffiness of the lives of its inhabitants, as May

Sinclair used the wild Yorkshire moors to suggest the harshness of the three sisters' lives. Again, in *The Sixth Beatitude* Hall uses the grim, wind-torn features of the Rye coast to point up the bleakness of Hannah Bullen's working-class life.

With her capacity for character delineation and for exploring personalities caught within a domestic framework Sinclair had an immediate influence on Hall's writing. Both writers shared an interest in the way personality is formed and family relationships work; in the way people deceive themselves and betray each other. And like Sinclair – and others of her period[40] – Hall introduced these themes into her stories, focusing on the effects of unconscious drives and impulses on daily routines.

Ladye, convinced that John's stories were worthy of publication, sent them in May 1915 to an acquaintance who had a reputation for discovering new talent. With unexpected swiftness, her respondent, the publisher William Heinemann, wrote back on 27 May to say the stories were of such excellence that he would like to meet the author.

On 1 June they drove up from Malvern to 32 Lower Belgrave Street to meet Heinemann for lunch. He was extravagant in his praise of her fiction. He singled out 'The Career of Mark Anthony Brakes'[41] as being the best short story ever submitted for his approval.[42] John with her characteristic bluntness said: 'Then you are going to publish my stories, Mr Heinemann?'

The reply was a shock:

> I will certainly do nothing of the kind. I am not going to present you to the public as the writer of a few short stories, however good they may be, and what is more, I do not want you to offer them to any periodical. You will set to work at once and write me a novel, and when it is finished I will publish it.[43]

Although Hall was already working on two novels, *The Cunninghams* and *Michael West*, she did not reveal this either then to the publisher or later to Una Troubridge who mistakenly records that John had not the faintest idea of how to set about writing a novel. To Heinemann Hall protested that she 'would never stay the course'. 'Oh yes, you will . . . You don't know it yourself yet, but I know it,' said Heinemann. 'You can and you will and you will bring it to me.'[44]

Radclyffe Hall was not yet ready to take Heinemann's advice, dispense with frivolities, and apply herself with the dedication required of a novelist. But he had convinced her that fiction was her forte.

From August 1915 onwards John resumed her friendship with Violet Hunt whom she saw on 29 August, six days after she wrote the last line of the final draft of 'The Woman in a Crêpe Bonnet'. It is highly likely that she took that manuscript, together with 'Mandalay', the story she had completed on 22 August, and the current version of *Michael West* for Violet to look at.

Ladye had woven Violet's new novels and those of her lover Ford Madox Ford, particularly Ford's *The Good Soldier*, into John's reading plan for the summer in Aspenden and London.[45] For the two years that John had been involved with Phoebe, Violet had been in serious trouble over her scandalous liaison with Ford Madox Ford. She had met him at the Galsworthys' in 1907, the year John had followed Ladye to Homburg. Violet and Ford became lovers in 1909. Ford's invalid writer wife, Elsie Martindale, set her face resolutely against a divorce. Despite public disapproval, Violet installed Ford at South Lodge where her weekly salons, attended by Radclyffe Hall and other writers, were now as well known for social tittle-tattle as for literary discussion.

Then, at the time John and Ladye were moving into Cadogan Square, Ford caused a sensation by telling the *Daily Mirror* that during his stay in Germany he had married that 'well known authoress Violet Hunt', having succeeded in divorcing his former wife on the technical grounds of desertion.[46] Violet was appalled. It was nothing less than a blatant lie: there were no grounds for Ford's claim that he was married to Violet. Certainly, Violet wanted to become, at last, a respectable married woman. But this story simply made her, once again, the object of gossip and scandal.

With extraordinary trust (some would say naïveté) and without viewing any official documents, Violet decided to accept Ford's assurance that he had obtained some kind of divorce and later, in a hotel room in France, she and Ford went through a form of marriage ceremony. When this proved to be bigamous Violet had great need of her women friends. With Ladye and John abroad, Violet turned to May Sinclair and later Rebecca West for support. But in 1915, when Ford discovered that Violet had syphilis, then in its tertiary stage, it was John who was there to sustain her friend. When Ford took a commission in the army, Violet saw it as a rejection of their relationship. On his stormy departure from London, Violet again turned for affection to Marguerite.

When Violet had read an early draft of 'The Woman in a Crêpe Bonnet'[47] the theme had been that of 'the outsider'. Hall poses the question of whether the blunt-fingered man who has committed murder is to be deemed 'the outsider' because of his crime or because he has been *caught*. In the final version shown to Violet, the theme has been amended to embrace the twin notions of infidelity and betrayal. Debating the meaning of 'infidelity' – a subject doubtless on her mind – Hall suggests that perhaps there is a faithfulness of the spirit even when the body has betrayed.

Her analysis of several types of betrayal is both complex and ironic. The prisoner indubitably has betrayed the girl who may or may not have betrayed him. He has certainly betrayed his now dead child. Outside the court, shoving and pushing her way to the front of the railings in her eagerness to see a villain hang, is a stranger, a woman in a crêpe bonnet, who will betray both God and the prisoner. She is a patronizing puritanical widow whose own son is, as she tells the crowd, 'as fine and God-fearing a young man as any you'll see in these parts'. She has no compassion for the man in the dock who they remind her is some other poor woman's child. 'Hanging's too good for the likes of 'im!' she says harshly. 'I could never 'ave no tenderness for the likes of 'im even if 'e was my own flesh and blood!'

The jury reach their verdict. The man is condemned. Two policemen pull him out into the yard past the waiting crowd.

> He was dragging backwards, they could not get him to walk properly, his knees were bending, he looked like a cripple . . . horrible . . . his knees looked like they had been broken . . . his face had fallen in, the cheeks sagging, the mouth dropped open, it was terror, naked and unashamed that stood revealed to the breathless crowd. The man was revolting, indecently afraid.[48]

Hanging's too good for the likes of him even if he was my own flesh and blood, runs the refrain. The finale is bitter. The likes of him was the God-fearing flesh and blood son of the woman in the crêpe bonnet.

This theme of the outsider and the matter of betrayal which so preoccupied Hall was the focus of Heinemann's favourite story, 'The Career of Mark Anthony Brakes'.

As a small black African-American boy Mark Anthony 'was . . . vaguely conscious of being somehow different'. At school he could not 'pass' as some of his kin could. He was not 'coffee-and-milk'. He was too clever to become a grocer like his father. 'His dreams were so much bigger than himself.'[49]

Fulfilling his dream of becoming a lawyer meant he would betray his African forebears. As he strove for success 'he could not resist the temptation to imitate the white man's speech'. In his intellectual aptitude, in his pursuit of a career, 'he knew he was white'. He also knew he was disloyal.

Racial prejudice prevents him from defending white clients, so he takes for no fee the case of a poor white actress whom no one else will represent. She will become his white advertisement. 'Well, I guess you're a white man, that's what you are,' she says as she accepts.

Given the period, her acceptance leads to an unacceptable situation. Their common bond leads him to contemplate what to her can never be contemplated: sex and marriage. She betrays him by appearing to lead him on.

Celibate for years, fastidious about sex, unwilling to marry a black woman, Mark Anthony had felt 'his isolation to the very depths of his being' until he fell violently in love with his client, the 23-year-old Rose Robins, whose likeness to Dolly Clarke is unmistakable. Now Mark Anthony 'began to find that the body is inevitably the battlefield upon which the great moral issues of life are fought out'. He contains his sexual feelings. He wins the case. Banner headlines shriek: 'Case for actress won by coloured lawyer'. Triumphantly he turns up at Rose Robins' bedsitting-room. In his agitation his voice takes on all the 'old tricks of intonation and dialect' so carefully hidden for so many years. 'I wants you to be my wife. I wants to take you into a cleaner life,' he stutters.

Rose is appalled. She begins to laugh hysterically. 'A cleaner life, did you say? What with a nigger? . . . Mad, you're stark staring mad . . . get out will you, black nigger, get out!'

Mark Anthony betrays everything he has taught himself about honour, compassion, decency. He lunges brutally towards her: 'He gloated over her like a beast over its prey.' There is blood on her face, blood in her mouth, blood on her dress.

He walks out of her room. He has paid the price. 'You were born black and black you have always remained. You have murdered your own ideal,' he says to himself. Then from the drawer of his writing desk he removes a revolver. He steps out into the night.

In the light of many years of radical black politics, it is hard to view this harsh yet simplistic story in the way that William Heinemann did. Una Troubridge tells us that the reason Radclyffe Hall did not include it in her 1934 collection of short stories (several of which dated from this early period) was that 'when she wrote it, [what] had been the originality of its theme . . . had since then been treated and exhausted by other writers, both white and coloured . . . her story had definitely missed the boat.'[50]

We can however still appreciate the powerful emotion that rushes through the narrative like its own spilt blood. Radclyffe Hall had no knowledge of what it felt like to be a black man outside a white society, but she certainly knew what it felt like to be a lesbian woman outside heterosexual society: thwarted, excluded, ostracized.

In these early fictions we see symbolic descriptions of the child at risk, the child abused, the child betrayed. Mark Anthony Brakes is as much a prisoner of his childhood as was Michael West or Marguerite Radclyffe-Hall.

We must be cautious of tracing facile links between Radclyffe Hall's writing at this time and her amorous preoccupations, if only because they so disarmingly invite such links. Yet connections do spring to mind. 'The Career of Mark Anthony Brakes', like 'The Woman in a Crêpe Bonnet', is excessive in its self-reproach for infidelity in its widest forms, excessive in its punishment for different kinds of betrayal.

The one characteristic Hall's biographers have so far agreed upon is that in most areas of her life Radclyffe Hall was an extremist. Although unable, or unwilling, to cease her affair with Phoebe when it was at its most hurtful to Ladye, she offered instead a splendid line in self-flagellation.

Una's own retrospective record of the Phoebe Hoare affair is interesting. She never mentions Phoebe by name. She calls her merely 'a passing emotional storm'[51] during a long period in which 'John's devotion burned with a steady light and was returned'. Una admits that John's 'fancy did stray once but it was a trivial, passing lapse, broke no bones and left no aftermath. It is hardly worth recording, Ladye dismissed the incident with a tolerant smile, and no one but John, scourging herself for infidelity, gave it any great importance.'[52]

It is obvious from Ladye's diary that, if it did not break the bones of their relationship, it splintered and fractured them to such a degree that they could not comfortably be reset. And aftermath there certainly was. The fact that the rubicon of mutual fidelity had once been crossed with Phoebe opened the way to a second adventure, this time with Una herself. That Una Troubridge should wish readers of her biography to think John's fancy for Phoebe unimportant may well have been in order to throw greater weight on to John's 'lapse' with her.

How long-lasting the 'passing emotional storm' with Una Troubridge would turn out to be surprised both of them, John in particular. When John met Una for the second time, on Sunday 1 August 1915, at a tea party in Cambridge Square, at the home of Ladye's sister Emmie Clarendon, that meeting foreshadowed a 'lapse' that was to become the lapse of a lifetime.

8

FROM A LAPSE TO A LIFE: UNA TROUBRIDGE

Una Troubridge labelled and tagged everything. Categories and classifications connect and construct her narrative, as naming and renaming constitute John's. Certain labels Una appropriated for her own use. Titles afford a good example.

Lady Troubridge was not born a Lady, though she seized on the title readily enough in June 1919, despite being already legally separated from Admiral Troubridge. During John's life, self-aggrandizement allowed Una to wield a handle that exerted considerable influence. She used it ruthlessly on any occasion she deemed useful for her partner's advancement and more discreetly for her own. When, in 1945, two years after John's death, she wrote her biography of Radclyffe Hall, she used as her author's credit 'By Una, Lady Troubridge'. She delayed publication (possibly for fear of libel from John's previous lovers Jane Randolph Caruth, Dolly Clarke and Evguenia Souline) until 1961 when all three were dead. In that more egalitarian age the fact that Hall's first biographer was a Lady did the book less service than her unladylike position as John's lesbian lover.

Lady Troubridge was not even born Una. On 8 March 1887, in a quiet Kensington square, the second daughter in the Taylor family was named Margot Elena Gertrude. Her family, given to pet names like her cousin Ladye's, immediately nicknamed her Una – the feminine of the Latin *unus*, and the Italian *uno*. A child of marked singularity, she soon became her name.

Una Vincenzo Troubridge, who borrowed her middle name from her Florentine relatives, the ancient Italian families of Vincenzo and Tealdi, first met John in June 1912: a meeting which appears to have left no impression upon either of them. Una, whose life as an Admiral's wife was to take her frequently abroad, did not keep in touch with John, though she continued to dine occasionally with her cousin.

On 1 August 1915 however, when Una met John for the second time at

Emmie Clarendon's, the impact on Una was decisive. The effect on Ladye can be seen in several gloomy diary entries: 'Una began to "drop in" on 15 August after which she was with us constantly.' On 23 August John finished writing 'Woman in a Crêpe Bonnet', but to Ladye's dismay the following day 'she went after dinner to read her MSS to Una Troubridge. After this date Una set in.'[1]

For Ladye this signified a ruthless rupture in their relationship. When John asked Violet to read her work she was seeking professional criticism. But a desire for Una's attentions tore at the fabric of their union. John's work had always been Ladye's primary concern. She corrected the spelling, did the copying, transcribed the manuscripts, orchestrated the readings. She had found composers to set the poems to music, had found a publisher to read the first fictions. Una, an interloper of a different magnitude from Phoebe, was a contender on a par with Ladye herself. What the impact of that second meeting was on John we know only through Una's description, a significant point.

Una Troubridge's particular power in relation to Radclyffe Hall is the power of depiction, of definition. Language is our means of classifying and ordering the world, our means of manipulating reality, of constructing myths which, if convincing, induce others to see the play and the characters from our point of view. From 1915 onwards, biographers have been hard put *not* to see the domestic and literary world of Radclyffe Hall according to Una's version. Una Troubridge after all was almost always *there*. She became the high priestess of facts and, judging from later evidence, facts were often for bending. The scarcity of autobiographical material, apart from notable glimmers within Hall's fiction, during the years 1915 to 1934 has meant that Radclyffe Hall's story has largely been told by Una.

John did not keep journals and, until her relationship with Evguenia Souline, wrote few personal letters. Una Troubridge on the other hand wrote a daily diary. For several years she also kept a fuller Day Book of events and personages. Una promoted Radclyffe Hall's books, tended the lamp of Radclyffe Hall's literary talents. She instigated their social invitations, dealt with publishers, agents, and later the press. John, it seemed, allowed – indeed, for some years appeared enthusiastically to endorse – Una's two inventions of 'John the Woman' and 'Radclyffe Hall the Creative Genius'. John herself began to believe in and act out the character depicted for her. Una and John became the twin heroines, that famous lesbian couple, in the colourful drama drawn and redrawn by Lady Troubridge, who after John's death consolidated her version of events with a hagiographic biography. It is therefore with caution that I view Una's depiction of Radclyffe Hall's middle years, attempting to balance it with reference to Ladye's few remaining journal entries, Souline's unpublished accounts, and Hall's fiction, autobiographical essays and, where possible, letters.

The world of 1915 had grown smaller as communications and travel were extended. Albert Einstein postulated his General Theory of Relativity, wireless service was established between the USA and Japan, and the first motorized taxis began to appear on the streets of London. It was however still a stereotypical society for women. In 1915, Margaret Sanger – who appeared with John's Paris friend Djuna Barnes at Mabel Dodge's salon in Greenwich Village – coined the term 'birth control', was jailed for writing *Family Limitation*, the first book on the topic, and was caustically designated 'the New Woman' by the popular press.* In 1919 Lord Beaverbrook was to buy up the *Daily Express* whose increased popularity gave wide circulation to traditional images of women. A stately carriage, a fine figure with abundant curves, flashing eyes under lowered lids were the appurtenances of feminine appearance. These, together with a proud or melting maternal role, became primary depictions.

In that period appearance and finery could dictate whether a woman was judged dull or decadent, shy or well-informed. Oscar Wilde (a good friend of Laura and Violet Troubridge, Una's future sisters-in-law) had already pointed out that it is only the shallow people who do not judge by appearance. It is thus hardly surprising that when the curtain went up that second time, on 1 August 1915, it was John's dramatic, androgynous appearance – almost brutal in its briskness, no child at heel, no languorous looks – that first entranced Una Troubridge: 'Her appearance was calculated to arouse interest. It immediately aroused mine.'[2]

Thirty years later Una recalled:

I can still see John as I saw her on that day . . . She was then 34 years of age and very good indeed to look upon. At that time short hair in a woman was almost unknown and she had not yet cut hers . . . It was silver-blonde . . . (it reached nearly to her knees and its growth defied frequent pruning) . . . in tight plaits closely twisted round her small and admirably shaped head. Her complexion was clear and pale, her eyebrows and very long lashes nearly as golden as her hair and her eyes a clear grey blue, beautifully set and with a curious fierce, noble expression that reminded me of certain caged eagles at the Zoological Gardens! Her mouth was sensitive and . . . could look very determined . . . but was liable to break into the most infectious, engaging but rather raffish smile . . . not the countenance of a young woman but of a very handsome young man. Like her father she was only of medium height but so well proportioned that she looked taller . . . Her hands, and here again they were not feminine hands, were quite beautiful and so were her feet.

Una goes on: 'for reasons much less obvious that interest was returned.'[3]

---

* In 1917 Sanger was listed with Margaret Anderson, Louise Bryant, Jane Heap, Elsa Baroness Von Freytag-Loringhoven and Mina Loy for the title of 'modern woman' by the *New York Evening Sun*. Djuna Barnes and Margaret Sanger mixed in the Greenwich Village crowd centred on the Provincetown Playhouse which produced important women writers and artists who created or sustained ideals of 'sex-antagonism'.

Una's appearance, dark curling hair, grey curious eyes, an energetic youthful figure, a young mother with a failing marriage, with the sharp vitality of a talented established artist, struck John rather differently. Still devoted to Ladye, though no longer erotically interested in her, still recovering from the agonized involvement with Phoebe Hoare, John was intrigued but cool. 'How do I know if I shall care for you in six months time?' she asked Una during an early conversation. Una was frank enough to report: 'John, I know, honestly believed that her feeling for me was just such another fancy as she had experienced before.'[4]

How John moved from viewing Una as 'just another fancy' to seeing her as a possible permanent partner was to some extent precipitated by the eventuality of Ladye's death. It was also assisted by Una's most pronounced characteristics: her gift for friendship and her relentless persistence. Though Una chose to remark first on John's appearance, in this respect her second comment carries greater import: 'Our friendship, which was to last through life and after it, dated from that meeting.'[5]

Sodality, staunch and tenacious, on Una's part was what enabled their platonic relationship to move steadily from August to November towards that of lovers; it enabled Una to endure John's sudden swings from manic moods to debilitating depressions; it allowed her to survive John's love affair in the 1930s with Souline. During the latter period, however, it is hard to separate Una's belief in and support for her lovesick partner from her need to control a dangerous situation. Evguenia Souline always represented to Una a disorderly item, an uncontrollable factor.

Control was as necessary to Una as was comradeship. Autocracy like art was rooted in her background. Her grandfather Henry Taylor had been a senior civil servant in the Colonial Office whilst also writing verse tragedies, articles and reviews. Her father Harry Taylor, placed in the army when his aim was to become a professional pianist, was appointed to the Consular Service in 1883 as a Queen's Foreign Service Messenger. His distinguished social companions included Sir Edward Burne-Jones, Rudyard Kipling, Sir Edward Poynter and Stanley Baldwin.

As a privileged junior member of this 'illustrious colony at Rottingdean',[6] Una's artistic confidence destined her to act as a skilled stage director carefully conducting the emotions and actions of her intimates. It is no surprise that her two idols were Sarah Bernhardt and Napoleon Bonaparte. When Una, then fourteen, saw the great actress play the great hero at Her Majesty's Theatre, she drew Bernhardt, painted her, modelled her, and finally persuaded her to accept several pencil drawings.

Una's alert artistic sense enabled her to keep pace with the avant-garde in art, just as her perusal of literature, though predominantly traditional, enabled her to move from Arnold Bennett and John Galsworthy to John Buchan,

Joseph Conrad and even D.H. Lawrence and to introduce John to *The Thirty-Nine Steps*, *Victory* and *The Rainbow*, all published the year John and Una's affair began.

Her talent for comradeship dated from Una's untroubled childhood when her sister Viola, five years her senior, became her most loving attachment, and was exemplified by her lifelong friendships with May Massola and Jacqueline Hope, the daughter of Laura Troubridge and Adrian Hope (cousin to Constance Wilde). Although prone to snobbery, she was loyal and honourable in her friendships. As a result she never lacked for friends. She had a sharp eye and where necessary an acid tongue which made her a keen observer and afforded her companions much amusement. She offered those closest to her her time, her energy and her unwavering support. She wrote to them, called on them, lunched and dined with them, dissected their causes, shared their cultural commitments, made herself available for their needs whilst still in pursuit of her own. Her cordiality made her an excellent companion, her sharp self-focus made her a successful singer and sculptor.

Una had a strong chameleon streak; it was thus easy for her to become whatever her friends wished her to be. This she did, not out of affectation, nor by playing a part, though she could do that too, but out of a desire to be the person they would most approve of.

Her sister Viola's approval was never in doubt. She was Una's acolyte as well as her closest confidante. From childhood Viola would write her letters marked in childish scrawl 'Private' that began: 'Dearest Blessed One and Only Una.' In later years she would always write to her as 'My Una' or 'My own Una' and sign herself 'Your own' or 'Your own Viola'. When Una, attending the Royal College of Art in 1900 as a precociously talented thirteen year old, felt overwhelmed at her success, Viola wrote: 'Your happiness, the happiness of your splendid young life is everything to me . . . I should be quite content to go softly all my years if you could live in a state of continual ecstatic joy . . . I pine to see you, I feel as if only half of me was alive without you . . . can't you draw me?'[7]

Their relationship grew in intimacy as the years progressed. In a letter from Salcey Lawn, Northampton, where Viola then lived with her small son Oliver Woods, she wrote: 'My Una, I have come to the conclusion that you are *absolutely* necessary to my existence.'[8] When the sisters were apart they corresponded frequently. As a letter which survives from Viola's stay in Limerick says: 'after all is said and done, it is you who comes firstly . . . sometimes I want you so, Oh how I want you – for I love you above and beyond them all.' Viola's affection for her sibling outstripped that for her men friends. When Viola was involved with Maurice Woods the journalist, she wrote from Dublin: 'The loneliness at first was awful . . . I miss you and Maurice as one misses sleep. The companionship of you both seems a joy undreamed of – a happiness, a soul's contentment, a depth beyond the things of this earth.'[9]

As children Viola had been robust while baby Una had been considered delicate. Childhood ailments had occurred at frequent intervals. They afforded Una considerable delight. 'It is a curious but undeniable fact that I look back upon almost all my childish illnesses with pleasure.' She was fed on calves' foot jelly and chicken broth while her sister ate shepherd's pie and Brussels sprouts. When Una developed diphtheria at the country house of the elderly painter G.F. Watts, she recalls the taste of 'large black hothouse grapes that were given to me peeled and bereft of their seeds'.[10]

This early pattern of gratification for sickness continued throughout her relationship with John, disarming criticism, deflecting difficulties, gaining her attention, provoking John's ever-ready protection.

Both Viola and Una were pretty children dressed by their mother Minna Taylor in Kate Greenaway styles. They wore muslin or cashmere dresses with puff sleeves, flounced hemlines and Empire line sashes under their armpits. Later, as Minna Taylor mixed with the Pre-Raphaelites and assimilated their ideas, her girls were garbed in turkey twill or butcher blue linen adorned with lace, while round their necks their mother hung amber strings or Venetian glass beads – a style that set off the Morris wallpaper, the unstained oak furniture and Minna's decided sense of superiority.

Viola grew into her prettiness, Una grew out of those designs. Una preferred boyish clothes to boys or young men irrespective of their regard for her appearance. At eight she blissfully became the 'fifth brother' to Lord William Cecil's four sons when on a holiday near Boulogne she wore one of the boys' suits. Her mother was shocked when at sixteen, like an early suffragette, Una appeared in a stiff collar 'attached to a flannel shirt with cuffs and cuff links', severely cut coat and skirt and low-heeled patent leather Oxford shoes.[11] When bored with this image she adopted the actor Fred Terry's highwayman's coat, white stock, three-cornered hat and gold lorgnette.

As an adolescent the richly theatrical and the impudently independent never failed to amuse her, as it never failed to dismay her mother. There was as little affinity between Una and Minna Taylor as there was between Radclyffe Hall and Marie Visetti. Born a great beauty of upper class Irish stock to the Hon. Robert French Handcock, second son of the 7th Baron Castlemaine of Westmeath, Minna was not fitted to become a poor man's wife nor his widow, which through her husband's straitened circumstances and early death became her moiety.

Unlike Marie Visetti she was never cruel, but she was snobbish, strict and often insensitive. She taught Una to respect the concept of freedom, then attempted to curtail her activities. Her mother's odd mixture of cosmopolitan cultivation with conformist views on the role of young women hedged Una's upbringing. Una, provided with a Belgian governess, spoke fluent French before she was seven, drew excellently, and wrote the Lord's Prayer on a threepenny bit. Young Una (like her older self) was ingenious, extrovert, egotistic and maddeningly patient. If she wanted something she would plot and plan with a quiet determination she believed she inherited from her father. Her will was like a slow burning flame that could not be extinguished. 'The girl was like some queer, unnatural fire, that gave out brilliance but no heat,'[12] wrote Radclyffe Hall later about Sidonia in *A Saturday Life*. Lady Shore's precocious young daughter Sidonia inherited the loneliness and alienation of young Marguerite Hall but the ice-and-fireworks of the youthful Una Troubridge.

Like Sidonia, Una was regarded as a child prodigy, and like Sidonia she 'usually did get what she wanted, by the force of sheer self-assertion'.[13] That Una was early able to discard her mother's chosen outfits, as later she discarded her mother's notions that she should wed well and stay married, was achieved through an unusual adolescent autonomy. Her scholarship to the Royal College of Art enabled her at thirteen to study for the Associateship of Modelling under the Professor of Sculpture and Modelling, Italian-born Edouard Lanteri who figured in Hall's *A Saturday Life* as Elinar Jensen, Sidonia's modelling professor, a 'queer little gnome with a crooked back' in shabby clothes, hand-knitted worsted socks, set apart from other men, 'successfully defying comparison' through his remarkable talents.[14]

Lanteri coaxed Una's exceptional abilities to professional heights, as Jensen triumphantly coached Sidonia's. By sixteen Una had rented an independent studio where she exhibited her figurines. Several expensive commissions came her way. The prima ballerina Adeline Genée posed for her in 1907. The completed statuette was exhibited at the Royal College that same year.

Under Lanteri's tutelage Una developed an authentic vision, yet twice she gave up her art in favour of a role as wife and nurturer. The first time, when she married Troubridge, the change afforded her so little satisfaction that she impatiently resumed her artistic endeavours. It is the second time, when she made a conscious decision to dedicate herself exclusively to Radclyffe Hall's art (at that stage embryonic), that invites investigation.

Una knew she was letting herself down. She knew she had baffled those who had taught her. She felt she had broken faith with Lanteri. In an essay written after Lanteri's death on 18 December 1917 Una says:

> He [Lanteri] became for me not only an instructor but my philosopher, guide and friend . . . He died of influenza while I was still a young woman but he lived long enough for me to disappoint him . . . He lived to see me throw overboard with complete indifference the talent that he had nurtured and on which he had built such high hopes.[15]

Those high hopes, those already acknowledged artistic achievements, that vivacious intellect, a trifle reminiscent of Violet Hunt, were part of what attracted John to her. Yet, like many writers before her (most of them male, for it is unusual for female writers to be given the opportunity), Radclyffe Hall was not averse to accepting Una's offer of artistic subservience in favour of the 'greater good' of their unit.

When Una later explained to John how she had felt, why she had done it, why it seemed worthwhile, Hall allowed herself to phrase the problem as Sidonia's when facing Jensen with her decision to give up modelling, first to sing then to marry.

> Elinar Jensen – such far-seeing eyes, such coarse woollen socks, and such faith! . . . His sort of faith was an outrage, she decided; he talked about leaving everyone free, and then chained them down with his faith . . . Faith was selfish too . . . What Jensen wanted was not her success so much as his own by proxy.[16]

Chains were Radclyffe Hall's recurring motif. The suggestion that devotion to another's talents was a way of ensuring success by proxy may have been an accurate appraisal of the motives behind Una's decision. Una herself said that she felt able to become John's 'lieutenant' and second-in-command because John invited rather than commanded devotion. By becoming Hall's lieutenant Una found an efficient way to run their ship.

If Lanteri was Una's professional guide, her domestic guide had been her father. Una's relationship with the man whom she usually called Harry was intense and affectionate. Between Harry Taylor and his younger daughter, whom he overtly favoured above the elder, there was an exclusive attachment.

Harry was a striking looking man, six foot two, with snow-white hair and vivid blue eyes alight with nervous energy. He exuded vitality, a characteristic Una inherited. The family were unaware that Harry Taylor had tuberculosis until he haemorrhaged one night in August 1906. Benevolently, King Edward VII sent his Messenger to a private sanatorium in Midhurst. During his convalescence in Pau in the foothills of the Pyrenees his condition suddenly worsened. Una was sent for. During February 1907, in order to attend her father, she left the Royal College of Art without obtaining the Schools Associateship, never to return. Three days before her twentieth birthday, on 5 March 1907, Harry Taylor died. He was fifty-two, the same age as Rat when he died. Una was bereft and distraught.

On the same day that Harry died, Ernest Troubridge, the brother of Una's friend Laura Hope, called 'the handsomest man in the British navy' by those outside it, and 'The Silver King' by those inside (for at forty-five Troubridge too had snow-white hair), was appointed Captain of the battleship *Queen* and Chief of Staff in the Mediterranean, based at Malta. During the previous two years, when visiting her friend Jacqueline Hope at the family home in Tite Street, Una had frequently met 'Uncle Ernest', a widower with three children. She had discovered him to be, if not 'the marvel'[17] Una and Viola deemed Jacqueline, at least a passably agreeable companion. Like his sisters, Ernest was interested in art and opera, and he sang and played the banjo. His cheerful company persuaded Una, who visited her Tealdi cousins in Florence immediately after her father's death, to pay a visit to him at Malta on her way back to England in 1908. On 8 March she attained her majority and with nothing to inherit she became engaged to Troubridge. That summer she and Viola returned to Italy to stay in Levanto with Una's English friend May, now married to the Italian Baron Cencio Massola. Una wrote to Jacqueline Hope that despite her engagement she felt gloriously free even though 'I don't ever dance' as 'the young men [sailors from Spezia] failed to interest me'.[18]

Her lack of interest in young men was the forerunner of her subsequent lack of interest in men of any age. It was this rather than money which afforded the motive for her marriage at the British Consulate in Venice on 10 October to the man only eight years younger than her father: '[I] married him chiefly, it must be admitted, because I discerned in his snow-white hair and rather Terryish cast of countenance a likeness to the beloved and for ever unattainable Scarlet Pimpernel of my dreams.'

Some people marry for money, some for mightier motives, some for snow-white hair. Una was impulsive. Snow-white hair was as reasonable a motive as any other. 'Having chosen a man old enough to be my father I set to work to look his age.'[19] She wore sweeping black velvets, looked ridiculous and failed lamentably. She took on his three children, aged fourteen, fifteen and sixteen, and failed them lamentably too. On 5 November 1910 Una gave birth to their daughter Andrea Theodosia – nicknamed, following the family tradition, Cub or Cubby by her and Zyp, her pet name for Troubridge (a name spelt both 'Zyp' and 'Zip' in her diaries). Pride in her status as a young mother, enthusiasm for her new role and genuine devotion to her daughter, particularly when Cubby was ill, further diminished the attention she paid her stepchildren. They became so resentful that by 1912 Ernest bought a separate house for his two unmarried sisters in order that they could care for his daughters Mary and Chatty. His son Tom followed him into the navy where Troubridge had been promoted in 1911 to Rear-Admiral. A year later he was appointed Chief of War Staff, after four months as Churchill's Private Secretary.

When Troubridge had been stationed at the Admiralty in London, Una, chameleon-like, had initially sublimated her personality to that of her husband, and allowed his interests to dominate her days; but in 1909 a near fatal ectopic pregnancy weakened and distressed her, and on her recovery she recognized that this self-abnegation was tedious and time-consuming. Imperceptibly she resumed a reinvigorated life of her own. She returned to her painting and sculpture, took daily singing lessons, pursued again her friendships with women. As Troubridge's career steadily advanced he began to resent any hint of marital independence. Una was now a naval wife. And as such, she suddenly became a prey to ill-defined discontents, recurring nausea, frequent headaches and insomnia. The aetiology was unfamiliar but the consequence would be consistent: disease rewarded.

Una was due to accompany Troubridge to Malta. Depressed and anxious she consulted doctors and specialists. Too nervous and lethargic to make love, to entertain, or to take any interest in her husband's activities, she was proving less than satisfactory for his needs. Her GP suggested she consult Dr Hugh Crichton-Miller, a specialist in psychosomatic disorders, neurasthenia, and most forms of neurology. He charged exorbitant fees, had a hypnotic effect on women patients, and was later to found the Tavistock Clinic. Una, accompanied by Viola, saw him on 10 January 1913. That night she wrote in her diary: 'He said he would cure me if I would stay in England and give him time . . .'[20] Crichton-Miller had supplanted Troubridge as a less dangerous mentor-successor to her beloved Harry. The psychotherapist had the additional advantage of both being more amenable to her own half-hidden feelings, and also more able to help her explicate them.

Troubridge saw Crichton-Miller and agreed to the plan. On 14 January Una was hypnotized for the first time. Four days later Troubridge went off alone to Malta. Miller's investigations slowly and delicately exposed her heterosexual antipathies as a partial reason for constant nausea, which he suggested might be aided by psychoanalysis. The treatment (or was it the expression of emotions she had for some time sublimated?) almost immediately began to make her feel 'much more cheerful'.[21]

Troubridge's absence left Una in no need of consolation. She spent her time convivially caring for Cubby, attending to her obligations to Minna Taylor, socializing with Viola, her husband Maurice Woods – the couple had married in December 1908 – their friends Jacqueline and Laura Hope, and renewing her artistic endeavours. She began a drypoint etching called 'The Wicked Voice', haunted Diaghilev's Ballets Russes at Covent Garden to draw Nijinsky, then obtained permission to attend his dance classes at the Drill Hall where she began sculpting him as Debussy's Faun. Initially she made the bust in wax, then cast it in marble, bronze and clay.

From her teenage years Una was impeccably organized and efficient. She made lists for everything and crossed items off as she achieved each task. She continued this habit throughout her years with John. In her diary for 1913–14 she recorded how many books she had read in Italian; idiosyncratically, she wrote a list headed 'My Earrings' which records sixteen pairs of earrings by colour, stone and length of dangle.

Her medical plan was equally orderly. She made almost daily visits to Crichton-Miller (by October she had had fifty-seven treatments), she learnt self-hypnotism (and was able within weeks to hypnotize both Viola and Troubridge's secretary), she read innumerable psychology books and began to understand her condition. On 23 January she recorded: 'Crichton-Miller –

epoch making visit.'[22] This may have been their first discussion of her inversion. Certainly they discussed it on several later occasions when she attended his hypnotherapy clinic at Bowden House in Harrow. So impressed was Una with Crichton-Miller that when her sister also became disenchanted with her marriage, Una persuaded Viola that she too would benefit from the Crichton-Miller treatment.

From her safe distance Una wrote often and warmly to Troubridge, detailing Cubby's antics as well as the more seemly of her own. His letters back were recorded in her journal as making her 'so so happy'.[23]

Her happiness receded as Troubridge's restlessness with their current separation increased. Every hint of pressure from her husband to rejoin him sent her fleeing for therapy to Miller. She attempted to leave for Malta on 18 March, then, overtaken by anxiety, recorded bitterly: 'Tried to leave.' Four days later she set off, leaving Cubby with a nanny and her in-laws.

In Malta, with Troubridge's superior Sir Archibald Berkeley Milne a bachelor, she found herself unwillingly in the position of First Lady. Though being asked to sing at Malta's Theatre Royal pleased her momentarily, calling on naval wives and hostessing functions brought on renewed attacks of boredom and seediness. On 8 May she wired Andrea's nanny Norah to bring the Cub to the Mediterranean. The child's arrival on 23 May was celebrated by tea with the Churchills and the Asquiths – in Malta in conjunction with meetings of the Committee of Imperial Defence – but eleven days later Cubby became seriously ill with an intestinal disease from which she almost died. The parents were united in their joint distress until Cubby's slow recovery swiftly demolished their own. Grateful for their return to England in July, Una rushed back to Crichton-Miller to find that her therapist was now regularly treating her sister Viola for her marital problems.

During this period Ladye, Una's cousin, became her particular confidante on emotional and sexual matters. It is probable, and in the circumstances highly ironic, that only Ladye, apart from Viola, was party to Crichton-Miller's suggestions of sexual ambivalence. As far as Una was concerned, Ladye was the safest possible listener, for her own *ménage à deux* with Radclyffe Hall was both open and accepted within their family. Although Una later said she had no memory of her first meeting with Marguerite Hall, what the occasion may have stirred in her was the memory of her own long forgotten relationship with another Marguerite with whom she had 'a short but intimate friendship'.[24]

The first Marguerite was Marguerite Michel whom Una had met in Florence after her father's death. Miss Michel was a governess employed to teach the children of her Tealdi cousins. The six foot tall 38-year-old tutor wore high cravats, ties and masculine attire which Una replicated in a statuette lovingly made of this woman with whom she became 'very intimate indeed'.[25] Una would reveal 'the most private matters of her life' to Marguerite who 'would hold, and as it were play with her hand'. The Tealdis, somewhat shocked at this intimacy, attempted to persuade Una that the governess might overwhelm or manage (or rather, mismanage) her. Later Una admitted to John her resistance against being 'in any way dictated to by this very dominant person'.[26] Yet something about their shared laughter and physical affection awoke a response in Una that would deepen when she met the other Marguerite for the second time.

It was during the visit to the Tealdis that Una converted to Catholicism. Thus, long before she had caught sight of the lover with whom she would spend twenty-eight years, Una was already acquiring those appurtenances that would fit her for a partnership which would bring with it inescapable arraignment. She had an ambiguous sexuality, a disdain for conventional heterosexual morality, an appreciation of a severe style in dress, a conversion to Catholicism, exceptional artistic abilities, literary discernment, a fierce organizing power, and despite her youthful intransigence a genuine appreciation of the compromises that friendship and love with a woman of Radclyffe Hall's relentlessness and restlessness would entail.

Una had need of every ounce of her newly acquired flexibility when in October Troubridge insisted that she, accompanied by the Cub and her stepdaughter Chatty, return with him to Malta. Suddenly Una had her own house, servants, coach, coachman, wealth and misery. As often as possible Una escaped to the Tealdis in Florence or to the Massolas in Levanto. When forced to reside in Malta, she devoted herself to opera singing and postal laments to Crichton-Miller, while Troubridge frequently slept aboard HMS *Defence*. In 1914 she wrote her diary almost entirely in Italian, though the English word 'seedy' occurs intermittently. She took up French translations with such skill that later she became Colette's first English translator; and she discovered that Troubridge had passed on to her a severe venereal disease from one of his 'adventures'. It did not endear him to her.

While Una was in Italy in August 1914 Germany declared war on France and Russia. When she returned to Malta with the Cub she found Troubridge had gone to sea; shortly after, he was suddenly recalled to London. Not until she met him again on 14 September in Naples did she discover the nature of the 'disgrace' into which her husband had fallen.

At the outbreak of war the German Commander in the Mediterranean, Admiral Souchon, had two fast ships, the battle cruiser *Goeben* and a light cruiser *Breslau*. Churchill ordered the battleships to be shadowed and entrusted this task to Troubridge, as Commander of the second squadron. Turkey, expected to remain neutral, had secretly negotiated with Austria and allowed the *Goeben* and *Breslau* a safe haven in the Dardanelles. Too late Troubridge realized that only his four armoured cruisers were fast enough to catch the German battleships. Intending to intercept them before first light on 7 August, Troubridge despatched his flotilla; but by 4 a.m. it had still not encountered the enemy, and, afraid of daylight attack, Troubridge ordered his ships back to their Adriatic station. The battleships passed unmolested from Messina to the Dardanelles. It was later said that 'No other single exploit of the war cast so long a shadow upon the world as [this] voyage' which brought about a chain of destruction and death.[27]

Criticism rained down upon Troubridge. His superior Berkeley Milne did almost nothing to help him, being primarily concerned to exonerate himself. Troubridge on the other hand went out of his way to avoid implicating Milne. On 30 August 1914 the Admiralty announced through the Press Bureau:

> The conduct and disposition of Admiral Sir Berkeley Milne in regard to the German vessels *Goeben* and *Breslau* have been the subject of the careful examination of the Board of Admiralty with the result that their Lordships have approved the measures taken by him in all respects.[28]

Three weeks later the Secretary of the Admiralty announced:

> Rear-Admiral E.C.T. Troubridge has been recalled to England from the Mediterranean in order that an inquiry may be held into the circumstances leading to the escape of the *Goeben* and *Breslau* from Messina Straits.[29]

After the extensive inquiry Troubridge himself requested a trial by court martial, feeling he had no other option if he wanted to clear his name. The court martial began at Portland on 5 November, Cubby's fourth birthday. Sittings were held daily. Una took to her bed. As Cubby was still in Florence staying with friends until their troubles were sorted out, Una had not even the solace of fussing over her child. On 10 November she recorded: 'In bed. Announcement evening papers.'[30]

Ernest Troubridge was acquitted. On 13 November Una, much relieved, got out of bed. However, despite his honourable acquittal, Troubridge never again held a sea command. He was given the humiliating post of Head of the British Naval Mission to Serbia, with naval forces and guns based in Belgrade to keep the Danube open for the Allies.

Although Una had a professional triumph at the end of 1914 when her bust of Nijinsky was displayed at a major international exhibition in Venice, she was under considerable stress. Expected to accompany Zyp into exile to Serbia in 1915 she managed to survive there only a short time before returning to England where she took a small house at 40 Bryanston Street, Marble Arch. From there she occupied herself by raising funds and volunteers for a hospital for British servicemen in Belgrade. Her Tealdi cousins wrote to congratulate her on her 'splendid hospital work' but for Una there was little splendour in her life. She could not see the rainbows for the rain. She was twenty-eight, still married to a man of fifty-two in whom she was uninterested and whose sexual overtures repelled her. She had a four-year-old daughter for whose sake, in the climate of the times, she felt she ought to continue some semblance of 'family life'. She had a finely tuned voice, a razor-sharp intellect and an untapped reservoir of erotic feelings. Lonely and less certain of herself than usual, she suddenly decided that if she couldn't yet make major changes she could certainly make minor ones – and make these dramatic. With characteristic impulsiveness she sheared off her abundant glossy hair until it was barely the length of a page-boy bob.

Her cousin Emmie, the gracious and conventional Lady Clarendon, probably felt shortened hair boded no good. Una needed distraction. The company of relatives would cheer her up. So on 1 August Emmie invited her for tea with her sister Ladye. It was there that she met John Radclyffe Hall for the second time. Una looked fragile, her expression melancholy. John's interest was aroused. That particular company of relatives did indeed take Una out of herself, and put her into the arms of her first – and last – woman lover. When Ladye looked back on that family tea party, it must have seemed more like the company of wolves.

The year 1915 was a treacherous one. The Germans sank the *Lusitania*; news came of the first Zeppelin attack on Allied troops at Salonika; Edith Cavell was executed in Brussels; and in the streets and homes of London, where John and Ladye still resided at Cadogan Square, tension mounted as Zeppelin raids over the capital intensified. Ladye's health worsened and her fear of raids grew in direct proportion to the number of times Una cajoled John away with her to Bryanston Street. Nor were Ladye's fears much allayed when John remained at home, for their private hours were increasingly shared with Ladye's charming but dogged young cousin.

In any *ménage à trois* there must be three versions of how a mild acquaintanceship becomes a grand passion, how the new pairing affects the established couple, how the triangle works or suffers.

Ladye's version is available. It is a haunting refrain of Una the ubiquitous, the pervasive predator who smoothly and skilfully infiltrates their life. Ladye details every event that hurts. The more it hurts the keener she is to record it. She appears almost glad that John's birthday on 12 August was spent with Phoebe as well as Dolly and Cara, for after that she finds little to be glad about.

During August Una came frequently to tea and stayed for dinner. John and Ladye met young Cubby, proclaimed 'a darling'. Cubby was soon playing with Cara's child Karen, while Viola's young son Oliver joined the youngsters. Una romped with the children. Una romped with John, the adult woman. John found Una's girlishness exciting. She took to calling her 'Squiggie' because she doodled on her drawings, and squiggled round her notes. John loved the squiggles, admired the drawings, avidly read the notes. Una moved to a flat with a studio in Hay Hill, Mayfair, where John became a frequent visitor, first in daylight, later overnight. John and Una exclaimed with delight over the coincidences of their fathers dying at fifty-two, of their Catholic conversions, of the fact that John had bought Una's statuette of Adeline Genée long before they knew each other. What a strange coincidence! What could it signify? Such phrases and more they shrieked to each other. And even to Ladye. No one was anxious to leave Ladye out.

Una and John revelled in each other's artistic gifts. Una gave John her Faun drawings; John had them framed. John read 'her two best stories' aloud to Una; Una reviewed and criticized them. Ladye quietly despaired. Una gave John an etching of 'The Wicked Voice': John had that framed too. Ladye even records the place of the framers, a shop in King's Road, as if detailing the nails may prevent them sinking deeper into what will literally be her coffin.

Towards the end of August John managed a few hours away from Una to see Violet Hunt and Phoebe Hoare but by September she was back with Una, this time in Brighton with Cubby and young Oliver. On 30 September Ladye gratefully chronicled that 'Una did some singing exercises with me', then more flatly recorded: 'she started a statuette of John'.[31] Ultimately Una gave up the statuette, preferring to talk to the woman who had modelled for it, but again according to Ladye's version she did draw 'a splendid head of John in profile'. Ladye's attempts at enthusiasm for anything connected with 'her Johnnie' show a generous gallantry that merited a return not on offer from Johnnie, who inexorably moved from being 'hers' to being someone else's.

In September the Hospital Unit which Una had been busy equipping left for Belgrade. Ladye's diary miserably reports that Una not only elected to stay behind in London, but decided to join John and Ladye on their annual holiday, this time in Cornwall's Watergate Bay. During this period John had offers both for the flat and the White Cottage which she decided to accept. While John and Una strode the beaches, intimacy growing, temperatures rising, Ladye, left in the hotel with Cubby and her nanny, became prey to violent nightmares: 'Had two frightening dreams . . . one that my eyes were being burnt – and the other that J was drowning on a river bank, whilst I was running to the bank shouting . . . There was a branch right over her head. I had a heart attack while dressing. Una photographed us.'[32]

On 11 October Belgrade fell to the Austro-Hungarians. John and Una, their holiday mood only slightly imperilled, went to Newquay for news. The following day they returned to London to discover that Troubridge had managed to escape. The unit was to be disbanded and sent home. Ladye knew there was now no prospect of Una departing. By 14 October fear of living alone during a raid sent Una scuttling to Cadogan Square for shelter. By this point Ladye's fears were for her own emotional well-being. Her tolerance overlaid by jealous rages, she gave vent to angry discussions with John which left them both depressed but the situation unchanged.

In November 1915 the inevitable happened. John and Ladye had moved into a suite in the Vernon Court Hotel in Buckingham Gate while sale negotiations for Cadogan Square and the White Cottage took place. On 29 November the romantic pair travelled to Malvern to take an inventory of the cottage. There in the afternoon, in John and Ladye's joint country home – which led Ladye to see it always as a double betrayal – Una and John made love for the first time. Thereafter Una never failed to cherish and record the date as the anniversary of their love, marking it with a circle in all her diaries.

In her biography Una recalls the way she fell in love with John in Cornwall:

I saw [her] for the first time in rough country clothes, heavy short-skirted tweeds unusual in those days, collars and ties . . . and day by day I fell more completely under the spell of her enthralling personality. She was so intensely alive, she could be so kind and tender, and she was also so wilful, so humorous, and in those days so intolerant! Her temper was so violent, so quickly spent, and her penitence, if she thought she had given pain, so extreme . . .

She found John moody, militant, prejudiced and passionate.

I remember saying to her: 'I believe you would be prepared to torture heretics . . . in another age you would have been a Torquemada' . . . and to this extent I was right: I had met for the first time a born fanatic. Not . . . one who would persecute others, but one who, if the need arose, would go to the pillory for the sake of her convictions.[33]

While John and Una grew closer, Ladye more and more often dined alone as she wearily repeated the same sad strategies she had used during John's affair with Phoebe. The Circle, including Adela, Gabrielle, Winaretta and Toupie, remained faithful, trying to support the older friend and understand the newer one.

It would be enlightening to view the events of Ladye's last months from Una's perspective but those two memories apart she has left us little evidence. The prolific journal writer who bequeathed posterity hundreds of Day Books and diaries chose to destroy her diaries for 1915 and 1916, the period when her affair with Radclyffe Hall began. But one feature is common to all her extant journals. Every one of them shows Una Troubridge in a favourable light, a worthy companion to Radclyffe Hall the martyred genius. One must assume that the two missing journals do not present so flattering a view.

If Una was at that time merciless, lacking in charity, a woman with no loyalty to her cousin, it is possible that she acted in the grip of passion rather than malice. Una's own verdict is delivered with frankness in her biography of John that promises to dwell 'in the palace of truth': 'I had at twenty-eight as much consideration for Ladye or for anyone else as a child of six.'[34] Dwelling still in that palace Una elaborates:

Kindly as she was towards me, Ladye most certainly felt no overwhelming desire for my incorporation in their daily life . . . as for me . . . I was swept along on a spate of feeling . . . and all I knew or cared about was that I could not, once having come to know [John], imagine life without her.[35]

Putting scruple behind her Una quickly took a new apartment with studio at 13 Royal Hospital Road almost next door to Dolly's house in Swan Walk. So placed, she could ensure that after she had dined with John and Ladye at their hotel, John could stay at the studio with her, have breakfast next door with Dolly, then go home nervous and irritable to Ladye. After a period of several weeks spent like this, culminating in a New Year's Eve spent with Una until a quarter to eleven, then with John for the remaining hour and a quarter, it comes as no surprise that Ladye's final entry for 1915 was: 'John and I saw the new year in and both felt depressed.'

If Una had failed to imagine life without John during 1915, she did no better in the first half of 1916. In January, although she continued to work at her studio during the day, she moved into the Vernon Court Hotel to be nearer her lover. Ladye confessed to her diary that she 'thought seriously of going to live by myself'.[36] By the time Troubridge wired to say he would be home to see her by 3 February, Una had contracted tonsillitis, thrown herself on John's protection, and retired to bed in their hotel leaving John to deal with her husband.

What then of John's part in this affair? Where can we look for her version of events? Even the sternest of Una's critics could not convince a balanced biographer that the affair was one-sided, that John was led handcuffed and roped away from Cadogan Square and into the young artist's studio. When Una was faced with Troubridge as a lover she was sick, seedy and often sour. On meeting John she was robust and ripe. John thought her beautiful. 'Her eyes look like the sea in a mist.'[37] Like Joan in *The Unlit Lamp* who suddenly sees Elizabeth as if for the first time, John suddenly notices Una's eyes, notices everything about her: 'Why haven't I noticed before how exactly like a tree she is . . . her eyes are like water, all greeny and shadowy and deep looking . . . a tree near a pool, that's what she's like . . . a larch tree just greening over.'[38]

It is certain that at the start of their affair John merely felt she was philandering; she intended nothing serious, was sure no lasting consequences would occur. Like Phoebe, Una was a married woman, temporarily available. Like Phoebe, the affair would flourish, fizzle, and founder.

But it did not.

John's careful calculations omitted two crucial factors: one was Una's unusual mixture of charm and persistence; the other was her own sense of commitment once someone depended on her. 'I can't bear to hurt things, especially things that seem to lean on me.'[39]

The Unlit Lamp, Hall's first completed novel, offers a fictional counterpoint to Ladye's diaries and Una's brief biographical details. Hall re-creates their triangular situation in the guise of the fight for love and possession of young Joan Ogden – so 'strong and protective',[40] 'so like a boy'[41] – by Mrs Ogden, 'the mother of headaches and secret tears'[42] who has Ladye's ageing illnesses and jealousy but none of her graciousness, and governess Elizabeth Rodney, like Una, 'a larch tree just greening over'.[43]

Elizabeth mirrors what for John must have been one of Una's most compelling qualities: her dedication to John's personal and literary interests. Elizabeth tells Joan/John that she no longer wants 'any triumphs myself, not now; I only want them for you. I want to sit in the sun and warmth of your success like a lizard on an Italian wall; I want positively to bask.'[44] Joan Ogden, like John, is disinclined to give up this offer. She is torn between two loves, the old and familiar and the new and vital. More attractive is the tidal wave rushing in, sweeping away debris.

Like many people in triangular situations, Joan/John wants to have it both ways. The hostility between the two women she loves threatens her foundations; she wavers between them.

> The antagonism between these two had never ceased to worry and distress her, not so much on their behalf as because she herself wanted them both. At all times, the dearest wish of her heart was that they should be reconciled, lest at any time she should be asked to choose between them.[45]

Una was in no position to ask; Troubridge, though absent, still loomed large in her life. Ladye was too frightened to ask.

Provoked by the crisis of Troubridge's return, John was no more willing to give up Una than Una was to relinquish John. Brutally John suggested to Ladye that they settle abroad, taking Una and the Cub with them. Fortunately for the protagonists, this idea failed to materialize. Guilt did not assist John in behaving well towards lovers she betrayed. She did not behave well towards Ladye. One night she argued and berated her for more than an hour and a half, leaving Ladye hysterical and emotionally exhausted. Yet when she made a final visit to Malvern to supervise the transfer of 'Our White Cottage' she was sufficiently overcome with nostalgia to write Ladye a loving note which temporarily brought them closer together.

Troubridge, frustrated and angry at being forced to reside at his club while his wife conducted an ambiguous liaison with a mannish woman, finally insisted that he, Una and Cubby reinstall themselves as a family in a home of their own. He leased a small house in Beaufort Gardens into which, despite tensions, the Troubridge trio moved on 6 May. John had already made an offer for a new flat for Ladye and herself at 22 Cadogan Court, a move that intimated strongly to Ladye that John had no intention of abandoning her. One motive was John's powerful sense of loyalty. Even had she wanted to leave Ladye she simply would not have known how to. This resistance was so deeply entrenched that it would reassert itself more forcibly in a later triangle, where circumstances would invite her even more strongly to make a break.

Another reason John did not seriously contemplate leaving Ladye was to do with Ladye's present state of health. Although she was only fifty-nine, her physical well-being was now greatly impaired. Swollen varicose veins were added to high blood pressure, attended by constant neck pains, and from April by a series of floating black specks across her vision which proved to be a blood clot in her left eye. Her renewed dependence on John called forth, as Ladye knew it would, her partner's protective instincts whilst simultaneously curtailing her freedom and bringing on the same claustrophobia she had felt at the time of her affair with Phoebe.

John felt imprisoned between her elderly partner's frail dependence and her young lover's insistent demands. Like Joan Ogden she wavered and fretted: 'If she loved Elizabeth [Una] she could not love her mother [Ladye] for one could not really love more than one person at a time, at least Joan was sure that she could not.'[46]

In John's life things came all too quickly to a head.

Ernest Troubridge's sudden sternness with Una had the same effect as Oliver Hoare's with Phoebe: the lovers saw each other less and longed for each other more. Momentarily Ladye's hopes rose. After she and John had gone together to listen to Agnes Nicholls sing at an Elgar concert she wrote, 'I felt tired but extremely happy.'[47]

Her happiness lasted less than two days, the final two days of her conscious life. On 14 May John and Una went to Taplow to find a replacement for the sickly French bulldog which John had given Una as a present the previous autumn. In John's absence Ladye visited Cara, then sang her composition 'Mother England' at a friend's tea party. When she arrived back John had not returned.

Having purchased the dog she and Una decided to spend the night of 14 May at the Skindles Hotel in Maidenhead so that the following morning John could buy a second bulldog for herself. Alone so rarely now, they lingered as lovers do, returning to London in the dark, and in John's case late for dinner. By the time Una reached home Ladye had made several anxious phone calls to Beaufort Gardens. On John's entry – doubtless made with not the best grace – she and Ladye began to quarrel. John had returned home, fearful of leaving Ladye alone to face the air raids, but she would rather have been with Una. Ladye knew this. Consumed by a sudden jealous rage she reproached John for spending time with Una while she was left fretting in the hotel. Violently, John lost her temper. Ladye, deciding on a dignified exit, rose from the table and instantly suffered an apoplectic seizure. Her doctor was away, so John, shocked yet as always composed in emergencies, made Ladye as comfortable as possible, then rang Una for her doctor's number. The doctor arrived at the hotel at the same time as Una.

Ladye was already unconscious.

For ten days Ladye lingered paralysed down one side of her body, unable to speak. John never left her side, waiting for a word, a sign, anything to show she was forgiven. Ladye appeared to recognize John and several times attempted to say something, but speech was beyond her. Once, feebly, she managed to grasp at John's hand and raise it to her lips.

On 25 May 1916 she lapsed into a coma and died without saying one word.

If Ladye had been able to speak, would she have reproached John or forgiven her? Had John been the cause of her lover's premature death? Those questions would torment Radclyffe Hall over the following years, and her contrition would echo throughout her mature novels in a variety of guises.

How she bore her self-reproach, how she sought salvation not merely through her own suffering but through Una Troubridge's also, forms the material of her Penitential Period.

PART THREE

SPIRITUALIST TO SPIRITUAL NOVELIST 1916–1927

9

THE PENITENTIAL PERIOD

After Mabel Batten's death, Radclyffe Hall the former philanderer was reconstituted as the griefstruck aesthete. She pencilled poems of mourning. She wrote to Rome requesting that Masses be said for Ladye at the Vatican. Daily she placed fresh delphiniums and lupins, Ladye's favoured flowers, by her framed photographs. Despair was the only luxury she afforded herself and on that she stinted not at all. She moved from the Vernon Court Hotel into Cadogan Court which she swiftly transformed into a shrine. Histrionic gestures and stormy rhetoric displayed but did not overstate her sorrow.

Unable to bear living alone in Cadogan Court, needing her family, John joined Dolly Clarke who was staying with friends at Purton in Wiltshire. Dolly, pregnant with her first child, was in as much distress as John, having learnt that Bobby had been killed in action. They wrapped themselves in mutual consolation, excluding those outside their grief. There might even have been some extra physical closeness in Purton during their sojourn, tightly sewn and seamed by sadness. It would add another layer to the intricate patterning of John's reliance upon and devotion to Dolly, for after Purton she accepted her cousin's suggestion that she let off part of Cadogan Court and become a paying guest at Swan Walk. It might also explain Una's growing jealousy of Dolly and the full measure with which that emotion was returned.

John's need to reassure herself that Ladye had been the love of her life was secondary to her determination to reassure Cara. If Una was made insecure by these reassurances, John had no room in her heart left over to care. She was not averse to sharing with Una some of the punishment for what she now saw as 'their sin'. Rapture tinged by death made intimacy ominous. Their lavishly gratified ardour at Ladye's expense now seemed to John treacherous. Expiation was necessary.

From Purton several impassioned letters burst from John's pen to Cara, the one person who she felt shared her sorrow. If justifications for her life with Ladye were needed, then justification she gave. Her love for Cara's mother, she said,

> was always the greatest emotion of my life while she was here, but now it has exceeded all bounds. I love her differently and with a sort of spiritual force . . . I gave to her the best eight years of my life – and although other people took my surface interest twice during that time, they never touched my soul . . . I think the only two intimate friends I had for a short space, namely Phoebe and Una, always felt that they got only my left over energy and thoughts. They used to say so in moments of annoyance . . . I am longing to go and join her . . . I never told her an untruth except once in all these years, and I never kept anything from her.[1]

It is possible that the one 'untruth' about an infidelity was a brief resumption of her affair with Dolly, when relations with Ladye were fragile, before Una 'set in'. That hidden indiscretion apart, the rest of John's letter was the truth as she believed it. John and Ladye for several years had succeeded in having an honest and loving relationship in which Ladye had performed three crucial functions: she had provided young Marguerite with the mother she desperately needed; she had been the first woman to return John's passion openly and fully; she had given Radclyffe Hall intellectual and artistic guidance. She had in effect reconstituted the lost child as the writer-woman.

John overlooked the fact that Ladye's motherliness had become inhibiting to her, that Ladye's sexual appetites had been blunted by habit and illness, that her own intellectual capacities were outstripping her mentor's. It was the death of her mother-lover she lamented; the fear that she had been responsible for that death with which she scourged herself. Once again as in her childhood she felt rejected and abandoned. She needed the understanding of Cara, the other daughter, 'your loving Mummy's Darling Child'.

But the Darling Child was in no mood to commiserate with John. Ladye's will destroyed that possibility. Under John's guidance, Ladye had changed her will after the Burford accident. John, feeling that Cara had not been sufficiently attentive to her mother's needs, had suggested she be given less formal responsibility at Ladye's death. Though the will designated Cara as Ladye's executrix, John was allotted the power to arrange the funeral and memorial and to dispose of many of Ladye's personal belongings. John was also bequeathed most of Ladye's library, all her photos, the furniture from the White Cottage, and several valuable paintings including the Sargent portrait.

The will charged Cara and John to act jointly and harmoniously in carrying out Ladye's wishes. John offered Cara some of Ladye's jewels and furniture but little appeasement seemed possible. Cara resented John's funeral arrangements. She wanted music in accordance with her mother's profession as a singer. John ordered only Gregorian plainchant. Ladye's body was embalmed and placed in an open coffin for the Requiem Mass which took place at

Westminster Cathedral on 30 May. John purchased a catacomb vault in Highgate Cemetery which contained four stone shelves, one for Ladye, two for John and Cara when they died. The fact that John had barbed wire erected around the tomb for fear of trespassers further upset and angered Cara. One night she broke into Cadogan Court. Seething with temper she woke John and demanded her mother's music scores which now legally belonged to John but which Cara insisted were hers by moral right. John handed them over but began to fear what else Cara might do to harm her.

In the matter of naming and acknowledgement, that consideration so integral to John's life, there were two curious occurrences. Though John was named as 'my friend' and favoured over Cara in the will, in all the obituary notices, presumably handled by Cara, John Radclyffe Hall was renamed Miss Marguerite Hall and in press reports of the memorial service at Westminster Cathedral, John was virtually invisibilized. Most gave greater space to Ladye's sister Emmie Clarendon than they did to Radclyffe Hall. On the published list of mourners, she was placed lower than relatives and immediate friends (if she was placed at all), so that a reader might have mistaken her for a distant cousin or passing acquaintance. The *Morning Post* of 31 May 1916 read:

A requiem mass for Mrs George Batten was held at the high altar in Westminster Cathedral at noon yesterday . . . Amongst those present were the French Ambassador, the Marchioness of Anglesey, the Dowager Countess of Clarendon, Lady Frances Bourke, Lady Young, Lord Cecil Manners, Lady Arbuthnot, Mr and Mrs Austin Harris, Miss Radclyffe Hall . . .

The magazine *The Lady* for 10 June 1916, who shared Cara's view on the lack of music, commented:

I went to the Requiem Mass for Mrs George Batten . . . She was so musical and so fond of Gregorian music . . . [but] we had Gregorian chanting and no music, which seemed to me very mournful. Her daughter Mrs Austin Harris was there with her husband and her tall young daughter Miss Honey Harris, and Mrs Batten's sisters Lady Clarendon, Mrs George Marjoribanks and Miss Hatch were all present as well as her nieces Mrs Burroughs and Mrs Whitbread, and others I saw there were Miss Marguerite Radclyffe-Hall (who was one of her greatest friends), Admiral and Mrs Troubridge etc. . . .

The Paris edition of the *New York Herald* for 2 June 1916 went even further in the process of invisibilizing Radclyffe Hall. They listed Rear Admiral Troubridge as being present at the Requiem Mass but did not list Hall at all.

It was Cara, not John, who cut out and kept the press cuttings.

A second incident in this business of naming and renaming is equally revealing. According to Cara Lancaster, in the three troubled years after the funeral

Cara Harris, Austin, Honey, Peter, Karen, Emmie and other members of the family who had long referred to her as 'dear Johnnie' slowly reverted to 'Marguerite'. In letters between family members she was referred to as 'Marguerite Hall'. From 1919, when she and Cara became permanently estranged, the family ceased to refer to her at all.

In 1916 John's hunger for absolution was intensified by the misunderstanding with Cara. Did Cara blame her for Ladye's death? Craving atonement, Hall's determination to punish herself grew. In a fundamental sense neither Radclyffe Hall nor her novels were ever free from this crusade. In her finest books, sexual sin, symbolic or actual, is always seen to produce death: 'In the days of her youth, at the time of the gathering in of the grapes, Teresa Boselli had passionately sinned [by having sex before marriage], and had for ever after hated her sin; but never more hotly than at this moment . . .'[2] That 'moment' of regret was the death of her daughter, which she saw as retribution. In *The Unlit Lamp* Joan Ogden's rebellion against her father's wishes brings on a heart attack which she believes hastens his death. Her intellectual and submerged sexual desire to share a life with Elizabeth is prevented by her fear that if she did so she might kill her sickly mother.

Radclyffe Hall's self-flagellation and relentless, if temporary, castigation of Una – a process recorded by Una in a succession of unhappy diary entries – is seen as part of a joint punishment. In *Adam's Breed* Teresa Boselli who 'was always repenting the sin that Fabio had helped her efface'[3] punishes her husband Fabio with sexual indifference just as John punished Una. Bitterly Teresa says to Fabio: 'Olga [their daughter] is dead . . . I feel nothing any more, neither love nor hate, my heart is broken. Can a broken heart feel?'[4]

Those were John's feelings. She had no heart left to give to Una, and no body either. A writer's words sometimes return to haunt them. Radclyffe Hall found herself speaking Mark Anthony Brakes' lines. 'The body is inevitably the battlefield upon which the great moral issues of life are fought out' – that would always be the plain on which her emotional fights were waged.

During 1916 and 1917 John underwent a steely transference of sexual longing from hot desire to erotic coldness. If Una attempted to renew their physical contact, John rebuffed her. For months Una was forced to skate across black ice:

> She [John] even reproached herself for that last day at Maidenhead. She turned to me instinctively in her despair . . . yet, paradoxically, her desire for expiation was such that I think there was a time when, had she only considered herself, she would have put me out of her life and offered me up as a sacrifice to loyalty.[5]

It would not be the last time that John used sexual abstinence both as punishment and as invitation. In a strange dance of celibate eroticism John shifted through a series of sensations. If she hungered for Una she made sure she held her at arm's length. She was excessive in her grief, formidable in her wrath. One minute she could be peremptory, the next mortified at having hurt Una. For hours thoroughly irritating, she could suddenly be immensely lovable. She was never carefree, though sometimes she acted the buccaneer of nervous high spirits. The next minute she might be found alone at her desk quietly sobbing to herself. The months affirmed Una's extraordinary staunchness and patience. Perhaps she understood John well enough to know that what she had to prove was that she would never abandon her. This she did, but the toll on her own sensitivities was considerable.

Throughout 1916, residing with Zyp and Cubby at 80 Beaufort Gardens, Una made herself ill with worry and reclaimed her old uncured 'heart condition'. Neither John nor Zyp took much notice, John intent on grief, Zyp intent on preparations for his return to a new position in Greece in September. It was sufficient for him that Una temporarily accepted a semblance of family life. On his departure however Una moved with the six-year-old Cub to the studio at Royal Hospital Road so that she could again drop in regularly to see John at Dolly's.

During the early part of 1917 John involved Dolly and Una in one of her less than companionable triangular situations. They dined, lunched and shopped together. Nobody was at ease. Controversial talk precipitated storms. 'Dolly came to dinner at 7.30 and staid till 11.15. John very depressed and in vile temper – not a nice evening and I cried much after I was left alone.'[6] On some nights John let Una sleep on the divan at Swan Walk; on other occasions she encouraged her to read aloud until past midnight, then turned her out. Una's response to sexual frustration and misery was a constant stream of ailments. John's response to several kinds of guilt was a vile temper. On 15 February 1917 Una was forced to move to 'another squalid little lonely abode' at 42 St Leonard's Terrace. Twelve days later, after an exuberant dinner with Violet Hunt, John graciously elected to sleep at Una's, merely a momentary reprieve. The following night Una woefully confided to her diary: 'Dined with John in her bedroom and read *Peter Ibbetson* to her until I finished it past 1 o'clock. Much upset at my walking home!'[7]

John and Una exasperated each other, disturbed each other, but never at any time did they bore each other. At first unwillingly, then sporadically, John made renewed sexual overtures to the younger woman. Una was greedy, over-eager, vulnerable in her desire. On 6 March John wrote a poem called 'Waking' depicting a moment of closeness.

> I shall wake in the half-light and I shall feel contented,
> I shall wake in the half-light, content, and wonder why;
> Til drowsily and drowsily my hand shall go to seek you,
> And drowsily and drowsily shall touch you where you lie . . .[8]

John admitted to missing Una when they were apart. When Una went to Edinburgh in mid-March 1917 to stay several days with her musical friends Mignon and 'Papa' Nevada, they corresponded twice daily; John even sent wires. Pent-up passion suddenly overtook them. They could not wait to see each other. Una broke her journey home at Birmingham. John raced up from London. They met on the station platform. Openly as a 'couple' renewed by love, they went to stay the weekend nearby with their psychic research friends the Oliver Lodges.

When John contracted German measles on 22 March, an event which made Dolly fear for her baby's health, Una seized her chance. She despatched the Cub to Jacqueline Hope's and persuaded John to stay for a time at St Leonard's Terrace to be nursed. She and Una, though again close, were not always calm. On Saturday 7 April Una's exhausted diary entry read: 'I howled most of the evening.'⁹

A brief convalescence in Bournemouth in April showed the same shifts. John bought a locket to hold Ladye's hair; Una's heart instantly played up. However, on her return to Swan Walk, John relented sufficiently to see Una on a regular basis without either Dolly's living presence or Ladye's ghost in attendance.

John and Dolly began to argue over John's visits to the celebrated medium Mrs Gladys Leonard. Dolly had asked John to try her out before Dolly herself attempted to contact her dead husband Bobby. Keen to communicate with Ladye's spirit, John had begun a series of psychic sittings, initially using Dolly as her note-taker, but later replacing her with Una. Dolly's resentment motivated John to move back to Cadogan Court on 1 May where she spent time with Peggy and making amends to Cara and Austin. It was almost a year since Ladye had died and she needed the support of those like her who had been closest to Ladye. Ironically Ladye's death, once imagined as a means of securing Una and John's joint future, now sharply divided them; only occasionally did John allow Una to stay at the flat. Ladye's flair, her easy-going style, and her quizzical sense of humour had kept John's stubborn intensity in check. Una had none of these attributes: she lacked a sense of humour, was over-sensitive and could become as histrionic as John.

Though still depressed at their uncertain future, Una, not by nature easily discouraged, determined to remain nearby and decided impulsively to lease a small house at 6 Cheltenham Terrace, a few minutes from John's flat. It would be ready for occupation in July. On 21 May, in Troubridge's absence, she signed the lease on his behalf. On 25 May, the first anniversary of Ladye's death, Una records that they did not sleep together. Symbolically John divided her day between her two 'families', the old and the new. She fetched Una for Mass at the Cathedral crypt where they were joined by Cara, Honey and Karen. After breakfasting at Cara's, John and Una then headed off with Cubby to Gamages, where John bought the child a tricycle.

Suddenly Una's fragile optimism was shattered. A telegram arrived from Troubridge announcing his return on 29 May. She took his civilian clothes out of Taylor's depository, then met him at Victoria.

Whatever welcome Ernest Troubridge expected, it was not what he received. During the remainder of May, June, July and August until his departure on the 26th, with her remarkable blend of ingenuity and perseverance Una contrived to persuade Zyp to join her and John for meals but never again to sleep or reside with her as her husband. Many evenings saw Zyp dining with his wife and her friend at Cadogan Court; sometimes he stayed the night as a guest of John's whilst Una went 'home' to St Leonard's Terrace. If Una stayed over at No. 22 she always slept on the divan in the drawing-room. Husband and wife frequently dined together at Cheltenham Terrace but Zyp, it seems, never exercised his marital rights.

How Troubridge was induced to accept this strange *ménage à trois* is not clear. Possibly John's open mourning for Mabel Batten went some way to extenuating the situation. He was in residence when John and Cara visited Highgate Cemetery in July. Possibly he made allowances for Una's 'nerves' or intermittent 'heart problems'.

For the time being, Troubridge chose to inquire into the matter no further. He insisted that Una accompany him to dinners with his family, to his sister Helen's wedding, to the reception at Jacqueline's, and to the Savoy or the Travellers' Club to meet his friends. These formalities apart, she was able to continue her shared life with John. This centred on their new interest in psychical research, which now involved them in commuting twice-weekly for seances to Datchet on the Thames where the medium Gladys Leonard rented a cottage.

Una's mounting conviction of the bond between them took strength from the discovery that their periods had started to coincide. From 1917 she illustrates her diary with funny little cartoons of their faces on menstrual occasions – John's face in profile with a longish nose, Una's shown full face with a small turned-down mouth. There was further proof in John's increasing concern for Cubby's welfare. When Cubby had her tonsils out in a nursing home on 6 July, it was John not Troubridge who was there with Una to comfort the child.

Una's own comfort was increased when John promised Una that 'if I died before her [I should] be buried at Highgate as near her as possible – so I am happier.'[10] When John wrote a codicil to her will leaving Una her clothes and 'little personal things' for her 'to have and hoard', Una felt headway was being made.[11] When John announced that she had obtained permission for Una to be buried with her and Ladye in the Highgate Cemetery vault, Una's grateful response ran: 'I feel I can never be *really* unhappy again & thank God's mercy.'[12]

Una (in Southbourne with John) returned to London for the day on 16 August to see Troubridge. Ten days later he left for Greece from where he sent batches of disturbing letters which began to put a strain on Una's relationship with John. Una's autumn diary entries reflect their tension:

> Cried most of the morning . . . then we made it up and worked til lunch . . . the alarm clock didn't go off . . . John furious . . . made it up at breakfast I being by then too miserable to bear it . . . I feeling mortally sad and discouraged . . . it all seems very uphill and hopeless today . . . neither past present nor future bear looking at and I feel almost too desolate sometimes to go on . . . [13]

John's view of events was somewhat more cavalier: 'When UVT's husband returns from the War it will not be possible for UVT to look upon herself as a free agent . . . under those circumstances she would find it difficult to be at MRH's beck and call.'[14]

Self-interest may have induced John to discuss their possible future together during the first of several successful holidays at the Cottage Hotel, Lynton. Whatever their separate motives, they made a joint decision to view houses which they could share. Over-hastily Una leased Grimston, a furnished villa in Datchet too small to contain herself, Cubby, the nurse and three dogs in permanent residence, with John as a constant visitor. However, it became their first communal home. They moved in on 25 November and John commuted between Grimston and Cadogan Court; Cheltenham Terrace was left empty. Less than a month later arguments broke out over servant problems, just as they had between John and Ladye. As both women were careful account keepers who retained amusing records of which bills were shared and which were joint they never argued about money.*

Finance however was the sole area of their domestic life free from anxieties. John's worries over her mother's health – Marie Visetti had suffered from both appendicitis and nervous strain – told on her own. The cook gave notice. Una retired to bed with stomach pains and Cub was in bed with a cough. John herself, like Una often prone to real or imagined illnesses, made a new will on 18 March, then took to cycling daily for miles to improve her health.

A further oasis of calm was provided by new Datchet friends Bill and Ida Temple, who at their house 'Ormonde' offered Cubby a home-away-from-home and offered John and Una carefree Christmasses for the next six years. Cubby joined the classes which Ida Temple ran for her own offspring, who were Cubby's age, as well as for the local children. Though Christmas at Ormonde was celebrated by Midnight Mass at the tiny village chapel, followed by dancing and songs round the piano, by 29 December the smallness of Grimston was beginning to irritate John.

---

* At the back of Una's 1918 diary is a cash account with calculations such as: 'March 23rd John owes me 17/7d. Food lunch 26, £1.7.0. total £2.4.7. Half of cheque to cook £1. John owes me £3.4.7. I owe John some tips to the servants.'

John awoke frightfully angry about the dogs, I wish they *could* all go, as their mis-
deeds seem to make her dwell on the other discomforts here which I *cannot* help:
Cub and her toys at close quarters, difficulties of food warmth and service. I am in
despair . . .[15]

Despite John's rages against burst boilers, dismissed servants and Una's terrible cooking, a 'marriage' of sorts was formulated. In discreet code on 30
January 1918 Una reports a declaration from her partner: 'J.s.I've m.L and I've
m.y.' Decoded it reads: John said I have married Ladye and I have married
you.[16]

John's view of marriage was traditionally masculist. Her disinclination to
cook or to engage in housework was written into their statutes. Una was
expected to share the psychic research work but also to run the home while
John herself performed only one job, either writing or research. Una's artistic
talents, formerly held in high esteem by John, were now relegated through lack
of time to one fine sculpted head of John herself. This was finished in October
1918, after which her sculpting was abandoned. John's pleasure in 'her head'
might well have led to more requests, had not Una tactfully insisted that John
sit instead for the well-known portrait painter Charles Buchel. The result, for
which Una paid the £35 fee, was the magnificent painting bequeathed by Una
in her will to the National Portrait Gallery where it hangs today.

When John decided that their union needed larger premises – which should
of course be purchased by her – Una wrote to Troubridge saying she wished to
move from Cheltenham Terrace to Datchet. Not only did Troubridge write an
angry refusal to Una, he also wrote two enraged letters to John.

To the lovers intent on each other it was almost as if he had not replied.
Paying him no heed, they proceeded with their plans. Una let Cheltenham
Terrace furnished. On 4 December she, Cub and John moved temporarily to
Swanmead in Datchet while they looked for a permanent residence. Ten days
later Troubridge wired from Salonika requesting that his greatcoat be sent to
Paris. The telegram sent Una first into despair, then over to see Crichton-
Miller. Nerved by his support she wrote to Troubridge on 21 December
announcing that she would not return to him.

The Kaiser had abdicated. The Armistice had been signed. The war was
over. Troubridge was about to come back to England. The lovers appeared
oblivious to all these events. On 2 January 1919 they settled on Chip Chase, an
eccentric secluded house in Hadley Wood, Hertfordshire, with mock battle-
ments like 'the sort of castle you would buy in Harrods' toy department'.[17]
Nearby in Oakleigh Park there was for sale a cottage suitable for the medium
Gladys Leonard which John decided also to purchase, a measure of the importance psychic work was taking in their lives.

On 9 January 1919 Troubridge was promoted to full Admiral. He wrote from

Paris to announce his return. Una's response was to retire to bed attended by Viola, Minna and Crichton-Miller. On 3 February as John was proceeding with negotiations for Chip Chase, Troubridge unexpectedly arrived at Swanmead. Una was in London. When she returned to Datchet she insisted on seeing her husband in John's presence. Her resolution bewildered more than angered him. He simply could not understand the situation. He had not been a cruel or difficult husband. He had attempted to sympathize with what he saw as his wife's 'nervous states'. That Una could purposefully wish to embrace domesticity with a woman rather than with him was beyond his comprehension. That this particular woman's image had transformed masculinity into a subversive and defiant desirability was beyond his imaginative grasp. A woman with an appearance as risqué as Radclyffe Hall was a woman who took risks.

It was a nasty meeting.

Troubridge now insisted on a legal separation, the only course open to Catholic couples. It had the advantage of being dealt with by solicitors out of court, thus avoiding unwelcome publicity. John instructed her own solicitors Hastie & Co. to act on Una's behalf in drawing up the financial settlement and arrangements for Cubby. By 6 February terms were agreed ready for Una to sign. Before she did so she took a taxi to Harrow to ascertain Crichton-Miller's advice. On 8 February Una was able to break the news to Minna and Viola that the Admiral had signed the document. She spent a long time with Cubby explaining the legal implications, including the fact that the child was now in Una's sole custody.

Troubridge however was not so easily satisfied. In March he threatened to renege on the separation order and regain custody of Andrea. He had changed his will the same day that he signed the separation order. In the event of Una predeceasing him, his sisters Laura Hope and Violet Gurney would become Andrea's guardians. 'My said daughter shall under no circumstances be left under the guardianship or care of Marguerite Radcliffe-Hall [*sic*].' Troubridge, like Ladye's relations before him, reverted to the feminine Marguerite. In his case he also returned to an earlier spelling of John's surname and reinstated the hyphen. Was he elevating her socially whilst keeping her gender carefully under his control?

Hastie, John's solicitor, and Sir George Lewis, the eminent lawyer whom John at once consulted, both felt Troubridge was bluffing and would not take the child. The deed was binding; he would not risk a public scandal by breaking a legal agreement.

Doubtless the Admiral's anxieties about the Cub, fed by his three children who had little love for their stepmother, were genuine. Una has been presented – both by her relations at the time and by biographers since – as an uncaring, neglectful mother. Yet she had a genuine fondness for her daughter whose health and welfare were always a priority. Whenever Cubby was ill Una would rush to her side with all manner of cossets and comforts. Una, John recorded, had 'an unreasonable tendency . . . to morbid anxiety where the child was concerned'.[18]

Una, however, was by no means completely absorbed in looking after her child. Cubby spent a great deal of time being cared for by her Troubridge relations, especially her Aunt Laura, her cousin Jacqueline and Hedley Nicholson, Jacqueline's new husband. There is no evidence at all that she suffered from these prolonged visits. Though Cubby was looked after by a nurse not merely during Una's absences but also as part of their routine existence, this was standard practice in middle-class homes of that period. Professional child-minders, nannies, nurses, governesses, were regularly employed to take children off parents' hands.

Where Una differed from many mothers of that period was in the conflict of loyalties she felt towards her daughter and her female lover. This has been in recent years a central issue in many lesbian relationships and emotionally healthy solutions do not come easily. A partial, and problematic, solution was found by Una after 1919. Following a 'foolish and childish row' that April, when John chose to resent the fact that Ida Temple was unable to take the Cub for a weekend, John and Una decided that Andrea should be sent to boarding school. The Convent of the Holy Child at Mayfield, Sussex, was chosen, and Andrea was despatched there in September 1919, shortly before her ninth birthday.

If John had been a more 'motherly' woman, then Una herself might have included the Cub in more of their outings. But John's own relationship to Cubby was ambivalent, her contradictory feelings evident in the great kindness she often showed to the child, making free with her time and attention, whilst at other times she might easily ignore or dismiss her.

She took her for walks, played outdoor games with her, bought her a wristwatch, cycles, toys, gave her a gold bracelet for Christmas 1918, paid all her school fees, and acted in an affectionate quasi-paternal manner. At one point she 'made up her mind that if the child showed any signs of having a good brain, the child must be sent to a University later on, and given a thorough scientific education, in order that she might become a useful investigator in Psychical Research'.[19]

On other occasions John displayed sternness, indifference or active resentment at the place Cub occupied in Una's affections. Within her lurked the hurt, rejected Marguerite/Michael figure who yearned for Una's undivided attention. If she could have utilized in her relationship with Cubby the sensitivity with which she re-created such a child's life in fiction, she might have healed her own loneliness and not increased that of the child in her charge.

That John herself may have wanted children is an interesting possibility. Several of her novels, most notably *The Unlit Lamp* and *A Saturday Life*, lament the symbolic sterility of the male partner in a lesbian relationship. When John and Una stayed in Florence in 1921 they visited the orphanage of the Innocenti where 'John [was] sorely tempted to buy a baby'.[20] In part this was an instance of John's desire to protect; in part it may also have betokened a wish to give Una an infant of 'theirs'.

Ironically, it was now that they were legally separated that Troubridge's elevation offered Una the chance of a title. In June 1919 while Una was in Bowden House nursing home recuperating under Crichton-Miller's care from 'nervous exhaustion', Minna Taylor rang John to say that her daughter was now 'a lady'. John passed on the news to Peggy, her companion at Chip Chase, then commented sardonically in Una's diary which she was keeping up: 'She [Minna] meant that Troubridge has had K added to his threadbare CMG.'[21] Although Una professed that the title was 'rather a bore', she was never above using and enjoying it. The Troubridges, loyal to the Admiral, believed she exploited it.[22]

Though Una saw Troubridge as the barrier to their felicity, and her separation from him as the reason for her resumed relationship with John, neither was the case. John's reaction to Ladye's death had been the impediment, and their adventures into psychical research – on which they were to be engaged for a number of years – were the real grounds for their renewed partnership. Had Ladye lived, John and Una would never have become a couple, for John's irascible loyalty would have prevented her abandoning her partner. What finally overcame John's guilt and strengthened the relationship with Una was their joint interest in spiritualism and the investigations they embarked on through the medium Gladys Leonard.

The First World War had occasioned such unprecedented numbers of deaths that it was hardly surprising that this cult had captured the popular imagination. Sir Oliver Lodge, pioneer of wireless telegraphy and a notable physicist, was a man who lent the highest respectability to psychical research and the alarming plethora of means by which it was pursued – including clairvoyance, table-turning, ouija boards, telepathy and the use of mediums. A former president of the Society for Psychical Research, he had written a bestselling account of his sittings with the medium Mrs Osborne Leonard who had successfully put him in touch with his dead son Raymond.[23]

John, seeking forgiveness from Ladye, had already experienced an unsatisfactory foray into the hereafter with a dubious medium called Mrs Scales, whom she suspected of cheating her. She was now anxious to pursue her psychical investigations in a more reliable manner. Una promptly wrote to Sir Oliver on John's behalf for advice. He recommended Gladys Leonard.

The mediumship involved four agencies: the sitter who sought to establish communication (in this case John); the medium, a largely passive 'switchboard', who stayed in a trance during each seance and through whose inert body the lines of communication passed (Gladys Leonard); the Control, a voice who possessed the medium's consciousness (Feda, the spirit guide who possessed Gladys Leonard during her trances). The fourth agent was the Ostensible Communicator from Beyond (Ladye). Feda purported to be a 13-year-old Indian, once married to an ancestor of Gladys Leonard's, who had died in childbirth in 1880. She spoke in a childlike squeak, had difficulty with her r's, and called Johnny Radclyffe Hall 'Mrs Twonnie'.

John went alone, anonymously, to her first sitting with Gladys Leonard. During a table-turning session the medium convinced her that it was Ladye who was trying to reach her.

MRH: Can you give me the name you always called me by?
Table: Yes. John.
Mrs Leonard: No, no, you must be wrong. John is a man's name.
MRH: It is correct.

John, impressed with this and other intimate details revealed by Gladys Leonard (such as the precise names of Mabel Batten, George Batten and the Watergate Bay Hotel), wrote to Cara to say she believed there was no cheating involved. Intrigued, John returned, first with Dolly as recorder and subsequently with Una. On 9 October 1916 she asked the crucial question that had haunted her since Ladye's death.

MRH: Something happened before she went over between us that made her unhappy . . . has she forgiven me?
Feda: She says: 'I've both forgotten and forgiven. You were not responsible . . . if you had known it would hurt me it would have been different.'
MRH: Tell her I didn't know she was ill, her passing was the shock of my life.

But John had known how much her infidelity had hurt Ladye; no amount of forgiveness from a disembodied spirit would easily assuage that guilt. On 15 November she said again:

MRH: Tell her I think I was very selfish before she died.
Feda: She says that at the time she sometimes wondered but now she knows you couldn't know she was ill.
MRH: That was no excuse for many of the things I did.

Occasionally the Control gave way to the Ostensible Communicator who then momentarily possessed the medium and could communicate directly with the sitter. John's excitement reached fever pitch when she and Ladye were able to communicate directly. Una, as the mere recorder, felt excluded. She was riled when Ladye repeatedly expressed the belief that John would join her, leaving Una and her troubled conscience still on earth. Una, ever inventive, suggested that 'several people might form part of the same ego, which would account for occasionally strong ties that sometimes seem inexplicable.' John agreed that the single selves of Ladye, Una and herself were probably unified within one ego and from then on she loyally dedicated each of her books to 'Our Three Selves'.[24]

Having replaced Dolly as John's chief supporter in this venture, Una was able to seek Ladye's approval for the position she had usurped. At a sitting on 13 October 1916 Una became the questioner for the first time:

Una: Tell my Lady she's got to help me to take care of Twonnie.
Feda: She says yes, she wants that, she puts her in your charge.
Una: Tell her I am honoured and will do my best.
Feda: She says she's afraid you hardly appreciate the magnitude of your task, it will be perfectly awful sometimes, terrible.
Una: Tell her I'll stick to it all right.[25]

Either Ladye from beyond or Gladys Leonard in the immediate vicinity had a nice sense of humour. An uplifting spirit became necessary as John in the early sittings vacillated between mournful declarations of guilt and sly remarks at Una's expense. Many of John's early questions when Una was present seem to be as much an attempt to punish Una as to exonerate herself. Their first joint sitting set the pattern.

MRH: Did she ever doubt my devotion?
Feda: She says 'No, I never, never doubted it.'
MRH: Does she love me more than anyone else?
Feda: She says 'Silly question, more than anyone – there is more in our love than there has ever been between two women before.'[26]

By that time John and Una were having several sittings weekly, taking extensive notes and engaging in voluminous correspondence with other researchers, including the writer L.B. Jacks and Sir Oliver and Lady Lodge whose home at Mariemont they visited twice.* Their psychic interests brought them the friendship also of William Butler Yeats who made frequent unannounced visits

---

* From 9 to 13 January 1917 Una sent Andrea to her Aunt Laura in Tite Street so that she and John could accept their first joint invitation to the home of Sir Oliver and Lady Lodge at Mariemont near Birmingham. Hero worship was in order and the new converts duly applied themselves. 'Such dear delightful people,' Una wrote. 'One could not long be shy.' Table turning and agreeable conversation left them 'honoured' to accept Lodge's hidden agenda of extra psychic research work. On the last night John retired early to bed with a nose-bleed while Una, who had worked hard on translating *Raymond* into French, entertained the Lodges. John felt pleased the great man had appreciated 'her Squig'.

to Una's studio at Royal Hospital Road to discuss plans for a proposed newspaper, the *Psychic Telegraph*, which despite their enthusiasm failed to materialize.

John's conversion to Roman Catholicism had given her a formal framework for the religious impulses which shaped her work. Now her susceptibility to instances of telepathy, coincidence, and paranormal forces made her an easy convert to spiritualism. She and Una both believed they had extrasensory perception and could communicate with each other telepathically. John's twin doctrines of Catholicism and spiritualism, with their separate vocabularies, nevertheless had certain links to which she attached herself. The passions of pity and awe were fundamental to each. The idea of reincarnation, which for John held beauty as well as necessity, was another common thread.

The extremes of religious fervour and elaborate ritual were endlessly appealing to her. However, as a Catholic, John had to deal with the fact that her Church condemned spiritualism. Several priests had heard her confessions on the subject and had taken her to task. Ladye from the Other Side reassured her that it was not the Church but its 'exponents' who condemned her. The implication was that if John looked hard enough she would find a confessor who condoned. However, even Father Norbert Wyllie of Cheyne Walk where John and Ladye had attended church was not prepared to offer approval. He left it to her own conscience – always a tricky business with John.

Una, the pragmatist, told Feda to give Ladye the message that she personally never confessed to spiritualist practices. For John, to whom salvation was won scruple by scruple, this was not satisfactory. She fretted and fumed. She even contemplated a break with the Church. Una, appalled at her incipient apostasy, hunted in vain for approving priests. When that failed, her zeal undeterred, she found several relevant articles by the Jesuit Father Thurston who had discovered a little known Decree of the Holy Office of the Roman Catholic Church which, though it condemned spiritualist practice by the ignorant, permitted legitimate scientific investigation of phenomena. With this in mind, and recommended by Sir Oliver Lodge, John joined the Society for Psychical Research to whose Council she was elected, after several battles, as its second woman member in 1918.

How far these proceedings were fraudulent or were genuine psychical manifestations is of course impossible to gauge. Certainly John's own early cynicism gave way to an earnest conviction in the reality of psychical phenomena, as a result of her many years of scientific research: research praised at the start of their career in the Society for its 'intelligent, cautious approach'.[27]

John and Una became particularly friendly with the Society's three most prominent women members: Helen Salter, the *Journal* editor, Isobel Newton, the Secretary, and Eleanor Sidgwick, sister of the philosopher and statesman Arthur Balfour and, later, second principal of Newnham College, Cambridge.

In the summer of 1917 Isobel Newton, who with Sir Oliver Lodge thought highly of John, asked John and Una to prepare a research paper on the accuracy of Ladye's ghostly revelations of her past life with John.

On 31 January 1918 John delivered the first part of their paper before a private audience of Council members. Most were impressed – sufficiently, indeed, to throw the second lecture in March open to the public. One male member however walked out. This was St George Lane Fox-Pitt. Once married to the daughter of the Marquess of Queensberry, who had done Oscar Wilde no good at all, Fox-Pitt was a friend of Troubridge and intended no good to Radclyffe Hall. Fox-Pitt's response to John's research was seasoned by his view of her provocative appearance and feisty attitude. At Society functions John wore an idly feminized version of a man's suit, with a severe skirt, in which she stood feet apart, one hand in her jacket pocket, the other holding a cigarette. Her wealth and class freed her from the constraints of public opinion but the sartorial indicators of a dashing masculine hat, bow tie and cravat readily enabled a viewer even subliminally aware of her relationship with Una Troubridge to read off her role within that partnership.

Dr E.J. Dingwall, a member of the Society at that period, recalled Radclyffe Hall as 'extremely aggressive in manner, and always [with] an eye for the ladies!' Dingwall, ninety years old at the time of his recollections, remembered the gossip in the Society about Miss Hall and Lady Troubridge. They 'loved shocking people', he said, 'and advertised the fact of their relationship'. On one such occasion, during a discussion of dreams, Dr Dingwall saw the Chairman's mouth drop open with shock as Lady Troubridge recounted a dream of hers starting with the sentence: 'Last night I had a most strange dream so I turned to John and said, "Darling, I've just had such a dream." '[28]

Fox-Pitt, who had serious reservations about Radclyffe Hall's style and manner, also had doubts about the nature of her research paper and about the scientific standing of the Council's newest and most volatile woman member.

The mercurial member meanwhile delivered part two of their paper on 22 March, this time to a ticket-holding audience at Steinway Hall. Its reception is open to varying versions. According to Una's account:

A big success, Sir Oliver in Chair. In the audience John's mother and mine, Emmy Campbell, Cara, Dolly, and Honey, Iris [Tree], Buchel and his wife . . . John read beautifully . . . Miss Newton said the audience [said] it was a flawless paper.[29]

Laura Hope, however, registered in *her* diary:

To Steinway Hall to hear Una and JRH's paper on spooks read out – it was so dreary that the three great ones on the platform, Sir Oliver and Lady Lodge and Mr Gerald Balfour, were all asleep![30]

But it was Cara's response to her paper which most disturbed John. On holiday in Lynton on 11 June they received a letter from Cara informing them that she had made an official complaint to the Society. She accused John of deliberately preventing her from attending sittings with her mother's spirit. Moreover she accused Una and John of being too 'emotional and excitable' to be reliable investigators. In her animus against Una she offered the Society the information that Ladye had quarrelled with John about Una just before her stroke, and that Una was unbalanced and was being treated for mental instability by Crichton-Miller.[31]

John, always quick to draw pen to defend her reputation or that of those she loved, wrote at once to Sir Oliver Lodge to refute Cara's charges point by point. She threatened a libel suit if Cara put her charges on paper. To avoid this Cara was asked to retract them in black and white. Sir Oliver Lodge gave Hall and the Society his full support. Eleanor Sidgwick offered to change Ladye's initials from MVB to AVB to protect her identity and appease Cara. Cara herself never pressed charges, nor did she give a written retraction, but the episode led inevitably to a growing estrangement between her and John.

That Dolly – her friend, cousin and ex-lover – should now encourage and stand by Cara wounded John much more. She saw this as a defection. When she and Dolly failed to come to an understanding, John felt she had no option but to view Dolly's conduct as perfidious. Dolly had shown disloyalty. John's treatment for traitors was always the same: she duly cut off Dolly's allowance. In doing so she lost her last affectionate link with her family.

Though Cara had survived the threat of a libel action, Fox-Pitt was not to get away so easily. In January 1920 he called at the Travellers' Club, and met Ernest Troubridge. Fox-Pitt had already passed on to him a copy of the research paper by John and Una that had so disturbed him. It disturbed the Admiral no less. He called the paper 'immoral'; he called Radclyffe Hall a 'vulgar climber' and a 'grossly immoral woman' who had come between him and his wife. He believed Hall had exploited the Society's work to gain a pernicious influence over his wife's mind. On 14 January, his suspicions confirmed, Fox-Pitt confronted Isobel Newton with his charge that Hall was a 'grossly immoral' woman. The following day he told Helen Salter that John had previously lived with Mabel Batten, another 'most objectionable person'.

John could not let pass a slur on Ladye's character. If Fox-Pitt would not withdraw his words, her lawyer Sir George Lewis would sue. Fox-Pitt remained implacable. Radclyffe Hall was forced to take him to court for slander.

Spiritualism had lost John the affections of Cara, the comradeship of Dolly, and would plunge her into the first (but not the last) court case in which her public reputation as a lesbian woman was to become an issue.

What then were the benefits of this interest? On a personal level it allowed

John to find ways to moderate if not entirely appease her sense of guilt. Not only did spiritualism reinstate Una as her approved lover, but it also incorporated Ladye, the deceased love, as a living partner in their shared daily life. On an intellectual level spiritualism had several benefits. John told Ethel Mannin that 'her psychic research work years ago did more for her in the matter of straight thinking and intellectual accuracy than any amount of ordinary educational mind-training.'[32]

Una Troubridge suggested that its effect on Hall's creativity was to train 'John in that infinite capacity for taking pains that she had so signally lacked, that became so salient a characteristic of her methods in later life and brought her natural genius to complete fruition'.[33] Una saw the transformation of 'the idle apprentice . . . metamorphosed by sorrow into someone who would work from morning to night and from night till morning, or travel half across England and back again to verify the most trifling detail'.[34] The literary dilettante had become a serious worker. When in 1919, aged thirty-nine, she finally realized that fiction was to be her vocation, she had evolved working methods from which thereafter she seldom strayed.

Until her death the other world fascinated her. The books she read and to which she returned (which included Du Maurier's *Peter Ibbetson*, Ford Madox Ford's *Ladies Whose Bright Eyes*, Alison Uttley's *A Traveller in Time*) all shared this concern with the metaphysical: as Una wrote, it fulfilled 'something in her nature that was dissatisfied with material life; the something that would occasionally make her say that she was feeling happy because for the moment she had a sensation that the veil between this world and another was very tenuous indeed'.[35]

This love of the mystical is present in her most sophisticated comic novel *A Saturday Life*. Although ostensibly the book explores the nature of artistic endeavour, Sidonia Shore's lightning changes of artistic skills become a commentary on Eastern religious ideas. Hall uses an Eastern theory of reincarnation to explain Sidonia's passionate enthusiasms and abrupt abandonments. The philosophical notion is that souls who live a 'Saturday Life' are destined to live through seven reincarnations on earth. Those who have reached the seventh embody all that was learnt or suffered in the previous six.

Research and redemption had finally released Hall from guilt and enabled her to write more freely. But despite her new energy 1917 was a lean year: she had written a war poem, composed music for several songs, published one article in *The World*, written one new story called 'Christopher Tennant'.

The following year was hardly better. Between June and December 1918 she merely revised old poems and wrote some new ones for the Bumpus publication of her *Collected Poems*. The start of 1919 was commercially successful for songs. She composed several for Mignon Nevada to sing, wrote a new poem called 'Jericho', revised two stories which she read to Peggy Austin in June, dabbled with a 'sketch' in October, in November attended the first performance by Mignon Nevada at the Central Hall of her composition 'Cuckoo', which a month later Chappells offered to publish.

This meagre output and its transitory nature dissatisfied her. By the end of 1919 she had put behind her the light-hearted world of salon-writing and versifying. Boxing Day was a crucial occasion. She returned to full-length fiction. She wrote all day. She wrote continuously for five days, hardly eating or sleeping. Penance was superseded by prose and perseverance.

Writing this novel was not a sudden decision. Towards the end of June and early July 1919 John had recorded in Una's diary that she was avidly reading May Sinclair's *Mary Olivier*, the story of an intense relationship between a mother and daughter. The nature of such a relationship began to obsess her. In December John read Clemence Dane's *Regiment of Women*, one of the few openly lesbian novels available at that time. She read it again a few months later. A conscious literary interest in lesbianism came also to preoccupy her.

As an account of erotic feeling between two women and of complex passions between mothers and daughters, these two books by May Sinclair and Clemence Dane had a singular influence on Hall's first completed novel. The specific genesis for the theme came during the summer holiday of 1918 which John and Una spent at Lynton. In the dining-room one evening they watched two guests make their way to the dining-table:

> a small wizened old lady and an elderly woman who was quite obviously her maiden daughter. The latter was carrying a shawl and a footwarmer and clutched a bottle of medicine. She fussed for several minutes round the old lady . . . John said to me in an undertone: 'Isn't it ghastly to see these unmarried daughters who are just unpaid servants and the old people sucking the very life out of them like octopi!' And then as suddenly: 'I shall write it. I shall write Heinemann's book for him and I shall call it "Octopi".'[36]

She did write it, though Heinemann was dead before she finished it. Given the interim title of *After Many Days* it would finally, after many trials, be published as *The Unlit Lamp*. Radclyffe Hall's apprenticeship was over.

10

STRIKING OUT

The years immediately following the war were significant years for Hall the writer and John the woman. She struck out on her first novel with its soft-hued but compelling lesbian theme. She fought her first court case with its muffled but potent lesbian sub-text. At the end of 1920 she finally cut her hair and took on her muted but powerful lesbian look. Her close-cropped Eton hairstyle with its exotic kiss curls like sideburns gave her an aura of highbrow modernism.

She now set her mind to writing. She did not yet know that as a serious novelist she would need to cut down ruthlessly on her commitments, to harness her chronic restlessness, to live the disciplined life of the desk. But she was able to make a start, ensconced with Una and Cubby in a secure base at Chip Chase, the first residence which she regarded as their joint home – not least because she was its owner.

Cheltenham Terrace had been let to the Crichton-Millers and John had finally sold Cadogan Court, the shrine to Ladye. She had however transferred all Ladye's photos, portraits and mementoes to Chip Chase where the Sargent portrait now hung in their baronial hall, with its growing collection of antique oak settles, chests and sideboards. It began to look like a scene from *The Forge* where Hilary Brent muses on the mania he shares with his creator: 'I'm an oak maniac, that's what I am . . . [I] have to collect something, it's a disease! . . . Why there's not a piece of furniture in this house that's not associated in my mind with some ripping acquisitive thrill.'[1]

Collecting it piece by piece, sometimes snatching it from another collector's hands, satisfied a certain lust within John. But behind the pleasure of acquisition lay another motive. When John felt empty or uncertain, she walked from room to room, touching the oak objects. The splendid strength of oak under her hands gave her a greater sense of security than anything she had yet felt since her uncertain childhood.

There was however one piece of furniture in Chip Chase that had associations of a different kind – Ladye's four-poster bed, which John took over for her 'solitary' slumbers. Fortunately, Una too preferred to sleep alone. Having been forced to share a double bed with Viola as a child, Una had grown up heartily disliking the idea: 'Why in the name of wonder . . . should anyone ever . . . wish for a bedfellow or desire to inflict one upon anybody else?' She did not feel that 'comfortable repose can really be achieved with one's head pillowed on another's breast'. Years later Una said she had always preferred to be 'master of one's bedclothes and captain of one's bed, not to mention lieutenant of the reading lamp and midshipman of the ventilation'.[2]

With John also preferring to be master of her own room in the matters of reading, writing and sleeping, they devised a system of proximity yet separation. An archway was built between Una's bedroom and the adjoining dressing-room. This in turn led into John's room.

The dressing-room became their breakfast room. There, each morning, still in nightclothes, they sat companionably over the toast, scanned the *Daily Mail* and the *Daily Telegraph*, and opened the post. Often beset by maladies, they would soothe each other's ills with diagnoses and discussion before John outlined which parts of *Octopi* she proposed to write that day.

If yesterday's writing had gone badly, one of her recurrent fits of depression would seize her, and she would sob miserably or vent her wrath on anyone in sight. Una's patience was not always equal to John's despair. Slight squalls not infrequently flared into grim rows in which one or other would threaten departure. Una, sunnier and more stoical, was sure that reconciliation would follow; John never felt sure of anything. She rocked inside to the malevolent rhythms of her childhood. Time had precipitated her into her first shared home with a lover, but 'home' brought with it the intensity of rows, reconciliations, recriminations, then rupture. It was never what she wanted; it was what she knew. If she was aware that she was repeating her parents' pattern and voiced that thought to Una, we have no record.

But when not in a rage, she clung to her lover as Hilary Brent did to Susan: 'It seemed as though he [Hilary/John] needed her all the time . . . he was worse than any child . . . He was such a queer mixture, so overbearing and yet so diffident.'[3]

The fact that John's emotions were so disorderly and tumultuous reinforced her desire for order and method in every aspect of her writing life. She wrote of her 'neatness complex' whereby 'anything in the nature of untidyness [*sic*] fidgets me to death'.[4] She became fastidious about where she worked and pernickety about what tools she used. There was a studied symmetry in her writing materials. Her study overlooked the large garden, and at her American roll-top desk, made of course of old oak, she wrote only with a gold-nibbed fountain pen to avoid 'writer's cramp neuritis'.[5] During the period of her early novels, 'though blue is my favourite colour', she recorded, 'I keep blue notepaper for letters. I always write my books on white paper.'[6]

The practical reasons for her methods were less important than the constraints they set. They kept her on the rails. One sees her as a child, gravely hopping in the squares, never on the lines. In the years ahead she became more rather than less particular about order. It was as if a certain narrowness of vision kept her sane.

In later years, Winifred Reed, who as Winifred Hales had worked as Hall's secretary on *The Master of the House*, recalled how Radclyffe Hall sternly insisted on 'Quaderno' lined notepads made in Milan, measuring 8 inches by 6 inches, with wide lines and a ruled one-inch margin: it was essential that the notebooks have an uncluttered look. Even her paper clips had to be a special shape: squat, oblong, and brass. Winifred Reed still treasured the paper clip holding part of the draft manuscript which Radclyffe Hall gave her above the writer's other more commercial gifts, which included an autographed copy of *The Unlit Lamp*, a small oak cabinet, a child's miniature oak chair, and a strange carved 'Cocky-Olly' bird, in memory of John and Una's live birds.[7] Radclyffe Hall was a stern employer – awkwardness often making her remote – but she was also generous.

Writing, though now a part of John's daily routine, was forced to compete with the other demands of running a home – among them the superintending of Cub's nanny, their personal maid Rosina, four house servants and two gardeners, as well as Miss Maclean, the daily typist who typed up their continuing psychical work in a small pleasant office near John's study. This was an extensive establishment for a woman who, like Hilary Brent in *The Forge*, was plagued by constant servant trouble, where 'maids came and went', where 'one dreaded getting up in the mornings to confusion consequent on new maids or no maids at all'.[8]

The couple had also decided to take up dog breeding professionally. They bred up to six Brabançonnes or griffons at any one time, of which the first was Fitz-John Minnehahah. He joined Olaf the Great Dane, the dachshunds Prudence, Ben and Una's favourite Thora, in the drawing-room, which John and Una had eccentrically converted into makeshift kennels by laying linoleum on the floor and fitting it out with wooden partitions.

Human visitors had to shift for themselves in a house where the presence of kennels in the drawing-room was no more quirky than the rest of the surroundings. Guests could sit around the oak refectory table, laid with pewter plates, in a stately dining-room perfectly attuned to this mock castle; or they could stroll through the minstrels' gallery, listening to the sounds of indoor birds. Una's two doves, Pelléas and Mélisande, and Karma, John's African grey parrot (a replacement for Ladye's Cocky) – purchased from Harrods who had acquired it from the comedian George Robey – all chattered inside, while in the gardens, more easily subdued, were Warwick the pet hedgehog, Hilary the donkey, and an ordinary rabbit dignified by the name Lady Dionissia.

In February 1920 Olaf their Great Dane developed epilepsy and had to be shot by the vet. John was almost as distressed as she had been by the death of her horse. When Una's dachshund Thora was put down on developing incurable follicular mange, they both wept. John bought Una a replacement cherry dachshund, called Thorgils of Tredholt (Thor for short), at a dog show in Guildford where they were exhibiting. Their enthusiasm and dedication, which had brought them success and appreciation in psychical circles, now brought them trophies and awards from the major English dog shows, and a certain resentment from other breeders.

Dressed in riding breeches, capes, big boots and fedoras, they were a formidable sight. John's appearance at dog shows was defiantly masculine rather than merely countrified. In the early twenties she developed her sartorial line in a manner which was conspicuously butch yet adhered firmly to certain class and gender conventions. Though she wore breeches to Crufts in 1923, this was due only to the gradual acceptance of trousers for women in a few very specific situations. There are photographs of John wearing trousers in private during the mid-thirties, when they were not yet generally worn by women; but she stuck to the convention of skirts for formal wear till the end of her life. Her gift was to make the skirt look almost more suitable for a racy member of the male sex.

For a woman often shy to the point of rudeness her extravagant way with clothes lent her an image quite the reverse of her nature. It was perhaps the desire for masks, that very theatricality, that led her towards Nathan's the stage costumiers for tricorn hats and swishing velvet capes. Add a monocle and the performance is unforgettable. You cannot wear a monocle and hope to be overlooked.

Fifty years later the guests recalled John and Una's clothes at a formal literary party: 'Radcliffe [*sic*] Hall wore a beautifully cut man's dinner jacket and skirt, a stiff shirt and bow tie . . . all in black, and wearing a monocle. Lady Troubridge wore the most glorious dress, and looked like a bride. It was an evening dress in cream coloured soft satin . . . They cut a tremendous dash as a pair.'[9] By then, in the mid-thirties, John and Una indicated their respective roles in the partnership through a fashionable masculinized and feminized dress code. But in the twenties, living together for the first time at Chip Chase, they were concerned to show themselves through their dress as a couple; their styles thus tended to coincide more than in later years. In order publicly to assert her new sexual identity and her partnership, Una adopted a style similar to John's, considerably more tailored than she wore later.[10]

In 1920 John went further. She purchased men's socks with garters and thick-soled shoes with a squat toe-cap. In August her tailor fitted her with a brocade smoking jacket; she had several photographs taken of herself wearing it. Later, as an established novelist, it became her regular writing outfit. She told the press:

> It has been suggested to me that I ought to have a picturesque corduroy coat and skirt to write in so that when surprised in the middle of a chapter I should at least look interesting, but I have flouted this idea with horror. The mere thought that I was putting on special garments would dry up the well of inspiration . . . I can never work in anything but old clothes although these must always be very neat . . . I usually work in an old tweed skirt and my velvet smoking jacket, a man's smoking jacket by choice because of the loose and comfortable sleeves.[11]

Now she saw herself like Stephen in *The Well of Loneliness* who had been guilty too long of 'indolence and folly, her illusion of safety where none existed'.[12] In 1920 John felt it was time to put indolence and the ephemeral behind her. She was learning what Puddle, Stephen's former governess, would tell Stephen: 'Work's your only weapon. Make the world respect you, as you can do through your work; it's the surest harbour of refuge . . . the only harbour.'[13]

As a poet Hall had been most comfortable writing when the mood took her. The psychical research work had not merely given her a regular writing routine, it also carried with it the stamp of professional approbation. She now spent long hours at her desk determined to write a set number of words, complete a section, plan a chapter. But despite her application and her passion for neatness and order, the author's need to apply herself did not come easily.

She had not yet learnt to shut herself off when necessary and leave to Una, that woman of practised intelligence and charm, the performance of social duties. That year, 1920, was prolific with distractions; the following year little better. On 8 January 1920 Phoebe Hoare came to lunch and stayed till 3.30, and according to Una, who appeared to feel none of the resentment she had felt towards Dolly, 'seemed to thoroughly enjoy herself'.[14]

Una's reaction was markedly more hostile when Jane Caruth, John's cousin and former lover, came to stay. Una admits that she 'awaited her arrival with a friendly interest and some curiosity'. John's description of the woman she had adored in her youth had been of a woman with long beautiful auburn hair, perfect figure and lovely hands. Una's depiction of the older Jane has the customary caustic tone she uses when faced with one of John's admirers:

> We found ourselves entertaining a stout, ageing American dame . . . Our guest had heavy jowls and an elaborately piled coiffure of hair that . . . had assumed that unpleasant brindle of auburn and grey that is almost mauve . . . Her conversation was a tissue of cranky, prim and hyper-critical strictures upon . . . life in general.[15]

Una was more relaxed about Peggy Austin's four visits in March, April, June and October. For John, the 17 October visit was a triumph for she had completed so much work on the novel that Una was able to read aloud from it 'all day' to Peggy and the contented author.

The Chip Chase lovers were a symbiotic couple. Together they frequently drove the twenty-four miles to and from London to meet Helen Salter and Isobel Newton on Psychical Society business. Together they paid duty calls on the Visettis, Minna Taylor (who had caused them great anxiety by a sudden illness in May) and, despite John's disaffection with Cara, on the Harrises. Together for pleasure they lunched at the Savoy with Toupie or Gabrielle, who since Ladye's death to John's delight had adopted Una into their circle.

Una, at her first meeting with Toupie on 29 March, was initially as captivated by her as John had been. With an intense almost frenetic enthusiasm they formed a close-knit trio, seeing each other several times a week for months in 1920 and almost as regularly in 1921. They would lunch either at the Savoy or the Hyde Park Grill, usually followed by a matinee, a recital, or tea with jazzy gramophone records at Toupie's flat in Egerton Mansions on the Brompton Road.[16]

When Toupie stayed at Chip Chase, coming down for dinner in flamboyant Chinese black satin mandarin trousers, she would sometimes bring her dog Priest, who was popular with John and Una, and sometimes her girlfriend Nellie Rowe, who was not. Toupie herself was beginning to tire of Nellie, but was nervous about ending the relationship. In August 1920 the lovers set off for a weekend to Brighton, where they and Nellie stayed at the Princes Hotel, while Toupie lodged more discreetly with her mother in Hove. One evening the Chip Chase pair waited until Nellie had gone early to bed, and thereupon crept out to join Toupie at a Brighton night-club, where they all 'talked and howled till 1.30 a.m.', Toupie appearing utterly indifferent to her lover's absence.

During the visit to Brighton John began to share Toupie's passion for cars. After Toupie had taught them both to drive, John, beguiled, purchased a black Singer saloon as a gift for Una. Toupie bought herself an Overland touring car. For the next few months the three women tinkered and coaxed the cars into action. Though John's car gave so much trouble that she sold it in October for £400, she had by then developed a definite taste for car testing, repairs, and mechanical badinage. Under Toupie's tutelage John also successfully tried out a motorbike and roared through London to night-clubs and bars.

From spring 1920 Una's journal refers to Toupie as 'Brother' and calls her 'him'. It is interesting to speculate upon the effect on the speaker as well as on the listener of constantly referring to a woman in male terms. Language itself is not neutral and served to invisibilize Toupie's femaleness.

In July when the trio were lunching at the Savoy, watching them curiously from a nearby table was Cencio Massola, the elegant Italian count married to Una's friend May. Una, who rushed across to talk to him, invited him back to Chip Chase for the weekend. It is possible that Cencio, seeing Una for the first time in the company of two obviously masculine women, may have viewed

Troubridge's wife in a new light. If he relayed this impression to May, it could explain why when John and Una visited Levanto the following year May and Cencio were noticeably cooler than had been expected.

From Una's viewpoint, one benefit from their friendship with Toupie was that it included Cubby. Toupie was that rare adult who knew how to befriend and pay attention to a child. Together she and Cubby joked and whispered secrets. Frequently she would invite Cubby to join the adults at the Hyde Park Grill for lunch. Toupie remembered to turn up on 5 November for Cubby's birthday, bringing greetings, treats and laughter. Not surprisingly it was Toupie who shared their relaxed family Christmas.

At this point John was taking her parenting seriously, encouraged in her attempts by the Cub's obvious dislike of visits to Troubridge and the fact that she 'almost tearfully rejoiced'[17] to be home. John played dominoes with her, took her and the dogs for walks, took her to the Temples to see the animals, and on 20 January she and Una gave her lunch at the Savoy before seeing her off to school.

Less than a month later, on 16 February, John and Una's writerly routine was interrupted with disturbing news from Mayfield that the Cub had a bad bout of influenza and abscesses in both ears. After much discussion they decided that when she had recovered they would remove her from Mayfield and send her to a convent at St Leonard's. Meanwhile Cub's condition worsened. An operation became necessary and she was moved to Dorset House nursing home. Una stayed by Cub's side until the surgery started.[18]

A child's illness can in an instant destroy a parent's happiness. Within even the slightest ailment there always lurks the danger of something more threatening. And so it was with Una. Her attention shifted sharply from her lover to her daughter.

This shift provoked a most curious reaction from John. As if in sympathy – or competition – she developed a sudden crashing pain in the head and bad earache. Dr Dan Mackenzie (Cubby's doctor), summoned to examine her, said it was merely neuralgia. 'Merely' was not a term to satisfy John, with her life-long susceptibility to ailments. But Una, wrapped up in her daughter's illness, for once had very little time for her partner.

In order to be near the nursing home they moved to Minna's uncomfortable flat. John lurked in bed ill, while Una paid daily visits to Cub. On 26 February, Mackenzie's verdict was that the Cub should be healed and back home in a fortnight, but Una could not stop worrying. 'I wasn't satisfied about Cub in my mind and didn't think Mackenzie was either.'[19] Una's intuition proved correct. Cub's temperature rose to 102° and another operation seemed necessary. By 1 March poor Cubby had developed chickenpox, and John and Una moved in to the Grand Central Hotel in Marylebone Road, where for seven days Una hardly sat still. She herself succumbed to renewed gynaecological problems;

when not at her own doctor's (Dr Sachs), she was rushing several times a day between John's sickbed in the hotel and Cubby's hospital bed. On 8 March, it was her thirty-third birthday – not one she wished to repeat. Her celebration was spent looking after the bedridden writer, making tea for Marie Visetti, John's unexpected visitor, and discovering that Cub now had infected adenoids. Not until 14 March did Cub recover. Finally, dressings and bandages removed, the child travelled home with John and Una to Chip Chase. 'At last,' said Una, 'a happy quiet evening.'

These events, reflecting as they do Una's concern for her daughter, show John just as clearly in an ambivalent light. Despite her concern for Cub, and her wish to provide the necessary marital support for Una, in the event she could not help assuming the child's sick mantle and in the process, if she lost a measure of Una's respect, succeeded in regaining some of Una's attention.

Curiously, when John became ill with stomach and gynaecological problems in June 1920, Una reported that 'Cubby's tummy [became] rather upset.' Poor Una was never able to deal with one of her sick charges without worrying in case the other came out in spots, scars or matching symptoms.

Cub's protracted illnesses and her own mimicry of them had severely interrupted John's writing schedule. However in May she returned to work on *Octopi*. With Cub restored to health, Una was restored to John as her literary assistant, though the demands on her time went way beyond editorial consultancy. She was expected to be nurse, confessor, lover and housekeeper, though Una was little better at housekeeping than her partner.

John would work obsessively, later and later into the night. As the years progressed and the books took over, this agonizing routine would often continue until dawn, at considerable cost to her health and eyesight. Her dismay at her own unhealthy schedules was often mixed with a self-conscious pride:

> When writing inspirational work . . . I frequently write twelve or fifteen hours at a stretch, but after these long spells I am apt to lie fallow for several days . . . yes, with inspirational work . . . [t]here are times when I can hardly understand my own words, so grotesque is the spelling.[20]

Radclyffe Hall had begun to play with the words 'inspiration' and 'art' in a somewhat self-regarding manner. She no longer simply 'worked' as she had done during her research period, nor did she now compose or write for pleasure as she had as a poet and songwriter. The enjoyment of her spontaneity was now seen as immature. Certain stringent forms must be adhered to if impulse and sensation were to be made to serve the ends of the imagination.

Radclyffe Hall's writing methods never varied. Una describes them prosaically: 'She never herself used a typewriter . . . she never learnt to type and the mere thought of dictating her inspiration to a typist filled her with horror. She always said that the written word was to her an essential preliminary.'[21]

Radclyffe Hall's own version is more lyrical: 'I must have a mystical marriage of pen and paper . . . I am not one of those authors who can dictate their work.' Then she relapses into a banal but more honest analysis: 'My manuscripts are so untidy they are difficult to read, so I always have to give them to my typist from dictation.'[22]

When Hall had completed a draft she would ask Una to read it aloud to her. From that reading she would dictate corrections to be incorporated into the next draft which was dictated back to the typist. John polished and changed as she read aloud. 'It was not an easy job,' admitted Winifred Reed, who at nearly ninety recalled the task she did at twenty with remarkable clarity:

> Radclyffe Hall was a perfectionist and she had a fiendish temper which was exacerbated by Lady T! I had to read and reread her chapters to her to check repetition of words, to look for words that rhymed, to ensure that no two characters had the same Christian or surname. All punctuation and lay-out had to be consistent. It was very easy to find yourself in the wrong with her. It behoved me, it behoved everyone to keep in with her, well, to keep in with the Couple.[23]

After the second secretarial stage, the typed version went back to Una to be further amended before being resubmitted to the typist. Radclyffe Hall made numerous drafts which she crossed through with a broad black pen line but never tore up.

The system taxed everyone involved and John knew it. When she wrote *The Well of Loneliness* she allotted to the character of Puddle Una's phenomenal patience. Stephen herself is almost a parody of Radclyffe Hall at her most tense and edgy.

> 'Stop embroidering that curtain, for God's sake, Puddle. I simply can't stand the sound of your needle; it makes a booming noise like a drum every time you prod that tightly stretched linen.'
>
> Puddle looked up: 'You're smoking too much.'
>
> 'I dare say I am. I can't write any more.'
>
> 'Since when?'
>
> 'Ever since I began this new book.'
>
> 'Don't be such a fool!'
>
> 'But it's God's truth, I tell you – I feel flat, it's a kind of spiritual dryness. This new book is going to be a failure, sometimes I think I'd better destroy it.' She began to pace up and down the room, dull-eyed yet tense, a tightly-drawn bow string.
>
> 'This comes of working all night,' Puddle murmured.
>
> 'I must work when the spirit moves me,' snapped Stephen.[24]

To work when the spirit moved her was Radclyffe Hall's cross also. Both Una and the secretary needed Puddle's tact and patience during this gruelling process, which in the case of *Octopi* lasted several years. If Una read aloud a chapter she considered of inferior quality, no matter how diplomatic she was, John would spot the flatness in her voice.

Having been asked whether I was tired and told that I was reading abominably and sometimes informed that my ineptitude was ruining the beauty of what I read, the manuscript would be snatched from my hands and torn to shreds or thrown into the fire. Physically and mentally exhausted, black depression would overwhelm her.[25]

John believed her inspiration had failed her. She would never write again. What she had written would shame a child of seven. 'Why had she ever imagined she could write? Nothing like this had ever happened to her before . . . and so on until, in spite of chronic insomnia, sleep would come, and days perhaps of stagnation and recuperation.'[26]

The tragedy was played out. The characters could leave the stage for the moment – but only until Radclyffe Hall wrote another chapter which fell below her own high standards. Then the exhausting 'acting of a drama which was essential to her processes'[27] would begin again. For the first time however it would be a beginning with a published end.

11

FINDING HER VOICE

During the early 1920s Radclyffe Hall began to see the writing of *Octopi* as her 'holy of holies' for whose sake 'it was right to endure'.[1] She began to compose a picture for herself of the writer as saint – ascetic, obsessive, tormented. Writing was a calling. Writing had a role to play in the improvement of society. She could set the world to rights, she could take up just causes, she could defend those in need of protection.

The first group she decided to champion, as had her fellow writer May Sinclair a year or so earlier, were the unmarried daughters unwillingly chained to the family home by the claims of elderly mothers. Even before the tragedy of these women's wasted lives was delineated, first in May Sinclair's *Mary Olivier*, then in Radclyffe Hall's *The Unlit Lamp*, some people had spoken out in fury. A correspondent to *The Times* on 12 May 1914 wrote:

> Every day a host of human vampires drain the life-blood of those who are their nearest and should be their dearest . . . the most usual species is the widowed mother with a daughter of any age from 20 to 50. The other children have gone out into the world to marry and to work . . . Clearly it is the duty of the one who is left to look after the little mother . . . The longer she stays on with her mother the more impossible it is for her to break away . . . Her opinions, her gifts, her ambitions she must keep in the background till they atrophy from want of use. She must . . . pay the wages, engage and dismiss the servants, count the linen, keep the books, and . . . run the house for the vampire's convenience . . .[2]

In an article about the genesis of *Octopi/The Unlit Lamp*, the novel which has Mrs Ogden as the vampire, Radclyffe Hall wrote:

> I knew that I was throwing down the gauntlet but in a way this made the book all the easier to write because I was fighting for others and not for myself . . . For a long

time I have felt that the Joan Ogden type never came before the public, never claimed the attention of writers, never voiced its grievances, and was therefore never championed ... They wither away for want of self-expression and encouragement because they are too refined, too sensitive, too unselfish or too timid or perhaps too noble ... to make a stand in defence of their rights ... A few years ago I came to the resolution that I would try and bring their grievances out into the light of day ... The idea possessed me so strongly that for three years I carried my manuscript wherever I went, abroad or in England.[3]

The novel's plot has its source as much in John's life as in society's structure and defects. Joan Ogden, like the young Marguerite, is a troubled adolescent, who sees herself as an 'unprepossessing freak',[4] interested in neither men nor marriage, who ultimately, after several attempted departures from the family home, is trapped by maternal needs and her mother's emotional reliance. Joan is both empowered to leave but also further constrained by her deep affection and growing sexual passion for Elizabeth Rodney who comes to tutor the academic Joan and her younger sister Millie, a musician. Mrs Ogden's hatred and jealousy of Elizabeth heightens as affection between the governess and her charge develops.

Joan is very like the young Marguerite. She is strong, energetic, with a brilliant mind and a defiant nature. Joan would never marry. 'Joan was so like a boy'[5] with a boy's hopes of success, of scholarship, of finding a society outside the confines of Seabourne. Her hopes are encouraged by Elizabeth, the singular, Sapphic, intellectually powerful New Woman, who suggests that Joan becomes a doctor and shares her house.

Joan, who deludes herself that she has the courage to seize the day, repeatedly turns down a marriage proposal from Richard Benson, who wishes to save her from being 'bottled' – though he never sees Joan's possible marriage to him as part of the bottling process.

The death of Joan's father and sister Millie, the misappropriation of Joan's trust fund, and her mother's clinging nature all conspire to sap Joan's will and prevent her achieving her goals. She gives up Elizabeth, and with her every chance of freedom and joy. The governess, her half-acknowledged sexual longing unrequited, her dream of sharing a life with Joan snuffed out, bitterly acquiesces in a marriage proposal from Richard's brother Lawrence Benson, 'the last person on earth that I could love'.[6] She moves away, leaving Joan to grow older and sadder.

With time, Joan ... had begun to weaken, and now she too took a hand in the church work ... developed quite a talent for arranging the flowers in their stiff brass vases ... Someone had to take Mrs Ogden to church ... so the task fell to Joan ... She would push her mother in a light wicker bath chair ... the combative instincts of youth had battered themselves to death in her.[7]

Joan ends her days, grey-haired, with varicose veins and unfulfilled hopes. Alone in the dismantled drawing-room, around her lies the wreckage and drift-wood of years spent in the service of others. She surveys the advertisements in the Situations Wanted columns. Typists, chauffeurs, ambulance drivers, uni-versity teachers, French and Italian speakers, farmers, book-keepers, those with degrees, those who had travelled, those who had served in the war, those who had a business education, those with hard won accomplishments – all those women were unable to find jobs. What chance was there for Joan Ogden, brilliant once, left with no skills, a woman who had not become what she might have been? Drawn and defeated, she agrees to act as companion to an elderly relative who has been in a state of arrested development since the age of six. Finding his doll for him and preparing his beef-tea Joan accepts that she now has 'Cousin Rupert to take care of instead of her mother'.[8]

Always she thinks back to a life with Elizabeth, a life she had been too afraid to take.

> Elizabeth, all in green, had reminded her of a larch tree . . . symbolic of growth, of fulfilment . . . Elizabeth had believed in her up to the very last. It was a blessed thing to have someone believe in you; it helped you to believe in yourself. She knew that now . . .[9]

What she knew now she knew too late. Her belief in herself, her belief in love, in a future with another woman had been sacrificed to a demanding mother and to her own lack of courage.

In a sense Joan and her creator Radclyffe Hall were trapped by the times they lived in. Society validated the chains which tightened around an un-married daughter's neck; society forbade the expression of such a daughter's erotic feelings for another woman who might offer her independence and love.

May Sinclair had outlined this process of entrapment in her novel *Mary Olivier*, with its portrayal of a similar woman in a not dissimilar situation, which Una had read aloud to John, and which John had reread eagerly. The novel's influence upon Radclyffe Hall is discernible in the twisted psycholog-ical relationship between mother and daughter. Mary Olivier is not what her mother wanted, any more than was Joan Ogden. Mary writes poems, reads books, enjoys the beauty of nature, and feels alienated from her mother's life of household duties. Mary's mother, like Mrs Ogden, is disillusioned by her rela-tionship with her husband, prefers her sons and enjoys a strange love–hate rela-tionship with her daughter. Mary's mother, like Mrs Ogden, is possessive. In later years Mary falls in love, has an affair, but refuses to marry because, like Joan Ogden, she cannot leave her now senile invalid mother.

Mary Olivier's rejection of her parents' repressive religion and her fears for her own destiny allow May Sinclair to conduct a metaphysical inquiry into the nature of God as well as an analysis of the issue of freedom and determinism. These are the same questions which preoccupied Radclyffe Hall not only in *Octopi/ The Unlit Lamp*, but in her subsequent novels. As *Octopi* moved towards a finished first draft, Hall suggests that although the natural forces which conspire against an individual's struggle for self-realization are strong, she is at least partly responsible for her own fate. The book's atmosphere of sexual ambiguity, real and imagined sickness, financial strain and emotional vulnerability forms the context for her view that individuals are trapped by their own destiny.

The context of both Sinclair's doomed daughter and Hall's crushed creature was middle-class middlebrow England where most young women were still brought up with the expectation that they would wait at home until claimed by men and marriage. This is the picture consistently presented by contemporary fiction. As Nicola Beauman points out, novelists of the time almost never represented women as workers, despite the fact that by 1914 some five million women were in employment, making up one third of the total labour force. The 1911 census listed 146,000 female clerks although very few made it into popular fiction.[10] Instead, novels of the immediate pre- and post-war period were still largely dominated by romantic themes and the ways in which women's lives were determined by men's interests. As a mainly middle-class art form, novels inevitably reflected middle-class expectations and showed married women with no particular function outside the home, and unmarried women with all the functions of the family slave within it.

Although Hall's original idea was to focus on these family dynamics, beneath her wider discussion of the commonplace tragedies of vampires and their daughters Radclyffe Hall was tracing a personal experience much nearer her heart. For the story hints at how crushed John's own life might have been had Ladye lived and become older and more dependent. The physical suffocation conveyed in some of the passages between mother and daughter reveals the claustrophobia John herself felt in the last two years of her relationship with Ladye. The choice of the original title *Octopi* is revealing. Love could crush its victim with its tentacles. In *Octopi* John used the same images of fetters and chains which she had bound and bonded into *Michael West*.

But almost as soon as she started *Octopi* Radclyffe Hall found she was not content with one theme. The emergence of a second, even more forceful subject, that of the growing love between Joan and Elizabeth, took over. The two women's love is not physically expressed but its restrained eroticism is intense as the situation is played out within its anguished triangle. The drama between Joan, Elizabeth and Joan's mother Mrs Ogden, mirroring that between John, Una and Ladye, operates against a background in which everyone appears to be at the mercy of sexual, psychological, cultural and economic forces they cannot control.

The book, published as *The Unlit Lamp*, is regarded by many critics as Radclyffe Hall's finest novel; but its structural weakness, as well as its psychological power, lies in its very presentation of these two competing themes which struggle for our attention.

Undercurrents from Marguerite's childhood now wove themselves into Radclyffe Hall's prose. The embryonic structure she teased out for *Octopi* between January 1920 and January 1923 united several shifting autobiographical strands which will recur in most of her major fiction. One theme is the parochial nature and conventional thinking of those who reside in English provincial towns: something well known to John from her time in Bournemouth and Southbourne. Another is the theme of the tomboy child who slowly recognizes her homosexuality, often developed into the character of the outsider alienated from a society intent on stifling or destroying her. Again, the child's conflict with her mother is shown to operate on two levels: the child fears and fights to get away from her, but simultaneously longs in vain for her love. Radclyffe Hall had already reworked several of these themes in the earlier novels *The Cunninghams* and *Michael West*.

As she progressed with *Octopi* Hall gave the gawky pugnacious Joan the aching vulnerability of young Marguerite. Initially Joan loves 'the little mother, the miserable, put upon, bullied mother, the mother of headaches and secret tears'.[11] Radclyffe Hall's own feelings, trampled on by her stepfather's violent overtures, become Mrs Ogden's, repelled by her husband's physical familiarities.

Joan Ogden's increasing disgust with her mother's physical embraces, even as she feels guilt at the way her fondness for Elizabeth is replacing her feelings for her mother, reminds us of John's physical disenchantment with Ladye in the last months of her life and her guilt at having replaced Ladye with Una.

We learn more about Radclyffe Hall's views on motherhood from *The Unlit Lamp* than from any of her subsequent novels. She had never known an ideal mother's love but she writes of it romantically both in early versions of *Octopi* and in an autobiographical essay that remains unpublished.

In the novel Joan Ogden muses on a maternal affection that

> ought to be a patient, unchanging love; the kind that went with making up the fire and sitting behind the tea-tray awaiting your return. The love that wrote and told you that you were expected home for Christmas, and that when you arrived your favourite pudding would be there to greet you. Yes, that was the ideal mother-love; it never waned, but it never exacted. It was a beautiful thing, all of one restful colour. It belonged to rooms full of old furniture and bowls of potpourri; it went with gentle, blue-veined hands and a soft, old voice. It was a love that kissed you quietly on both cheeks, too sure of itself to need undue demonstration.[12]

In her unfinished autobiographical fragment, composed a few years before the start of *Octopi*, Radclyffe Hall writes even more openly of her needs.

Some devilish and possibly misplaced sense of humour makes me want to write my idea of a mother . . . the sort of mother I wished I had had. I see her as upright but gentle, a woman of dignified repose. Her ideals are simple, wise and unshakeable . . . ideals that the world no longer admits but which I could have cherished for her and guarded . . . in a word, a woman one longed to protect, while coming to her, in turn, for protection. I see her grown tired of the noise of cities . . . her home is far away in the country. She loves flowers and her garden shows forth her love. She welcomes me there when I am tired with work. Does she know me for what I am? I wonder. If she does she must often be bewildered, must be at a loss to understand . . . She may understand for she had kept her faith in the things of the spirit . . . She has met old age half way as a friend – and they walk together she and old age, hand clasped in hand . . . When her time comes to die she will die unafraid, believing that many she loved will be waiting.[13]

Marguerite the child and Joan Ogden the girl need the understanding of imaginary mothers, having not received it from their own. Marguerite's mother controlled her child through displays of dislike, contempt, anger and violence. Joan's mother exercised control by means of possessiveness, jealousy, suffocation and hypochondria.

Marguerite's damaged childhood mapped the contours of this novel and gave it its sense of impending disaster. From those painful early years, John knew that damaged people are dangerous. They have learnt how ordinary cruelty is inflicted, and have learnt to survive that infliction. Writing out of that internal landscape was hard. Unlike the writing of her next two comic novels, *The Unlit Lamp* afforded her no relief; she needed constant breaks, becoming high-spirited sometimes to the point of hysteria.

Music helped, as did drinking and dancing in the company of like-minded women. Foxtrotting to gramophone records was in vogue and Toupie, John and Una spent hours dancing and smoking, sometimes at Chip Chase, where Toupie and her cousin Claude, Ladye's friend, stayed weekends, sometimes at Toupie's flat. They began to mix openly in the company of other lesbians, among them Gabrielle, Nellie Rowe, Enid Elliot and her lover the Hon. Eileen Plunkett from Ireland, who had both been drivers in the ambulance unit organized by Toupie and her colleague Norah Desmond Hackett. They were later joined by a riotous couple nicknamed Poppy and Honey and with them they danced their nights away at the Orange Tree Club, a straight but bohemian night-club similar to the Cave of Harmony and the Ham Bone Club in Soho, all of which became fashionable haunts in the twenties patronized by artistic or wealthy lesbians. The shortage of men after the war had made the sight of women dancing together familiar and unthreatening.

The summer faded away and with it frivolity. By October 1920 the gaiety and fun were over. November brought news that the Fox-Pitt slander suit would be heard mid-month. John fretted, but unlike Una whose anxieties were personal, hers were mainly professional.

Although the good name of Mabel Batten had been called in question, although allegations of a sexual nature had been imputed, it was her professional reputation as a 'fit' investigator and Council member which concerned her. That her worries lay in that direction surprised her, but confirmed the fact that she had begun to think of herself more and more as a public person: a woman who wrote, a woman who was a respected researcher – in the phrase of Ladye's circle, a woman who 'did things'. She had, progressively as a poet, rigorously as a researcher, acquired a professional reputation which could be tarnished. She had been expecting her co-option to the Council, but Sir Oliver Lodge suggested that she postpone the appointment until after the court case. Reluctantly John agreed.

Her position in relation to Fox-Pitt's allegations of immorality was problematic. She was aware that the most solid line her counsel, Sir Ellis Hume-Williams, could take would be to refute the slightest hint that she was a homosexual woman. As she was proud of her sexual orientation, though not yet ready to defend it in public, she was placed in a deceitful position which was anathema to her nature. She still placed her reliance on male 'experts', or at least she was not yet ready to challenge them, so she allowed her solicitor Sir George Lewis and Sir Ellis Hume-Williams to construct her case as they saw fit.

Apprehensions may have been increased by the fact that a move was afoot to bring lesbian relationships within the purview of the criminal law: an offence of 'gross indecency by females' was mooted for introduction in the Criminal Law Amendment bill due for passage through Parliament in 1921. Though dropped in the Lords, the proposal was part of a growing public awareness of the subject and likely to increase the threat from Fox-Pitt's allegations.

Una's anxieties were of a different order from John's. Worried that Troubridge would be called to give evidence, and would publicly back up his allegations – for Fox-Pitt had assured Mrs Salter that 'Admiral Troubridge is not afraid of anything, and would be quite willing to make this statement publicly' – Una grew tearful and succumbed to several bouts of sickness. Her 'marriage' as well as her marriage was under threat. Feeling unsafe, Una ensured that she and John took precautions not to see Troubridge either privately or publicly. When they needed to take Cubby to visit him at Cheltenham Terrace they carefully arranged to do so only when the servants would be present. Once they made an error and the Admiral came to the door to greet his daughter. Seeing him they resolutely refused to speak and rushed away, leaving Cubby confused and Troubridge furious.

Nervous tension brought on a renewal of Una's ailments. The gynaecological troubles from which both she and John had suffered in October, when they had been treated by Dr Sachs, returned. When Sir George Lewis told them on 9 November that the case might be heard in two days' time, Una's symptoms and John's bad temper got worse.

To everyone's relief the case was finally listed for midday Thursday 18 November. It was heard in the King's Bench Division before the Lord Chief Justice and a Special Jury. It was to be a two-day ordeal for John and Una, who found that even a sense of being in the right did not dispel their fears.

The Times followed the case. John avidly followed the *Times* reports. The case was given wide publicity which John both relished yet abhorred. This tangle of emotions was to be a keynote in her future dealings with the law. The plaintiff's complaint against the defendant was that Fox-Pitt had slandered her by speaking and publishing these words:

Miss Radclyffe-Hall is a grossly immoral woman. Admiral Sir Ernest Troubridge has recently been home on leave and has in my presence made very serious accusations against her. He said she had wrecked his home. She ought not to be co-opted as a member of the Council. I didn't like to be hostile to her at first, but my own feelings about her have been confirmed by what Sir Ernest Troubridge told me.

Miss Radclyffe-Hall is a thoroughly immoral woman. She lived for many years with the woman mentioned in the paper which she and Lady Troubridge wrote, a woman who was a most objectionable person . . . She [Hall] has got a great influence over Lady Troubridge, and has come between her and her husband and wrecked the Admiral's home. I am quite determined to oppose her election to the Council. If I cannot persuade Mrs Sidgwick to withdraw her proposal of Miss Radclyffe-Hall for the Council, I intend to bring the matter before the Council myself and put it strongly so as to carry my point, as she is quite an unfit person to be on the Council.[14]

Two slanders were alleged: first, that Radclyffe Hall was a thoroughly immoral woman; secondly, that in consequence she was an unfit person to be on the Council. Sir Ellis Hume-Williams began the proceedings. Suavely he told the jurors of John and Una's 'friendship', without giving any hint of its lesbian nature. Delicately his words emphasized John's wealth and Una's breeding and social class.

A friendship sprang up between them with the entire approval of Admiral Troubridge. In 1916 Lady Troubridge had been very ill, and Miss Radclyffe-Hall, whose means were much larger than those of the Admiral, offered to take her away for a holiday. The Admiral approved, and in 1919, he suggested that, for the future, Lady Troubridge should make her home with the plaintiff. In the summer of 1916 the plaintiff and Lady Troubridge became interested in psychical research . . .[15]

When Hall's counsel turned to a consideration of Fox-Pitt's statements to Miss Newton and Mrs Salter he became bolder. Those remarks, Sir Ellis Hume-Williams said, could only be understood to refer to Radclyffe Hall's sexual immorality. He told the court that there was

> abundant evidence that the defendant had used what he had heard for the improper purpose of venting his animosity against the plaintiff and making against her as horrible an accusation as could be made against any woman in this country. The words used by the defendant could only mean that the plaintiff was an unchaste and immoral woman who was addicted to unnatural vice and was consequently unfit to be a member of the Council.[16]

John was the first witness. She walked into the court passionate but self-composed, dressed in a sombre outfit that offered the merest hint of the stricken creature within. Her coat and skirt were black and brisk. A white neckcloth and a high stiff collar emphasized her pale cheeks. She spoke steadily, keeping the traces of anger out of her voice. She thrived on combat though it wore her thin.

She was cross-examined by Fox-Pitt who had unwisely decided to dispense with the service of lawyers and conduct his own defence. A most eccentric showing he made. In an extraordinary move he had changed his original defence. First, he said that he did not admit he spoke or published the words complained of. Secondly, he stated that he did not mean and was not understood to mean what was alleged, and that in any case the words were no slander on the plaintiff. Thirdly, with Alice-in-Wonderland logic he told the court that the words did not describe the plaintiff or her character, her sexual morality or her chastity, but merely described the papers which she had read and her method of treatment of psychic investigation. Lastly he pleaded that the words were spoken, if at all, on privileged occasions.

The defendant addressed the Lord Chief Justice, and in a further linguistic volte-face, said he had not used the word 'immoral' in a popular but in a special sense. This special sense turned out to be the use of immoral only in relation to Hall's work within the Society.

In order to maintain such an upside-down defence he had to prove that Radclyffe Hall was a dubious, fraudulent or at the very least an incompetent scientific researcher. He asked her questions about her training in science, psychology, physiology and psychic matters, all of which she handled sensibly and to the jury's satisfaction. Then Fox-Pitt began to lose his temper:

The Defendant: 'This paper of yours is scientific rubbish, quite unworthy of the Society, and its publication is extremely harmful. It has produced a condition of mind which I consider immoral.'[17]

At this point the Lord Chief Justice intervened to point out that the charges against Fox-Pitt went considerably further than whether Radclyffe Hall's work was against the public interest. From this point on the Lord Chief Justice's constant interventions began to pinpoint the very real weaknesses in Fox-Pitt's case. However the absurdities attaching to the spirit world as presented in John's paper, laughable as these were when taken out of context by the Lord Chief Justice, hardly helped Hall's case.

Lord Chief Justice: 'How does a spirit bathe? I see later on that the lady has a private bathing pool in the spirit world.' (Laughter in the court.)[18]

The first day's proceedings having been adjourned, John and Una, tired and tremulous, talked far into the night debating the issues, still uncertain whether John would win over the jury. Una, due to appear in the witness box the following day, hastily purchased a dark veil to tone down her violet silk hat. She offered her evidence in a discreet and respectable tone but at one point unwittingly yielded to the temptation to pull rank.

Counsel: 'Who was A.V.B.?'
Witness [*Una Troubridge*]: 'A lady who is now dead; she was my cousin. If his Lordship would allow me I should like to say that in life she occupied a high social position and lived in perfect amity with her husband.'

His Lordship did not allow her. Tartly he responded: 'How does this affect the case?'

When Sir Ellis Hume-Williams suggested that an allegation had been made by the defendant that Ladye was a person of low and immoral character, His Lordship grew more acid: 'Her high position in society would be no answer to the charge that has been made.'[19]

Fox-Pitt appeared highly antagonistic not only towards John and Una but also towards their female friends, Miss Newton, Mrs Salter and Mrs Sidgwick, the formidable trio who effectively ran the Society. Fox-Pitt claimed that these women were part of a 'conspiracy' which to the amusement of the court he called a '*junta*'. It would appear that the acrimonious defendant was not merely anti-homosexual but also anti-feminist. It was to John's advantage that his defence was muddled as well as manipulative, contradictory as much as combative.

The beleaguered jury retired in great confusion. Returning their initial verdict they found as a fact that the words were uttered, but that they were not intended to apply to the plaintiff's personal character, but to her research work which was calculated to influence the character of the Psychical Society. His Lordship's suggestion that this might be seen as a verdict for the defendant was hotly refuted by John's junior counsel, St John Field, who argued that the question of intent was immaterial. Wearily His Lordship despatched the jury to reconsider the wording of their verdict: that is, whether the words 'were not intended to apply' actually meant 'did not apply'. On their return the jury offered a verdict for the plaintiff Radclyffe Hall, awarding her damages of £500.

Fortunately for Una, who had no wish to see her marriage exposed in public, Troubridge was not called to the witness stand. Nevertheless the case reaped so much adverse news coverage that according to members of his family the Troubridge name became 'an unending source of embarrassment'. He himself was seen as 'the laughing-stock of Europe' and Una's photographs were cut out of the family albums in Runcton, the Troubridges' house in Norfolk.

Una's diary entry the night of 19 November was unequivocal: 'Home to a much relieved and happy evening.'[20]

John's relief however was tempered by the knowledge that her victory was hollow. If Fox-Pitt had been defended by a counsel of similar standing to Sir Ellis Hume-Williams, or even if he had attempted to prove rather than to deny that John was 'immoral' in a sexual sense, he would probably have won his case. As it was, Radclyffe Hall had won by what she saw as a highly manipulative method. Her own counsel had taken great pains to ensure that Fox-Pitt shied away from the implication of his allegations that her sexual behaviour lay within the realm of 'unnatural vice'. As Hall believed her lesbianism to be neither vicious nor 'unnatural', and as jurors, witnesses and spectators, who possibly did, were in no doubt as to what was meant by 'grossly immoral', she felt she had won on terms incompatible with her integrity. As a woman who cut through hypocrisy and evasion, the legacy of this strange case was a disturbed conscience. She affected insouciance but it overlaid a brooding vision.

Although Fox-Pitt resigned not only from the Council but also from membership of the Society, he decided to appeal against the verdict. In March 1921 when the appeal was heard, he won on a point of law (that insufficient attention had been paid to his defence of privilege) and a new trial was ordered. Sir George Lewis advised John to take no further action. For once she sensibly accepted his suggestion.

For several months John had frequently asked Ladye's spirit if she could bob her hair and Ladye had adamantly refused. However in November Ladye had relented. John had waited until the court case was over to make her next rebellious move. On Friday 17 December 1920 Una wrote in her diary: 'After tea I cut off John's hair and we washed it!'[21] Radclyffe Hall was forty when the luxuriant waist-length plaits fell to the scissors. The following day they drove into London so that John could have it professionally trimmed and waved. She now looked the part she was about to play.

12

THE TWENTIES

The Twenties – the Jazz Age, the age of speakeasies in New York, a new-fangled flippancy in London. Pent-up energy after the war drove insurgent youth into wild dance routines – the Charleston, the Blackbottom, the Tango. There was a fever in the air, and with it a lighter spirit, an air of frivolity. Yet at the same time a darker undercurrent, a restless intensity came to infect writers on both sides of the Atlantic.

Though the novel Radclyffe Hall was currently engaged on, *Octopi/The Unlit Lamp*, was moody, filled with forebodings and images of chains and fetters, she was writing the darkness out of her system, and some of the scintillating spirit she put into her night-life was ready to surface in *The Forge* when *The Unlit Lamp* was finished. It is not surprising therefore that her first, darker novel took longer to find a publishing home than her second, which was lighter, zestful, merry, much more in keeping with the tone of the twenties and with that of other writers.

In the early years of the twenties, among the new voices emerging in America were Scott Fitzgerald and Sinclair Lewis. While Lewis satirized small town America in his novel *Main Street*, Scott Fitzgerald heralded the new age in *This Side of Paradise* (published March 1920), in which he caught the frenzied fever of fast-living youth, decorative, desirable, ultimately doomed for its decadence. The same prevailing principle, amusing, abandoned, iconoclastic, was to be found in Radclyffe Hall's London, amongst the young and arty at Prince's in Piccadilly, on the Criterion Roof, at Romano's in the Strand, down at the Hammersmith Palais de Danse or for the smarter set (John, Una and Violet's circle) dancing between supper courses at the Savoy. Like Scott and his friends in New York, John and her companions in London, called by Ethel Mannin 'the Bohemians', alternated between the latest jazz craze and Paul Whiteman's dance band. They frequented the densely packed Ham Bone Club in Ham

Yard, Soho, once a harness room above a stables, where for a guinea a year subscription (with a two-thirds discount for writers and artists, which appealed to John) they kicked their heels on the pocket-handkerchief dance floor, felt they were witty, daring, and striking a blow for social freedom.

> All those short haired girls sitting about unsentimentally on men's knees, all the cocktails and cigarettes and adventures that made up their lives . . . their lives were cocktails and they had spiritual indigestion. But didn't they get something out of life, too, something that pre-war youth missed? Their lives were amusing, colourful. But they were hard, these children of the Jazz age; they had Jazz souls.[1]

Radclyffe Hall and Scott Fitzgerald shared that hard edge, that bitterness beneath the innocence, and it showed in their novels. John and Una shared other characteristics too with the Fitzgeralds, who were known and would be admired in the twenties by John's friends Rebecca West and Natalie Barney. Scott, like John, was a writer in constant need of a constant 'wife', a spouse who read and listened. While in London Una read and analysed John's *Octopi/The Unlit Lamp*, over the water Zelda Fitzgerald, who epitomized the liberated flapper, the playgirl with moral courage, performed the same role for Scott. When Zelda told friends that her husband thought she was 'a lazy woman', Scott confessed that her kind of 'unemployment' was as useful to him as we know Una's was to John. 'I think you're perfect. You're always ready to listen to my manuscripts at any hour of day or night . . . You do, I believe, clean the icebox once a week.'[2] Una Troubridge, unlike Zelda, had a succession of servants to clean the British icebox.

In an era which saw the opening of the Eighth Congress of the International Woman Suffrage Alliance at Geneva in June 1920, John still conformed to Scott Fitzgerald's hard-hitting model of 'male writer with intelligent listener wife', an image that despite the mild remonstrations of feminist friends John never entirely lost.

As Zelda and Scott Fitzgerald left New York to head for Europe, Zelda summed up John's own restlessness when she said: 'I hate a room without an open suitcase in it, it seems so permanent.'[3] John, suitcases at the ready, felt the same. The year 1921 was to be one of John's most flurried. It was the year that she sold Chip Chase in January, rented an apartment at 7 Trevor Square, Knightsbridge, in February, purchased a house at 10 Sterling Street in May, then escaped from pressures in London by going to Levanto for September and October and Florence from November until the start of the following year.

In England they had not found it easy to settle on a house. At one point so uncertain had they been that Una had even written for particulars of a lighthouse for sale. In December 1920 John had nervously asked Una how she would feel if they ever left Chip Chase. 'I don't care where it is as long as we are together,' Una stoutly reassured her diary. A month later on 20 January 1921

John accepted an offer of £5,000 for the house from a dog owner called Mrs Thomas. Content that Chip Chase should be in an animal lover's hands, John lost no time over the move. She and Una were on the wing again.

By 14 February the British pair had sorted, destroyed and stored what was left of their possessions. On 9 February, preparing for the move which took several days, they walked the dogs on the golf links where they encountered Ladye's old friend Ethel Smyth, who lived nearby. Despite the fact that this was Una's first meeting with Ethel, impulsively she told her that she 'was suffering from an unmentionable disease given to her by the beast of a husband' from whom she had fled.[4]

Throughout 1919 Una had been treated by Dr Sachs and Dr May who had taken several blood tests which proved conclusively that venereal disease was present. Dr May had told her that 'said innards would always be sensitive but three years extreme care might make me relatively sound. I think it so damnably hard on John and an uphill lookout!'[5] Una's constant medical problems were indeed to become a source of depression and difficulty for both of them. Nor did Una make light of them. Illness, though an annoyance, was a fascinating preoccupation. This particular malady provided an additional reason for their separate bedrooms at Chip Chase, and sometimes fuelled their quarrels. That Una was prepared to make such a candid confession to Ethel Smyth may tell us something about Ethel's own accessible and open-hearted nature, or it may point to the conversational boldness of these self-avowed Bohemians.

When Ethel came to tea with John the following day, John lost no time in giving her up-to-date information on Ladye's discourses from the spirit world, for Ethel like John held a strong belief in communication with the dead.

Ethel, well-known as a feisty feminist, had just created a modest storm in Hull where one of her works was being performed. So incensed had she been by the conductor's lack of skill that she had snatched the baton from his hand. Lent a sympathetic ear by John, Ethel talked of her continuing struggle in the male-dominated musical world to get her operas performed, and of her new collection of essays *Streaks of Life* in which that struggle was described. In her new book, Ethel had also reviewed *Mount Music*, a novel by Edith Somerville with whom Ethel had spent a magical spring in Sicily. Edith, who with her cousin Violet 'Martin' Ross formed the famous literary partnership Somerville and Ross, was a writer Ethel was very keen John should meet.

On her return home Ethel informed Edith that 'they [John and Una] told me thrilling things and are simply dying to meet you.' Whether John and Edith were as anxious to meet as Ethel was to perform the introductions is unclear, but on 24 March Ethel arrived for tea at Una's bringing Edith with her. John however was ill in bed. Una told her diary later, 'I entertained them as best I could.'[6] She probably did far better than her modest record suggests. She was after all an expert in the social graces, and she and Ethel had in common books, music and art, and doubtless discussed among other novels the American writer everyone in their circle was talking about, Sinclair Lewis.

John's attention was drawn again to Sinclair Lewis later in the year, by the Australian novelist Ida Wylie, a new literary friend five years older than John. Before John and Una set off for Italy in the autumn, Ida wrote and gave them her view of Sinclair Lewis's *Main Street*: though 'frightfully long and dull in parts . . . it gives a perfect picture of American life in the Middle West and makes one so thankful that one doesn't live there that it is quite worth buying.'[7] Ida's generous offer to give them her copy of Lewis's book was the start of a long and supportive friendship which proved of great professional benefit to John.

Ida recommended other books, including *Joanna Godden* by Sheila Kaye-Smith, who would later become a good friend of John's, and A.S.M. Hutchinson's *If Winter Comes* over which Ida herself had 'wept copiously'. She added however that she had been 'in an emotional mood and perhaps on second reading I shouldn't like it so much'.[8]

A year later, in September 1922, at a tea party given by May Sinclair, John met A.S.M. Hutchinson's sister Vere, whose book *Sea Wrack* had just been published by Cape. John and Una got on particularly well with Vere Hutchinson and her illustrator partner Dorothy Burroughes-Burroughes, known as 'Budge', not least because both couples had parallel interests in writing and art. The couples began to see each other frequently.

Ida Wylie, as enthusiastic about Vere Hutchinson's writing as she was about John's, was surprisingly self-effacing about her own work: 'My own addition to the World's Masterpieces is not due till next spring and I wouldn't ask my worst enemy to read it. It makes me blush every time I think of it. It's most painful . . . this really knowing what's what and not being able to live up to it.' In fact during her lifetime she had a very large readership and by her death in 1959 she had published over two hundred short stories and fifteen novels. Today the novels that are best known are those with Indian settings such as *The Daughter of Brahma* (1912) and *The Temple of Dawn* (1915), both of which were selling well by the start of her friendship with John.

John's first meeting with Ida and her lover Rachel Barrett had been accidental. In June 1921 they had all four attended a dog show where a fire occurring in the tent had burnt several of the dogs. Ida, whose passion for English bull terriers equalled their own, was as distressed as Una and John. Though Ida's interest in animals attracted Una, as she got to know Ida better she despaired of what she deemed Ida's pathological promiscuity. John however was intrigued by exactly that quality. Ida's captivating mixture of literary intellectualism and a racy sexuality meant that she took risks. Those were risks which John fantasized about but nowadays seldom took. Volatile, funny and erotically daring, Ida returned John's affection immediately. 'I do hope you won't forget me,' she wrote soon after they met. 'Because I count meeting you both as one of the really nice things that have happened to me.'[9]

Both John and Ida had courageously broken out of the closet to lead open – and public – lesbian lives, though Ida's bid for independence was made at a younger age and she ventured more, most especially her father's disapproval. In 1904, at the age of nineteen and in defiance of her father's wishes, she went to Karlsruhe in Germany to pursue an intense lesbian affair which lasted for eight years and gave her material for her novel *Towards Morning*, published in 1918. When Ida returned to England in 1911 she became a militant suffragette and through the women's movement met her lover Rachel, who became another ally of John's. John envied Ida, as she had envied Toupie, not only for her boldness but also for the war work Ida had carried out first in London then in France. Ida's feminist view of lesbianism as well as her war accounts influenced certain situations and characters in John's novels, most particularly *The Well of Loneliness*.

John and Ida shared a fascination with 'dear abroad' dating from childhoods spent travelling through Europe and America. During the war years England was a less fertile place for new female short story writers than the USA, so by the time of Ida's meeting with John, Ida was commuting regularly across the Atlantic, where she had achieved considerable literary success. Each time Ida was in England, however, she helped John make new literary contacts.

It was through Ida that John got to know May Sinclair better, and through their influence gained an entry into several writing associations. May Sinclair and Violet Hunt were founder members of a newly formed international organization for poets, essayists, editors and novelists, the PEN club, whose first president was John Galsworthy. In the spring of 1922 May and Violet ensured that John was elected to join the company of distinguished women writers from around the globe. Ida herself was elected in June. John went to her first PEN club dinner on 2 May and accompanied Ida a month later to her inaugural meal. John took her other new writer friend Vere Hutchinson to the next PEN dinner. Again at Ida's suggestion, John became a member of both the Writers' Club and the Women Writers' Club where she began to meet other novelists and editors. At last she felt she had a niche in the writing world.

Although Violet Hunt's place in John's life had settled comfortably to that of loyal writing friend, nevertheless some hint of their former flirtation occasionally lurked beneath their literary banter. It seems that Violet had told Ethel Smyth that John was extraordinarily handsome, 'like a Roman empress'.[10] On 21 May Violet confided 'her troubles' to Una and the Roman empress.[11]

Those troubles had increased. During his time in the army Violet's not-quite-husband,[12] Ford Madox Ford, had secretly been writing love letters to Stella Bowen, a woman younger than Violet. Unbeknown to Violet, Ford and Stella planned to set up together in a country cottage once he left the army in 1921.

Having publicly proclaimed for years her somewhat uneasy status as Ford's 'wife', Violet, discovering his defection, became insane with desperation. When in 1920 Ford and Stella moved to Scamell's Farm in Bedham, Sussex, a friend leaked the address to Violet who, accompanied by May Sinclair, followed them to the village and watched him as he went about his work.*

When Violet returned to London she paid the wife of a carpenter working for Ford to send her regular reports on her 'husband'. She learnt to her chagrin that on 29 November Stella had given birth to a daughter. Violet had little choice but to resettle to the life of a single woman writer. The early use of arsenic for her complexion plus the natural processes of ageing meant that she was already losing the exquisite appearance that John had been so taken with. The consequences of syphilis had thinned her once abundant hair, for which she now needed constant scalp massages. In 1917 Violet had written in her diary that her love for Ford was 'an unholy passion that will last till I die'.[13] The loss of that love together with the loss of her looks decided her against further affairs. Her women friends, including John, May Sinclair, Rebecca West and Ethel Colburn Mayne, continued to sustain her, and Una too was drawn not unwillingly into the circle.

On 11 June 1921 Violet invited John and Una to dinner, 'a very pleasant quiet evening'.[14] Violet, still obsessed with Ford, gave them several of his books, including *The Good Soldier* which Ladye had read aloud to John in 1915. By the end of January 1923 John would have read Ford's *Ladies Whose Bright Eyes*, dedicated to Violet, five times.

Like John, Violet led both a social and a literary life. At night she appeared at fashionable artistic night-clubs and often in rowdy lesbian bars; by day she hosted elegant literary luncheons and tea parties at South Lodge in Campden Hill. After Una had attended her first South Lodge party on 25 July she decided it was useful for John's career to be seen at such events and subsequently pushed her into going.

The other side to Violet's life mirrored the other side to John's. Steadfast at her desk, Violet was indefatigably professional as a writer, a good role model for John. Her private unhappiness at this time stimulated her into writing her most interesting novels to date. Following a frank autobiographical novel, *Their Lives*, about three sisters, she wrote an equally candid sequel, *Their Hearts* (1921), dealing like Hall's *Octopi/The Unlit Lamp* with mother–daughter relationships.

The book, obsessed with sexuality, expresses a view with which John, still

---

* The two women made no attempt to hide themselves. Ford, distressed and angry, wrote to Ezra Pound on 30 August 1920: 'Violet . . . has planted herself in the neighbourhood and runs about interrupting my workmen and generally making things lively. I fancy she had you followed by a detective when you came down and so got the address. But I may be wrong about that.' See Richard M. Ludwig (ed.), *Letters of Ford Madox Ford*, p. 39.

traumatized by her father's abandonment and her stepfather's violence towards her, was all too familiar: that men, even the best of them, were dangerous animals, and a little of them went a long way. Castigating the effect on daughters of keeping them in ignorance about sexual matters, Violet showed a candour not apparent in fiction written by other women at that time, which would be emulated and surpassed by Radclyffe Hall within a few years. Violet's novel had little of the spiritual beauty of even the earliest of Radclyffe Hall's fiction, but its grim defiance was a quality John respected. Their friend May Sinclair summed it up:

> If you care for nothing but beauty, beauty of subject, beauty of form and pattern, beauty of technique, you will not care for the novels of Violet Hunt. But to the lover of austere truth telling, who would rather see things as they sometimes are than as they are not and cannot be, who prefers a natural ugliness to artificial and sentimental beauty, they will appeal by their sincerity, their unhesitating courage, their incorruptible reality.[15]

Sincerity, courage, and incorruptible realism were phrases later applied also to *The Well of Loneliness* and its author, epithets which depicted characteristics John and Violet shared in abundance.

In the years 1921 to 1923 John's writing, like Violet's, explored the conflict young women faced between their need to conform to parental and social expectations and their wish to use their intelligence to strike out on paths of their own. It was a new era for women, the age of the New Woman, caught poignantly by Radclyffe Hall in *Octopi/The Unlit Lamp*.

What were they like, these New Women? It is 1921. John, writing furiously at her American oak desk, remembers the hotel in Lynton where she and Una have spent two summer holidays. She places the older Joan and the needy Mary Ogden in the same hotel. Mrs Ogden, fatigued from their journey, has retired to rest. Joan watches two young girls with bobbed hair and well-tailored clothes who had come on to the veranda from the garden. One of them was in riding breeches. Their voices drift in through the open window.

> 'Have you seen that funny old thing with the short grey hair?'
> 'Yes, you mean the one at lunch? Wasn't she killing? Why moiré ribbon instead of a proper necktie?'
> 'And why a pearl brooch across her stiff collar?'
> 'I believe she's what they used to call a "New Woman",' said the girl in breeches with a low laugh. 'Honey, she's a forerunner, that's what she is, a kind of pioneer that's got left behind. I believe she's the beginning of things like me.' . . .
> Joan laid down her newspaper and stared after them . . . Yes . . . that was what she had been, a kind of pioneer, and now she had got left behind . . . Active aggressively intelligent women, not at all self-conscious in their tailor-made clothes, not ashamed of their cropped hair; women who did things well . . . women who counted

and who would go on counting; smart, neatly put together women, looking like well-bred young men. They might still be in the minority and yet they sprang up everywhere . . . the boots they wore were thick but well cut, their collars immaculate, their ties carefully chosen. But she, Joan Ogden, was the forerunner who had failed . . . the prophet who had feared his own prophecies. These others had gone forward, some of them released by the war . . . and if the world was not quite ready for them yet, if they had to meet criticism and ridicule and opposition, if they were not all as happy as they might be, still they were at least brave, whereas she had been a coward . . . A funny old thing with grey hair, who wore moiré ribbon instead of a necktie . . . yes, that was what she had come to in twenty years.[16]

Impulsively her heroine Joan dashes out of the hotel, throws the pearl brooch into the bushes, and rushes into a tailor's shop where she purchases the newest pattern stiff collars and a set of contemporary neckties. But halfway back to the hotel her ebullience drains away:

> [She] stared incredulously at her purchases; she had spent considerably over thirty shillings – she must have gone mad! . . . Pioneers that got left behind didn't count; they were lost, utterly lost in the desert . . . one could not catch up with the young when one was forty-three.[17]

John, writing in 1921 about the 43-year-old 'forerunners', was recalling the first wave of New Women, the elderly version of those unashamed cropped-headed young things who now stormed through the twenties. During John's childhood and adolescence those pioneers had already appeared in a handful of Victorian novels, some of which she and Ladye had read together. Olive Schreiner's *The Story of an African Farm* (1883), Sarah Grand's *The Heavenly Twins* (1893), George Egerton's *Keynotes* (1893), George Gissing's *The Odd Woman* (1893), Grant Allen's *The Woman Who Did* (1895) and George Meredith's *Diana of the Crossways* (1895) all had heroines who struggled to cast away the stereotyped image with which women were encumbered.

Those New Women of the 1890s were trail blazers for the second wave of New Women in the 1920s, in their carefully chosen ties and immaculate collars, women who faced new challenges, like Hall's heroine Joan Ogden who defies her father in order to study medicine.

> 'I'm going in for medicine.'
> 'For *what*?'
> 'For medicine. Other girls have done it.'
> Her father rose unsteadily to his feet . . . he pointed a fat shaking finger at his wife.
> 'Mary, what did I tell you . . . My God! . . . Does she ask my permission? No, she states that she intends to be a doctor. A doctor, my daughter!' . . .
> He turned on Joan: 'You must be mad,' he told her. 'It's positively indecent – an

unsexing, indecent profession for any woman, and any woman who takes it up is indecent and unsexed. I say it without hesitation – indecent, positively immodest!'[18]

Indecency, immodesty and immorality were refrains running through the twenties. Yet as if in battle against them some serious young women were becoming doctors, others were taking matters of pregnancy and birth into their own hands. Joan Ogden worried that, after her sister Millie's first slip into 'sin', Millie might become pregnant. While Radclyffe Hall depicted such conventional attitudes in fiction, in the world outside radical reformers campaigned to get contraception accepted. Three years after Margaret Sanger, Djuna Barnes's friend, had coined the term 'birth control', Dr Marie Stopes caused a sensation when her book *Married Love* first appeared in 1918, and in March 1921 she founded and opened England's first birth control clinic in London. She faced bitter opposition from clergymen and doctors who feared it would encourage immorality.

Immorality: that word again. No wonder the twenties has been characterized as the age of gin-and-sin. It was a new era framed by a new look, a look that caused mounting alarm amongst elderly men. Almost everywhere, intoned the newspapers in horror, the corset was in decline. Critics claimed that women's clothes had become – yes, immodest and immoral. Skirts had been steadily rising since the war but by 1921 thousands of women were showing their calves. Fashionable creatures who preferred *less* revelation caused greater controversy by trying to emulate men. Suddenly John did not look so outré. Rather she looked absolutely in touch with the new models with their flat chests, straight clothes and brisk back and sides. Many women, like Radclyffe Hall's Miss Ogilvy, who had done men's jobs in the war wanted styles that reflected their new freedom. Designers were quick to catch on to the economic advantage of making shorter styles that took less material. Guardians of traditional values however were worried that mock-masculinity led to loose behaviour, especially if combined with other disturbing feminine trends such as smoking small cigars, puffing jewelled pipes, or wiggling to the Camel Walk. New York and London night-clubs teemed with unblushing flappers eager to learn Creole jazz steps which churchmen on both sides of the Atlantic condemned as 'a return to the jungle'.

John's friends flourished in the jungle. They were the ones who smoked jewelled pipes, who danced the exuberant Elfreda. They were the hard drinkers, the lesbians. Many of them were in the theatre. It was a modish company John kept. English actress Gwen Farrar and through her American actress Tallulah Bankhead and revue star Teddie Gerard joined John's established crowd (Poppy and Honey, Susan, Toupie, Nellie, Gabrielle and Violet) at the Ham Bone or the Cave of Harmony. Teddie pioneered the first backless evening gown to gasps of admiration and dismay. By 1923 John and Una in John's new six-cylinder Buick Philadelphia frequently drove to Teddie's Orchard Cottage in Gloucestershire where they met Teddie's lover Etheline, her friend Jo Carstairs, the American woman speedboat racer, and Michael Arlen, author of *The Green Hat*. Though Teddie's wildness, her hard drinking and excessive drug taking, were a world away from John's own moderate habits, something about Teddie and her gang drew John towards her. Perhaps it was Teddie's pronounced Americanism and the memory of John's own reckless period in the States with her cousin Jane. Perhaps it was the tantalizing feeling of being very near to someone on the edge.

Later, through Ladye's actor friend Ernest Thesiger, John and Una changed their night-time haunt to the fashionable Eiffel Tower restaurant in Fitzrovia – that area between Soho and Bloomsbury that served the artistic generation of the twenties – where the set included Nancy Cunard, Lady Diana Manners and Iris Tree.

This heady mix of the rich, the famous, the artistic and the boundary-breaking seemed to release channels of vitality in John which, once stimulated, kept going for days on end. Then just as suddenly her energy, even her patience with this frivolity, would give out, and the channels would run dry. What never ran out was her ability to soak up incident and atmosphere and utilize it in her novels.

Costume balls were in vogue. In *The Forge* Radclyffe Hall amusingly describes the first such event that Susan Brent attends. The ball

> was a swirling, heaving, undulating sea of colour, that drifted now this way and now that to the loud thudding rhythm of the band . . . A tall Oriental, naked to the waist, walked slowly across the floor, followed by a harem of six veiled women . . . A youth dressed as a peacock gyrated proudly all alone. His magnificent tail furled and unfurled at will . . . Round and round the room he pranced in imitation of the peacock's display . . . a kind of grotesque mating dance . . . A couple of grey friars shouted disrespectful compliments to . . . a Cleopatra, whose breastplate on the left side had a tendency to become displaced . . . A man completely covered in silver paint and very little else danced gravely with a woman in crinolines . . .[19]

It was a scene John knew well. In July 1922 in Paris, she and Una had accompanied two new friends, the American painter Romaine Brooks (whom they had met in 1921 through Toupie) and her American lover Natalie Barney, to a costume ball of which the one in *The Forge* is a mirror image. John and Una, like Romaine and Natalie and like Vita Sackville-West and Violet Trefusis, loved dressing up, playing parts, holding daggers, acting slave girls, becoming masters. For six months from January to July, John who wrote all day was determined to party all night. In March she even insisted they attend Toupie's fancy dress ball the day after she had been diagnosed by Dr Sachs as suffering from 'extreme exhaustion' for which the prescribed invalid diet was port, oysters, champagne, beef tea, ovaltine, turtle soup and a great deal of *rest*.

But rest she would not. She alternated intense spells of writing with concentrated spells of dancing, smoking and talking, interrupted by debilitating patches of dreadful fatigue. One week in that famous steamy summer of 1921 tells us everything. On Saturday 18 June Violet called for John and Una and took them to the Orange Tree Club where they dined and danced till midnight. On the 22nd Violet found John and Una back at the Club, this time with Susan and Honey. They left the club only to reconvene at Susan's place where Honey taught them the Jog Trot and the Vampire. They reached home at two a.m. After several such nights, when Susan accompanied by Nellie Rowe or Violet would arrive after dinner and stay till midnight, John was too exhausted to work properly, and too anxious to give herself the quiet break she needed. Even when she went for a weekend at the end of April to Gabrielle Enthoven's magnificent Gloucestershire home Eastington Hall in the hope of rest, she insisted they dance every night.

Though too much socializing wore John out, it was not the only pressure. New tensions arose in 1920 from the Society for Psychical Research. Despite Fox-Pitt's resignation and John's vindication, several members felt that the court case had soiled the Society in the eyes of the public and that this warranted keeping John off the Council. When Una discovered that John's name had been excluded from the annual general meeting the following January, she at once telephoned Isobel Newton and threatened their joint resignations. Mrs Sidgwick hastily restored John's name, proposed her co-option, and on 7 February 1921 John was finally appointed a Council member. Although she never lost interest in the Society she was beginning to feel that if her future career was to be as a novelist, she might have to consider resigning.

During 1921 she began to suffer eyestrain and an undiagnosed pain. She saw an optician who pronounced her sight 'perfect' but by her birthday on 12 August Una recorded that John was still 'very unhappy and tired all day and her eyes very painful'.[20] Although reassured by the oculist and somewhat cheered by Una's birthday present – the Sargent drawing of Ladye made in advance of the Sargent portrait – John's eyes continued to trouble her, and this would have frightening repercussions in later years.

Another pressure on John, as well as on Una, came from Cubby, who was suddenly sent home from St Leonard's Convent in January 1921 for 'naughtiness' jointly perpetrated with her friend Cicely Coventry. Although Cubby's conduct report in January was 'fairly good', John and Una lectured her severely before breakfast on 5 January and followed this up with another lecture ten days later. Una recorded in her diary for 15 and 16 January: 'We had Cub in and heard the facts about her naughtiness at St Leonard's.' Then (after Mass the following day), 'John and I had it out with Cub . . . I forgave Cub before dinner.'

John, it seems, was perhaps less forgiving for she accompanied Una and Cub back to the school on the 28th and talked to both Mother Emmanuel and Mother Theodore, after which Una reported: 'Cicely Coventry to be expelled.' John and Una had tea with Cub, who narrowly avoided expulsion, then as Una put it, 'by train and car home and to bed worn out'.

Cub was in fact a bright and talented child who at the end of the summer term brought home two prizes, one a good conduct medal, the other an award for first class exam honours. Sadly Una and John rarely attended her school functions, nor did they often take Cub and her young friends out for treats or holidays. Una and Zyp's separation had distressed Cubby, but as she disliked her visits to her father, John could, had she wished, have slipped into the role, if not of father, at least of loving older friend.

Instead John adopted an often authoritarian, paternalistic attitude to the child. She failed either to be consistent or to intersperse her rigour with any regular show of affection, and Cub suffered undeniably from the lack of it. This inconsistency was a major failure in John's dealings with Cubby. The irony was that Cub thoroughly enjoyed her times with John and Una but did not see enough of them to develop relationships of real depth.

On 31 August, their last day at Trevor Square, when they broke the news to the child that they intended to spend several months abroad, Cub sobbed and sobbed inconsolably. Una wrote in her diary: 'Cub went off after breakfast in floods of tears poor lamb . . . John got up and we went to Whiteleys where she sent Cub a postcard album.'[21] On this occasion as on others John showed a singular lack of imagination in thinking that her standard device of buying people off (this time at a vulgarly cheap price) would work on a highly distressed child of ten who was her lover's daughter.

During their absence in Italy Una arranged for Cub to spend holidays with Minna, and the Troubridges, to have a holiday governess called Miss Lynn, and to spend Christmas with her father at Cheltenham Terrace. Troubridge, although remaining President of the International Danube Commission, officially retired in August 1921. His retirement caused a drop in his annual income from £2,555 to £1,275, which substantially affected the allowances to Una and Cubby. Una now had to rely financially almost entirely on John, who paid all major bills and bought most of Una's and Cubby's clothes. There is no evidence to suggest that John minded this, but with those payments came a strong suggestion that she as much as Una should determine Cubby's welfare. Problems occurred when Cubby's best interests were incompatible with John's. Cubby might have been happier staying with Viola and young Oliver Woods, but this was not possible at present. While John and Una were abroad Viola finally married J.L. Garvin, the editor of the *Observer*, an elderly widower with six children. For a while at least Viola could not give her niece the attention Cubby needed.

John's restlessness, and another illness in August, drove them abroad that year, neither of them it seems feeling any undue responsibility for Andrea. On 1 September they left for Italy, arriving in Levanto on 10 September where Una was eager to introduce John to her friend May Massola. Initially the meeting seemed set to succeed. Una wrote in her journal at the Hotel Stella: 'May came round almost at once – just the same perfect darling creature.' But the darling creature soon showed a less perfect side after witnessing John and Una's open devotion to each other. Perhaps the tales Cencio had brought back with him from London, where he had met John and the rakish-looking Toupie Lowther, had also taken root in May's mind. Cencio himself took off on his yacht. May, no doubt also a trifle jealous, began to resent John's exclusive hold on Una's affection. By October signs of strain were evident. 'May came out with us and was peevish,' reported Una.

The local custom of keeping birds in tiny cages was another feature of Italian life which upset them both. They began to purchase as many birds as they could afford in order to set them free. But when they spotted a canary cruelly imprisoned, John, remembering the canary Visetti had forced her to abandon, insisted on buying it, this time holding it safe. She purchased a large cage and christened the bird Gabriele after Gabriele d'Annunzio. It accompanied them everywhere.

Cencio returned in time to see them off at the station for their journey to Florence, on 6 November. The parting of the two couples was perfunctory and Una never resumed her close relationship with May. For Una, who had been remarkably fortunate in having her relationship with John accepted by her sister, mother and friends, it was a first hint of how others might regard it.

John had visited Florence with Ladye, and Una had wandered romantically through the city with that other Marguerite. Now 'our Florence', as they soon termed it, became a shared place of joy, each mingling her own memories of the city with those of her partner.

In the city itself the political situation was tense. On the first night in their hotel they heard repeated rifle shots. The next morning when they anxiously enquired about the incident, the concierge dismissed it as a routine Fascist-Socialist brawl and of no consequence. Fascists and Communists were roaming the streets and coming to blows day and night with little restraint. Una and John, who in England staunchly voted Conservative, sided firmly with the Fascists, largely for reasons of class and religion. The Communist party, atheist in tone, horrified them as Catholics; the Communist slogans on the city walls they found disturbing. Una was particularly keen to join the crowd rushing to the bridge at Santa Maria Novella to hear the young Benito Mussolini speak. John, more cautiously, insisted that they both stay out of the way in the hotel.

In Florence John wrote furiously at *Octopi/The Unlit Lamp*. Una frequently had to beg her not to overtax herself. It was a heated rehearsal for what would be a lifelong argument about John's work and its effects on her health. It was probably in Florence too, redolent with memories of Ladye and their last visit there together in April 1914, that John recalled another source of inspiration of her novel *The Unlit Lamp*, a source that Una was not party to and so never recorded. In 1910 Ladye had read aloud to John a book called *The Devourers* in which a clever mother is preyed upon by her grasping daughter, who gradually 'swamps' the mother's mind. The plot is the reverse of *The Unlit Lamp* but the theme is identical. John had been so impressed by the tentacled passions of the mother–daughter relationship that later she gave Ladye a copy of the book inscribed: 'To Ladye from John. How we loved this book when we read it together at Sidmouth!'[22]

Back home in England in the spring of 1922, in the quiet of their new small house in Sterling Street, Knightsbridge, John continued work on the first draft of *Octopi*, finishing it on 26 October that year. On 20 December she changed the title to *After Many Days*, an allusion to the biblical text: 'Cast thy bread upon the waters for thou shalt find it after many days.'

Meticulous in her record keeping Una reported that the final draft was completed on Christmas Eve 1922 at five past ten at night. All it needed now was a professional reader and a publisher. Ida Wylie had introduced John to J.D. Beresford, a reader for Collins, who offered to read the completed manuscript and also her short stories. The manuscripts were corrected after Christmas and handed to him on 6 January 1923.

Ida also read the novel and pronounced herself 'most enthusiastic'. She was interested in the fact that Radclyffe Hall like their friend May Sinclair, along with many novelists of the first quarter of this century, was concerned to capture reality by means of naturalism and psychoanalytic portraiture.

In Radclyffe Hall's case, what emerges from her novel *The Unlit Lamp* is a psychoanalytic study of two women passionately attached to each other, in which is implicit the suggestion that homosexuality can be a conditioned phenomenon. This forms an interesting counterpoint to Hall's later views on homosexuality as inborn.

It is ironic that Radclyffe Hall, author of the world's best-known lesbian novel, never set out to be consciously identified as a lesbian writer, though homosexual characters appear in almost all her novels, whilst at the centre of *The Unlit Lamp* is an unconsummated lesbian relationship (although Hall did not at the time appear to consider that she was writing a novel of lesbian love). As Zoë Fairbairns makes clear, when Radclyffe Hall later decided to write *The Well of Loneliness*, it was in response 'to a deliberate decision to describe and vindicate lesbianism to a hostile public'. When John told Una that in her view 'the time was ripe' in 1926 for a lesbian novel she did not feel she had already written such a book.[23] This poses the interesting question of how the homosexuality/lesbianism of an author affects her work even when that work either has nothing specifically to do with lesbianism or, as in the case of *The Unlit Lamp*, when the work was certainly not intended to be 'a lesbian story'.

Yet if we use a wider and more sensitive measure, which could include Adrienne Rich's still-debated idea of a 'lesbian continuum',[24] then the passions between Elizabeth and Joan, though not as explicitly 'sexual' as the passions between Stephen and Mary in *The Well of Loneliness*, are no less strong. *The Unlit Lamp* offers an alternative reading of love between women and is as useful a contribution to the 'cause of sexual understanding' as *The Well of Loneliness*.[25]

It helps to understand Radclyffe Hall's theoretical stance and literary position to see that she used both the idea of lesbianism as environmentally 'encouraged' as well as the idea of the lesbian-as-born, expressing them equally well in two major novels. That several lesbian literary traditions can co-exist with each other in a single *œuvre* is a useful example of how lesbians (Radclyffe Hall and her characters included) are too diverse to share a single sensibility.[26] Such diversity encourages her readers to confront the idea of who exactly is a homosexual and what constitutes sexual identity.

To a contemporary reader *After Many Days/The Unlit Lamp* is probably her most accessible and sensitive novel, its psychological portraits going deeper than those of her later novels. But when shown to J.D. Beresford in 1923, it presented him, as a professional reader, with certain problems. The author was known as a poet rather than a novelist; the book was lengthy and the vision grim nor did it sit easily with the prevailing ethos of the times.

Beresford returned the manuscript on 10 January, indicating diplomatically that in its present form it was not a commercial proposition for Collins, though he said that they had read it with 'intense interest'. He made useful suggestions for shortening and changing it which John implemented.

Ida Wylie came up with an even better suggestion. What John needed was a clever literary agent, and within days Ida had persuaded Audrey Heath, her own agent, to meet John and read *After Many Days*.

Audrey was small, shy and birdlike, and although she did not yet know it, she would soon answer to John and Una's nickname of 'Darling Robin'. But only the pet name and her size were diminutive. Nothing else about her was small, petty or insignificant. A former Cambridge University classicist, she had a razor-sharp business brain, a keen literary sense, and a mind like a vice. She was going to need all that strength if she planned to handle Radclyffe Hall. And handling Hall meant dealing with Una – a formidable task.

Audrey Heath had worked with the Hughes Massey–Curtis Brown literary agency before they separated. When the split occurred between Brown and Massey, Audrey set up her own agency, A.M. Heath, in 1919, taking many of the eminent Massey–Brown authors with her. As the large American agency Brandt and Brandt, with whom Massey–Brown had been linked, did not wish to favour either Massey's clients or Brown's, Audrey shrewdly utilized their services for her own list. A meeting between Audrey and her proposed clients was set up.

Holding the precious manuscript, John and Una, torn between nervousness and confidence, climbed to the top of a winding spiral staircase to reach Audrey's cramped offices above London's Burlington Arcade. Audrey knew she must size up not merely the novel in their hands, but also this already well-known, eccentric and litigious couple. Speedily she scanned a few pages. She liked what she saw on paper. She then had to consider the person. For she would be taking on not only this manuscript but also the handsome woman before her, with her neat head of hair shiny with good hard brushing, her imposing carriage, her fierce eagle eyes, with their intense caged look – a look which could quickly become vulnerable. In accepting Marguerite Radclyffe-Hall, she would need to accept also the complexity of someone who had renamed herself John, with all that signified. Audrey realized quite quickly that she might have to deal with the vulnerability beneath the fierce façade, the sensitivity of the girl Marguerite beneath the dashing exterior of the woman John. The two were not likely to be separated in her writing. She would need careful handling if there were to be more novels after this one.

After Many Days, the book Audrey placed on her desk, was as much the girl Marguerite's as the adult John Radclyffe Hall's. Marguerite had always known she was different. She had lived in her body differently from other girls; she had wanted to do different things in the dark. Gossip in her childhood told her she was different. John never outgrew that feeling, though she acknowledged it, used it, shaped it in her writing. In her adult life John faced up to that gossip. A good agent had to understand that difference – there in *After Many Days* as it would be in Hall's subsequent novels – and reckon with the gossip that might accompany it.

Audrey was a good agent. She saw that John had shortened *After Many Days*. She approved its length, style and content. She knew, as had Beresford, that it would be hard to sell. She also knew that this odd woman, one minute effusive and excitable, the next gruff and shy, was that rare creature, a writer of genuine talent. She agreed to handle her.

She felt, as John had felt, that Heinemann was the obvious publisher. Unfortunately John had waited too long to show her book to her mentor. William Heinemann had died while she was finishing the final draft. Audrey decided even so to send it to Heinemann's. They turned it down. Nine more publishers turned it down. Audrey's faith in the novel and in John did not waver. John's faith in Audrey remained constant. They were now a team. Someone suggested that if John could write a second, shorter and more light-hearted novel and get that accepted first, the challenge of selling *After Many Days* could be met.

In mid-January 1923 John began to write a bright novel for the twenties. She wrote to order and wrote fast, determined to succeed. Her working title was *Chains* but the novel was submitted to Audrey Heath on 19 June 1923 under the title *The Forge*. Audrey loved it, sent it immediately to the London publishers Arrowsmith who in September, after only minor revisions, offered her a contract to include options on her next two novels. John insisted that her credit on the cover should read 'Radclyffe Hall' to eliminate any feminine associations. On 24 January 1924 *The Forge*, dedicated 'To Una, with love', was published. The author's name duly appeared for the first time as plain Radclyffe Hall – no hyphens, no feminine *prénoms*. Her grandfather Charles would have been proud of her.

The book was highly autobiographical. Hilary Brent, the writer, was based on John, Susan Brent, the former art student, was based on Una, their marriage and mishaps reflected the Hall–Troubridge ménage. But that said, the skill with which she satirized their situation, commented ironically on her characters, and utilized personal emotions for a general theory about the struggle between art and life was that of an accomplished – and to everyone's surprise a comic – novelist.

Although her second book was a comedy it deals irreverently with the same theme which had preoccupied her during her work on *The Unlit Lamp*: the connections and ties which bind people to one another. In effect Radclyffe Hall stands her first novel on its head to produce her second. In the first book human relationships are seen as potentially destructive and annihilating. The chains of love can bind too tightly; people can be imprisoned; their spirits can suffocate and die. In the second novel, bonds are seen as interdependent. The imagery of chains is there in both novels, but in the first it symbolizes those forces which restrict self-development, while in the second it symbolizes the power of commitment to enhance people's lives.

The more optimistic book matched the tenor of the times and was an instant success. It was written in a mere five months and had been accepted by the first publisher who saw it. By contrast, *After Many Days*, now finally retitled at Una's suggestion *The Unlit Lamp* (from Browning's poem 'The Statue and the Bust' with its famous phrase 'the unlit lamp and the ungirt loin'), had taken nearly three years to write, and took a further two years to find a publisher. Cassells, the eleventh publisher to whom it was shown, finally accepted it and published it in September 1924, eight months after her second novel.

Radclyffe Hall was now forty-four. She had two novels on the bookstalls and had started her third – *A Saturday Life* – for which a publisher had already offered her an option. The most important phase of her professional life had begun.

13

FORGING AHEAD

Radclyffe Hall had discarded her dilettante devil-may-care attitude to writing. Now the devils drove her to success. She was shrewd enough to realize that making a début with comedy could be advantageous. The torrent of rejections for her first 'serious and sad' book had forced her to become pragmatic.[1] It was a pragmatism she would not lose.

With a new pride in herself as a comic novelist, she looked for a wider circle to appreciate her material. Una of course was on hand, but Una alone proved insufficient. John needed appraisal from outsiders, especially other novelists. Fortunate in the group of literary women friends around her, she was now able to call on Ida and Rachel, who had smiled supportively through passages of *The Forge*, to red-pencil *A Saturday Life*. Vere and Budge did the same.

Budge, an artist herself, understood the visual imagery by which John invoked her characters' inner vision, the myriad sights their souls could see. John, duly appreciative, bought one of Budge's paintings at the private view of Budge's exhibition on 3 November 1923.

John began to take part in public discussions with fellow novelists. Since February 1923 she had seen more of May Sinclair, whose novels *Mrs Neville Tyson: Two Sides of a Question* and *A Cure for Souls* she and Una had admired. She asked May to read her poems and some new stories. Finding a niche with Audrey Heath had increased John's confidence and brought a new facility to her writing. Between the end of *The Forge* and the birth of *A Saturday Life*, she finished 'The Scarecrow'[2] and restarted *The Cunninghams* which she worked on intermittently throughout 1923. This was to become what Una called a 'trolley book': 'the books she herself well knew would never see publication . . . [they] served merely as trolleys to carry her from a fallow period to one of renewed production.'[3] Sometimes John wrote as much as 25,000 words before discarding a trolley book. Sometimes, as in the case of *The Cunninghams*, she would keep the book going on and off over several years.

In an attempt to relax, John might take a holiday with Una, she might meet Toupie, Gabrielle, Poppy or Princess Violette Murat (a lesbian friend of Natalie Barney and the Princesse de Polignac) for a round of gaiety at the Cave of Harmony; she might join the acting crowd, Marie Tempest, Ernest Thesiger, and his friends composer-conductor Eugene Goossens and his wife Boonie at a dance given by actress Gwen Farrar or for dinner at the Eiffel Tower.

More frequently John hung around in the company of Teddie Gerard, her lover Etheline, and Teddie's friend Tallulah Bankhead. The American stage vamp, one of Zelda Fitzgerald's set in Montgomery, Alabama, had early established a reputation as being even more wild and wilful than Zelda. Tallulah's husky Southern drawl was first heard on the London stage in 1923 in a play called *The Dancers*. Two years later she appeared as the daredevil heroine of the hit play adapted from Michael Arlen's *The Green Hat*, which was seen by both John and Una and Scott and Zelda Fitzgerald on the Fitzgeralds' trip to London.

Tallulah had a unique following amongst young working-class women, mainly shopgirls and typists, who stormed the gallery to see her – a cult the press condemned as 'The Hysterical Gallery Girl Syndrome'. What they found threatening, John found intriguing: hundreds of young women publicly idolizing a sensationally sensual woman who smouldered through her stage parts.

Reputedly bisexual, Tallulah preferred boyish women to men.[4] Like Teddie, Tallulah fascinated John because she was American, reckless, drank to distraction, risked drugs and slept with whom she pleased. From the moment *The Forge* was in the bookstores, John nervously lavished her attentions – and her wealth – on Tallulah.

At the opening of Tallulah's new play *This Marriage* in May 1924 John filled her dressing-room at the Comedy theatre with extravagant bouquets. She and Una frequently took Tallulah to dinner at the Eiffel Tower. John danced with her till dawn at Bretts. But even vamping it up with Tallulah could not allay John's tensions.

She could not settle to anything. She watched Una take dancing lessons at Guy Allen's studio. She learnt new steps to the foxtrot. She and Cubby watched Toupie fence; she joined Guy, Eugene Goossens and Romaine Brooks for a dance at Margaret Morris's – queen of the body and soul movement and fashionable teacher of eurhythmics. It shook her up but it did not settle her down. Even showing her dogs in the aristocratic dog-breeding world (Una was now on the Committee of Cruft's) did not bring her the usual pleasure. Lunching with Audrey Heath or going for drives with Ida and Rachel in her new Buick nicknamed Phillida calmed her slightly.[5] On those drives she could explain to Ida, as she had to Audrey, her worries about her last book, her next book, her current inability to write. Ida at least would understand.

She exhausted her friends as she exhausted herself. Suddenly she would become ill, anxious, sleepless. Una might have to read aloud to her at night for as long as eight hours. As reviews came in, John would grow agitated. Perhaps the reviewers did not mean what they said; perhaps the underlying message of a good review was bad. She had no new ideas; she was not getting any younger. Ultimately, to Una's relief, John would seek consolation in a trolley book.

While John was writing, she read only 'shockers' – detective novels, mysteries, thrillers and other lightweight books. Now Una suggested adding to their reading list more novels by John's contemporaries. They chose Hugh Walpole, Aldous Huxley and Arnold Bennett, paid particular attention to Rose Macaulay's *Orphan Island*, Michael Arlen's *The Green Hat* and Osbert Sitwell's *Triple Fugue*. John had met the Sitwells in June 1923 at a lunch given Mrs Sidney Schiff. A few days before the luncheon she and Una had attended a memorable performance of Edith Sitwell's *Façade* after which Una laconically reported: '[Had] a bad pain afternoon of Miss Sitwell shouting down a megaphone and we early to bed.'[6] The Sitwells' literary experiments seemed to John pretentious and unreal.

Several of their 'bedtime authors' were her fellow members of the PEN club, where John took Audrey Heath to dine for the first time on 5 June 1923. Una had long encouraged John to build up literary contacts. Now she was glad to have Audrey's support in a process which was to pay off when many of those established writers later stood witness for her at the trial of *The Well of Loneliness*.

On *The Forge*'s publication day, 25 January 1924, John, in proud receipt of her six complimentary copies, lunched at her publishers Arrowsmith, then hurried Una round as many bookshops as they could, counting the copies, and watching for sales. With every subsequent publication they would perform this same ritual.

They dined with Vere and Budge to celebrate, Vere sadder than usual as her mother was dying. The following day John and Una walked to the Visettis' so that John could give her mother a copy of the book. Whatever praise or affection she was hoping for she did not receive. Her mother took the book and said nothing. Whether she ever read it, John never knew.

Una wrote cards to all their friends encouraging them to buy the novel before stocks subsided. Una was not above writing cards to enemies if she thought it might improve sales. This time she did not have to worry as the book reached a second printing on 1 March. On 20 February Una had begun a press cuttings book for John with the words: 'Eleven reviews so far and all good.' Ida Wylie reviewed it for the *Sunday Times*, enthusing about the scenes of 'genuine gaiety'. She also pointed to Hall's accurate character portrayals and descriptions 'which insist on being read and remembered for their light-handed delicious rightness'.[7]

Violet Hunt wrote to John, 'you are a "clever cat" as we used to say at school – a dog in your case.'[8] Vere Hutchinson, whose own novel *Great Waters* had just been published by Cape to heartening reviews, and generous praise from John and Una, was even more enthusiastic:

> Johnnie dear, I was so overwhelmed by all the generosity you and Una showed over the old book, I never said a word of *The Forge* . . . but you took my breath, – tongue, bowels and heart clean away! Honest to God you did . . . Both Budge and I simply love the book. I want to say right away, I think the wisdom lying beneath the light-ness is quite remarkable. You have a perfectly delightful way of touching on the comic and making one not so much laugh as *think*. I believe the only other being who could manage that was that delightful creator of Elizabeth and her German Garden. Well I loved it Johnnie.[9]

Vere, who with Budge later became models for Jamie the composer and her consumptive lover Barbara in *The Well of Loneliness*, saw something of herself in the portrayal of Hilary Brent: 'I have never for years been so sorry for anyone as I was for Hilary in Italy. Of course I am exactly like Hilary . . . my poignant sorrow for him therefore really very funny!!'[10]

The *Field*'s reviewer thought Radclyffe Hall was a man, which did not dis-please John. She was more irritated by the *People* who knew she was a woman, but concentrated on the fact that the author owned a wardrobe without frocks rather than on the merits of the book.[11]

Several reviewers noticed that despite the book's comic focus it contained several serious motifs which were to recur throughout Hall's fiction – among them the difficulty of achieving self-awareness, which Hilary and Susan Brent both strive for, and the conflict between the rival philosophies they try out in their lives. For the one, the self is the only thing that can be known to exist; for the other, a belief in human effort must involve others as well as self.

Another recurrent motif is the conflict between ambition and the demands of a day-to-day existence. This is epitomized in *The Forge*'s preoccupation with the role of the artist, where the novel's most ruthless character is Venetia Ford the painter, artlessly (or heartlessly) modelled on Radclyffe Hall's artist friend Romaine Brooks, who was six years her senior. Hall began this treatment with Millie Ogden, the musical daughter in *The Unlit Lamp*. From that point onwards, an artist occurs as a significant protagonist in almost every novel. In *A Saturday Life* Sidonia Shore is a multi-talented prodigy, her mentor Elinar Jensen a sculptor. Ugo Doria, the hero's unrecognized father in *Adam's Breed*, is a poet. 'Upon the Mountains' presents a pianist and composer Tino della Valda. *The Well of Loneliness* provides us with Hall's most sensitive exploration of an artist's aspirations in the character of the writer Stephen Gordon. The fact that this novel is as much the story of a struggling artist as it is the tale of a stigmatized lesbian has often been obscured by the crushing fame the novel attracted as a result of the court case.

Hall's depiction of both successful and failed artists reflects her own ambivalence towards her talent, her achievement, and the motives that drove her. She dwells repeatedly on three ideas: first, that artists are always thwarted; secondly, that art is not an end in itself. Thirdly, she sees art as ambivalent, artistic success being impossible without human deficiency (so Venetia Ford, the artist figure, is drawn as brilliant but lacking in humanity) whilst failed creativity is often offset by human and emotional involvement.

Contemporary writers such as James Joyce, Marcel Proust and Virginia Woolf were similarly preoccupied with issues of artistic sensibility versus mundane experience. Unlike them, Hall never suggests that there can be a synthesis between the two.[12] Radclyffe Hall, for whom this conflict was an intense personal struggle, seems to enjoy the polarity of extremes which she offers her artist-protagonists. Although *The Forge* is a much slighter book than her later ones, within it this paradigm is well worked out and bears investigation.

Susan and Hilary Brent, married, rich, relatively compatible, nevertheless feel trapped by each other and by their environment. He wants to write, she to paint, each needs love. They move from urban to rural surroundings looking for an ideal artistic setting. They openly procrastinate. They covertly blame each other. No paintings or novels get done. Seeking the elusive ideal of 'freedom', they separate to pursue their careers. Hilary travels in North America, to discover that Susan's absence preoccupies him more than the writing of books. Susan, in her voyage of self-discovery, abandons woman's traditional role, believing marriage restricts her art – a view reinforced when she meets her idol, the ruthlessly independent painter Venetia Ford. Susan embarks on a sensually ambivalent relationship with Venetia which falters because of her need for social approval. Venetia, as a lesbian and a great artist, believes she can and must do without it. Underlying this development is the suggestion that great art was Venetia's proof of the lesbian's worth to society, which, if we substitute writing for art, was becoming Radclyffe Hall's own personal position.

In the novel, Venetia's finest painting is 'The Weeping Venus' in which she portrays the Goddess of Love as a woman, tired of life, whose body is 'languid with too much pleasure, emaciated by too much suffering'.[13] Subject and title were borrowed straight from Romaine Brooks, among whose most notable paintings was 'The Weeping Venus' (1915).* Romaine intended a strongly feminist theme for her painting: that women's reproductive capacities condemn them to second class citizenship, a fate from which they can only be released by death. Hall uses the title of the painting but sanitizes and individualizes the theme so that the painting merely represents in Susan's awestruck view 'a terrible conception of love'.[14]

---

* Romaine's model for this extraordinary nude portrait was her lover, the dancer Ida Rubinstein. The portrait remained unfinished because Ida grew tired of the arduous sittings and Romaine never found another model with legs as delicate and long as Ida's.

Susan examines Venetia's studio:

> The walls were hung with this woman's pictures . . . Grey, always grey or fawn or
> black, on the walls, in the restful furniture, in the pictures. The place was a study in
> monotones, and yet it was ruthlessly, terribly alive with the dominating personality
> of Venetia Ford herself.[15]

'Grey, always grey.' Is that what John saw in Romaine Brooks' work? Is that
what Romaine was?

At Romaine's first meeting with Gabriele d'Annunzio, at a luncheon where
fellow artist Capiello was displaying his dazzling coloured canvases, the poet
gazed at the multicoloured selection, then whispered to Romaine: 'And to think
how much can be expressed without any colour at all!' That comment summed
up Romaine's artistic philosophy with such accuracy that she invited him into
her studio and into her life. D'Annunzio's verdict on her art, after her first
exhibition in Paris in 1910, was that Romaine Brooks was 'the most profound
and wise orchestrator of greys in modern painting'.[16]

Romaine, whose character Hall drew on for Venetia Ford, was both grey and
never grey. She saw her life, which she considered hardly worth living, in terms
of black and white. Yet her life itself, turbulent and troubled, was techni-
coloured with emotion – indigo with passion, red-hot with torment, on green
alert for the dangers that started, as John's did, in her childhood. It was hardly
surprising that her melancholy was monotone, as were her paintings.

In her autobiography *No Pleasant Memories* Romaine's mother is her chief
tormentor, her brother St Mar vicious, demented and dependent, her home
suffused with supernatural evil and childish terror.* There were several
similarities between Romaine's life and John's.

Romaine's parents divorced and her alcoholic father deserted her. Her
mother Ella Waterman Goddard – besotted by Romaine's brother, the mentally
deranged St Mar, who looms like a gargoyle out of Romaine's nightmare childhood – abused Romaine, then abandoned her. Unpredictability, which had
menaced Marguerite's childhood, overshadowed Romaine's also. Romaine's
mother, like Marie Visetti, was completely unpredictable. Sometimes she made
Romaine her personal whipping-boy; sometimes she would insist that the child
tickle the soles of her feet for hours at a time until the mother-gaoler fell asleep.
The child was either half-starved or fed in the small hours of the night –
psychosis the inevitable consequence of sleep deprivation.

---

* Those who read Romaine Brooks' memoir backed away. Carl van Vechten, the novelist and
photographer, a friend of John's, whose portrait Romaine painted, refused to believe such savage
memories. It was less the barrage of unpleasant (but largely proven) facts he could not credit than
the vindictive tone of the woman bent on bringing at least literary justice to the people who tried
to destroy her. See Meryle Secrest, *Between Me and Life*, p. 11.

Whereas Marie Visetti insisted on frills and frocks for Marguerite, Romaine's mother dressed her in her brother's old clothes. Not content with the implied suggestion that it would have been better had she been born a boy, her mother openly declared her contempt: you are uglier than your brother; you are not loved like your brother; you are not loved. In a home life very like Marguerite's, Romaine was not loved by anyone except the servants.

Like John and Una, Romaine's mother employed mediums. Unlike them, she saw ghosts, had forebodings, talked to the crouching figures of unseen crazed girls and scared Romaine with hellfire, psychic spirits and murderous monsters. When Ella conducted seances she would imagine Romaine was spying on her, and would descend, whip in hand, raging at the child.

Like John who turned to writing as a bulwark against misery, Romaine began to draw out of self-preservation.

In the early awakenings to love there was another curious coincidence. Just as Marguerite had first fallen in love with a voice, so too did Romaine. In place of Agnes Nicholls the voice was that of the young Clara Butt, the famous English singer, who came to lodge in the same house as Romaine in Paris. Sensual feelings reinvigorated the faith of the painter in her talents as it had the writer in hers. Professionally, like John, Romaine tried other artistic forms before settling finally to her serious work. Privately, like John, she inherited a fortune in her twenties.

There were so many similarities between John and Romaine that their some-times stimulating, sometimes uneasy alliance becomes easier to understand. Parents had broken their spirits in childhood. They felt under-valued; to be of worth they felt they had to be someone else. 'Doing art' became their way of being. Although John could not grow artistically without 'chains' whilst Romaine could not develop if encumbered by them, their retreat into art was integral to their autonomy. But neither could become too close to anyone else who had suffered in the same way. Thus there were echoes in John's friendship with Romaine of her edgy relationship with Cubby.

Romaine and John both needed loving mothers and secure havens. It was something neither of them found. The grey generalities of Romaine's early life matched John's, the damaging details left a similar mark. Romaine's solitary life ensured her total dedication to her painting and a freedom of spirit which John envied.

She envied also Romaine's life with D'Annunzio in Venice, with Somerset Maugham, Norman Douglas and Axel Munthe in Capri,* with the dramatic and dazzling group that was at the centre of artistic life in Paris. When Romaine talked of her work in Paris where she painted Ladye's friend Winaretta Singer,

---

* It was in Capri that Romaine met the English homosexual poet John Ellingham Brooks, whom she married.

where she was presented to King Edward VII, and where she met the American writer Natalie Clifford Barney, known for her wealth, social connections and outrageous lifestyle, John recalled the international whirl with Ladye.

If there was a slight tameness to her days with Una, meeting Romaine at a party given by Toupie in June 1921 added an exotic flavour. She and Una spent the weeks before their departure to Italy mainly in her company. Romaine suggested they visit her at her house, the Villa Cercola on Capri. The villa had a wooden dance floor, a Decca portable gramophone and Romaine employed a Chinese manservant to play it.

Capri was noted for its flamboyant women and exotic happenings. Residents included society beauty Mimi Franchetti, she of the knotted cane and the long jade cigarette holder; her lover the throaty pianist Renate Borgatti, and the Marchesa Casati, who greeted Compton Mackenzie on his arrival at her villa completely naked on a bearskin rug, attended by a sapphire parrot, a golden gazelle, and a huge Negro servant in blue breeches and plush tailcoat. John and Una were sufficiently entranced by the stories to consider a visit. But trouble arose when Toupie became infatuated with Romaine, who encouraged her advances then treated her coldly. Versions differ at this point. But whatever the truth, Toupie became increasingly quarrelsome because she had not been invited to Capri. Anxious to avoid conflict, John and Una cancelled their visit.

They were however glad to see Romaine in Paris after their Florence trip on 7 January 1922. In Paris Romaine Brooks was as much an icon of style as Radclyffe Hall in London: tuxedoed, monocled, crop-headed, elegant hands swirling a cigarette in a holder, at first glance seeming to be male.

The two women, the writer and the painter, offered the most pervasive image of lesbianism to be found in either country. Romaine and John's distinctive appearances led to the assumption in both France and England that these transvestite tendencies signified a 'disease' in which women's bodies unhappily housed male desires. This led to a further assumption, often quite incorrect, that their lesbian relationships would be disordered, promiscuous and destructive. John, whose affectionate, loyal, though often tempestuous partnership with Una lasted twenty-eight years, and Romaine, whose passionate lesbian attachment to Natalie Barney survived their separate infidelities to span half a century, gave the lie to this assumption.*

---

* Some contemporary feminist historians are disturbed by the Romaine–John cross-gender cult because of its associations with the pathological medical model. For them, the First Wave of 'innocent' nineteenth-century loving-friends is a more disarming lesbian 'herstory' to look back on. But for Romaine, as for John, and for many of their generation, that model may have seemed more restrictive than liberating. It did after all appear to leave out 'sex'. Esther Newton, who carefully analysed the myth of the 'mannish lesbian', argued that 'Hall and many other feminists like her embraced, sometimes with ambivalence, the image of the mannish lesbian and the discourse of the sexologists about inversion, primarily because they desperately wanted to break out of the asexual model of romantic friendship.' Esther Newton, 'The Mythic Mannish Lesbian', in *Signs*, 1984.

For Romaine, as for John, there was something romantic as well as highly sexual about dancing out their desire for another woman whilst attired in male clothing. This visual replication of heterosexuality within a lesbian relationship was bold, provocative. The sexual ambiguities, the erotic posturing, the veils and cloaks that could be thrown off to expose the hidden lusts, appealed to the writer in Hall, the artist in Romaine.

But when John and Romaine met in Paris in January what each saw was merely the polished performer, the stylish, mannish woman who mirrored their own image. Subliminally they recognized themselves in each other.

The meeting was casual enough. Romaine breezed up to their hotel in her open top car. She drove them to her apartment at Avenue Victor Hugo, where she was particularly gracious and warm towards Una. John rightly began to suspect that Romaine found Una more than a little attractive. How would Una respond? When Romaine said provocatively she did not approve of the wave Una had put in her hair, Una instantly washed it out. The following evening John became curt about the wave. Una obediently curled it back in.

Three days later they dined with Romaine to meet the legendary Natalie Barney. The American millionairess, who spoke perfect French in the classical eighteenth-century manner, appears as a character in half a dozen works of fiction. She was herself a writer who between 1900 and 1963 published over a dozen books – verse, drama, fiction, essays – chiefly in French. Her fame however stems from her being without doubt the most famous lesbian of her time. She was not a lesbian in the mould of John and Una. Her reputation was secured by her emancipated ideas and the defiance with which she lived them. Not all her male biographers perceive her in this light. One of them called her 'a female Don Juan'[17] in 'recognition' of her numerous affairs with women as diverse as the celebrated courtesan Liane de Pougy, the poet Renée Vivien (who some say destroyed herself for love of Natalie) and the Duchess of Clermont Tonnerre, whose relationship overlapped that with Romaine Brooks.

Natalie's enduring value, however, to contemporary women is as a pioneering feminist ahead of her times. She was a woman who resolutely refused to subordinate her life to the demands of men. Thus when Rémy de Gourmont called her 'The Amazon' the title signalled more than her habit of riding in the Bois de Boulogne every morning, carrying a cane, dressed in a bowler hat and a black bow tie. Natalie, who presided over the most powerful literary salon in Europe which she had established in 1909 and which endured creatively for nearly sixty years, invited John and Una to become 'regulars' at the famous Friday salons. If John wished to feast her eyes on people who 'did things', this was the place. Over the years Jean Cocteau, Tagore, Renée Vivien, Colette, Djuna Barnes, Dolly Wilde, Zelda Fitzgerald, Gertrude Stein, Alice B. Toklas, Paul Valéry, André Gide, Ezra Pound, James Joyce, Janet Flanner, Mata Hari,

Isadora Duncan, and other illustrious writers, artists, diplomats and intellectuals spun in and out of her doors; circulated wildly within her elegant seventeenth-century mansion. On any given Friday the guest parade at 20 Rue Jacob looked like Times Square during Theatre Hour.

Natalie was to play a central role in Radclyffe Hall's life as her intellectual, lesbian-feminist mentor, her good friend, and the model for Valérie Seymour in *The Well of Loneliness*.

During that Paris trip John and Una lunched with Natalie's notorious ex-lover, Elizabeth de Gramont, Duchess of Clermont Tonnerre, at her villa in Passy. Called Lily by her friends and the Red Duchess by those who felt strongly about her Communist leanings, she short-sightedly used a lorgnette which contrasted oddly with her tall, imposing figure and aristocratic manner. Her husband had ancestral holdings and reactionary views. 'He thought a woman's place was in the home, doing tapestries and receiving 300 cousins.' The Duchess's attempts at rebellion were not always successful. 'When people first had cars it was considered daring for women to drive . . . The Duchess stole the Duke's car and went out for a joy ride and he spanked her.'[18] John and Una were captivated by Lily's voice and laugh. They were in good company. Proust had said Lily's laugh was like the notes of a bullfinch, her voice the freshest and most ravishing he had heard.

On 27 April 1923 Romaine returned to London hoping 'to find you both glad to see me'.[19] They were and spent most of their time in her company, and Romaine gave Una a valuable sketch of D'Annunzio.[20] Occasionally Romaine became fierce and temperamental. After they had been to a concert at the Aeolian Hall, Una recorded: 'Romaine was damnably rude and we left at once and came home and talked it over.' The following day Una says pompously: 'To luncheon at HP Grill where we kept Romaine in disgrace!'[21]

A few Romaine-free days followed, during which they attended the speech day at Cubby's new school, St George's at Harpenden, where Una, resplendent in a new mother's hat, watched Cubby dance and act in a French play.

When Romaine asked if she could paint Una she was forgiven. Una helped her track down a suitable studio in Cromwell Road, but pointed out that before she would agree John's goodwill was needed. Meanwhile there lay between John and Romaine the not insignificant matter of John's literary portrait of her in *The Forge*. Romaine was the one person who did not find the book amusing. The character of Venetia Ford was not even thinly disguised and Romaine felt the depiction was a travesty, utterly lacking in depth. She told Natalie angrily that John had watched her 'with the eye of a sparrow who sees no further than the window pane. I find myself . . . chirping, pecking, hopping, just as she would do herself.'[22]

In order not to displease John however she wrote her a relatively diplomatic letter. She said that the book had amused her '. . . but I don't like laughing when I read, so do hurry on the sad and disagreeable volume [*The Unlit Lamp*]. Fatigue makes me long to hear of another's woe.'[23] John was sufficiently appeased to allow Una to start her nine sittings in May 1924.

Una decided to wear a monocle, a severe black jacket with a manly cut, a white starched shirt with a stiff wing collar. Amused by Una's get-up Romaine wrote to Natalie: 'Una is funny to paint. Her get-up is remarkable. She will live perhaps and cause future generations to smile.'[24]

Future generations have smiled because Romaine wickedly posed Una standing up, so that her legs vanish under pinstripe skirt, hidden by a table on which are plopped Thor and Wotan, Una's two fat dachshunds. The dogs look up adoringly while one of Una's monstrously lengthened arms stretches down until a jumbo hand clutches one of the dogs by its collar. Una's body becomes elongated, angular, and as if seen through a distorting mirror.

Romaine and Una had already exchanged sharp words over the painter's unflattering verdict (to others if not to John) on *The Forge*. Romaine, called by Robert de Montesquiou 'the thief of souls',[25] cleverly caught Una's exasperated expression under her cropped helmet of hair. Despite her affection for Una the woman, Romaine rendered Lady Troubridge at her most arrogant and least appealing. Though assuring Romaine she was pleased, to several friends Una remarked wistfully: 'Am I really like that?' She let slip something of her disappointment to Toupie who repeated it to Romaine. The sittings caused a strain in their friendship.

Romaine probably expected John to purchase the painting. John, shown the portrait on 9 June, had no intention of buying it. Even after it had been shown to great acclaim and amusement on both sides of the Atlantic the following year,[26] John would not change her mind.

During John and Una's next visit to Paris on 25 June, Romaine provoked an extraordinary scene. Natalie, affectionate and charming, asked Una to read passages of *The Forge* aloud. Halfway through the reading Romaine rushed in 'and made a hideous scene abusing *The Forge*, John and Natalie like a fishwife'.[27]

The incident revealed to John what she had not wanted to recognize: that beneath Romaine's insouciant exterior she was as insecure and as hypersensitive to criticism as John herself. It taught John a lesson. From then on she made sure that the sources for her fictional characters were better disguised and issued a disclaimer that none of her work was autobiographical.

When *The Unlit Lamp* came out, John sent Natalie a copy, but assured her there were 'no portraits drawn from life'. Natalie, much amused, sent back a mischievous note:

> I have no quarrel with portraits drawn from life! Will get Romaine to read some parts aloud to me – though I think she may feel that you have treated an even more serious subject lightly and that she was more worthy of the serious book.[28]

John and Una left Paris for Bagnoles where throughout July they took daily baths and corrected proofs sent out by Cassells. On their return Vere helped London to lionize the new writer. In the summer of 1924 she and Budge gave a party where the guests included Violet, Michael Arlen, Margaret Irwin (whose books John read repeatedly) and Leonard Rees, Editor of the *Sunday Times*, who, with his wife Molly, was instantly taken with John. Rees was well aware that Newman Flower, Cassells' newly appointed director, had been sufficiently impressed by *The Unlit Lamp* to buy it for his firm. Since his appointment Flower had swiftly built up the imprint with several highly successful writers, including H.G. Wells, Compton Mackenzie, Louis Bromfield, Arnold Bennett, Sheila Kaye-Smith and Ernest Raymond: John was joining an impressive company in June 1924.

As Newman Flower's praise for *The Unlit Lamp* circulated over drinks, Leonard Rees watched John's sharp or witty responses to other people's flattery delivered in her shy, almost inaudible voice. As *The Forge* had reached the best-seller list of *John O'London's Weekly* in mid-March, the book was already a talking point, its author suddenly the centre of attention. John, who hated small talk, did not quite know what to make of this, and many of the guests did not quite know what to make of her.

Leonard Rees also watched Una as she attempted smoothly to shield John from the vulgar curiosity of the acid-edged crowd. Una, who was never in doubt about other people's response to her charm, worked hard in social situations at encouraging people to admire in John qualities that lay beneath her unconventional appearance and often abrupt manner.

Even without Una's skilful exercise in public relations, Leonard Rees decided that he liked what he saw of John. He became tireless in helping her to make useful literary contacts, and she adopted his suggestion that she should see and be seen at theatrical first nights, then cultural high spots of the London social calendar. Sometimes she and Una attended as many as four matinees and evening performances in a week. John in her man's stock, high stiffened collar and romantic sweeping cloak made heads turn. She never carried a handbag but had special pockets sewn into her skirt. In her box she often cut a figure more dramatic than the plays she attended.

In Molly and Leonard's home she relaxed sufficiently to feel at ease with Augustus John, E.V. Lucas, Edmund Gosse and Rebecca West, with whom, once she got over her awkwardness, she became good friends. By the time Molly and Leonard Rees's daughter died suddenly in May 1925, John had become sufficiently close to spend the morning with Molly, helping her to deal with her shock and grief.

Some closet homosexuals in Leonard's circle felt threatened by John's openness, by what they perceived as her brash claim to be what they took great pains to hide. Alec Waugh, elder brother to the as yet unpublished Evelyn Waugh, held a markedly different opinion of John. Alec's father had directed Chapman & Hall during the period when his firm published Marguerite Radclyffe-Hall's poetry, so he viewed her with an affectionate, slightly paternalistic eye. Waugh saw her as discreet, even strictly conventional:

> We met quite often and entertained each other. She was not a woman who let down her hair! She and Una struck me as an austere Edwardian couple who expected conventional behaviour from their guests and hosts. She said once of Francis Lakin: 'If you want to have a properly run house, you can't have people like him around. The servants won't stand for it.' She never in my presence referred to her own amatory relations any more than a Victorian couple would. It was assumed that intimacies took place in darkened rooms when the world was silent.[29]

Newman Flower asked John to produce more short stories. In an age of excess, an age of satire, an age of exotic intimacy, Radclyffe Hall scoured its grimy underside, prodded its dark belly. She chose a new framework for her stories, focusing on the doomed side of people's natures and their desperate search for spiritual fulfilment.[30]

Beginning that August with 'The Lover of Things',[31] which took as its theme the self-destruction brought about by a man's fanatical appreciation of art, she finished it in two days. It was published in 1934 by Heinemann (not Cassells) in her collection of short stories *Miss Ogilvy Finds Herself*, with several more that dealt with the limiting effects on people of compulsions and obsessions.

Her anti-hero, Henry Dobbs, is obsessed with beautiful bric-à-brac; things arouse his lust and break his heart. He has nothing left over to offer his wife. Driven to stealing an exquisite statuette his action, according to Hall, is one of frustrated artistic and spiritual ambition. His spirit seeks liberation, transformation. Dobbs, the exile, the trapped individual, is on the same quest for freedom as Hall's other loners: Alan Winter in *The World*, Miss Ogilvy, Tino and Matteo in 'Upon the Mountains', Charles Duffell in 'The Rest Cure'. They all fail because of their doomed psychological compulsions.

While writing these dark stories for Newman Flower, John still occasionally consulted Gladys Leonard, who was also employed as a medium by Flower. But in March of that year after a bad bout of influenza John decided to cut down on commitments and finally resigned from the Council of the Society for Psychical Research after eight turbulent years.

Free to commit herself to writing, she awaited developments with *The Unlit Lamp*. With the novel now reduced to 108,000 words, Audrey Heath was able to negotiate an excellent contract that gave her for the first time an advance of £50. Her royalties were to be 15 per cent on the first 3,000 copies and 20 per cent thereafter. The novel would be a six shilling hardback.

Cassells took out an option on her next two novels, not including *A Saturday*

Life. Arrowsmith, who had turned down *The Unlit Lamp* in January 1924, had offered by way of compensation to waive their option on Hall's third novel, but John who always honoured her word, whether legal or informal, insisted that Arrowsmith retain their option on *A Saturday Life*. By May 1924, a month before the contract with Cassells was signed, John had already finished her first draft of *A Saturday Life*.

The Unlit Lamp was published at the end of September 1924 and dedicated 'To Mabel Veronica Batten, in deep affection, gratitude and respect'.

Una felt John should be photographed at this critical stage in her career so the writer posed for the elegant Lafayette studio. This time she liked being bathed in flashlight. A hint of a smile plays about her lips.[32]

On publication day a carnival feeling was in the air. John and Una swooped on St Pancras Station where a giant display of *The Unlit Lamp* was advertised on the clock. John gazed up, swung round wildly. Maybe it would disappear. No, there it was: her novel, set high above the time, in a crowded station where disorderly commuters rushed about, late for trains. Let them be late. The clock told the time by her *Unlit Lamp*.

They lunched with Minna at the Berkeley. John could never afterwards recall what she ate, or even if she ate. They raced to the Times Bookshop and Harrods to discover that both had sold out. 'Home and found five reviews all magnificent.' 1 October brought three more good reviews. But Alec Waugh's review in the *Sunday Times* was a let-down. Alec had congratulated her on her interesting subject matter, but he admitted that he was disturbed by the feminine focus of the novel. How strange it was to find a book in which men were merely incidental![33] John always found weak or ambivalent reviews from friends hard to take. This time was no exception. However, she barely had time to brood before *The Lady* and the *Daily Telegraph* praised it, to be followed by Ida with a magnificent critique in *Queen*.[34]

With rosy reviews and the sound of money in the air John was riding high. The British literary establishment wanted to meet her. At the Reeses she dined first with St John Adcock and publisher John Murray; there followed meals with Rebecca West, E.V. Lucas, Netta Syrett.[35] As glasses clinked over jubilant banter, as they teased her and roused her to a new vital self, she forgot her old sadnesses, her intermittent depressions. At the PEN club dinner in December, when members crowded to congratulate her, she flourished, her Greek profile pink with pleasure. She was louder at home, with awkward bursts of nervous wildness, when first Peggy then the café crowd, Rachel, Ida and Gabrielle, piled up the dinner invitations. Violet made a festive meal for John, Una and May Sinclair. Minna, gracious for a change, told them at lunch on 14 October that Viola and Garvin were 'wildly enthusiastic' about *The Unlit Lamp*.

Only Vere and Budge were not behaving as usual. On 1 November Una records: 'Dined Vere and Budge and felt an atmosphere.' Though John and

Una tried tactfully to discover the reason, the other couple were strangely reticent. On 4 November, the night before Cubby's fourteenth birthday, Una and
John dined at the PEN club where to their consternation they found 'Vere very
odd.' Two days later they returned from seeing Gabrielle, who now directed
the Victoria and Albert Museum's important Theatre Collection, 'to find
Budgie's bomb'.

The bombshell contained tragic news. To their horror Budge's note revealed
that Vere was desperately ill with an unspecified virus which was likely to leave
her paralysed and subject to periodic bouts of insanity. Her new book *Great
Waters* had just been published and excellently received but there was little
hope of many more publications. How long would she live? Would she be able
to write at all? How could Budge maintain them both on her meagre illustrator's salary? The following day, 7 November, Una rang Audrey to ask if anything could be done about Vere's prospects, but Audrey was as gloomy as
everyone else. In 1925 Vere managed to write a new book, *The Naked Man*, but
by the time it was published she was almost permanently paralysed. John, Una,
Teddie Gerard and Violet remained constant, but as the situation worsened
Vere and Budge began to isolate themselves.

Their isolation, Vere's dwindling ambitions, her unfulfilled hopes in the face
of irrational forces beyond her control, troubled John who had been dwelling
for some months on the theme of lost and lonely people seeking spiritual
release. Vere's situation wove itself in and out of her thinking. In October she
began writing *The World*.*

The book was started as a series of vignettes but, at Audrey's suggestion,
developed as a novel. It is set in Mrs Raymond's seedy London boarding house,
a setting given the same detailed malicious quality that permeates Katherine
Mansfield's *In a German Pension*, which John had read soon after it appeared
in 1911.

Hall's protagonists, like Mansfield's, are helpless, pathetic, looking for something brighter and more beautiful than can be found over greasy suppers of
beef, red currants and spinach accompanied by black bread.[36] In Mrs
Raymond's bedrooms, 'the one armchair sagged badly . . . its back bore traces
of brilliantine where Alan's own head and others had rested.' Alan Winter,
Hall's asthmatic bank clerk, is as worn out and respectable as his surroundings.

Hall in this novel prefers the role of observer. Like Christopher Isherwood,
she is a camera with its shutter open, passive, recording, watching, waiting to
develop and print her characters: Mr Pitt, physical trainer, 'in modest duck
shorts and sweaty singlet'; Colonel Blakeney of 'doubtful antecedents';

---

* *The World* was started *c*. 28 October 1924. The first five important chapters including the
chapter that became 'Fräulein Schwartz' were written between October 1924 and March 1925.
It was taken up again in 1927 and 1928 after *Adam's Breed*. The central themes that feature in
all the *Miss Ogilvy* stories are in this unfinished novel.

Fräulein Schwartz who so 'frequently sighed [that] her blouse creaked in sympathy'; and asthmatic Alan Winter, who is another Henry Dobbs rendering to possessions (in Alan's case, to hide-bound ledgers) the love he cannot give to people.

From 26 January 1925, while drafting *The World*, she wrote 'Upon the Mountains', a short story with a similar theme, completed in a mere nine days, which Audrey 'adored'. In this story of two brothers and the woman one of them loves we again find the notions of limitation, aberration, isolation. Hints of homosexual suffocation, and John's guilt over Ladye's death, infuse this triangular story of two brothers whose passion for each other refuses to allow a woman's love to intervene. When the married brother dies, the widow and the surviving brother compete for a sign from him from the beyond. Raw as is the contest, the story struggles to an almost optimistic conclusion in which the surviving brother is redeemed by suffering and granted the blessing he looks for. In writing it, John was struggling with enormous pain in order to survive. It is a pain she stores up, and a survival technique she is going to need.

On Thursday 4 December 1924 John and Una had moved into 37 Holland Street, where they would live for the next four years, the high point of John's literary career. Curiously Una, who had always preferred sleeping alone, was 'enchanted' when, following the move, they gave up their separate communicating bedrooms to share 'our bedroom'. Several entries along the lines 'we early to bed', as well as Una's reiteration of the fact that vaccines from Dr Sachs had stopped, implies that her disease was cured and that their lovemaking resumed.* Although Una's own ambitions were now largely sublimated to John's she seemed wholly secure, feeling that her place in John's life was central and indispensable. For the moment it was so.

They spent a relaxed tenth Christmas together with Cubby and the Temples at Datchet after paying their respects to Ladye at Highgate Cemetery. In London for New Year's Eve they despatched Andrea to her father and saw the New Year in with Toupie, her girlfriend Fabienne and Gabrielle.

Una, who had started working on translations, book reviews and dustjackets, designed the jacket for John's third novel *A Saturday Life*, published on Wednesday 1 April 1925. The book was 'Dedicated to Myself' by John who saw aspects of her own personality in the character of gruff-voiced Frances Reide, the lesbian companion of Lady Shore. Hall gave the supernaturally talented Sidonia Shore several of Una's childhood traits.

The book had already sold nearly 700 advance copies. Arrowsmith decided to capitalize on John's growing reputation by bringing out a cheap second edition of *The Forge* the following month. Sales in the bookshops John and Una

---

* There is conflicting evidence as to whether or not Una's malady was a sexually transmitted disease. This biographer has followed the line suggested by Una's own diaries and her conversations with friends such as Ethel Smyth and Violet Hunt.

visited on publication day were brisk. Over dinner with Ida and Rachel at the Hyde Park Grill John and Una drank the book's health. A 'fine review' four days later in the *Sunday Times* by Leonard Rees was matched by good reviews in early June in the *Times Literary Supplement*, *Punch* and the *Bystander*. Universally good reviews followed elsewhere.[37]

A.E. Coppard confirmed most critics' view that characterization and description were Hall's strengths. The theme of reincarnation was said to be 'interesting' but plot was still her weakness.[38] The novel's theme looked back to *The Unlit Lamp* in its focus on a trio of women (Sidonia, Frances, Lady Shore) with its echoes of the guilt-torn triangle of John, Una and Ladye; it reflected *The Forge* in its scrutiny of the conflict in a woman's life between her roles as unconventional artist and conventional wife and mother. Like its predecessors the new novel asked the underlying question: can the central character (Joan/Susan/Sidonia) fully realize her potential within a stereotypical context, or does she have to sacrifice an essential part of herself for the sake of a socially defined 'femininity'?

The book looks forward to Hall's later novels in its preoccupation with spirituality. Like *Adam's Breed* and *The Master of the House* it has a strong religious base. The child-heroine Sidonia's existence is governed by a legend called the 'Saturday Life Myth' from an Eastern theory of reincarnation, which suggests that certain people are fated to live seven times on earth but in the last incarnation all previous existences are repeated at high speed. Sidonia's mentors – Frances, Elinar Jensen and Liza Ferrari – teach her to strike a balance between creative inspiration and everyday life, a balance that Hall endlessly tried to achieve in her own life.

Sidonia's quest for identity leads her inevitably to self-denial, a theme Hall will use and re-use. Unexpectedly Sidonia gives up first her brief possibility of love with Frances, then her long struggle for independence as an artist, finally capitulating to marriage and motherhood with David, one of Hall's most stunningly dull characters – interchangeable, as Hall herself tells us, with any Eton-Oxford chap who lacks intellect, originality or imagination. Fortunately she allows Sidonia to see his defects also. Why then should Radclyffe Hall offer her extraordinary heroine such a dreary fate?

Several theories have been advanced. One is that Hall merely fell back on a conventional comic-fiction formula of her time, that heroines of Sidonia's class and background would ultimately sink into wifehood.[39] A second theory suggests that in moving progressively down the path of self-denial, Sidonia by marrying David consecrates herself to a life of service.[40] A third believes that beneath the seemingly conventional ending Hall implied that Sidonia's vitality would continue because she had learnt from her mentors to balance self-expression and the values of home-and-hearth.[41]

There is something to be said for all three assertions. Certainly at this point

Hall was not prepared to make radical statements about a life opposed to the heterosexual norm. The notion of service is also integral to her *œuvre* – though marrying David seems rather to be overdoing it. And Hall herself struggled to find a way of living that offered stability without sacrificing creativity.

However, I believe Hall was attempting something else. In *A Saturday Life* she had no intention of writing a traditional male–female novel with a stereo-typed finale. She wants her heroine to find what is true in herself, to express that truth, even if that truth changes at different stages in her life. Like all Hall's protagonists Sidonia must act according to her deepest nature. Sidonia will never lose her imagination, her creative soul; but she is now ready emo-tionally to produce a new life, in the shape of a child, without sacrificing her own. On the last page of the book Sidonia holds her new 'gold-medal baby' and tells Frances, her older unmarried friend with whom she had briefly fallen in love: 'I'm in my last act now Frances.' The older woman's eyes fill with tears 'because of her [Sidonia's] beauty, lying there – a woman with a child at her breast'.[42]

For Radclyffe Hall as for Frances that image was erotic and mysterious, but also unattainable. Within John's inherited framework of beliefs maternity was the quintessential expression of womanhood. Forgoing that was the price paid by congenital inverts.

As Alison Hennegan wisely points out, we need not lament Sidonia's mar-riage for as we leave Hall's heroine her infant son has already replaced her husband in her affections. The novel ends with marriage and a baby. But, as Una knew, in life that is not necessarily the end of the tale. Once Sidonia dis-covers this, as Hall firmly suggests she might, anything can happen.[43]

Ida Wylie's review in *Queen*[44] fastened intelligently on the novel's central notions. Of all the fine reviews hers was the most perceptive. She defined John as an author 'who sets out with no apparent intention at all of being funny but who surprises the chuckles out of you with the nonchalant air of a conjurer pro-ducing rabbits from the pockets of an astonished schoolboy'. Ida felt that John's early poetic career gave her prose exquisite economy: 'Laughter lurks in her description of a sofa. She can conjure up Italian memories in a line.' She predicted that Radclyffe Hall would soon write a major novel. Her prediction was to come true with John's next book.

Within a fortnight of publication of *A Saturday Life* John began work on a book called *Food*. It was to become *Adam's Breed*, the novel which brought her prestige, critical acclaim and two major literary awards in one year.

14

CRITICAL ACCLAIM

John's inspiration for *Adam's Breed* occurred, like that for *The Unlit Lamp*, while she was nonchalantly observing strangers in a public dining-room. The genesis for her first novel took place in a hotel, for her fourth in a restaurant – or so the legend runs.

According to Una inspiration struck suddenly. A bolt of creative lightning flashed across their table in the Pall Mall restaurant. Una, fifty years after the event, tells a good story.

It is 14 April 1925:

> [Over a] pleasant tête-à-tête luncheon John became abstracted and inattentive. Her eye was following our obsequious waiter and presently she told me with quiet decision, 'I am going to write the life of a waiter who becomes so utterly sick of handling food that he practically lets himself die of starvation.'[1]

The next day, according to Una's over-tidy recollections, John began to write *Food*.

Subsequent biographers have accepted this story of the novel's sudden genesis, a tale which subtly suggests that Hall's plot for *Food* was the start of her process of reflection on the theme of service and sustenance. However, such a process had been going on for some years and had been reflected in her poems and short stories.

More significantly, among the Rossi-Lemeni papers in Rome, undiscovered until now, are some yellowing nicotine-stained notes, execrably typed, scored through and misspelt, which date *Adam's Breed*'s inception to the time Hall was writing *The World* some six months before the Pall Mall occasion.

> I wrote *Adam's Breed* because I could not help writing it. It started as an obsession and grew. I have been looking at the people who serve me silently in various capa-

cities . . . I have speculated as to what they really felt and thought about me and my doings . . . what their real lives were like. I felt this especially in the case of waiters and all those connected with the preparation and serving of food . . . to me a hateful service. From these obsessive speculations grew the idea of a waiter who might get so utterly sickened by the constant overwhelming nearness of food that . . . he would eventually starve to death in the midst of plenty. Not realizing at the time that Gian-Luca was lying in wait for me . . . I thought at first I would use the idea for a short story . . . then I realized no short story would relieve me of my obsessive idea . . .

I was actually trying to write another book (*The World*) . . . I was quite a quarter of the way through.[2]*

In April 1925 at a small dinner for May Sinclair and Rebecca West, John talked for hours about her obsession.[3] Then she began to transcribe it: 'It simply would not let me alone. I worked every day and all day and often most of the night, but though I was very tired in body I never seemed tired in mind or ready to leave off the writing.'[4] She wrote almost without a pause until the beginning of June. Not even Ladye's ghost was allowed to interrupt her work: on 25 May she suggested that Una go alone to the cemetery to put flowers on Ladye's grave.†

Only John's literary friends were encouraged to call, among them Ida, Rachel and a newer friend, novelist Eileen Bliss. Eileen's conversation was peppered with remarks about Etheline, Teddie Gerard's lover. John had already noticed the pair together while Teddie was away in New York.§ If the gossip had reached Teddie's ears, she remained remarkably cool. Writing to John and Una, Teddie exhibited a certain sang-froid about lesbian love-life, her own included: 'I am wondering who is with who amongst our bright young friends – I suppose the cards have been shuffled and re-shuffled by now.'

Teddie enquired affectionately after Vere and Budge. John found it hard to reply for daily the news worsened. Nowadays Budge lunched with them on her own as Vere was too ill to leave the house. John found the lunches unnerving. Secretly she wondered how Una would cope if she was struck by a debilitating illness. Una wondered the same. Neither of them dared say it aloud. At least their wealth, social status and relative openness as a couple meant that if one of them fell ill no authoritarian figure was likely to part them – though this was not always the case for lesbian couples.[5] In *The Well of Loneliness*, Jamie the musican and her dying partner Barbara, modelled on Budge and Vere, voice

* *The World* was not quite buried. Though it did not survive as a published novel, a whole chapter became the story 'Fräulein Schwartz' and passages from several more chapters can be discerned in other stories.

† In her diary that night Una misspelt her deceased cousin's name as 'Ladie', an indication perhaps that Mabel Batten was now taking a back seat in their lives.

§ It is possible that Teddie Gerard's lover Etheline replaced Constance Spencer in Eileen Bliss's affections. Eileen Bliss had taken Constance Spencer to see John and Una in early June 1925.

these fears. A nurse sees Jamie 'squatting on the floor by [Barbara's] bed, like a dumb, faithful dog who endured without speaking'; she turns to Stephen Gordon: 'Is she a relation?' Stephen hesitates then shakes her head. The nurse continues stoutly: 'That's a pity, in a serious case like this I'd like to be in touch with some relation, someone who has a right to decide things.'[6]

Lesbians less lucky than John and Una did not have this right. Spending bitter hours with Vere and Budge, John perceived that she could use a novel to bring the plight of such women out into the open. She thought back to Ladye's death. In *The Well of Loneliness* she shows Jamie and Barbara quarrelling before Barbara falls into a coma, just as John and Ladye had done. Barbara dies without being able to speak or forgive, just as Ladye had done.

By January the following year (1927), Budge was telephoning them in despair, lamenting that 'Vere had gone out of her mind.'[7] In March they asked Budge to join them in Boscombe where they walked the cliffs, knowing as they talked that no solution was possible.[8] In July they went to tea with Vere, by then according to Una 'a tragic and well-nigh hopeless sight'.[9] She could no longer walk; suffered frequent epileptic fits; they had begun counting the days.

Every day Vere struggled from bed to wheelchair to write. Later, propped up, she wrote in bed. She succeeded in getting two more novels published by Hutchinson's in 1928, but John found her friend's anguish almost more than she could bear. Was she only thinking of her own possible future? Or was it the painful privilege of her inner 'seeing-eye' which made her unable not to see suffering everywhere, and to intensify it where it existed? Pain, need and fear, whether in animals or people, always called forth her strongest responses. This could make her a taxing companion.

Seeing birds trapped in tiny cages, John had paid to release them. Seeing beaten dogs, she had taken them home and cosseted them until their whimpers ceased. What could she do now for Vere? Nothing, except stand by her side, as her friend's whimpers increased and her writing diminished.

Even earlier Vere's plight, added to her own tough writing schedule, had wrung John out. Una had persuaded her to slip away to the Cottage Hotel at Lynton. She idled away a few days, tried out her new Brownie camera, began to pull round, when Newman Flower wrote to say he declined to contemplate *Food* as the title; he was sure the novel would be mistaken for a cookery book.[10]

Already on edge, John panicked. Una left her frenziedly muttering unsuitable titles, swooped on the local W.H. Smith's bookstore, ransacked the shelves, then hit upon Kipling's poem 'Tomlinson'. In this a dead man's soul is denied entrance both by St Peter at the gates of Heaven and the Devil at the gates of Hell: the man's living has been secondhand; he has no soul to call his own. Finally the Devil, who speaks Scots, shows more pity than St Peter, because being 'all o'er-sib [intimately related] to Adam's Breed', he deems it better not to mock another's pain.

Writing was now indisputably central to Radclyffe Hall's life. Fortunate beyond a writer's reasonable dreams, John knew she was central to Una's life. Single-minded, she focused on her words to the exclusion of much else, able to do so in the knowledge that Una would furnish her with the best surroundings to write in. How quiet could the house be kept? How could the servants – a chauffeur, a cook and two maids – be made to drive carefully, cook properly, clean thoroughly? Above all could Una's diplomacy persuade them not to have rows with the hot-tempered author or, worse still, give in their notice? The cook and one maid survived the rigours of the regime through 1925 but the parlourmaid was swiftly replaced and the chauffeur sacked.

To Cubby the place was like a house of cards. Occupants were reshuffled so often and the location changed so frequently that sometimes at the end of a term with the King, Queen and assorted Jacks ever moving on, she hardly knew which house she was going back to. Like a well-brought up Cheshire Cat she kept on smiling as she resettled herself and her schoolbooks somewhere new, but often inside she must have felt as uncertain and wide-eyed as Alice.

Between 'proper' houses there were often temporary basecamps, such as Swanmead at Datchet, between Cheltenham Terrace and Chip Chase when she was nine; Trevor Square between Chip Chase and Sterling Street when she was eleven, and a suite at Kensington Palace Mansions between Sterling Street and Holland Street when she was fourteen.[11] Hardly had she pitched her tent than the campers moved on. Now on the margins of another new home whose centre was her mother's lover, who was to be central to Cubby's life? Who was to make her feel at home in Holland Street?

Her new home was attractive: large rooms with casement windows opening out from wide ledges filled with bulbs, freshly tended, winter and summer. Solid oak furniture stood around new gasfires set in old English red-brick hearths. The bright golden yellow drawing-room on the first floor seemed perpetually bathed in sunshine. As Cubby moved shyly around it, it must have seemed an attractive house for a young person to bring home their friends. But her mother never encouraged her to do so – John is writing, darling; visitors would be such an intrusion!

At home during the holidays most of Cubby's moments were spent cooped up in the smallest room which served as a guest room during term time. Those guests, she supposed, did not fuss or fret John in the way that she and her friends did. Once John genuinely embarrassed her by suggesting she might want to call her 'Uncle'.[12] Whatever Cubby privately thought, she knew how her friends would react. She did not take up John's offer.

In February and March of 1925 John had made an effort. She had taken several days off work to paint Cubby's room, but the only outsider who saw it was Cubby's maths teacher who came to give her extra coaching the day after her arrival home from St George's Convent. She had arrived on 30 March in time for dinner, but then discovered her mother and John were going out to a first night without her.

Easter for Cubby held no holiday spirit though she went to church a lot. On Sunday 5 April her mother and John pored over a review of *A Saturday Life*,[13] while she went to the Zoo with Dickie, the maid. Only at Datchet, with the Temples, their children and animals, where no one wrote books, was she truly herself.

John too felt rooted in Bill and Ida's company, rather as she did in Peggy Austin's. At Datchet she found too that she was more relaxed with Cubby. On their return she and Una made an effort to spend two days with their charge before sending her on 20 April to her father. They took her to see John Barrymore playing Hamlet at the Haymarket, then the following day they drove her to Audrey Heath's. But even when John and her mother did include her, it was often to attend events to which Cubby was indifferent, or to meet people with whom she had little in common.

In Una's diaries there is a noticeable absence of invitations to Cubby from schoolfriends. Whether she received them and was not allowed to go, or whether no one invited her, is not recorded. One can only wonder whether the increasing fame or notoriety of her mother's lover had anything to do with it.

In July Cubby attended her first Guide camp, possibly catching some infection there for by August Una was again worried about Cubby's health. Una as usual became solicitous. When Cubby asked to go to Datchet Una willingly drove her. On a Sunday after regaining her health Cubby was taken once more to the Zoo: 'Andrea [went] with the maids but [joined] John and me for tea at the aquarium.'[14]

Changes for the better in Cubby's routine were always slight, and seldom lasting. But despite her unsettled and unconventional upbringing she was growing into an affectionate, usually sunny-spirited young woman. Thrown so often onto her own resources, she learnt independence and tough-mindedness from an early age, and if pushed too far by her mother, had a will (not unlike Una's own) which would strongly assert itself.

If John felt able to treat Cubby as the whim took her, she was less able to do this with her own mother or Una's. During the next three years Marie Visetti's health started to falter. This, together with her hysterics and several false alarms, left John shaky with subdued resentment and concern.

Nevertheless John managed to complete four chapters of *Adam's Breed* in the spring and summer of 1925 and signed a contract with Cassells by 30 July. The terms, including the £50 advance, were identical to those for *The Unlit Lamp*. What she needed now was an American publisher. In September Russell Doubleday, fleetingly in London, read her almost finished manuscript, liked it, and wired Audrey Heath in October with an offer from Doubleday Page and Company to publish it in America.[15] A month later John jubilantly signed the contract. Although the terms were not as good as Cassells' she did receive a £250 advance, and the knowledge that for the first time her work would cross the Atlantic.

At two p.m. on Saturday 7 November she wrote the last sentence of *Adam's Breed*. She hand-delivered the finished typescript to Cassells on 17 November. It took her only three more days to prepare a version free of Anglicisms for the American market. Eccentrically she celebrated by purchasing a cockatoo called Not from Gamages.

John, usually prey to doubts on finishing a book, this time felt an optimistic charge of elation. Una purred like a contented cat. While writing John saw only 'the steadies': the Temples and Peggy Austin, or her literary friends (May, Violet, Rebecca West, Sheila Kaye-Smith, Eileen Bliss and, when she was well, Vere). A book complete, she would be swept up again by Gabrielle, Toupie, Fabienne, Poppy, and Rachel into the iridescent artifice of London's café society. Only the novelist Ida Wylie bridged both circles and thus enjoyed a unique place in John's writing life.

Marie Visetti again ensured the rapid demise of John's hard-earned enjoyment. Inevitably her next *cri de cœur* came the day after John had delivered *Adam's Breed* to Cassells.[16] For more than a week John ministered to the Visettis, taking Marie for four consultations with Dr Martisius. Marie's illnesses, coinciding as they did with the publication or delivery of John's novels, displayed the same attention-seeking pattern as did the coincidences of John and Cubby's illnesses in relation to their calls on Una. Interestingly, in September of that year John and Cubby were both ill at the same time, both taking to their beds and awaiting Una's ministrations.[17]

Minna Taylor too had interrupted John's writing. In the spring she had become, in Una's words, 'very tiresome'.[18] Minna, currently writing her memoirs, was probably reluctant to include in them her daughter's lover of whom she had never approved. John suspected that Minna was still in contact with Zyp and quietly hoped for a reconciliation between him and Una. When they had fought the Fox-Pitt case, Minna had given them very little support – a fact Una could not overlook.

Little support had also been forthcoming from Viola, whose husband J.L. Garvin was Editor of the *Observer*: a paper which in Una's view had failed to do enough to back John. But keen to patch up their relationships, Minna and Viola joined John and Una in Brighton in October, all four of them dancing at the hotel that night – Una dancing with John and 'two unknown young men!' – and dining off oysters at Cheesemans.[19]

During the summer Una and John's relationship with Minna had improved sufficiently for her to become, with Audrey Heath, one of the first two readers of *Adam's Breed*. Una read the growing novel to her in three instalments during July, August and September, while John, hawk-like, watched her every expression.[20] In Minna's opinion: 'it is a great book, fine and more interesting than *The Unlit Lamp*.'[21] Audrey's reaction was even more intense: '[Audrey] says she cried all the way home after *Adam's Breed* and can't bear to think how dull she will feel when it's finished.'[22]

Galley proofs of the finished novel came on 3 December. On 1 December John and Violet Hunt had attended the PEN club dinner, John nervy, Violet reassuring. She had read large portions of the manuscript and may already have been considering submitting it for the Prix Femina Vie Heureuse, although she said nothing yet.

Inevitably a few days later John collapsed, this time with influenza. Her recovery was slow, necessitating a gentle end to 1925.

Only one matter marred New Year's Eve. Una had intercepted a mysterious letter addressed to Cubby. Angrily she and John had called Cubby in to question her. They were still questioning her severely on New Year's Day. It is possible that Cubby's letter had been from an 'unsuitable' friend. Una appeared to allow only young Oliver Woods, Cubby's cousin, access to her, a relationship encouraged by Viola and Garvin: 'Don't forget that we [hope to] have Andrea a little . . . that is [,] as much as you can spare [her] – these next weeks when Oliver is home.'[23]

In the next few days Una told Minna and Viola about Cubby's disgrace, and called in Dr Grant from St George's Convent. Una's excessively stern treatment of her daughter was becoming a talking point within the family. Earlier that month James Garvin had written to her: 'Don't repress my little favourite Andrea too much. She's full of sap and must follow nature. She will follow it more or less reasonably if emancipation comes by rather liberal degrees. Otherwise the pent-up bursts its barriers some day and there is unnecessary devastation . . . I want Andrea to be happy.'[24]

Cubby meanwhile, glad to leave such a heavy atmosphere, was packed off to her father's for a week. It was the last time she saw him.

On 28 January 1926 Una's diary recorded one single flat statement: 'Admiral Troubridge died at Biarritz.' No emotion was expressed, no event recalled from what had once been a shared life. That life was so far behind her, so alien from her present, it seemed like a half-remembered chapter in someone else's novel.

Minna broke the news to them on the telephone. It seemed that Troubridge, who had retired in 1924, had collapsed with a heart-attack at a tea-dance. Una's prime concern was her pension. Troubridge's total estate amounted to only £452 18s. 11d. Una's naval widow's pension would only be £225 per year and Andrea's maintenance allowance a mere £24 a year. Una was devastated. Cubby, now nearly sixteen, wished to continue at St George's until she could go to university. Tom Troubridge as the sole executor, who to say the least did not feel warmly towards his stepmother, would be responsible for such financial decisions. When Una told her family, 'Viola [was] very nice, Minna intoler-

1. The infant Marguerite's family group, early 1880s. *Left to right*: her great-grandmother Jane Jones of Huntingdon, New Jersey; Marguerite Radclyffe-Hall; her grandmother Sarah Diehl; and her mother Marie Diehl Radclyffe-Hall

2. Marguerite and her cousins, c. 1903: Marie Diehl Visetti (in flowered hat); Marguerite Radclyffe-Hall with her arm round the shoulder of her cousin-lover Jane Randolph; Jane's sons Thomas and Decan Randolph (in sailor suits); Aunt Emma Jones Reade; and Aunt Lode Diehl

3. Marguerite's mother, Marie Diehl Visetti

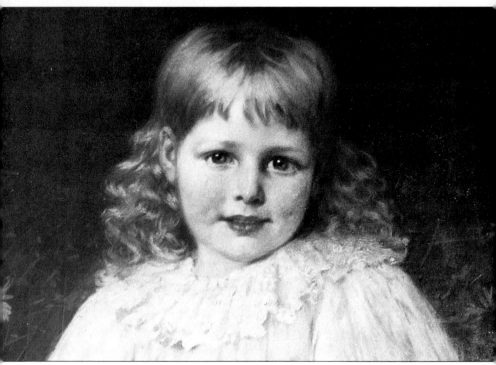

4. Marguerite with curls: a portrait of Marguerite aged 5 by Katinka Amyat. The curls were later painted out by Clare 'Tony' Atwood at Una Troubridge's request

5. Radclyffe Hall as a young woman

6. The April
Grandmother: Mabel
'Ladye' Batten with her
grandchildren, Peter
aged 2 and Honey aged
6 months

7. Ladye (*left*) and John
paddling, *c.* 1910–14

8. May Sinclair, suffragette, 1910: outside the 'Votes for Women' shop in Kensington, London

9. Violet Hunt, c. 1907–16

10. Clemence Dane, 1923

11. Toupie Lowther (*second from left, second row*) and her all-women ambulance unit, formed in 1917

12. The Medium: Gladys Leonard

13. Una Troubridge, 1915

14. Una, husband and child, 1914.
Left to right: Ernest, Andrea ('Cubby') and Una Troubridge

15. Una, John and the dachshunds

16. Romaine Brooks, c. 1925

17. Colette, 1909

18. Djuna Barnes (*left*) and Natalie Barney, Nice, France, c. 1928–30. Natalie was the model for Valérie Seymour in *The Well of Loneliness*. Radclyffe Hall appeared in Djuna Barnes's lampoon, the *Ladies Almanack*

19. Havelock Ellis, 1931, by William Rothenstein. He wrote an introductory commentary for *The Well of Loneliness*

20. Audrey Heath, Radclyffe Hall's literary agent

21. The Smallhythe Trio and Vera, *c.* 1921. *Left to right*: Edy Craig and Christopher St John (top step); Clare 'Tony' Atwood and Vera 'Jack' Holme (bottom step)

22. Naomi 'Mickie' Jacob at Casa Mickie, Sirmione, Italy, with her dogs Prince Carlo China and the Hon. Perci Plate

23. Vita Sackville-West, photographed by Virginia Woolf for *Orlando*, 1928

24. Vera Brittain, 1936

25. Compton Mackenzie with friends in Ireland, 1924: (*left to right, top row*)
G. K. Chesterton, James Stephens, Lennox Robinson; (*bottom row*) W. B. Yeats,
Compton Mackenzie, Augustus John, Edwin Lutyens

26. Virginia Woolf and Ethel Smyth in the garden at Monk's House, Rodmell, Susse

27. Radclyffe Hall at the time of *The Sixth Beatitude*, 1936.
Inscribed 'Evguenia from John'

28. Evguenia Souline as a young woman

29. Radclyffe Hall with Fido, *c.* 1939–41

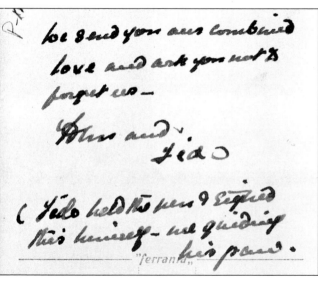

30. Inscription by Radclyffe Hall on the back of the snapshot of her poodle Fido

able'. Una's mother attempted to persuade her to remarry a man of means. While her stepchildren Chatty, Tom and Mary attended the funeral in Biarritz on 1 February, Una, at home with John and Cubby, went to Minna's in a fury where 'Viola again nice. Minna more damnable than ever . . . Home to dinner and wrote my mind to Minna.' She would never marry any man. Moreover she would never, never, leave John.[25]

On 13 February she and Cubby did attend Troubridge's Memorial Service at Westminster Cathedral. John stayed away and walked the dogs. For several months, as Una tackled the Ministry of Pensions, the Officers' Families Fund and Sir George Lewis, she seethed with anger at her deceased husband. Her perseverance finally paid off. She won her case at a Pensions Appeal Tribunal and her niggardly pension was increased. Some of the Troubridge clan never forgave her for continuing to draw that widow's pension until the day of her death; in Una's view, having never divorced, she was legally and morally entitled to it.*

On 4 March *Adam's Breed* was published. Newman Flower wrote to say that it was the finest book that had been submitted to him in twenty years. Later he admitted that though he was proud to publish it, he had not expected it to sell.[26] His firm however put all their big guns behind it, billing it as 'the book that has set the literary world talking'. Even before publication, praise for the book (and gossip about the author) was on everyone's lips. Alfred Noyes, given a review copy, telephoned to say 'it was unquestionably by far one of the finest books he had read in the last ten years'.[27] Every critic who followed him commented on its originality, power and strength. The *Sunday Herald* labelled it a novel of 'sympathy, strength and skill in craftsmanship rare in these hurried, novelty-seeking days'. The *Observer* felt it only just fell short of greatness. *The Times*, according to Una, gave a 'splendid account'. John, who wrote to Jane Caruth that it was 'far and away the best thing I have ever written', found her sentiment echoed in the *Sunday Times*, its reviewer announcing that *Adam's Breed* stood 'head and shoulders above the general run of contemporary fiction'.[28]

Five days after publication, the Times Bookshop, Hatchards and Fullers all re-ordered copies. On 12 March Audrey reported that the first edition of 3,500 copies had sold out within a week, and Cassells were already printing a second edition of 1,500. The reprint of 1,500 copies was followed by a third and fourth reprint of 1,500 each.[29] Between news of the third and fourth impressions, they discovered that only two copies were left on the Times Bookshop shelves. Both vanished while John and Una stood and watched.[30] That same week in Charing Cross they gazed up in wonder at a huge banner advertising *Adam's Breed*.

In March the novel had been published in the Dominions;[31] by June they learnt it was selling furiously in Toronto and Melbourne. On 31 March, John

---

* Radclyffe Hall, who already paid most of Una and Andrea's expenses, may have felt that as 'head of the family' she should become fully financially responsible.

posed for her now statutory post-publication photograph, this time taken by the fashionable photographer Douglas.

Doubleday, who were not publishing the book until July, reported in May that American subscriber sales already stood at 2,000. Cassells told John on 21 May that *Adam's Breed* was going too well to need extra advertising. Indeed the firm had postponed a G.K. Chesterton title in order to print 3,000 more copies of Hall's novel. Una began to keep a careful record of sales in her journal. By the end of June her reckoning suggested that 9,400 copies had been sold in England, while John estimated she had already made £637 in royalties – a considerable sum in those days.

At midnight on 3 May the General Strike had begun. Transport and railway workers and other unions downed tools in support of the miners' campaign against drastically reduced wages. Swayed by the Conservative press, John and Una saw it as a class war, even Communist-inspired, and hastened to put their jewellery into store. Immediately they offered their help transporting patients to and from Charing Cross Hospital. On 5 May they had their first wireless installed and were able to listen to the news. When the strike was over, at the Women Writers' Lunch at the Rembrandt Hotel on 18 May, John found it hard to believe that almost all the women there had already read *Adam's Breed*.

During these weeks of publicity and sales statistics, she had, almost as a talisman, begun writing again. She had finished two short stories, 'The Blossoms' and 'Saint Ethelfrida', and had begun work on 'Miss Ogilvy Finds Herself' – not only her most significant story but one which would provide the impetus as well as some of the characterization and wartime descriptions for *The Well of Loneliness*.

The renewed burst of writing on top of what Una called 'bizzing around' brought on severe exhaustion. Her throat seized up; she trembled with fatigue. Una decreed that a space was needed for John to 'vague around'. Since John had just bought Una a Standard motor car, nicknamed (like Una) 'Squig', Una suggested they took the vehicle, plus Dickie the maid, Bradley the chauffeur, Nut the dog and the luggage – ah, the luggage! – for a short break to Burgh Island in Devon.

'Vaguing around' did John so much good that within days she was obsessively visiting estate agents and dragging Una to view several impossible cottages. At the same time, she decided to use Burgh Island as a setting for 'Miss Ogilvy' – an idea which Audrey, who was visiting them, approved. The story was finished on 8 July.

While in Devon John heard that her former lover Jane Caruth was briefly in London. Hoping to waylay her, though in vain, she wrote:

Adam's Breed is supposed to have made my reputation . . . Isn't it amusing that I should have become quite a wellknown writer? I sometimes can't understand it myself, but there it is, it has certainly come to pass . . . Why go home so soon? I think you are being very rude to England. Yours affectionately, Marguerite.[32]

Back in London John lunched with Noyes, then went to a PEN club dinner where she 'was much lionised and very sick'.[33] Another sore throat loomed. On 23 March Violet Hunt had written to John to tell her she had put *Adam's Breed* up for the Prix Femina Vie Heureuse–Bookman award. At the PEN club everyone buzzed with the news. The Femina was the only literary prize awarded annually in both France and England for the best work of fiction. The English and French committees each included an array of distinguished women writers who shortlisted three novels by female or male writers from their own country. The final award to the English novel was made by the French Committee and vice versa.

The English Committee included Clemence Dane, Violet Hunt, Sheila Kaye-Smith, May Sinclair, Rebecca West, Professor C. Spurgeon, and two friends of Ladye's, Ethel Colburn Mayne and novelist Alice Perrin, who had come with Violet to a literary dinner at John and Una's in April.

Audrey now decided it was time for John to meet Carl Brandt, whose New York literary agency had a reciprocal arrangement with A.M. Heath. Maxwell Perkins, Scott Fitzgerald's legendary editor at Scribner's, described Brandt as shrewd, sociable, somewhat partial to drink, 'perhaps a little bit slick' but excellent with writers. At their meeting on 14 July John felt negotiations with Brandt might work. Five days later she invited him to dinner at Holland Street, always a sign of her approval.[34]

Having given a successful broadcast for the BBC on 3 August, John left for Paris with Una on their way to Bagnoles and Monte Carlo. In Paris they planned to dine with the Brandts. Dinner, easy for the socially skilled Una, was something of an ordeal for John, who was glad to slip away to see Natalie Barney, Mimi Franchetti (pianist Renate Borgatti's lover) and the poet Anna Wickham, a trio with whom she could say what she liked and be who she was.[35] Bagnoles proved peaceful, Monte Carlo a disaster and Paris memorable for meetings with Djuna Barnes and Colette.

The *succès fou* in Paris since 1920 had been Colette's *Chéri*, the lyrical story of an ageing courtesan's final love affair with the young son of a friend. John and Una had read and admired most of Colette's novels, and hoped that Natalie would introduce them to her. Una felt passionate about the idea of translating Colette, who was as yet untranslated in England.

On 19 October Natalie took them to Colette's apartment in the Rue de Beaujolais. At fifty-three the French novelist was thirteen stone, twice divorced, and in love with a 36-year-old pearl broker, Maurice Goudeket. John and Una were captivated by her rolling brassy voice and her verve. She autographed their copies of her *Chéri* books and lunched with them at Prunier's in the company of Natalie and Lily de Clermont Tonnerre on 22 October. John thought her a great literary stylist with a wise understanding of human nature, but admitted later that she had some reservations about the sensual side of Colette's nature.

> Colette, who loves good food and too much of it; Colette who loves the sexual act and too much of it; Colette who has a peasant's outlook on money the while she over-indulges herself. Yes but Colette who adores the wind and the rain, the sea and the earth and the fruits of the earth . . . a great woman . . . and a masterly writer.[36]

While John wrote, Una saw Colette again and put forward her plan. Colette agreed enthusiastically and suggested Una start with *La Maison de Claudine*.

After their arrival home on 2 November, John took to using blue stationery exactly like Colette's and named her new dog after her. They had been absent throughout the whole of Cubby's holiday. Now, more concerned with news about the imminent Prix Femina shortlisting, Una failed to record her daughter's sixteenth birthday on the 5th in her otherwise meticulously maintained diary. On the 24th Violet telephoned John to say that *Adam's Breed* had been shortlisted for the Femina alongside Liam O'Flaherty's *The Informer* and Sylvia Townsend Warner's *Lolly Willowes*. With previous winners including Katherine Mansfield for *Bliss*, Rose Macaulay for *Dangerous Ages* and David Garnett for *Lady into Fox*,[37] Radclyffe Hall suddenly found herself in the league of major writers and facing stiff competition.

Sylvia Townsend Warner's first novel, *Lolly Willowes*, had just caused an 'excited bustle' in London. There were a striking number of similarities between Sylvia and herself. Though thirteen years younger, Sylvia like her was a lesbian, monied and upper middle class. She too would publish five books of poetry and seven novels, as well as short stories, translations, a biography and numerous pamphlets. She lived for nearly forty years with the poet Valentine Ackland, a Catholic, first lapsed, then reconverted. Like John and Una the pair were inseparable. When Valentine went off on a journey even for a few hours she would leave a note; when parted for longer, they wrote to each other twice a day. Then suddenly Valentine fell in love with a wealthy American, Elizabeth Wade White, who for more than a decade formed an intimate and troubling part of Sylvia and Valentine's lives. Such a triangle was all too familiar to John.

Sylvia's whimsical style matched her eccentric characters, who existed amongst the most startling events. Unlike John's novels, Sylvia's were characterized by highly original plots but there were certain themes common to the two women's novels which could account for their massive popularity in the mid-twenties.

Like *The Unlit Lamp*, *Lolly Willowes* – as Wendy Mulford emphasizes in her biography of Sylvia Townsend Warner and Valentine Ackland – pointed up the oppressive ways in which English bourgeois families exploited unmarried women. In the shortlisted novel Lolly the heroine lodges in a Chiltern village, where lurks a coven of witches and warlocks. Lolly, who becomes a safe white witch, finds the devil's casual power over her and other witches more agreeable than the aggressive power of men.[38]

Where *Lolly Willowes* differed profoundly from *Adam's Breed* was in its use of witchcraft as a metaphor for the power of spiritual change in people's lives, whereas Radclyffe Hall threw off all masks and confronted spiritual problems openly.

Hall's preoccupation with a spiritual essence in *The World*, 'The Lover of Things' and *A Saturday Life* now fully manifested itself. It was *Adam's Breed*'s other-worldly symbolism, its search for meaning written with the intensity of poetry, which impressed readers and critics. But it is the accumulation of realistic and imaginative details which grounds the other-worldliness and carries readers along.

It was the first book Radclyffe Hall had researched. She based Fabio and Teresa's pasta factory on a macaroni factory Una discovered in Old Compton Street. Soho, where much of the action takes place, John 'knew in her bones'. The Doric Restaurant in the novel was born 'after an exhaustive tour of the underground regions of the Berkeley', once Ladye's favourite Grill. During October, John accompanied pathologist Dr Bronte to a public mortuary. During an October weekend in Brockenhurst, Una recalls, 'we followed Gian-Luca step by step to the New Forest'. They were hunting for a charcoal burner, similar to one Marguerite had met in Bournemouth as a child. Years later Una wrote: 'I am not likely to forget our hunt for that charcoal burner; we trudged and waded in abominable weather and found him at last . . . and she [John] listened for hours while he expounded his lore.'[39]

The research was worth the effort. In what is Hall's most complex novel, the variety, texture and denseness of naturalistic detail is the first of three vital components which Hall skilfully blends together.

We see her sift and stir the ingredients, at her best when, like her characters, she is handling food. She takes us among the predominantly Italian community in Soho, into the Soho Salumeria which belongs to Fabio, grandfather of Gian-Luca, her melancholy boy hero – technically English, emotionally belonging nowhere.

All his life Gian-Luca remembered those first impressions of the shop; the size of it, the smell of it, the dim, mysterious gloom of it – a gloom from which strange objects would continually jump out and try to hit you in the face – but above all the smell, that wonderful smell that belongs to the Salumeria. The shop smelt of sawdust and cheeses and pickles and olives and sausages and garlic; the shop smelt of oil and cans and Chianti and a little of split peas and lentils; the shop smelt of coffee and sour brown bread and very faintly of vanilla; the shop smelt of people, of Fabio's boot blacking, and of all the boots that went in and out unblacked; it also smelt of Old Compton Street, a dusty, adventurous smell . . . Providing as he [Fabio] did a smell for every nose, he also provided a taste for every palate. Huge jars of plump, green olives, floating in turgid juices . . . a galaxy of cheeses, all approaching adolescence, rolled or sprawled or oozed about the counter. Tomatoes . . . huddled in cans along a shelf; there were endless sauces, endless pickles, endless pots of mustard, endless bits of split and dried and powdered peas. There were endless bottles containing ornate liquids – Menta, Arancio, Framboise, Grenadine, Limone – beautiful gem-like liquids, that when a sunbeam touched them glowed with a kind of rapture . . .[40]

There is a kind of rapture in the richness, the redolence, the teeming vividness of these details. They are sensual, material, grounding the book in a specific place and time – first the streets of London, then the Genoese countryside, finally in England's New Forest, at the start of the century. Located within these settings, and viewed with similar insight, are a series of characters who 'jump out' at the reader like her 'strange objects'.

There is Gian-Luca himself, the lonely child, illegitimate, unhappy, who never discovers he is the son of his poet-hero. From birth Gian-Luca is rejected by his grandmother Teresa who will never forgive him for the fact that her beloved daughter Olga died in labour, refusing to disclose the identity of her child's father. Teresa never forgives her Roman Catholic God either. She sends her grandson to the Board school open to all denominations rather than to the Roman Catholic school. The English exclude him because he is not as they. The Italians mock him for thinking he is English.

Gian-Luca is stateless, churchless, fatherless, motherless, a small misfit with ashen-fair hair. Other children 'set him apart as a kind of unnatural freak'.[41] He will be followed by Hall's other 'unnatural freaks': Malise, Miss Ogilvy, Stephen Gordon. Teresa, 'a barricade of steel', feeds his body but starves his soul. At eleven years she tells him, 'you are not quite as other children.' She offers him only one bleak creed: 'Remember . . . that you always have yourself, and that should suffice a man.'[42]

Gian-Luca spends half his life attempting to live by this stern philosophy, his self-reliance enabling him finally to become the highly respected headwaiter at the Doric. Adoring the aloof Teresa he bows to her bleak edict. But Teresa loves no one – certainly not her husband Fabio, who is one of Hall's strongest yet gentlest portraits, a man who will give and give against any odds.

These portraits set amidst a cornucopia of exquisite detail would have left *Adam's Breed* as no more than another finely wrought example of the mainstream traditional novel. But Radclyffe Hall lent her story a wider theme, transforming what would otherwise have been merely the sensitive story of

Gian-Luca's odyssey from lonely boy to distinguished head-waiter to starving beggar into a heavily textured allegory of the soul's quest for God.

Gian-Luca's quest starts slowly and gains impetus through a number of setbacks, of which the most moving is his meeting with his idol, the poet Ugo Doria, who unbeknown to him is his father.

Gian-Luca, head-waiter at the Doric 'with that rarest of all gifts, the instinct for perfect service', strengthens his barren life with poetry. One day Doria makes a restaurant reservation. Gian-Luca plans every detail of the meal, reads and rereads the great poet's poetry. 'He pictured Doria as slender and tall, with the strong, lean flanks of a race-horse; his eyes would be inspired, the eyes of a poet, but above all the man would convey a sense of bigness, bigness of mind, bigness of spirit.'[43]

Doria arrives. He is a fat, elderly man of sixty, with a self-willed mouth that had weakened and coarsened, with pale eyes, small and screwed up, because of the skin gathered in bladders beneath them. Only his hands were part of Gian-Luca's and Hall's dream – hands long, white, still elegant. But the hands were around the waist of a courtesan; became greasy with food and wine; flicked through the menu but fawned on the coarse, painted woman.

This shallow creature was Gian-Luca's idol – and his father. That neither of them know this is a fact revealed by Radclyffe Hall in what is without doubt a narrative *coup de théâtre*.

Driven out of his mind and on to the streets of London at the sight of his fallen idol, Gian-Luca comes upon a beggar woman and her blind son selling matches. That experience becomes the first step in what is to be his complete spiritual transformation. As in 'The Blind Ploughman' and her later *The Sixth Beatitude* the device of 'seeing' and 'sight' is used in the double sense of both inner and outer vision, as is the notion of service: service both in this world and to the divine. Gian-Luca begins his pilgrimage alone in the New Forest, where he stumbles towards a deepening insight into this life and the next. Teresa had taught him that he had himself; experience has taught him that without God, he has lost himself.

In the Forest he asks an old Romany woman: 'What is the Romany word for death?' 'Merripen,' she says gravely. He asks her what is the word for life. 'Merripen,' she says gravely. That life is death and death is life was learnt not only by Gian-Luca, but more painfully by his creator. Exile is again the keynote of this book.

In looking at Hall's complete *œuvre*, we can see that *Adam's Breed* is at one with the novels that preceded and followed it. Within her compassionate vision, Gian-Luca is another protagonist who attempts to resolve the needs of his soul with the demands of a material world.

If Hall's 'lesbian' novels (*The Unlit Lamp*, *The Well of Loneliness*) fit her spiritual scheme, so do her 'spiritual' novels (like *Adam's Breed*) find their place within her lesbian framework. Not only is the misfit, the outcast, central to their theme; but the search for spiritual wholeness is inseparably tied into Radclyffe Hall's belief in the nature of sexual identity and its place in God's plan. (She herself derived comfort from the belief that inversion was part of nature – a belief which she expounded in *The Well of Loneliness*.)

The novel's astounding popularity[44] brought John numerous invitations to address literary gatherings. In January 1927 she spoke to the Writers' Circle of the Institute of Journalists where the columnist Wilhelmina Stitch chaired the meeting and afterwards hosted a dinner in John's honour at Gatti's restaurant, where the entire menu comprised dishes described in *Adam's Breed*.[45]

At Zion College on 16 March she lectured to the Bookman Circle on 'True Realism in Fiction'. She praised the imaginative realism of Jane Austen and the Brontës. She lovingly surveyed Dickens, Thackeray and George Eliot, gave Ida Wylie an approving mention then applauded the Americans Sinclair Lewis and Fannie Hurst, he for *Babbit* and *Main Street*, she for *Lummox*.* John crossed swords with Vita Sackville-West when she suggested that 'accumulation of finely observed detail' led to artistic creation. Mrs Nicolson (as the reporter termed her) said tartly that we should beware that wealth of detail did not obscure significance. When John told the Circle that it was never legitimate for writers to deal with 'unpleasant' subjects because of their unpleasantness, it was the motive behind the books that counted,[46] we can smile wryly in view of the later accusations of 'unpleasant realism' levelled at *The Well of Loneliness*.

Among her listeners was Grace Spencer, one of a number of women correspondents who had recently showered her with fanmail. Many were lesbians who had begun to recognize themselves in John's earlier novels.[47] Grace and the rest of the Circle's audience felt *Adam's Breed* was more powerful and beautiful than any of Hall's previous works. The judges of the Prix Femina Vie Heureuse agreed. On 8 April 1927 Mlle Claudel telephoned to tell John she had won the coveted prize.

Letters and cables of congratulation flooded into Holland Street. Those that particularly touched her were from other writers and artists including Ethel Smyth, Ernest Raymond, Cunninghame Graham, and Ellen Glasgow who wrote to the publishers she shared with John: 'Why didn't you tell me you had published the most beautiful novel of the year, an amazing book, *Adam's Breed*?'[48] Two letters were special, one from Peggy, the other from Violet. Her old Malvern friend wrote: 'Johnny darling . . . How I lick my lips over the juicy bits of praise I read about you in the Press . . . I feared to find myself . . . in a

---

* Fannie Hurst was America's highest earning fiction writer throughout the 1920s and '30s. On that occasion Radclyffe Hall reserved her highest praise for the Norwegian Knut Hamsun's *Growth of the Soil* which had won him a Nobel Prize in 1920.

bevy of intellectual representatives of all nations laying laurels at your feet. So well deserved Johnny dear, and so applauded by your loving Peggy.'[49]

Violet's letter is curious. Instead of opening as usual with 'Dear Marguerite', she started with her friend's professional pen name:

> Dear Radclyffe, Well. I congratulate you. I am pleased that it has turned out so well . . . and I shall like to see you 'translate' . . . it really *would* be nice to see it in French dress . . . I want to see your new one. I believe I shall like it better than A. B. You gave me an idea of it once.

The concluding lines of Violet's letter may have hidden an intimate memory of their time together in that hotel in Edinburgh: 'I suppose you go away for Easter? I don't go away. I never do. I hate being alone in hotels.'[50] How far Marguerite had come since that weekend.

Sales spun. *Adam's Breed* was on show in every London bookshop, John on show in every newspaper and magazine. Her photograph was everywhere. American and Continental newspapers captioned their pictures: 'Man or Woman?' The *Houston Chronicle*'s caption ran: 'You Are Wrong – It's Not A Man'.[51] John's cousin Winifred sent her a cutting from the States headed 'Male or Female?' depicting 'Miss Radclyffe Hall well known in British literary circles who affects the masculine in her dress'.[52]

The English press were slightly more discreet. Their brief biographical sketches mentioned John's international travels, dog breeding, psychic investigations, collections of oak furniture, and her status as an indefatigable first nighter; but they too focused on her masculine appearance and her mannish clothes. Her monocle got more mileage than the Femina. The *Westminster Gazette* on 12 April labelled their photograph 'Award to Monocled Writer'. The following day, they informed any laggard who had missed the description of Hall as having a flaxen Eton crop and masculine attire that her 'only concession to feminine costume seems to be silk stockings'.[53]

Although not one photograph showed her with the monocle in her eye, it became her media trademark. Suddenly an intelligent journalist from the *Lancashire Daily Post* intervened. She pointed out that she had known Hall for years; Hall rarely if ever wore a monocle, but her 'close friend' Una Troubridge did. 'Possibly she has been confused with her very close friend.'[54] Perceptive though this was intended to be, the remark did smack of the notion that once you have seen one lesbian you have seen them all.

The *Birmingham Post* not only told readers she had 'the best shingle in London' it also pointed out: 'It is, alas, not often that one meets an established woman novelist who goes out of her way to encourage and praise the work of other women who are yet beginning.'[55] Other women journalists were keener to promote Radclyffe Hall as a model of domesticity despite her outré wardrobe. The *Auckland Star* wrote: 'Culinary genius is the feminine writer's special domestic gift . . . George Sand always declared she was far prouder of her pastry than her novels. One of the most outstanding contemporary examples of brainy domestication is Miss Radclyffe Hall.'[56]

Evelyn Irons of the *Daily Mail* interviewed her for a series on 'How Other Women Run Their Homes'. John, who always let Una look after the house, or rang for the maid, gave a hilarious picture of her domestic routine.

> Lady Troubridge sees to the food. I am not really interested in that side of housekeeping . . . My province is the house itself. I am a fussy housekeeper with a perfect mania for cleanliness . . . I often write for twelve hours at a stretch. If during that time I spy specks of dust I have to control my itch to remove them, for I have the housewife's 'seeing eye'. After that my housework comes as a relaxation. But I cannot let the house run itself – I must supervise it personally and do my accustomed 'chores'.[57]

Anyone who still felt Radclyffe Hall did not have a sense of humour should reread that article. Evelyn Irons herself chuckled at the interview and became a chum of John's. A sporty, intelligent Oxford graduate in her mid-twenties, she lived with Olive Rinder, a bookish leftish young woman subject to tuberculosis, in a flat in Royal Hospital Road. The pair got on so well with John and Una that they soon met frequently, first over tea and dinner, then going together to films and first nights and to meals at the Hyde Park Grill. Una saw the Irons–Rinder relationship as a 'marriage', which afforded her great satisfaction.

On 16 May the Prix Femina prize-giving took place at the Institut Français. John was nervous, needed the support of May Sinclair and Violet Hunt. Other literary friends including Sheila Kaye-Smith and Leonard and Molly Rees were in the audience with Una. John Galsworthy presented the prize. Hall's book, he said, had given him enormous personal pleasure; although he had written 'one or two' novels himself, he added, he had never ceased to wonder how it was successfully done.[58]

The engagements were not yet over. Indefatigably on 1 June John took Alfred Noyes' chair at the Writers' Club Dinner. The sheer number of events was giving her a skin; she was becoming less awkward in public. Though she had her own eccentric style, it was obvious to people that she cared about books and cared for other writers. She had known what it was like to be out on a limb.

Suddenly it was July, and though she was approaching exhaustion there was still the party she and Una had planned to give. It seemed from the guest list that half of London's literary establishment were coming to Holland Street to hear Rosamund Johnson and Taylor Gordon sing Negro spirituals. In the front row of improvised stalls sat John Galsworthy and Robert Cunninghame Graham. Sybil Thorndike, Lewis Casson, Ernest Thesiger, Gerard Hopkins, Wilhelmina Stitch, Margaret Irwin, John Adcock, Sheila Kaye-Smith, the Newman Flowers, and the rest crowded the drawing-room and hung from the stairs. Those faithfuls on whom she relied, Gabrielle Enthoven, Violet Hunt, Leonard and Molly Rees, Viola, Minna, Toupie, crammed themselves excitedly on to cushions. The press couldn't get enough of it. John wore a man's dinner jacket and Mrs Galsworthy favoured a crinoline skirt; each had their followers, enabling the press to report that 'half the ladies present favoured the masculine mode and half the latest Victorian effect.'[59]

The quiet trip to Paris and Bagnoles that followed was a necessity. They had baths, massages, quiet talks and meals with Colette and Natalie, and stayed until late September.[60]

On 22 December 1927, only eight months after winning the Femina, Hall heard that she had won the James Tait Black Memorial Prize worth £250 for the best novel of the year.[61] In the history of the two prizes it was a 'double' that had occurred only once before, in 1924, with E.M. Forster's *Passage to India*. Hall stoutly told all male reporters: 'I consider women writers not only are, but always have been, the equal of men writers.'[62]

Even this was not the end of the awards for *Adam's Breed*. In 1930, while fallout continued from the *Well* explosion, *Adam's Breed* received the American Eichelberger Gold Medal for outstanding achievement in the field of humane work. Such serious critical attention gave Radclyffe Hall an established place in the literary world of the twenties and thirties. *Adam's Breed* sold successfully for twenty years and, seventy years later, still sells well.

In July 1926, the previous year, John had quietly begun to make notes for a new book.[63] Discreetly she embarked on a reading plan which included the works of Havelock Ellis. Una records:

> It was after the success of *Adam's Breed* that John came to me one day with unusual gravity and asked for my decision in a serious matter: she had long wanted to write a book on sexual inversion, a novel that would be accessible to the general public who did not have access to technical treatises . . . Her instinct told her . . . she must postpone such a book until her name was made; until her unusual theme would get a hearing as being the work of an established writer.
>
> It was her absolute conviction that such a book could only be written by a sexual invert, who alone could be qualified by personal knowledge and experience to speak on behalf of a misunderstood and misjudged minority . . .
>
> In her view the time was ripe, and . . . although the publication of such a book might mean the shipwreck of her whole career, she was fully prepared to make any sacrifice except – the sacrifice of my peace of mind . . . Therefore she placed the decision in my hands . . . I told her to write what was in her heart . . . I was sick to death of ambiguities, and only wished to be known for what I was and to dwell with her in the palace of truth.[64]

John listened, nodded, probably smiled – if only at the line 'the palace of truth'. She went straight back to her study. She had work to do. She was about to start *The Well of Loneliness*.[65]

Throughout October and November she wrote, using the working title *Stephen*. Shortly before hearing that *Adam's Breed* was up for the Prix Femina on 24 November she read Audrey the first four chapters. In December she read Minna Taylor the same four chapters revised. In her view *Stephen* was obviously fit for her mother-in-law's ears. Would it be equally fit for the ears of the world she believed was awaiting it?

PART FOUR

CRUSADE AND MARTYRDOM
1928–1933

15

BOLDNESS

In 'Salvation', a poem Radclyffe Hall wrote several years before *The Well of Loneliness*, she thunders out these lines:

> I will be bold and unafraid
> And great with high endeavour;
> And all the trumpets men have made,
> And all the drums that men have played,
> They shall be mine for ever.
> There'll be a noise, a mighty noise
> Of bugling and drumming
> When I go out to Jericho,
> Across the plains to Jericho,
> In the good time that's coming![1]

This song-poem acted as a theme for her writing of *The Well of Loneliness*, which she saw more as the waging of a biblical campaign than the writing of a novel. The book itself is filled with biblical resonances and Old Testament rhythms which irritated some of its critics.

Hall was Joshua leading her people to the Promised Land, the land of freedom. She was Joshua, hoping to take the city of Jericho for her people. As the months went on, and the publishing battles grew harder, she did indeed call them 'my people', 'my persecuted people', 'my misunderstood people'. Bold and unafraid she was, and great with high endeavour; not one person, whether for or against her, denied her that. And indeed there was a noise, a mighty noise – though it was not a good time that was coming.

Stephen Gordon, the heroine of *The Well*, was born 'a narrow-hipped, wide-shouldered little tadpole of a baby', marked out from birth by her appearance. As she grows up, her likeness to her father strikes her mother Lady Anna 'as an outrage – as though the poor, innocent seven-year-old Stephen were in some way a caricature of Sir Philip; a blemished, unworthy, maimed reproduction'.

The reader has been warned: already it is clear that there is no good time coming for Stephen. Tarnished and crippled, she is soon identified as an invert of the masculine type. Sir Philip encourages Stephen in fencing, riding astride and exercising with dumb-bells.

At seven Stephen becomes infatuated with Collins the housemaid who, preferring the opposite sex and an older age, resolutely kisses the footman. Stephen is driven wild with jealousy. Her mother, appalled by her unruly behaviour, grows ever more distant. Stephen's loneliness increases after she meets young Martin Hallam, on holiday in England from Canada, who sees in their friendship the stirrings of love while she sees it as comradeship between two boyish pals. When Martin declares his passion she is struck with a 'kind of dumb horror, staring at his eyes that were clouded by desire'.[2]

Hall makes it clear that although Stephen learns that the 'loneliest place in this world is the no-man's land of sex'[3] many of her troubles stem as much from desiring male prerogatives (such as independence, acknowledgement of talent, a university education, power) as they do from same-sex feelings.

The tragic death of Stephen's father compounds her isolation. Only Puddle, her closeted lesbian governess, who looks like Granny Diehl, understands her.

Stephen becomes besotted with the calculating married Angela Crossby, who rocks a dangerous seesaw between encouragement and rebuff. Angela betrays Stephen to her mother Lady Anna, who is so disgusted that she banishes Stephen from Morton, the family home.

Stephen becomes a writer, her first book a major triumph. It is significant that only after acknowledging her lesbian desire is Stephen able to write successfully. An exile in Paris she is introduced to the exceptional Valérie Seymour, modelled on Natalie Barney, beautifully at ease in her own lesbian nature, who exerts a profound influence on Stephen.

With the start of the First World War, Stephen (like Miss Ogilvy who was the model for this section of the novel) finally finds her community within a women's ambulance corps, where 'side by side with more fortunate women, worked Miss Smith who had been breeding dogs in the country; or Miss Oliphant who had been breeding nothing since birth but a litter of hefty complexes'.[4] These scenes are lifted almost verbatim from her short story 'Malise', probably written the previous year.

While serving with this group, Stephen meets her great love, Mary Llewellyn, an innocent young orphan from the Welsh valleys. Stephen suppresses her desire for Mary until after the war, when, like John and Una, they take a joyous vacation in Orotava and Stephen's resolve melts. She takes Mary in her arms 'and that night they were not divided'.[5]

This is the high point of the novel, and the only overt line about lesbian sexual fulfilment – if such a modest statement can be called 'overt'.

Stephen becomes the protective writer-husband, Mary the attentive nurturing wife with far too little to do. Valérie Seymour introduces them to Paris's homosexual café society, where they form firm friendships with Jamie, an unsuccessful composer, and her consumptive lover Barbara. At Alec's bar the homosexual clientele have lost all self-respect and drink despairingly night after night:

> [It was a] meeting-place of the most miserable of all those who comprised the miserable army. The merciless, drug-dealing, death-dealing haunt to which flocked the battered remnants of men whom their fellow men had at last stamped under; who, despised of the world, must despise themselves.[6]

Of course there were bars and night-clubs as miserable as this in Paris, and Hall had sampled them. But she had also sampled energetic lively salons and cafés where homosexuals felt less apologetic about themselves. That Hall deliberately chose to depict only one side of the 'inverted' life of the period was part of her fictional plea for understanding.

The darkness gathers as the novel concludes. Barbara dies (as Hall knows Vere will surely do) and Jamie, unable to live without her, commits suicide. Lady Anna refuses to recognize Mary's existence and shadows hang over Stephen and Mary's once ecstatic relationship.

Martin Hallam re-enters the picture, resumes his friendship with Stephen, then falls in love with Mary. Stephen, tormented that she cannot protect Mary, prepares to give her up for what she mistakenly believes is Mary's own good. She pretends to have an affair with Valérie Seymour which sends Mary fleeing in distress into the waiting arms of Martin Hallam. Stephen, distraught, makes the novel's final desolate (and melodramatic) plea: 'Acknowledge us, oh God, before the whole world. Give us also the right to our existence!'[7]

Hall started her research in two widely different directions. To fill out the character of Stephen, Hall turned first to the works of the sexologists Havelock Ellis, Karl Ulrichs and Richard von Krafft-Ebing.[8] Hall relies heavily on the theories of Ellis and Krafft-Ebing that homosexuality was inborn and that the female 'invert' was typically masculine and tended to seek relationships with feminine women. She also used the notion of a 'third sex' or an 'intermediate sex' found in works by Magnus Hirschfeld and Edward Carpenter. Carpenter drew on and extended Ulrichs' conception of 'a male soul in a female body', positing a category of people who belonged distinctly to one sex as far as anatomy was concerned but who belonged mentally and emotionally to the other.

Both Ellis and Carpenter saw themselves as libertarians, questioning the moral censure which society attached to homosexuality. Ellis declared that 'inversion [is] not a disease or a "degeneration"' while Carpenter claimed that 'men and women of the exclusive Uranian [homosexual] type are by no means necessarily morbid in any way.' Both advocated the decriminalization of homosexuality while Carpenter went further, insisting that homogenic affection was a valuable social force, and linking social change with feminism, lesbianism and sex change.[9]

Krafft-Ebing is incorporated directly into Hall's narrative when Stephen finds a copy of one of Krafft-Ebing's books – probably his *Psychopathia Sexualis* – in her father's study after his death. Evidently Sir Philip had been aware of Stephen's homosexuality, but had remained silent, either from shame or from a wish to 'protect' her. Shame and protection, as Hall was aware, were the underside to the sexologists' ideas of 'freedom' and 'erotic options'. Stephen Gordon's father displays an understanding of the negative as well as the positive consequences of the sexologists' work. Ellis and his colleagues had brought homosexuality into the open but at the same time, by pathologizing same-sex desire, had the negative effect of encouraging the belief that homosexuality was diseased.

Sir Philip, well read in the current psychological literature, knew that if his daughter fell into this new category of 'homosexuals' she would be likely to be stigmatized. From the shame accompanying it she would need protection. Stephen feels similarly about Mary. She can adore her but she cannot protect her: 'The world has deprived me of my right to protect; I am utterly helpless, I can only love you.'[10]

It is Valérie Seymour who argues angrily and powerfully against Stephen, as Natalie Barney argued with Hall. Valérie, like Natalie, has established an international feminist literary salon which stands, as she does, as a courageous 'lighthouse in a storm-swept ocean' to bring comfort to Stephen's distressed friends. Valérie, like Natalie, is at ease with her sexual identity. She tells Stephen briskly that to talk of 'protection' is merely to ape male heterosexual standards that are old-fashioned, anti-feminist, and inappropriate to lesbian lives. In Valérie's eyes, Stephen's notion that ultra-feminine inverts should assume they have the right to be protected is outdated. She tries to encourage Stephen to find a way of living that is self-sufficient and outside male standards. When Stephen reveals her plan to force Mary to leave, Valérie, outraged, says Stephen was 'made for a martyr'.[11]

Throughout the narrative, Valérie tries to raise Stephen's low self-esteem. She believes that, in the words of Hall's theme-song, a good time is coming: recognition is at hand, inverts must merely 'bide their time'. They must be bold and unafraid, must play their trumpets, bang their drums, 'cultivate more pride . . . learn to be proud of their isolation'.

Valérie stands in the novel as a rational optimistic balance to Stephen's pessimistic perspective. To present her character and to give the novel its alternative standpoint (which has too often been ignored)[12] Hall researched in quite a different direction.

She was already well read in the homosexual writings of Emile Zola, Guy de Maupassant, Clemence Dane, Rosamond Lehmann and Colette. To these she now added Oscar Wilde, Renée Vivien, Djuna Barnes, Virginia Woolf's *Orlando* and Natalie Barney's *Pensées d'une Amazone, Quelques Portraits-Sonnets de Femmes* and her other works. Natalie probably pointed John in the direction of her former lover Liane de Pougy's *Idylle Sapphique*, and was doubtless influential in suggesting the hundreds of books which Una lists between 1926 and 1929 on 'Women's Progress'.

Radclyffe Hall also utilized her own experience for the portraits of both Stephen and Valérie but as Una Troubridge makes clear the novel is not an autobiography, for although many of Stephen Gordon's feelings and reactions were Hall's, practically none of her circumstances or experiences were. Though Hall felt out of step, unlike Stephen she had learnt to accept her 'otherness'. Accepting her exclusion fostered qualities of introspection and enabled her to delineate her exiles from a revealing, sometimes ambiguous, perspective. As Puddle says to Stephen: 'Why, just because you are what you are, you may actually find that you've got an advantage. You may write with a curious double insight.'[13]

Hall had warned Una that 'publication of such a book might mean the shipwreck of her whole career.'[14] Una had taken this statement seriously. Given the period in which she wrote, this was a realistic statement. Yet Lovat Dickson, an early biographer of Radclyffe Hall, who later admitted how his own unconscious homophobia had permeated his research, says derisively: 'As she [Hall] was completely secure financially, talk of the shipwreck of her career was overdoing it. She was risking nothing except a year or two of work on a book which in the end she might not be allowed to publish.'[15]

For a professional author that in itself is a considerable risk. In Hall's case it was only the least of the risks. The label 'invert' then, like 'lesbian' now, was still a term to which one attached oneself at great risk. It may be hard for us today to credit just how bold was Radclyffe Hall's first overt onslaught on the taboo of homosexuality.

But though bold, because of the times she lived in, she was forced by social, even by literary pressure to make a kind of contract, a compromise, in the way she wrote her novel. There is a suggestion that when Hall 'represents the lesbian as scandal and the lesbian as woman-who-is-man' she was 'making an implicit, perhaps unconscious pact with her culture'. Being a more straightforward, traditional novelist than her fellow writers Djuna Barnes, H.D. or Gertrude Stein, who all wrote coded or satiric lesbian texts, and unlike them rejecting both silence and encoding, Hall claimed 'her right to write for the public in exchange for adopting the narrative of damnation'.[16]

She allowed herself to write openly about her lesbian heroine Stephen and the other homosexual characters in Paris; she allowed her women to desire each other; but that was as far as she allowed the narrative to go. The rest is darkness. In a profound sense her inverts *are* doomed; it is a narrative of damnation. And this for highly pragmatic reasons: she believed the law would allow no more than this, if indeed even this was permissible. She believed (correctly) that if at her novel's conclusion two women who shared an 'abnormal passion' walked off into the sunlight holding hands and heading for the nearest bedroom, she would alienate heterosexual readers and antagonize critics. The book, after all, was aimed at a twin audience: a middle-class heterosexual audience whose attitudes she wished to change, and an audience of guilty and voiceless inverts whose suffering she hoped to reduce. Sympathy needed to be invoked through involvement with her heroine. Her realistic style was more suitable for such involvement than the Modernist experimentation of Djuna Barnes. Characterizing the lesbian as a 'freak' yet born so, and paradoxically 'normal' or 'natural' in the eyes of God, was her way to win that sympathy. To that end she backed up her imaginative ideas with the pseudo-scientific theories of male 'experts'. This also increased her own confidence, for to wage this campaign she needed every ounce of bravery she could muster. Courage incidentally is the key virtue in the novel, and is esteemed by all its protagonists.

Hall began writing in Paris in October 1926 at the Pont Royal Hotel, Rue du Bac, where she and Una had a suite of three rooms one of which they converted into a study. John's work was well known in France. *Adam's Breed* was on show in all the Paris bookstores and by May 1927 Paris, Menton and Nice had all reordered. When she needed to relax several British friends were visiting Paris. Accompanied by Eileen Bliss, Etheline, Toupie and Fabienne, she spent evenings gathering material in the Left Bank's homosexual bars and clubs or with Natalie Barney, who continued to impress her. She translated their conversations into those between Stephen and Valérie.

On 8 October John and Una had visited the grave of the lesbian poet Renée Vivien, three years John's senior, who had been born in London as Pauline Tarn in 1877. Something about Renée's tragic story was weaving itself into the fabric of *The Well*. She wanted to know more about Vivien from Natalie, who had been her lover.

Pauline Tarn's mother, like John's and Romaine's, had made her life unbearable. On reaching her majority, like John she left home, rechristening herself with the male appellation René Vivien in order to pass herself off in Paris as a male poet who, like Natalie, wrote only in French. Her success was instantaneous. She won a reputation as one of the best second-generation Symbolist poets. When well established, she altered her name to the feminine Renée for her third volume of poetry which John had already read and found moving.

Natalie, who profoundly affected John's life and work, had had an even greater effect on Renée. Many of Renée Vivien's love sonnets, some of her invocations to death, were inspired by their relationship. The despair John felt rising from those poems, with their melancholy images of purple violets, may have come from her torment over Natalie's infidelities. On one occasion when Natalie was away, Renée, hearing a false rumour that she was about to marry, tried to commit suicide. After two further attempts she was given emotional and financial security by a rich baroness, but when Natalie suggested in 1904 that Renée run away from the Baroness and escape with her to Lesbos, Renée did so. Restless like John, Renée wandered through Europe, Asia, Turkey, Hawaii. Turbulent affairs did not interfere with her prolific writing: between 1901 and 1909 she wrote fourteen volumes of poetry, most of which John read, three volumes of short stories, two novels, and a translation of Sappho into modern French. Towards the end of her life she shut herself up in her apartment at 23 Avenue Bois de Boulogne, nailed the windows down, filled the rooms with Buddhas and incense, and became increasingly alcoholic and anorexic.

Report had it that Renée had actually died less from starvation than from love of Natalie. Janet Flanner,* whom John met at Rue Jacob, was a particularly harsh critic:

> Once Natalie had been out all night and thought about Renée Vivien on the way back home: 'Oh, she's been so ill, I'd better stop and say good morning to her.' And she found a florist shop open . . . she bought an enormous bouquet of *white* violets . . . The butler [at Renée's] eventually answered the bell . . . She said: 'How is she this morning?' offering the white violets. And he said: 'Oh, what tact Mademoiselle has. She has just this minute died, and they're *white* violets. *Quelle chance pour vous, Mademoiselle, ça tombe si bien.*'[17]

Other close friends believed that Natalie never got over Renée's death. Whatever the truth, John's interest in Vivien lay above all in her literary rendering of the lesbian as outcast. Fascinated by her, she went with Una to Vivien's grave on 20 October to take photographs. And as she wrote, the sense of Renée Vivien's tragic vision, centred on alienation and exile, powerfully permeated her own novel.

During her Paris research for *The Well*, a lighter and more caustic view of lesbian life was revealed to John by her meeting with Djuna Barnes at another of Natalie's parties.[18] In the self-referential manner of many of Barney's literary circle Djuna used most of Natalie's friends, including John and Una, as characters in her satirical *roman à clef* of the Parisian expatriate lesbian set, *Ladies Almanack*.

* Best known for her famous 'Letter from Paris', signed pseudonymously Genêt, contributed to the *New Yorker* between 1925 and 1975.

Natalie herself figures as Evangeline Musset whose biography this *Almanack* purports to be. Patience Scalpel is Mina Loy, the token heterosexual in the Barney crowd. Senora Fly-About (One of Buzzing Much to Rome) is John's friend Mimi Franchetti, the black sheep daughter of a noble Italian family. John's other friend Dolly Wilde, Oscar's niece, becomes Doll Furious. Journalist Janet Flanner appears with her lover Solita Solano, drama editor of the *New York Tribune*, as Nip and Tuck, a pair of plucky journalists. Cynic Sal, who wore a man's top hat, was Romaine Brooks, and John and Una take the stage as the two British women in the *Almanack*'s month of March. Una becomes Lady Buck-and-Balk who sported a Monocle and believed in Spirits and John is satirized as Tilly-Tweed-in-Blood, who sported a Stetson and believed in Marriage. According to Barnes' lampoon Lady B-and-B and Lady T-T-in-B believed in Matrimony but only between women, and would do away with Man altogether.[19]

Barnes' characters speak in a curiously formal yet mocking way. There are verbal similarities between lines in *Ladies Almanack* and James Joyce's *Finnegans Wake*, parts of which Joyce had read aloud to Djuna Barnes during the twenties. Like Virginia Woolf's *Orlando* (the fourth lesbian narrative about to be published the same year as *The Well of Loneliness*, *Ladies Almanack* and Compton Mackenzie's *Extraordinary Women*) Barnes experiments with language. The way in which she plays with gender and explores sexual identification is diametrically opposed to Radclyffe Hall's realistic depiction.

The publication of homosexual texts at that time depended not only on their stylistic mode but also on their envisaged audience. A book like Djuna Barnes', whose audience was the same as its subject matter, could be printed in the equivalent of a limited edition. Underground lesbian documents of a 'cult' nature found publication more easily than straightforward novels like Hall's, which were written for a mainstream readership. As Djuna Barnes' satirical extravaganza addressed the women who were themselves the subject of the satire, she had less problem than Hall in finding a publisher. Robert McAlmon not only produced 1,050 copies in his Contact Editions, but as a gift to the author he also paid for the printing – done at the Darantière Press whose owner Maurice Darantière had printed *Ulysses* six years earlier. Natalie Barney also helped Djuna with the printing costs. It is possible that if John had run into serious publishing trouble Natalie might well have come to her aid too.

When John returned to England to continue the planning of *Stephen*, she intended to work calmly and carefully through 1927, but as January dawned, and she increased her output to twelve hours a day, Marie Visetti produced one of her costly emotional interruptions.

On 2 January John received an urgent phone call to say that her mother was ill with pneumonia at a Brighton hotel where she and Alberto had been staying for the New Year. John and Una rushed down to Sussex to discover that Marie's 'pneumonia' was merely bronchial catarrh. Unfortunately however she would need nursing care for some time. As Marie had just fired her servants, John could not send her home but had to hire a specially heated ambulance to take Marie to a nursing home in Kensington.

Una had always felt that the 'ghastly old folk' interrupted John's work and drained her pocket, but this time they taxed to the limit John's considerable patience. Alberto and Marie's affairs were in chaos. No bills had been paid at Phillimore Terrace, the lease had expired, there was no life insurance policy, Marie had spent £70 a time on clothes, and to John's horror the Visettis had used up most of the capital left to them by Granny Diehl and Aunt Mary. John did all she could to set matters straight, only to be harangued, yet again, by Marie.

John allowed some of her repressed anger to seep into a bitter letter to her cousin Winifred:

> The whole business has shocked me beyond words . . . Albert is just frankly dishonest and . . . always has been . . . my mother has developed into a worse fury than she used to be and that's saying a good deal . . . Are they both mad? I don't know. I only know that their house has such a dreadful name that no decent servant will go near it . . . I literally feel in despair.[20]

As Marie recovered so did John, but it was only a temporary respite. On 23 January Alberto's temperature reached 104° as severe flu set in. When Marie refused to nurse him, and with no 'decent servants' to hand, John felt impelled to hire and pay for two nurses before she and Una started taking a precautionary look at hotels and flats for Marie. When they returned to Phillimore Terrace in the evening, according to Una, 'all seemed well except Marie's temper'. Alberto's relapse on 25 January forced them to suffer that temper. Hardly had they arrived home when Marie's nurse rang to say that Marie had been so vile that she was leaving at once. When John telephoned her mother, Marie put the phone down.

That was it! John had suffered enough. She talked to Marie's doctor to see if Marie was going insane. He assured her that Mrs Visetti was well this side of sanity but that her already uncontrollable temper was inflamed by jealousy over John's literary success. Any word of it brought on her mother's towering rages. The doctor advised John, if possible, to avoid seeing her mother. John wrote furiously to Winifred: 'No grown up woman could allow herself to be abused & insulted as I have been lately – such a state of affairs is unseemly between mother and daughter, and I'm done with it for good and all.'[21]

For one of John's compassionate nature, it was difficult to make the complete break she now planned. In her letter to Winifred, who was often at odds with her own mother, Jane Caruth, John said: 'I want her [Jane] to love you, because I have so often felt the bitterness of having no mother.'[22] That said, she employed one of her habitual strategies for dealing with difficult situations. She paid her mother off. She told Marie and Alberto that she would pay them a monthly allowance on condition that all communication between them ceased. The Visettis did not argue the point.

As always, writing became John's salvation. By the end of March 1927 she had almost finished nine chapters. Una herself had for some time been producing a great deal of skilled literary and artistic material, including book jackets, book reviews, and regular editing work. Her translation of Charles Pettit's *Le Grand Eunuque* had been published in America, had run to a second edition by 26 July 1927 and would be published in Britain in August. A few months later, in demand as a translator, she agreed to translate Pettit's *La Chinoise Qui S'Emancipe* for the New York publishers Boni & Liveright. At its successful publication she was interviewed by the press. By birth and education more intellectual and artistic than John, she must have appreciated getting some of the limelight, her own career as a sculptor and writer long since subordinated to her partner's work.

During the summer of 1927 John and Una returned to Bagnoles and Paris, saw Natalie and Colette, while John collected more material. She had now written twenty-seven chapters of *Stephen* which by November had become *The Well of Loneliness* – a title which, as Lovat Dickson says, was 'another of Una's inspirations'. As 1927 drew to its end, Carl Brandt arrived to talk enthusiastically to John about *The Well*'s chances in America.

As John's writing patterns grew more intense in the first few months of 1928, Una and Andrea were thrown together more than usual. On 5 April they arranged Masses for Ladye, then attended the first night of *Thunder in the Air*. On their arrival home they found that John had finished *The Well*. Una took Andrea to Datchet the following day so that John could revise in peace. The revisions were completed on 10 April. They bound four copies, took three to Audrey on the 17th who delivered them the next day to Newman Flower. John felt none of the doubts or misgivings which often attacked her at a book's conclusion. She was in high spirits, ready for battle.

John's negotiations with publishers for *The Well* were wary but defiant. On 16 April she wrote to Flower:

> No doubt had I wished to I could have signed on with Cassells prior to your reading *The Well of Loneliness*. But . . . since you were the first publisher to appreciate my serious work, and also because of our personal friendship . . . I did not want you to put your name to a contract before you had fully grasped the nature of the book with all its serious import . . . the more so as . . . *I could not consent to one word being modified or changed*.

She went on to say that she had undertaken the novel at the promptings of her heart; it was a book she had 'long had in mind'. Now that she had 'attained literary success' she felt she could put her pen 'at the service of some of the most persecuted and misunderstood people in the world'. 'Nothing of the kind,' she believed, 'has ever been attempted before in fiction.

> Hitherto the subject has either been treated as pornography, or introduced as an episode as in [Rosamond Lehmann's] *Dusty Answer*, or veiled as in [Clemence Dane's] *A Regiment of Women*. I have treated it as a fact of nature – a simple though, at present, tragic fact. I have written the life of a woman who is a born invert, and have done so with what I believe to be sincerity and truth; and while I have refused to camouflage in any way, I think I have avoided all unnecessary coarseness.[23]

John added persuasively that she might be able to obtain a foreword from Havelock Ellis who had written to Carl Brandt to say that if her book 'could do anything to help the cause of these unfortunate people it would have his very sincere good wishes'. John had recently met Havelock Ellis through publisher Roger Scaife, and since that meeting had corresponded with Scaife who had sent her a volume of Amy Lowell's poems which John exclaimed over: 'I think many of the poems quite beautiful . . . Her real genius comes out in the unrhymed verses, some of which remind me of Sappho.'[24] Their shared appreciation of Lowell encouraged John to think – misguidedly as it turned out – in terms of Houghton Mifflin, Scaife's company, as an appropriate American publisher.

John told Flower that she needed a fast decision because she wanted her novel published in England in the autumn to avoid interference from the forthcoming General Election:

> I need not say how sorry I should be to sever my connection with Cassells, but unless you feel . . . that you are prepared to go all out on it and to stand behind it to the last ditch, then for both our sakes, as also for the sakes of those for whom I have written, please don't take it.[25]

Flower wrote back to Audrey on 23 April: 'As a piece of literary work this is one of the finest books that has gone through my hands, but unfortunately it is not a book we can publish. It would, I feel sure, do a lot of harm to our other books here.'

He tried to soften the blow in two ways. Firstly he pointed out that Cassells was not an appropriate house. As it mainly supplied circulating library fiction, this was doubtless justified. Secondly he assured Audrey, knowing his words would be passed on:

> I cannot tell you how distressed I am that she should be passing from us. I have had great pride in her work . . . but naturally Miss Radclyffe Hall writes what she feels she wishes to write, and one cannot blame her. She is a great artist and I take my hat off to her.[26]

The great artist meanwhile was hunting down an elusive Havelock Ellis. John wrote a persuasive letter asking Ellis to give her novel 'in a few words the support of your unassailable knowledge and reputation'. It would, she felt, prevent the book from being taken up as a 'salacious diversion'.[27] When Ellis met John and Una, whom he described as formidable, fierce, 'terribly modern & shingled & not at all Faun's style', his personal interest as well as his professional curiosity was aroused.[28] He agreed to write an 'Opinion' that John could quote provided he liked the novel.

Audrey sent the book next to Heinemann. Charles Evans declined with the words: 'We have arrived at this decision . . . very reluctantly . . . *The Well of Loneliness* contains some of Miss Radclyffe Hall's best work . . . indeed, dealing with the childhood of Stephen is as fine a thing as has been done in our time.'[29] Although neither Evans nor his colleagues found 'anything to object to' in the way the subject was treated, they knew the book would be regarded as propaganda and that its publisher would meet a chorus of fanatical abuse which, though unjustifiable, would undoubtedly harm them. He asked Audrey to tell John that the novel had profoundly moved them and that he really regretted 'our courage is not as great as hers'.[30]

Martin Secker also lacked courage. He said he was immensely impressed with John's gifts, and would willingly publish a future novel of hers, but not this one. The reason he gave was that it was not 'a commercial proposition'; the reason he slyly withheld was that in the autumn he intended to publish another lesbian novel, *Extraordinary Women* by Compton Mackenzie.

Mackenzie's novel is a virulent satire on the lesbian colony he had observed in Capri. Each chapter is headed ironically with a quotation from Sappho and Mackenzie proceeds to mock the cult of the lesbian goddess as followed first by Natalie Barney and Renée Vivien and later by Ethel Smyth, who is wickedly depicted in the novel as composer Olimpia Leigh. Mackenzie himself admitted that most of his characters were exact depictions of real people, with John and Una at the forefront.[31] Madame Hermina de Randan has the 'finely cut profile', the inherited wealth, and hobbies like 'spiritualism and gardening and collecting old furniture' of Radclyffe Hall and is an intimate 'friend' of Madame Anastasia Sarbecoff, based on Una.

To the portrait of Hall, Mackenzie adds several spurious suggestions: that Hermina/John 'displays openly the animosity and scorn she had always felt for a man'; that her work for the Society for Psychical Research had to be rescued from the 'aspersions of male investigators'; and that she, Madame Hermina de Randan/Radclyffe Hall, was 'deficient in humour'[32] – the last a criticism still regularly applied to lesbians, and one which brings as little consolation to women today as it did to Radclyffe Hall at the time.

Mackenzie's misogynist romp in no way conflicted with John's serious intentions in *The Well* but, although Martin Secker knew that, John did not.

Audrey decided to send the manuscript next to Jonathan Cape who with his partner George Wren Howard had launched the company in 1921. By 1928 Cape had a prestigious list, including among his authors Sinclair Lewis, Ernest Hemingway, Mary Webb and Henry Williamson, who were guided by London's finest editor Edward Garnett. Unlike Cassell or Heinemann they did not rely entirely on library sales but sold directly to the public through book-stores.

Jonathan Cape, self-made, with a sharp instinct for a commercial proposi-tion, also had literary flair and a persuasive manner with authors. He it was who captured the writers, whilst Wren Howard, a shy Hampstead man with excel-lent taste, gave the Cape books their distinctive elegant appearance. Agents admired Cape's profitable, adroit, albeit unpredictable strokes which had fast become a legend in publishing. A typical move had been his success in pub-lishing an abridged version of T.E. Lawrence's *Seven Pillars of Wisdom* which sold over 30,000 copies in under three months. Radclyffe Hall's novel was made for Cape's list.

On 8 May John, Una and Audrey met Cape for lunch at the Berkeley Grill where he set out his noticeably cautious strategy for publishing *The Well*. He agreed to John's autumn date; offered a larger than usual advance of £500 (compared with £100 paid by Cassells for *Adam's Breed*); but proposed a limited edition of 1,250 copies priced at twenty-five shillings each, three times the cost of an average novel. If the book 'caught on' (by which he meant, though he did not say, without attracting the attention of the police) he would produce a larger cheaper edition. He pointed out that he was taking a huge financial risk, but that this exceptional price would keep the book out of reach of sensation mongers. On those grounds John accepted his offer and signed the contract with Cape on 11 May.

That same day Havelock Ellis told John he had read half the book and was sure he could write an 'opinion' in its support. On 15 May Ellis's 'opinion', now termed a 'Commentary', arrived.

> I have read *The Well of Loneliness* . . . Apart from its fine qualities as a novel by a writer of accomplished art it possesses a notable psychological and sociological significance . . . it is the first English novel which presents, in a completely faithful and uncompromising form, various aspects of sexual inversion as it exists among us today . . . The poignant situations . . . are here set forth so vividly . . . yet with such complete absence of offence, that we must place Radclyffe Hall's book on a high level of distinction.

John's verdict was that it was 'perfect'. One can see why. Ellis had praised her literary talent and her 'scientific' accuracy, which would be the two fronts on which she fought for her novel. Jonathan Cape agreed it was good[33] but sug-gested changing the phrase 'various aspects of sexual inversion' to 'an aspect of sexual inversion' on the grounds that Ellis's term could be interpreted as including male homosexuality which was a criminal offence. On Ellis's agreement Cape, agitated about the word 'inversion', amended the phrase to read 'one particular aspect of sexual life'.

When Cape placed Ellis's 'Commentary' at the front of the novel like a Preface, Ellis took umbrage. John apologized to Ellis. All parties diplomatically declared it had been a misunderstanding. Cape meanwhile changed his plans again and decided to print 1,500 copies of an unlimited edition, reducing the price to fifteen shillings and leaving the type set up for more copies if necessary.

In America as in England it had been hard to find a publisher. Bernice Baumgarten in the Brandt office suggested Doubleday, who had done 'everything they could to put over *Adam's Breed*',[34] but Doubleday turned it down. Audrey Heath thought there was 'a moral obligation to let Scaife have a chance on it for Houghton Mifflin, as it was through him that John got in touch with Havelock Ellis'.[35] However neither Brandt nor Heath held out much hope, as Houghton Mifflin was based in Puritan Boston where – after Scaife had reluctantly turned it down – Carl told John 'the Boston Watch and Ward Society would make it impossible for him to publish'.[36] Roger Scaife, 'honestly distressed', wrote to John suggesting that although she doubtless welcomed the hostility that her novel was bound to arouse, his company would do her a 'poor service' by publishing.[37]

Wearily Brandt tried Harpers who 'came close to taking it' but not close enough.[38]

Suddenly Blanche Knopf, the small dynamic wife and partner of American publisher Alfred Knopf, appeared in London, where at a Heinemann reception she met Radclyffe Hall. Blanche, who scoured Europe for intellectually adventurous novels, liberal non-fiction, poetic or experimental literature, immediately asked Hall who was publishing *The Well* in America. When Blanche learned that no contract had yet been drawn up, she asked if she might have a two-week option. That night John and Una delivered the manuscript to her at the Carlton Hotel. The book, though it handled sex, which Knopf generally did not, was very much an avant-garde novel, which was just in Knopf's line. Knopf offered Carl Brandt a contract on 8 June.

Four days later there were 'a thousand alarms and excursions'. The contract contained a clause by which the author was to be held solely responsible, financially and legally, for any difficulties, delays or expenses arising in connection with publication. In other words, in return for her 15 per cent royalty and no advance (considerably lower terms than usual) she was to be held legally responsible for any action taken against the book by the American authorities.

John's condition for any publisher of this novel was that they should stand heart and soul behind her book. Knopf were not doing so. The vista of endless legal costs and waste of time flew before John's eyes, minutes before she herself flew into a rage. She instructed Audrey and Carl to give Knopf until 22 June to withdraw the offending clause. If they failed, the novel would be submitted to Harcourt Brace. By 21 June Knopf had not yielded. John's anger expressed itself in an extraordinary letter to Brandt:

> My patience is completely at an end. It is not that I do not like Mrs Knopf person-ally, I do; but I am accustomed to dealing with men in business, to going perfectly straight for a point, and above all to sticking to essentials. I find it both difficult and tedious to deal with a woman, and this I have several times told her quite frankly, asking her to settle all business details with my agents. The trouble is she has a great hankering for 'the personal touch', and this I consider a great mistake . . . if her methods are somewhat unusual and tortuous, I put it down to the fact that she is a woman, and that in many cases it is better for women to keep out of business negotiations.[39]

Had John forgotten that her 'beloved Robin', the highly esteemed Audrey Heath, was a woman? – that she herself was a sharp business woman as well as a successful writer? She had certainly forgotten anything she had learnt from Natalie Barney about sisterly solidarity. That night, in martyred mood, John asked Una to read aloud the unpublished parts of Oscar Wilde's *De Profundis*, the long poem he had written in Reading Gaol.

Before any further histrionics could occur, Knopf complied with the dead-line. John then instructed Bernice Baumgarten to check all the Knopf proofs to ensure that not one word was different from the original. Her novel, she believed, was too important to be softened or changed. Usually when she deliv-ered one novel she had already embarked on the next. Her immersion in the present book was total: she oversaw the smallest detail of its production.

On 8 July John sent Alfred Knopf a crayon head of herself – drawn by Charles Buchel – for publicity purposes. She asked them to avoid the black profile silhouette used by Doubleday: 'I became superstitious about the black thing and began to think it unlucky.' She also enclosed some lines about her reasons for writing *The Well* and hoped they would 'consider it wisest and more dignified to confine your publicity rather to matters connected with the book, than to such things as my dress, appearance, recreations and personal habits'.[40]

Knopf planned the American edition to coincide with Cape's publication in the autumn, but in July, again without warning, Cape changed his plans. He now intended to move publication forward to 27 July, a mere three and a half weeks away. He had discovered Secker's scheme to bring out Mackenzie's *Extraordinary Women* in Britain with a simultaneous publication in America by Vanguard Press.

Even prior to September 1928 (when Mackenzie's novel was published and to John's chagrin no legal action was taken against it) John felt threatened. She assured Cape that she trusted him to 'do the best . . . to defeat our rivals and steer *The Well of Loneliness* to success'. She made clear that in general she 'despised authors who paid for publicity and thus took an advantage over their poorer brethren' but because of these 'exceptional circumstances' she was prepared to make an unprecedented deal with Cape by adding £150 of her own money to Cape's £300 publicity budget. 'I thought on this one occasion it seemed only fair to myself, to my book and its courageous publisher.'[41]

The courageous publisher wrote to Audrey that 'it would be unwise to give it [the book] undue prominence . . . [as it] might have the effect of creating a wrong impression in the minds of the public.' The pragmatic Cape then swiftly accepted John's offer.

John's second protective measure was to cable Carl Brandt urging him to persuade Knopf to hasten their American publication. Carl did not believe *Extraordinary Women* would harm *The Well* whilst an early publication date might damage their publicity prospects. John remained firm. Reluctantly Knopf agreed to publish in October.

On 10 July – at precisely the point when Cape switched his plans and John was at her most fragile – with the Visettis' usual nicety of timing John's once feared, always despised stepfather Alberto Visetti died. John went to see the corpse moved and was 'abominably received' by her mother. Despite this she was left to handle the funeral arrangements for the body of the man whose hands on her own body she had never, in all those years, forgotten. Her misery during those few days was somewhat offset by a joyous telegram from Andrea on 9 July to say she had passed Responsions. She was ready for Oxford.

In the few weeks left before publication John worked hard on her literary friends to contribute reviews that showed a 'proper spirit, the spirit of desire for impartial justice and understanding towards an unhappy and very unfortunate section of the community'.[42]

Leonard Rees responded by asking Ida Wylie to submit a review for the *Sunday Times*. John admitted to Una's brother-in-law J.L. Garvin that it 'would be childish of me to pretend that I do not know how much your support in the *Observer* would contribute'. Her subject might be met with prejudice but she felt that prejudice could not 'enter into the judgement of a mind such as yours'. Her parting note was wistful: 'Whatever may be your attitude as Editor of the *Observer* towards *The Well of Loneliness*, I shall be most anxious as a writer to hear from you as to your personal reaction to my two years of work.'[43]

The Well of Loneliness was published on 27 July. There were large advertisements in seven dailies. The novel blazed from the windows of all the bookshops diligently toured by John and Una. Andrea sensibly went off to Guide camp.

In accordance with Cape's policy of sober and careful publishing, he had sent review copies only to the quality dailies and serious periodicals. The first review, by novelist L.P. Hartley, was published in the *Saturday Review* on 28 July. The author's appeal, he said, 'is a powerful one, and is supported by passages of great force and beauty', but he felt she had spoilt it with her polemical passages.[44] On 2 August the *Times Literary Supplement* called it 'sincere, courageous, high-minded and often beautifully expressed'. Una the relentless diary-keeper said stoutly: 'a fine review'.

Meanwhile the novel was selling fast. W.H. Smith, Truslove and the Times Book Club had already run out of stock, a second edition was reprinting, when on 4 August Leonard Woolf reviewed it for the *Nation*. 'She is obviously a serious novelist who asks to be judged by high standards.' He judged the first part, Stephen's childhood up to her father's death, as very fine indeed but then he felt it lost its way, its emotional strength sacrificed to its propagandist goal.[45] Ida Wylie's review in the *Sunday Times* the following day, hardly surprisingly, was more complimentary. 'Radclyffe Hall writes with distinction, with a lively sense of characterisation, and with a feeling for the background of her subject which makes her work delightful reading. And, first and last, she has courage and honesty.' Ida did however share Leonard Woolf's reservation: the novel's controversial nature ran the risk of overshadowing the book's literary skill.[46]

On 9 August Arnold Bennett reviewed it in the *Evening Standard*. He mentioned that Havelock Ellis 'praises it for its fictional quality, its notable psychological and sociological significance, and its complete absence of offence. I cannot disagree with him.'[47]

John and Una however did not see Bennett's review that day for they had decided to motor to Rye at the invitation of Anne Elsner, a devotee of John's writing. They fell in love with Rye almost instantly. Its cobbled streets and historical associations, its quiet atmosphere was to become immensely important to John during the next decade. On their return they read the *Morning Post*'s 'fine review' which said:

> There can be nothing but respect and admiration for the author's handling of it [the theme]. Mr Havelock Ellis's brief commentary was not required to establish its challenge, which from the first pages emerges with a frankness free of offence and an increasing passionate sincerity.[48]

They drove over to Vere and Budge, intending to show them the reviews, but Vere's condition was in Una's words so 'very distressing' that literary excitement seemed inappropriate.

Another important review came through the intermediary of Winifred Holtby. Holtby, as well as being the author of three successful novels, was a director of the influential magazine *Time and Tide*, and intimate companion of Vera Brittain. Responsible for the periodical's book reviews, during the period 1927 to 1931 Winifred gave Vera Brittain seventy-five weekly book columns to write. Among the 1928 selection was Hall's book. Under the heading 'Facing

Facts' Brittain described Hall's story as a non-offensive, passionate yet restrained plea for the extension of social toleration, compassion and recognition to the 'biologically abnormal woman', who, because she possessed the tastes and instincts of a man, was often undeservedly treated as a moral pariah. With uncompromising force she continued:

> It may be said at once that *The Well of Loneliness* can only strengthen the belief of all honest and courageous persons that there is no problem which is not better frankly stated than concealed. Persecution and disgusted ostracism have never solved any difficulty in the world.

In the sanctimonious atmosphere of 1928 these were brave words, but Brittain, although she and Winifred stood unwaveringly by John before and during the trial, was also an acute and critical reviewer. In her detailed critique she raised concerns similar to those voiced by Leonard Woolf. John had attempted to dismiss Woolf's critique as an example of male disregard for lesbians (an odd remark in view of Leonard's wife Virginia's open love affair with Vita Sackville-West) but she was not able to level such a charge against Vera.[49]

Brittain questioned Hall's over-simplistic reliance on the Ellis model of inversion, and pointed out that there was much in the novel which could equally well account for a psychological or environmental basis for Stephen's inversion. She also focused on what is implicit throughout the novel: that Stephen's 'abnormal' boyishness could also be seen as the healthy preferences of any intelligent girl.

Among serious magazine reviews Con O'Leary in *TP's Weekly*, on 11 August, was sure 'the reader will agree with Mr Havelock Ellis . . . that "the poignant situations are set forth with a complete absence of offence"'.[50] It was becoming obvious that Ellis had done certain reviewers as well as Hall a good turn. On 17 August came the best review yet. The *Daily Telegraph* called it 'truly remarkable', and praised it as 'a work of art finely conceived and finely written'.[51]

Thus far the critics had treated the book seriously as a fine novel which attempted with honesty to present a subject otherwise taboo. Her prose had been accounted neither coarse nor trivial. Although discerning reviewers cavilled at the author's insistence on the reader's sympathy for those marked with the brand of Cain, not one critic expressed alarm that such a doctrine should be openly propagated.

Una felt surprisingly comfortable, John less so. She knew her talent only gave her a limited immunity. She was ready to be a great figure, a saviour of the persecuted, doomed by an unjust fate. Doom however seemed to be deferred. The literary winds seemed set fair for a moderate artistic success.

But not for long. On 18 August 1928 there was a notice in the *Daily Express* announcing that in the next day's *Sunday Express* the Editor would call for a certain book by a certain author to be suppressed. Names were coyly omitted. Excitement built up inside and outside Fleet Street. It was an anniversary like no other: one that John and Una had no wish to repeat.

The following day, 19 August, on the main features page of the *Sunday Express* appeared a startling photograph of the author. She was dressed in her gentleman's silk smoking jacket, her collar stiff and high, her bow tie black. One hand was in the newly constructed pocket of her skirt. The other hand held a burning cigarette. Readers knew she would let it burn to the end. She looked languid, elegant – with a hint of the haughty, the decadence of the dandy, a lingering memory of Beardsley and Wilde.

Alongside the photograph was a banner headline an inch and a half high: 'A BOOK THAT MUST BE SUPPRESSED'. Beneath it, James Douglas, *Sunday Express* Editor, launched himself in large type, ran to almost a whole page, and took five full-blown indignant columns to demand that the book, an 'intolerable outrage', be withdrawn from circulation.

His article was a disgusting display of sensational journalism. It was tub-thumping and sexually titillating, carrying biblical overtones not unlike passages from *The Well of Loneliness* itself. But where Hall's intentions had been sincere and sensitive, Douglas's motives were mercenary and malicious.

He called upon his readers to defend their country, to defend their religion, to protect their children and protect England's tradition of fine literature. He labelled homosexuality a plague, youth and children its victims, the British press its scourge. Douglas had sent Jonathan Cape a copy of the forthcoming article the Friday preceding the *Sunday Express* denunciation:

This pestilence [homosexuality] is devastating the younger generation. It is wrecking young lives. It is defiling young souls.

I have seen the plague walking shamelessly through great social assemblies. I have heard it whispered about by young men and young women who do not and cannot grasp its unutterable putrefaction . . .

This novel forces upon our society a disagreeable task which it has hitherto shirked, the task of cleansing itself from the leprosy of these lepers . . .

It is a seductive and insidious piece of special pleading designed to display perverted decadence as a martyrdom inflicted upon these outcasts by a cruel society. It flings a veil of sentiment over their depravity. It even suggests that their self-made debasement is unavoidable, because they cannot save themselves . . .

If Christianity does not destroy this doctrine, then this doctrine will destroy it . . .

It is meet and right to pity them, but we must also pity their victims. We must protect our children . . . I would rather give a healthy boy or a healthy girl a phial of prussic acid than this novel. Poison kills the body, but moral poison kills the soul . . .

Finally, let me warn our novelists and our men of letters that literature as well as morality is in peril. Fiction of this type is an injury to good literature. It makes the profession of literature fall into disrepute. Literature has not yet recovered from the harm done to it by the Oscar Wilde scandal. It should keep its house in order.[52]

There was no precedent in mainstream English literature for the sympathetic presentation of lesbianism. Many writers had written acceptable novels with lesbian themes, but all had carefully ensured that either the lesbianism was condemned or the mode of sexuality satirized. Douglas's outrage simply ran ahead of that of the presiding Chief Magistrate.

As Sir Chartres Biron would soon make clear to her, Hall's fatal flaws were that she had elected to make her characters attractive; that she had produced a document in which no lesbian was considered blameworthy, and had illustrated 'horrible tendencies' and 'unnatural offences'[53] as in need of sympathy, and moreover neither horrible nor unnatural.

As John had hoped, there was a noise, a mighty noise – in the press, in the courts, in the publishing houses, among the men and women of letters. As she had feared, she would have to be bold and unafraid, for the sounds and effects of that noise would not subside for years.

16

THE WELL

When the storm broke, an American journalist friend wrote to Radclyffe Hall: 'You have torpedoed the ark . . . therefore you mustn't be surprised that Mr and Mrs Noah have come out to see what's happened!'[1] She was not surprised, for as she told Gorham Munson, a literary scholar, six years later: 'I felt that I was about to undertake the task of a pioneer, and that I must therefore be prepared to face the consequences – frequently unpleasant – that accrue from most pioneer work.'[2]

Critics and defenders came out of the ark, two by two, four by four, growing in numbers, strength and vociferous chorus. Some brayed. Some howled. The *Sunday Chronicle* gulped: 'Amazing Story by a Woman'. Then it chattered incoherently about 'one of the hidden cankers of modern life' before it relapsed into modesty over who exactly the woman was or what exactly the book was called.

The *People* decided fantasy was far more intriguing than any attempt to keep a grip on truth. They invented a superb spy story about Scotland Yard secretly examining the country's lewdest book. One of the *People*'s daredevil reporters, who had tracked down and perused, at severe cost to his own pure soul, the book in question, was so appalled that he felt 'nothing could justify its publication'. Not a library in Great Britain, he was sure, would be able to face stocking it.[3]

But he was wrong. An immediate consequence of Douglas's condemnation was that the first printing sold out. Libraries and bookstores throughout the country demanded more copies. One library in London received six hundred inquiries on a single day.[4]

The *Daily Herald*, a Labour newspaper, strode confidently out of the ark ready to calm the raging waters and change the face of the debate. On 20 August Arnold Dawson, the literary editor, boomed:

> In this book there is nothing pornographic. The evil-minded will seek in vain in these pages for any stimulant to sexual excitement . . . Miss Radclyffe Hall has entirely ignored [the] crude and violent figures of sexual melodrama. She has given to English literature a profound and moving study of a profound and moving problem.[5]

Dawson countered the vitriol of the *Sunday Express* by suggesting that, if standards of hypocritical stunt journalism were invoked, then writers of the calibre of Sterne, Smollett, Swift, Defoe, even Shakespeare himself, would all have to be banned.

Two days later a respectable female chorus from the *Lady's Pictorial* piped up in Hall's defence: 'There is absolutely nothing in it to offend anyone; except, peradventure . . . the man or woman who is ready and willing to condemn everything they do not understand.'[6] On 25 August from the Great Outdoors came the sanguine voice of *Country Life*: 'The mature, the thoughtful and the open-minded will find in it much food for reflection, a window giving upon understanding, and a psychological study of profundity and pathos.'[7]

John, who was photographed in every paper – raffish cigarette between her teeth under wide-brimmed blue Montmartre hat – was devastated by Douglas's attack on inversion even more than his attack, by implication, on her. She wrote to her friend Fabienne:

> I know that those words have wounded many who cannot afford to be further wounded. If the result of the article is . . . to cause certain weaker souls to feel despair, perhaps even to drive them out of existence, then I hope that his day of reckoning will come when he stands face to face with his and their Maker.[8]

This letter firmly reiterated her view that inverts were normal in the sight of God. In her eyes, and in the eyes of her Maker, Douglas's attack was unChristian. In her first public interview with the *Daily Herald*, she enquired whether Douglas's conception of Christianity led him to think that because God permitted 'certain types' to be born they should be 'thrust aside or ignored'. In those few words lay the core of her defence. As sexual inversion existed it was a fact of nature. Inverts therefore must be offered the same compassion and toleration as non-inverts.

As her detractors took up arms against her sexuality, her fight took on the aspect of a religious crusade. There was a significant moral difference between her position and that of Douglas who believed that homosexuality was a 'contagion' that infected innocent people.[9] Her moral stance mattered not a jot to journalists but was everything to Radclyffe Hall.

The wily Cape, always one step ahead, remained the man of action not of reaction. The previous week he had ordered a second impression of 3,000 copies. On Monday 20 August he wrote to the *Daily Express* to defend his decision to publish *The Well*. His next step appeared to be impulsive but like the man himself was highly calculating. He wanted to clear himself with the law whilst keeping public interest focused on the novel. With this intention, he had submitted the book to the Home Secretary together with Douglas's article, a selection of the best reviews, and the suggestion that Sir William Joynson-Hicks give his opinion of *The Well*. If Sir William felt the publishers had been at fault, he, the obedient public servant, was ready to withdraw the book.

What the loyal citizen failed to do was to discuss his approach with John, or even to notify her of his plan. That Monday Cape was forced to tell her what he had done.

She was furious. In a towering rage she insisted on a heated meeting in his office. Cape pointed to the beneficial sales that would result from the publicity. John pointed to ethical considerations and the necessity for consultation between publisher and author. However there was little either of them could do except seethe silently and await the Home Office verdict.

When it arrived, signed by the obscenity authority himself, popularly known as Jix, its contents were not a surprise. He was a Christian fundamentalist who hated Communists and had a trigger reaction to 'immoral' literature. In submitting the novel to him Cape had made a grave misjudgement. Jix had concluded that no matter how 'well and artistically [the book] may have been written', it was 'inherently obscene . . . It deals with and supports a depraved practice . . . its tendency is to corrupt, and . . . it is gravely detrimental to the public interest.'[10] He reminded Cape that the book could be suppressed by criminal proceedings, but said he preferred, in view of Cape's letter, to allow him to withdraw it.

This unambiguous threat went beyond the Home Secretary's legal powers. Jonathan Cape, however, hoist on his own petard, had no option but to send a telegram to the printers to stop work on the reprint. Then he wrote to *The Times*:

> We have today received a request from the Home Secretary asking us to discontinue publication of Miss Radclyffe Hall's novel *The Well of Loneliness*. We have already expressed our readiness to fall in with the wishes of the Home Office . . . we have therefore stopped publication.
>
> I have the honour to be your obedient servant,
>
> Jonathan Cape.[11]

Such abject humility, such prompt obedience, seemed somewhat out of character. But the humble Cape had other plans up his sleeve. On 22 August he wrote to his printer: 'Please make moulds of the type as quickly as possible, and deliver them here. The type should be kept standing after moulding until further notice.' Cape then flew moulds of the type to Paris, sub-leased the rights to John Holroyd-Reece, an English language publisher, and proceeded through Holroyd-Reece's firm, the Pegasus Press, to solicit orders from English booksellers.

Cape's deviousness did Radclyffe Hall few favours. When the book came to trial, Cape's contradictory intentions and actions, unearthed by a sharp detective inspector who stolidly revealed them in the witness box, weighed heavily against *The Well*.

John, though beset by misgivings, gave in to Cape's plan. One reason was her determination not to allow her book to be suppressed, a purpose reinforced by the massive – and supportive – mailbag she was daily receiving from heterosexuals as well as homosexuals. Previously she had written to Gerard Hopkins, who had praised her novel, that she wanted to be the first person who had 'smashed the conspiracy of silence'.[12] Suddenly she saw herself as someone standing up for the freedom of the pen. 'On behalf of English literature,' she said firmly in her second interview for the *Daily Herald*, 'I must protest against such unwarrantable interference.'[13]

Her second reason for agreeing to Cape's new plan was that through Ida and Bill Temple she already knew John Holroyd-Reece socially. Even before Cape's proposal John had received a sympathetic call from Holroyd-Reece about *The Well*. On 28 September the book was reissued by Pegasus Press.

In England *The Well*'s withdrawal had motivated four major figures of English literature – Arnold Bennett, E.M. Forster, Virginia Woolf and Leonard Woolf – to rally to Hall's side. Arnold Bennett in his *Evening Standard* review had called the novel 'honest, convincing and extremely courageous'.[14] Forster, as the author of *Maurice*, a then unpublished (and unpublishable) homosexual novel, written in 1913, had a special interest in Hall's case. He visited her with a proposal. He and Leonard Woolf would be prepared to draft a letter of protest to be signed by as many influential literary personages as possible. Hall, appreciative, even a little overwhelmed, agreed with alacrity.

Behind the scenes Bennett and Forster gathered an impressive list of signatories, including Bernard Shaw, T.S. Eliot and Lytton Strachey.* John also acquired the support of Naomi Royde-Smith, author of the lesbian novel *The Tortoiseshell Cat* which, with Rosamond Lehmann's *Dusty Answer*, Gertrude Atherton's *The Crystal Cup* and Sylvia Stevenson's *Surplus*, was on a list of lesbian literature found amongst the trial papers.[15] Evidence suggests these novels were submitted by John and Una from their own extensive homosexual reading list.

Despite Bennett and Forster's hard work, John was distressed at the draft

---

* Other signatories included Lascelles Abercrombie, James Agate of the *Sunday Times*, Laurence Binyon, Vera Brittain, Ivor Brown, John Buchan MP, Robert Cust JP, John Drinkwater, Gerald Duckworth, Ashley Dukes, Edward Garnett, Victor Gollancz, Harley Granville-Barker, H.D. Henderson Editor of the *Nation*, A.P. Herbert, Laurence Housman, Professor Julian Huxley, Storm Jameson, Sheila Kaye-Smith, Rose Macaulay, Desmond MacCarthy, Violet Markham, John Middleton Murry, Eden Phillpotts, Sir Nigel Playfair, Logan Pearsall Smith, Dame Ethel Smyth and Hugh Walpole.

letter which stressed the legal aspects of literary suppression rather than the merits of her book. Always over-sensitive to criticism, she now saw traces of it everywhere. Had the *New Statesman* not appeared that week with a poor review of *The Well* by Cyril Connolly and an odious comparison of *The Well* with Compton Mackenzie's *Extraordinary Women*, she might have been more flexible in her dealings with Forster, or at least calmer. As it was she was neither.

The *New Statesman* reviewer had angered her most particularly with the words: 'It would be hard to find a novel more fanatical than *The Well of Loneliness* . . . What literary interest it has . . . is obscured by the constant stream of propaganda.'[16] Although the review of Mackenzie's book also contained some sharp barbs, calling it 'as dreary a tale as it is possible to imagine', nevertheless Mackenzie was congratulated for having 'the courage to offer a faithful description of a modern social disease'. Summing up its inquiry into which, if either, book should be withdrawn, the *New Statesman* concluded: 'The withdrawal of Miss Hall's book is not a very great loss, but the withdrawal of Mr Compton Mackenzie's book – so discreetly priced at one guinea – would be in our view a minor public misfortune.' In the mellifluous phrases of the *Statesman*, 'The Lesbian cult exists, but it is like those anaerobic bacilli which cannot endure fresh air.'[17] Hall saw the journal as preaching the same hostility as the *Daily Express*, and she was outraged.

It was at this point that Forster went to discuss with John the Bloomsbury Plan. Hall, still smarting from Leonard Woolf's tepid review of *The Well*, rejected his proposal outright. They clashed over intention, quibbled over words, bickered over meaning. Their argument spread through Kensington and Bloomsbury. Other writers were drawn in, forced to take sides. Virginia Woolf in an amusing letter to her lover Vita Sackville-West, who consistently urged her to support Hall, complained that her own inability to write at that moment was due to the eruption about 'your friend Radclyffe Hall (she is now docked of her Miss owing to her proclivities)'.

Virginia gave Vita her own version of events:

Leonard and Morgan Forster began to get up a protest, and soon we were telephoning and interviewing and collecting signatures – not yours for *your* proclivities are too well known. In the midst of this, Morgan goes to see Radclyffe in her tower in Kensington, with her love: and Radclyffe scolds him like a fishwife, and says that she won't have any letter written about her book unless it mentions the fact that it is a work of artistic merit – even genius . . . and now we have to explain this to all the great signed names – Arnold Bennett and so on.[18]

Forster and the Woolfs *did* explain but, as Virginia told Vita, 'our ardour in the cause of freedom of speech gradually cools, and instead of offering to reprint the masterpiece, we are already beginning to wish it unwritten.'[19] On Saturday 8 September Virginia, keeping Vita abreast of affairs, wrote:

She [Radclyffe Hall] drew up a letter of her own, protesting her innocence and decency, which she asked us to sign, and would have no other sent out. So nothing could be done except indeed one rather comic little letter written by Morgan Forster, which he asked me to sign; and now it appears that I, the mouthpiece of Sapphism, write letters from the Reform Club![20]

A letter to the Editor protesting against the banning of *The Well of Loneliness* signed by E.M. Forster and Virginia Woolf did in fact appear in the *Nation and Athenaeum* of 8 September. They used *The Well* as a stepping stone to alert readers to other themes that might be rendered taboo, such as pacifism, birth control and suicide. Both Woolf and Forster felt strongly that to create great literature a 'free mind' was a necessity and their major objection was to the obstacle suddenly posed to free minds. About the negative response to lesbianism, they were (in Hall's view) far too detached. In fact they downplayed its effect, even its occurrence: 'It enters personally into very few lives, and is uninteresting or repellent to the majority.' A sentence of that ilk from two literary lions, who happened to be a homosexual and a lesbian, could only seem to Radclyffe Hall as niggardly backtracking.[21]

Hall next complained to Arnold Bennett that the Forster version not only omitted the moral integrity of the book but also compromised Bennett's published perception of *The Well*. 'I do not *want* the support of anyone who will not vouch for the decency of my book,'[22] she told Bennett. This put her fellow author in a quandary. Remaining supportive in public, to Forster he was less enthusiastic about *The Well*'s long-term literary value. To Hall he hedged his bets. He told her that although he stood by both the merits and decency of the book, he felt comfortable signing the Forster draft 'because it enabled certain other, more timid persons to sign'.[23]

Although Hall and the Bloomsbury writers believed in many of the same principles, their methods of dealing with them, even of thinking about them, were diametrically opposed. Bloomsbury's writers and philosophers held most things at bay with an amused and abstract detachment. They liked spinning ideas, juggling truths, catching evasions, netting improprieties, ridiculing the establishment. Hall, though a complex creature herself, was by comparison simplistic and straightforward. The notion of overlapping truths did not interest her. The barbarity of suppressing 'the Truth' did.

Several things are clear. First, Hall's unambiguous stand on lesbianism, both in personal terms and as a literary theme, conflicted with the intellectual complexity of Bloomsbury's multi-layered sexualities. Secondly, Hall's openness rattled both Forster and Woolf. Forster was a discreet homosexual and an indiscreet misogynist, while Virginia Woolf was a 'married lesbian' whose marriage protected her public image, despite the important love affair she was conducting at that very time with Vita Sackville-West, also married. The significant difference as lesbians between Virginia Woolf and Radclyffe Hall was that Woolf felt her lesbianism as an emotional and sometimes sexual orientation but not as a political identity. For Radclyffe Hall, her inversion was both a personal and increasingly a political identity.[24]

Forster's support was also complicated by a compound of literary arrogance and homosexual insecurity. Under the influence of too much alcohol at a weekend party at Rodmell, the Woolfs' Sussex home, Forster allowed his equivocal feelings to erupt. He complained that Hall had 'screamed like a herring gull, mad with egotism & vanity'. Then he let slip that he was far from tolerant towards lesbianism. He told Virginia that it disgusted him and that he knew a Dr Henry Head* who could 'convert' lesbians. When Leonard Woolf challenged him about his own homosexuality, Forster admitted that *he* would not want to be converted. His distaste for lesbians it appeared was rooted in his disapproval of the idea that 'women should be independent of men'.[25]

It says much for Virginia Woolf's sang-froid that she remained ironic. For she was after all one of those discreetly 'disgusting' creatures, then in the throes of her complex relationship with that other 'disgusting' creature for whom she had composed *Orlando*.

Virginia Woolf did not think *The Well* was a great book. Her reaction to Hall's novel was ambivalent and changeable. She told Roger Fry that Hall's novel was 'so pure, so sweet, so sentimental, that none of us can read it'.[26] To Lady Ottoline Morrell she wrote: 'The dulness of the book is such that any indecency may lurk there – one simply can't keep one's eyes on the page.'[27] To her sister Vanessa Bell, she wrote: 'I think much of Miss Radclyffe Hall's book is very beautiful. There is the old horse – that is wonderful . . . she shoots the horse herself. That is beautiful . . . she is wonderfully clever.'[28]

Whatever their private misgivings, both Forster and Virginia Woolf staunchly opposed the banning of *The Well*. In their letter to the *Nation and Athenaeum* they quibbled with the authorities, defiantly seeking loopholes in the official stance. Although lesbianism was forbidden as the central focus of a novel, could novelists allude to it? Would it be possible to ascribe lesbianism to one's minor characters? Hermione Lee in her biography of Virginia Woolf emphasizes that both Virginia Woolf and Forster were protesting against the Home Secretary's censorship on the grounds of the novel's lesbian theme rather than for its supposed 'indecency'.[29] She and Forster attempted to widen the issue. 'What of the other subjects known to be more or less unpopular in Whitehall, such as birth-control, suicide and pacifism? May we mention these? We await our instructions.'[30]

Public support for Hall's cause continued to pour into Holland Street. Private support came as always from Ida Wylie, and from her chums Toupie,

---

* Coincidentally, Dr Head had earlier been consulted by Virginia in his role as a neurologist during her depressive illness in 1913.

Fabienne, Susan and Etheline. In and around Rye they called on newer friends Noël Coward, Sheila Kaye-Smith and a lesbian couple Wilma and Dickie. With these friends they talked over the case and read the fanmail. John told Oliver Baldwin, the homosexual son of Prime Minister Stanley Baldwin, that her postbag (400 letters on one day alone)[31] encouraged her 'to stand the racket of having told the truth'. She would go on 'telling the truth and the truth and the truth whenever opportunity offers'.[32]

Opportunities were about to present themselves, for the Knopf edition in America was scheduled for publication in October, and by 28 September large shipments of the Pegasus Press edition were reaching England from Paris. Then suddenly Knopf, in Una's phrase, 'ratted' on them. In mid-September Blanche Knopf, *en route* back to America from Europe, had sent John a postcard which promised 'full steam ahead'.[33] But in her absence Alfred Knopf became anxious that the British ban on the book had irrevocably changed the novel's image. The Knopfs, afraid of the fire, wished to remove themselves from the heat. Blanche wrote to John:

> I am convinced that . . . we could never avoid selling it as a dirty book, which is the last thing you or any of us want to see happen . . . We are thus faced with the hopeless prospect of attempting to defend a book which has not been defended in its author's own country.[34]

'Darling Robin' was despatched to New York to help Carl Brandt extricate their author and her rights from the collapsed contract. Jonathan Cape negotiated to take over *The Well*'s American rights and eventually settled on a progressive publisher Donald Friede, head of a new American firm Covici Friede. On 27 November John accepted the offer from Covici Friede who published *The Well* on 16 December.

When John and Una finally met Donald Friede, Una wrote to Audrey Heath: 'I do like Friede very much and think that as US publishers go he is quite decent and honest . . . He . . . seems very staunch about *The Well* and their determination to fight to the end.'[35]

In Paris, orders from English booksellers had exceeded Holroyd-Reece's expectations so he appointed Leopold Hill, a London bookseller, to act as his agent and distributor. A shipment of 250 copies sent to Hill was impounded as pornographic by the Customs at Dover, who had been tipped off by the *Daily Express*. John and Una rushed to Cape's office and insisted he telephone Holroyd-Reece, who assured John that he would fight the case all the way. John then engaged the services of Harold Rubinsten, a writer-lawyer, to defend the case of Pegasus Press if it came to a prosecution.

The *Daily Herald* again headed the field in Hall's support. In their 6 October edition, the literary warriors Bernard Shaw and H.G. Wells fiercely attacked the Home Office and the Customs seizure. Hall, also interviewed in the *Herald*, called the Customs' action 'an outrage against literature and an attack on personal freedom'. The newspaper pointed out that as no ban had yet been imposed on *The Well* and as no legal action had been taken against Compton Mackenzie's *Extraordinary Women* the Government had some explaining to do.

On 18 October, probably after consultation with the Metropolitan Police, Customs released the shipment. There was however little time for Hall to relax. A few days later, the police, using the 1857 Obscene Publications Act, obtained search warrants and reconfiscated the copies of *The Well* from the premises of Leopold Hill and another London bookseller.

Within days Cape's offices were raided too. This time the police only made off with one Cape edition and six Pegasus copies. When Hill and Cape came forward to claim ownership of the books, the police had already applied to the magistrates for summonses against both men to show cause as to why these books should not be destroyed. Cape and Hill had no recourse but to defend the book in the Magistrates' Court.

In London a warrant was served demanding Jonathan Cape's appearance at Bow Street on 9 November. In Paris at the Pegasus Press offices, orders for *The Well* poured in from all parts of the globe.

The trial of *The Well* for obscenity in 1928 focused the attention of the literary world on the question of literary freedom, but its open discussion of aspects of sexuality central to feminism made it also a watershed in cultural history.

Obscenity cases were not a new phenomenon in America or Britain. For several years publishers, editors and some authors had suppressed literary material even before it was published in order to avoid prosecution. James Joyce's *Dubliners*, with its implicit homosexual content, had been subject to many delays before its publication in 1914. The following year, D.H. Lawrence's *The Rainbow*, which contained a significant lesbian scene, was suppressed. In 1921 Lawrence produced a sequel, *Women in Love*, which narrowly avoided prosecution for its scene of Japanese wrestling between two naked men which, given the times, contained startlingly frank language and heavy homoerotic undertones. The paper *John Bull* called it 'A Book the Police Should Ban'. The same year had seen the trial for obscenity of Jane Heap and Margaret Anderson, who published the 'Nausicaa' episode of James Joyce's *Ulysses* in their *Little Review*: a case which showed that even heterosexual material was not above attack by the authorities.

In the Paris of the twenties, publishing, like art, had undergone considerable change. In 1922 Sylvia Beach, the owner of a small but imaginative radical Paris bookshop Shakespeare and Company, had brought out a limited edition (1,000 copies) of James Joyce's banned novel *Ulysses*. The New York Society for the Prevention of Vice seized copies of the literary magazine which serialized it and obtained its conviction. Such was Joyce's reputation that the book quickly became a cult, as Radclyffe Hall's *The Well of Loneliness* was about to become. Copies of *Ulysses* were smuggled into Britain from Paris by the intelligentsia, a foretaste of what would happen to *The Well*.

Lord Northcliffe, the pioneer of popular newspapers, the man responsible for many of the media prejudices against books like those of Joyce and Lawrence, had stated publicly that 'most of the ordinary man's prejudices are my prejudices and are therefore the prejudices of my newspapers.' Although he died in 1922, most of his prejudices lived on.

In view of these events Hall knew that the choice of defence lawyer was crucial. The *Ulysses* trial had shown her that defence counsel in obscenity trials were not necessarily tolerant of lesbianism. John Quinn, engaged to defend the allegedly lesbian editors Margaret Anderson and Jane Heap, told Ezra Pound that he had

> no interest at all in defending people who . . . stupidly and brazenly and Sapphoistically and pederastically and urinally and menstrually violate the law, and think they are courageous . . . The bugger and the Lesbian constantly think in terms of suits and defences.[36]

The 'Lesbian' Radclyffe Hall, like the 'Bugger' Oscar Wilde, had several times thought in terms of suits and defences, there being little other recourse open to her. However, an aspect of the problem which overshadowed Wilde's trial and came to the fore in the *Ulysses* trial was repeated in the case against *The Well*. Several eminent people prepared to defend liberty of expression did not wish to be seen to champion homosexuality; many who proclaimed liberal views in private were not prepared to stand up for them in public.

Of more than a hundred individuals in the arts, literature, medicine, science, the Church and Parliament whom Harold Rubinstein and John approached for support, half of them, in John's view, lacked the necessary spunk. Those who declined saying they had not read the book included the Bishop of Birmingham, Lord Beauchamp, the Archbishop of York, Robert Baden-Powell, Sir William Beveridge, Frank Swinnerton, and John's writer friend May Sinclair. Arthur Conan-Doyle had 'left for South Africa'; H.G. Wells had 'gone abroad', John Drinkwater declined on grounds of 'practical difficulties'.

Geoffrey Faber replied: 'I have publicly expressed my dislike . . . of any interference with the liberty of the press and of literature.' However, he added lamely, 'my position as the Head of a Publishing House prevents me from exercising the same freedom of expression where a particular book is concerned.'[37] Professor Gilbert Murray felt the novel had insufficient literary merit. He disliked police prosecutions of literature but thought this one might succeed. So he withdrew. Evelyn Waugh had not read the book and disliked legal proceedings. So he withdrew. Eden Phillpotts claimed to be a recluse and that the harsh light of a witness box would do him no good. So he withdrew.

Margaret Kennedy, author of *The Constant Nymph*, said her testimony, or indeed anyone else's, would be useless because the law on obscenity was ill-defined. Harley Granville-Barker said he did not feel 'sexual perversion a fit subject for art'.[38] G.B. Stern and James Agate both claimed illness as a reason for not volunteering. Lascelles Abercrombie, who believed 'the action taken against it . . . stupid and oppressive', declined to stand because of ill-health. He did not even read it.[39]

Bernard Shaw, despite his written views in favour of John's case, said he was too immoral to appear as a reliable witness for the defence. Arnold Bennett was another who did not follow up his written protests with a public stand, seeking his excuse in the lack of a clear definition of the word 'obscene'. The Act which then governed the matter defined as obscene any book that tended to 'deprave or corrupt' those whose minds were open to immoral influence. Bennett like Shaw felt such a definition was so broad that it could apply to the entire British public and would render any defence inadequate or impossible.

Virginia Woolf in a letter to Quentin Bell on 1 November summed up the literary scene:

> At this moment our thoughts centre upon Sapphism – we have to uphold the moral-ity of that well of all that's stagnant and lukewarm and neither one thing or the other . . . I'm just off to a teaparty to discuss our evidence. Leonard and Nessa[40] say I mustn't go into the box, because I should cast a shadow over Bloomsbury. Forgetting where I was I should speak the truth. All London, they say, is agog with this. Most of our friends are trying to evade the witness box; for reasons you may guess. But they generally put it down to the weak heart of a father, or a cousin who is about to have twins.[41]

The 'teaparty' was held at the studio of the architect Clough Williams Ellis. Among those present were Bernard Shaw, Rose Macaulay, Vita and Virginia herself who despite her caustic comments was loyally prepared to give evidence on behalf of the book. Her course of action was much influenced by Vita who remained throughout a staunch defender of John's. At some level her defence of Radclyffe Hall's public lesbian cause was a conspiratorial rose offered to her private lesbian lover Vita.

Not so loyal was John Galsworthy. 'I am not prepared to go into the witness box on behalf of Miss Radclyffe Hall's *The Well of Loneliness*,' he said. 'I am too busy a man, and I am not sure that the freedom of letters is in question.' This was a statement of appalling cowardice from the man who was not only a writer-friend of John's, but also the President of PEN, whose charter is based on the freedom to write and speak one's opinion. Hermon Ould, General Secretary of PEN, himself a homosexual, said he was 'sorry he could not make a stand' because to do so would imply that he was speaking for the whole of PEN.[42]

John's anger over what she saw as the PEN betrayal led her to resign from the PEN club on 20 November 1928.[43] Five days later her fury with Galsworthy and Ould had subsided sufficiently for her to reconsider. It was not until 19 September 1931 that John permanently resigned from PEN.

A major disappointment was Havelock Ellis. Her mentor's refusal to testify was couched in these words:

> I never have been in the witness box. There are two good reasons against it. The first is that I do not possess the personal qualities that make a good witness and would probably make a bad impression . . . The second is that being the author of a book on this very subject that has been judicially condemned, I am 'tarred with the same brush' . . . It is people of the highly conventional and respectable kind, & occupying a high position . . . who will be really helpful.[44]

Ellis's behaviour was characteristic. He was not a resolute man when faced with the full power of the law, as had been seen in the trial of his own *Studies in the Psychology of Sex* which had been banned from publication in Britain thirty years before. He had been happy to lend his supportive commentary to John's book but preferred to allow his mistress Françoise to attend the Bow Street hearing on his behalf while he stayed at home and read. That John tolerantly accepted his excuses and even judged them to be reasonable shows her great measure of respect for him.

Several of John's writer friends had reservations. Rebecca West was appalled at the Home Office action but did not feel this was a good case on which to fight censorship.

Fortunately there were many prestigious people who allowed their names to go forward without reservation. Violet Markham thought 'it a scandal that so fine and serious a work should be banned, especially in view of the amount of corrupt and degraded literature which circulates without hindrance'.[45] Hugh Walpole wrote directly to Cape: 'I admire Miss Hall's courage in writing [the novel] and would have admired yours in publishing it if you had stuck to it . . .'[46] To John and Rubinstein he was positive and enthusiastic: 'I am ready to go anywhere and protest against any censorship and if you want me at the court for that purpose I will gladly come.'[47]

Other writers and critics who followed the example of the Woolfs, Markham and Walpole included Vera Brittain, Winifred Holtby, E.M. Forster, Edward Garnett, A.P. Herbert, Sheila Kaye-Smith, Rose Macaulay, Naomi Mitchison, John Middleton Murry, Naomi Royde-Smith and Storm Jameson. Miss Jameson, one witness assailed by doubts, visited Virginia Woolf, whom she did not know, to enquire nervously whether or not they were expected to testify that *The Well* was great literature. 'No, there will be no need for that' was Virginia's sombre response.[48] Virginia, who wished that her protest rested on a more 'literary' book, had bouts of nervousness which made her ask whether 'for temperamental reasons' she could be one of the last witnesses to appear. She said she would appear if she was 'absolutely indispensable'.[49] Although in the event she and the other witnesses never gave testimony, depositions were taken from them which are still in the trial papers, Virginia Woolf's recording: 'In my opinion, *The Well of Loneliness* treats a delicate subject with great decency and discretion.'[50]

Other prominent figures from the Church and politics came forward. From publishing and journalism those willing to stand included Victor Gollancz, Gerald Barry, Editor of the *Saturday Review*, Desmond MacCarthy, Editor of *Life and Letters*, Caradoc Evans and Con O'Leary of *TP's Weekly*, and Arnold Dawson, Literary Editor of the *Daily Herald*. Laurence Housman of the British Sexological Society supported her. His Society invited John to speak after the trial but she declined on the grounds that her Catholic beliefs might conflict with some of their goals.[51]

Others seen as valuable to the cause included Robert Cust JP, Member of the London Morality Council, Charles Ricketts the Royal Academician, Oliver Baldwin MP and Professor Julian Huxley.

Among academics, Sir Michael Sadler, Master of University College, Oxford, declared the book a 'masterpiece'. To suppress it would, he thought, 'be contrary to the public interest. It is poignant, vivid, deeply felt. It is in the same category as Rousseau's *Confessions*.'[52] Psychologists, doctors and sexologists were also represented, among them Vaughan Sawyer, Kenneth Walker, Norman Haire and Una's Harley Street specialist Dr R. Gruber.

The trial papers reveal that attitudes towards lesbianism among scientists and psychologists differed widely. In September 1928 the *Lancet* had said: 'The fallacy of the book lies in the failure to recognise that strong attachments between members of the same sex occur as a phase of normal development.'[53] By contrast Dr Norman Haire testified that the invert is 'anatomically distinguished from the normal person'. He also suggested that 'homosexuality tends to run in families.'[54]

Sex reformer Dr Stella Churchill was passionate in John's defence. She had dined with John and Una on 26 October to discuss the case. Later, together with the Woolfs, she agreed to stand surety for Jonathan Cape and Leopold Hill should that be necessary. She also started a Defence Fund and sent John £30, which John, though appreciative, returned.

The views of many were summed up by psychiatrist Dr Karen Stephen. The novel, she said, was 'a seriously written piece of literature, and ought not to shock the ordinary novel-reading public. The fact that it deals with inversion in a serious spirit does not seem to me reason for suppressing it.' She did however feel that 'the support of a Freudian would probably be harmful rather than helpful.'[55]

To strengthen her case John had also solicited support from 'working people'. With the aid of the *Daily Herald* she had obtained signed protests from the South Wales Miners' Federation and the National Union of Railwaymen.

When the case came to court on 9 November between forty and sixty eminent personages sat in the well of the court willing to give evidence.* They were not called upon to do so. Sir Chartres Biron, the Chief Magistrate, an elderly man whom Harold Rubinstein later called 'pathologically boorish',[56] autocratically disallowed their testimony as irrelevant. Writers, artists, lawyers, doctors, scientists, politicians, and church officials were each and every one denied an opportunity of expressing an opinion.

One witness, one witness only, was allowed to give his views as to the merit of Radclyffe Hall's novel. That man was Chief Inspector John Prothero of the Metropolitan Police – hardly a literary hero.

Under the 1857 Act, potential defence witnesses did not have to be called. It was the owners of the books, and the premises where they were found, who were prosecuted, not the author, who could neither be directly represented nor summoned to give evidence. The onus of proof lay on the defendants, Cape and Holroyd-Reece having 'to show cause why the articles seized should not be destroyed'. And the Bench gave the verdict, as publishers did not gain the right to a jury trial until 1967.

The fact that John's counsel advised against her going into the witness box disturbed and angered her. She had a great deal she wanted to say. In a long document to Rubinstein she explained her reasons for writing *The Well* and for choosing fiction as her means, and emphasized her belief that the book contained not a single obscene word: 'I do not regret having written the book. All that has happened has only served to show me how badly my book was needed . . . I would not alter so much as a comma.'[57]

Since it was her book on trial she saw herself as the defendant. Oscar Wilde had declared, after the trials which had destroyed him were over: 'All trials are trials for one's life.'[58] That is exactly how Hall regarded this case.

Reluctantly she agreed not to appear, after extracting a promise that the defence would ensure the court knew she was not ashamed of her inversion, nor afraid of giving evidence in front of her fellow writers.

In the week preceding the trial, Una and John had tried to keep their spirits up. They went to Rye and walked on the Marsh on 5 November, then on the 7th they attended the opening night of their new friend Noël Coward's *This Year of Grace*. During that week, John read Virginia Woolf's *Orlando* (dedicated to Vita Sackville-West) which had just been published. Virginia Woolf's biography-novel attempted with serious playfulness to analyse and deconstruct the way literature shapes our expectations of life, at the same cocking a snook

---

* According to Una Troubridge there were 'fifty-seven witnesses in our favour'. Michael Howard, historian of the Cape firm, gave the number as forty.

at masculist notions of female sexuality and female creativity. Orlando, who changes sex and lives through several centuries, is a female erotic who cannot be tied down, either by gender or by time. Rebecca West hailed *Orlando* as a beautiful exploration which turned a 'dark jungle into a safe habitation for the spirit'.[59] If the dark jungle was antique male-dominated literary traditions or dark undiscovered places in psychology,[60] then Woolf was set on the same course as Radclyffe Hall, who had plumbed dark places in *The Well*, and Djuna Barnes who was exploring new areas of the jungle on her way towards *Nightwood*. Hall, Barnes and Woolf were all venturing through hitherto unexplored territory within the male literary world.

Radclyffe Hall must have puzzled at length as to why *Orlando* (like *Extraordinary Women*) did not come under the censor's ban. Called 'the longest and most charming love letter in literature',[61] it was an overt Sapphic portrait which even included photographs of the author's lover. But the difference between Woolf's sexual presentations and Hall's was that although same-sex desire in the form of eroticized relationships between women is fundamental to Woolf's writings, it is always emotional, elusive, imaginary or symbolic. The presence of Vita in *Orlando* is as much symbolic as real. For Hall realism is the core. Both Hall and Woolf explored gender and the role of the artist; both writers were in league against authority. But Woolf was a satirist, a fantasist, an experimentalist. Authority left her alone. They allowed her to be judged by her literary peers and by posterity.

Hall's book had no such good fortune. It was to be judged within a few days.

On the day itself, John and Virginia had a brief conversation concerning costs. The Woolfs, not realizing that there was no personal defendant in the case, offered to stand bail for John should that become necessary. Later Virginia described John as 'lemon yellow, tough, stringy, exacerbated'.[62] Virginia had a stronger connection with Una than with John, which gave her an additional motive for support. As children they had met frequently at parties, and their families were connected by friendship through Virginia's great-aunt Julia Cameron.

Bow Street Magistrates' Court on 9 November looked like a first night. So great were the crowds that a notice was placed on the door saying 'Court Full' long before the proceedings began.

John looked far from lemon yellow and stringy. Her cheeks were flushed, her hair newly cropped. She sat conspicuously at the solicitors' table wearing a blue-black Spanish riding hat, made familiar in many photographs, and a leather coat with an astrakhan collar and cuffs. The *Daily Herald* breathlessly described her features as 'refined and well-chiselled, the expression in the eyes being one of mingled pain and sadness'.[63] The sense of doom which had hung over Marguerite's childhood now seemed settled firmly on her shoulders. She would not have chosen to be a martyr but stood determinedly behind her cause.

Una sat in the public seats which were mainly occupied by women. According to Storm Jameson she looked 'abominably over-dressed and over-made-up'.[64] Perhaps she needed to hide behind some war-paint. This case would be hard too for Una; it placed their kind of love, as well as John's book, on trial. She hardly took her eyes off John.

Sir Chartres Biron, 'white-haired, clean-shaven, tight-lipped', who used a quill pen which sat neatly on his copy of *The Well of Loneliness*,[65] took the Bench. Virginia Woolf later described him as 'a Harley St specialist investigating a case. All black and white, tie-pin, clean-shaven, wax coloured & carved, in that light, like ivory.'[66] Rumours circulated through the court that Biron had been overheard at his club saying he thoroughly agreed with James Douglas.

Before him appeared the prosecution team Mr Eustace Fulton and Sir Archibald Bodkin, Director of Public Prosecutions, whose very presence indicated the seriousness of the case. Opposite them, the defence team was headed by Norman Birkett KC, the eminent red-headed counsel who with Mr Herbert Metcalfe represented Jonathan Cape. A young and eloquent left-wing barrister, James B. Melville, appeared for Leopold Hill, seconded by Mr Walter Frampton. The defence counsels had all been instructed by the solicitors Rubinstein & Nash.

It must have been apparent early on which way the judgement would go, for the term 'horrible practices' was used continuously as both magistrate and prosecution made it clear they strenuously objected to the idea that 'depraved' sexual experiences could elevate the spirit.

Chief Inspector Prothero was called first by Fulton. He described the seizure of the books, then was cross-examined by Metcalfe. When asked if he agreed with the *Times Literary Supplement* review which called *The Well* 'sincere, courageous, high-minded and often beautiful' he conceded courage and sincerity but changed beautiful to offensive. The offence lay in Hall's dealings with unnatural physical passion. That, thought Prothero, should be dealt with only by scientists and doctors. When asked by Metcalfe whether his views might alter if offered the evidence of the line of distinguished witnesses, Biron interrupted: 'I do not think that the OPINION of the witness would be of any great importance.' This was a clear indication of the magistrate's intended perspective.

Since under the Act the prosecution had to prove their points from the novel's text as well as its subject-matter, Fulton on re-examining Prothero discussed with him the parting between Mary and Stephen at a railway station. Although there was almost no evidence of physicality, Prothero remained firm in his belief that the parting conveyed 'a Lesbian and physical passion'. By this point the entire prosecution team and most members of the court were seeing lesbian passion skulking in every corner.

After the prosecution's closure, it was the turn of Birkett who had arrived at the court two hours late and never fully recovered his position. For a man at the top of his profession he displayed incredible ineptitude throughout the case. He both exceeded his brief and overturned his own defence by suggesting that *The Well* described only 'normal friendship' between two women: sentimental, not physical. Mary's was 'a schoolgirl crush transferred to adult life and innocent of sexual implications'.[67] Those who had read the novel were amazed. John was livid. Not only was it a claim impossible to substantiate, but it also undermined her whole purpose in writing the book.

Biron himself was equally incredulous: 'Do you say that [the novel] does not deal with unnatural offences at all?' Birkett answered: 'I say not.' Then possibly recognizing the hole into which he had just dug himself and his client, he switched positions. What he had meant was that 'nowhere is there an obscene word, a lascivious passage.'[68]

When Birkett attempted to call his notable witnesses he produced more trouble for John. He called Desmond MacCarthy to the stand, having failed to find his first witness Sir Julian Huxley. When he asked MacCarthy: 'Having read *The Well of Loneliness*, in your view is it obscene?' he was stopped by the magistrate. Biron refused to allow the question and ruled out 'opinions' or testimony from any other eminent witness. Virginia Woolf at least was relieved. Biron's view was that 'opinions' could not constitute evidence; his ruling alone would decide if this book was obscene. Perhaps if Birkett had asked a question that did not elicit an opinion, other witnesses might have been called. As it was, Birkett, the man of muddle and mistakes, was forced to listen to John haranguing him bitterly over lunch at the Waldorf Grill.

John, inflamed with rage, tearful and agitated, was vigorously supported by Una, John Holroyd-Reece and Harold Rubinstein. Birkett was to be allowed no further opportunity to wreck her case. John, galled into control, insisted that after the break he retract his words. She wrote later to Gerard Hopkins that Birkett's action had filled her with 'horror and despair'. That he had given a 'blatant denial of the physical aspects . . . [of] my study of inversion' made her feel her work 'was both shamed and degraded'. She told Hopkins that she had threatened Birkett that if he did not publicly retract his assertion, 'I would get up before anyone could stop me and tell the Magistrate the truth.'[69]

After the recess Birkett was obliged to issue a retraction – doubtless a humiliating procedure – concluding his remarks with a plea that the treatment of the book's theme 'is one which singularly accords with good taste and high artistic and literary merit'. Young James Melville made a better showing. He quoted George Moore on the difference between literature and pornography: that 'real literature' is concerned with 'description of life and thoughts about life rather than acts. It is the very opposite with regard to pornography.' Hall's book in his view was literature.[70] He suggested that *The Well* dealt 'straight with the matter but in a spirit of reverence'. It was not a book which 'glorifies indecent practices' but rather a book 'with a serious intention worked out properly' which does not 'excite libidinous thoughts but is an attempt to deal with a social question that exists'. The core of his defence was that phrase 'it exists'. Inversion is with us whether we like it or not. In Hall's novel

> there is not a word of praise or apology; the book accepts inversion as a fact in life, as a fact of nature, more, as a fact of God's own creation . . . It is a fact – as truly a fact as is the fact that in the law of nature the greater body attracts the less.[71]

Melville was a consummate performer and a hush fell as he finished. Una and John hoped he had swayed Biron to their side. The lawyers suspected that he had not.

Biron adjourned the case for a week to consider his verdict. John and Una dined with Audrey and John Holroyd-Reece at the Hyde Park Grill and discussed the possible outcome till late into the night. John had already decided that if they lost she would press on with an appeal. 'This thing has got to be fought out to the end.'[72]

The case resumed on 16 November. This time John cut an even more colourful figure by tucking a sprig of her favourite white heather into her sombrero. To Hall it was no ordinary flower: twenty years earlier, in 1908, she had penned the lines:

> And all alone on the side of the mountain
> I spoke to the new born day,
> Oh! Help me gather some rare white heather,
> Sweet Morning, show me the way!

White heather, the substitute for happiness, the symbol of luck. No longer a promising young poet, she was an established novelist on trial for her book's life. She was still in need of the white heather for luck. She touched the sprig in her hat carefully, then waited for the court to fill up.

Crowds flocked to Bow Street to hear the verdict but many of the defence witnesses stayed away, believing (correctly) that it was a foregone conclusion. Biron's repugnance to any form of homosexuality was evident throughout his hour-long judgement speech which was bedevilled with references to 'filthy sin', 'horrible practices' and extreme 'acts of the most horrible, unnatural and disgusting obscenity'. Hall and her book did not have a chance.

Biron, of course, made the most of Birkett's clumsy retraction and Cape's deviousness. He kept meticulously to the definition of obscenity under the Act. Although defence counsel had shown indisputably that *The Well* contained no indecent words, nevertheless according to the 1857 Act the book's intention could still count as obscene. The focus of his outrage was the novel's failure to chastise 'unnatural vice'; rather it saw it as admirable, and solicited society's compassion and toleration for such proclivities.

Biron used passages from Hall's text to demonstrate his points. When he reached Stephen and Mary's meeting at the French front, the magistrate said: 'according to the writer of this book, a number of women of position and admirable character, who were engaged in driving ambulances in the course of the war, were addicted to this vice.'

At this point John, burning with rage, sprang up shouting: 'I protest! I am that writer!'

Biron, in a low well-modulated voice said: 'I must ask people not to interrupt the court.'

John was not to be put down. She burst out again: 'I protest. I emphatically protest!'

Sir Chartres rebuked her: 'I must ask you to be quiet.'

But she would not be quiet. 'I am the author of this book . . .' she began, but was not allowed to finish.

'If you cannot behave yourself in court,' he asserted, 'I shall have you removed.'

'Shame!' she shouted from her seat at the solicitors' table.[73]

What provoked this outburst was Hall's anxiety that any slur on the fictional ambulance unit would be interpreted as a slur on the real women in Toupie Lowther's unit on whom (despite the disclaimer at the front of her book) she had based her characters.

Minutes before Biron delivered his verdict Melville asked permission to speak. He told the magistrate that Miss Radclyffe Hall wished everyone to know that she would have gone into the witness box had she been allowed to do so. In a sense she had the last word.

Biron came to his inevitable conclusion. The novel was obscene. It would indisputably tend to corrupt those into whose hands it fell. He ordered the seized copies to be destroyed. Costs were set at forty guineas for Cape and Hill.

The *Daily Mirror* reported Hall as saying: 'Long passages in my book were misinterpreted in the most amazing and shocking manner'[74] – a remarkably restrained comment given the criticism to which it had been subjected. Una's caustic diary entry read: 'Sir Chartres Biron lied solemnly for more than one hour and condemned *The Well of Loneliness* to be burnt as an obscene libel.'

Biron and the legal system had won on points. John had won on honour.

She, of course, was determined to appeal. She felt that no one had understood her purpose in writing *The Well*. In her letter to Gorham Munson written six years later – an important document, being the only general account by Hall of *The Well*'s publication – she stressed her threefold purpose:

Firstly I hoped that it would encourage the inverted in general to declare themselves, to face up to a hostile world in their true colours . . . with dignity and courage.

Secondly, I hoped that it would give even greater strength than they already possess to the strong and courageous, and strength and hope to the weak and the hopeless among my own kind . . . to make good through hard work, faithful and loyal attachments . . . this against truly formidable odds.

Thirdly, I hoped that normal men and women of good will would be brought through my book to a fuller and more tolerant understanding of the inverted; that those parents who had chanced to breed male or female inverts would cease from tormenting and condemning their offspring . . . would cease destroying that self-respect which is the most useful and necessary prop to those of all ages . . . particularly to the young invert.

She also hoped that her book would reach any who had the care of the young, as well as doctors and psychologists who generally met inverts who were 'physically or psychically unfit . . . who owing to persecution have become the prey of nervous disorders'.[75]

The year 1928 was not only that of the censorship battle; it was also the year when women in Britain finally got the vote on equal terms with men. To bolster the process Bernard Shaw published his *Intelligent Woman's Guide to Socialism and Capitalism*, while only a few weeks before women received the franchise on 2 July, Vera Brittain published *Women's Work in Modern England*, her powerful plea for abolition of sex differentiation in the labour market.[76] For Brittain, her participation in *The Well* proceedings had not been without its uses. Her review of Hall's novel followed by her nomination as a prospective defence witness enhanced her own opportunities for publicizing her views on the urgent need for moral and social reform.

Hall's novel in fact had some less well-documented effects on Vera Brittain and Winifred Holtby.* Despite Vera Brittain's denials she and Winifred were constantly 'entangled in the public imagination'. Vera became exasperated, and at the League of Nations Assembly in Geneva[77] became furiously embroiled in 'a tremendous and vehement argument . . . about feminism and homosexuality' with Monica Whateley, who since *The Well*'s publication could not accept that Vera's relationship with Winifred was not homosexual.

Initially Winifred treated the notion as a joke, and would say 'Look she's got my hair' as she cradled little Shirley, her friend's baby, in her arms. Later, following the furore over *The Well*, an unpublished letter of Winifred's reveals hints that only her self-control prevented her erotic feelings for Vera from surfacing: 'Radclyffe Hall has taught me a lot. She's all fearfully wrong, I feel. To love other women deeply is not pathological. To be unable to control one's passion is.'[78]

---

* In their biography of Vera Brittain, Paul Berry and Mark Bostridge point to *The Well* and the post-war vogue for subsequent 'deviant literature' as reasons for what they call the 'myth' of the alleged lesbian relationship between Vera Brittain and Winifred Holtby.

Vera's involvement with *The Well* continued a long time. Thirty-eight years later, in 1966, as a director of the new publishing company Femina Books launched by the film director and writer Muriel Box, she agreed to contribute a book on Radclyffe Hall and the obscenity ban for a series called *Women on Trial*.*

In the autumn of 1928 Radclyffe Hall's trials continued. Notice of appeal was given on 22 November. The hearing itself on 14 December at the County of London sessions was virtually a formality as the same arguments were reiterated. To John's relief Birkett had withdrawn, leaving Melville, with Walter Frampton's help, to make his spirited defence. The prosecution was led by the Attorney-General Sir Thomas Inskip KC, MP with Eustace Fulton and Mr B. Purchase as Counsel. Sir Robert Wallace KC chaired the Bench of ten men and two women, none of whom, according to Una, had read the book.

The prosecution made a great deal of Jonathan Cape's deceitful dealings with the Home Office and Pegasus Press. The speech was again riddled with terms like 'unnatural tendencies', 'abnormal character', 'abhorrent practices'. In their view the worst aspect was 'the assumption that indulgence in unnatural physical passion is not merely lawful but may be even noble and virtuous'.[79]

It took the Bench only ten minutes to consider their verdict. Sir Robert Wallace summed up by saying that the character of the book could not be judged from the isolated passages read, though they gave an indication as to the general tenor. But the book had to be taken as a whole. It was a 'dangerous and corrupting book', also 'a very subtle book . . . which is insinuating in the way in which it is propounded and probably much more dangerous because of that fact'. Sir Robert Wallace's final comment was that it was 'a disgusting book when properly read . . . an obscene book and a book prejudicial to the morals of the community'.[80]

The Appeal Court upheld the order made by the Magistrates' Court and the appeal was dismissed with costs.

John's instant reaction to the case was bitterness and a feeling of betrayal. Many fellow writers had let her down. The PEN club on whose executive committee she had sat had lamentably failed to send her a letter of support signed by every member. She tendered her resignation (although this was afterwards withdrawn). Her government and country had let her down. She felt that

---

* According to her biographers, the book, *Radclyffe Hall: A Case of Obscenity*, came to fill her 'with despair'. The law in 1928 having prevented witnesses from testifying to the novel's literary merit, the limited material available to her led to insurmountable difficulties. After 'endless boring research in nooks and crannies', Brittain's manuscript amounted to less than 22,000 words, which she then had to fill out with essays about the legal aspects of the case from other contributors. Published in 1968, by which time severe arteriosclerosis had affected both her perceptions and her aspirations, this last book is a sad reflection of fifty years of excellent writing. She said of it: 'I really didn't put very much work into RH . . . It didn't interest me enough, and I only hope it's readable.' (P. Berry and M. Bostridge, *Vera Brittain*, pp. 514, 517.)

Baldwin's government had made an example of her case, confiding to Vita Sackville-West her belief that the government had secretly instructed the Appeal Court not to allow the appeal.[81] Even before the verdict she had written to her friend Fabienne:

> I have been a Conservative all my life and have always hotly defended that party. When people told me that they stemmed progress, that they hated reforms and were enemies of Freedom, I, in my blindness, would not listen. I looked upon them as the educated class best calculated to serve the interests of the country. And yet, who was the first to spring to my defence, to cry out against the outrage done to my book? Labour, my dear, and they have not ceased to let off their guns since.[82]

Six years later she was still bitter: 'Had I required proof of the blind and bitter antagonism that exists against the inverted . . . then I had that proof as I sat in the police courts and listened to the conducting of those two cases.'[83] Suddenly she felt displaced from her own society in a way that was different from any previous feeling of alienation. That had been personal; this was public. As a lesbian Radclyffe Hall had always been positioned on the boundaries. The trial and its verdict formally outlawed her.

How does a lesbian writer's sense of outlaw status affect her literary vision? Her marginal position in society before and after the trial both helped and hindered her novel-writing. It gave her a certain flexibility and freedom; she could write what others could not. But the knowledge that many homosexual men and women were far from free was one reason for the running metaphor of imprisonment and chains to be found in all her novels culminating in *The Well of Loneliness*. The suggestion that there may be a 'dialectic between freedom and imprisonment that is unique to lesbian writing' shows itself in Hall's writing, but it is important to remember that *The Well* follows a series of novels in which her childhood had given her just cause to deploy such symbols.[84]

Patently the trial had deep significance for Radclyffe Hall not only in her professional but also in her personal life. It became her constant reference point. She measured even the torn loyalties in her love life by it. When she fell desperately in love with Souline, Una's reminder of her own support through the *Well* crisis was enough to keep John hanging on to the partnership. When Souline threatened to leave if John did not give up Una, John herself used *The Well* as her reason for continuing their tortured triangle.

The trial had been highly detrimental to John's finances. For only the second time in her life she found herself in urgent need of 'ready money' to meet the legal costs. The unlooked-for support, financial as well as moral, of ordinary people was one of John's deepest satisfactions. As she told Gorham Munson:

> One very rich man, unknown to me personally, generously offered to pay the whole of my expenses himself . . . while . . . a number of poor working class men wrote

. . . saying that if a subscription was started they would like to contribute their hard earned shillings . . . Indeed the sympathy of the British working classes was one of my greatest supports.[85]

The trial had engendered widespread sympathy, particularly from miners' and railwaymen's groups. Public collections were made. A subscription was started to pay her legal expenses. But as Hall said to Munson: 'I could not very well accept in view of the fact that I possessed certain assets . . . I was able to sell my London house and thus procure the necessary ammunition.'[86]

Thus on 13 November 1928, after residing at Holland Street for only four years, she was forced to sell it. She and Una decided to lease a small flat in London but to make Rye their home. Initially they stayed at Rye's Mermaid Inn. Three days later they saw Journey's End, a cottage in the cobbled row of houses known as The Hucksteps which five years later John bought for Una and renamed The Forecastle. Currently it was let furnished to their friend Anne Elsner, who generously decided to loan it to them for six months. With the cottage went Mabel Bourne, 'an admirable servant'. The cottage became their haven, Mabel their heroine. They would flee from stressful police, politics, magistrates, and meetings, hurry down to Sussex 'where the faithful Mabel Bourne would be there to greet us with blazing fires and her genius for cooking'.[87]

In those days the cottage had none of its later beauty. Its Tudor charms were disguised almost beyond recognition by masses of heterogeneous junk. It rocked and swayed in the great south-westerly gales while Mabel hung up blankets to keep out the draughts. The bathwater was temperamental. They read by oil lamps. But to John and Una 'it was a heavenly haven of peace in which we pulled ourselves together for the next round before plunging back into the battle.'[88]

There *would* be a next round. Another battle awaited them. Covici Friede's American edition of *The Well*, published on 16 December, was far from safe. But meanwhile there were compensations. The trial and the ban had turned the novel into an underground best-seller. Pegasus continued to print it in France. Una calculated that by the end of 1928 *The Well* had sold over 7,500 copies outside America, of which 4,000 had been sold since James Douglas's condemnation. By the following February Pegasus alone had produced sales of 9,000 and was ready to reprint.

John and Una spent their first quiet Christmas at Rye. With them were Andrea, Audrey, Audrey's assistant Patience Ross and her friend Morny. Una and Audrey went for drives while John, Andrea and the others went for long wet walks through the incomparable Rye marshes.

John was gathering strength.

17

THE TROLLEY YEARS

For Radclyffe Hall the years 1929 to 1932 were trolley years. A trolley book was Hall's term for a book taken up and worked on between two major novels. If we scrutinize her life we can see how closely, in this respect, it mirrors her art. A trolley passage could be a period between two great love affairs (which might include a less important relationship), or it could be a stage between two significant spiritual awakenings or simply a phase between two periods of vital living marked by those impulses and connections that distinguish life from mere existence.

Radclyffe Hall had passed through trolley passages before. Phoebe was a trolley affair between her love for Ladye and her new feelings for Una. The aeon after Ladye's death was a trolley period – a stage of penance, apprenticeship and growth.

Perhaps she needed trolley passages every few years to mark time, to tread water, to regroup her forces. But for John a trolley, whether in literature or life, was in no sense a rest. The trolley years, like the books, took energy, commitment and infinite pains. Yet, with all that, they were but a semblance of living, an episode in which she went through the motions. The vigour, the vim that enlivened her major fiction were simply not there.

So it was after the trial of *The Well*. On the surface John worked, entertained, was companionable with Una. But underneath she was in retreat. The years were marked by stillness, a state of suspension.

She vacillated between withdrawn moodiness and wild hilarity. She knew it was more urgent than ever to write another book. Her stubborn sense of purpose had not deserted her but momentarily she had been deflected by the deep depression that often follows drama, exacerbated this time by her sense of betrayal and growing isolation. During 1929 in Paris she worked intermittently on the trolley novel *The World*, finally making a decision to rework several chapters as short stories to be used in her 1934 volume *Miss Ogilvy Finds Herself*.

She watched Herbert Hoover become thirty-first President of the USA. She saw a second Labour Government under Ramsay MacDonald take office in Britain. James Melville, John's impressive young barrister, had received a post in the new government, and Cape expressed hopes of republishing the novel which came to nothing. Melville failed to answer John's letters. 'I am afraid that Labour is going to rat on me,' John said sadly to Audrey.[1]

She felt ill at ease with both governments, discomforted in both countries where her books still sold extraordinarily well. The world economic crisis began with the collapse of the US stock exchange. John kept a tight rein on her purse, drove a hard bargain with publishers, but something inside her had also given way.

Her friend Noël Coward had his play *Bitter Sweet* produced. The title summed up her feelings, she sent him flowers, and sat in the audience. Coward had become a close friend in recent years, more particularly since acquiring a house, Goldenhurst, in Romney Marsh, which he had bought in 1926 and which brought him within easy reach of John and Una in Rye. He and John, according to Terry Castle in her study of the pair,[2] appear to have been introduced to each other by their theatrical friends, Gabrielle Enthoven or Teddie Gerard, in the early twenties, and certainly knew each other by the time John's friend and idol Tallulah Bankhead was starring in the London production of Coward's *Fallen Angels* in 1925.

There may well have been reciprocal influences too. Not only might it be said that John acquired much of her idiosyncratic clothes sense from Coward, but Terry Castle suggests that the portrait of the mercurial homosexual playwright Jonathan Brockett in *The Well of Loneliness* was based on Coward (who may have repaid the compliment in his later play *Blithe Spirit* whose vigorous medium Madame Arcati may well owe something to Hall's spiritualist leanings).

But the heady pleasures of earlier years had now passed. The fate of *The Well* weighed on John's mind and she continued to brood. She listened to the British literati talking about William Faulkner's *The Sound and the Fury* and Ernest Hemingway's *A Farewell to Arms* but did not share their excitement. She marvelled at how D.H. Lawrence, who had survived *The Rainbow*'s prosecution for indecency in 1915, had managed to get *Lady Chatterley's Lover* published without it so far being brought to trial.

She was interested in Lawrence partly because his work expressed his belief in emotion and the sexual impulse as both creative and true to human nature; and partly because Lawrence had been encouraged to write by Violet's lover Ford Madox Ford, one of her favourite authors. Lawrence, who had learnt fast from the scandal of *The Rainbow* and from his own forced expulsion from Cornwall following its prosecution, had taken refuge near Florence where he had privately published *Lady Chatterley's Lover*. The unexpurgated edition of his novel would be banned in Britain until 1960. That would bring Radclyffe Hall no consolation. She never wanted other writers to be forced to face what she had faced.

An experimental television service began in Britain but John was content to sit listening to the wireless in the quiet cottage in Rye. Constitutionally melancholic, John found some of her lowness of spirit seep away as she sat at the cottage window watching timber ships with tall masts and brown sails make their way along the Rother. Like Hannah Bullen, her heroine in *The Sixth Beatitude*, John stood staring seaward: 'Romney Marsh stretched out between her and the sea, more than two miles of greyish-green marsh with cattle upon it, sheep and strong steers – for a long time ago the sea had left Rother.'

John stared as Hannah Bullen and her forebears had stared when keeping watch for enemy ships. In Rye, as in the fictional Rother, 'people would pause at their work, shading their eyes and staring at nothing but the Marsh'. John too would pause at her work and watch the herons' heavy powerful flight, the plovers circling and screaming above their young, the moorhens paddling in and out of rushes, the larks dropping like plummets over the thorn trees heavy with blossom at the Marsh's edge.[3] Sometimes, having less heart for people, she would turn to old fictional favourites like *Ladies Whose Bright Eyes*. If she did pick up a new book, it was one written by a staunch supporter such as Naomi Royde-Smith or Storm Jameson.

Once again the long-suffering Cubby had arrived back at a place she called home, this time Holland Street, to find the official 'sold' sign displayed. Though her mother and John had decided to live permanently at Journey's End, keeping only a small rented apartment in London, as John's health deteriorated in the early weeks of 1929 they felt that living abroad for a while might help her recover. John and Una planned to curtail their stay in Rye, return to London, then leave for Paris in February. John just had time to make Mabel a generous offer of three weeks' wages. They would not see her again until November.

In London, John continued to answer her fanmail. Since *The Well*'s publication she had received over 5,000 letters of which only five were abusive.[4] She showed her gratitude to the miners, who had protested in her defence to the Home Secretary, by selling her treasured Sargent portrait of Ladye to Glasgow Art Gallery. She gave the £1,000 to the Lord Mayor of London's Fund for the Relief of Distress in the Coalfields.

John gave several lectures on sexual inversion.* At one lecture was novelist

---

* One, on 25 January 1929, to the Southend branch of the National Council of Labour Colleges' Students Association, was given as a gesture of appreciation to the Labour Party for their support.

Naomi 'Mickie' Jacob, who had asked Una, whom she barely knew, for a ticket as the hall was sold out. Though Mickie had written to John in support of *The Well* they had never met, but she was to become one of John's closest friends in the years up to her death.

On 28 January John heard from Covici Friede in America that *The Well* was still selling well. However, several weeks later the New York police arrested Donald Friede and seized over 800 copies of the book on a charge of obscenity. A complaint had been made by John Sumner, secretary of the local Society for the Suppression of Vice. Covici Friede were not taken totally unawares, for, expecting such a complaint, they had already hired attorney Morris Ernst, an expert in censorship battles. Described by John as the man who 'fought the forces of retrogression on behalf of my American publishers . . . that brilliant lawyer and champion of literary freedom',[5] he was given hero status.

Unlike the craven Cape, Covici Friede continued to sell the book with a ferocious sales pitch while awaiting the official verdict. Meanwhile Ernst solicited an impressive array of endorsements from America's most distinguished writers and artists, including Ernest Hemingway, Scott Fitzgerald, and Sinclair Lewis who found the novel 'almost lugubriously moral'.*

Women writers and artists who joined the protest included Ellen Glasgow, Edna St Vincent Millay and, most strongly, Ida Wylie, now working in America. Edna Ferber, like Virginia Woolf, supported the principle rather than the book. She allowed her name to be used because she said she was worried that the New York Vice Society might track down the Old Testament.

The Sumner case was heard before the Manhattan Magistrates' Court on 29 February. Friede was pronounced guilty, *The Well* judged obscene because it 'idealized and extolled' perversion, and was 'anti-social and offensive to public morals and decency'. The Judge stated: 'The book can have no moral value since it seems to justify the right of the pervert to prey upon normal members of the community.'[6]

Ernst's stance differed from the British defence as he soft-pedalled the homosexual issue and asked whether the law should condemn what he viewed as an otherwise unobjectionable book simply for its theme. Unfortunately the court did not share his view. Ernst appealed immediately and the publishers stepped up publicity. By February sales had reached 50,000 and the book was judged a runaway success.

John had to wait until 19 April to hear, to her relief, that a special Appeals Session court of three judges had decided in favour of *The Well*. She wrote later to Gorham Munson recording her

---

* Among other supporters were Sherwood Anderson, John Dos Passos, Theodore Dreiser, H.L. Mencken and Upton Sinclair.

great cause for gratitude . . . towards those eminent American men and women who came forward in defence of the book, and great cause for gratitude towards the three American judges who conducted the last case in so seemly and so eminently just a manner.[7]

At the time, with excitement bordering on hysteria, she wrote to Audrey asking her to tell 'all the nations of the earth' who would be likely to translate *The Well* of the successful verdict.[8]

When the verdict arrived, John and Una were already in Paris, where they heard that Friede planned a Preface to a new Victory Edition that would include reports of the two trials. At one of Natalie's soirées, Ezra Pound suggested to John that the full text of Britain and America's obscenity laws, which made such 'humorous reading', should be included.[9]

Suddenly John no longer had money worries. By June 1929 she would make £6,000 in royalties from the American edition of *The Well* alone. Arrowsmith reprinted *The Forge* and *A Saturday Life*. In Britain, by 25 March 1929, *The Forge* had sold 2,600 copies since the previous December, while *A Saturday Life* had sold 1,700. *Adam's Breed* sold even better, and *The Unlit Lamp* sold with 'amazing strength' because readers now identified its lesbian undertones. The US appeal verdict had had the effect in most countries of increasing sales of all Hall's books. Before the appeal the wily Cape had set up a sister company in America. From Doubleday he cleverly purchased the American rights of *Adam's Breed* and under his new imprint, Cape & Harrison Smith Inc., he produced an American edition of *The Unlit Lamp*. By October 1929 this US edition had sole over 15,000 copies.

When John and Una had arrived in Paris on 5 February copies of *The Well* and photographs of the author were in all the bookshops. The Pegasus edition was selling over a hundred copies a day. Gallimard invited Una to work on a French translation, which would make John the first female author on their prestigious list.*

The Well of Loneliness was also being translated into Dutch, German, Norwegian, Italian, Czech and Polish. The Danish translator Karen Michaelis wanted to make some small changes in order to ensure that the novel was not suppressed in Denmark. Initially an irritable John barked 'no' but when Karen told her that the book had caused her to change her views on homosexuality, John instructed Audrey to allow her the concessions. Translation rights of all John's other books were selling fast too. *Adam's Breed* was translated into Dutch, German, Swedish, Norwegian and Italian, and *The Unlit Lamp* into Italian, Dutch and Czech.

John, ambivalent about this success, wrote to Audrey: 'Do you remember the

---

* Radclyffe Hall later reclaimed the English rights in 1938 but it was not republished in England until 1949, six years after her death.

time when no publisher much wanted John Hall, and now they're all at each other's throats – oh, well, as long as we get the dollars!!!'[10]

But the money gave her no security. She felt infertile, lacking in fluency. She was strained, wrung out. Celebrity status both suited and exhausted her. It intensified her inner loneliness. Another writer who knew how she felt, Virginia Woolf, that same year had written: 'This celebrity business is quite chronic – and I am richer than I have ever been . . . and for all this, there is vacancy and silence somewhere in the machine.'[11]

John's retreat into that silence had not a little to do with the ambivalent response *The Well* had received from other women writers in Britain. Violet Trefusis, in a letter to her former lover Vita Sackville-West, declared the book 'a loathsome example' of homosexual literature. She proposed that she and Vita write in response a story of same-sex love that would be better than *The Well*.[12] Unfortunately, lacking Hall's persistence and dedication to the topic, they never actually did so.

May Sinclair expressed dispproval not so much of the book but of the non-platonic ménage at Holland Street, which, she told gossipy novelist Netta Syrett, came as a shock to her. May, who felt she knew John and Una very well, said: 'I don't believe what is said of them is true,' to which Netta replied, 'I believe it but I don't mind.' May retorted: 'You wouldn't like it if it happened to *you*.' May had told fellow writers Rebecca West and G.B. 'Peter' Stern that what *had* happened a few years earlier was that the 'lesbian poetess Charlotte M[ew]' had chased her upstairs into the bedroom. 'And I assure you, Peter, and I assure you, Rebecca,' she said, 'I had to leap the bed five times!'

According to Netta Syrett, May finally leapt off her perch and, using a nursery phrase that might have described 'perfectly good bread and butter' that someone else would be grateful for, said stoutly to Charlotte: 'My good woman, you are simply wasting your perfectly good passion.'[13]

More than ever John saw herself as a literary exile from a traitorous country.

Paris was freezing so John and Una spent their first few days huddled over the fire in John and Jeanne Holroyd-Reece's apartment in the Rue Boulard. Though the cold outside drained John's diminishing energy and left her cold inside too, she did not stop seeing people, but they emptied her. She spent her leisure hours with Natalie, Romaine, Colette, Lily de Gramont and the rest of the Paris circle. It did not raise her spirits to learn that certain members of the group were less than enamoured of *The Well*.

Hall's portrayal of the Paris homosexual community had deeply disturbed many of her friends. The Parisian counterparts to her depressing fictional bars – the Ideal Bar, Le Narcisse and Alec's Bar – were by no means the only homosexual communities in Paris. That frequented by Natalie, Romaine and the others was considerably less wrapped up in self-loathing than the one Hall invented. Many club-goers saw 'the lesbian' as a more romantic figure than

Hall's depictions, particularly Natalie Barney who with Renée Vivien had modelled her identity on nineteenth-century French literature, from which she derived a strength and pride in her sexual identity.

Barney's group were singularly less interested in writing propaganda pieces about tolerance for inverts than in fostering the growth of a positive identity and sense of community amongst lesbians themselves. An American sociological study of attitudes towards *The Well* by lesbians in the twenties and thirties found that 'almost to a woman, they decried its publication' believing that it 'puts homosexuality in the wrong light', thus doing more harm than good for their community.[14] Romaine Brooks called the novel 'a ridiculous book, trite, superficial', though she didn't say so to John's face. Behind her back she called her 'a digger up of worms with the pretension of a distinguished archaeologist'.[15] As Romaine could not be frank with Una, their friendship faltered, and sharp-eyed Una was quick to notice.

The attitudes of the Parisian group were not dissimilar to those of some harsh American literary critics today. Lillian Faderman believes *The Well* has helped 'to wreak confusion in young women' and that Hall's 'popular rendition of "congenital inversion" further morbidified the most natural impulses and healthy views'.[16] Some critics ask why Hall has not provided lesbians with a more appropriate role model. Others are uncomfortable with the way Hall's novel focused on explaining the lesbian 'problem' to heterosexuals.

But if we look to writers to establish a tradition, then it is sensible to remember that no tradition fostered by outsiders is likely to be comfortable. No doubt the Paris Modernists recognized that Hall's decision to make Stephen's open lesbian sexuality the central conflict was unprecedented, but they could not have contemplated such a decision turning the book into what has been called 'the lesbian novel'[17] and 'the lesbian Bible'.[18] That it was for years the single fiction by which all other lesbian novels were measured has secured the book its historical and socio-cultural place. But its power resides in the fact that it is many-layered, and open to wider interpretations than a polemical cry for homosexual understanding.

Its lasting value stems only partly from its portrait of a spiritual exile and more significantly from its portrait of the way an artist's imagination develops. In suggesting that writing is also Stephen Gordon's weapon against a hostile world, Hall connects her two themes of the artist cut off from other people and the invert disallowed a place in society. Yet Stephen the unconventional writer is also Stephen the woman who longs to conform and who venerates marriage, just as John did.[19]

Hall's newly entrenched views on marriage and adherence to the existing social system for inverts, who were outside both, also gave rise to amusement amongst her Paris friends – Natalie, Romaine, Lily, Djuna and the others. John, who had always wished to be an 'insider', generalized from that experience to the feelings of other inverts. She saw them as 'honest, simple souls who long to live honestly and to live as themselves, they desire to form part of the social scheme, to conform in all ways to the social code as it exists at present'.[20] Writing to Gorham Munson in 1934 John talked of their secret wishes: 'Such inverts desire to legalize their unions. Preposterous, do you say? And yet it may come, though I may not be here to welcome its coming.'[21] These inverts did not see same-sex 'marriage' as preposterous as John's Paris friends did. But interestingly, nearly seventy years later, moves towards legalized marriage for gays and lesbians illustrate the extent to which we are inheritors of her vision.

'Such inverts' certainly did not include Romaine, Natalie, Djuna, Lily, and those others proud of a community that lay outside the traditional social scheme. Nor were they based on her English friends like the rebellious, sophisticated Ida, Rachel, Toupie, Fabienne or Gabrielle, several of whom had tried marriage, found it wanting, and were taking great pains to avoid any such replication.

It was as if the publication, defamation and suppression of *The Well* had spawned a million offspring – the readers, the fans, a collective body of 'honest, simple-souled' homosexuals who were obliged to want what Hall wanted for them. But striking even at the time was the significant effect Hall's ideas on legalizing unusual unions had on other women writers. At the Third Congress of the World League for Sexual Reform, held in London in September 1928, her influence was strongly felt. Vera Brittain put forward six 'sweeping innovations' which she advocated as the essential basis for the establishment of successful monogamous marriages, one of which took up Hall's suggestion of the legalization of experimental unions.[22]

Ironically while John publicly advocated legalized unions for inverts, privately she found her own 'marriage' to Una daily more stifling. Una was beset with gynaecological problems; was constantly seedy or 'cheap'. She enjoyed being looked after: illness for her had always smacked of reward. But had Una forgotten John's irritation with Ladye's ailments? Memories of Ladye as an invalid stirred John, if not Una, most uncomfortably. Loyalty kept her by Una's side but she did not relish the prospect of increasing frailty clouding their future. Small infirmities ensured that passion had flown. Not every night but often enough, John began to retreat behind locked doors. The warning signs were there. Once John began work on her next novel, she would settle determinedly on celibacy.

To Souline on Easter Sunday 1935 she described how she had felt in those last few years before she met Souline: 'As you know before I met you I was dry – as dry as bones – then I fell in love and that stirred the fluid again, that awoke me, energised me, made me come alive.'[23]

Did Una really not notice the dryness? The crack of splintering bones? Her Day Book keeps reaffirming John's 'undoubted' love for her. Her diary reiterates her view that she and John would be a pair-until-death. But determination was one of Una's strongest characteristics. And loyalty and her need to exercise control. These qualities filled her with a sense that she could override all setbacks, overlook all disappointments, achieve all goals.

Very occasionally during these years Una admits to unquiet thoughts, but each time she puts them down to her own ill-health, or more often to John's work, and each time she returns for comfort to their united stand over *The Well*. In Una's eyes the trial had made their union an unbreakable fixture.

She had not grasped the very different meaning the trial had had for John. The bravado with which they fixed their colours to the mast and flaunted them had indeed drawn them closer together. For John, however, that shared stimulation was less a symbol of future unity than a present, as erotically irresistible as sex – possibly, after fourteen years together, more irresistible. It *was* sex.

But now that stimulus was over. The last orgasm had been the US appeal verdict. The novel had brought John financial success but not critical acclaim. The book was still banned in her own country, and interest in it and in its author had dwindled. She minded her book's fate more than she minded her dwindling erotic interest in Una.

What did Una do? What compensations did she find? Ever resourceful, Una turned increasingly to her own writing. She became highly professional, insisted on credits and royalties. She wrote to Audrey's assistant, Patience Ross: 'Dearest Patience . . . *Yes. I want my name on everything now* so as to get known in case the Colette translations materialise.'[24] She was as generous as usual with the royalties she received for translations, buying John in Paris two presents: a pair of sapphire and diamond cuff links and a tiny Brabançonne bitch called Tulip.

As John became more detached, Una clung ever more closely, and discouraged intimacies with other people. Ironically it was at this point that they suddenly lost four valuable friendships.

When Evelyn Irons did not use her position as deputy editor of the *Daily Mail* women's page to promote *The Well*'s cause, John saw her as a traitor. Tarred with the same brush were Viola and Garvin. Despite John's request to Garvin to review her book in a 'proper spirit', the *Observer* failed to review it at all. Once their intellectual friends moved to support John, the Garvins tried to do likewise, but for Una and John their offer came too late.

The saddest loss was that of Toupie, John's sporting friend since 1910. Eighteen years' solid comradeship was a lot to throw away but when several people told Una that Toupie Lowther resented *The Well* 'as challenging her claim to be the only invert in existence', John let herself be persuaded. It was a curious statement because in later years Toupie told people that she herself was the model for Stephen Gordon.[25] Had John not been so wrapped up in herself she might have talked matters over with Toupie. In the past she had confronted rumours, sorted out the truth. Now the slightest hint of a betrayal fuelled her growing paranoia. When Una reported that the once flagrantly masculine Toupie had begun to disguise herself in scarlet silk 'confections' with low necks and accordion-pleated skirts, John did not doubt her. When Una insisted that Toupie was shunning 'her own ilk', John let Una write her friend off with the words: 'She was essentially a crank. A compound of the very male and very feminine.'[26]

The losses however perturbed John who valued friendship as much as she valued love. Una shrugged them off: 'Somehow we don't seem to be intended to have any *very* intimate friends, though, thank God, plenty of valued and delightful friends of moderate intimacy . . . When anyone looks like crossing that barrier, something always seems to step in quite unexpectedly and put an end to it.'[27] Often, and expectedly, that something, or someone was Una herself. She did not want anyone else to become intimate with 'her John'.

On 13 February in France they learnt of a more grievous loss. 'Our old dear friend Ida Temple has died,' Una told Robin, 'but mercifully of heart failure . . . So while we are very sad and tearful . . . we try to remember how mercifully she has been spared a painful and frightening end but it is pretty awful to think of those three young girls . . . left on their own and possibly prey to fortune hunters.'[28]

Ida's death marked the end of the Datchet days so beloved by John and Cubby. When they returned to Rye John determined to re-create a Datchet country atmosphere. But for Cubby it would never be the same. If anyone had mothered her it had been Ida. If any place had been a home it had been Datchet. In Paris on 31 March John and Una heard that Andrea had won a scholarship to Oxford. Young Cubby was about to take her own tentative first steps in a new world.

Ida's death brought John the recognition that life was fragile. People shifted, shuffled, then fell through the veil. She felt more alone than ever. Her distress over the loss of her friends was paralleled by her anger at three professional incidents. The first concerned an American actress, Wilette Kershaw, who while working in Paris had bought an option on the stage rights to *The Well* and wished to play Stephen. John accepted the £100 option fee but when she and Una saw her act they were horrified. Wilette was a pink fluffy ingénue! That was the first hitch. Worse came when they couldn't find a dramatist. John was not interested in adapting it for the stage but hoped Clemence Dane might be. Dane declined because she felt the novel would not make interesting theatre. The contract was tricky and Wilette Kershaw failed to sign. Furiously John returned the fee and said she was cancelling her option. Unfortunately John's letter crossed with one from Miss Kershaw saying she had now signed. Lawyers told John she was unable to cancel. John fumed until October when she took out an injunction against Kershaw who, despite having tried to send the option money back to John, finally agreed to rescind her rights. But in August 1930, Kershaw, despite legal opposition and Audrey Heath's intervention, put on a pirated production with a script unseen by John. On 2 September 1930 Kershaw's play opened at the Théâtre de la Potinière as '*The Well of Loneliness* from the novel by Radclyffe Hall'. No dramatist received credit. Kershaw's ploy was to mislead the public into thinking it was Hall's own work.

John Holroyd-Reece went to see the play on his irate author's behalf. 'Nauseating is no word for it,' he wrote to John. '. . . When you consider the obvious vulgarity and an excess of the greatest extreme of American sloppy sentimentality, you will be able to form an idea of what the performance must have been like.'[29] For her finale, the sentimental Miss Kershaw changed out of her stage clothes, modelled on John's, into a cute white number (lots of frills, plenty of leg) and made a treacly appeal on behalf of the world's inverts.

John issued a press release to the French newspapers disclaiming responsibility and threatening legal action. Wilette hit back with a vulgar interview for the *New York Times* stating that she had given John a 'substantial cheque' (doubtless the returned £100) in return for permission. Fortunately the critics panned the play, which closed hastily, so legal wrangling was suspended. The episode boosted sales of her novel, so sensibly John decided to take no further action.

The second incident concerned the ubiquitous *Extraordinary Women*. While John could still not get her book published in England, she heard that Compton Mackenzie's novel was about to be published in a cheap popular edition with no harassment from the Home Office. As if to rub salt in her wound, Macey's, promoters of the Vanguard edition of Mackenzie's book, had placed an advertisement in the *New York World* maliciously linking Mackenzie's novel to *The Well*. The advertisement proclaimed that Radclyffe Hall 'herself . . . an EXTRAORDINARY WOMAN' was one of the major protagonists in Mackenzie's 'brilliant satiric fictional divertissement'.[30]

John, angry and exhausted, recognizing that she was the model for Mackenzie's Hermina de Randan, instructed Carl Brandt to do everything possible to persuade Macey's to withdraw the advertisement. Although she believed she had reasonable cause to sue Mackenzie for defamation, she was too weary to take legal action. Instead, fastening her attention on the Home Office's inconsistency, she wrote wrathfully to Audrey: 'I renounce my country for ever, nor will I ever lift a hand to help England in the future.'[31]

The third incident caused her so much pain that for several years afterwards she was barely able to discuss it. In the late summer of 1928, Hermes Press published an anonymous but biting satire of the trial of *The Well of Loneliness* called 'The Sink of Solitude'. A mock-heroic poem accompanied by caustic cartoons by Beresford Egan, it lampooned James Douglas and Jix for their high-handed

'St Stephen'
Beresford Egan's cartoon of The Well of Loneliness

hypocrisy, and chicken-hearted Cape for his moral cravenness. One cartoon savaged Stephen Gordon and John herself. Egan drew Radclyffe Hall nailed to a cross like Christ, wearing her black Spanish sombrero, her body touching that of a naked woman dancing round the cross. In the bottom right corner Jix looks disgustedly away from Hall while in the top left corner a baby cupid makes a rude gesture at John. Watching this lewd scene with cold distaste is another Eton-cropped woman.

John was outraged. Egan felt that as lesbians, unlike male homosexuals, could not be prosecuted, John's anguish on the subject of their sexuality was unjustified.[32] That she never considered her lesbian identity as in conflict with her Catholic practice was most evident over this issue. In deep spiritual pain, she saw Egan's cartoon as nothing less than blasphemy. She felt, as Virginia Woolf had written some years earlier, that 'peculiar repulsiveness' for 'those who dabble their fingers self-approvingly in the stuff of others' souls'.[33] In Egan's case his fingers were spiteful as well as self-approving. John hated him and his cartoon and the small-minded verse it accompanied. She had been engaged on larger issues, a campaign of emancipation, something elevating, noble. Now he had taken a crack at it, at her, at her God. Terrible guilt, neither necessary nor rational, swept over her. She felt she had been exploited in order to offend her Maker.

This feeling was the strongest motive for her decision to write a new novel that would make 'amends for that insult to her Lord and to her Faith'.[34] In the moment that she viewed Egan's cartoon, the idea for _The Carpenter's Son_ took root. She told Una that

> she was haunted by the desire to write a book about a boy of our own times, the son of a carpenter, who, as he grew up in the carpenter's shop, would have memories and impulses that he did not understand, that linked him with the Carpenter's Son of Nazareth.[35]

This book, written as a gift for God and to gain forgiveness, was, Una said, 'nearer and dearer to her heart than anything she wrote before it or afterwards'.[36]

As the choice of setting was essential to John's creative process, and as she could not decide where to set the story, she did not immediately begin writing the novel. Instead she blundered back into _The World_, brooding on brutality and injustice. The book's theme of alienation, isolation, made it sympathetic to her in her present mood. She tackled it with tenacity and industry but without intoxication. That would come with _The Carpenter's Son_.

John began to long for anonymity. The notoriety which had befallen her disturbed the awkward, self-effacing side of her nature. Writing to Gorham Munson six years later she recalled it vividly:

I could not escape it [notoriety] then nor can I even now six years after the book's publication. I do not like notoriety, it embarrasses me and makes me feel shy, but I realise that it is the price I must pay for having intentionally come out into the open, and no price could ever be too great in my eyes.

Her openness had brought her a measure of spiritual release: 'Nothing is so spiritually degrading or so undermining of one's morale as living a lie, as keeping friends only by false pretences.' What she hated was 'the lies and the conspiracy of silence that a ruthless society . . . forces on them [inverts]'.[37]

In Paris lethargy and depression again caused John to sink further into ill-health. When Una realized that her partner was 'far past any enthusiasm' she determined they should have a real vacation. Colette suggested St Tropez where she had recently bought a villa. John called Una cruel and crazy to 'think of dragging her, tired to death as she was, to the ends of the earth and . . . landing her somewhere in the unknown'.[38]

The unknown proved to be the beautiful Côte des Naures. John's tired nerves relaxed once they settled into the Golf Hotel, Beauvallon. Throughout June and July they explored Provence and swam daily in the small coves. John grew 'brown as a berry and her hair got bleached and her eyes were clear and her teeth very white in her tanned face . . . All the lines of strain and anxiety seemed to disappear and her smile grew rakish and carefree again.'[39]

On their journey down to St Tropez, when they reached Fréjus John suddenly called to their chauffeur Pierre to stop. 'What had caught her eye was a low stone archway and under the archway, half in and half out of it, a carpenter's bench and a carpenter at work. "Look," she said, "there is my carpenter's shop. That's where Christophe Bénédit was born." '[40]

After this, John could not laze for long. *The Carpenter's Son* must be started. Using Pierre, who had been born in the area, as her guide, she learnt the local customs and became acquainted with the local dialect which would be a prominent feature in the fictional St Loup-sur-Mer based on St Tropez. They toured the area, collected data, visited Colette's house, met up with Natalie, Romaine and Etheline.

Marie Visetti's compulsively bad timing interrupted John's rest cure. Marie needed an operation. John spent hours in 'much writing and telephoning' from Bagnoles, then went to Paris on 12 September to be on hand in case her mother's operation the next day necessitated her speedy return to London. John's anxiety over her mother resulted in her being taken ill in the middle of the night and left her for several days with a roaring temperature. Snail-like she regathered strength and began to work. With John needing more time on her own, Una invited Andrea over to Paris for company.

Andrea arrived on 1 October and stayed for a week, before going up to Oxford on the 12th. Though she was nearly nineteen, Una still treated her as an ill-disciplined child. She told Audrey: 'John and I are paralysed to realise that she will next week be wearing a cap and long (scholar's) gown! She looks about thirteen!'[41]

For once Una spent most of her time with Andrea, and for her daughter it was one of the pleasantest times she had ever spent with her mother. While John worked, Una met Andrea at the Gare du Nord, drove her through Paris and the Bois, took her sightseeing to Sacré Cœur, Versailles and St Cloud. They went shopping, walked in the Champ de Mars, and dined out together. On her last evening both John and Una took her to a night-club. Una was able to report proudly: 'Andrea blissful.'[42] Una even helped her pack before she and John saw her off. If only Una and John had managed to spend more days like that with Andrea, a relationship beneficial to all of them might have ensued. Sadly, Una's sudden attentiveness towards her was instigated by John's growing isolation.

Una cheered up when on Andrea's departure John discussed the new novel with her, which was begun on 14 October. John wrote feverishly and by 26 October was able to dictate the first chapter to Una. At last John had real work; the exile was over. They decided to return to England and reached London on 1 November.

In their absence Virginia Woolf had utilized the trial of *The Well of Loneliness* in *A Room of One's Own*, her newly published book. Following the award to Virginia Woolf of the Prix Femina for *To the Lighthouse*, the notoriety attached to Virginia Woolf's *Orlando* had led to unprecedented sales for her work.[43] Although this was fuelled by its *roman-à-clef* associations with Vita Sackville-West, the match had been lit by *The Well of Loneliness* controversy.

Virginia Woolf recognized that *The Well* described a realm of experience which was part of her own agenda in *Orlando*, an experience which society did not wish to hear lest it be threatened. Her reflections on Hall's trial were now incorporated in coded form in *A Room of One's Own*.[44]

Virginia Woolf's book was based on two lectures delivered in October 1928 to young women at Girton and Newnham Colleges, Cambridge, many of whom had copied Hall's Eton-cropped hairstyle. Woolf's heroine, Judith Shakespeare, the dramatist's fictional sister, has been identified as Radclyffe Hall.[45] Virginia's academic audience would have known that Radclyffe Hall claimed descent from Shakespeare's daughter and that some supporters of Hall had tried to use Shakespeare's Sonnets as evidence in the trial.

Shakespeare's sister becomes the oppressed woman artist in any age but, in the context of the times in which Woolf was speaking, she also becomes 'Radclyffe Hall'. Woolf tried to achieve two things: to connect non-feminist lesbians like Radclyffe Hall's circle and Vita Sackville-West with women's political cause, but also to link all women with the suffering of lesbians.

With her ironic request to the Cambridge women students to check that Sir Chartres Biron was not eavesdropping, it was clear that Hall's obscenity trial was still in progress. Subtly, Virginia Woolf invited her audience to join her in a conspiracy of sexual and verbal transgression, which both echoed Hall's trial and transcended it – a conspiracy first with her live audience, and later with her readers, of women in league against authority over the matter of sexual choices and women's freedom.

Openly accompanying her to the lectures was Vita Sackville-West, who was known to have devoted much energy to organizing support for Radclyffe Hall. Lesbianism itself therefore was seen to be as much on trial as literary free speech. The precise words of Virginia Woolf's lecture – an oblique commentary on *The Well* case and on its presiding magistrate – took up and focused these implications:

> Are there no men present? Do you promise me that behind that red curtain over there the figure of Sir Chartres Biron is not concealed? We are all women you assure me? Then I may tell you that the very next words I read were these – 'Chloe liked Olivia. . . .' Do not start. Do not blush. Let us admit in the privacy of our own society that these things sometimes happen. Sometimes women do like women . . . 'Chloe liked Olivia,' I read . . . All these relationships between women, I thought, rapidly recalling the splendid gallery of fictitious women, are too simple. So much has been left out, unattempted . . . Almost without exception they are shown in their relation to men . . . Now if Chloe likes Olivia and they share a laboratory . . . it . . . will light a torch in that vast chamber where nobody has yet been.[46]

As Virginia Woolf discusses her fictitious novelist Mary Carmichael, whose twin heroines Chloe and Olivia share a laboratory, and 'like' each other, she allows that liking to serve as a sign for lesbian desire. As she suggests that women can exist in relation to each other, as she posits the nature of female homoeroticism in terms of that vast chamber where nobody has yet been, she also acknowledges that Radclyffe Hall has been there before her. Hall knows that these things sometimes happen, that women sometimes do like women. Hall's book was struck off the literary register for just that knowledge.

In the holograph notes for *A Room of One's Own*, after the phrase 'Chloe liked Olivia. They shared a . . .', Woolf wrote:

> The words covered the bottom of the page; the pages had stuck. While fumbling to open them there flashed into my mind the inevitable policeman . . . the order to attend the Court, the dreary waiting; the Magistrate coming in with a little bow . . . for the Prosecution, for the Defence – the verdict; this book is obscene + [sic] flames sing, perhaps on Tower Hill, as they compound (?) [sic] that mass of paper. Here the paper came apart. Heaven be praised! It was only a laboratory. Chloe–Olivia.[47]

In this draft, Virginia Woolf patently feels anxious about whether her own book with its coded references to Hall's trial could, like the banned book, go up in flames.

Of course it did not. That Hall was forced to make a stand whereas Woolf was not was as much to do with their politics as their literature and not a little to do with the conduct of their personal lives, the profound differences in the way they each 'liked' other women. When Virginia Woolf wrote: 'These Sapphists love women; friendship is never untinged with amorosity,'[48] Vita and John were among those she termed 'these Sapphists'.[49] It was a group in which she did not include herself.

The two writers however had one thing in common. Like John, Virginia felt she was not quite one thing or another. Virginia, 'not a man nor a woman',[50] used this notion creatively in her fictional biography. Orlando, inhabiting two gender worlds, highlights Virginia's own dilemmas. But where Virginia had concerns about her sexual identity, John had concerns about her gender identity. John loved and emulated the power of men but she distrusted their destructiveness. The burdens of the past would always trigger some confusions for her as they did for Virginia Woolf. But unlike Woolf, Hall the spiritual realist either fiercely stamped them out, shut them down, or let God deal with them. She was God's creature. He would know what to do with her and others like her, even if the world did not.

If Virginia Woolf was reluctant to embrace knowledge about those Sapphists, her mother-in-law Marie Woolf claimed to have no knowledge at all of the practices that *The Well of Loneliness* had recently brought to her attention. Mrs Woolf, who had acquired the banned book at Harrods because her daughter Bella had been at school with Marguerite Radclyffe-Hall, said to Virginia:

> It is a dreadful pity . . . that such a book should have been published . . . What I mean is that there are many unmarried women living alone. And now it is very hard on them that such a book should have been written . . . you may think me very foolish – I am 76 – but until I read this book I did not know that such things . . . went on at all . . . When I was at school there was nothing like that.

Leonard impatiently assured her that it went on at his school: 'It was the most corrupt place I've ever been in.' Even Leonard, liberal champion of *The Well*, called school homosexuality 'corrupt'.[51]

That John's world view had been severely shaken by those who saw homosexuality as 'corrupt' made her more firmly entrenched in her Sapphist position. Una too became increasingly intolerant of closeted inverts, commenting about a departing Rye neighbour who had remained closeted: 'Rye will be well rid of her . . . we have no use for an invert who is ashamed of her kind and cowards can only do harm.'[52] Both John and Una felt that wealth or independence bred an obligation in lesbians to be open: 'I have very little sympathy indeed with the woman invert of independent means who resorts to camouflage,' wrote Una on behalf of them both.[53]

Returning to Rye in late November, their loan of Journey's End having expired, they booked into the Mermaid Inn where they stayed for several months while they househunted. On their first day in Rye they viewed The Black Boy, an ancient house with leaded windows and a crooked oak door in the High Street. Its name came from 'Black Charles', the nickname given to King Charles II who was reputed to have stayed in the house. Una, the hero-worshipper, felt a deep affinity with him. John generously decided to buy The Black Boy, put it in Una's name, and give it to her for Christmas.

Andrea joined them after her first term at Oxford, and on Christmas Day they took sweets and sixpences to the twenty-nine children living at Hucksteps Row, then walked on the Marsh in 'a gale and rain'. A new pattern of life in Rye had begun.

The Black Boy inevitably needed a complete overhaul and major renovations, so while these were in progress they moved out of the Mermaid Inn the following March and took a short lease on a furnished house at 8 Watchbell Street.

In Rye John would atone for Egan's blasphemous cartoon, for Mackenzie's outrages, for the world's injustice to inverts. Hall and her book *The Well* had in some dreadful way been used to insult God but through her writing would come absolution. She felt safe and at peace in Rye. She believed that in this small town with its cobbled streets, 'where you can get away from this hideous age of progress',[54] she was about to create her greatest novel, *The Master of the House*.

18

THE RYE RELATIONSHIP

One of Radclyffe Hall's most intense relationships was her relationship with Rye. A fortified Cinque Port trapped by the sea, Rye in the thirteenth and fourteenth centuries was bustling with merchants, sailors, smugglers, pirates. The sense of the sea is still there, though the waters have receded and broad stretches of marshland have replaced the ebb and flow of the tides. In this place encircled by three rivers, John still felt the missing sea in her bones and recaptured its past in her writing.

When she stayed at the Mermaid Inn, whose black and white timbered façade and distinctive sign hung over the steep cobbled street, she would sit near the bar, where in the past the notorious Hawkhurst smugglers kept their loaded pistols beside their tankards. She would drink in their adventures, soak up the atmosphere, reproduce it ineffably in one of her finest novels, *The Sixth Beatitude*.

She would listen to the tale of the ghost of a serving maid who lost her heart to one of the smugglers and who was said to return just before midnight. Was it to her room? Was it to Una's? It could have been. Ghosts were an ordinary part of John's existence. She felt comfortable with ghosts, content in Rye. The town was recondite, secretive; it held her close.

She liked what she saw. The brushwood, the rock, the strangled river beds. The silence, the desertion, the dozy afternoons. Those who lived around Romney Marsh were impatient of interruption. They stood with their backs to the community, looking away from gossip, detached from the world's concerns.

The constant sight of masts and sails at remote distances offered John the presence of the sea more powerfully than when she was close to it. The lines of light – she lived inside the lines of light, the ever-changing light that quickened the flats of the rivers and canals. She felt the Marshes were organic, alive, and the sun lifted her misery when it shone with a double lustre over Romney

Marsh. She could use that sun in a novel about Rye – Turner's sun, Patmore's sun.[1] It became the light in *The Sixth Beatitude* that 'suddenly brightened and deepened, so that the cattle that grazed on the edge of the marsh . . . looked as though magicked', looked as though changed 'into glowing enamel'.[2]

She walked on the Marsh – often with Una or the dogs, but often on her own – watching the sun settle above the shingle, listening to the wind music that slipped into her writing and shut out the world. While she consciously thought about *The Carpenter's Son*, every day she imperceptibly gathered material for *The Sixth Beatitude*.

In the latter novel she recalls (in Rother) the Rye of 1930, the year of her passionate attachment:

> [It] would sometimes seem more than a town of old, decaying black-and-white houses huddling inside an ancient town wall – Rother would almost seem like a person. Rother could draw unto itself lovely colours: soft greys and soft browns and soft, dark purples; and at sunrise and sunset its red roofs would blaze, and so would the leaded panes of its windows; and after a storm all its cobbles would shine . . . And then there were the tall, straight masts of the ships that lay at the bottom of Anchor Street where the sea had once washed against the Strand, and where now there was only a tidal river . . . Rother would seem to stare down at those ships with old, thoughtful eyes very full of affection.[3]

Rother seemed almost like a person, and it seemed to be the only person John needed that year – and the next – though she did not say as much. She hugged it to herself much as a silent lover. She would stand beneath the church clock, and read the plaque on the clock face between the Quarterboys. 'For our time is a very shadow that passeth away.'* Time in Rye took on a different meaning for her, slower, older. She adopted its rhythm in both *The Carpenter's Son* and *The Sixth Beatitude*.

Little wonder, she thought, that Coventry Patmore called it 'a town in a trance'. It lay as though under an enchantment which John quickly succumbed to, like Ford Madox Ford before her. He had trodden her Marsh. He had regarded it as 'an infectious and holding neighbourhood': 'once you go there you are apt there to stay.'[4] Ever since reading his books, which Violet had first loaned her, she had felt a strong link with Ford. Now she knew it to be this secret love.

Rye's recondite charms had laid a spell on many writers before Radclyffe Hall had arrived there. Ford (at twenty-four known as Hueffer), then living at Aldington Knoll, had enticed the American writers Stephen Crane and W.H. Hudson to Rye, and rented out Pent Farm to the 40-year-old Joseph Conrad.

---

* The Rye church clock is believed to be one of the oldest in the country. On each side of the clock face are two figures, the Quarterboys, so called since they strike the quarter hours only.

In February 1899 Stephen Crane and his wife Cora rented Brede House with its lurid reputation as a smugglers' haunt. Cora wrote to Edward Garnett expressing her hopes for Stephen that 'the perfect quiet of Brede Place and the freedom from a lot of good, dear people, who take his mind from his work, will let him show the world a book that will live.'[5] Una knew what Cora Crane meant. Too many dear good people were 'anxious by their friendliness to express their appreciation of John's "good fight"' so she, like Cora, had to keep people 'at bay until the book [*The Carpenter's Son*] is ended'.[6]

In 1898, when Henry James was fifty-five and John but eighteen, James came to live permanently at Lamb House in Rye. Between 1898 and 1914 James corresponded with H.G. Wells, later a supporter of John's, who lived at Spade House at Sandgate on the Kentish coast. It was on Wells and Conrad that James depended for literary companionship, though he frequently saw the Rudyard Kiplings and intermittently socialized with the young Ford Madox Hueffer and with Lady Maude Warrender, daughter of the Earl of Shaftesbury, who with her lover the singer Marcia van Dresser was to become a good friend of John's.

From 1909 Violet Hunt, then in the early stages of her scandalous liaison with Ford, visited James regularly until James heard that Ford's wife Elsie intended to sue Ford for divorce, at which point he broke off hospitable overtures.

John appears to have shared Henry James's love–hate relationship with town and country, London and Rye. When she, like James, was in the marshlands, her cosmopolitan soul longed for London; when she, like James, was in the city, she pined for Rye. It was partly James's presence that beckoned his contemporaries and successors like the American poet Conrad Aiken, T.S. Eliot's friend, to this literary retreat.

In the early thirties John met the 41-year-old Aiken, then currently mentor to the young Malcolm Lowry. In 1924 Aiken, like John, had lost his heart to the circling jackdaws and the vast intricate Marsh map of green around Rye. It was his childhood home of Savannah, Georgia, in microcosm. He bought Jeake's House (where he lived for twenty-three years), a remarkable listed building in Mermaid Street. Once a wool store, it had wood panelling, oak beams and an eighteenth-century galleried former chapel. His study, which John surveyed with envy, overlooked a mile of green marsh and the blue edge of the Channel.

Jeake's House became the site for voluble literary gatherings to which John and Una were soon invited. The brilliance of Bernard Shaw, Arthur Bliss, and the poet H.D. which had rung through the gallery had given way, by John's time, to a medley of eccentric talents that set Rye tongues wagging. In this company, John regained some of her old fire. Una traded ideas with the artists Edward Burra and Paul Nash, while John indulged in literary gossip with the writer Francis Yeats-Brown, former assistant editor of the *Spectator*, his girlfriend Rosalind Constable and the novelist E.F. Benson (called Dodo by his friends after the title of his first novel).

Malcolm Lowry, young, dishevelled and on the edge of dipsomania, regarded by Aiken's second wife Clarissa as 'a caged lion . . . never been house-broken', constantly widened the eyes of John's staid neighbours with his revelries. His worst antic was to induce Aiken to join him in a javelin-throwing contest across the Rother river. Too drunk to release their weapons properly, they both fell in and emerged like bloodied, mudstreaked apparitions.

In comparison with these exploits, John and Una, called by Aiken the 'Roaring Girls', behaved with relative decorum, although one anecdote of Aiken's has it that the 'astonishing pair . . . could be heard almost every morning bawling out the wretched little tailor in the High Street, or flinging back at him, all publicly, a badly made pair of breeches'.[7] Though Rye did not take kindly to either breeches or breaches of social propriety, the fact that John felt she could wear the first and handle the second, showed her ease in the town.

In 1930 E.F. 'Dodo' Benson, author of the Mapp and Lucia novels (popular in the thirties and still read today), had taken over James's Lamb House. As one-time Mayor of Rye, he was the first of this new literary coterie to welcome John and Una, and thereafter John began to lunch with him regularly.

Sheila Kaye-Smith, who had been one of John's witnesses, in between writing books farmed with her husband Penrose Fry in a converted oast-house called Little Doucegrove at near-by Northiam. Initially Una called the 'Small Frys' 'affectionate and dear' and regarded Sheila's 'quite remarkable talent in *Tamarisk Town* [as] almost amounting to genius'. Later events soured her appreciation, though not John's.[8]

In 1931 John involved another Rye resident, the writer J.D. Beresford, who lived in West Street, in her endemic hobby of buying and selling houses. She purchased Santa Maria in West Street from Beresford for £1,000 as an investment, but for once her financial acumen deserted her and when she sold it in 1937 she received only £900.[9]

She did not mind. During her years in Rye she purchased more properties in one town than at any other time or in any other area. It was as if she wanted a stake in the earth near Romney Marsh.

In the January of 1930, snow blew thickly over the Marsh. Rye was 'as white as a bridal veil with soft folds of snow on its roofs and cobbles'.[10] In the world outside Rye's falling snowflakes even harsher weather prevailed. In the United States the great Depression worsened. Unemployment was rife. In India, Gandhi's civil disobedience campaign sought independence from British rule. The Allied occupation of Germany finally ended, but the Nazi party won a third of the seats in the German Reichstag. There was a steely change in the political climate.

John, usually alert to political issues, seemed to view them as if at one remove. Temporarily she reposed in Watchbell Street* where Mabel Bourne was re-interviewed as a permanent housekeeper, as The Black Boy would not be ready to receive their furniture until 6 August. Mabel, who stayed with them longer than any other servant, did not live in but for years maintained the house and the two women with great dedication. As Sybil Thorndike came to tea and Axel Munthe dined,[11] John juggled social niceties with the growing feeling that she was engaged on a pilgrimage with *The Carpenter's Son* and should not brook interruptions.

Una, meanwhile, continued to pursue her own ambitions. Between June and September she finished the French translation of *The Well*. In October her stage version of Colette's *Chéri* was produced by the Stage Society at the Prince of Wales Theatre, largely thanks to Gabrielle Enthoven's intervention as a member of the Society's council.

Both Una and John constantly interfered with the production. Tempers grew short. Finally a blazing row about costumes took place between Gabrielle and Una. 'Gabrielle Enthoven behaved disgracefully,' fumed Una, who took months to forgive her. The first night was weak and 'The press for *Chéri* unspeakable.'[12]

Earlier that year, 1930, Una had begun a Day Book, her second journal. In it she gave vent to her greed for gossip, and her malicious wit focused on catty descriptions of Rye residents. An increasing number of entries mentioned John's 'seediness' or her self-withdrawal. This became most noticeable during Andrea's visits.

On 13 January Andrea missed her train, did not arrive until after luncheon, and Una felt she should be admonished.[13] John was too weary to intervene. 'I lectured her all afternoon and she left after tea,' Una noted resignedly.[14] When Andrea returned in April to spend the Easter vacation with them, John hardly spoke to her.

John hungered to re-create the glorious energy which had streaked through her days on *The Well*. Una wondered if a trip to London would stimulate her. Periodically they used a Daimler and chauffeur to drive up if they needed hair-cuts, spectacles for John, or new clothes. They also used it for their regular sessions with Mrs Leonard who now had a cottage at Tankerton near Canterbury. Una had begun to rely on the spiritual Ladye's 'enduring affection and near-ness'[15] for more comfort than she was currently receiving from the material John.

John agreed to a ten-day trip to London in June during which she summoned her strength in order to be sociable with Ellen Glasgow, Gabrielle Enthoven and Axel Munthe. On 3 July they dined at 56 South Eaton Place with

---

* Watchbell Street was so named in 1499 after the Mayor erected a bell at the lookout to warn of invasion from France.

Ida, the writer with whom John maintained perhaps her firmest bond. John and Ida discussed the sales of *The Well* which between January and the end of December 1929 were reportedly 73,900.[16] By the end of June over 100,000 copies had been sold in America alone, which gave John royalties of $60,000.

Time with Ida did not entirely help to reconcile John to London life. A moody paranoia was beginning to take possession of her. Despite a pleasant Christmas spent earlier with Patience Ross and Robin, this paranoia had begun to affect her relationship with both of them. Patience had shown them a bright young writer's manuscript whose theme, John decided, had been stolen from *The Unlit Lamp*. She complained to Audrey of Patience's 'impudence' and insisted that Patience no longer deal with her affairs. John was becoming obsessed with plagiarism. Audrey had already been forced to listen to John's wild idea that Galsworthy had pirated one of her plots.[17] Even Darling Robin was accused of 'muddles'. The London visit was not a success.

Fortunately in July, at a pageant staged at the Barn Theatre in Smallhythe, John met three local residents who immediately raised her spirits with their pranks and theatricals and would rank amongst her closest friends in the coming years. These were Edy Craig, Ellen Terry's daughter, the writer Christopher St John and the painter Clare 'Tony' Atwood – known locally as the Smallhythe Trio, called by John Gielgud (Ellen Terry's great-nephew) 'the famous trio' and by Una 'Edy and the Boys'. They lived in the Priest's House, a timbered cottage which had been a present from Ellen Terry to Edy. It was a few minutes' walk from the Barn, which was next to Smallhythe Place, the cottage where Ellen Terry had seen out her days. On the actress's death in 1928, the Trio had turned the Place into a memorial museum which became the centre for artistic schemes, craft shows, jumble sales and wild flings that amazed the locals.

Edy, who had acted at the Lyceum under Henry Irving with some of her mother's brilliance, had converted the barn in order to stage annual performances in Ellen Terry's memory. Although Edy could be bossy and difficult, she was a woman who radiated warmth and generosity. Unflinchingly loyal, she had an earthy charisma to which John responded.

Chris, a fervent Catholic convert like John, changed her name from Christabel Marshall to Christopher St John after John the Baptist to whom she felt a special devotion. Edy and Chris had met as a result of Chris's 'crush' on Ellen Terry, whose biography she later wrote. The great actress brought her home and asked Edy to look after her. Their sexual intimacy was quickly established and they lived together for forty-eight years from 1899 until Edy's death.*

---

* Initially Edy Craig and Christopher St John lived together in Smith Square, Westminster, where their friends dubbed them 'the Squares' because they were not. Subsequently they moved to Smallhythe.

Like Edy, Chris had become actively involved in the militant suffrage movement, on leaving Oxford, and in 1909 she was arrested for setting fire to a pillar box. She collaborated with Cicely Hamilton on several witty propaganda plays including the famous *Votes for Women*.*

In 1911, together with Gabrielle Enthoven and Laurence Housman, Chris and Edy founded the Pioneer Players, an important theatre club specializing in foreign, feminist and avant-garde plays, which in 1912 had given the first performance of Shaw's banned play *Mrs Warren's Profession* which John and Ladye had attended.

In 1928 Edy and Chris formed a *ménage à trois* with Clare Atwood (1866–1962), known as Tony. It had been Edy's idea which Chris, hesitant and awkward at first, finally accepted. It was made easier by Tony's sweet-natured presence and peace-keeping qualities. Tony and Chris both wore masculine jackets and trousers, topped in Tony's case by an aged Panama hat. Edy, the undoubted leader, called Chris 'Master Baby' and Clare–Tony 'the Brat'.

Tony was a figurative artist of distinction who painted interiors, portraits, architectural subjects, landscapes and still lifes; exhibited at the Royal Academy, and was one of the first women commissioned as a war artist during the First World War. Like Christopher and John she was a devout Roman Catholic and one of her gifts to John was a relic of the True Cross. John kept it safe all her days.

John took at once to the Trio, who instantly reciprocated her affection. These three women cemented her attachment to Rye. John would smile to herself at the threesome who lived life to the full and outraged everyone's expectations. She knew what that felt like.

Una found Chris an 'interesting and rather tragic figure' though she was initially somewhat taken aback by her looks. Chris, Una felt, was 'ugly as few are ugly, to deformity, physically a sort of "ugly Duchess" with a sort of impediment in her speech that must have been near to being a cleft palate'. But she fastened on to Chris's intellect: 'Her mind and personality are so brilliant and honest and fine that the ugliness is eclipsed and forgotten, by all but herself. Violent too and incapable of compromise, she falls out with those who would have her do so and one loves her for her intransigence.'[18] In her inability to compromise Chris somewhat resembled John, and perhaps it was that familiar characteristic to which Una responded with a mixture of respect and irritation.

Sometimes the Trio were accompanied by their lesbian friend Vera 'Jack' Holme, who helped with Barn theatricals, a woman two years younger than John, whom Edy and the Boys had known since their suffragette days. In the

---

* Produced in 1909. Chris was not only a playwright, but also a novelist and music critic; she wrote several biographies, including a well-reviewed one of Ethel Smyth.

years 1910–11 she was arrested and charged with obstruction three times and like Ethel Smyth was imprisoned in Holloway Gaol. As a young woman Vera/Jack was described by Sylvia Pankhurst as 'a noisy, explosive young person, frequently rebuked by her elders for lack of dignity'.[19]

That explosiveness is what attracted her to John who envied her the training she had had with the WSPU guerrilla army. From 1909 when she was twenty-seven she was the WSPU chauffeur who drove Emmeline and Christabel Pankhurst round Britain. One of the WSPU publicity postcards sold to raise funds for the vote was of Vera/Jack in her uniform.*

At a Barn gala in July John and Una re-established their acquaintance with Clemence Dane,† who delivered the address on Ellen Terry before a performance of scenes from Shakespeare by John Gielgud, Violet Vanbrugh and Edith Evans. Dane, a former Slade art student, had briefly been an actress, and became involved in Barn theatricals in the same manner as John and Una. A committed feminist, she had written a collection of essays, *The Women's Side* (1926), aimed at encouraging women to think about matters of political and social policy.

Through the Smallhythe jumble sales where, according to Una, 'we gazed with rapture . . . Christopher's shrunken vests jostled things of such unthinkable dilapidation that they seemed only ready for decent cremation', John met several more lesbian writers, such as G.B. 'Peter' Stern, and many ex-suffrage workers including Isobel 'Toto' Goldingham.

Those palmy summer days at Smallhythe remained in John and Una's memories as cloudless, rose-strewn, bewitched. When Edy was away on holiday she lent them the key to the Priest's House. Blissfully they lounged in hammocks in the garden, momentarily at ease, chattering idly, listening to sounds drifting in from the Marsh.

The Smallhythe zinnias faded as autumn replaced summer. On 28 November Toto Goldingham invited them to her house to meet her friend Mary Allen, then the country's best known policewoman. In 1914 she had helped her lover Margaret Damer Dawson (who died in 1920) establish the Women's Volunteer Police Force, which during the war became the Women's Police Service, with Mary Allen as Commandant.

Although today we do not usually envisage the women's police as either politically radical or feminist in focus, for Mary Allen, a former militant suffragette, the setting up of such a force was an explicitly feminist goal, with which John and Una were in absolute sympathy. As Mary Allen pointed out, 'many of the women attracted by the idea of women police had been prominent

---

* A photograph of Vera 'Jack' Holme (1882–1969), taken in 1960 and found among her private papers after her death, shows her wearing full male dinner dress.
† Clemence Dane was the pen name of Winifred Ashton (1887–1965).

workers for women's suffrage . . . their efforts . . . had brought some into close, sometimes painful, touch with the police, teaching them how very unpleasant it is for an alleged woman culprit to be handled by men.'[20]

Under Margaret Damer Dawson, Mary Allen and Toto Goldingham, the WPS had been effectively run. But massive opposition to its prominent lesbian composition had led the Home Office to disband it after the war and it was not until after the Second World War that an official women's police force was formally constituted. In the meantime, Mary Allen continued campaigning, lecturing widely on the subject of the women's force, founding the *Policewoman Review*, and setting up a Women's Emergency Corps during the General Strike. But it was only by these unofficial means that the force survived between the wars. John and Una believed that the authorities were hostile to Mary because she was an invert. All they wanted was 'fluffy policewomen', scoffed Una.[21]

Certainly Mary, known as Robert, and her companion Miss Taggart looked anything but fluffy. Mary's lesbianism was flamboyantly indicated by her monocle, Eton-cropped hair and addiction to police uniform on both public and private occasions. Her passion for police dress, knee-high boots, breeches and peaked cap was shared by Miss Taggart, a former sub-Inspector in the WPS, who lived with Mary and their two St Bernards at Danehill, the house originally owned by Damer Dawson at Lympne in Kent.* Their appeal to Una was that they were 'both alike intensely friendly and in very obvious personal sympathy with John and with our views'.[22]

In Rye, John and Una saw more of Wilma and Dickie, who lived in the Hucksteps. They were lesbian but not feminist, more like one of Havelock Ellis's stereotypical couples. When over made-up, Wilma looked, according to Una's uncharitable pen, as though 'she had been buried and dug up just as decomposition set in!'[23] Dickie, beefier and more staid, watched Wilma chase other women, even bring one, a certain Pat Chambers, back to their ménage at Hucksteps Row. Distraught, Dickie confided in Una, who sternly decided that Pat and Wilma should be debarred from their home. Though Una was more intransigent than ever on the matter of loyalty, John knew all too well just how easily a *ménage à trois* can occur.

Having moved into The Black Boy on John's birthday, 12 August 1930, they spent their first Christmas there. Though Una's relationship with John had changed and diminished she wrote sturdily in her Day Book:

> This, our first Christmas at The Black Boy, was the happiest we have ever spent together . . . on Christmas Eve Sheila and Penrose Fry dined . . . and went with us to Midnight Mass, the 15th in succession for which John and I have been together

---

* The fact that after Dawson's death Mary Allen continued to live at Danehill with a new partner indicates that she had been the major beneficiary under Dawson's will.

. . . John gave me a gold identity disc bracelet and I gave her a gold (country) watch chain.[24]

For the second Yuletide running they went to Hucksteps Row to give out sweets and sixpences to the neighbours' children. This year however their own child, now a young woman, was not with them. By December 1930, relations between Andrea and Una and John had deteriorated dramatically.

It is hard to know how Una felt. Anger with Andrea tended to displace distress. She seemed composed enough on 28 December, when Noël Coward and two friends turned up at The Black Boy after lunch. She revelled in showing them round and discovering that Noël 'adored every inch of the house'. He told tall stories so that they 'all howled with laughter', Una describing it as 'harmless and not ill-natured laughter such as Noël excels in. He is one of the only people . . . who succeeds in being chronically and excruciatingly witty without victimising anyone or making anyone feel that his next excess will be at one's own expense.'[25]

Their sixteenth year together closed with John writing till one a.m. in the study where Una patiently sat with her until she heard 'the midnight bells coming down the great chimney'.[26]

By 1931 John had developed a debilitating pattern. Most nights she worked till 2.30 a.m. Una, unable to sleep, would creep down to find John in a 'bitter cold room, fire out'. Una was aware that 'it distresses and sometimes annoys her that I should stay awake but I cannot help it . . . my nerve is shaken . . . All my eggs, dear Lord, in that one basket, and not my earthly love can make it stronger or protect it from harm.'[27]

John drove herself without mercy. While engrossed in writing the life of a modern Christ-figure, not only did she live chastely but her involvement with the sanctity of her subject caused her a curious medical condition. She had written the first four chapters when she was struck by continual pain first in the palm of her right hand, then in her left. When an angry red stain appeared in the centre of each palm she consulted a distinguished radiologist. Deep ray treatment did nothing. Una believed the stains were stigmata. John, sure that they were, simply endured the pain until the book was finished, whereupon the blemishes vanished.

Forced to write with both hands in bandages, she now firmly believed that if she was to achieve fine literature the writing process itself would necessarily involve pain. It was as if John had suddenly discovered that the secret of life was suffering. Some of her arrogance had dwindled away. Like her hero Oscar Wilde she saw humility as the honest acceptance of all experience. Wilde had learnt that kind of humility in Reading Gaol. John had learnt hers through the trial.

But John's desire to make the novel an act of penance, similar to her penitential abstinence after Ladye's death, affected Una badly. Having worked through the night, John was often too exhausted to eat breakfast, so they seldom ate together. Worse in Una's view, John had insisted on separate bedrooms, and consistently locked Una out. Gossip from the servants reveals that rows would often take place around midnight outside John's bedroom. Una would be desperate for sexual affection, John steely and indifferent. Bessy, a maid sent to work for Una at The Black Boy, reported: 'It was very difficult last night – Lady Troubridge was lying outside Radclyffe Hall's door saying "John darling, let me in!"'[28]

From 12 January for nearly a month, they stayed at the Royal Crescent Hotel, Brighton, for John to regain her strength.[29] The stratagem came too late. Six days after their arrival she sank into another depression, 'brooding upon the exile of *The Well*'.[30] Then she fell ill and stayed ill.

The economic crisis had brought down the Labour Government in Britain and a National Coalition had been formed. Staying in their hotel was the Labour Home Secretary, J.R. Clynes. Seeing Clynes served to remind John 'of the way in which the Labour people used her case as a whip to flog the Conservatives and then threw it overboard when they came into power . . . with a word he could wipe out the stain that rests from the book.'[31]

If John had been revealed as an open lesbian then her society had been revealed as smug, two-faced and hypocritical, but for John nothing mattered more than that stain of having her honestly undertaken work branded as obscene – a stain which in her eyes had wiped out the novel's mass circulation in a dozen languages, with sales at 150,000 in the English language alone.

Pragmatically Una pointed out that John's sickness was a reasonable response to having written ninety thousand words in fourteen months; if John, she said, chose to 'write on controversial subjects . . . an inevitable consequence is a controversial press'. But John still hungered for 'universal approval'.[32]

She was somewhat cheered by several pieces of optimistic news. She received the Czech translation of *The Well* 'beautifully produced'. She heard from Tauchnitz that *The Unlit Lamp* had sold 5,400 copies between its first appearance on 18 November and 31 December.[33] Harrison Smith cabled from New York that sales of *A Saturday Life* up to date were 4,275 and that it was 'still selling' in spite of the 'atrocious book season'.[34]

John told Una she was pleased, but a bitter edge tinged her pleasure. Outside the wind howled, storms blew up, and both John and Una succumbed to a bad attack of influenza.[35] During her bout John lost her appetite, apart from a wild craving for bath buns which 'turned out a dry snare and a delusion'. The only preface to a meal that gave her 'the ghost of an appetite' seemed to be a dry martini 'with a dash'. 'We both felt subhuman,' recorded Una's Day Book, John greatly 'down and discouraged'. Though Una's remedy as always was 'to stay close by her and try and cheer her',[36] John more often preferred to be left alone to read Edgar Wallace shockers.

Marie Visetti's age and frailty began to worry John. Did she, at seventy-five, as Una believed need a constant companion? Impossible, thought John; Marie 'flies into insane rages at the smallest sign of opposition . . . and uses physical violence to all and sundry'.[37] Should she herself care for her mother? Lunacy, thought Una.

Though John still hankered for a mother whom she would 'want to keep near us', Una dismissed the problem with characteristic brusqueness: 'We are so utterly sufficient to one another that I doubt whether we should have had much room for parents . . . or children, and if one of us died and the other survived, no outsider would be of any consolation.'[38]

Una had already short-sightedly relegated her sister Viola, her mother Minna Taylor, her close friends Jacqueline and May, to positions of unimportance. It was her relationship with Andrea, however, which proved beyond any reasonable doubt that she had 'no room' for children and that Cubby would always remain an 'outsider' who could never prove a consolation.

On 5 February 1931 Una received a letter from her stepdaughter Chatty Gurney asking for Andrea's present address and lamenting that Cubby had failed to answer letters from the family. Una remarked tetchily: 'It really is outrageous of Andrea . . . her stepsisters have been quite kind to her . . . and without her brother's allowance she could not live on the Admiralty pension of £36 a year – but she has never seemed grateful.'

Perhaps unspoken doubts about her relationship with John caused Una to feel less in control of events than usual. Her tactic now was to try and take control of her daughter's life. On 9 February she instructed Harold Rubinstein to ascertain officially whether Andrea was really living at the address she had given and with whom. 'Until she is 21 – another nearly 9 months – I must know something of her whereabouts and activities – it is all very depressing.'[39] By 12 February Rubinstein reported back to Una that Andrea was living where she had affirmed, the place was 'quite respectable' but when he called at 9.40 a.m. Andrea's two flat mates were still in bed and 'Miss Troubridge was not dressed and would not see him!!'[40]

As spring settled over Rye, and the thorn trees grew heavy with blossoms, Una tried to entice John out into the burgeoning sun. But the hours dragged on as John silently secreted herself away with Winifred Hales, her new secretary, using Una less as a reader now. It comes as no surprise that Hales, the pretty secretary from Iden, became the next target for Una's wrath.

In September 1931 the young and bonny Hales fell ill and Radclyffe Hall sent her home. This fact is established by everyone. Thereafter the version given to me by the elderly Winifred Reed (formerly Hales), who still had a vivid recollection of events, is very different from the irascible account left by Una in her Day Book.

20 September: Mrs Hales, the secretary's mother, having waited 18 hours before the girl was due to resume work, rang up to say that her daughter 'was not progressing as well as had been expected' etc. . . . Having prevented me from making other arrangements, she lets us down at the last hour! John terribly upset and no wonder . . . What an iniquitous letdown . . . the girl has always been purely hysterical.

The Day Book for 21 September continued: 'I have rung up Hales . . . she comes this morning to hand over her work so is not too ill to be on the move. I only wish I could have the pleasure of boxing her ears.'

Hales arrived at 11.30 that morning. Una, furious, says that Hales had announced:

a) that she had received and never given notice
b) she was a monthly servant
c) she claimed wages and insurances in lieu of one month's notice.

All of which fictions were duly demolished and she left somewhat subdued.

Nowhere in the Day Book is there any evidence that Hales was paid wages by Una. Nor is any reason given as to why Hales was either fired or 'released' other than that she went home ill with John's permission. There are two more curt entries in Una's hand:

22 September: . . . My beloved is sitting by my bed at work polishing the chapter that I typed for her yesterday. She tells me she met Miss Hales this morning romping around in the rain just in her ordinary mackintosh minus the muffler and heavy over-coat of yesterday. When one thinks of how the girl has chucked up her work in such an emergency!

The 'girl' who was seen 'frisking up West Street' continued to anger Una who had difficulty finding a replacement as local girls (like Hales and horses) needed 'breaking in'.

23 September: . . . Oh if I had my hands on that devil Hales, but she will get no reference for reliability after two years' employment, so I do not think she scores . . . In an emergency I can quite decently take on . . . my results are not decorative and my hesitant touch is annoying to John but I shall get better if I do it often.[41]

That is the authorized version, biblical in its pronouncements.

The unsteady tones of Winifred Reed, nearly ninety, offer us the alternative version of that 'devil Hales', her youthful self: 'I had worked for two years on *The Carpenter's Son* . . . I was proud of the work. I felt it an honour to work for Miss Radclyffe Hall, even though she was remote.'

Radclyffe Hall was not always remote. Sometimes she was fierce.

Once she punished me for leaving a key in the outside of the door . . . she took the key away from me like a naughty child . . . I've still got a note of the date she gave

it back to me . . . It was very undignified to have to ring the bell to get into work . . .
But she was only like that when she was writing. Whenever she was writing she
would get het up. She would swear at me. I was brought up not to swear . . . If she
wasn't writing she would be very generous and kind to me.

That day, that September, she *was* het up. I felt I was bordering on a breakdown
because although I got on well with *her* it was difficult working because Lady
Troubridge was jealous of me. I feel sure she was at the bottom of my leaving. She
felt Miss Hall had a particular affection for me.

According to Winifred Reed, Radclyffe Hall was not angry when she sent her
home that September day; she could see she was ill.

My mother took it into her hands and rang up and said I wouldn't be going in the
next day. So she, Lady Troubridge, turned it around and said: 'Don't come in. Don't
come back.' I didn't get paid. I never got paid. When I went there she made me sign
something to say I wouldn't claim any more money, or that I was paid . . . I went to
a solicitor afterwards but of course it didn't do any good . . . if it is something
unpleasant like that you try and forget it.

But the former Hales seems not to have forgotten much at all: 'I was useful
while I lasted, I did so many things. But they had trouble keeping people . . .
servants or secretaries. Lady Troubridge was the one who got people worked
up, or got Radclyffe Hall against you . . . She could stir up trouble or she could
exacerbate any sort of trouble . . .'

Had Radclyffe Hall felt a 'particular affection' for the young and bonny
Hales? Winifred Reed thought not.

She was always completely 'right', you know right and proper . . . She liked me best
when I was reading her work back to her. One day, just before I got the sack, I was
reading *The Carpenter's Son*, it was beautiful. I didn't cry, but I had a catch in my
voice. She said 'It's only a book Hales, don't be ridiculous.'

Within a few weeks the ordeal was over. John completed *The Carpenter's Son*
on 25 November 1931. Una changed the name of the book to *The Master of the
House*, the title taken from St Mark's Gospel: 'Watch ye therefore: for ye know
not when the master of the house cometh' (13:35).

Their second Christmas in The Black Boy approached. Last year they had
spent it without Andrea. Would she join them this year? At the end of her first
year at Oxford she had taken Pass Moderations in Greek literature, logic and
French but, exhilarated by her performances in university drama productions,
she was set on being an actress. In November, Una had ignored her daughter's
twenty-first birthday, merely recording in her diary: 'Andrea comes of Age.'[42]
She did not see her; there was no celebration. For a woman given to anniversaries, treats and surprises, this was harsh dealing. On 11 December Andrea

arrived in Rye with a bombshell. She intended to leave Oxford without a degree and go on the stage: 'We received Andrea at 11.30 in the library. She went at 3.30, leaving us appalled.'[43]

Una refused to understand Andrea's genuine dilemma. She had no sympathy with her new-found aspirations. There was to be no reconciliation. John acquiesced in Una's attitude. Andrea was not invited for 'family' Christmas.

Instead John and Una's new family, Chris, Edy and Tony, spent the Christmas period with them. They all went to Midnight Mass, opened their presents together, and entertained the 'Small Frys' for Christmas dinner. Una recorded the respect the Trio felt for John. Andrea, in Una's view, had never shown sufficient respect for John. That was Andrea's undoing. It was also Una's loss.

Early in the new year John's close friend Vere Hutchinson died aged only forty-one. During the previous two years Vere had become almost totally paralysed and her bouts of insanity ever more frequent. Budge continued to look after her until she died, managing at the same time regularly to exhibit her linocuts, paintings and pastels.* From 1932 until the end of her own life in 1963, as if she could no longer bear the pain of adult life, Budge began to specialize in illustrating children's books, including Elizabeth Gorrell's 'Bear Bus' series. Budge, who had always been closer to Una, withdrew from John, as if Vere's death had cast a shadow over their relationship. Budge immersed herself in work for the Society of Women Artists, while John let Vere's shadow gather with the others as she set about her work correcting proofs for *The Master of the House*.

A prestigious Foyles luncheon had been arranged to coincide with the publication of her book. Sheila Kaye-Smith annoyed John and Una when she admitted that she had 'wangled herself and her book into the Foyles luncheon'.[44] John, irritated, went to see *Mädchen in Uniform*, a film about 'one of her kind'. Then, calmer, she polished up her tarnished image by having an exceptionally sleek pre-publication photograph in tweed suit and check bow tie, taken by society photographer Howard Coster.†

She decided to be generous to Sheila. At the Foyles luncheon on 17 March John, in Una's phrase, 'eclipsed' Sheila when she was fêted as the guest of honour. She 'spoke most admirably' to an audience of 700, then signed books for more than an hour. Subsequently, John being someone, in Una's view, who 'surpasses the normal human', praised Sheila's book and gave her a signed copy of *The Master of the House*. Una, who rarely surpassed the 'normal

---

* 'Budge', Dorothy Burroughes-Burroughes (1890–1963), trained at the Slade, Heatherleys and in Paris. She was a member of the Royal Society of British Artists and was involved in the Society of Women Artists.

† That particular photograph, taken by Coster on 25 February 1932, now in the National Portrait Gallery, has become one of the most familiar images of Radclyffe Hall.

human', said she 'would oh so gladly have torn [it] out of her mean little hands'.[45]*

John really had a good heart. She followed up every demonstration of fierce impatience, every flare-up, by contrition, compassion and a genuine display of 'niceness'. In *The Master of the House* her protagonist Christophe Bénédit also has a good heart, compassion, inexhaustible charity. Unfortunately Christophe does not share John's flaws or foibles, which are what make her contradictory and compelling.

In terms of a novel, the problem with perfection is that it is boring, and Bénédit is as near perfect as an ordinary man can be. So overwhelmed was Hall with the idea of creating a boy in the image of Christ that she failed to draw on her greatest talent: that of psychological exploration. In *The Master of the House* Hall engaged her heart, even her soul, but not her sharp critical imagination.

On 29 February Cape published *The Master of the House* in two editions: an ordinary 7s. 6d. edition, for which there were 7,000 subscribers, and a de-luxe special edition limited to 150 author-signed copies, with photographs taken by Howard Coster, costing two guineas. John received excellent terms: a £1,500 advance and a 20 per cent royalty on the first 30,000 copies, 25 per cent thereafter, and 25 per cent on all limited edition copies. The terms, John believed, reflected her increased standing since *The Well*. Una, more cynically, felt Cape, who was also publishing the novel under his US imprint Cape & Harrison Smith, was trying to make amends.

Again John insisted on no alterations or omissions to the text. She also forbade any serializations, feeling it would be disrespectful to her theme. A week before publication, the special limited edition was sold out. Two weeks after publication, total sales reached 9,000 and the book was top of the *Observer* best-seller list.

The omens looked good, deserved a significant memento. With relief and delight, for Una's birthday John gave her Ladye's gift to her of a diamond and platinum haircomb.

Their excitement however was premature: the book's theme and the critics' response would drastically change the pattern of events.

If we look at other literature being produced that year, it is clear that *The Master of the House* was out of tune with the times. In the States Ernest Hemingway had written *Death in the Afternoon*, whilst Damon Runyon's *Guys and Dolls* was running on Broadway. In Britain Aldous Huxley had just published *Brave New World* and Noël Coward's play *Cavalcade* was produced,

---

* This incident is reminiscent of an earlier instance of John's generosity of spirit, when, having harangued the ineffectual Sir Norman Birkett for his defence at *The Well* trial, she then warmly forgave him and presented him with a signed copy of the banned novel.

which John and Una saw on 5 March. At the cinema Shirley Temple was making her début in *Red-Haired Alibi*. The arts reflected an inter-war intensity but were considerably more light-hearted than Hall's new novel.

The Master's theme of the relation between a Provençal carpenter's son and the one born two thousand years earlier was, in the telling, simply too heavy and overladen with dull goodness. Although Christophe is the central protagonist, the unseen hero of the novel is Christ himself, God's Son of 'Indestructible Compassion'.[46] Matching the invisible ever-present hero is a theme which, though treated in virtually all Hall's previous novels, received here its clearest exposition.

Although John had used similar religious motifs in *The Unlit Lamp*, *Adam's Breed* and *The Well of Loneliness*, she had used them more obliquely so that they underlined or emphasized aspects of the characters. Nothing was leaden or flat in the previous narratives as it was in her new novel.

In *The Well*, for instance, when Stephen first meets Valérie Seymour she feels Valérie 'was seeing before her all the outward stigmata of the abnormal – verily the wounds of One nailed to a cross'.[47] Because Stephen is portrayed as a fanatic this overblown description becomes credible. When Stephen decides to hand over Mary to Martin Hallam as an act of metaphorical 'crucifixion', the readers' sympathies are engaged. We care that Stephen's social victimization should lead to her martyrdom.

If we look at a parallel incident in *The Master of the House* what is missing is that feeling of engagement. Christophe, in Palestine during the Great War, makes his way across enemy lines in a fit of exaltation and, unarmed, attempts to persuade hostile soldiers to end the war by loving one another in the name of Christ. Five ragged and starving soldiers, 'demented by blood and appalled by defeat', spit in his face, strike him and strip him bare. Forcing his body back onto the wooden planks of a timbered door they run nails through his hands and crucify him. In the novel's closing words: 'presently he became very still and his dying eyes gazed out to the east – to the east where the flaming, majestic dawn rose over the world like a resurrection.'[48]

Hall attempts with her last line to save the readers' souls, as she was saving Christophe's, with an exultant message of spiritual awakening. What she does not save is her literary reputation. Five hundred pages of unremitting virtue attached to a protagonist who never stumbles is simply too much to take. The ending fails dismally. The *Observer* critic at the time remarked mournfully: 'We do *not* feel in the mood for a last wild protest of suffering humanity against untold agonies.'[49]

The agony was to be John's, as disappointing review followed disappointing review. The *Sunday Times*, no longer edited by John's friend Leonard Rees, who had died in January, featured a critique by Ralph Straus, who told readers he was baffled by the author's intentions, none of which he felt were effectively carried out. The *Times Literary Supplement*, in Una's pithy phrase, 'went for' both the novel and the author. As for *The Times*, its 'vicious review', which emphatically stated that the novelist's serious spiritual aims were unsuccessful, also contained two misstatements about the Palestinian campaign which John had meticulously researched.[50]

Immediately the enraged author hustled off first to Cape then to Rubinstein to draft a denial which was published in *The Times* the following day. It did not help. By April sales barely touched 10,000, and the book was no longer on the best-seller lists.

Worse was to come. At the end of the month Cape told John that his American company, now called Cape Ballou, was bankrupt. Circulation of *The Master of the House* ceased. Copies were seized by Cape's creditors. John raged at Cape, called him 'a dirty blackguard' and a 'skunk', and said that having killed *The Well* in England he was now doing the same for *The Master of the House* in America.

That afternoon Cape, 'the colour of weak lemonade', released his rights to *The Master of the House*.[51] In May the rights were sluggishly taken up by Houghton Mifflin. Though good reviews appeared, all momentum had been lost and by September the American sales were a mere 7,000 copies, a fraction of her previous novel sales for the same period.

Worries of a different kind were in the air when at a Barn performance in September 1932 John sat next to Vita Sackville-West, whom she hadn't seen since the trial, and who greeted her warmly. Then several of their friends gave John the news: Vita, it seemed, had been playing havoc with the emotions of Evelyn Irons, Olive Rinder and Christopher St John. Virginia Woolf had suffered too and a state of nervous tension prevailed in London, at Sissinghurst and at Smallhythe.

Chris had fallen helplessly – and hopelessly – in love with Vita just as Vita was recovering from a passionate affair with Evelyn Irons. Edy, Chris and Tony needed John's attention, and though John's friendship with Evelyn had cooled since her ineffectual stand over *The Well* at the *Daily Mail*, she was concerned for the state of her 'marriage' to Olive.

Vita's affair with Evelyn started in 1931 when Evelyn interviewed Vita for a newspaper feature. Vita invited Evelyn to Sissinghurst for the night, and walked with her by the lake in the moonlight. Later Vita swept in to a party at Evelyn and Olive's Chelsea flat, whereupon Evelyn told Vita she was 'desperately in love' with her. Within a few days they were lovers. The initial idyll turned sour over the issue of commitment and deception. Evelyn, like John, was used to being open while Vita thrived on concealment. As a 'married lesbian' Vita was dedicated to publicly protecting her marriage, an aspect John, as well as Evelyn, found hard to accept.

Olive became ill, gave up her job, came down to Sissinghurst one day, was 'wholly fascinated' by Vita and recklessly told her so. A triangle of the sort all too familiar to John was set in motion.[52]

The Irons–Rinder marriage, so admired by John and Una, was now badly damaged. In January 1932 Olive had, in the words of Vita's biographer, 'abandoned herself childishly to Vita's will . . . [saying] "I am absolutely yours"'.[53]

Evelyn, exhausted by the quarrels and betrayals of the past months, began to look elsewhere.[54] Olive, who perhaps suffered most, was forced to move out of the flat, and was found a bungalow near Sissinghurst and given financial protection by Vita. In August when Vita finally recognized that Evelyn had defected she sent her an anguished poem called 'Valediction', which begged her to remember

> That passion once went naked and ungloved,
> And that your flesh was startled by my touch.[55]

Vita's concealment of her powerful emotions towards Evelyn was so practised and so effective that neither her husband Harold Nicolson nor her ex-lover Virginia Woolf realized their depths. But John's friend, 60-year-old Christopher St John, who visited Vita, then only forty, the day before she posted her 'Valediction' poem, *did* realize. As she told John and Una, she instantly recognized that Vita was 'a tragic figure': 'Contemplating a worn piece of green velvet on her dressing-table, I felt my whole being dissolve in love. I have never ceased to love her from that moment.'[56]

John, whose experience encompassed several such moments, understood at once. Tony tried to dissuade Chris. But once Vita had held Chris's hand, given her a string of blue beads from Persia and a great deal of hope, no amount of dissuasion was possible. Vita at first responded to Chris's wild intensity, which provoked terrible scenes with Edy at Priest's House. John and Una were drawn into the tensions and reconciliations.

Vita told Chris that the list of those she really loved was a short one but Chris was now on it. 'I do love you, for all you give me,' Vita said. But though they consummated their relationship with a night of passion, what Chris actually gave Vita was consolation. The emotional vacuum left by Evelyn Irons seemed insupportable to Vita. Unfairly she filled it with Chris's adoration, which John found unjust.

In a biblical analogy that had echoes for John, Chris saw herself as St Christopher to Vita's Christ and swore to 'carry her over' for ever.[57] In 1933 Chris became demanding; Vita withdrew. By October Christopher, bereft, was in great need of John and Una's comfort. By December she was suicidal. Edy and Tony were pretty near the brink too. While John and Una struggled to support all three members of the Smallhythe Trio, Edy and Tony finally rallied round Chris, who ultimately came to terms with Vita's rejection of her as a lover. She got on with her life in Rye, and steadfastly remained friends with Vita. John, who would try to act similarly, found this last trait admirable.*

John had stood as a concerned outsider watching the break-up of two relationships which she had assumed were solid. Edy and Chris had already weathered thirty-four years together. Olive and Evelyn similarly had seemed set to spend their lives together. One lightning flash and those edifices had crumbled. At the edge of the abyss, John surveyed her friends and wondered about herself.

She did not say much to Una. Her thoughts about her own relationship were too fragile, too confused. Una was sanctimoniously harsh about Vita, calling her a 'snoop' for breaking up two established couples (had she forgotten her own intrusion on John and Ladye?). John, hypersensitive to triangular situations, did not assent. She and Vita, united in their predilection for destructive triangular relationships, also shared the feeling that moments of ecstasy can relieve depression. In John's writing and in her life she empathized with Vita's self-admitted creed: 'To thine own self be true'. Both of them knew that sometimes the consequences could be devastating for other people.[58] John knew also that being true to herself had twice before involved her in triangular love affairs. She could not rule out the possibility it might happen again.

She pushed the distracting thought away but still felt uneasy. Her ennui was aggravated from May 1932 when her eyes began to trouble her again. She and Una took the waters in Bath but though a doctor there examined her he could find nothing wrong with her eyes.[59] Then her own frailty was succeeded by Una's falling ill. For nearly three months Una was laid up.[60] In Bath Una had suddenly been confined to bed with fibroids. An emergency hysterectomy proved necessary. She was operated on at the Welbeck Clinic in London on Tuesday 5 July, while John stayed round the corner at the Welbeck Palace Hotel. John saw Una before she went down to the operating theatre and was there when she woke up. She continued to visit her daily, bringing bedjackets, peaches, pale and dark red carnations, a Victorian posy of multicoloured flowers in a silver basket.

All Una's family sent flowers, as of course did Ida. Rye excelled itself. Her room looked like a first night as bouquets streamed in. At the back of her diary Una recorded the names of those who had remembered her, their floral tributes listed according to the number of bunches they had provided. The numerous list included:

---

* Even more moving were Vita's actions after Edy's death in 1947. After nearly half a century as Edy's partner, Chris was at her wits' end, and Tony, then over eighty, was not much better. They had run out of joy and palpably out of money. Vita gave them sufficient funds to carry on while negotiations went ahead for the Ellen Terry house to be acquired by the National Trust. Her generosity meant that Chris and Tony could finish their lives together, until Chris's death in 1960, in what had been their home without having to finance its upkeep.

Andrea 3. [Andrea was particularly solicitous and concerned.]
Audrey 3.
Viola 3.
Mother 3.
Ida 2. [On 28 July Ida came to see Una bringing yet more flowers, thus upping her score on Una's hidden check list.]
Sheila 1 (2 dead sweet peas and a withered rose)

At the end of the list, underlined, it said: 'John so many times I could not possibly count.'

On 2 August they went to Brighton where John pushed Una's wheelchair along the front to Hove and became mightily fed up. For Una her illness had forged a new intimacy between them. John, though dutiful, attentive and caring, remained troubled.

When they returned to Rye on 24 August they found more flowers from the Smallhythe Trio's garden, as well as roses from Dodo. Ida visited again on 2 September, this time with her new American lover Dr Jo Baker. Una had long felt Ida was irresponsibly promiscuous, but this time she was glad to see her. When Sheila and Penrose called, however, Una refused to see them.

A sudden mood of restlessness followed Una's recovery. In November they headed off for London where to their delight they found Edy and the Boys also in town for Christmas. The five of them had Christmas dinner in Edy's flat in Bedford Street. Andrea came on Christmas Day and again on Boxing Day, probably from Camber Sands where she was temporarily living in a caravan. And not alone! This time she received a warm reception. In conciliatory spirit Una noted: 'Andrea lunched and we talked over her problems poor child.' Andrea, stunned at such a sympathetic response, stayed for tea.[61]

Andrea had joined a repertory company. Early in 1933 John and Una bought her a fur coat at Harrods, attended her rehearsals, and went to her first night at Wimbledon. John, buying a furnished flat at 17 Talbot House, St Martin's Lane, of which she took possession on 18 May, began to spend more time in London, moving in the theatrical circles of John Gielgud, Lillian Braithwaite and Gladys Calthrop. John and Gielgud talked about collaborating on a play based on *Adam's Breed*. Though the project did not materialize their friendship flourished. Una described Gielgud as 'wild, like a stag that has just broken cover and stands erect and watchful. You wonder, if you move, will it be gone in an instant?'[62] John found him as charismatic as she had found Teddie Gerard and Tallulah Bankhead.

Once again they tried to live in two places simultaneously, commuting back to Rye for John to finish her work on the *Miss Ogilvy* short story collection.

Andrea, who had begun courting Lord and Lady Warren's son Toby, a man 'like a Greek god',[63] brought him to tea several times. They all survived the first two occasions on 29 June and 6 July but when Lady Warren and Toby lunched with them on 2 September something went disastrously wrong. Lady Warren smoked all their cigarettes. She condoned the fact that Toby and Andrea were living 'like gypsies' in a caravan. She encouraged them in their wild ideas of a country cottage, a town flat, two cars and several dogs. Toby upset Una by saying he expected Andrea to keep working and now she had 'pull' to go into films. When they left, Una asked John who would look after 'the unfortunate dogs'?[64] When Andrea visited again, bitter recriminations broke out, Andrea screaming at Una: 'If you like to go about saying I'm living with Toby, I don't care!'

On 3 October 'Andrea lunched and left very insolent'. On the 21st from Andrea came another insolent letter. The brief and balmy time between mother and daughter was over. Una washed her hands of Andrea's wedding and instructed her bank to pay over the £267 nest-egg she had been saving for her daughter.[65] 'She never was really flesh or spirit of mine and this affair has been the last illusion and the last disillusion I shall endure on her behalf,' ran the bitter entry in her Day Book.[66]

On 7 November 'Andrea sent ME an invitation from Tom [Troubridge] to her wedding.' As the invitation did not include John, Una saw it as a deliberate insult. Wherein did the problem lie? Had John not agreed to pay for the wedding perhaps? That seems unlikely in view of her generosity. Had her clothes, manners or lesbian identity offended Toby's mother? We cannot know. What we do know is that Andrea's wedding took place at St Mary's Catholic Church, Cadogan Street, with a reception given by Tom and his wife Lily Kleinwort. Una did not attend.

Una's illness, her growing dependence on John, the scenes and panics with Andrea, the failure of *The Master of the House*, her inability to get *The Well* republished in Britain had taken their toll of John's energy. They were but precursors to the heart-breaking years that were to follow.

As a result of severe losses on the American stock market John's income had fallen by nearly half. She was forced to put The Black Boy up for sale. In December 1933 Journey's End, the cottage which had been their first Rye home in 1928, was up for sale. John bought it for a mere £750, put it in Una's name, and rechristened it the Forecastle. It lay at the end of Hucksteps Row, hanging and dipping over the cliff with wondrous views of the river Rother, Romney Marsh, and the sea in the distance. It would be their final home in England.

To Una's distress John began working through the night again, distilling the bleak vision prevalent in the *Miss Ogilvy* collection. The five stories, several of which were reworked, matched the black and desolate mood of their author.* The book was published on 5 March 1934 simultaneously by Heinemann in

---

* They included, apart from the title story, 'Upon the Mountains' (written 1925), 'The Lover of Things' (1924), 'Fräulein Schwartz' and 'The Rest Cure – 1932'.

London and Harcourt in New York. Despite good advance sales it attracted poor reviews: more evidence, John thought, of the hostility towards her since publication of *The Well*.

Like the anguished exiles in *Miss Ogilvy*, John herself became almost totally self-absorbed, and retreated further into Rye. She wanted to settle into the Forecastle but when her hunting leg started paining her again, Una suggested they took a short break at Bagnoles-sur-Mer.

John had a feeling of doom. She told Una several times that she felt anxious. Something was going to happen, she was sure of it. Una took no notice. She insisted they went abroad. In years to come Una was to wonder whether her life might not have been different had she heeded John's warnings:

> I always remember how earnestly she opposed me and how I overbore her protests in my anxiety for the good of her health. She told me afterwards, many times, that she had an almost overwhelming instinct against leaving England . . . and had been unable to understand her own forebodings.[67]

Ironically, within days of arriving at the Hotel des Thermes in Bagnoles it was Una, not John, who became ill. Struck with severe enteritis she pleaded with John to get a nurse from the American Hospital; this, she thought, would leave John free to enjoy the sun and sand. John agreed.

A competent nurse, moon-faced with spectacles, slanting eyes and high cheek-bones, arrived at their hotel. She was a White Russian who spoke little English. Evguenia Souline had entered their lives.

PART FIVE

THE BOOK OF LETTERS
1934–1943

19

SOULINE

Souline was improbable. She should never have happened to an ordinary probable pair like John and Una. The probability of her happening to them must have been one in a thousand. She did not inhabit their world. She hardly lived in the same sphere.

John and Una lived in an orderly world. Rhythms and routines were regular resonances. Though John was eccentric and her fashions bizarre, her suits came from Savile Row; no debts were incurred. Though John's sexual behaviour was outré, though she lived with a woman, that woman was orderly, that woman was a Lady. The Lady and John took care of each other; read aloud from reasonable books; paid the grocer who generally delivered; had their clothes pressed, placed things in drawers and knew where to find them.

Souline could never find anything. She was paid to care for other people. Her friends whom I have talked to, many of them White Russians like herself, now resident in England, said she was lovely – lovely and lost, a lost soul, passionate, impetuous, intelligent. She saw life askew. A trifle anarchic, subversive, quick-silvered, she glimmered and glinted, was here for a moment then gone. Her friends found her mercurial, Una labelled her an hysteric.

Souline's world had changed violently with the Russian Revolution, and she had changed with it, was still changing, was changeable. Una, once she knew of John's wild and passionate attachment to Evguenia Souline, saw the young woman as 'a creature of impulses and violent surface emotions; she was indeed as violent and uncontrolled as a savage.'[1] All you could rely on about Souline, so Una believed, was that she would change her mind. Souline however, despite the obstacles, despite the traumas, never changed her mind about loving John.

John thought Souline vague, found her vulnerable. Ariadne Nicolaeff, a close friend of Souline's during her last sixteen years, including the significant period of John's final illness and death, said of Souline: 'I'd call her an innocent, a naïve . . . she was too thin-skinned.'²* John too found her innocent. In a letter a few weeks after they had become lovers she wrote: 'I ought to kneel before your innocence, that innocence which I have already changed.'³

John made and remade her memories of their first meeting, their first kiss, the first time she refrained from making love with Souline, the first time they made love, and within those inventions and re-inventions innocence becomes their emblem. Their form of lovemaking is innocence exchanged. At the end of 1934, after a few tremulous months as lovers, John wrote to Evguenia: 'We found each other in 1934 and therefore let it always be remembered . . . It's strange, but I feel as though I were you, as though I had lost my innocence to love, as you lost yours, Souline.'⁴† The idea of an innocent, lonely, sexually elusive Russian refugee, for whom she could spin words as gifts, whom she could encircle with largesse, was more prepossessing than its tormented reality would turn out to be.

Those qualities of innocence and vulnerability were not wholly surprising given that Evguenia Souline was a young victimized Russian who in 1920 at the age of eighteen had fled for her life. But they were entangled with other qualities which made her, in John's view, disorderly, disorganized, a young woman who went desperately awry. She slipped through your fingers, had ends that untied. She did not always say where she was going or what she was up to. For nine years John tried to keep tabs on the woman she saw as her greatest (and most tormented) love. But Souline slid out of her box, vanished up a sleeve. Her friends told me that more than anything else she hated control, yearned for independence. More than anything else John yearned to control, needed someone to depend on her.

What intrigued John from their very first meeting was Evguenia's mysteriousness; the mystery both fascinated her and irritated her profoundly. Souline, the text, was often indecipherable. John could not translate her, though she felt that their souls were in close conspiracy. Souline's flights, her elaborations, their battles, all stemmed from John's hot and imperfect struggles to hedge Souline in. You cannot fence in a mystery but John was painfully slow to accept this idea.

Una noticed the mystery and labelled it deceit. But then Una thought her own daughter deceitful and allowed *her* no mystery. Remember the solicitor

---

* Ariadne Nicolaeff first met Souline at Evesham during the war, when they both worked for the BBC, Souline working for the European Service while Ariadne monitored Russian broadcasts.
† Though John frequently referred to her as Souline (or, at the start of their relationship, Soulina: the Russian form of her surname), both John and Una consistently spelt her first name Evguenia in their correspondence with her (the 'u' inserted to make the 'g' hard, although the Russian transliteration is Evgenia). Souline too signed herself Evguenia in the one letter of hers to John that survives (7 June 1939). However, Souline used the French version of her name, Eugenie, on official occasions, and this is the spelling which appears on BBC staff records and also on her will, which she signed Eugenie Makaroff. This book follows its predecessors in using the spelling favoured by Radclyffe Hall at the time of their friendship. (My thanks to Ariadne Nicolaeff for information on these points.)

sent to spy on her. In a jealous rage, Una one day shouted to John that Souline was 'as secretive as Andrea and looks it'.[5] When Andrea visited Rye, Una regularly if accidentally called her Evguenia.[6] Maybe if you were Andrea or if you were Souline, you would not want to be constantly open to Una's carping and criticisms, to John's seasonal swings from proprietorial protection to colossal indifference. You might want to preserve your identity, strike out for independence, cultivate secrecy.

Even in their first days together in July 1934, Souline tried to tell John how important independence was to her. She explained that paradoxically she also felt very insecure, which indicated to John how much she needed care: 'My apparent loneliness and my circumstances invoked in her [John] a sense of pity and protection which she always possessed in excess . . . I felt she wanted to protect me and give me all her consideration.'[7] Souline never managed to make John understand that though she valued being protected she abhorred being controlled. As Ariadne Nicolaeff underlined: 'Zhenya [as her friends called Souline] told me again and again she didn't want to be controlled by money, she wanted her own independence . . . Zhenya's final break from Radclyffe Hall was an assertion of her own independence.'[8]

John, whose own insecurities drove her thus to dot the i's, cross the t's, bolt the doors and call the world to heel, assumed that other people behaved similarly. When they didn't she would shake her head in bewilderment as she did over Souline whose behaviour was diametrically opposed to her own. Souline was unable to plan because she never knew if anything would last. As a girl on the run during the Russian Revolution her constant refrain had been that 'it can't last, it won't last.'[9] But the earlier times, the prosperous times, had not lasted either. They might come again, but perhaps they too would not last. This idea was imprinted on her brain, becoming a refrain that runs through every scrap of her writing, a permanent condition of life. If you don't believe in security, you don't put return addresses on envelopes, you don't put string round parcels, you don't form firm edges yourself. For nine years John constantly begged Souline to wear galoshes so that her tubercular condition did not worsen. But if you have been a fifteen-year-old girl under sentence of death, if you have seen your classmate Xana die in the train compartment before your own eyes, if you have been forced to travel with that corpse while wondering if you were to be the next to be shot, you don't wear galoshes. They may keep out the rain but they won't protect you from life.

If you have shivered at Voronezh Station and watched people shot at random, if you have listened to priests on their knees beg for mercy, if you have seen deserters hanging on trees, if you have survived all that but were forced for months to live in tents without proper rations, you make a decision never to be hungry. You take any food you are offered. You take any money you are given. It can't last. It won't last. There is only today.[10]

Una thought that Souline was mercenary, that she hung on to John for the allowance John gave her. Previous biographers who had seen none of Souline's writings, met none of Souline's friends, talked to none of Souline's intimates, also considered her grasping, or frivolous, or not worthy of John. Souline's friends thought otherwise. Their phrases echoed each other: 'Zhenya told me again and again she didn't want to be controlled by money, she wanted her own independence.' 'It was independence not money Zhenya hankered after.'[11]

Ariadne, who was close to her, said of Una's biography: 'Troubridge turned Zhenya into a grasping little bitch. Her friends were appalled. She absolutely wasn't . . . She was naïve yes, but she had never been in any way avaricious or mercenary.'[12]

John accepted that. John trusted and believed in Souline right from the start. John felt they were two parts of what she and Evguenia called the 'Same Heart'; they were bonded spiritually, emotionally, as well as physically. They were soul-mates from a former life. Souline felt the same. She wrote later of their first meeting: 'There was a[n] unseen link between her heart and mine, that could be broken off at any time and then anything could happen.'[13] Improbable as their push-and-pull partnership was, they shared this Same Heart which they thought would be enough to sustain them.

Even Una at the start had held a different impression of Souline. She liked her; but she was not in possession of all the facts. To be frank, she had been told nothing at all. In July 1934 Una's journal records one set of facts, while behind the scenes another narrative is taking place. While the first hints of passion prevailed between John and Evguenia, Una saw Souline merely as a 'charming Russian and admirable nurse', as 'an extremely nice woman'.[14] Una wrote: 'I like her immensely and feel the greatest confidence in her.'[15] Una knew that during her own illness John found Souline interesting to talk to, and was glad of it. Perhaps Souline might become their young friend? If 'innocence' is the same as being kept in the dark, did Una's own innocence make her more, or less, clear-sighted about Souline's character? It is an intriguing question.

At Bagnoles, where it started on 2 July 1934, Una records: 'Nurse Souline came from the American Hospital and took over . . . a White Russian refugee, more efficient than either of us would have believed possible . . . quite unmistakably of our own class.'[16] Una's estimate was correct. Souline's father was a General in the Imperial Cossack Army. Born on 5 January 1902,* Souline was

---

* By the earlier Julian calendar Souline was born on Christmas Eve, which was celebrated on 5 January. She herself habitually used the Gregorian calendar as it is used in the West, which was not adopted in Russia until 1918. BBC staff records give the year of her birth as 1902, although recent writers on the subject tend to assign it to 1904 – perhaps on the strength of a statement of John's in a letter to Souline of 17 August 1934: 'Oh you funny adorable innocent woman, and you thirty years old!'

his only daughter.* She had two brothers, both of whom had followed their father into the Imperial Army. One was killed in the Revolution, the other, fifteen years her senior, who had been an officer and interpreter in the army, was forced as a refugee in France to become a gym instructor and taxi chauffeur. He died some time after Souline met John.

Souline told John that she 'had a total lack of preparedness for this kind of [nursing] life . . . Like many of my own people who had been thrown out of their own country by force of historical events I tried my luck in finding something to do to earn a living.'[17] Earning a living was new to the sheltered young Russian girl.

> I was educated in the famous . . . Smolny Institute . . . a boarding school for girls where only children of high rank officials were admitted. No democratic notions of any kind were allowed to enter our heads. Our life was sheltered . . . We did not know what work meant, we were fed, clothed, bathed and waited upon hand and foot . . . young and irresponsible . . . we had the best of everything . . . until the revolution . . . then no money, no clothes, just what one had on one's back . . . One thought hammered on my head; it can't be true, it can't be real . . . the fact that one had no money, no food, no food at all, no clothes, just what one had on one's back did not disturb the serenity of mind, one had one purpose just to survive . . . it can't last, it won't last.[18]

Lenin had evicted the cosseted daughters of Russian aristocrats, taking over their school for his headquarters, sending the school south to Novocherkassk. On the frightening train journey the Revolutionary Forces threatened to shoot Evguenia and six other 15-year-old schoolgirls on the pretext that they did not have the correct documents: 'It was like a bad dream . . . not even wanting to escape . . . meekly waiting to be sentenced to death.'

Though one schoolchild died, the rest lived – 'a miraculous escape' Evguenia called it, the miracle due to the mercy of the Commissar in charge.[19] Evguenia's school somehow survived until 1920, 'the year the Red Army came to stay for good'.[20] Then, as she later recorded, 'my father . . . at that time already retired – had to leave Novocherkassk as they were looking for him and besides my stepmother did not wish to stay there alone when the Soviet army would enter it'.[21] Evguenia and her family fled on south, her father and stepmother in a droshky, Evguenia on a haycart. Reaching Novorossisk on the Black Sea, they were just in time to catch the last British freighter leaving for Constantinople. There insanitary conditions dragged Evguenia down with

---

* There are several conjectures as to the place of her birth. Joan Slater's two decades of scholarly research on Radclyffe Hall and Souline have led her to believe that Souline was born in St Petersburg: the girl's education at the Smolny Institute would seem to confirm this. Ariadne Nicolaeff also assumes that St Petersburg was the place of Souline's birth. Hall, however, appears to believe that Souline was born 'a little squealing baby . . . a very long way away in Poland' (RH to ES, 5 February 1939). In her novel *Emblem Hurlstone* Hall's heroine, Felia, who shares many of Souline's characteristics, is also described as Polish.

fever. Eventually she and the other refugees landed on the Greek island of Lemnos where they were sheltered in tents and fed minute rations of corned beef. Evguenia, very sick, was transferred to improvised hospital barracks run by the British medical authorities. On her recovery she began to help the nurses. This was her introduction to a profession for which she had an unmistakable talent but a deep dislike.

Gale conditions suddenly blew roofs off the barracks and forced the refugees off the island and on to Serbia. For a few months Evguenia worked there happily as an interpreter to the American Commission. Despite her gift for and enjoyment of languages it was a nursing career which the American Commission in Serbia chose to encourage. They helped to place her at the American Hospital in Paris. The gruelling nursing work was badly paid, left her without sleep, and within months of her training she contracted tuberculosis and was twice sent to sanatoriums, first in the Pyrenees, then in the Alps.

'Decidedly the work in the Hospital did not suit me but the more I disliked it the harder I worked. I was a model theatre nurse it appears.' By then her father and stepmother were living with her in Paris, but within a short time of each other both of them died. By the time she came to graduate as a nurse and was ready to start earning her living she was alone once again. 'I did not know what to do or where to turn.' When a chance came for her to try something different in America she took it, but it was slump year in the decade of the Depression. Unlucky, unemployed, she returned to Europe and her reluctant profession. 'The days dragged . . . there was no relief from everyday drudgery, from watching people dying . . . it can't last,' she thought.[22]

And it did not. A call came from the American Hospital which sent Evguenia Souline to Una Troubridge's bedside and ultimately into Radclyffe's Hall's bed.

> The hospital rang to say I was wanted on a case . . . 'Can you go immediately . . . to Bagnoles to take care of Lady Troubridge, friend of Miss Radclyffe Hall?'
>
> 'Yes of course I can,' I said matter of factly.
>
> 'Miss Radclyffe Hall is a friend of the patient, you understand, her name is Miss Radclyffe Hall . . .'
>
> On my way I thought hard who on earth Miss Radclyffe Hall could be . . . why did Miss Thevoz repeat her name twice? Vaguely but only too vaguely did I have the impression of hearing or seeing this name somewhere before . . . I could not place it and gave up trying.[23]

At the Hotel des Thermes, the woman with the unmemorable name was expecting Nurse Souline.

> No sooner did the receptionist telephone than down the stairs came a very great personality . . . It was the head that took my breath away: its perfect poise, its short hair of beautiful golden colour enhanced by the last rays of the late afternoon sun which seem[ed] to follow the descending figure all the way down.

She gave me one look over and said: 'Not English eh?' There was a tinge of annoyance in her voice.

'No I am Russian.'

'White of course,' said she sternly.

'Yes,' I said timidly.

She interested me at once enormously. She was so unusual in her manner of speech, of approach . . . of behaviour. As it was almost dinner time she took me first to the patient her friend Lady Troubridge, who had not seemed to be very ill, and then down again to the dining room.

It was the first of many dinners they had together in that restaurant – an unusual action of John's in the 1930s when employers seldom invited employees to dine. John did not behave like an employer. She insisted that Evguenia (whom she quickly and affectionately called Soulina or Souline, it being a prettier name) was served first, ordered her favourite dishes, plied her with a stream of questions about her life. 'I knew right away that I liked her and all her questions which she put to me to find out more about my antecedents . . . amused me . . . [she had] such a direct way,' Souline later wrote.

They sat at a table with potted palms waving behind them while the hotel dance band played hit songs of the period. In September when John was in Sirmione and Souline in Paris they would listen separately to Ray Noble's 'The Very Thought of You' and remember the band playing it that first lunchtime in Bagnoles. In November 1934 Souline, again alone in Paris, will write to John, back with Una at the Forecastle in Rye, to say that the song on her radio makes her feel sentimental and wretched. The tune continues to haunt John for nine years until her long last illness. As late as 1939, when Souline, unable to bear their triangular situation in Viareggio for a moment longer, leaves for Paris, threatening to disappear from John's life, John writes desolately to her: 'Something very intimate has gone from my life . . . it is childish perhaps, but many very little and happy things have gone together with one great big thing. There are foolish songs that I cannot bear to hear, or even to think of: "The very thought of you".'[24]

But such a possibility was not in their minds the day they first heard it played. In the dining-room of the Hotel des Thermes John was very smartly dressed. Souline never forgot John's appearance.

This was the first time I saw someone of my own sex almost in masculine attire and who did not look ridiculous. Her shirt and tie were impeccable. Her tweed of light brown colour suited the colour of her lovely hair. She wore low heeled shoes made of crococile leather. But it was the shape of her head, the perfect line of the cranium, the harmony of that line that struck me spellbound. She held her beautiful head very erect as though she was always right in whatever she thought and did. There was a sort of defiance in her whole attitude, and yet if you said anything that appealed to her emotional senses or her sense of humour – the whole face would mellow into a glowing warm smile.[25]

It was the smile that did it. 'When she laughed, no one could resist it and had to laugh with her.'

Souline laughed. They both laughed. But beneath the opening sentences of their conversation something confused her: 'There was something definitely not quite ordinary and normal. She roused my instinct in some perturbing way.'[26]

Souline pondered her perturbation as she ran errands. 'When I had to do errands for them or rather for their animals because they had a canary and a dog ... I did them with trembling heart because I knew she [John] was extremely pleased with me.'

Yet, while Una rested upstairs, in between Souline's tasks and her nursing care she and John were increasingly drawn together. They walked, they talked. The words spilled out, rapt and focused – the talk of people feverish to find out everything there is to know about one another.

Souline described the first stirrings of a nameless emotion for John: it was, she said:

> like being on the edge of a precipice and not knowing which direction the weight of life is going to pull . . . If we went for a walk, that is when the patient was much better, she always wanted me to be near her. Her mood changed completely, as she said to me in her letters afterwards, because she fell in love with me and I suppose I with her.[27]

The line 'she always wanted me near her' is used repeatedly in Souline's autobiographical writings. It was rooted in John's continuous demands for her presence.

> John wished me to be a child, a Chink child as she said, and she would not let me go away from her even for an instant. She wanted me to be constantly with her, near her. She said everything tasted better, everything seemed brighter when I was there and yet at the same time she coerced me and did not wish me to see anybody else for a long period.[28]

This need to have Souline at her side is depicted in even the earliest of the hundreds of letters that poured from John's pen for nine years. During their first five years, except when they were together, John wrote devotedly to Souline every day, sometimes (neurotically) twice or three times daily. Had she received the previous letter? Why had she not yet replied? Was she ill? Had she caught a chill? Was she seeing someone else? Would she just send a postcard to say a letter was on its way? Yes, a postcard was imperative. John was fretting. John could not write until the postman came with a letter.

Several letters tell us in retrospect how John saw Souline in those first trembling days. In a letter later in 1934, John's first recollection of meeting the young Russian matches Souline's almost exactly:

> 'You're not English,' I said, feeling rather dismayed; and you answered 'No, I'm Russian.' 'White?' I asked sternly and you answered 'Yes'. My God how little I knew what would happen – beloved I am thankful indeed that you are white, but if you were red as Hell I'd have to love you.[29]

Another letter picks up another first memory, one she will return to:

> How I used to watch your face at Bagnoles when I fancied that you didn't know what I was doing . . . One day when I stood before you at the chemists I lost my head a little and I said: 'Aren't you a darling!' I'm certain you heard but your face remained quite expressionless . . . Of course you were right, I was being cheeky.[30]

Imprinting her new feeling for Souline on those same sheets of blue paper used by her friend Colette, John wrote: 'Love is a strange thing, my Soulina, it intensifies all beauty, turns joy into pain and pain into joy.'[31]

In a letter written on 18 September from Sirmione she told Souline that the first thing she had noticed was her 'queer, unusual and very darling face'.[32] At first sight the face with its slanting eyes and unfathomable expression was striking, but less so than her slim white hands. In November of that year, after Souline had made her first visit to the Forecastle in Rye and had returned to Paris, leaving John, attended by Una, a prey to unusual loneliness, John wrote:

> Souline, you are not a beautiful woman – I suppose I was right when I thought you ugly but while I thought that I fell madly in love and now I see no face but yours, no face seems beautiful to me but yours . . . I can't write any more, my poor exasperated physical body is too tormented. After all God made me and made me as I am. He also made you as you are, a passionate loving woman.[33]

But in July Souline was not yet passionate; she was taken aback, apprehensive, stumbling a little in her broken English. John assured her they should speak English together. She wanted to hear Souline speak her language, but she did not want her to improve. 'Never learn to speak English quite properly, will you?' John wrote.[34]

Almost instantly John desired Souline's friendship, desired an entrée into Souline's mind. Later she will rework this and say that almost instantly she desired Souline physically. Later still, towards the end of the nine years, she will chide herself for almost throwing away the chance of friendship by so much hot desire. By then she is scared that even friendship may be forfeited. 'If it must be friendship, all right, but write to me, I am one of those who cannot be starved.'[35]

Starvation too of the sight of Souline's unusual face with its flickering elusive expressions was to beset her over the years, recurring in her daily letters and intruding in her fiction. That same 'unusual darling face' with its slanting eyes belongs to Felia,* the strange foreign wife of Paulo the doctor in *Emblem Hurlstone*, the novel John began in Sirmione on 10 August after first meeting her puzzling young Russian.

Emblem, the scholarly writer who concentrates his mind on Greek civilizations in order to escape contemporary pain and misery, becomes intrigued with Felia/Souline. Emblem's first words to Felia echo John's to Evguenia.

'You are not Italian, what are you?' he asked sternly.
'I am from Poland' she answered timidly.[36]

Emblem cannot make the woman out. Like Souline she has the innocence of a child but the mystification of a mature woman. Her husband Paulo tells him 'she has always been silent . . . yet she has so many things on her mind, so many very terrible things. She and her mother escaped from Poland when the army took Warsaw.' Paulo confides in Emblem that they sleep in separate rooms and begs him to become Felia's friend.

Felia and Emblem go bathing. They sit afterwards in the garden, watching the sun go down. He tells her they will speak English together. He likes to hear her speaking his language. But he does not want her to improve.

Felia has Emblem's dead mother's hands, white slim exquisite hands, which draw Emblem towards her. Emblem had been so afraid of pain that he had been unable to watch his mother die. He takes one hand in his, he looks at Felia's face. He does not initially find it as beautiful as her hands.

She stared at him with her slanting grey eyes.
'You have my mother's hands,' he said to her. 'She had beautiful hands. Are you glad your hands are so like my mother's?'
'Yes, Emblem, if you are glad.' . . . She looked away from him across the lake . . .
'This lake is cruel.' She shivered a little . . .
She looked at the hands that resembled his mother's. 'Were you very fond of your mother?' . . .
'Yes, my dear, she was all my life,' he said simply.
'Why are you afraid of me, do you think? . . . Is it my hands?' . . .

He hears 'was it because of her hands.' The hands make him afraid.

---

* Of the several names, Celia, Felia, Yelia, and once Jelia, which Hall gives her heroine I have used Felia as the one occurring most often and in later drafts. Also in a manuscript book labelled Sirmione that I found in Rome, Hall refers several times to 'Felia', the name she found in a diary entry of Prince Wolkonski's memoirs of 1920. The first two versions of *Emblem Hurlstone* use the name Celia, but are then heavily scratched out – the name perhaps being too close to Souline.

'No, Felia,' he says. He knows that it is not entirely because of her hands.

'I think it's your voice and perhaps your face. My mother was beautiful. You are not. Do you know you are very ugly Felia?'

   She laughed very seldom, but now she did laugh. 'So you find me ugly?'

   'Very ugly,' he smiled.

   'I know that I am ugly,' she told him . . . Then she glanced at his wristwatch. 'Paulo is late . . .'[37]

Souline herself believed that her own 'ugliness' had shattered an early dream to be a ballet dancer or a stage star. 'I knew I had a great ability . . . and surreptitiously behind the backs of my parents I had taken lessons . . . I managed to join some company and was drafted in but my parents would not hear of anything of the kind.'[38] She might have fought her parents but she was unable to fight her ill-health. When she contracted tuberculosis she wrote:

> Alas for the idea of becoming a star . . . My first sanatorium! The beginning of the crumbling down of my dreams to be ever on the stage again. Besides I was not good looking, if not to say ugly. Who would care to take me on with that kind of Mongolian, almost, face. Men liked only pretty pretty girls and the stage was still wrapped up in the old tradition . . . Some kind of despair set in me and I resigned myself to my fate.[39]

Later she recognized that she *was* attractive. At the time 'I could not imagine myself changed merely with a makeup. How wrong I was . . . Later years have proved how wrong I was then.'[40]

However the myth of the manipulative mercenary Russian girl has had ugliness woven into its fabric. In her official biography of Radclyffe Hall Una describes Souline as having a 'curious face';[41] in her private Day Book Una was more forthright: 'She has no looks or real brains with which to do much for herself and she has a completely negative character.'[42]

Richard Ormrod, in his biography of Una, depicts Souline as a woman with 'the slanting eyes and facial features of the Mongolian races . . . [who] wore glasses, and was far from beautiful'.[43] Michael Baker in his biography of Radclyffe Hall tells us that Souline was 'a plain woman, moon-faced, bespectacled, with slanting eyes and high cheek bones' who constantly played a tactical game of 'the innocent child in order both to lead her [John] on and to restrain her'.[44]

No one, however, who knew Souline well thought her manipulative or described her as ugly. Monica Still, who researched Radclyffe Hall's life and relationship with Souline for over a decade, said: 'I met a great many people who knew Souline and there is not one who has not said she was lovely, she was sweet, she was cultured . . . She had beauty of the spirit.'[45]

Professor Bob Smith, a friend of later years, who as a student at the School of Slavonic Studies lodged with Souline for three years at her house in Kilburn and helped her with her pronunciation for the BBC, described her as having 'a broad face, sometimes she wore glasses, a nice face, vivid and friendly'.[46] Ariadne Nicolaeff is even firmer: 'Ugly no. She was not an ugly person. She had a funny little tilt on her nose . . . It didn't have a bump in a place bumps are on noses. Not exactly a split or a dimple near the tip, but a sort of funny mark . . . Not ugly no. Lots of people thought she was really attractive and she *was* attractive.'

Photos of Souline show the tilted nose, the wavy hair, an intense haunting expression in the eyes behind round black spectacles. Her features seem less important than the attractive warmth of her expression. Souline in her nurse's uniform becomes an erotically charged image to John, a password to intimacy. As late as 3 March 1939, more than five years after their meeting, John recalls:

> I can see you now sitting there at Bagnoles in your white coat and cap, poring over my book [*The Master of the House*]. I can see how you flushed to the eyes with plea-sure when I wrote your name in it and gave it to you. You were thinner in those days and very pale, you looked delicate and tired and you were very silent, and one day you found the courage to come all the way upstairs to find out if I was ill because I was rather a long time coming down. 'I have come on my own initiative' you said . . . I laughed because the words sounded so pompous. And one day in the motor you suddenly said: 'May I take off my cap please?' . . . All that you were then . . . seemed to me intensely appealing, I felt the whole of me reaching out to you, crying out that I must and would protect you, you who despised being protected.[47]

On 6 July 1934, far from indifferent to the solicitous friendship on offer, Souline sat downstairs and poured out her life to John. Upstairs Una, feeling efficiently cared for by her nurse, recorded: 'Everything much more cheerful.'

John and Una had been invited by novelist Naomi 'Mickie' Jacob to visit her at Sirmione on Lake Garda. Welcoming letters now arrived from Mickie. Cheerfully Una felt 'our Italian trip may after all materialise and do her [John] all the good I had hoped for.'[48] Unaware of events around her Una herself was making excellent progress: 'I lunched downstairs with John and the nurse . . . I am leading a practically normal for Bagnoles life . . . [Dr] Joly came at 5 and said I could gradually resume normal life.'[49]

Una, unlikely ever to resume 'normal life' again, felt by 10 July that John looked 'less worried in the face and smoother . . . I think the cure is taking hold on her.' She trusted the efficient Nurse Souline sufficiently to decide 'to keep the nurse a few days longer as she reassures us with her experience'.[50]

While Souline in Una's eyes had become 'a treasure' and was 'obviously friendly' she displayed 'sudden inhibitions and reserves which baffle one'.[51]

Some of those baffling inhibitions were almost certainly related to the extraordinary and impetuous behaviour of the 'admirable nurse's' employer, Miss Radclyffe Hall. Una however put Souline's perplexing behaviour down to the fact that 'she saw much horror in Russia during the Revolution until she left it in 1922 . . . it has left complexes that she fears to stir up.'[52]

So sorry did Una feel for 'the poor child who is lonely and not happy' that she went out of her way to help Evguenia.[53] Freelance nursing being precarious and badly paid (Souline received 50 francs a month), Una furnished a recommendation to the American Hospital as a result of which Souline was taken on to their permanent staff.

By 14 July John's charisma had started to work its effect on the young Russian. She was suddenly troubled and swept by doubts.

> Being on the edge of a precipice . . . that very veiled uncertain feeling dwelt within me and gave rise to my subconscious mind the knowledge that all was not altogether right . . . I decided that I must go as soon as I can so as not to be engulfed in this contradictory mass of feelings . . . The matter only grew worse when I said I had to go now that the patient was so much better. But Miss Radclyffe Hall did not oppose my desire and took me herself to the station and put me on the train.[54]

So absorbed was Souline in John that she appears to have had eyes for no one else. She does not recall Una accompanying John to see her nurse off to Paris on the 6.11 train. 'The excellent nurse goes this evening and we are sorry to see her go,' wrote Una on 14 July. 'John really wonderfully better, her face smoother and fuller.'[55]

Una decided to read aloud to John from their favourite Mazo de la Roche books *Jalna* and *Whiteoaks* and was puzzled when John failed to concentrate. Her partner was silently planning her first letter to Souline which she wrote on 17 July. She told Evguenia that she and Una would leave Bagnoles for Paris on 24 July. She was desperate to arrange a meeting with Souline for the 26th.

> *Please* may I come and see you . . . don't ask anyone to meet me, you know by now that I am shy of people, also there are things that I want to say to you – not frightening things – I don't know why I always have a feeling that you are scared of me . . . I don't want you to be scared . . . I hear you thinking a very ridiculous thought about your room being just one room . . . but one room is large enough for me . . . I am really a very humble person. The letter you promised to write when I shouted at you in an agitated voice yesterday has not arrived . . . I waited until the morning post . . . before venturing a long-distance call which I hate . . . trying to hear your fading voice . . . to know that all was well with you. I heard myself shouting: 'Don't go away Souline!' Did it make you laugh? . . . Somehow I expected a letter today, felt I had a right to a letter today, and because it has not come I am enormously downhearted.[56]

This letter sets the pattern for the hundreds that would follow. John took the initiative, impatient always to hear from her beloved. Her pleasure or misery would be formed by Souline's responses and communications. John already had the 'right' to those letters and, she hoped, to that love.

Souline was amused by her urgency:

> John was very impatient and if she wrote a letter she wanted the answers to her questions almost the next day before the letter could even reach the addressee. She was impatient in most of the things but very touchingly pitiful of any suffering she encountered.[57]

On arriving in Paris Souline had flown straight to the apartment of her close friend Lisa Nicolsky, another Russian refugee, to tell her what had transpired. 'I asked her advice and protection against something that was not definitely drawn in my mind.'[58]

The following day John telephoned her. Souline felt trapped, entranced, agitated.

> I fought like anything within myself not to fall under her spell and repeated to myself over and over again: no, no, I do not wish to. But namely what, I did not dare telling myself [*sic*]. It was an uneasy feeling and yet it was so absorbing that I could hardly do anything without thinking again: no, no, I must not let myself be carried away by this undetermined emotion.

Then she wrote back what John called 'a darling stiff little letter'. John congratulated her on her English but said: 'My very dear . . . in my country one would not – in the circumstances – have begun "My Dear Miss Hall!" Try to get it into your head that never again can I be "Miss Hall" to you.'[59] In the same letter John reiterated her need to see Souline on the 26th when after a 12.30 lunch they would go back to John's hotel where they would be 'quite alone and able to talk undisturbed'.

Not for a moment was Souline deceived about the controlling nature of John's affection.

> John was obviously very determined. Her letters became at once strong and emotional. She just could not hear of any reason on my part not to accept her affection, not to write to her, not to see her. I was still very indecisive . . . I turned to my loyal friend Lisa, who rightly said that I must not wave away such a feeling as John probably had for me. I already knew I could not go against her wishes. John was too dynamic in pursuing her goal. She swept me off my feet by writing beautiful protective letters, although I resented that a little, having to look after myself for a long time by then and was proud of my independence.[60]

On 24 July John and Una left for Paris and settled into the Pont Royal Hotel. John wrote immediately to Souline.

It seems so strange that only a few weeks ago I did not know that Paris meant you . . . It's red hell to be here and not to be able to see you until the day after tomorrow . . . No, you can't do anything for me except to think of me a very great deal . . . take a taxi on Thursday, I insist upon this, and you will pocket your pride and let me pay for the taxi too . . . You will pay him and I will pay you later – that is how it will be done, says John.[61]

John's letters acted like a tide overwhelming Souline: 'Innocent as I was, I was also a round fool, one does not argue, nor fight against something which is beyond one's power to arrest, to check.'[62] Redrafting this account many years later and with the benefit of hindsight, Souline changes 'I was also a round fool' to 'I was no round fool'. Then in a third version, scratched through and pencilled and torn, she crosses out 'no' and reverts to the state of round foolishness. What she felt at the time may have been something quite different. What is clear is that she had few illusions about John. She understood, though for reasons she was unaware of, that John was ready to embark on a new emotional undertaking.

John was obviously ready to fall in love, she was waiting for her ideal . . . I was unprotected, a lonely pathetic figure, a refugee on whom she could bestow her reserve of deep affection and love, whom she could treat a little like a child. Yes, very much like a child, as time went on it proved itself to be so. All of a sudden again she was instilled with creative energy having found the force and power in the love itself.[63]

This last notion she may well have picked up from John's own writings; John certainly told her so often enough.

What were Souline's emotions as she received these outpourings?

I could not resist any longer. I could not fight, although I knew she was not free, which only added to the confusion of the state of my mind. I only wanted . . . that it should be a success, that the third person would also be kind and affectionate, understanding the situation and above all be kind, very kind to a Russian refugee. But, alas, that was not to be, alas![64]

That third person would have to have been more of a saint than Una to try and make the triangle a success. Yet, for all her anger, grief and distress, when Una discovered the situation she did, at least at the start, make valiant attempts to understand John and to help Souline. From whatever mixture of motives, she consistently offered practical aid to the Russian refugee who had, in her eyes implausibly and capriciously, become John's lover.

On 26 July, Evguenia Souline and John met in Paris and had lunch. Aware of their meeting, and thinking it inconsequential, Una wrote laconically in her diary: 'July 26th. John gave my ex-nurse luncheon at Lapeyrouse.'[65]

After lunch John took Souline back to the Pont Royal Hotel in the Rue du Bac. In John's room they kissed for the first time. In a letter from Sirmione, John reminds Souline of how silly, shy and awkward they had both been: 'I had kissed your mouth many times already but you suddenly said "Do you want to kiss my mouth?" '[66] John's version depicts Souline's first kiss as that of a chaste child's. Later she reminds Evguenia how she, Souline, had faltered, moved away from John and said shyly: 'This is the only way I know how to kiss.'

> You said that to me in Paris, do you remember? And your darling lips were so firm and protective, so chaste, so unwilling to give, so unwilling to respond . . . Why you kissed me like a sister or a child – or were you really experienced and not intending to do otherwise? I have so very often wondered. But once, just once, your lips gave way a little.[67]

Souline's written recollection of that meeting omits the kiss entirely: 'John invited me to the hotel and we had . . . a long talk.' John asked her about her attitude to men. What experiences had she had? 'I was young . . . full of vitality . . . very vivacious. I certainly had some admirers of the opposite sex and liked being courted. In the sanatorium of Praz-Coutant in the Alps, I was to have married a promising young artist.' This was Zema Otchakowsky, a fellow patient. Women and men were strictly segregated so the courting was romantic, platonic, not much more than a series of supervised walks and Christmas festivities. The idea of marriage did not outlast Souline's stay in the sanatorium. 'Our romance did not last long. I was discharged and went to the States. Otchakowsky became very ill and had to live in the sanatorium . . . I was free from any romantic ties, and therefore ready to accept any given affection.'[68]

On that memorable occasion John was more than ready to give it. 'Her [John's] love, her affection, her nearness drove me almost to a kind of ecstasy which only comes once in one's own life . . . I felt like giving my own life for her.'

Souline perceived John on that disquieting occasion as 'so kind . . . so distant yet so near.' She records:

> They were leaving the next day and she wanted me to write to her. I was elated . . . came home in a state of mind when I did not know anything but that I was in love with Radclyffe Hall the famous writer, the writer of *The Well of Loneliness* which Mrs Baker [one of her clients] gave me once to read.

Souline had read it, years before, but had 'not quite understood the gist of it perhaps through my lack of knowledge of the language'.[69]

On parting from John on 26 July Souline's last words to her were: 'I can't believe that this is the last time I shall see you.' In her next feverish letter, from the hotel on 27 July, John responds:

I woke up almost before it was light with those last words of yours hammering on my heart . . . This is going to be a day of deep pain – and there will be many such days of pain – and I am tormented because of you, and this torment is now only partly of the senses . . . it is a torment of tenderness, of yearning over you, of longing to help you – of longing to take you in my arms and comfort you innocently.

She tells Souline her flesh is consumed 'by reason of your flesh', yet so subjugated and curbed by her pity that the whole of her would gladly melt into tears, 'becoming as a cup of cold water for your drinking'. Momentarily she picks up some of Souline's moral anxieties: 'If this is wrong then there is no God . . . but there is a God . . . and I have my rightful place in His creation and if you are as I am you share that place.'[70]

The biblical resonances running through this agonized letter are remarkably similar to those spoken by Stephen in *The Well of Loneliness*. It is as if John were reliving her heroine's tempestuous emotions. John wrote as Stephen would: 'I am close beside you, and your hand is in mine and your pain is my pain, and your need is my need.' Halfway through her missive a letter comes from Souline. John is released into greater fervour:

It is a beautiful letter. It is as though I had struck the rock with the staff of love and at last the spring has gushed out, out of your heart into mine, beloved . . . all this was meant to happen . . . that our love will last, that our mutual desire . . . is only the physical expression of a thing that is infinitely more enduring than our bodies . . . Otherwise why did I let you go from me even as you came – I who needed you so and who could have made you incapable of resisting? . . . For you are not a woman of ice . . . my little virgin, and I agonized to take your virginity and to bind you to me with the Chains of the flesh because I had and have so vast a need that my wretched body has become my torment – but through it all my spirit cries out to you Souline.

John continued to dwell on this notion of spirit. 'The flesh may be weak but the spirit is strong – yesterday it was my spirit that saved you. Must I always save you? . . . God help me, I ought not to write like this for our time is not yet . . .' John ended the letter with the words: 'I dare not write any more, and since you have your living to earn and I am a marked woman . . . I beg you to lock up this letter.'[71]

Yet again, in this letter, as in so many others, Souline's innocence forms the undercurrent to John's passion. From Sirmione on 12 September she wrote to Souline:

My dearest, I will let you call the tune and if you are frightened of love itself, the physical side of love . . . Dearest I shall not do you any hurt . . . There's nothing to fear, there's nothing to dread, except in as much as all intense feeling is rather a terrifying thing . . . I marvel at your innocence, I am humble before it, I kneel down and kiss the feet of your innocence.[72]

She broods ceaselessly on Souline's sexual inexperience. It will always remain a route to their intimacy. At the end of 1934 she wrote of their first meeting in Paris: 'Dear innocent passionate woman that you were – you don't know how tender I'd felt, and still feel when I think back to the first time and remember.'[73] In June 1935, the same memory haunts her: 'How virginal and innocent you were, how ignorant of physical passion, you the most passionate of all women.'

On 29 July, John and Una arrived at Sirmione on Lake Garda. There they stayed at the Albergo Catullo, a modest hotel with a view of the lake, close to Mickie Jacob's house – known locally as 'Casa Mickie'. 'They came up every morning to my villa before luncheon,' Mickie Jacob wrote later. 'John pounced on *The Times* and immersed herself in it.'[74] The three friends went for excursions, gathered with wine and laughter in the Piazza. Mickie Jacob took some photographs of the 'blue and gold days' when around Lake Garda 'the wonderful old castle seemed to lose its grim air, the lake round it danced and sparkled, the youth of most of us seemed to assert itself, and laughter came easily'.[75]

For Mickie, her two nieces Felicia and Audrie, and Gladys Faber, widow of the producer-actor Leslie Faber, who was staying at John's hotel, Sirmione that summer was a tranquil place. But on 31 July for John and Una the tranquillity was shattered, and thereafter their laughter was forced.

John decided that, after almost nineteen years of fidelity to Una, she had no choice but to tell her of the new feelings she had for Souline. How Una would respond she had no idea.

20

SAME HEART AND SEVERE DIFFERENCES

Those involved in a crisis tend to offer versions of reality whose 'reliability' is notoriously tricky for biographers. To gauge from Una's own writings she would seem to have been unperturbed by John's shocking piece of news. Una the meticulous recorder of details almost entirely glosses over the incident.

In her engagement diary for 31 July she wrote: 'John and I breakfasted in our room, John with a migraine. I stayed with her all day.' In her usually detailed Day Book she merely scribbled: 'a very anxious day.' The following day the Day Book stoutly recorded: '19 years today since I met John.' On 2 August, still maintaining the pretence that nothing had changed, she penned: 'Mickie, Gladys Faber and the two kids [Felicia and Audrie] dined with us to celebrate our 19th anniversary and entry into our 20th year together.'[1]

In her biography of Hall she wrote: 'It never for one moment entered my mind that this young Russian woman with the curious face . . . was to be anything in our lives but a bird of passage.'[2] In Una's literary log, birds of passage were given short shrift, either for reasons of pride or self-preservation, or, if our lives are what we *think* they are, because this was the truth as Una saw it. She may also have been concerned to ensure that John's public image as 'a faithful partner within an inverted union' remained untarnished.

Though Una wished posterity to believe that John's news had left her untouched, nothing could be further from the truth. Unlike Una's self-censored diaries, John's letter to Souline of 31 July tells of a terrible scene that raged all night:

> she [Una] suddenly hurled herself onto the floor and behaved as though she were demented . . . she reminded me over and over again until I have nearly gone mad, that I have always stood for fidelity in inverted unions, that the eyes of the inverted all over the world are turned towards me, that they look up to me . . . that for years

now they have respected me because of my own union that has been faithful and open.

This was a cleverly calculated move. John's response, as Una knew it would be, was: 'And when she says this I can find no answer because . . . I have tried to help my own poor kind by setting an example . . . and thousands have turned to me for help, and found it . . . she says I want to betray my inverts.'

While John looked for an answer to Una's first line of attack, her partner came up with a second: 'She has reminded me of her operation, of every illness she has had through the years. She has told me that she is very ill now, that if I do see you . . . she will never be happy again and will fret herself until she died.'

John had counted on seeing Souline in Paris on their way back to England in September. But now she wrote:

> I cannot see you in Paris . . . I thought Una would consent, for she knows how it is with me, with us . . . [but] she means to keep us apart . . . She says she will not toler-ate our meeting, when I said that I should control myself if only I could see you again, she would not believe me.

John acknowledged the reasonableness of Una's seemingly unreasonable response even as she wrote hopelessly to Souline:

> I dare not blame her, I do not blame her. She and I have been together for 18 years. When all the world seemed to be against me at the time of *The Well of Loneliness* persecution, Una stood shoulder to shoulder with me, fighting every inch of that terrific battle. She has given me . . . all her life ever since we made common cause, therefore she has the right to do what she is doing and she will not ceed [sic] this right, but insists on it with all her strength which lies – as she well knows – in her physical weakness.[3]

The one concession Una would allow was that John and Souline should con-tinue to correspond. A day later Una had relented sufficiently to give John per-mission to see Souline in Paris provided that John promised not to be unfaithful 'in the fullest and ultimate meaning of the word'.[4]

With that, temporarily, John had to be content. Although she wrote repeat-edly that Sirmione was 'hell' without Souline, in fact she was charmed by its streets crossed by old stone arches that stretched between tumble-down houses. From her table on the pavement where she ate her food under an arbour of vines was 'the lair of a certain fruit vendor . . . his stall is always a joy . . . great slices of water-melons, red with black seeds and very green rind . . . bunches of lemons with their stalks and leaves – one is hanging up in my bedroom.'

The descriptions in this letter to Souline immediately evoke the tastes, the colours, 'above all the . . . wonderful smell that belongs to the Salumeria' stuffed with Fabio's foods in *Adam's Breed*.[5] She told Souline she could not endure the beauty of the mountains that turned pink at sunset; they gave her the most 'intolerable heart-ache . . . because of the longing I have for you'.[6]

Though Souline longed for John she asked cautiously: 'Can't love be only spiritual?' John's reply that 'I scourged myself but spared you . . . I spared you because I love you intensely . . . if you demanded it I could put my poor body in chains' is a refrain that will echo through their nine years' correspondence.[7] When Souline worried that their love was 'wrong',[8] John reassured her that profound love not only cannot be wrong but could be stronger than the other love that begets children:

> The other day . . . I thought . . . 'Would Souline like to have a child?' Dearest I can't give you that I am afraid . . . you mustn't laugh at me, my Souline, I suddenly saw you with a child and the child was our child and we were very happy. Would you love me even more if I were a man? In some ways I should probably love you less. I'm not trying to lessen the obvious importance of normal love between men and women – and this love can of course be terribly strong – only I think that the other love is stronger.[9]

When Souline worried that Una might read her letters, John reassured her they were locked away in a dressing-case and the key hung round her neck.[10] When Souline agonized about not having enough time to write letters, about not always *wanting* to write letters, John's manipulative reply suggested that if Souline stopped writing her creative inspiration would fail her:[11] 'Surely my love – and I hope our love – gives me a very clear claim upon you . . . do you know who I am? I am really a very well known author whose career is watched by a very large public . . . You have fallen in love with Radclyffe Hall, not with Mary Jones or anyone like her.'[12]

John made her first attempt to send Souline money, initially 200 francs to cover postage and stationery. 'Souline you must let me help you. It will be doing me such a service – such a great charity you will be doing, and if you love me you will not refuse me.'[13] As Souline recorded: 'That first time [in Sirmione] . . . she fretted that I was not eating well, had no money to buy shoes and dresses with . . . She sent me a generous cheque. I resented it at first but really who could resent it for long when one is in dire need of everything, starting with a pair of pyjamas.'

Later John will buy Souline's winter clothes, pay many of her fares, subsidize her rent. Later still she will give Souline an allowance. In 1935 John encouraged her to leave the American Hospital and return to freelance nursing, because she felt hospital work exhausted Evguenia's frail health. As a defence against periods of unemployment, John paid her £10 a month as living expenses plus a quarterly sum of 3,500 francs towards her rent. This became an annual allowance of £250, paid in monthly instalments.

One consequence was a reduction in the necessity for Souline to find employment, which brought her greater security but tighter bondage. John, who worked hard and productively all her life, had a blind spot about Souline's psychological and practical need to work. 'As time went on I *had* to work, although John did not wish me to . . . It was better for my moral[e] and besides the cost of living was quite high . . . I don't think John realised it.'[14]

Over the years, as Souline shared, on a part-time basis, John's wealthy life-style, she more acutely felt their differences in financial status and security: 'It is one thing to work just for pocket money when you have your own country, home and place where to sleep but it is quite another thing to start earning from scratch, uncertain of present, not knowing what awaits you in future.'[15]

John's 'gentlemanly' notion of aid was that she should provide and Souline should obey. In several letters John calls Souline her 'obedient servant'[16] and treats her like an affectionate master. Yet paradoxically she ends her letters: 'Your slave (that's what I am), John.'[17] For John there was but one model of loving which necessitated constant communication, acceptance of finan-cial protection and a bondage which took no account of Souline's need for autonomy.

Consistently over the next nine years of their correspondence the same themes were reiterated: her responsibility to her 'inverts'; her responsibility to Una whose past loyalty prevents John from abandoning her. At the same time John is filled with an overwhelming desire for Souline, which is in turn counterbalanced by their spiritual love, her perception of Souline as an inno-cent in need of protection. This love, and the suffering it brings, is pre-ordained by God. There is no renouncing it. It must be sustained by daily contact – by letter, postcard or telegram.

Initially, Una was consoled by John's reluctance to abandon her, recording in her Day Book in January 1935:

> it is a poor outlook really for any third person . . . there is so little left over from her [John] except the physical impulse . . . the best is always for me, she [John] would if she obeyed her impulse make the other one serve me, and while she discusses her [Souline] with me . . . my name is only allowed to be mentioned with . . . gratitude and respect . . . her 'amie' knows less than nothing of me save that I allow this thing because I cannot . . . make John miserable.[18]

But that Una, even in a private diary, felt able to use the word 'allow' illustrates the level of deception or self-deception under which the affair proceeded.

Before long the constant stream of letters between John and Souline was mirrored on Una's side by a constant series of ailments: rapid heartbeats, diar-rhoea, 'tedious dysentery', biliousness, 'a week of ill health, acute worry and distress' culminating in entirely sleepless nights.

However Una's resolute denial that anything was wrong co-opted John into a silent conspiracy of acting, at least publicly, as if they were in perfect accord. Mickie Jacob's young nieces Felicia and Audrie certainly noticed nothing amiss. Though only fifteen at the time Audrie (now Atcheson) has, sixty-two years later, a bright recollection of absolute harmony. She recalled Una trying to 'tempt John with things to eat . . . she fussed like a mother hen.'[19]

Audrie recalls Una looking 'distinguished' with her 'pale gold hair which she wore straight and cut short with a fringe . . . like a mediaeval page . . . clothes . . . reminiscent of the twenties . . . Grecian sandals, a long string of amber beads and one or two bone ivory bracelets high up on her arm.'[20] John, with her 'fine sensitive face, artistic hands and sleek hair which she brushed back behind her ears' by contrast looked severe, handsome, her stress also imperceptible.

John gave Felicia a copy of *The Well of Loneliness*. 'We vaguely knew it was about lesbianism . . . my opinion of it then as a fifteen year old was much the same as it is today,' said Audrie. 'I found it deeply moving and strangely pathetic. It was impossible to be shocked by writing so full of sincerity and sensibility.'[21] Mickie's nieces 'accepted without question . . . that both Mickie and John had masculine personalities. There seemed nothing sinister or unnatural in the way they behaved . . . We treated Mickie as we would a favourite uncle; John, as a brilliant, rather shy and sensitive man.'[22] They became attuned to the 'sympathy, understanding and comradeship between Mickie and John . . . John was the sensitive intellectual caring deeply about . . . all sad humanity. Mickie responded by pretending to be far more low-brow and broad humoured than she really was.'[23]

John wrote at length to Souline of the woman who remained her close friend until her death: 'Mickie Jacob . . . has somehow become a kind of King in this place, loved and respected by the whole town, for Mickie has a most merciful heart, and though poor herself gives much to the poor.' In John's eyes, Mickie, nine years younger than herself, born in Yorkshire, the child of a bohemian middle-class Jewish family, was one of 'the most remarkable people' she had ever met. She taught people how to cook, lectured on the theatre and literature, worked ceaselessly for animal causes, and rarely took any exercise.

John's visual description of her fellow author as a woman with 'short very curly black hair', who 'wears glasses and is more than average fat . . . dresses like a man, except for Mass, when she shows her respect for God and the priest by putting on a skirt', when 'the result is not good nor is it convincing', is borne out by photographs of the period.

Mickie loved the limelight and treasured applause. When she joined the WSPU in 1912 and immediately asked if she could be involved in illegal suffragette activities, Sylvia Pankhurst said: 'You might be a useful person if you would overcome your idiotic love of popularity, Jacob.'[24] Evidently she overcame it sufficiently to work productively with John's other militant suffragette friends, Vera 'Jack' Holme, Mary Allen, Chris St John and Rachel Barrett.[25]

John respected and envied Mickie's war work, as she had envied that of Mary Allen, or earlier Toupie Lowther. During the First World War Mickie had joined the Women's Legion where she ran a munitions factory in London supervising 500 men and women. During the Second World War, while John, safe in the West Country, pined bitterly at being excluded from war work by ill-health, Mickie would work with ENSA, the Services' entertainments unit, providing essential supplies and entertainment for military hospitals and factories.

Though John laughed at Mickie's 'very coarse stories' she saw her as a 'tragic soul, very emotional . . . very courageous'.[26] Mickie was particularly brave about her tubercular ill-health. In the twenties she had become an active Labour Party campaigner and prospective candidate for Sevenoaks, but consumption had forced her withdrawal. She had spent three years in a sanatorium, but had never completely recovered, which is why she had left England for Italy in 1930.

When illness forced a change of career from acting to writing she had an instant success with her first novel, *Jacob Usher* (1925). Between then and John's death in 1943 she wrote thirty-two best-selling novels, mainly middle-brow fiction or romance, at the rate of two a year.* During John and Una's stay, she was bravely trying to finish another book before returning to hospital for another serious operation. Una recorded that Mickie's 'miserable lungs have gone again in three separate places. God alone can foresee the end.'

Despite her ill-health Mickie surprised Una with an erotic confession: 'Now she tells me she has been desperately in love with me for weeks which of course means fretting – no appetite, feelings of guilt and misery [over] Miriam [her lover] . . . only 32, quite penniless,' and arriving imminently.[27] Perhaps the declaration was not a total surprise, for a few days earlier Una had written pro-phetically: 'I could not be in love [with Mickie] in a hundred years if there were no-one else in the world, but I do love her.'[28]

Mickie was not the only woman during that period to find Una desirable. Around Christmas in Rye at the end of 1934, Olive Chaplin, Edy Craig's 48-year-old niece, spent time 'casting an eye' on Una who found her 'a darling and very attractive' but stoutly affirmed, 'my focus is fixed and has been since August 1st 1915.'[29] A month later in Paris, Natalie Barney's young Chinese sec-retary-lover, Nadine (known as Whang), who for years had cross-dressed and passed for a man and a soldier, made 'a gentle but quite unmistakable advance'

---

* After Radclyffe Hall's death Naomi Jacob produced a further twenty-eight novels as well as twelve volumes of autobiography, but continued to regard her output with modesty.

to Una which amused but did not tempt her: 'I am incorrigibly faithful and never could sample anyone new, however attractive.'[30]

After Una had turned down Mickie Jacob's offer of 'unrequited love' she wrote: 'What a damnable thing really is this sex element that crops up and spoils everything. I wouldn't ever have wanted poor old Mickie that way if she had been "the only boy in the world" but I did like her tremendously as a friend . . . now just because she [made] me declarations that she ought not . . . all our friendship is spoilt.' Over the incident with Olive she wrote: 'So far all is well with Olive . . . [but] I feel and fear the same thing may easily happen . . . [because] I am a fixed star and see no one but John . . . so it's difficult to see why anyone feels me to be attractive when I have nothing to give.'[31] Although Una remained 'fixed' in her affections, perhaps her vulnerability and her need to feel she was still sexually desirable subtly conveyed itself to these women.

News of John's work had reached Sirmione, including the fact that her collection of stories published that March, *Miss Ogilvy Finds Herself*, had made the best-seller lists.[32] Also on sale in Sirmione were Italian translations of *The Well* and *Adam's Breed*, though by 21 September the former was to be confiscated and prohibited in Italy.

In a summer of incessant thunderstorms, shattering gales and torrents of rain, Una made no mention of those other daily storms about when and if John could see Souline and in what ways she would be 'allowed' to kiss 'the white and adorable teeth' or any other parts of her body. Once John began to dedicate herself to writing *Emblem Hurlstone*, Una thankfully deluded herself into thinking that renewed novel writing would launch John into recovery.[33]

John set *Emblem Hurlstone* in Alcione, a fictional Sirmione that had 'witnessed the love of a pagan poet'.[34] In early September the former lover of the pagan poet D'Annunzio appeared briefly in Sirmione. Romaine Brooks looked

> incredible and exceedingly dirty. On a deeply sunburnt face she had splashed quantities of orange rouge and a smear of crimson lipstick. Her hair, ragged and untrimmed . . . much too long, hung in greying wisps from under a tiny grubby boat-shaped hat that looked as if she'd picked it up in the road . . . she, cinerina of the soft greys and blacks, was rigged out in a brilliant blue silk blazer, crimson sweater, smoke-blue skirt and pastel coloured scarf.

As if that was not enough to shock and offend, Romaine had become 'very fat and her nails smeared with bits of bright red varnish on top of weeks of neglect'. Shown to her room, Romaine changed without washing, then to John's dismay 'disclosed discoloured old stays and doubtful underwear'. She spent much of her time with John and Una divesting herself of a litany of complaints against Natalie, against mosquitoes, against the lavatory conditions.[35]

Despite the awkwardness of that incident, later that year Romaine, who was leaving for America, generously sent them two paintings as a Christmas gift. One was 'The Charwoman of St Ives', according to Una 'one of the three best [paintings] she ever painted' which 'John bagged . . . at once as she has always adored it'. The other was the oil sketch of D'Annunzio which Una had long coveted: 'A portrait of a great man by a great woman.'[36]

Romaine was still close friends with D'Annunzio who lived at Il Vittoriale, a palatial villa across the lake. Audrie Atcheson talked of 'the strange and scandalous stories of his frequent and colourful love affairs' which circulated about the village of Gardone Sopra that summer.[37] D'Annunzio, now in his seventies, was almost a hermit. Una, long his admirer, who had read his work in Italian, was determined to meet him. Romaine warned her that access nowadays was only achieved through literary status so Una persuaded John to purchase an Italian version of *The Well of Loneliness* to be sent to the poet.

After a breathless eleven days' silence a waitress who had taken a message on Sirmione's single public telephone ran to John's hotel to report that the Commandante would send a letter by car on the morrow. The next day, delivered by Alfa Romeo, came an envelope sealed in bright blue, addressed in letters one inch high to Radclyffe Hall. With it came ruby, sapphire and platinum bracelets, rare copies of D'Annunzio's work inscribed to John, a large porcelain bowl of golden grapes decked out with primrose rose petals. Towering above these impressive gifts was a bouquet of cerise carnations. D'Annunzio had been overwhelmed by John's book. Una told everyone that D'Annunzio was the only man in the world whom she would never refuse sexually. John laughed at her. 'Well, he is 74 now darling.' As D'Annunzio wished to see John alone Una was denied the opportunity of either conversation or congress.

At D'Annunzio's villa on 16 September John discovered they shared a love of the past and a rejection of contemporary values. John's lasting respect for the poet impelled her that October to read his works, and led her for years to correspond with him. Several times they arranged to meet but owing to his growing reclusiveness the meetings were always put off. When he died in 1938 John sent a huge laurel wreath and wept bitterly as if for a close friend.

A vehement nationalist with Fascist links, D'Annunzio influenced John's attachment to Italy and pushed her further to the right politically. United to this was her developing antipathy to Russian Communism which was sharpened as a result her relationship with Souline whose views in the thirties were also frighteningly anti-Semitic. Later Souline admitted that 'my political views were non-existent but if anyone said something silly about Russia it was always galling for me to hear.'[38] At the time John may have overstated her own anti-Communist attitudes in order to accord with Souline's.

During John's second summer in Sirmione in 1935, accompanied by both Una and Souline, some hasty and ingenuous anti-Semitic remarks by Evguenia in front of Naomi Jacob caused such a thoroughgoing row between John and Mickie that Mickie threw all three of them out of her villa. Gradually the bonds of lesbian sympathy and the dwindling of John's pro-Fascist sympathies enabled their relationship to be repaired, but it took considerable time.

After the 1934 visit to Sirmione John had planned to return to Paris with Una on 5 October, but on 29 August Souline wrote a letter filled with 'bewildering hints' to say she might be leaving for the States on 3 October as nurse-companion to a nameless client – in fact, the Mrs Baker who had been the donor of *The Well of Loneliness*.

Hysterical with jealousy John penned a tyrannical torrent of words. Souline had not told her who the client was. Why was Souline unable to 'refuse this woman anything – that whatever she demands of you you have to grant her, even if by doing so you hurt yourself, and me you hurt very dreadfully indeed'?[39]

Mrs Baker was to become something of a *bête noire* to John, for a year later, when she had again attended Mrs Baker, John wrote to Souline (whom she had taken to calling Royal Chink Pig or Piggie, often abbreviated to RCP):

> Now listen . . . she has no claim whatever on you . . . you flattered her vanity my little Cossack . . . you thought of yourself as her second lap-dog. Well now you are not a lap-dog . . . but a Royal Chink Piggie with a crown over one ear and a wide gold collar around your neck on which are engraved these protective words: 'I am I and I belong to Johnny'. And on the other side of the collar, on the side that no one is allowed to see, are the words: 'I love Johnny, Johnny loves me and Johnny is the one who NEEDS ME'.[40]

Souline was to learn that John's jealous rages could be aroused by even a hint of infidelity. In June 1936 John suddenly became suspicious of a romance between her RCP and Souline's Russian friend Lisa Nicolsky. She rushed round to Souline's Paris flat and ripped the place apart. She smashed and tore every photo of herself, every memento, all her own novels, every etching and picture, even the crocodile bag she had given Souline the previous Christmas. Then she 'systematically hunted the flat for any evidence of some other presence, demanded Evguenia's keys as an alternative to breaking open her wood cabinet' but found nothing suspicious at all. Distraught and contrite she subsided into a weeping child, desperate for reconciliation.[41] John, repentant, was almost as great a trial as John the tyrant.

But all that came later. In September 1934 John's Royal Chink Piggie was not yet tied to her sexually, and John panicked. She wrote that she was willing to rush to Paris earlier than arranged, as long as Souline would put an entire ten days at her disposal. Souline was to take on no work, arrange no engagements, set her life aside.

Radclyffe Hall has a standard to uphold. I am so madly in love with you that you can force me to lower the standard by worrying me . . . by making me utterly unfit to work, by your own inability to stop being vague . . . Are you going to help . . . by giving me those ten days? . . . Can I possibly do more than meet your wishes by coming . . . sooner? . . . Were I free I would naturally be with you now . . . But if I do my bit then I expect you to do your bit also.[42]

But John was not free and she failed to recognize how crucial that was to Souline. Instead, she did 'her bit' by insisting Una change *her* plans so that they could be in Paris on 22 September. Una, dedicated to John's interests even when they conflicted with her own – or perhaps unable to cope with John's rages, nerves and hysterical outbursts – ensured they arrived by the 21st.

On the 22nd John and Souline met at Souline's lodgings at Passey. John and Souline could hardly believe that they were at last in each other's arms. The floodgates opened, Una's strictures were swept away. For once Una was not in John's thoughts; she was certainly not present in Souline's lodgings. After tentative starts and halts, after protestations of passion from the one and timorous rebuttals from the other, Souline and she made love. After eighteen years, and with what she would afterwards swear was the craziness of first love, John had been unfaithful to Una 'in the fullest and ultimate meaning of the word'. And she revelled in it, relived it, and rewrote it time and again.

On 30 December 1934 John excitedly recalled that meeting:

I felt the first day when I came to your room as nervous and shy as a boy of sixteen – and oh what a thing you gave me – good God, I shall always remember 1934 if only for that – what a thing you gave me! . . . I was torn in half by desire and pity. Do you remember how I fed you that night? I fed you from my plate as though you were a baby. I can see you now, sitting hunched up at the table, all broken and sorrowful and terribly anxious, and you were spoiling everything through sheer nerves and through being so terribly over-excited yet apprehensive . . . Darling, darling, you must have suffered like Hell – I could have wept over you my Soulina.[43]

A year later John, tremulous with feeling, recalled it again:

Oh Souline, it is a wonderful thing that has come to me through you, for I was your first lover. Through me you are no longer a child. Wonderful . . . but also terrible because so achingly sweet . . . I found you a virgin, I made you a lover, a most blessed responsibility . . . a most sweet and dear burden that I shall bear to the end and beyond . . . I find that to take an innocent woman is quite unlike anything else in life. It is perhaps the most perfect experience in life if real, deep love and tenderness goes with it, if with it goes the will to protect, the will to hold and the will to keep. Your innocence was a revelation to me. I had never met anything quite like it before.[44]

The passage points up John's pride in her sexual prowess, her predatory toughness, which will continually play with Souline's innocent but intense physical magnetism. John will play and replay, but she will not harm: sex was important for John, but carried responsibilities.

Sex and in particular their first lovemaking appeared to be so important to Souline that she talked about it on several different occasions to her friend Ariadne Nicolaeff. Souline described to Ariadne what she called her 'seduction' as a 'shock' but 'not shocking'. Ariadne said: 'Lesbian homosexuality at that time was not talked about . . . but we all knew, and we all had homosexual and lesbian friends . . . I was Zhenya's friend. I took it for granted.'[45] The reverberations of their first sexual encounter on Souline caused her later to write an essay focusing on that aspect which she showed to her friends Bob Smith and Ariadne Nicolaeff. Ariadne said: 'Most of all she wrote about the seduction of her physically . . . She had to write it down. Nothing in her life had ever happened like it before.'[46]

In Paris John talked at length to Souline about *Emblem Hurlstone*, which she saw as a novel inspired by their love, their 'mental child'. Souline has been criticized for hindering Hall's writings, being ignorant of her novels, or believing that Hall's writing was unimportant. Chief exponent of this viewpoint has been Una Troubridge:

> Intelligent as she [Souline] was and capable in many ways . . . John's work was to her a matter of no interest and could, in her view, be a very subsidiary consideration, and indeed a matter for resentment . . . She did not like to feel herself overshadowed by John's established literary eminence. She had less than no appreciation of the conditions essential to the production of creative work and was intensely bored whenever John was immersed in it . . . Even after a number of years Evguenia hardly knew the names of the characters that John had created.[47]

There is much internal and external evidence to suggest the reverse. Souline's Russian friends, who supported her both during her relationship with John and thereafter, give no credence to such an idea: 'It is not true at all that she [Souline] never took an interest in Radclyffe Hall's books. She read them and understood them, she made comments about them. She felt the fact Radclyffe Hall was a writer was very important.'[48]

Souline herself writes frequently in her autobiographical essays that central to her elation is that she loves and is loved by 'the writer of *The Well of Loneliness*'.[49] She read each work carefully and made comments, often from a very different standpoint based on her youth and Russian background. Part of Evguenia's willingness to become John's lover was due to her sense of Hall's prestige as a writer:

> Part of the importance of the seduction for Zhenya was that Radclyffe Hall was an eminent writer. That importance comes from the fact that Zhenya was a Russian and Russians are complete idiots about writers. They adore writers. Writers are more

valued in Russia than in England, so to say, as Troubridge and other people have said, that Radclyffe Hall's writing and the fact that she was a writer was unimportant to Zhenya is complete nonsense.[50]

Una Troubridge's view of Souline as 'a difficult case, efficient but without talent or initiative', a girl who was 'spoilt and tiresome . . . moody and capricious',[51] who lacked sufficient intellect to comprehend John's work, has been, until now, the authoritative version. Given the lack of alternative biographical evidence Evguenia Souline's character has been at the mercy of such descriptions. This has acted not merely to the detriment of Souline's image but also to the demeaning of a relationship John herself respected and yearned for till the day of her death.

Una's perception that 'both John and I knew that she [Souline] felt it [Hall's writing] to be an interference with the agreeable aspects of life as she wished to live it'[52] was not borne out by Radclyffe Hall herself. John frequently said that she found Souline's criticisms useful, though not always as flattering as Una's. She used Souline as well as Una as a sounding board for her literary ideas. Though she received an immediate verbal response from Una, she would anguish until a postal reply came from Souline.

Hall believed that Souline had reawakened her creative impulse: 'This book [*Emblem Hurlstone*] is entirely the result of our love, the result of its joy and its desperation . . . Out of ourselves I will make a book, I am making a book for you, Soulina.'[53]

Souline appears to have been proud of *Emblem Hurlstone* and later of *The Sixth Beatitude* which Hall called 'their books' or 'their child'. 'It's your book I'm working on now so don't be jealous of the time I give it,' she reported on *Emblem Hurlstone* in the autumn of 1934. By 5 December she told Souline: 'Our child is sleeping . . . Its trouble lies in the cutting of its third tooth . . . I want every smallest sentence to be very tidy . . . This child – since it's ours – must have very special care.' On 10 December, with three chapters of *Emblem Hurlstone* written, she told Souline on the phone: 'Our child has at last cut its third tooth.'[54]

When in April 1935 she finally abandoned *Emblem Hurlstone* and began writing *The Sixth Beatitude*, it was to Souline that she wrote, somewhat anxiously:

I have a great surprise for you – it is not the book about Sirmione, no . . . this is a story . . . about the very poor of this Sussex . . . the book is my best work . . . Why could I not get on with the book that came to me after that terrible first parting with you in Paris? . . . oh heart of my heart, I am too near it all . . . You have filled me with love to overflowing but it must overflow back onto you. It can't and won't overflow onto paper . . . before I met you I was dry – then I fell in love and that stirred the fluid again – made me come alive – and I began writing, but not the right book . . . You are my inspiration, it is owing to you that I can work hard.

Then recalling how tetchy she could be when she was writing hard she asked Souline: 'How would you endure being with me when I am working at this terrific pressure? I am irritable, I can't eat my food, and sometimes I just fly out over nothing . . . Una has had to endure it for years . . . Are you sorry that you have fallen in love with an Author?'[55]

Even before Souline could send the necessary reassurance, John drew renewed breath: 'My book continues to prosper grandly. I wonder what you will think of it? . . . I think it's the best thing I've ever written . . . its all, all YOU.'[56] In May, she wrote from Beauvallon: 'Rejoice when work comes easily and splendidly . . . say to yourself I the RCP have made John able to do this.'[57] On 28 October 1935, when *The Sixth Beatitude* was finished, John wrote instantly to Souline: 'the finest book I have so far written.'[58]

The central character, Hannah Bullen, an impoverished cleaning women, is strong, generous and, more than any of Hall's protagonists, has that clear inner vision that enables her to see beauty and creativity in a life of disorder, poverty and unending disasters. Hannah lives in Hall's very own Hucksteps Row, called in the novel Crofts Lane. From the viewpoint of those with impure vision it was 'a small, cobbled alley full of crouching, decrepit, decaying houses', but from Hannah's and Hall's perception it had those 'links with life – with loving and mating, with birth and death, with sorrow and joy' which had indeed a 'certain beauty'.[59]

The story probes beneath the usual conventions of morality. Hannah herself, the mother of illegitimate children, could be seen as 'immoral' or as a 'loose-living, shameless woman who had taken her pleasure where she could find it' but readers are gently led to see that the gravest faults of Hall's heroine 'were one with her highest and noblest virtues; that the life-force, be it ardent enough, may flow into many and diverse channels, so that her fine generosity, her will to work, her will to endure, her will to indulge the desires of her flesh, her will to be fruitful, her will to mother were all one and the same.'[60]

Compassion is the keynote to Hannah's character. Inevitably the finale shows us Hannah's terrible courage when she dies attempting to save her neighbour's children from a blazing house. At one with nature, Hannah was at one with the best of humanity. A child of nature she was at one with the Marsh, with the waters that crept through its dykes, with the water fowl hidden in its reeds. Nature itself, the changing seasons, and the Rye marshland are among the best descriptions Hall ever penned.

The Sixth Beatitude was published by Heinemann in April 1936 to mixed reviews. By July only 6,000 copies had been sold in Britain and only 2,000 copies in the USA. Perhaps the critics found the sense of loss and change within the novel too fatalistic for their tastes. Perhaps they were not ready for the overturning of suburban notions of fidelity.

Since *The Master of the House* Radclyffe Hall had learnt to accept reviews that did not accord with her own faith in her novels. With Hannah's own courage, and Souline's cherished support, characteristically she began a new book, about a Merano shoemaker called Otfried Mahler. She started it on a trip to the Italian Tyrol. So immersed did she become that she stayed in Merano for seven months from September 1936 to March 1937 to work on it.

John retained – and would repeat – her gratitude to Souline for rekindling her creative fire after several years of what had looked like slow extinction. In the remaining nine years of her life, Hall wrote only two more formal novels, one of which, *The Merano Shoemaker*, was destroyed by Una after Hall's death, but she also wrote what amounted to a Book of Letters.

By turns, this is 'A Portrait of the Artist as an Older Woman' (a highly reveal-ing autobiographical sketch of Hall the writer from fifty-four to sixty-three); a story of a passionate and agonizing love affair; portraits of selected contemp-oraries; and evocative descriptions of people and politics in the places she resided, most notably Italy.

The Book of Letters, which mingles the personal and the political, the fictional and the socio-cultural, was Hall's monumental literary work during the last passion, the last sickness and the drama of the last disease. It is essen-tial that a biographer neither overlooks it nor consigns it to the realm of 'mere love letters'.

While John constructed this final work, Una began a painful examination of her feelings. On 21 September 1934 she wrote from Milan: 'There seems no end to the upheavals this summer.' On reaching Paris there was no entry at all for the 22nd when John and Souline made love. Each day for the next eight days, was entered the single word: 'Paris.' Thereafter most entries read: 'We talked till two a.m.' or 'we talked till three fifteen a.m.', following such bitter lines as: 'Worked alone all evening' (26 September), 'John bought flowers for Souline and took them there' (30 September) and later that day: 'Went out alone this afternoon to Our Lady of Victories . . . and prayed long and desper-ately for help.'[61]

Una's fears of being abandoned by John for a sexually more exciting young woman were aired on their return to London in October 1934, when she spent time with Ida Wylie and Jo Baker.

Ida had returned from Moscow, where she had been sent by the *Saturday Evening Post* to collect copy for an anti-Bolshevik novel. She had become ill with dysentery and had to be returned to England on a stretcher assisted by Jo Baker and Rachel Barrett. In an extraordinarily irritable outburst against Ida for her 'unreliability' and sexual infidelities (now mirrored by John) Una exploded:

Ida [is] still living with Jo in New York and travelling with her, but the first fine care-less rapture has not lasted 18 months! Two years ago with tears in her eyes she was telling John that she could not live unless Jo left her friend of 25 years' standing and made a home for her . . . already Ida has so completely 'got over' her passion that she says that such things are long over . . . all she asks of life is to have her house kept by someone who does not get on her nerves, so that she wants to shy things at them at breakfast!

Though Una admitted she still found Ida 'intellectually remarkable' she despaired of what she called Ida's 'selfish irresponsibility, which makes her at 50 as reckless a home-wrecker as any boy of 22'.[62]

In an attempt to ensure that her own home was not completely wrecked in 1934, Una helped Souline secure an entry visa to come to England.[63] Souline doubtless already held a French Nansen (a passport issued by the League of Nations to stateless persons), otherwise Una – or indeed anyone – would have been unable to procure her an English visa. But the following year Una went further. In January 1935 she wrote in her journal: 'I have arranged on my personal guarantee an annual visa which will enable her [Souline] to come to England as many times as she wishes during the year for not more than a month at a time.' She added wryly: 'So there is another obstacle removed by me!'[64] The following day Una and John took Souline to renew her passport, completing the formalities at the British Passport Office for Souline's annual visa.[65]

Una's loyalty to John over the matter of Souline's visa bears out her own words the next day: 'Truly we are like no other living couple, John and I. It seems quite crazy but in some strange way this episode which should by all the laws of custom and probability have made a rift between us has only drawn us closer.'[66] As John wished 'to benefit the girl in every possible way' Una decided that she should have 'my assistance'. Una's realistic appraisal came in the words: 'Already she is in a better financial case as of course John is supplementing her earnings. Now I have got her the annual visa and it seems we will get her a country.'[67]

That same month Una saw a French solicitor in an attempt to speed up Souline's French naturalization papers on the grounds that 'the more they see of each other the sooner I suspect the thing will work itself out.'[68]

In February 1935 Una procured Souline the facility to obtain a visa at twenty-four hours' notice by showing a letter of invitation from Lady Troubridge. Una wrote in her diary: 'I cut my own throat.'[69] Asked by John why she was kind to Souline, Una did not reply but wrote in her journal: 'Such a difficult question . . . one side of me can hardly bear to see her: I am profoundly and unhappily jealous of her and of every sign of John's feeling for her, and part of me feels that to be unworthy and a thing too small for my vast love for John and that makes me want to be kind . . . so as to force the better side of me uppermost.'[70]

Though Una certainly showed her better side in this, her actions also allowed her a measure of control over John's involvement with Souline. Her 'willing' help put John even further into her debt and perhaps, she felt, saved her home from wreck a little longer.

Meanwhile John acted more deviously than Ida. Alternately fearing that in fighting for Souline she would lose Una, or that in cleaving to Una she would lose Souline, she began a pattern that would last almost a decade of spending time with one woman whilst desperately trying to console the other. She made love with Souline but telephoned Una while still in her lover's company. She heaped azaleas, bouquets, and messages of eternal love on Una, then fled to Souline, her everlasting and future soulmate. Overwhelmed by love, intemperate with desire, she clung to Souline, then, overwhelmed by guilt, offered reassurances for Una to cling to: 'She [John] said to me yesterday: "Remain with me for ever and ever".'

John allowed Una the consoling delusion that 'in spite of everything we are close, close, one spirit and one flesh, indissoluble and indivisible for ever,' whilst at the same time she wrote to Souline:

> I am not and have not been for years the least in love with Una. I feel a deep gratitude towards her, a deep respect and a very deep affection – also an enormously strong sense of duty . . . for you I feel . . . a consuming need that is not the need of our bodies only . . . the strong vital love – the combative love, the protective love, the anxious yearning, restless love . . . My love for you is more like 'first love'.[71]

Between 1934 and 1936, John attempted to get the two women to live with her in harmony. On 4 November 1934 when Souline arrived for her first visit to England, Una took herself to Rye while John went to meet Souline at Folkestone. As Souline recalled: 'I remember . . . John meeting me standing on the very edge of the pier. She would have come nearer were it at all possible. Yes, she saw the Chink face . . . a very green Chink face . . . her thrill of meeting me on her own soil [made us] both mad happy.'[72]

They spent a rapturous three days alone at the Grand Hotel. John spoke and wrote a dozen variations on the line: 'You have taken me body and soul in your hands.'[73] Their senses were heightened, the sea looked a deeper shade of blue, drops of rain fell upon them warmly like a cloak, three days might have been three minutes or three centuries. What was time when it was on your side, when you felt ridiculously young, when you believed it would last for ever? 'Were we not always waiting we two for our meeting?' John had written and would write the same thought again and again.[74]

If John had needed greater proof that their love would flourish only if they were on their own, she had it in Folkestone. If John had needed further proof of her complete physical, even emotional separation from Una, she had it in Folkestone. But, greedy for suffering, she insisted that she and Souline join Una for three wretched days in London. In 1928 John had written prophetically in *The Well of Loneliness*: 'Thus the bitter nights slipped into the days, and the anxious days slipped back into the nights, bringing to that curious trinity neither helpful counsel nor consolation.'[75]

If Una felt it, so too did Souline. If John noticed it, she allowed it to slip by unremarked. She did however ask Una to return to Rye, in order to leave her and Souline together in London. Then, further humiliating Una, John decided she wanted to show Souline the Forecastle. Una trailed miserably back to the London flat, while John took an excited young Russian to Sussex. The garden in the Forecastle was still 'a mass of red and purple zinnias dahlias chrysanthemums and salvias'. Una, that autumn, described the house as 'warm and dear and smelling of wood fires, breathing the curious peace that has always haunted it'.[76] Though Evguenia felt its peace she also understood that it was Una's home. John too felt torn and guilty, sensing Una's presence, but she would take no decision that would release one or other from this well-appointed prison.

On 20 November Souline returned to Paris. John wrote immediately: 'Now I possess you and you possess me and distance cannot separate us.'[77] Though John refused to recognize it, distance often helped the trio recover from the suffocation of their triangular relationship. Souline herself wrote: 'I had more freedom for studying and thinking away from them . . . John did not quite understand that.'[78]

John asked a lot of herself but she asked far more of Una and Souline. In a rare moment of honesty she told Una: 'I think I should like a harem with you in command of it.'[79] It was her fantasy that the trio could comfortably coexist. She and Una had family, friends, books and literary life in common as well as a past. She and Souline shared a sensual passion, a tenderness and a spiritual kinship that went beyond their bodily truths. She wished to be able to give a different kind of affection to each of them. She wished for the ecstasy of new desire without the agony of discarding the comfortable old slippers. She wished to abolish jealousy, find peace, and write another damn book! Souline wrote: 'She knew she was asking too much, I suppose, in the very deepest of her heart but she would not admit it to herself.'[80]

The demands John made caused Una to wonder whether she was being punished for her cruelty to Ladye who 'holds my hand day and night. I feel her presence . . . I am oh so deeply humbly grateful to her for giving me what I do not deserve.'[81] She believed that all she had done to hurt Ladye 'she has repaid by helping me in almost exactly similar circumstances'. For the first time Una acknowledged that she had been 'utterly selfish and cruel to her . . . in the crude egotism of youth and personal desire'.[82]

That first Christmas of 1934 Souline stayed away. John and Una spent a strained and polite few days at the Forecastle. December had seen the French translation of *Miss Ogilvy* and the American two-dollar edition of *The Well of Loneliness*. There was also interest in a proposed translation of *The Unlit*

Lamp.[83] But John's mind was elsewhere. Two letters from Souline helped her to struggle through Christmas Day. Nothing helped Una except for the dry fact that John was there. Since she couldn't be with Souline, John declared uncharitably that she was glad Evguenia was on duty at the hospital where she had a new job among new people.

'Personally I have a secret liking for all new things,' John wrote to her on Boxing Day, 'fledgling birds, puppies, kittens and babies! . . . Had I been a man I would have given you a child – as it is I am angry that I cannot do so – I much long for an independent chink-faced brat. Jolly for you if I had been a man! . . . Don't be scared, it will never happen – or at least not through me, more's the pity!!'[84]

A New Year's Eve letter and a journal entry sum up 1934. On New Year's Eve John wrote to Souline to say she wanted to touch her. Una wrote to herself: 'The last day of a very unhappy year . . . the road ahead of me looks very steep and rough.'

In 1935 John toyed restlessly with the idea of leaving Rye and settling in Paris for the sake of joining Souline. She considered selling the Forecastle – it was filled with the wrong memories; the past and Una were always there. Then Una's heart began to 'murmur'. Tests proved negative but several doctors warned Una to avoid undue strain. John decided instead to sell the London flat with its five flights of stairs.

In 1935 family matters impinged on John's attention. In October Marie Visetti contracted pernicious anaemia and became violent. 'I cannot pretend that this seriously effects [*sic*] my heart as she and I have been so wide apart,' John wrote to Souline. 'The poor, angry, cruel old woman . . . anyhow I forgive her faults towards me and I hope she forgives me my faults.'[85] John placed her in a nursing home but her mother's violent outbursts meant another removal to a hotel, paid for of course by John.

In November, Andrea and Toby Warren had a son, Nicholas Vincenzo Warren. John and Una read the notice in *The Times* and sent a congratulatory cable. When Toby was away, Una went to visit Andrea, but the sight of her daughter must have reminded her painfully of that other 'difficult' young woman who was to arrive for Christmas.

If Andrea had achieved her independence with too small a struggle, Souline was already finding the cost too great. In the summer of 1935, after five days in Paris visiting Evguenia at a clinic where the young woman had undergone an operation on her sinuses, John spent a single night alone with her lover at a hotel in St Raphael, then coerced an unwilling Souline to join her and Una first in Beauvallon then in Sirmione.

Souline desperately desired privacy but John was able to have her close at hand, Una having conceded that she would 'sooner have her in the same hotel as myself. It is better for John than coming to and fro late at night . . . it is against all so-called decent custom, but once a thing exists I can't myself see that such details matter.'[86]

Such details mattered painfully to Souline. They began to matter more to Una when at the Albergo Catullo in Sirmione John went every night to Souline's room. Rows rent the peace of the village.

Souline loved Sirmione. 'Almost continuous sunshine, the blue sky, the lake sinister in the storm, the tall cypresses making beautiful shapely avenues . . . it was a continuous poetry and John was happy.' But Souline could not share John's happiness. 'The atmosphere was not . . . healthy being a triangle . . . it was almost unbearable.'[87]

She was asked to bear it on many more occasions. In January 1936 the trio spent time together in Paris. In March that year they travelled tensely to Grasse, then in July abrasively to Alsace, then in September amid sullenness and scenes to the Italian Tyrol, until April 1937 when a bitter trio – together almost uninterruptedly for over a year – reached Florence. On the occasions they did spend in England, shared Christmasses were claustrophobic. After the first one in 1935, Souline wrote: 'I wanted my independence because I could not do much for her [John] but be there. She needed me like water, like air, it seems and yet she would not give allowance to my own feelings when I was cooped up with them both.'[88]

Souline's view of the triangle as unhealthy is borne out by the trio's recurrent symptoms: melancholy, agitation, depression, heart murmurs, resentment, violent rage, feverish excitement, jumping pulses, lethal fatigue, intermittent weeping and – one might add – severely impaired judgement. If this was love it reads like torture.

Determined to maintain the illusion of a harmonious love triangle, John did not allow herself to investigate the mounting tensions. Una and Souline however were not characters in search of an author. Radclyffe Hall could not rearrange the scenario, as she could with Stephen Gordon, Mary Llewellyn or Joan Ogden. Una and Souline had plots of their own which they intended to work out.

21

SICKNESS, DEATH AND BEYOND

Between 1937 and the end of John's life, Una's decisive actions revolved around a curious delusion. She saw Souline less as a woman than as a symptom of John's sudden 'malady'. John's feelings for Souline were an affliction that had to be borne by both of them. Una, stalwart and reliable, would see the writer through this health crisis, this passing madness. Somewhere she was sure, beneath the besotted obsessed woman, blown this way and that by storms from Souline, lurked the steady John, *her* John.

John, of course, had never been steady, and in the form in which Una envisaged emotional possession had probably never been 'hers'. If John had ever 'lost herself' in someone it was patently Souline. The very equality that gave strength to John and Una's relationship also forbade those troughs and heights. As for steadiness: for some years, John's intemperate rages, her wild moods, her sudden excitements, her morose depressions, had been focused on and around her writing and her God. Now, with the passions centred on Souline, the tempests were let loose on Una.

Una survived by holding hard to two shaky beliefs. She believed that the difficulties John was encountering with the slow-moving *Shoemaker of Merano* were due to its impoverished emotional base. Her stumbling block with this novel was similar to the one she faced with *Emblem Hurlstone* for this novel also borrowed aspects of Souline's character and fictionalized John's suffering and ecstasies. She also believed that John was not writing anything else of consequence.

She could not see as important (though she was shown enough of it) John's 'factional' Book of Letters which she considered merely a self-indulgent outpouring on a worthless object. Indeed it would have been hard for anyone in Una's position to regard as 'literature' the account of a dramatic love affair between doomed lovers one of whom is your partner; or to notice how the snapshots of landscapes formed the backdrop to that action; or to relish the way in which other writers and artists were turned into malicious minor characters; or to admire the insightful self-portrait of the blocked artist as heroine.

Later, more detached readers, however, can see that Hall was simultaneously living her life and transforming it through a book, some of which was still at the stage of raw material, some a careful second draft (her numerous post-scripts act as different versions), the best of it fine-tuned like her formal novels.

Radclyffe Hall's heroine John does not hide from the worst of her selves any more than did Joan Ogden. John-the-heroine's spiritual reliance on her God invokes the same hot power that Christophe's did in *The Master of the House*. The John figure is as controlling as Mrs Ogden, as arrogant as Stephen Gordon, on occasion as icy as Teresa Boselli, yet at the same time she is imbued with Fabio Boselli's great compassion.

The narrative of the Book of Letters shows a craggy honesty. It is jagged, spiteful, morbid and funny. The story leaves John-as-heroine little to be proud of except her own brutal candour but the narrative's magnetic sharpness pos-sesses and is possessed by a mesmeric voyeurism. The Letters are private, and raw.[1] The reader must read on.

That privacy, that rawness is part of this book's compulsion. The invasion of privacy invited by the author-correspondent was worked and reworked over the years. The Book of Letters stylistically repeats and plays with the same nar-rative themes that occur and recur in her other books: self-deception, betrayal, human affection, the healing power of natural beauty, the alienated individual, the incorporation of spiritual belief into mundane reality. In this last poetic drama, where some of the lines have the feel of her later poems, Hall worked with the same metaphors, the same themes, that had preoccupied her life's writing.

During John's last six years, Souline – both the person herself addressed in the book, and also its other central character – had intentions incompatible with John's (and with Una's) but just as strong. Souline's determination to become a *somebody* drove itself hard against her lover's egotistic desire to control her movements with money as if she were a nobody, though that is not how John put it.

In Souline's view, 'I just thought I shall DO something. I shall achieve some-thing, and it will be alright. I won't need John's money. I love her for herself and not for the money.'[2] John's version came from a writer bent on asserting authority, invoking the name that gave her the greatest self-esteem:

> Dearest you have the love of Radclyffe Hall but maybe that's just Dead Sea fruit to you . . . Apparently you are not one of those who take pride in being the star that follows the bigger star. You do not like 'following in the tail of a comet' . . . well then sweet own heart, you should have fallen in love with a humble *nobody*.[3]

Souline ignored the *de haut en bas* attitude at the start of the letter and hurled John's words back at her. She had every intention of studying, to do something to occupy what John called her 'eternally restless mind'. The doctor who had nursed her through TB had told her she needed 'good conditions in order to survive'. But now, with John beside her and those conditions at hand, it was impossible to settle. 'I was always tempted to do something with John and I never had the courage to say no.' First she would study in Florence – a course perhaps in history of art – but there were so many reasons against it – the language, her age. It would be better, she thought, if she studied at the Sorbonne. But that only made John unhappy. Even Oxford and Cambridge had once been within her sights – to study medicine, perhaps – but at every turn, as she knew, there was always Una at John's side to thwart her plans.[4]

Errant tendrils of their love caught on the branches of their argument. The awkward lopsided fact of Evguenia tugged at John's throat. 'Don't worry,' John made an attempt at reassurance. 'Una shall not have any hand in your studies, nor shall she even advise if I can muzzle her.'[5]

Una was not to be muzzled. Souline was not to be placated: 'The atmosphere was full of nervous tension . . . the air itself was impregnated with heavy forebodings and I had to go away in order not to be broken down under the strain of it,' Souline wrote later.

John had already written *her* lines in *The Sixth Beatitude*. Like Hannah Bullen, she 'was all on edge these days; everyone got on her nerves . . . restless she was: something stirred in her blood, something very defiant and very persistent.'[6] That something was the awareness that Souline was slipping away. She could forget about John for hours at a time though it did not mean she no longer cared. John would have liked to parcel Souline up but there was no way of tying the string so that it stayed tied. John asked for markers of permanence. Souline, who viewed life as a process, saw the relationship as a place in which she shed skins and renewed them. Their two positions were virtually irreconcilable.

In the summer of 1937 John signed the lease for an apartment at 18 Lungarno Acciaivoli with a view over Florence's Ponte Vecchio.[7] She planned to leave Souline in Paris during their summer break in Rye but for the trio to return to Florence in the autumn. Evguenia expressed her unease about a plan they both knew was untenable. Look upon me 'as a man who was already married when we met,' John said weakly.[8] She hoped there was a way by which she and Souline 'could find happiness even in the circumstances'.[9]

Souline was adamant: there was no way she would join them. 'The circumstances were such that they made me ill.'[10] It came as no surprise when in July Souline issued her ultimatum from Paris. She would rather leave John than go to Florence for the winter if Una was there.

For eight hours John sobbed, sulked, screamed and raged. In hysterical fury she vented her wrath on Una. 'I feel as if a harrow had passed over me,' Una cried into her Day Book.[11] The lovers parted. Una consoled John. The lovers reunited. Una consoled herself. Later John would try a new refrain: variations on a theme that ran: 'Try hard to LOVE me more than you HATE Una.'[12]

Several tries ended in failure. Una, 'exhausted in spirit, mind and body', with John only marginally less so, returned to Rye on 14 July 1937 after eighteen months abroad. John wrote to Souline:

It is almost as though a part of my life has come to an end, a period of our life lived closely together, the period you hated and longed to be released from . . . maybe your half [of our heart] is singing and shouting 'Free! free! free!' – I can only say to your half of our heart: 'Love me, cling to me, understand me. Understand my love, my desire to protect.'[13]

Souline understood all too well. For years she had suffered a siege of over-protection. That August John, in mackintosh mood, sent a list of injunctions 'for the care of an RCP by itself'. The page was headed: 'These instructions to be taken with the RCP. I mean it. I am not joking.' The list included:

No vodka or spirits.
No climbing.
A warm wrap always to be taken sunset or evening.
A short lying down every day if possible without too much boredom.
A sunshade to be taken, YES.
Good wine may be drunk with meals.
No drinking on an empty stomach.
By order of John S. H. [Same Heart]
Turn over.
Seven pairs of stout shoes to be taken including those with rubber soles.
Always change shoes and stockings if the least damp.
Take your magnificent umbrella.
Remember always to love John.[14]

The 'wise good and careful Piggie Hall' who was expected to keep 'its hoofs dry' and never go out 'without an enormous big umbrella' was suddenly wearied by the game.[15] 'I usually gave in . . . She was obsessed . . . with the healing of my weak lungs.'[16]

John's concern by then had a manipulative ring: 'I know I'm fussy and make you feel impatient . . . [but] if you get ill I shall die I tell you.'[17] She refused to count as admissible Souline's evidence that 'it was mostly the unhappy mood of my mind combined with the unfortunate surroundings that made me ill . . . I started some kind of a flare up after our living together *à trois* . . .'[18]

Interminable discussions throughout August finally led John to accept that 'her little Russian disaster'[19] should never again have to live *à trois*. 'I know that you must have your life because you cannot find happiness in mine.'[20] On the strength of that reluctant admission Souline acquiesced to the Florence plan.

It was however still her own torn feelings that preoccupied John: 'My poor broken life . . . had things been different my life might have been so contented . . . could there have been friendship between you and Una . . . But never again will we live three together, this I have promised, so do not fear it.'[21]

In John's mind the idea of Florence became a place of erotic contemplation. It would be the backdrop for their second honeymoon. A rising moon, pale silver, would outline the city, constellations would glitter, they would whisper nonsense, they would retell their coming-together stories, they would taste each other, they would lose themselves in desire and possibility.

Paradoxically another fantasy raced in tandem through her mind. Florence would also be the city where one more time they would enact their child and mother romances. One more time, John yearned for her adult lover to play 'the little Chink child'. Integral to John's eroticism had long been the feeling that Souline was the child she longed for; a feeling not unusual in lesbian relationships where mother–child roles intermingle with those of female lover. That year it struck John with strange intensity. (Was it because her child was growing up? Growing away?) 'You are my love and my desire but also . . . the child that through some unkind trick of fate you cannot give me . . . Since you cannot give me a child you must sometimes become one in order to pacify me.'[22]

Souline did more than merely accept this; she nestled inside it. 'John often said that we had probably met before . . . that we were related to each other in one or other form, most likely as father or mother and child . . . and that I feel very strongly too.'[23]

John had a deep desire for children, not necessarily to bear them, but to rear and protect them as a parent: had she not tried to 'buy' a baby in Italy in the early years with Una? At moments of depression with her work she would become highly emotional about her childlessness. Feeling a genuine bitterness at not having experienced motherhood, John nonetheless produces some of her most moving portraits of very young children: delicate Millie and robust Joan Ogden, tempestuous Sidonia, the small scared Stephen, Christophe and his teething baby cousin Jan.

By associating childbirth with creativity, her books at one level became offspring, but Una and Souline were invited to play very different roles in their parenting. It was crucial to John that Una saw John as the sole progenitor of the novels. Una's task was to provide favourable conditions for their conception, then following each birth she was to act as midwife and caretaker. She would listen to the 'children's' stories (drafts), she would christen them, help them find homes in the publishing world.

With Souline, John clung to a fantasy that she was *not* the sole progenitor.

The novels written after 1934 come out of her bodily union with Evguenia. They are flesh of their joined flesh, *their* children, who cut their teeth, have birthdays (chapters), misbehave (get writer's blocks), must be kept in check. And as mother of the child they could not have, Souline willingly played out her fantasy role.

Before the reality of Florence broke those dreams, Andrea, the only child John had attempted to rear, came to stay twice that summer, bringing her own child Nicholas, now nearly two.[24] John told Souline that Andrea's husband Toby Warren (designated by John as a 'flop'), as well as antagonizing her, Una and Viola, had also antagonized his family, from whom 'no help was forthcoming' despite the fact that Andrea had produced their only grandchild and 'a boy at that'.[25] It was a tell-tale remark from John at precisely the point when she herself desired a child – and 'a boy at that'.

Andrea, so John continued, though despising Toby, was 'loyal to him which is as it should be' – a curious remark given John's own infidelity. But even as an alternative family, John remained tied to the image of virtuous domesticity, and whatever allegiance she offered to Souline in private, she was determined to maintain the public role of loyal partner to Una.

Andrea was thin, down at heel and, as Una remarked tartly, out of work. She just bit back the word 'again'.[26] Andrea, in fact, was to find success at work very soon. The BBC, intrigued by Andrea's varied careers in film, theatre, advertising, journalism and as Axel Munthe's secretary, commissioned her to write for their programmes, initially as a freelance. Andrea had first approached the BBC for an audition in 1935. She told them of her film parts and about playing a 'period ingénue' in a show of Ernest Milton's called *Paganini*. She had acquired her post as secretary to the author Axel Munthe, she said, 'because I could read to him as he wished to be read to . . . in French and Italian'. It seemed that Radclyffe Hall's and Una Troubridge's upbringing of Andrea paid off in at least one way. After her divorce from Toby Warren in 1941, the BBC employed her for seven years as a lively radio announcer and studio manager, and she worked for them again as a freelance between 1953 and 1958.[27]

John felt unusually relaxed with Andrea and reported to Souline: 'Andrea has become rather a darling and she is quite goodlooking these days. She is also quite without affectation.' Indeed, her good looks were soon to become nationally known. In 1943, after she had compered Forces' Choice, a sexist writer for *Woman's Journal* described Andrea as 'far too pretty and vital to be wasted on the desert air'.[28]

Unable to keep her mind for long from Souline's singular looks, John was relieved when Andrea spotted 'a Chink photograph'. Andrea, John reported, thought 'you had an amazing face: Tartar! I thought to myself "scratch a Russian and you find a tartar!"'[29]

In the course of Andrea's visit John wrote decisively to Souline: 'Let us resolve never again to quarrel.'[30] That resolution was easier to keep when they were apart from Una. There was a joyful time when John wanted Souline to meet Colette and threw a lunch party for her Russian lover, Maurice Rostand and Natalie Barney. 'The lunch was . . . in one of the numerous . . . Russian restaurants . . . John wanted it that way in my honour.'[31] Souline, 'very excited', watched Colette. 'I shall never forget [her] appearance . . . she was bare feet wearing sandals . . . in the middle of winter. Round her rather plump figure was thrown a scarf of vivid blue which matched her gentian eyes . . . her hair was standing in all directions . . . much tinted.' The shy young Russian watched the eminent French writer but recorded with satisfaction that 'John only looked at me.'

The next occasion Evguenia met Colette was the summer she and John spent time with Romaine and Natalie. The four of them played table tennis. 'There was no end of laughing. John just could not stop. She had what she wanted.' They were invited to a party on the roof of Trait d'Union, Romaine's villa hidden among 'pinewood that smelt heavenly':

> We all lay down on cushions and looked upwards: the sky was sewn with glittering stars . . . Colette in her pink organdie pyjama-slacks . . . drinking the orangeade, lying near John . . . whenever anybody ventured to tease John, she used to say: '*Il ne faut pas tourmenter John.*'[32]

Peaceful pinewood days became more rare. In August 1937 John took up the question of Souline's visa with Humbert Wolfe, whom John described as 'almost a Minister'. Wolfe approached the Home Office on Souline's behalf with the request for a 'come and go' annual visa.[33]

John, never a patient person, fretted and fumed for a week. But on 25 August she was able to write to Souline from Rye:

> Darling, darling, darling, this morning came a letter from Humbert Wolfe saying that the Home Office has granted you an annual visa allowing you to come and go and to stay in England for 6 weeks at a time. This is the greatest possible triumph . . . You may imagine that I am pleased with myself – the idea of asking Humbert for help was entirely my own.[34]

Despite this good news, their resolution not to quarrel grew harder to sustain as John's health took a blow. On 25 August, John had fallen, twisted her ankle badly and maintained a triple fracture. She was still in the London Clinic when Souline arrived. Later John said ruefully: 'The day I was really pretty bad with that broken [ankle] bone you fell out of love – my long illness did it.'[35]

The cause was less John's long illness than the disastrous way it was conducted. Souline was excluded from all serious discussions yet was criticized for not being sufficiently informed or attentive. John, who seemed unaware of the psychological consequences, constantly used Una as her go-between, almost as her gatekeeper.

It started that September when Una, not John, met Souline at Victoria, carrying a note that read: 'Welcome to England my darling Heart, John.' Souline was forced to receive it from Una's hand. This destructive pattern of communication was to operate through every stage of John's many illnesses.

Souline stayed at the Clifton Hotel, Welbeck Street, and visited the clinic in the mornings. Una stayed at John's side all day every day. Another malevolent pattern took shape: Una, custodian of the bedchamber, monitored visitors, encouraged as few as possible, stood as a hostile barrier between Souline and John.

John was forced to stay in the clinic until 13 October when she finally left on crutches, her leg still in a plaster cast. An irritated Una was sent to Rye as John moved into the Clifton Hotel to be with Souline. Later Una was compelled to return to London to allow the two lovers together with a nurse to go to the Forecastle. Una was distressed and angry at this changed situation but John had kept her promise to Souline. The triangle was formally at an end.

The October nights closed in. By now John was well enough to go in a wheel-chair to Paris where, towing an eager nurse, the trio set off for Florence. Although Souline demanded and received a separate flat in Via dei Benci with a personal maid, Angeline,[36] she felt excluded when John and Una visited old friends. She ached for Paris.

In the spring, John's health began to deteriorate further. Her ankle was so bad that she needed sticks to walk. Anticipated as an opportunity to pursue their passion, their time in Florence had been filled with the habitual fights; there had been little time together. Passion remained a flat word on a printed page. John threw her sticks into a corner, stuffed her ears against the clatter. Where was her wild brilliance? What had happened to that first innocence when they believed they could speak in tongues, light up the days? In January and February she signed sad letters to Souline 'your lame dog'.[37] Would Souline, who tired swiftly of ideas and people, grow tired of a sick animal?

John came close to a frightening inner edge. She called the condition '"nerves", "grumpiness", and a dozen different names'[38] and kept the blank empty spaces at bay with a continuous stream of lists, instructions, timetables, minute and detailed plans for a book on which she could not concentrate. Incoherence was a form of madness she dared not engage in. She forced her thoughts into tramlines. She categorized emotions; graded her writing; scored *The Shoemaker* against *The Master of the House*. This semblance of order allowed her to breathe until new rows broke out again in June 1938 between Una and Souline.

The trigger this time was John's continued admiration for Una as a woman who 'did things' and her reluctance to ensure Souline a comparably active role.

'I knew what I wanted of life. I wanted to make good, to find something that was worth working for. I was looking for it. John only helped me to try and find *myself*.'[39]

John asked only one thing of Souline: to become half of 'their' heart, to breathe the same air, to melt body into body, to assign her soul to John's. A more damaging request it would have been hard to invent. 'John only wanted me to be there at her side . . . I loved her but I knew I could not stay in those circumstances. The moment I could get away I did so and went to the Sorbonne'[40] whose entrance exam she was determined to take.

John tried bribes. She offered her a job as her secretary for £300 a year. Souline refused. Reluctantly John agreed to Souline taking the exam. She raised her allowance to £300 a year. There was of course a catch. 'All Piggies have most excellent memories and mine has not forgotten the terms on which it gets its Piggie allowance.'[41] If Souline wanted her Pig portion she was never to live in an 'unsuitable' climate. 'Florence seems as though it had a gaping wound in its side because you are not here.'[42]

Wounds abounded. Souline's departure for Paris that June had disastrous effects on them both. John suffered what was virtually another nervous breakdown. Souline failed her exam, and went to St Malo with Lisa on holiday.[43] Rows and reconciliations became their way of life.

While Souline was in St Malo John received another blow. Peggy Austin, her oldest friend, had been killed. 'I saw it in the *Daily Mail* . . . [She] has been killed together with two other women when their motor crashed into a ravine near Bordeaux,' she wrote to Souline in St Malo. John recalled how she and Peggy had 'never lost touch with each other through the years . . . she was associated first with such a happy carefree time in my life, and her death has made me look back . . . one must never look back, but always forward . . . beloved I look forward towards you . . . be gentle with my heart.'[44]

Souline could not both be gentle with John's heart and achieve her own ambitions. In June 1938 John had said to her: 'I do understand your wish to work,' and later: 'As you say, you love me in your own way. Everybody can only love in their own way. There can be no hard and fast rules, beloved.'[45] She sympathized with her failing the Sorbonne exams, but at the same time could not bear the separation that success would have entailed:

> I know the Sorbonne has the name of being one of the most devilish exams in the world. I wish you had not wanted to go in for the thing, but as you did, that's that. Oh, I suppose I ought not to have said that – you will tell Lisa . . . I am going to stop you educating yourself.[46]

She had uttered the correct lines but she could not bring herself to act on them. She became so distraught she even threatened suicide.

You can face quite calmly life without me but I simply cannot face life without you – I don't want to do myself in. It's against my every religious belief, a great sin and a terrible sign of cowardice, but I feel I am nearing the end . . . I am turning from side to side in my prison of circumstances that you know of and knew of before I took you.[47]

Souline could not tell whether John was genuinely ready to pull down the final curtain or whether it was another scene in their drama. It is likely that John herself at that stage could not tell.

That suicide note may however have been the impetus behind John and Souline's decision to try another period together in August. Ironically (or was it maliciously?) they chose Malvern, the town where John and Una had consummated their love affair. 'Unmerciful they were the one to the other. Their mating was harsh and unmerciful – a scourge, a relentless combat of bodies, when at last they parted they did not embrace, because neither felt the need to embrace.'[48]

Body promises were wearing thin. They tore each other apart physically, then abruptly 'all of a sudden life seemed to go bad – these bodies – their hot lusts, the clamours that they awoke in each other' were no longer enough.[49] At Christmas Souline proposed that they cease their lovemaking for a while. Perhaps a physical space would help them come to a better psychic understanding.

Previous biographers have used December 1938 as a crude marker for the end of their sexual partnership. It is tempting but far too simplistic as an interpretation of lesbian sexuality. We must not be beguiled by the standard heterosexual assumptions about what takes place in a lesbian relationship and how it can be measured. Genital sex traditionally has been the indicator by which heterosexual society polarizes lesbians into 'couples' and 'non-couples' and by which it measures the beginning and ending of lesbian relationships. To some extent, some lesbians have internalized this idea, but not all, since this is not necessarily either an accurate temperature reading for the nature of coupledom or, as in John and Souline's case, the measure of their sexual feelings for each other. Lesbian cultural history does not reserve the label 'sexual' for relationships that are genitally consummated or genitally maintained.

Souline's highly charged sensual and physical interest in John, and her erotic susceptibility to John's caresses continued to imbue John's writing long after Christmas 1938, as it continued to imbue their lives.

De-emphasizing genital lovemaking did not render their relationship asexual. Their playful secret life of pet names and animal games, their fantasies of Piggies wearing crowns, and Piggies wearing nothing at all, of kisses being fed through iron bars, is evidence of an ongoing cuddled and cosseted sexual intimacy. The language of their erotic relationship continued to be the language of play: 'Sometimes we are rather like two ships that get blown about for a while by winds, or washed apart for a while by tides . . . Piggie cannot put out to sea all alone and I cannot put out to sea without Piggie.'[50]

For a time 'something far deeper' than 'the physical side of our life',[51] epitomized by their 'little Piggie prayer that Piggie's so small and the world is so large',[52] held them both safe. When John felt secure within this safety net, she was able to act straightforwardly: 'Our bodies are so much part of each other . . . [but] there must never be anything between us . . . unless you desire me.'[53]

But when she was struck by the 'awful illness called the Pig-Pine',[54] the absence of sexual contact as well as the absence of Souline herself played on her sense of insecurity.

> I myself have been a great lover – I have loved and then grown weary . . . and put an abrupt and brutal end to the thing just as you have done . . . perhaps I am paying for my past and the price is high . . . You no longer desire me, you have made that quite plain and you had a perfect right to do so. Am I jealous and suspicious? Of course I am.[55]

She began to be suspicious of everything Souline did. In June Evguenia wrote to tell John that she planned to spend some weekends with Lisa at Lisa's weekend cottage. John became hysterical. Was Souline going to vanish? Would she live there permanently? Did she prefer Lisa's company to John's? What about England? What about love? For once as readers we are fortunate. There exists just one letter of Souline's which escaped destruction. It is her affectionate rational answer to John:

> Darling Johnnie . . . I can't understand what you are fretting about? My plans are unchanged . . . I shall come to England for a month . . . I shall keep my promise . . . I have explained to you twice . . . our desire to go in the country, but if you prefer to take it as a drama then do it. I can't prevent you . . . Johnnie it can't be the reason of your upheaval – there must be the . . . reason in it that you never can accept me to have my own opinion or action, or else it is Una who is hoofing it up.[56]

Both of Souline's assumptions were correct. It says much for her patience and good will that she concluded:

> No Johnnie darling, don't take everything so hard. You have done all you think you have and I thank you but don't coerce me too much in my own innocent little plans . . . Let live and you shall be happier yourself . . . Be happy, be happy. Piggie asks you to be happy. Your Evguenia.[57]

In analysing that year's troubles, any conflicting views on sexual expression seemed less significant than their conflicting goals. John had a life to which she wished to add on Souline. Evguenia wanted to form a new life together with

John. Souline was invited, beguiled, finally ordered, merely to 'be'. It took John until 1942 to comprehend that this would never be enough for any self-respecting, talented woman like Souline. Where there is a functionless existence there is a bereaved person. Souline showed John her bereavement on countless occasions but John failed to see it.

The most critical theme in Radclyffe Hall's novels, most particularly *The Sixth Beatitude*, is that of seeing with the inner eye. Yet in this, her most demanding relationship, she simply did not see. She did not see, because she could not face, the fact that for Una the situation 'hurts and hurts and hurts and is never for one waking moment out of my mind and heart'.[58] She did not see, because she could not face, Souline's deep bitterness at Una's increasingly contemptuous treatment of her as the affair continued.

You make too much of it, John had said in 1937; Una does not count, John had said in 1938; I cannot see what the problem is, John said in 1939. Viewing John's health symbolically as she did herself it is not surprising that when her body began to crumble, limb after limb, what faltered first were her eyes. They gave her great trouble even before her ankle broke. Since Merano she had suffered an uncontrollable nervous spasm in the lower eyelids which turned the lashes inwards against the eyeballs. In August 1937 her eyes, 'none too good', were said not yet to need an operation. Painful spasms were mistakenly put down by a London specialist to wrong spectacles. Chronic conjunctivitis was diagnosed, regular eyedrops advised. Her painful sight did not prevent her working sixteen hours a day and through the night. The condition worsened and would return in a dangerously threatening form.

The body politic too was falling apart. War was brewing. 'Everyone is worried . . . These are mad bad days,' John wrote in August 1938.[59] Her especial concern was for her lover: 'These are grim and anxious days for us all but more especially for those who own RCPs.'[60] She wrote in September to reassure Souline in Paris: 'Remember that if you are in even the smallest trouble of any kind I will come to you at once.'[61]

In September 1938 Chamberlain had flown to Munich to see Hitler at Berchtesgaden and Bad Godesberg. John expressed her hatred of Hitler: 'he is an hysteric, I think an epileptic . . . a fanatic,'[62] but at the same time, at that stage, she also expressed her dislike of the Jews. This stance which she had imbibed from D'Annunzio was maintained in letters to Souline, now reinforced by the fact that Italy had become Germany's partner under the Axis pact. As rumours of imminent war grew, her feelings rocked: 'As for me John Radclyffe Hall what do I feel? I scarcely know, beyond amazement and spiritual horror. I cannot seem to envisage the horror and yet I am haunted by it. No mere words can express this madness that has suddenly stricken Europe.'[63]

Her protective instincts towards her child-lover caused her to draw up a new will.[64] In a desperate desire to draw Souline permanently to England she pointed out to her that as under its terms her eventual inheritance would be equal to Una's and would be in English money, England was 'the right and proper country' for her to reside in. Regarding the changed will she assured Souline: 'I have made you ample provision after my death and even some day a substantial income unless you do something entirely outrageous which you will not, will you, my darling?'[65]

This promise of security was believed by Souline for all time: 'John . . . never stopped saying that I can whistle with my hands in the pockets, I was provided for the rest of my life. I believed it or when I did not believe it there was no cause for disbelieving it.'[66] After John's death, when there was cause enough, it was that promise, that will, which lit the flare on an already inflammatory situation between her and Una.

With war threatening, John hoped to provide for Souline an unconditional visa which would allow her much greater flexibility than the 'come and go' visa already obtained. This would mean that Souline could work in England, stay for an indefinite period, and come and go as she liked.[67] John talked to officials at the Home Office and by mid-September the Secretary of State had authorized Souline's unconditional visa. By 21 September 1938 Souline in Paris had had the visa put on her French Nansen. John was jubilant.

[T]he getting of that unconditional visa was a miracle. It is scarcely ever given to anyone who has only a Nansen – indeed I was told by Collinson [an official at the British Passport Office in Paris] that it would be *very* hard to obtain, if indeed it could be obtained at all of which he seemed extremely doubtful. And now you have actually got it in a few weeks and at a time like this! A miracle![68]

John had prayed to St Thomas More, who she felt 'must realize how urgent it was to you to get this England's protection . . . And now beloved do something for me . . . Write to me and say "The unconditional visa is actually on my French Nansen". Am I childish?'[69] Once she got to England Souline would retain her French Nansen with its new unconditional English visa until the Nansen expired. A helpful official at the Home Office had suggested to John that she would then be able to get her English Nansen.

'What an effort it was to get any visas for anywhere for me!' Souline later wrote. It was 'like moving 10 tons of bricks', John told her. Indeed it was. 'John had to exert all her energy and pull all the strings to have some concrete results.'[70]

John was all the more surprised at her success since it was well known that the Home Office was under immense pressure on all sides from refugees, legal and otherwise: 'Jews! Jews! Jews! Millions of them trying to push their way into England and dozens and dozens are managing to slip in without papers or passports via Ireland or by arriving at small villages on our coast in fishing boats.'[71]

Two years later, in 1940, John's closest Jewish friend Mickie Jacob arrived in Britain somewhat in the manner John had professed to scorn. When Italy, previously neutral, came out on the side of the Axis, Mickie, her lover and lover's two daughters moved temporarily to southern France. Within weeks of arriving, they were evacuated on cargo ships with no washing facilities to Gibraltar where their ship was attacked by German submarines. Miraculously unscathed, Mickie returned to England with only the clothes she stood up in.[72]

Under Mickie's influence, John began eventually to comprehend the extremity and barbarity of her own views. But in 1939 John's crusade on behalf of lesbians had not yet led her to empathize with other persecuted groups, as her letters, which at that stage make shameful reading, patently show: '. . . Jews. Yes. I am beginning to be really afraid of them: not of the one or two really dear Jewish friends that I have in England, no, but of Jews as a whole. I believe they hate us and want to bring about a European War and then a World revolution in order to destroy us utterly.'[73]

At this point English upper-class anti-Semitism was sufficiently standard as to be hardly remarked upon in the circles in which Radclyffe Hall moved. Virginia Woolf for instance, who married the Jewish Leonard Woolf in 1912, recalled many years later to Ethel Smyth: 'How I hated marrying a Jew – how I hated their nasal voices, and their oriental jewellery, and their noses and their wattles – what a snob I was.'[74]

That Radclyffe Hall shared that class and racial prejudice does not excuse her but it does set it within its context. Her increasing sense of lesbian exclusion, and her preoccupation with the social position of the exile, led her with a stubborn slowness eventually to acknowledge that her inhumane views stood in contradiction to her other deeply held principles. By 1942, when genocide was proposed as an appropriate response to the so-called 'threat' posed by Jews, she recoiled with horror as news of the mass deportation of Jews from Vichy France to the gas chambers filtered through:[75]

> [T]he wholesale slaughter of the Jews is too fearful, the more so as one feels help-less to do anything for the poor devils . . . Bad Jews there certainly are and always have been, but *this* . . . I cannot excuse her [France] . . . a woman is a woman and a child is a child, and both should be protected.[76]

The moderating of her views ran parallel with her increasing fatigue and her resignation over the separation from Souline. In spring 1939 she began to believe she and Souline had 'only met to part'. She knew Souline blamed her for not being able to 'offer [her] a home together with myself',[77] and suspected that Evguenia was 'now very anxious to marry'.[78] Like Stephen Gordon, sacrificing herself for what she saw as Mary's rosier future, John wrote dramatically: 'Perhaps that is why I came into your life, to give you the freedom and time to look about you. A strange mission for R.H., a very strange mission, but it is not for me to question heaven.'[79]

This morbid philosophizing coincided with the onset of another severe illness in the summer of 1939. X-rays showed scars on John's lungs – evidence perhaps that the unnamed illness in her adolescence may well have been tuberculosis – an over-active thyroid and an enlarged aorta. A Rome specialist decreed she should give up smoking and advised against a return to England's damp climate with its possibility of pneumonia. With an iron will John, a life-long chain-smoker, at once obeyed. Her hot temper however did not improve.

Too ill to write, she resigned herself to settling permanently abroad but returned to England that summer to sell the Forecastle. 'I am beginning to wonder what I am worth . . . very little . . . if I cannot get back to my new book . . . but one goes on somehow.'[80]

Despite decisions to separate, the lovers again wrote daily. In August Souline even agreed to stay *à trois* in Rye. Bruised in spirit, tense and sedated, John had no strength for the worst row ever to take place between Una and Souline. During their argument Souline tried to prevent Una from leaving the room. She pushed and grabbed at her, fighting like a cat with years of pent-up resentment and frustration. John screamed at her: Apologize to Una, you should apologize to Una. Souline hung on, apologized to no one. Only when Una's maid rushed in to help did Souline let Una go.

On 1 September Hitler invaded Poland. On 3 September the three of them sat in the Forecastle parlour – two of them hardly speaking – and heard Chamberlain announce the outbreak of war. The trio were trapped in England.

The Forecastle was sold for £1,650. The homeless threesome went to Lynton where they hoped the temperate Devon climate would begin to pull John round. Ironically that year the West Country suffered one of the worst winters on record. By the autumn Souline, suffocating at such close quarters with Una, decided to leave and, despite John's opposition, took a nursing job in Exeter. Though John bought two horses and taught Una to ride, an adventure that briefly brightened her spirits, depression descended again at Christmas when renewed pain in her eyelids halted her work.

In 1940 John suffered from a bad bout of influenza, failing eyesight, unbearable lid and lash spasms, and severe colitis.[81] Fearing for herself, John begged Souline to ensure that 'we must never put too great a distance between us in these dangerous days.'[82] Souline agreed that wherever she was she would come at once if John grew very ill and needed her.[83] When the fall of France confined Souline permanently to England, she agreed to turn in her nursing badge, return to Lynton and take up lodgings near John at a house called Spraytonia. John perceptibly relaxed. 'It really is a mad bad world, but Piggie will keep close to its Johnnie and will be safe.'[84]

Tired of hotel life John and Una, together with their menagerie of pets, including John's favourite dog Fido, also took rooms in Lynton at The Wayside, a cottage owned by friends situated near a Catholic church and the convent of the Poor Clares. John wanted to do war work, but in May her gums started bleeding constantly, new digestive problems beset her, and she was reduced to such a low state that between Christmas and the New Year she sobbed every day.

During 1941 John bound Souline more closely to her by acting as her referee and guarantor to the Secretary of State in matters connected with her visa. In practice this meant that before Souline could get police permission to holiday in another county unaccompanied by John, the police would check first with John. As every day Souline sought new ways to assert her independence, this guarantorship symbolized John's increasing need to tie Souline to her formally. From the same motive she suggested that Souline should appoint her as her next of kin.

That summer, consulting a Dr Tizzard in Bath, John was diagnosed as having a 'dry gritty catarrh' in her eyes. Tizzard feared that this catarrh could lead to an ulcer which might cause blindness. As John and Una were installed at the Francis Hotel, he suggested that operations to the lower lids of both eyes could be done at a near-by nursing home at 8 Upper Church Street, Bath.

'He advises me to be operated on at once,' John wrote to Souline, 'as Hitler is quietish at the moment.'[85] The operations were expected to involve only five days in bandages; stitches were to be removed on the sixth day, then the process was to be repeated for the second operation, with a further week at least at the Bath hotel. Fido's vet sent John an amusing message via Una: 'Tell her that it is quite an easy operation, we are constantly doing it for dogs.'[86] Even so the idea of being 'totally helpless for a week . . . at such a time' appalled John.[87] Had she known how long she would in fact be helpless, she might have made a different decision. As it was she felt 'a just fearful chance of going blind had to be put against a just possible blitz – I have chosen the operation.'[88]

Souline, deeply concerned, wanted to be with John in Bath. But John was too ill and Una too busy (and ill disposed) to find Souline a room. 'Better stay where you are and I will send for you if absolutely necessary,' John wrote, adding: 'Una wants me to say she'd do her best in an emergency.'[89] Most of all in a time of danger, John protected and excluded her adult lover as she would a child, and left the practical responsibility to Una who was invaluable on these occasions and undoubtedly came into her own.

On 29 August, installed at the Church Street nursing home, John dictated her letter to Souline for Una to write: 'Darling, Una writes this for me as I may not use my eye.' It was the first of dozens Una was asked to write and Souline forced to receive. When John became too sick even to dictate, Una dutifully took control, devising curt notes containing up-to-the-minute medical information. In Una's hand 'Darling Piggie' is ordered to go to church, light candles for eyes that 'need a lot of praying for',[90] and write letters daily. Una read aloud Souline's replies; wrote replies in return. The inbuilt masochism of such a system lent itself to constant distrust and misunderstandings.

As for Souline she must have felt rejected, silenced, a prey to all the emotions Radclyffe Hall drew so well when depicting her cast of exiles, but which she failed to recognize in her dealings with her lover. The effect on their relationship was so damaging that it never recovered.

The surgery on John's left eye caused a haemorrhage which provoked terrible pain and great fear of permanent disfigurement. 'I am not allowed to see my own eye in case I should pass out!!' wrote the John–Una duo.[91] After the haemorrhage the eye looked so gruesome that 'even the nurses flinched.'[92]

John's first bid to save her sight had not gone well. But the writer recuperating in Bath was determined on a second. 'The threat of possible blindness makes me quite capable of leaping onto the operating table!'[93] That threat made John realize 'how much beauty is still left even in this war-hideous world'. The fact that she was using Una as her medium did not stop John from reminding Souline, though perhaps more temperately than before: 'Do you remember the three bridges at sunset in Florence? . . . you are much in my thoughts.'[94]

Souline sent roses by return. They bloomed by John's bed as she learnt that 'a bit of what they call a running stitch has refused to part with me.'[95] By 22 October she had been in Bath for nine weeks, bandaged for seven weeks, and her eyes did not yet match in size. There was however 'now no gaping corner or other horror to shock expectant mothers into miscarriages', and she could at last write shakily to Souline herself.[96]

She told her that Tizzard and his staff had pronounced her the bravest woman they had ever known. But when she finally returned to Lynton, renewed, and predictable, disputes with Souline took the edge off her courage. Perhaps unwisely, Souline broke the news that she was taking a typing and shorthand course in Oxford. John now had her illness as well as her money to barter with.

> Evguenia, This evening you quite deliberately and with full medical knowledge of the state of my heart, did your utmost to make a scene, and then to force upon me your scheme for Oxford . . . This being so when your next month's allowance comes due . . . it will be less by £5. I regret having to resort to such a method. Radclyffe Hall.[97]

Here was the old fighting Radclyffe Hall, regretting very little about her chosen methods and making light of Souline's anxieties over her lover's ill-health or the resentment she might have felt at her exclusion.

Souline shrugged it off and went to Oxford from where as usual friendly relations were soon restored. John's health unfortunately was not. The eyelid spasms reappeared, the ingrowing lashes again proved troublesome, her teeth and gum trouble worsened. Tizzard admitted botching the eye operation.

Though saying feelingly, 'I think he had better drop eyes and become a butcher,'[98] John was magnanimous: 'I do feel that the unhappy surgeon did his best and that this is the last thing he would have wished.'[99]

His best was so far from being good enough that another operation proved necessary for which John went to London to consult the Royal Physician, Lord Dawson, about her general state of health and 'ability to stand up to a *fourth* operation',[100] and to see two eminent eye surgeons, Sir Duke Elder and Dr Williamson Noble. The secretary at first told John that Elder was not taking any new patients, 'but when she grasped that it was me (poor half blind Radclyffe Hall) she said he surely would see me'.[101]

John's sense of humour outranked even her generous spirit. From the Rembrandt Hotel awaiting Lord Dawson she wrote to Souline: 'Tomorrow I am expecting to hear from him as to whether I have *no* teeth out, one tooth out, *all* my teeth out or *my head cut off* – which latter would of course solve many problems.'[102]

Once more she was forbidden to use her eyes. John anguished over 'whether it will ever be possible to obey the rules and produce inspirational work'.[103] But the eye operation had to be postponed because suddenly her entire system collapsed. She had abscesses on her gums, several tooth extractions, pleurisy, double pneumonia, haemorrhoids. She lay in a coma for weeks at London's Rembrandt Hotel while in Oxford Souline began her typing course. John suffered a London Christmas of yellow fog, raging germs and damp cold. Her lungs became a 'mess of grating sounds',[104] she contracted severe influenza, kept her lover away for fear of flu germs on Souline's lungs, and with raging toothache she wrote to her: 'keep your tail curl [Piggie] . . . and for heaven's sake find a good dentist.'[105]

It took another six months before John was well enough to get up. Meanwhile Una resumed writing John's letters to Souline. As John's eyes deteriorated, in a savage parody she told Pig that she had foreseen the problems of communication at long distance between them by reason of 'having the gift . . . of "Second Sight"'.[106]

In 1942, struggling for new brave lines and amusing scenes, John fought off an ache in her left lung, and stabbing pains when she drew deep breaths. Cultivating irony as a strategy to control her fear she resigned herself to more eye operations, as the surgeon was 'practically certain that he can give me an eye with which I can do my literary work'.[107]

John's world had shrunk to the size and shape of her illnesses. Her only interest outside was the thought of seeing Souline first for a rare visit to the Rembrandt in April and then a few days later when she planned to return to Lynton. She was filled with apprehension about her health but her hopes of that special meeting ran high. She had deluded herself into thinking that once Souline finished her typing course she would settle near at hand in Devon.

Her lover arrived at the hotel and stood at the end of John's bed. She had a piece of news. She knew exactly what effect it would have on John, but she knew the consequences for herself of once more renouncing her own life to be with a woman who lived with someone else.

I have been offered a typing job with the Red Cross at Basingstoke, she said. I intend to take it. The next line was inevitable. I shall cut your allowance, John said. I know, Souline said. I don't think I care any more. Una, who witnessed the scene and wrote it all up, said Souline told John she had given her the best years of her life and had received nothing in return.

Later Souline wrote more calmly:

> I just thought I shall do something. I shall achieve something and it will be alright. I won't need John's money. I still love her for herself and not for the money. It was a kind of defiance. During the war I had to do something and I went in search and found some work against John's wishes who always wanted me to stay near her.[108]

At the time neither of them was calm. Souline shouted; John shrank and turned grey. That evening Una wrote self-righteously to Souline, addressing her coldly as 'Evguenia' and signing herself 'Una V. Troubridge'.

> I think it only right to repeat what I have already told you: that Lord Dawson warned me that [John] had been in a very low state when she fell ill, that she had been 'very very ill' . . . He is sending her to Lynton to recuperate for the further operation & if, in such circumstances, you decide to go away without keeping her informed of your address . . . and if the strain breaks her down & she dies it will be your doing & on yr conscience all yr. life.[109]

By the time the ambulance took John back to Lynton she hoped desperately that Souline would be there. There was no Royal Chink Piggie snuffling by the gates. 'Oh Lord, Lord! Who would have an RCP rooted into the fibres of one's heart?'[110]

John did of course cut her allowance. Half angry with Souline, half angry with herself, she invented a new rule. If Souline agreed to live and work in the same county as John she would continue to receive £250 a year. If she refused, it would be cut to £100 a year. Even that was dependent on her always letting John know 'honestly' her address. This harsh game of control and evasion had become a ritualized contest. Even the allowance nowadays represented a complex interplay of ownership and fear of ownership, submission and fear of submission. The push and pull of money had become the currency of their love affair.

In July 1942 Souline told John she had got a job with the BBC Foreign Service at Evesham in Worcestershire at a salary of £300. By Christmas she had changed jobs to a department of the Foreign Office near London, but gave John only a poste restante address. John supplemented her salary of £156 by continuing the allowance of £100 and adding £24 for heating expenses. It was to be continued in perpetuity on the condition that Souline always informed John of her whereabouts. 'Caring for you has become a habit – in this case one of those habits of the heart that because their roots are both deep and strong are apt to be rather dangerous to uproot lest the heart starts to bleed to death in the process.'[111]

Souline's work meant long absences. On 12 December John wrote: 'It is as though a dark thick curtain had dropped between us.' She pleaded for Souline to join her at Christmas; begged her not to take work till afterwards so that she could count on her arrival. 'Do not imagine that I have hidden chains with which to keep you prisoner in Lynton because there are no chains.'[112]

Occasionally a writer is destined to pen some lines that presage 'coming events [which] cast their shadows before'.[113] In 1908 Radclyffe Hall wrote of 'The Quest of the White Heather', a rare and precious plant sought as a symbol of happiness.

> And all alone on the side of the mountain
> I spoke to the new born day,
> 'Oh! help me gather some rare white heather,
> Sweet Morning, show me the way!'[114]

Hall was then twenty-eight, young, healthy, launched on a career and wildly in love with Ladye.

Thirty-four years later Ladye was long dead. John was sixty-two, almost blind, dying with cancer, still wildly in love, still in quest of the white heather – this time with Souline, who was expected to join them for Christmas.

Unable to come, Souline sent John a glorious white heather plant. As John sat without her on Christmas Eve she wrote:

> Darlingest RCP . . . I am touched to the heart . . . indeed I am touched to tears – only I am forbidden by the occulist [*sic*] to shed any . . . I have had very many disappointments in my life but I can honestly say, never one quite so bitter . . . Remember that your John, once so active and all over the place, is in the Lynton Prison Camp asking you to feed it once in a while through the prison bars.[115]

John spent Christmas Day with Una, missing Souline like a prisoner deprived of light, her eyes fixed on the rare white heather. On Boxing Day she wrote again to Souline, describing the Christmas dinner that had been cooked in 'the wild hope that you would share it'. It is the last letter to Souline in Radclyffe Hall's own hand.

John's wild hopes almost at an end, she blessed Souline, asked God to keep her safe, and wrote: 'I miss you even after all these years. Your John. Enclosed is a bit of the white heather you gave me.'[116] Souline kept the white heather after John's death and until her own. When she lay dying she pressed it on to a white card and kept it with John's letters.*

For years John had used calculations, tallies, orders, itineraries to stave off her fear of chaos, to frame her illnesses, to keep death at bay. But in the spring of 1943 Baedeker and Bradshaw could no longer guide her health nor timetable her last months. Sickness tore her apart. She required day and night attention. Measuring the cosmos was no longer possible. Una took adjoining rooms at the Ritz Hotel in London and hired a nurse.

On 11 April 1943 John left Lynton in a Daimler ambulance and was never to return. 'In bed at the Ritz in her silk pyjamas', she was examined first by Dr Armando Child, and then by leading cancer specialist Dr Cecil Joll. It was confirmed that she had cancer and needed an instant colostomy. It was arranged that the operation would take place the following day at Lady Carnarvon's nursing home in Hadley Wood.[117]

At once John ceased fretting and became wise and brave: 'Do I set my affairs in order?' she asked. To Una she said: 'You know, don't you, it may be cancer, and if so, it is God's will and we must not only accept it but welcome it.'[118]

The following day, the day of the operation, Souline and Mickie Jacob arrived at Hadley Wood. Dr Joll performed the operation, but without success. John had inoperable cancer of the rectum. She went through a second operation with enormous courage. Physical suffering did not embitter her, she saw it as one of her dues. 'One must pay for most things in the world, for lasting joys and for joys that pass,' she had written in *The Sixth Beatitude*.[119]

Her final trial came with the approach of death. When Dr Child, her consultant, faltered at delivering bad news at her bedside, John grinned at him and said: 'Stop trying to think how to tell me I've got inoperable cancer, I know it quite as well as you do.'[120] Though she fretted and fussed over minor ailments and irritations, in any major crisis John was heroic. Grace under pressure and a gallantry that she had always wanted to show in wartime were now her means of facing her last trial.

She asked Souline to visit her. She told Una how much she appreciated her constant presence and practical help. However, with hindsight we can see that one of Una's actions was not helpful to John's health, was indeed injurious. After seven weeks at Hadley Wood, with the hospital about to close down, Una moved John to a nursing home at Primrose Hill, where the conditions were appalling and where John, despite being so ill, was obliged to take exercise.

---

* In 1995 in Texas, I read Hall's poem: 'He who seeks white heather/Must find it deep in his heart!' then opened John's last letter to Souline. Out of it dropped the same faded sprig of white heather that had been placed there fifty-two years before.

Fortunately, a vacancy came up at the London Clinic where they were given a single room with a divan for Una.

Mickie Jacob visited every Sunday. Andrea and Viola came constantly. Souline visited all the time but Una did not always allow her to see John. In August, with John growing weaker but not wanting to remain in hospital, Una rented a flat, 502 Hood House in Dolphin Square, with day- and night-nurses in attendance, so that John should die in comfort.

John, too weak to hold a pen, was still writing letters to Souline in her head. They would become conversations never to be completed. Years before she had written, 'if you go on tormenting me I may suddenly not love you any more . . . love is as fragile as glass and must not be roughly handled.'[121] They had handled each other awkwardly, often roughly, yet their bond had never broken. 'The same heart can never be torn quite asunder, otherwise it stops beating.'[122]

Souline, not always a kind ghost, still haunted her.

During her final days, that first week of October 1943, there was an air raid on the Saturday, 2 October. John, drugged by heroin, pulled herself back to the present, listened to the boom of guns, and said, 'Well, I can't do anything about it.'[123] Her tasks were nearly over.

Seven days before her death John suddenly, without apparently planning it in advance, made a new will drafted by Harold Rubinstein. In the 1938 will it was assumed by both Una and Souline that John had divided her estate equally between them. Between 1934 and 1943 John had many times assured Souline that she would make 'ample provision after my death' for her. Souline's friend Ariadne remembers that John 'reassured Zhenya and promised to look after her. There was talk of wills and adoption.'[124]

In this new twelve-line will there was a radical alteration. She appointed Una as her sole executrix and stated:

> I devise and bequeath to her all my property and estate both real and personal absolutely trusting her to make such provision for our friend Evguenia Souline as in her absolute discretion she may consider right knowing my wishes for the welfare of the said Evguenia Souline.

The will, witnessed by Dr Child and a nurse, gave Una the power over Souline's future that none of the trio had ever previously anticipated.

It is a curious document for though it certainly acknowledges John's long-term responsibilities to Una, it uncharacteristically breaks a solemn undertaking to the young woman whom she had not stopped loving. For the first time she reneged on almost a decade's worth of promises to protect Souline up to and beyond her death. Perhaps John's change of heart was due to Souline's absences and her desire for independence; perhaps to John's residual guilt over the pain she had caused Una. It is equally possible that a woman fluctuating between a heroin delirium and a pain-racked rationality may have been more vulnerable than usual to pressure from Una. It is impossible to calculate John's motives. Like Una and Souline we are left with the consequences. For John the matter was settled. There would be little left for her to do.

On 5 October, waking from now semi-permanent unconsciousness, she looked up at the nurse with a ghost of her old jaunty grin and murmured: 'What a life!' Then she threw back her head, and made her last coherent statement: 'But I offer it to God.'[125]

As dawn broke on 6 October she sank into a coma. Souline arrived at 6.30 p.m. We do not know what Una said to her. We know that Souline looked down at John, guarded by the vigilant Una, not yet lifeless but with her life and loves behind her, unable to say a last word to her last lover. There was no room at the bedside for both of them and Souline left quietly before the hour was up. Una wrote in her Day Book: 'John does not want her or anyone but me.'[126]

We do not know what John wanted – perhaps peace, perhaps to be alone at last with her God. The sense of foreboding and doom that she had never entirely shaken off may have reconciled her to suffering. But finally, she had had enough of suffering. The next night, 7 October, John achieved her peace.

Radclyffe Hall's death at 502 Hood House, Dolphin Square, SW1, was recorded by her earthly time-keeper Una Troubridge as taking place at seven minutes past eight in the evening.[127] The disease was officially described as death from carcinoma of the sigmoid colon.

Hall died believing with T.S. Eliot:

> What we call the beginning is often the end
> And to make an end is to make a beginning . . .
> The end is where we start from.[128]

She died conspicuously and with courage, as she had lived. After her death there were only the words that came after.

22

AFTER WORDS

The first words were Una's.

It was 8 October. Una slept next to the corpse all night and awoke refreshed to find that Mickie Jacob had arrived. Mickie, who had been calling regularly during John's illness, asked if she could see her friend's body and say goodbye. Una was resolute. 'No, Mike,' she said. 'You have no right, Una!' flared Mickie. 'I have every right,' said Una. 'Now Mike, please go.'[1]

Death became Una. She was collected, firm and in full possession of herself. She was also for the first time in full possession of the writer she had lived with for twenty-eight years. More significantly, as literary executor, she had been left in charge of Hall's words.

Souline's words were written much later:

> That spiritual and physical link which existed between us was never really broken
> . . . as I write these lines, I feel John's spirit very near me. No matter where I was, I
> could always come back to her. John was holding me by the invisible thread which
> used to get tight . . . very tight . . . when the atmosphere was full of nervous tension.

Souline's personal epitaph emphasized their 'bond of union'. She dwelt on John's repeated line that 'we had met before in our lives': 'I feel that idea very strongly . . . If there is another life beyond this one I think we are bound to meet each other again . . . amend all that was to be amended between us and make the union foolproof happy.'[2]

Those were words that John would have understood.

The press offered their own words on Monday 11 October with a long analytical obituary in *The Times*. Hall's work, it said, notably *Adam's Breed*, was 'sympathetic and finely written'; *The Well of Loneliness* was 'dignified and restrained'; her other novels 'had real merit and originality'. The obituary emphasized her 'abundant sympathy and pity' and suggested strongly that controversial views on *The Well of Loneliness* should 'not be allowed to rob her of credit for her sterling literary qualities, her well-controlled emotional pitch, her admirable prose style'.[3] Other complimentary obituaries followed, though Peterborough in the *Daily Telegraph* could not help remarking, one more time, on Miss Radclyffe Hall's 'decidedly masculine appearance'.[4]

Naming and misnaming, which had beset John's life, haunted her also in death. Her very death certificate recorded her name as 'Marguerite Antonia Radclyff-Hall' reinstating the hyphen and dropping the 'e': the misnaming had gone full circle. *The Times* called her 'Margaret' Radclyffe Hall. Her mother, Marie Visetti, when she wrote to Jane Caruth to complain that John's will did not mention her, misspelt her own daughter's name 'Margarite', a linguistic rejection in line with others throughout John's life. Marie's main concern was to safeguard her £200 annuity, her chief emotion that of bitter resentment against her daughter. Yet, in the personal column of *The Times* on Monday 18 October 1943, she inserted these words:

> Mrs Albert Visetti, 48, St Aubyn's, Hove, thanks those who have so kindly written to condole with her on the death of her daughter Marguerite Radclyffe-Hall.

The Times, unable themselves accurately to name their controversial author, corrected Marie's misspelling of Marguerite but then inserted an elevating hyphen between her two surnames. John's grandfather Charles Radclyffe-Hall would have approved.

Marie, eighty-nine when John died, lasted a further two years as a chronic invalid ageing painfully with arthritis and, till her own death silenced her, nursing grievances about her child.

John's body was embalmed and placed in a mahogany coffin. The words on the brass name plate came from a favourite sonnet by Elizabeth Barrett Browning:

Radclyffe Hall
Author
1943
'. . . And if God Choose I Shall
But Love Thee Better After Death.'[5]

On Thursday 14 October 1943 a Low Mass was held at Westminster Cathedral. Later the coffin was transferred from the Cathedral to the vault in Highgate Cemetery where behind an iron grille Ladye's coffin had lain since 1916 reposing longitudinally on the stone bench at the right. John's coffin was placed horizontally facing the entrance. Una had the same quotation from Elizabeth Barrett Browning inscribed on a marble slab with Radclyffe Hall's name above and the name 'Una' underneath the inscription.

Una planned that her own coffin would eventually take the third place in the vault, to bolster her by now somewhat shaky belief that 'Our Three Selves' still meant Ladye, John and Una, and excluded Souline.

Una gave complex written instructions to Harold Rubinstein in 1944 for her own interment. This included embalming like John, an attire of blue silk pyjamas, the adornment of jewellery and crucifix, a coffin plate with the inscription that she was 'The Friend of Radclyffe Hall' and a dedicatory plaque that told the world she had 'shared a home' with the author 'for nearly 29 years'. Chance however does not always listen to human directives. Una's careful injunctions were not discovered until after her death and burial in Rome several thousand miles away.

On Tuesday 26 October 1943 a Requiem Mass was said for Radclyffe Hall at the Church of the Immaculate Conception, Farm Street, London W1.[6] In place of John's first love Agnes Nicholls, who was too ill to sing her solo, a tenor from the resident choir sang César Franck's uplifting *Panis Angelicus*. More than a hundred people attended the Mass, including Souline, Andrea, Audrey Heath, Patience Ross, Viola, Harold Rubinstein and the Holroyd-Reeces. Very few of John's friends were there, attesting to her isolation during these last years with Souline.

Una continued for a time to live in the flat at Dolphin Square. She slept in John's bed and wore John's clothes, huddling sadly under her lover's blue beret.

John had left her a wealthy woman. Una inherited Radclyffe Hall's estate of £118,015 19s. 0d. (which excluded royalties on Radclyffe Hall's books) but her prime concern was to ensure the future of John's literary property, to which end, a few days after John's death, she redrafted her will. Initially she entrusted Radclyffe Hall's literary copyrights to John Holroyd-Reece whose kindness when she left Dolphin Square in 1943 encouraged her move to a flat belonging to him above his own. When she discovered that John's so-called 'friend' was solely interested in gaining control of her money, she revoked her will, and asked Rache Lovat Dickson, a publisher friend of Harold Rubinstein's, to become first her literary executor and later to write an 'impartial' biography of Radclyffe Hall based on information Una would provide.

Una continued to pay dutiful visits to Minna Taylor who finally died aged eighty-six on 30 January 1947, the same year as Viola's husband J.L. Garvin and Edy Craig who had been a constant support to Una. Minna's will, as idiosyncratic as Una's, directed that her funeral be as inexpensive as possible and that no one should wear mourning. It was, and no one did.

Una, in a state of 'sheer dull desolation ... with recurrent waves of unendurable misery',[7] renewed her friendship with Jacqueline Hope (now Hope-Nicholson) who gave her a key to their house in Tite Street to make her feel at home. Una, who needed to grieve for John in the company of women who had also loved and respected her, maintained friendships with Colette and

Lily Clermont Tonnerre until 1954 when they both died. She saw Romaine regularly in France and entertained her in Italy, and kept up a correspondence that spanned forty years with Natalie who outlived all their set to die in 1972 at the age of ninety-five.

Mickie Jacob forgave Una her brusqueness at the time of John's death and they were reconciled. Naomi Jacob, in the words of *The Times*, had become 'a lively, sympathetic and deservedly popular novelist' who by the fifties was a lesbian media star.[8] In the sixties the Lesbian Minorities Research Group claimed Mickie as an over-eighties supporter, and through her Radclyffe Hall. In a letter to the lesbian magazine *Arena Three* she said: 'One saying of Radclyffe Hall's often comes back to me: "A great many women can feel and behave like men. Very few of them can behave like gentlemen."'[9] Mickie missed her friend Gentleman John. 'I only wish that Radclyffe Hall . . . [was] here so that [she] might read your magazine with me.'[10]

Despite Una's continuing friendships, she had 'a strange feeling of belonging to nobody'.[11] Perhaps it was this, together with Andrea's warmth and kindness to her after John's death, that drew them closer together. In 1943 Una described her daughter as 'an admirable unselfish generous woman' who frequently offered her 'really sumptuous meals'.[12] Yet when Andrea remarried, this time the 46-year-old divorced Brigadier Douglas John Tulloch Turnbull, known as 'Bull', on 4 October 1948 at Kensington Registry Office, once again Una did not attend her daughter's wedding.

From Ethiopia in 1950, where Bull Turnbull was Military Attaché to Emperor Haile Selassie, Andrea wrote Una affectionate letters signed: 'Love and bless you, darling, Andrea.' At this point she got into what John and Una would doubtless have called 'a scrape'. The Emperor became so enamoured of Andrea, and so conspicuously indulgent, that the Foreign Office, severely embarrassed by their 'great friendship', removed Turnbull from his post.

Despite the scrape and their varying locations, Una kept in constant touch with Andrea. Six years after John's death Una, still restless and unsettled, decided to settle in Florence, where she became immersed in opera, a passion she had shared with John. By chance she met the 31-year-old bass, Nicola Rossi-Lemeni, in whose work and life she submerged herself as she once had in John's. Rossi-Lemeni became to her 'the son I never had'[13] whom she followed across the globe wherever he sang. It was to Rossi-Lemeni she left her hundreds of day books and diaries, later inherited by his son and Una's godson Alessandro. When the Rossi-Lemenis settled in Rome, Una decided to make that her final home from 1957.

By July 1963 the 76-year-old Una was so frail that Andrea wrote to Rossi-Lemeni offering to come and look after her mother if she was needed. Una however managed to rally for a final two months. She made a new will, which left the Charles Buchel portrait of John to the National Portrait Gallery and appointed Lovat Dickson and Harold Rubinstein executors of Radclyffe Hall's literary materials. The residue of her estate of £57,274 13s. she left to the Community of the Poor Clares at Lynton. When Una died on 24 September 1963, the generous-spirited Andrea received £2,000, a pearl necklace and some pearl and diamond earrings. It is unlikely that Una had ever entirely forgiven Cubby for not adoring John as thoroughly as Una herself had.

Tragically Andrea, aged fifty-six, died in a car crash three years later, in 1966. At the BBC Andrea was remembered with amused affection as the announcer who failed to go on the air at 6.30 one morning and who announced to the world some twenty minutes later that she had overslept. Her punctual step-parent John Radclyffe Hall doubtless turned uneasily in the world beyond that morning.[14] Despite this *faux pas*, Andrea became one of the few women radio announcers to make the transition to television.[15]

Her only child Nicholas joined a Cistercian order at Nunraw in East Lothian. When asked about John and Una, he said his mother had been 'exceedingly reticent'.[16] To her professional colleagues at the BBC and in journalism, Andrea, equally reticent, always said she had 'a shady past'.[17] It was a past, and a childhood, like that of Radclyffe Hall's, filled with restless uprootings, loneliness and parental indifference. That Cubby survived and overcame it so that 'after she was grown up [she] grew to be very fond of Una'[18] speaks of some of John's own compassion. Perhaps living with Radclyffe Hall, though an enormously difficult experience, afforded Cubby some guidance in 'pity and sympathy' not on offer from her mother.

Una's treatment of Andrea was mirrored in her treatment of Souline after John's death. It was not expansive, it held no warmth, but it was scrupulously fair and meticulously dutiful. She honoured until Souline's death the terms of John's will which asked her to provide for Evguenia. One gains an impression however that Una was not displeased at her powers of control.

Within a few days of John's death Evguenia, who wanted to lease a flat in London, went to Una for 'advice' (her words) or 'financial sanction' (Una's words). A violent row blew up. It was to be the first of many over the years.

John had left a deplorable situation to be handled by two women each bitterly resentful of the other. Souline believed, on the strength of John's previous will and her deceased lover's endless assurances, that she was entitled to more than she was ever allotted by Una. Una was honest enough to admit that Souline's 'advantage lies with keeping on good terms with me, since her allowance is and will always be, at my discretion'.[19]

Una continued Souline's allowance and supplemented it with three small 'gifts' a year. Later she covenanted the allowance, renewing it every seven years. She did this, firm in her belief that John wanted Evguenia to be 'taken care of' but did not want 'her so provided for that she is idle, as this in the past only led her to degenerate into discontent, ill-temper and misery'.[20]

Souline did not in fact allow herself to become idle. She had worked for the BBC European Service at Evesham during 1942. Later in the war she joined the Allied Army as a linguist and left for Europe. In Paris she met and married Vladimir Makaroff, a fellow Russian who spoke no English. He had been a cavalry officer in the First World War who like Souline had left Russia after the Revolution. He had settled in Czechoslovakia, taking work in an insurance office until the partition of Europe forced him to flee again. Their marriage created a bureaucratic fuss that John would have abhorred. Souline had no valid passport nor had she asked her commanding officer for permission to marry. She was chucked out of the army. John who had already reflected sadly on the possibility of Souline marrying would have been horrified at the style in which it happened. Perhaps she would have been mollified by Souline's words to Ariadne that she married Vladimir 'because he wrote such marvellous letters'.[21]

Vladimir was small, brisk and restrained. A man who assumed 'an air of jaunty gallantry', he was withal 'a sad person with few friends' who 'underneath was tinged with a Hall-like melancholy'.[22] Like John, the one woman Makaroff was never restrained about was Souline. Her unpredictability drove him mad, but he was obsessively attached to her during her lifetime and fanatically devoted to her memory until his own death in 1980.

Marriage to Makaroff did not prevent the violent collisions between Souline and Una. Between 1947 and 1950 Souline, then forty-six, approached Una to lend her £3,000 with which to purchase a boarding house as 'security for the future', as 'the thought of growing old without any security . . . is frightening.' Una declined. Souline said: 'You seem to disregard the fact that she [John] in her lifetime was inordinately attached to me, and promised me more than once that I shall be well provided for after her death.' Then with some truth Souline added: 'John if she were alive would have come to my rescue.'[23] Una's anger at such a likely supposition increased when Souline reminded her of a scene that had taken place over John's bedside during her final illness. According to Souline, John had clasped their hands together and said: 'I want you to be friends. There will be enough for both of you if not to live in luxury – in comfort. But you, Evguenia, shall ask Una's advice.'[24]

Una, beside herself with rage, denied the scene. She protested that it was an invention of Souline's. If it was an invention, it had the authentic stamp of John's misguided hope for her two lovers and her careful appraisal of their characters.

With no rescue in sight, Souline and Vladimir worked hard turning a small house in Kilburn into bed-sits. A crowd of White Russian intellectuals and English lecturers from the School of Slavonic Studies moved in among the rolls of lino. Vladimir practised his English on the lodgers, played chess and found a job in a Russian bookshop behind London's Hanway Street, an occupation which was later to serve the interests of Radclyffe Hall's literary materials.

When the boarding house went under, Una did send Souline an extra payment of £150 to help repay the loan Souline had drawn to set it up. Next, Souline and Makaroff moved to a chilly flat in Lancaster Gate, where Souline's failing health began to suffer; then to another flat, less cold, in Sussex Gardens. Souline got a variety of jobs, including work with the UN in Geneva, and ultimately to her immense satisfaction as a radio broadcaster for the Russian Service of the BBC, where she remained until her death in 1958. Finally Souline had become a woman who 'did things'. She hoped John would have approved.

Una never approved of Souline or of anything she did. In one of the hundreds of Letters to John which Una continued to write every day, she told John that she now saw her role as '"guardian of the lamp" of your genius and our enduring love'.[25] These duties involved presenting Radclyffe Hall as a faithful partner and an unqualified genius and, in the process, accommodating but minimizing Souline's existence.

Even during Souline's lifetime Una attempted to dismiss her from the public records. As copious references to Souline in her day books might illustrate John's 'weakness', Una left an instruction in the front of volume 22 that nothing was to be published after 28 June 1934, the day Una hired Souline as a nurse. (It seems that in this matter her memory let her down: according to her diary written at the time, Souline entered their lives on 2 July 1934.)

Una decided that she must protect John (or herself) by leaving behind a definitive record of their life 'to cheer and encourage those who come after us'.[26] During four weeks in 1945 she wrote at one go her biography of John's life. In it Evguenia Souline, the woman who occupied almost the last decade of John's life, is reduced to three unimportant pages. Hardly surprisingly, Una elected not to publish it until after Souline's death.

Moreover Una also destroyed John's last half-completed novel *The Shoemaker of Merano*. She told the press she had burnt it at John's request. Later she revealed that the true reason for burning the book was that Hall had 'almost unconsciously allowed . . . her personal suffering and natural resentment', pertaining to someone who during the 'closing years of her life' had 'very deeply hurt her', to permeate its pages.[27] Exactly how it presented Souline or Souline's effect on John, we shall never know, but the novel's destruction was consistent with Una's desire to expunge Souline from the official literary record.

Una never admitted to destroying all Souline's letters to John but as only one of Souline's letters was ever discovered, we must assume that they were burnt as part of the censorship process.

Una knew all too well of the existence of John's last literary achievement, the Book of Letters, but she did not know it had survived. Souline kept every one of John's letters to her. She even restuck the one that John tore into pieces the day she ransacked her flat in a jealous rage. During her last severe illness,

Evguenia spent her time typing out John's letters from the handwritten originals, dating, categorizing, and filing them. 'She wanted them published,' said Ariadne. But she believed that 'Radclyffe Hall's literary executor had control of the copyright. Zhenya [felt] she owned only the paper and ink.'[28]

Souline started her massive task in August 1957, when living at 76 Lancaster Road; she continued it in September at 227 Sussex Gardens, then, becoming ill, she carried out the work in the outpatients department between hospital appointments. As a patient later in several hospitals she was still wearily immersed in John's letters. She approached a Mr Wilenkin to see if she could sell them so that posterity would have a record of Radclyffe Hall's last love letters. Souline sent covering notes to Wilenkin attached to the top copies which described her own state of mind as she reread and typed out John's love letters.

Though after her death her husband sold the letters to Bertram Rota, a London bookseller, who in turn sold them to the Harry Ransom Humanities Research Center in Texas, Souline's personal notes were never sold to or filed at Texas. They turned up in 1996 with copies of the originals given by Vladimir after Souline's death to their friend Iris Furlong. They offer a fascinating last glimpse of Souline's frame of mind.

Souline started, with wry humour, by pointing out to Mr Wilenkin that John 'often makes mistakes' and in a later note: 'Radclyffe Hall was rather a bad speller and in some I left the words as they were written by her.'[29] As she went on to type one of the letters dated 16 August 1934, and reread John's lines – 'My heart, my very, very little lonely Child who has been so mishandled . . . by life . . . you should trust me . . . believe me . . . I am indeed your friend . . . I am very terribly in love' – she added to Mr Wilenkin: 'I feel terribly sad . . . It is such a torment to write them because naturally I re-live those past years again.'[30]

On 25 November 1957 Souline wrote to Wilenkin: 'Herewith some more copies of letters . . . I shall need a good rest . . . because it has made me very despondent and sad, "heavy of heart", as RH used to say to me.'[31] The following day Souline sent another batch but said she needed to pause for a few days, 'otherwise I shall have another nervous breakdown'.[32]

By the time she reached the Darling Piggie letters from Florence – John writing to her in June 1938 that 'Una does not hate you . . . even if she did . . . what does it matter as long as we two love each other . . . if you leave me I break completely' – Souline was only capable of writing a short note to Wilenkin. It ran: 'For me it is a very gruesome task, I am almost breaking under it.'[33]

She continued until the final letter was typed on 18 February 1958. Then she broke off and her entire system broke down. It was a mirror image of John's final months. Souline died on 16 July 1958 of the same disease John had been broken by, cancer of the bowel.

Same Heart was what John had always said.

NOTES

The following abbreviations are used in the accompanying notes:

MVB   Mabel Veronica Batten
RH   Radclyffe Hall
ES   Evguenia Souline
UVT   Una Vincenzo Troubridge

Life and Death   Una Lady Troubridge, *The Life and Death of Radclyffe Hall*, Hammond, Hammond, London, 1961.

Cara Lancaster   Collection of Cara Lancaster, London.
Ottawa   Lovat Dickson Collection, National Archives of Canada, Ottawa.
Rome   Collection of Dr Alessandro Rossi-Lemeni, Rome.
Slater/Still Collection of Joan Slater and Monica Still, England.
SPR   Society for Psychical Research.
Texas   Harry Ransom Humanities Research Center, University of Texas, Austin.

Publication details of all works cited are listed in the Bibliography on pages 408–15, unless otherwise shown.

INTRODUCTION

1. Sales figures 1982–October 1996 supplied by Virago, October 1996.
2. In seventeen episodes, 21 February–18 March 1974.
3. Key works of the new criticism are: Lillian Faderman, *Surpassing the Love of Men*; Toni A.H. McNaron, 'A Journey into Otherness: Teaching *The Well of Loneliness*' in M. Cruikshank (ed.), *Lesbian Studies: Present and Future*; Sonja Ruel, 'Inverts and Experts: Radclyffe Hall and the Lesbian Identity' in R. Brunt and R. Coward (eds.), *Feminism, Culture and Politics*; Esther Newton, 'The Mythic Mannish Lesbian: Radclyffe Hall and the New Woman', *Signs*; Beverley Brown, 'Talking about *The Well of Loneliness*', *Hecate*; Gillian Whitlock, 'A Martyr Reluctantly Canonised', *Hecate*; Jean Radford, 'An Inverted Romance: *The Well of Loneliness* and Sexual Ideology' in *The Progress of Romance*, Routledge, London, 1986; Angela Ingram, '"Unutterable Putrefaction" and "Foul Stuff"', *Women's Studies International Forum*; Gillian Whitlock, 'Everything Out of Place: Radclyffe Hall and the Lesbian Tradition', *Feminist Studies*.
4. Rebecca O'Rourke, *Reflecting on The Well of Loneliness*, p. 96.
5. 'For Miss Ogilvy had found as her life went on that in this world it is better to be one with

the herd, that the world has no wish to understand those who cannot conform to its stereotyped pattern.' *Miss Ogilvy Finds Herself*, p. 7.

6. In 'The Lover of Things' Henry Dobbs, imprisoned within the claustrophobia of human relationships, turns for liberation to the possession of antique objects, but this compulsion defines him as a loner. Fräulein Schwartz, similarly disaffected, 'was the friend of all the world, a fact which naturally made her feel lonely, since the world had no time for Fräulein Schwartz, nor had it expressed the least wish for her friendship'. *Miss Ogilvy Finds Herself*, p. 140.

7. In 'The Rest Cure – 1932' businessman Charles Duffell suffers a nervous breakdown after the New York stock exchange crash in 1921. As his business disappears so his psychological existence vanishes. His sense of alienation leads him to reincarnate himself first as a horse, then as a tree, finally as a stone. In a world where stones and people are seen to be distinct, it is not surprising that he is carried away to a mental hospital. Charles Duffell, like Joan Ogden, Stephen Gordon, Wilhelmina Ogilvy, Henry Dobbs and Fräulein Schwartz before him, is an outcast.

1: EARLY NAMING

1. RH, *Miss Ogilvy Finds Herself*, p. 6.
2. Ibid., pp. 187–8.
3. RH, unpublished essay 'Forebears and Infancy', second draft. Rome.
4. RH, 'Why I Wrote Adam's Breed'. Rome.
5. 'Forebears and Infancy', second draft. Rome.
6. RH, 'I Must Have Been a Tiresome Baby', unpublished essay. Rome.
7. RH, Stuart Song 1 in *Rhymes and Rhythms / Rime e Ritmi*, Edizioni Orsa Maggiore, Milano, 1948, p. 71.
8. While in Bristol he addressed the British Medical Association (of which he became President in 1860) on natural cures for arresting tuberculosis.
9. Lovat Dickson suggests that a confirmation of this claim can be found in *Shakespeare's Son-In-Law: A Life of Dr John Hall*, by C. Martin Mitchell, Cornish Bros., Birmingham, with a preface dated 1947. Lovat Dickson, *Radclyffe Hall at the Well of Loneliness*, p. 26.
10. 'Forebears and Infancy', third draft. Rome.
11. RH, *The Forge*, p. 41.
12. Ibid., p. 249.
13. RH, early essay 'Ancestors', second draft. Rome.
14. *Life and Death*, p. 9.
15. 'Forebears and Infancy', second draft.
16. Ibid.
17. RH, autobiographical essay written after *The Well of Loneliness*. Rome.
18. Ibid.
19. Ibid.
20. 'Forebears and Infancy'.
21. RH, 'Antecedents and Infancy', second draft. Rome.
22. RH, unpublished essay on infancy. Rome.
23. Marguerite Radclyffe-Hall, *'Twixt Earth and Stars*, p. 41.
24. 'My Love is a bird with a broken wing', ibid., p. 20.
25. RH, *Emblem Hurlstone*, unfinished novel, 1934. Rome.
26. Sidonia Shore in *A Saturday Life*, Gian-Luca in *Adam's Breed*, Henry Dobbs in 'The Lover of Things', the brothers Matteo and Tino in 'Upon the Mountains' and Hannah Bullen's daughters in *The Sixth Beatitude* all grow up without fathers. The girls Joan Ogden in *The Unlit Lamp* and Stephen Gordon in *The Well of Loneliness* are devastated by the destructive tensions between their parents.
27. RH, several versions of unpublished essay, later part of publicity article 1928. Rome. (Underlining Hall's, italics mine.)
28. Author's conversation with Winifred Reed (formerly Hales).

29. Marie Visetti to Jane Caruth, from the Viennese Hotel, 48 St Aubyn's, Hove, Sussex, 13 October 1943. Texas.

30. 'Forebears and Infancy'.

31. RH, early autobiographical essay (untitled). Rome.

32. RH, unpublished essay. Rome.

33. Completed first but published second, in 1924.

34. RH, *Michael West*, unfinished novel. Rome.

35. RH, 'Antecedents': a draft. Rome.

36. Ibid.

37. *Life and Death*, pp. 13–14.

38. Ibid.

39. Ibid., p. 15.

40. *Miss Ogilvy Finds Herself*, pp. 37–8.

41. Ibid., p. 11.

42. *The Unlit Lamp*, 1981, p. 11.

43. Ibid., p. 35.

44. RH, *The Well of Loneliness*, 1982, p. 33.

2: IN THE NAME OF THE FATHERS

1. RH, 'The Lover of Things' in *Miss Ogilvy Finds Herself*, p. 37.

2. *Life and Death*, p. 13. Also marginal notes in RH's hand on Psychic Records of sittings with Mrs Leonard mid-1916–mid-1921. See also Richard Ormrod, *Una Troubridge*, p. 84.

3. The marriage was not dissolved until 4 December 1888.

4. RH, *Michael West*, unpublished novel. Rome.

5. Essays include 'A Tiresome Baby', 'Forebears', 'Autobiographical Fragment 1912'. Rome.

6. RH, *The Well of Loneliness*, 1982, p. 7.

7. Ibid., p. 59.

8. RH, *Michael West*.

9. RH, 'I Must Have Been a Tiresome Baby', unpublished essay, written spring 1926. The verse which she somewhat shamefacedly records went:

> No wonder the birdies love you,
> No wonder the butterflies hover near,
> No wonder the roses grow above you,
> No wonder the birdies love you dear.

She adds unnecessarily: 'I was a rank sentimentalist even at that age and somewhat precocious!'

10. RH to the Editor of *America* (date uncertain, but after 1924) written after the publication of both *The Forge* (1924) and *The Unlit Lamp*. Rome.

11. Ibid.

12. RH, publicity piece written after *The Well of Loneliness*. Rome.

13. RH, 'Forebears and Infancy', first draft.

14. *The Unlit Lamp*, 1981, p. 59.

15. *The Well of Loneliness*, 1982, p. 59.

16. Ibid., p. 65.

17. Ibid.

18. Ibid., p. 67.

19. Nigel Nicolson (ed.), *A Change of Perspective*, p. 520.

20. *Michael West*, early draft.

21. See Claudia Stillman Franks, *Beyond the Well of Loneliness*.

22. *Life and Death*, p. 21.

23. Lovat Dickson, *Radclyffe Hall at the Well of Loneliness*, p. 131.

24. *Life and Death*, p. 21.

25. RH in a letter to her cousin Winifred Macey, 15 February 1927, from Holland St, Kensington, London. Texas.

26. UVT, Day Book, 13 July 1936. Rome.

27. UVT, 'Letters to John', unpublished letters to Radclyffe Hall, written after Hall's death in 1943. Rome. This 'sexual incident' was also confirmed in a private conversation with Monica Still who had seen additional Day Books and material by Una Troubridge describing the incident, originally in the collection of Dr Rossi-Lemeni, Rome.

28. UVT, 'Letters to John' from 1943, *c.* 1947. Rome (currently on loan to Richard Ormrod). Confirmed in conversation with Joan Slater whose written records of these parts of the 'Letters to John' I was able to view.

29. UVT, Day Book, Monday 13 July 1936. (Emphasis mine.)

30. *Life and Death*, p. 19.

31. Ibid., p. 16.

32. Ibid., p. 20.

33. RH, notebooks with drafts for 'The Career of Mark Anthony Brakes', 'The Woman in a Crêpe Bonnet' and an early version of *Michael West*. Rome.

34. Notebooks with drafts of *Michael West*.

35. RH, *Emblem Hurlstone*, unfinished novel, 1934, with earlier drafts. Rome.

36. RH, 'The Career of Mark Anthony Brakes' and 'Malise', notebook drafts. Rome.

37. 'The Career of Mark Anthony Brakes', first and second drafts.

38. 'Malise', unfinished story.

39. 'Forebears and Infancy'.

40. 'The Lover of Things' (written 1924) in *Miss Ogilvy Finds Herself*, p. 37.

41. *The Unlit Lamp*, 1981, p. 123.

42. 'Forebears and Infancy'.

43. RH to ES, 27 November 1934. Texas.

44. RH to ES, 1 August 1934. Texas.

45. Alice Miller, *Thou Shalt Not be Aware*.

46. Judith Lewis Herman and Lisa Hirschman, *Father-Daughter Incest*.

47. Florence Rush reports that there was a frightening increase in sexual assaults upon children in the Victorian era: *The Best-Kept Secret*.

48. *Life and Death*, p. 16.

49. Joanne Glasgow (ed.), *Your John*, p. 10.

50. *The Well of Loneliness*, 1982, p. 207.

3: RENAMING LOVE

1. *Musical Times*, 1 April 1895 and 1 January 1897.

2. Professor Stanford, who conducted the opera class at the Royal College, spoke of her fine dramatic sense. Parry Jones in *Opera*, vol. 10, no. 11, November 1959.

3. *Life and Death*, p. 25.

4. The society journal *Madame* in 1905 praised her early achievements in *The Ring* and as Donna Elvira in *Don Giovanni*. The reviewer reported that 'Miss Nicholls has, at the age of 25, achieved an amount of success, of which many a singer of fifty has sighed in vain . . . while still a student . . . she received many flattering invitations to sing at festivals, she also, before quitting the institution at which she studied, appeared by command of the late Queen Victoria – once in opera, twice in oratorio.' Quoted in Parry Jones, op. cit.

5. *Life and Death*, p. 25.

6. RH, *The Unlit Lamp*, 1981, p. 192.

7. Ibid., p. 196.

8. Ibid., pp. 196–7.

9. RH, *The Well of Loneliness*, 1982, p. 15.

10. Ibid., p. 20.

11. Parry Jones, op. cit.

12. *Life and Death*, p. 26.

13. Ibid.

14. UVT, Letters to John, 6 December 1943. Rome.

15. *The Unlit Lamp*, 1981, pp. 72, 100.

16. Lillian Faderman, *Odd Girls and Twilight Lovers*, p. 1.

17. Lillian Faderman, *Surpassing the Love of Men*, p. 16.

18. Karl Ulrichs (1825–95), Richard von Krafft-Ebing (1840–1902), Edward Carpenter (1844–1929) (who coined the term 'uranism' for homosexuality), Magnus Hirschfeld (1868–1935) and Havelock Ellis (1859–1939), the British psychologist and writer whose works included *Studies in the Psychology of Sex* (1897–1928).

19. *Life and Death*, pp. 18–19.

20. Una Troubridge, 'The Tyranny of Home' in 'I Remember', Manuscripts and Essays, Lovat Dickson Collection, vol. 3. Ottawa.

21. *Life and Death*, p. 22.

22. Ibid., p. 23.

23. Ibid.

24. Ibid., pp. 22–3.

25. Ibid., p. 23.

26. Ibid., p. 25.

27. Ibid., p. 24.

28. Ibid., p. 27.

29. Ibid.

30. Ibid.

31. RH, *A Sheaf of Verses*, Bumpus, London, 1908; Gaby Goldscheider, Windsor, 1985.

32. From 'Remember' in *'Twixt Earth and Stars*, p. 59.

33. *'Twixt Earth and Stars*, p. 65.

34. *Life and Death*, p. 27.

35. RH, *The Forge*, pp. 11, 12.

36. *Publisher and Bookseller*, 28 July 1906.

37. *The Lady*, 5 July 1906.

38. *Queen*, 4 July 1906.

39. Hubert Bath set four poems: 'A Song', 'Italian Spring', 'On the Lagoon' and 'A Sea Cycle No. XV', all love lyrics embracing nature and the sea. Cuthbert Wynne set to music 'Let Not the Morning Break'. Easthrope Martin composed a tune to match 'Shall I Complain?' and Dolly's lover Robert Coningsby Clarke wrote a score for 'Gentler Dame Priscilla', as he would later set the cousinly poems to Dolly to music.

4: THE SWEETEST VIOLET

1. Joan Hardwick, *An Immodest Violet*, pp. 25, 26, 27, 28.

2. Ibid., p. 19.

3. Ibid., photograph captions between pp. 112 and 113, and Alan Judd, *Ford Madox Ford*, p. 175.

4. Brigit Patmore, *My Friends When Young*, p. 50.

5. Ibid.

6. Hardwick, op. cit., p. 9, and photographs of Violet Hunt during this period.

7. Violet Hunt, *Affairs of the Heart*, Freemantle, 1900.

8. Violet Hunt, *Sooner or Later: The Story of an Ingenious Ingenue*, Chapman & Hall, London, 1904.

9. Violet Hunt, *The Workaday Woman*, T. Werner Laurie, London, 1906.

10. Ibid., usefully analysed in Hardwick, op. cit., p. 51.

11. See Sheila Jeffreys, '"Free from all uninvited touch of man": women's campaigns around sexuality, 1880–1914', in L. Coveney *et al.*, *The Sexuality Papers*, pp. 22–44.

12. Sheila Jeffreys, *The Spinster and Her Enemies*, p. 1.

13. Violet Hunt, Diaries, 1906. Cornell University, USA.

14. Hardwick, op. cit., p. 51.

15. Violet Hunt, Diaries, May 1906.

16. Ibid.

17. Marguerite Radclyffe-Hall, *A Sheaf of Verses*, Bumpus, London, 1908; Gaby Goldscheider, Windsor, 1985.

18. 'Malvern: July 3rd 1906', *A Sheaf of Verses*, 1985, pp. 58–9.

19. Violet Hunt, Diaries, 7 July 1906.

20. Ibid., May 1906.

21. 'A Pearl Necklace', *A Sheaf of Verses*, 1985, p. 81.

22. Judd, op. cit., p. 174.

23. Hardwick, op. cit., p. 52.

24. Violet Hunt, Diaries, 12 September 1906.

25. Ibid., 14 September 1906.

26. John Sutherland, 'Not Exactly an Ideal Husband', review of Max Saunders, *Ford Madox Ford: A Dual Life*, Oxford University Press. *Sunday Times*, 4 February 1996.

27. Quoted in Elizabeth Longford, *A Pilgrimage of Passion*, p. 152; also in Michael Baker, *Our Three Selves*, p. 34.

5: THE APRIL GRANDMOTHER

1. *Life and Death*, p. 30.

2. Ibid.

3. Lovat Dickson, *Radclyffe Hall at the Well of Loneliness*, p. 37.

4. MVB, Diaries, 1911. Cara Lancaster.

5. MVB, Diaries, 1910, 1912, 1913. In May 1910, she practised part-songs at Percy Grainger's, on 7 June in return she heard Percy Grainger's musical practice, in July she took Marguerite to see Mischa Elman performing at the Ritz with Melba, the following day she took Percy Grainger and singer Edmund Burke with Marguerite to the opera *La Bohème*. By 1912 when Mabel had been living quietly and comfortably with Marguerite for over a year she ensured they never missed a concert or recital of Percy Grainger's. They accompanied him to the Albert Hall for an important concert on 4 February; went to hear his Balfour-Gardiner concert at the Queen's Hall on 27 March; took Cara, Mabel's daughter, and Mabel's sister Emmie to his concert on 21 May. The following May they went with Dolly and Bobby Clarke to hear his music performed at a private soirée.

6. Elizabeth Longford, *A Pilgrimage of Passion*, pp. 152, 153.

7. Ibid. Blunt wrote disparagingly of one that 'she has ceased altogether to be a pretty woman, and has become instead a "woman's delegate".'

8. Ibid.

9. *Life and Death*, p. 30.

10. Ibid.

11. Ibid.

12. Ibid., p. 31.

13. RH, letter to Newman Flower, Cassell, 17 April 1928. Ottawa.

14. 'Fruit of the Nispero No. XIII', *Poems of the Past and Present*, 1910: from early draft, 1908.

15. Cara Lancaster, in conversations with the author, January, February 1996.

16. George Batten to Cara Harris, 4 August 1909. Cara Lancaster.

17. Ibid., 6 August 1909.

18. Ibid., 23 August 1909.

19. II Samuel 1:23.

20. *The Well of Loneliness*, 1982, p. 316.

21. Cara Lancaster, in conversations with the author, January, February 1996.

22. Rupert Hart-Davis to Michael Baker, 22 April 1981. Michael Baker, *Our Three Selves*, p. 177.

23. Author's conversations with Cara Lancaster, January, February 1996.

24. MVB, Diaries, January, February, March, April 1910.

25. Ibid., 17 October 1910. Earlier entries May, October 1910.

26. Ibid., 24 October 1910.

27. Ibid., 14, 24 January, 2 March 1911.

28. MVB to Cara Harris, 25 April 1911. Cara Lancaster.

29. MVB, Diaries, 12 May 1911.

30. Claude J. Summers, *The Gay and Lesbian Literary Heritage*, p. 743.

31. Ibid., p. 744.

6: SAPPHISTS, SUFFRAGE AND CATHOLIC CONVERSION

1. MVB, Diaries, 12 June 1913. Cara Lancaster.

2. James Laver, 'Gabrielle Enthoven and the Enthoven Theatre Collection'.

3. Ibid.

4. Emily Hamer, *Britannia's Glory*, and Michael Baker, *Our Three Selves*.

5. RH, unpublished story 'Malise'. Rome.

6. *The Well of Loneliness*, 1982, Author's Note preceding p. 7.

7. Baker, op. cit., pp. 125, 126.

8. MVB, Diaries, 1910, 1911, 1912, 1913.

9. See Jessica Douglas-Home, *Violet*, p. 112 and p. 106, citing Ethel Smyth's memoirs *A Fresh Start*.

10. *Life and Death*, p. 38.

11. RH, *The Forge*, p. 129.

12. Cara Lancaster, in conversations with the author, January, February 1996.

13. RH to ES, Letter no. 34, 6 September 1934. Texas. See Joanne Glasgow, *Your John*, pp. 44–5.

14. RH to ES, Letter no. 48, from Talbot House, London, 4 October 1934.

15. There is a good analysis of suffrage in Maggie Humm, *The Dictionary of Feminist Theory*.

16. Douglas Goldring, *Life Interests*, p. 51; Joan Hardwick, *An Immodest Violet*, pp. 66, 67.

17. Hardwick, op. cit., pp. 66, 67.

18. *The Unlit Lamp*, 1981, p. 11.

19. Ibid., pp. 59, 60, 61.

20. *Pall Mall Gazette*, 4 March 1912.

21. MVB, Diaries, 1912.

22. MVB to Cara Harris, 14 August 1912. Cara Lancaster.

23. Margaret Lawrence, *The School of Femininity*, pp. 329–30.

24. Marguerite Radclyffe-Hall, 'Incompatible' in *A Sheaf of Verses*, 1985, p. 39.

25. 'Faith' in ibid., p. 107.

26. MVB, Diaries, 4 January 1912.

27. Richard Ellmann, *Oscar Wilde*.

28. Joanne Glasgow, 'What's a Nice Lesbian Like You Doing in the Church of Torquemada?' in Karla Jay and Joanne Glasgow (eds.), *Lesbian Texts and Contexts*, p. 242.

29. MVB, Diaries, 21 January 1912.

30. Ibid., 7 November 1912.

31. *Life and Death*, p. 36.

32. Glasgow, op. cit., p. 251.

33. Ibid., pp. 241–52.

34. Richard Ormrod, *Una Troubridge*, p. 37.

35. Ethel Mannin, *Young in the Twenties*, p. 54.
36. Glasgow, op. cit., p. 242.
37. Ibid., pp. 242, 243, 244.
38. *A Sheaf of Verses*, 1985, p. 21.
39. Ibid., p. 67
40. Ibid., p. 34. (My italics.)
41. Ibid., p. 29.
42. Ibid., p. 35.
43. 'I Must Have Been a Tiresome Baby'. Rome.
44. 'North and South', 'A Night in Italy', 'My Castle', 'Brother Filippo', in *A Sheaf of Verses*, pp. 100, 95, 57, 45.
45. Ibid., pp. 36–7. (My italics.)
46. Ibid., p. 108. (My italics.)
47. Marguerite Radclyffe-Hall, *Poems of the Past and Present*, Chapman & Hall, London, 1910.
48. Ibid., p. 45.
49. Virginia Woolf, 'The Speaker', 21 April 1906.
50. 'Be of Good Cheer' in *Poems of the Past and Present*, p. 7.
51. Ibid., p. 43. (My italics.)
52. There is an excellent discussion of these motifs in Claudia Stillman Franks, *Beyond the Well of Loneliness*.
53. RH, *The Sixth Beatitude*, 1959, p. 7.
54. *Poems of the Past and Present*, pp. 52–4.
55. *Daily Telegraph*, 16 November 1910; *The Times*, 6 October 1910; *Pall Mall Gazette*, 2 December 1910; *Sussex Daily News*, 26 October 1910.
56. MVB, Diaries, 23 November 1913.
57. Mignon Nevada to RH, from Songdell, 72 Carlton Hill, St John's Wood, London, 10 June 1918. Ottawa.
58. Marguerite Radclyffe-Hall, *Songs of Three Counties and Other Poems* with Preface by J.B. Cunninghame Graham, Chapman & Hall, London, 1913. *The Lady*, 13 March 1913; *Daily Telegraph*, 14 March 1913.

7: FIRST FICTIONS, FIRST INFIDELITIES

1. MVB, Diaries, May, June, July 1913. Cara Lancaster.
2. Ibid., July 1913.
3. 28 July–16 October 1913.
4. MVB, Diaries, July, August 1913.
5. Ibid., 25, 30 August 1913.
6. Ibid., 4, 9, 13, 22, 25, 30 September, 2, 4, 6 October 1913.
7. Ibid., 19 September, 11 and 15 October, 22 and 26 November 1913. On 18 December 1913 Ladye records that they 'bought a matchbox for Morena'.
8. Violet's biographer certainly thought so: see Jessica Douglas-Home, *Violet*, p. 136.
9. MVB, Diaries, 31 December 1913.
10. RH, essay 'I Must Have Been a Tiresome Baby'.
11. See Florence Rush, *The Best-Kept Secret*; Diana E.H. Russell, *The Secret Trauma*; Louise DeSalvo, *Virginia Woolf: The Impact of Childhood Sexual Abuse on her Life and Work*; Judith Lewis Herman and Lisa Hirschmann, *Father–Daughter Incest*.
12. MVB, Diaries, January, February, March 1914.
13. MVB to Cara Harris, from Tamaris, 24 March 1914. Cara Lancaster.
14. MVB, Diaries, 2–5 May, 4 June 1914.
15. Ibid., May, June, July 1914.
16. MVB to Cara Harris, 20 July 1914.
17. MVB to Cara Harris, 18 August 1914.

18. Adela Maddison to MVB, enclosed with letter to Cara Harris, 18 August 1914. Cara Lancaster.

19. MVB, Diaries, 12, 17, 22, 23 August 1914.

20. MVB to Cara Harris, 18 August 1914.

21. MVB, Diaries, 4 September 1914.

22. *The Unlit Lamp*, 1981, p. 284.

23. *The Well of Loneliness*, 1982, p. 271.

24. MVB, Diaries, 19 September 1914.

25. *Life and Death*, p. 43.

26. Douglas-Home, op. cit., p. 136.

27. MVB, Diaries, 29 January, 2 February, 28 April 1915.

28. RH, *The Forgotten Island*.

29. Douglas-Home, op. cit., p. 138.

30. RH to Douglas Sladen, undated (probably *c*. June/July 1914). Sladen Collection, Richmond Library, vol. 66, p. 32.

31. MVB, Diaries, 15 May 1915.

32. RH to the Editor of *America*, undated but written after *The Forge* and *The Unlit Lamp*. Rome.

33. Copied out by Ladye, 19 June 1914. MVB, Diaries, 19 June 1914.

34. Ibid., 3, 10, 17 January 1915.

35. Ibid., review at front of journal, and entries 21, 22, 23 February, 9, 10, 14 March 1915.

36. Ibid., red diary, 26 March 1915.

37. *Life and Death*, pp. 38, 39.

38. RH to the Editor of *America*, op. cit.

39. Cited by T.E.M. Boll, *Miss May Sinclair, Novelist*.

40. Claudia Stillman Franks points out that RH's writing was 'fairly typical of the Georgian psychological novel' and that her work shows exposure to 'the same network of ideas' as does May Sinclair's: *Beyond the Well of Loneliness*, p. 38. See also Hrisey Dimitrakis Zegger, *May Sinclair*.

41. RH, 'The Career of Mark Anthony Brakes'. Rome.

42. *Life and Death*, p. 40.

43. Ibid., p. 41.

44. Ibid.

45. On 11 August Ladye finished reading aloud to John, Violet's 'wonderful book' *The House of Many Mirrors* (Stanley Paul, London, 1915), followed on 5 and 6 September by *The Good Soldier* (published in March, before Ford left London and Violet to enlist in the army), which merited Ladye's verdict of a 'wonderfully clever book'. MVB, Diaries, 11 August, 5 September 1915.

46. Joan Hardwick, *An Immodest Violet*, p. 104.

47. RH spells this 'crape' in the original drafts.

48. RH, unpublished story, 'Woman in a Crêpe Bonnet' (several versions including final version). Rome.

49. RH, 'The Career of Mark Anthony Brakes'.

50. *Life and Death*, p. 40.

51. Ibid., p. 42.

52. Ibid., p. 38.

8: FROM A LAPSE TO A LIFE: UNA TROUBRIDGE

1. MVB, Diaries, 23, 24 August 1915.

2. *Life and Death*, p. 46.

3. Ibid.

4. Ibid.

5. Ibid.

6. UVT, 'I Remember', undated unpublished autobiographical essay. Ottawa.
7. Viola Taylor to UVT, undated.
8. Viola Taylor to UVT, from Salcey Lawn, Northampton, undated.
9. Viola Taylor to UVT, from Salcey Lawn, Northampton, undated.
10. UVT, 'I Remember'.
11. UVT, unpublished essays 'Holidays' and 'Clothes'. Ottawa.
12. RH, *A Saturday Life*, 1987, p. 64.
13. Ibid., p. 59.
14. Ibid., pp. 93–4.
15. UVT, undated unpublished essay 'Teachers'. Ottawa.
16. *A Saturday Life*, 1987, p. 129.
17. Viola Taylor to UVT, undated.
18. UVT to Jacqueline Hope, 25 August 1908. Quoted in Michael Baker, *Our Three Selves*, p. 65.
19. UVT, 'Clothes', op. cit.
20. UVT, Diaries, 11 January 1913. Ottawa.
21. Ibid., 14 January 1913.
22. Ibid., 23 January 1913.
23. Ibid., February 1913.
24. RH, Notes to Psychic Records, 3 January 1920. SPR.
25. Ibid., 3 January and 12 June 1920.
26. Ibid., 12 June 1920.
27. B.W. Tuchman, *August 1914*, Constable, London, 1962.
28. Ottawa.
29. Ibid.
30. UVT, Diaries, 12 November 1914.
31. MVB, Diaries, August and September 1915.
32. Ibid., red diary, 9 October; blue diary, 9 October 1915.
33. *Life and Death*, pp. 48, 49.
34. Ibid., pp. 46, 47.
35. Ibid.
36. MVB, Diaries, 28 January 1916.
37. RH, *The Unlit Lamp*, 1981, p. 108.
38. Ibid., p. 34.
39. Ibid., p. 119.
40. Ibid., p. 21.
41. Ibid., p. 55.
42. Ibid.
43. Ibid., p. 34.
44. Ibid., p. 131.
45. Ibid., p. 107.
46. Ibid., p. 69.
47. MVB, Diaries, 13 May 1916.

9: THE PENITENTIAL PERIOD

1. RH to Cara Harris from Purton, undated, probably *c.* 1916. Cara Lancaster.
2. RH, *Adam's Breed*, 1985, p. 13.
3. Ibid., p. 11.
4. Ibid., p. 17.
5. *Life and Death*, pp. 54, 55.
6. UVT, Diaries, 4 February 1917. Ottawa.
7. Ibid., 28 February 1917. Ottawa.

8. RH, 'Waking', March 1917.
9. UVT, Diaries, 17 April 1917.
10. Ibid., 16 September 1917.
11. Ibid., 6, 10 October 1917.
12. Ibid., 1 December 1919.
13. 9, 24, 21 September 1917.
14. RH, Notes to Psychic Records, Sitting 22 November 1917. SPR.
15. UVT, Diaries, 29 December 1917.
16. Ibid., 30 January 1918.
17. RH, Notes to Psychic Records, Leonard Sitting, 1 January 1919. SPR.
18. RH, Notes to Psychic Records, 27 December 1917.
19. Ibid., 19 June 1918.
20. UVT, Diaries, 14 November 1921.
21. Ibid., 3 June 1919.
22. RH, Notes to Psychic Records, Sitting 2 August 1919. SPR.
23. *Raymond, or Life After Death*, 1916.
24. RH, Notes to Psychic Records, Sitting 6 July 1918. SPR.
25. Ibid., 13 October 1916.
26. Ibid., Leonard Sitting, 15 November 1916.
27. Sir Oliver Lodge, quoted in Michael Baker, *Our Three Selves*, p. 93.
28. Dr E.J. Dingwall to R. Ormrod in Richard Ormrod, *Una Troubridge*, p. 103.
29. UVT, Diaries, 22 March 1918.
30. Laura Troubridge Hope, Diary, 22 March 1918, in Ormrod, op. cit.
31. UVT, Diaries, 25 July 1918.
32. Ethel Mannin, *Confessions and Impressions*.
33. *Life and Death*, pp. 59, 60.
34. Ibid., p. 59.
35. Ibid., p. 149.
36. Ibid., p. 69.

10: STRIKING OUT

1. *The Forge*, p. 27.
2. UVT, undated essay 'Beds'.
3. *The Forge*, pp. 51, 52.
4. RH, publicity article. Rome.
5. RH, publicity article about writing methods. Rome.
6. Ibid.
7. The author's conversations and taped interviews with Winifred Hales Reed, 1994, 1995. Also W.H. Reed's own diaries, articles, essays.
8. *The Forge*, p. 45.
9. Richard Ormrod, *Una Troubridge*, pp. 247–8.
10. For an interesting commentary on John and Una's dress codes, see Katrina Rolley, 'Cutting a Dash', *Feminist Review*, 1990.
11. RH, publicity article. Rome.
12. RH, *The Well of Loneliness*, 1982, p. 343.
13. Ibid.
14. UVT, Diaries, 8 January 1920. Ottawa.
15. *Life and Death*, p. 23.
16. Lovat Dickson, *Radclyffe Hall at the Well of Loneliness*, p. 103.
17. UVT, Diaries, 5 January 1920.
18. They fetched Cub from school on 18 February and took her straight to Dorset House, where the operation took place on 22 February 1920. UVT, Diaries.

19. UVT, Diaries, 28 February 1920.

20. RH, article 'How Novelists Work'. Winifred Hales Reed.

21. *Life and Death*, p.70.

22. RH, publicity article, undated but *c.* early 1920s.

23. Conversations and taped interviews with Winifred Hales Reed, 1994. Also W.H. Reed's own diaries, articles, essays.

24. *The Well of Loneliness*, 1982, p. 216.

25. *Life and Death*, p. 72.

26. Ibid., pp. 72–3.

27. Ibid., p. 72.

11: FINDING HER VOICE

1. *The Well of Loneliness*, 1982, p. 217.

2. *The Times*, 12 May 1914. Analysed in Nicola Beauman, *A Very Great Profession*, pp. 53, 54.

3. RH to the Editor of *America* (undated, but between *The Forge* and *The Unlit Lamp*). Rome.

4. RH, *The Unlit Lamp*, 1981, p. 183.

5. Ibid., p. 55.

6. Ibid., p. 261.

7. Ibid., p. 271.

8. Ibid., p. 314.

9. Ibid.

10. Beauman, op. cit., p. 42.

11. *The Unlit Lamp*, 1981, p. 55.

12. Ibid., p. 141.

13. RH, autobiographical essay, undated but *c.* 1915. Rome.

14. Reports in *The Times*, 19 November 1920 and 16 March 1921 (when the slander case against Fox-Pitt went to the Court of Appeal).

15. *The Times*, 19 November 1920.

16. Ibid.

17. Ibid.

18. Ibid.

19. Ibid.

20. UVT, Diaries, 19 November 1920.

21. Ibid., 17 December 1920.

12: THE TWENTIES

1. Ethel Mannin, extract from her novel *Sounding Brass*, described in Ethel Mannin, *Young in the Twenties*.

2. Scott Fitzgerald to Zelda Fitzgerald, quoted in Andrew Turnbull, *Scott Fitzgerald*, p. 131.

3. Ibid., p. 134.

4. Louise Collis, *Impetuous Heart*, p. 163.

5. UVT, Diaries, 17 November 1919. Ottawa.

6. Collis, op. cit., pp. 164, 165. Also UVT, Diary, 24 March 1921.

7. Ida Wylie to UVT, from 6 Blenheim Rd, London, 28 September 1921. Ottawa.

8. Ibid.

9. Ida Wylie to UVT, 28 September 1921.

10. Ethel Smyth to RH, 16 February 1921. Ottawa.

11. UVT, Diaries, 21 May 1921.

12. It appears that their marriage was never legally authenticated.

13. Joan Hardwick, *An Immodest Violet*, p. 154.

14. UVT, Diaries, 11 June 1921.

15. May Sinclair, 'The Novels of Violet Hunt', *English Review*, p. 118.

16. RH, *The Unlit Lamp*, 1981, pp. 284–5.

17. Ibid., p. 285.

18. Ibid., p. 110.

19. RH, *The Forge*, pp. 120, 121, 122.

20. UVT, Diaries, 12 August 1921.

21. Ibid., 31 August 1921.

22. Richard Ormrod, *Una Troubridge*, p. 146.

23. Zoë Fairbairns, Introduction to Radclyffe Hall, *The Unlit Lamp*, 1981, pp. 6, 7.

24. This may include a range of sensual and sexual women-identified experience, rather than simply the fact that a woman has had or has consciously desired genital sexual experience with another woman. This term was first suggested by Adrienne Rich in *Compulsory Heterosexuality and Lesbian Existence*. It is a notion elaborated on and developed by the present author in Sally Cline, *Women, Celibacy and Passion*.

25. Fairbairns, op. cit., p. 8.

26. Useful on this subject is Claude J. Summers' introduction to *The Gay and Lesbian Literary Heritage* and several discussions throughout that book.

13: FORGING AHEAD

1. Her pragmatism was not always revealed in her public letter writing. She had learnt the knack of self-presentation, though sometimes this conflicted with her honest nature and tripped her up. She wrote letters to newspapers explaining her craft. New to the game, she was often a little pompous. In her letter to the Editor of *America* she wrote:

> I have often been asked how it is possible that the same author can have written a humorous book like *The Forge* and a serious, not to say tragic, book like *The Unlit Lamp* . . . Life, as I see it, is a mixture of comedy and tragedy, with a few intermediate tones. Occasionally I am impressed by both at once, as happened in the case of my two novels . . . I had practically completed it [*The Unlit Lamp*] . . . when certain aspects of postwar existence in England struck me forcibly one evening while I was undressing. These aspects were humorous and I sat down the next day and started to write *The Forge*. During my serious and sad moments I completed *The Unlit Lamp*.

What this public version skilfully omits is the torrent of rejections for her first 'serious and sad book' which forced her to become pragmatic.

2. 'The Scarecrow' remained unpublished and was lost.

3. *Life and Death*, p. 73.

4. The suggestion that Tallulah liked boyish females comes from Brendan Gill, *Tallulah*, p. 37.

5. UVT, Diaries, February–August 1924.

6. Ibid., 12 June 1923.

7. *Sunday Times*, 10 February 1924.

8. Violet Hunt to RH, undated. A.M. Heath.

9. Vere Hutchinson to RH, 1924. Ottawa.

10. Ibid.

11. *People*, 2 March 1924.

12. Claudia Stillman Franks in her review of Hall's literature, *Beyond the Well of Loneliness*, is very interesting on this point.

13. RH, *The Forge*, p. 138.

14. Ibid., p. 140.

15. Ibid., p. 139.

16. Meryle Secrest, *Between Me and Life*, pp. 226 and 193.

17. George Wickes, *The Amazon of Letters*, p. 8.

18. Bettina Bergery, quoted in Secrest, op. cit., p. 337.

19. Romaine Brooks to UVT, 1923. Ottawa.

20. UVT, Diaries, 7 June 1923.

21. Ibid., 30 June, 1 July 1923.

22. Secrest, op. cit., p. 291.

23. Romaine Brooks to RH, undated letter. Ottawa.

24. Romaine Brooks to Natalie Barney, letter 1924. Ottawa. Also in Secrest, op. cit., p. 292.

25. Secrest, op. cit., p. 199.

26. At the Wildenstein Galleries, New York; the Art Institute, Chicago; the Alpine Club, London; and the Galerie Charpentier, Paris.

27. UVT, Diaries, 25 June 1924.

28. Natalie Barney to RH, from 20 Rue Jacob, Paris, 20 October 1924.

29. He wrote to Rache Lovat Dickson with this description of their meetings between 1924 and 1926. Alec Waugh to R. Lovat Dickson from Boulevard de Paris, Tangier, Morocco, 26 May 1970. Ottawa.

30. On Wednesday 13 August Una records that Hutchinson took 'Mark Anthony Brakes', William Heinemann's favourite story.

31. Started 14 August, finished 16 August.

32. 3 October 1924. Una was also photographed by Lafayette.

33. *Sunday Times*, 28 September 1924.

34. *Daily Telegraph*, 15 October; *The Lady*, 25 October 1924.

35. On 11, 17 and 14 November 1924, respectively.

36. Katherine Mansfield, *In a German Pension*, p. 11.

37. *Times Literary Supplement*, 3 June; *Punch*, 13 June; *Bystander*, 14 June 1925.

38. A.E. Coppard, review found in scrapbook kept by RH's secretary Winifred Hales Reed. Copy also in Radclyffe Hall Collection, Texas.

39. Suggestion made by Rosalind Miles in *The Fiction of Sex*.

40. Suggestion made by Michael Baker in *Our Three Selves*.

41. Suggestion made by Claudia Stillman Franks in *Beyond the Well of Loneliness*.

42. RH, *A Saturday Life*, p. 224.

43. Alison Hennegan, Preface to *A Saturday Life*, 1982.

44. *Queen* magazine, 29 April 1925.

14: CRITICAL ACCLAIM

1. *Life and Death*, p. 79.

2. RH, 'Why I Wrote *Adam's Breed*'.

3. UVT, Diaries, 14 April 1925.

4. RH, 'Why I Wrote *Adam's Breed*'.

5. See Sally Cline, *Lifting the Taboo*, pp. 304–19.

6. *The Well of Loneliness*, 1982, pp. 405, 406.

7. UVT, Diaries, 29 January 1927.

8. Ibid., 12 March 1927.

9. Ibid., 21 July 1927.

10. Ibid., 16 June 1925.

11. 1919, 1921, 1924.

12. Anecdote told to Michael Baker by Beresford Egan, 22 December 1981.

13. Review in the *Sunday Times*, 5 April.

14. UVT, Diaries, Sunday 9 August 1925.

15. Russell Doubleday to Audrey Heath, 15 October 1925. A.M. Heath.

16. UVT, Diaries. *Adam's Breed* was finished 7 November 1925; sent to Cassells 17 November. Visit to Visettis and first consultation with Dr Martisius 18 November; second consultation 19

November. Delivery of US section of *Adam's Breed* to A.M. Heath and purchase of cockatoo 20 November. Third and fourth consultations 23 and 27 November.

17. UVT, Diaries, Tuesday 15 September 1925.
18. Ibid., 9 April 1925.
19. Ibid., 4, 5 October 1925.
20. Ibid., 28 July, 1, 2 August 1925.
21. Ibid., 28 July, 17 August, 1 September 1925.
22. Ibid., 1 September 1925.
23. J.L. Garvin to UVT, from Gregories, Beaconsfield, 10 March 1927. Ottawa.
24. J.L. Garvin to UVT, from Gregories, Beaconsfield, 22 December 1926. Ottawa.
25. UVT, Diaries, 28, 30 January, 1 February 1926.
26. UVT, *Life and Death*, p. 79.
27. UVT, Diaries, 20 February 1926.
28. *Sunday Herald*, 21 March 1926; *Observer*, 14 March 1926; *Sunday Times*, 14 March 1926; *The Times*, 22 March 1926. RH to Jane Caruth, 22 January 1926. Texas.
29. Third impression 25 March; fourth impression 23 April.
30. UVT, Diaries, 13 April 1926.
31. UVT, Diaries, 25 March 1926.
32. RH to Jane Caruth, 13 June 1926.
33. UVT, Diaries, 6 July 1926.
34. A. Scott Berg, *Max Perkins*, p. 465. Brandt invited to dine 19 July. UVT, Diaries.
35. UVT, Diaries, 13 August 1926. Paris–Bagnoles–Monte Carlo trip, 12 August–2 November 1926.
36. RH to ES, 12 April 1935. Texas.
37. Mansfield won 1921, Macaulay 1922, Garnett 1923, Percy Lubbock for *Roman Pictures* 1924, Mary Webb for *Precious Bane* 1925. *New York Publishers Weekly*, 10 March 1928.
38. Wendy Mulford discusses this in depth in her book *This Narrow Place*, p. 105.
39. *Life and Death*, p. 80.
40. RH, *Adam's Breed*, 1985, pp. 27, 28.
41. Ibid., pp. 52, 53.
42. Ibid., pp. 57, 58.
43. Ibid., p. 258.
44. Doubleday, who had decided to republish *Adam's Breed* with a new jacket, told Audrey 'they will never let go'. UVT, Diaries, 1 April 1927.
45. Ibid., 17 January 1927.
46. *Bookman*, April 1927.
47. Grace Spencer to RH, 23 January 1927. Ottawa. Grace Spencer, 'a friend of Joan (Ogden), Frances (Reide) and Gian-Luca', had suggested that 'Frances should be the patron saint of all we happily unmarried women – wise, gallant, full of that detached and dry humour which can transform life and keep alive the spirit of adventure.'
48. Ellen Glasgow to Cassells, 1927. Ottawa.
49. Peggy Austin to RH, from 49 Cambridge Mansions, 1 May 1927. Ottawa.
50. Violet Hunt to RH after *Adam's Breed*. Lovat Dickson Correspondence, vol. 4, no. 15. Ottawa.
51. *Houston Chronicle*, 8 May 1927.
52. Winifred Macey Duenner to RH. Rome.
53. *Westminster Gazette*, 12, 13 April 1927.
54. *Lancashire Daily Post*, 13 April 1927.
55. *Birmingham Post*, 11 April 1927.
56. *Auckland Star*, 12 February 1927.
57. *Weekly Press*, Christchurch, New Zealand, 28 July 1927, which published *Daily Mail* London interview by Evelyn Irons.
58. *Newcastle and Northern Mail*, 17 May 1927.
59. *Manchester Daily Journal*, 14 July 1927.

60. Paris–Bagnoles trip 11 August–25 September 1927.

61. The adjudication was made by Professor Grierson, Professor of English Literature at Edinburgh University. Her notification of the award came from Robert Welsh at 21 Wellington Square, Ayr, on behalf of the James Tait Black Memorial Trust.

62. RH, syndicated press statement to outlets in USA through *Paterson Press Guardian, Eastern Express, Farago Forum, Picayune Times,* etc. February, March, April, May, June 1928.

63. UVT, Diaries, 22 July 1926.

64. *Life and Death,* pp. 81, 82.

65. Ibid.

15: BOLDNESS

1. Radclyffe Hall, 'Salvation', poem used as frontispiece to Una Lady Troubridge, *The Life and Death of Radclyffe Hall.* 'Salvation' was set to music and sung by Paul Robeson. Jane Marcus called it a feminist hymn to the overthrow of all patriarchal Jerichos: J. Marcus, *Virginia Woolf and the Languages of Patriarchy.*

2. *The Well of Loneliness,* 1982, pp. 96, 97.

3. Ibid., p. 77.

4. Ibid., p. 274.

5. Ibid., p. 316.

6. Ibid., p. 393.

7. Ibid., p. 447.

8. There is a short analysis of these theories, their usefulness to Radclyffe Hall's work, and the impact on lesbian women in Chapter 3 above.

9. See Havelock Ellis, *The Psychology of Sex,* p. 224; Edward Carpenter, *Love's Coming of Age,* Labour Press of Manchester, 1896, and *Intermediate Sex,* London & Manchester, 1908, quoted in Sandra M. Gilbert and Susan Gubar, *No Man's Land,* vol. 2: *Sex Changes,* ch. 6, pp. 216–17, for detailed discussion.

10. *The Well of Loneliness,* 1982, p. 304.

11. Ibid., p. 443.

12. One critic who did not ignore it but gave an interesting detailed analysis is Alison Hennegan in her Preface to *The Well of Loneliness,* 1982.

13. *The Well of Loneliness,* 1982, p. 208.

14. *Life and Death,* p. 82.

15. Lovat Dickson, *Radclyffe Hall at the Well of Loneliness,* p. 125.

16. Catharine R. Stimpson, 'Zero Degree Deviancy: The Lesbian Novel in English', in Elizabeth Abel (ed.), *Writing and Sexual Difference.*

17. Janet Flanner, New York, 8 June 1972, in George Wickes, *The Amazon of Letters,* pp. 261, 262.

18. UVT, Diaries, 26 October 1926.

19. Djuna Barnes, *Ladies Almanack,* originally published 1928.

20. RH to Winifred Macey, 23 January 1927. Texas.

21. RH to Winifred Macey, 15 February 1927.

22. Ibid.

23. RH to Newman Flower, 16 April 1928.

24. RH (from Holland Street) to Roger Scaife of Houghton Mifflin.

25. RH to Newman Flower, 16 April 1928.

26. Newman Flower (Cassell & Co.) to Miss A.M. Heath, 23 April 1928.

27. RH to Havelock Ellis, 18 April 1928. Ottawa.

28. Phyllis Grosskurth, *Havelock Ellis,* p. 398.

29. C.S. Evans of William Heinemann to A.M. Heath, 27 April 1928.

30. Ibid.

31. Compton Mackenzie, *My Life and Times,* p. 138.

32. Compton Mackenzie, *Extraordinary Women*, pp. 13, 14, 15, 16, 17, 18.
33. UVT, Diaries, 16 May 1928.
34. Bernice Baumgarten to Audrey Heath, 22 March 1928. Ottawa.
35. Audrey Heath to Carl Brandt, 11 May 1928. Texas.
36. Carl Brandt to RH, 8 June 1928. Ottawa.
37. Carl Brandt to RH about Roger Scaife, 3 June 1928. Ottawa. Roger Scaife to RH, 5 June 1928. Houghton Library.
38. Carl Brandt to RH, 8 July 1928. Ottawa.
39. RH to Carl Brandt, 21 June 1928. Ottawa.
40. RH to Alfred Knopf (from 37 Holland St, London), 8 July 1928. Texas.
41. RH to Jonathan Cape (written in UVT's hand), 29 June 1928. Ottawa.
42. RH to James Garvin from Holland St, London, 15 July 1928. Texas.
43. Ibid.
44. *Saturday Review*, 28 July 1928.
45. *Nation*, 4 August 1928.
46. *Times Literary Supplement*, 2 August 1928; *Sunday Times*, 5 August 1928.
47. *Evening Standard*, 9 August 1928.
48. *Morning Post*, 10 August 1928.
49. *Time and Tide*, 10 August 1928.
50. *TP's Weekly*, 11 August 1928.
51. *Daily Telegraph*, 17 August 1928.
52. *Sunday Express*, 19 August 1928.
53. *The Times*, 17 November 1928, p. 5.

16: THE WELL

1. RH to Gorham Munson from The Forecastle, The Hucksteps, Rye, Sussex, 2 June 1934. The Munson Letter, Lesbian Herstory Educational Foundation, New York. This letter, which was written in response to a request from Gorham Munson and Professor George Willis for use in their proposed history of contemporary English and American fiction, appears to be the only formal writing by Hall about her experiences relating to *The Well*. It came to the notice of the Foundation by way of a New York city man who found the letter in his deceased parents' closet. A lesbian co-worker urged him to donate the letter to the Archives which he did in spring 1994. The letter reflects Hall's notions on love, sexuality and society and bears evidence of anti-Semitism, racism and classism, but is of great interest to Hall scholars.
2. Ibid.
3. *Sunday Chronicle*, 19 August 1928; *People*, 19 August 1928.
4. Monday 20 August 1928.
5. *Daily Herald*, 20 August 1928.
6. *Lady's Pictorial*, 22 August 1928.
7. *Country Life*, 25 August 1928.
8. RH to Fabienne, 27 August 1928, referred to in Michael Baker, *Our Three Selves*, p. 226.
9. *Daily Herald*, 21 August 1928.
10. W. Joynson-Hicks to Jonathan Cape, 22 August 1928.
11. Jonathan Cape to Editor of *The Times*, 22 August 1928.
12. RH to Gerard Hopkins, 15 August 1928. Berg Collection, New York Public Library.
13. *Daily Herald*, 24 August 1928.
14. *Evening Standard*, 9 August 1928.
15. For this information I am indebted to Jane Marcus.
16. *New Statesman*, 25 August 1928.
17. Ibid.
18. Virginia Woolf to Vita Sackville-West, from Monk's House, Rodmell, 30 August 1928.
19. Ibid.

20. Virginia Woolf to Vita Sackville-West, from Monk's House, Rodmell, Sussex, 8 September 1928.

21. *Nation and Athenaeum*, 8 September 1928.

22. RH to Arnold Bennett, 27 August 1928. Bennett Collection, London University.

23. Arnold Bennett to RH, 23 August 1928. Bennett Collection, London University.

24. There is a useful discussion of married lesbians in Suzanne Raitt, *Vita and Virginia*.

25. P.N. Furbank, *E.M. Forster – A Life*, vol. 2, p. 155. A good analysis of this is to be found in Bonnie Kime Scott, *Refiguring Modernism*, vol. 1, p. 244.

26. P. Berry and M. Bostridge, *Vera Brittain*, pp. 227, 228.

27. Virginia Woolf to Lady Ottoline Morrell, from 52 Tavistock Square, London, WC1, early November 1928, before the trial. See Nigel Nicolson (ed.), *Letters*, vol. 3.

28. Virginia Woolf to Vanessa Bell, from Monk's House, Rodmell, Sussex, 2 September 1928. Ibid.

29. Hermione Lee, *Virginia Woolf*, p. 526.

30. Virginia Woolf and E.M. Forster, letter to *Nation and Athenaeum*, 8 September 1928. See P.N. Furbank, op. cit., p. 154.

31. 1 September 1928.

32. RH to Oliver Baldwin, 2 September 1928.

33. UVT, Diary, 27 September 1928, and Blanche Knopf to RH, undated and 20 September 1928. Formerly A.M. Heath, currently with Jonathan Lovat Dickson, Toronto, Canada.

34. Blanche Knopf to RH, October 1928.

35. UVT to Audrey Heath, November 1928. Ottawa.

36. John Quinn to Ezra Pound, 16 October 1920. Letter held at Northwestern University. Discussion of letter in Bonnie Kime Scott, *Refiguring Modernism*, vol. 1, pp. 243, 244.

37. Richard Ormrod, *Una Troubridge*, p. 181.

38. Letters formerly in the possession of Michael Rubinstein, currently with Jonathan Lovat Dickson, Toronto, Canada.

39. Ormrod, op. cit., p. 181.

40. Virginia Woolf's sister Vanessa Bell.

41. Virginia Woolf to Quentin Bell, from 52 Tavistock Square, London WC1, 1 November 1928.

42. Lovat Dickson, *Radclyffe Hall at the Well of Loneliness*, p. 157.

43. RH to PEN from Holland St, London, 20 November 1928. Texas.

44. Havelock Ellis to RH, 20 October 1928. Ottawa. See also Michael Baker, *Our Three Selves*, p. 235 on Ellis's earlier confrontation with the law.

45. Ormrod, op. cit., p. 180.

46. Hugh Walpole to Jonathan Cape, date smudged, 1928. Original owner Michael Rubinstein, now with Jonathan Lovat Dickson, Toronto, Canada.

47. Ormrod, op. cit., p. 181.

48. Anecdote told to Michael Baker by Storm Jameson, 27 March 1981.

49. Defence counsel documents. Ernst Collection. Texas.

50. Jane Marcus, *Virginia Woolf and the Languages of Patriarchy*, p. 179.

51. Papers relating to the British Sexological Society and George Ives and their correspondence with RH are in the Harry Ransom Humanities Research Center, Texas. The BSS was not the only organization of its type at that time. There was also the secret homosexual rights organization called the Order of Chaeronea run by George Ives. During this period there is some correspondence between RH and Ives which suggests that she and Una applied for membership. Ives however was not approached as a defence witness, possibly because he would be seen to do her cause no good.

52. Quoted in Lovat Dickson, op. cit., p. 158.

53. *Lancet*, September 1928.

54. Quoted from the trial papers in Marcus, op. cit., p. 213.

55. Quoted in Lovat Dickson, op. cit., p. 159.

56. Quoted in Vera Brittain, *Radclyffe Hall: A Case of Obscenity*, p. 87.

57. Defence counsel documents. Ernst Collection. Texas.

58. Oscar Wilde, Letter no. 509, quoted in Richard Ellmann, *Oscar Wilde*, p. 409.

59. Rebecca West, 'High Fountain of Genius', in B.K. Scott (ed.), *The Gender of Modernism*, pp. 592–6.

60. Woolf had identified this as an important topic in her book *Modern Fiction*.

61. Suzanne Raitt, *Vita and Virginia*.

62. Bonnie Kime Scott, *Refiguring Modernism*, vol. 1, p. 246.

63. *Daily Herald*, 10 November 1928.

64. Storm Jameson to Michael Baker, quoted in Baker, *Our Three Selves*.

65. *Daily Herald*, 10 November 1928.

66. Anne Olivier Bell (ed.), *The Diary of Virginia Woolf*, vol. 3, pp. 206–7.

67. This was Sheila Kaye-Smith's description in *All the Books of My Life*, p. 137.

68. *The Times*, 10 November 1928.

69. RH to Gerard Hopkins, 14 November 1928. Berg Collection.

70. James Melville's speech. Transcript of shorthand notes of Barnett, Lenton & Co., 9 November 1928.

71. Ibid.

72. RH to Gerard Hopkins, 14 November 1928.

73. Brittain, op. cit.

74. *Daily Mirror*, 10 November 1928.

75. Radclyffe Hall to Gorham Munson, op. cit., pp. 2, 3. The author has viewed several other (unpublished) articles by Hall relating to her purpose in writing *The Well*.

76. Paul Berry and Mark Bostridge, *Vera Brittain*, pp. 227, 228.

77. September 1929. Quoted in ibid., p. 273.

78. Ibid., p. 276.

79. Transcript of the shorthand notes of Barnett, Lenton & Co., *DPP v. Jonathan Cape & Leopold Hill*, 14 December 1928.

80. Ibid.

81. RH to Vita Sackville-West, 16 December 1928. See Nigel Nicolson (ed.), op. cit.

82. RH to Fabienne, 27 August 1928.

83. RH to Gorham Munson, op. cit., p. 5.

84. Martha Nell Smith, 'American Literature 1900–1969', in Claude J. Summers (ed.), *The Gay and Lesbian Literary Heritage*, p. 39.

85. RH to Gorham Munson, op. cit., pp. 6–7.

86. Ibid.

87. *Life and Death*, p. 92.

88. Ibid.

17: THE TROLLEY YEARS

1. RH to Audrey Heath, 23 August 1929. A.M. Heath and Lovat Dickson.

2. For more on this relationship, see Terry Castle, *Noël Coward and Radclyffe Hall*, pp. 10, 11, 13, 20, 33, 38–42, 73–8.

3. RH, *The Sixth Beatitude*, 1959, pp. 7 and 61.

4. RH gave this information to Laurence Housman. Quoted in L. Housman to George Ives, 16 January 1929. Housman–Ives Papers. Texas.

5. RH to Gorham Munson from The Forecastle, The Hucksteps, Rye, Sussex, 2 June 1934. The Munson Letter, Lesbian Herstory Educational Foundation, New York, p. 5.

6. Vera Brittain, *Radclyffe Hall: A Case of Obscenity*, p. 43.

7. RH to Gorham Munson, op. cit., p. 6.

8. RH to Audrey Heath, 20 April 1929. Ottawa.

9. RH to Donald Friede, 4 May 1929. Ottawa.

10. RH to Audrey Heath, 28 March 1929.

11. 11 October 1929. Leonard Woolf (ed.), *A Writer's Diary*, p. 146.

12. Quoted in Philippe Julian and John Phillips, *The Other Woman*, p. 228.

13. This incident between Charlotte Mew and May Sinclair is said to have occurred in 1914. Rebecca West sent to May Sinclair's biographer Dr Theophilus Boll a copy of a letter from G.B. Stern detailing the conversation heard by herself and Rebecca West. Marjorie Dawson Scott (Mrs Marjorie Watts) heard details of the story from her mother who discussed it with Netta Syrett. A witty exploration of the event is to be found in Penelope Fitzgerald's *Charlotte Mew and Her Friends*, pp. 132, 133, 134.

14. Lillian Faderman, *Surpassing the Love of Men*, p. 322.

15. Quoted in Meryle Secrest, *Between Me and Life*, p. 291.

16. Faderman, op. cit., p. 323.

17. It was novelist-critic Jane Rule who first pointed this out.

18. Del Martin, co-author of *Lesbian/Woman*, called it a 'lesbian Bible'. Del Martin and Phyllis Lyon, *Lesbian Woman*, p. 17.

19. *The Well of Loneliness*, 1982, p. 438.

20. RH to Gorham Munson, op. cit.

21. Ibid., p. 6.

22. Paul Berry and Mark Bostridge, *Vera Brittain*, pp. 227, 228.

23. RH to ES, Easter Sunday 1935. Texas.

24. UVT to Patience Ross, 10 February 1929.

25. *Life and Death*, p. 113.

26. Ibid.

27. UVT, Day Book, 1 February 1931. Rome.

28. UVT to Audrey (Robin) Heath, from Osborne Hotel, Paris, undated but probably February 1929.

29. John Holyrod-Reece to RH and UVT, 2 September 1930. Texas.

30. *New York World*, 25 April 1929.

31. RH to Audrey Heath, 7 April 1929. Ottawa.

32. Michael Baker, *Our Three Selves*, p. 257.

33. Leonard Woolf (ed.), *A Writer's Diary*, p. 19.

34. *Life and Death*, p. 104.

35. Ibid., p. 100.

36. Ibid., p. 104.

37. RH to Gorham Munson, op. cit., p. 7.

38. Richard Ormrod, *Una Troubridge*, p. 190.

39. Ibid., p. 192.

40. *Life and Death*, p. 101.

41. UVT to Audrey Heath, 3 October 1929.

42. 7 October 1929.

43. 8,104 copies were sold in England and 13,301 in the USA during its first six months. James King, *Virginia Woolf*, p. 423.

44. Ibid., pp. 427, 439.

45. Jane Marcus, *Virginia Woolf and the Languages of Patriarchy*, pp. 163–87.

46. Virginia Woolf, *A Room of One's Own*, 1929, p. 78; 1992, p. 106.

47. Monk's House Papers B6, quoted in Marcus, op. cit., p. 173.

48. 21 December 1925.

49. King, op. cit., p. 399.

50. Virginia Woolf to Vanessa Bell, 23 July 1927. Nigel Nicolson (ed.), *Letters*, vol. 3, p. 401.

51. Virginia Woolf to Vanessa Bell, 2 September 1928. Ibid., p. 525, quoted in King, op. cit., p. 419.

52. UVT, Day Books, 16 February 1931.

53. Ibid.

54. UVT to Jacqueline Hope-Nicholson, 22 April 1930, quoted in Michael Baker, *Our Three Selves*, p. 261.

Notes 399

18: THE RYE RELATIONSHIP

1. Iain Finlayson, *Writers in Romney Marsh*, gives a good survey of several writers' appreciations of Romney Marsh, including Henry James, Joseph Conrad, Ford Madox Ford, E.F. Benson, Stephen Crane, Conrad Aiken and Radclyffe Hall.

2. RH, *The Sixth Beatitude*, 1959, p. 14.

3. Ibid., p. 91.

4. Finlayson, op. cit., p. 15.

5. Ibid., p. 17.

6. Una believed that the number of potential visitors meant that John 'who dreaded ostracism for me, can feel she has helped and not harmed me'. UVT, Day Book, 4 January 1931.

7. Finlayson, op. cit., p. 147.

8. UVT, Day Book, 10 January 1931.

9. On 7 April 1931 RH made an offer for 17 West Street. Offer accepted 8 April; contract signed 15 April; house called Santa Maria 19 April; balance of money paid 6 May; keys to property received 9 May; renovations undertaken May, August, September; shown to Audrey Heath 25 September and to agent 17 November.

10. *The Sixth Beatitude*, 1959, p. 26.

11. 1 July 1930.

12. UVT, Diaries, 23 October 1930.

13. Ibid., 13 January 1930.

14. Ibid., 14 January 1930.

15. UVT, Diaries, 17 February 1931.

16. John had received news of the sales on 15 January.

17. UVT, Diaries, 4 July 1930.

18. Ibid., 24 February 1931.

19. Sylvia Pankhurst, *The Suffragette Movement*, 1977, p. 225, quoted in Emily Hamer, *Britannia's Glory*, p. 53.

20. Mary Sophia Allen, *The Pioneer Policewoman*, p. 13. A good description of the work of Allen, Taggart and Goldingham is given in Hamer, op. cit.

21. UVT, Diary, 9 January 1931.

22. UVT, Day Book, 27 December 1930.

23. Michael Baker, *Our Three Selves*, p. 269.

24. UVT, Day Book, re December 1930 (written in retrospect 14 January 1931).

25. Ibid., 28 December 1930.

26. Ibid., 31 December 1930.

27. Ibid., 7 January 1931.

28. Incident reported by Mrs Lawrence-Jones to her niece Marya Burrell who told Una's biographer Richard Ormrod.

29. Until 6 February 1931.

30. UVT, Day Book, 18 January 1931.

31. Ibid.

32. Ibid., 19 January 1931.

33. Ibid., 4 February 1931.

34. Ibid., 16 February 1931.

35. Ibid., 1 February 1931.

36. Ibid.

37. Ibid.

38. Ibid.

39. Ibid., 9 February 1931.

40. Ibid., 12 February 1931.

41. Ibid., 20, 21, 22, 23 September 1931.

42. UVT, Diaries, 5 November 1931.

43. Ibid., 11 December 1931.

44. Ibid., 18 February 1932.
45. Ibid., 27 March 1932.
46. RH, *The Master of the House*, 1952, p. 393.
47. *The Well of Loneliness*, 1982, p. 247.
48. *The Master of the House*, p. 394.
49. Gerald Gould, *Observer*, 28 February 1932.
50. *Sunday Times*, 28 February; *Observer*, 28 February; *The Times*, 4 March 1932. *Times Literary Supplement* quoted in Richard Ormrod, *Una Troubridge*, p. 205.
51. UVT, Day Book, 30 April 1932.
52. Victoria Glendinning, *Vita*, p. 242.
53. Ibid., p. 246.
54. Ibid., pp. 248, 249.
55. Ibid., p. 249.
56. Ibid., p. 250.
57. Ibid., p. 237.
58. Ibid.
59. The pain in John's eyes started 5 April; she felt run down 3, 8 May; was examined by doctor in Bath 18 May. John and Una stayed first at the Grand Pump Hotel, then at the Empire Hotel.
60. 25 June–31 August.
61. UVT, Day Book, 26 December 1932.
62. Ibid., 15 July 1933.
63. Ormrod, op. cit., p. 212.
64. UVT, Day Book, 2 September 1933.
65. Baker, op. cit., p. 287.
66. UVT, Day Book, 3 October 1933.
67. *Life and Death*, p. 114.

19: SOULINE

1. *Life and Death*, p. 116.
2. Author's conversation with Ariadne Nicolaeff, 20 January 1996. Also Ariadne Nicolaeff, 'The Love Letters of John Radclyffe Hall to Evguenia Souline', unpublished article, 1985.
3. RH to ES, Letter no. 44, 18 September 1934. Texas.
4. Ibid., Letter no. 115, from Rye, 30 December 1934. Texas.
5. UVT, Day Book, 5 September 1935.
6. Mentioned in RH to ES, 18 July 1937.
7. ES, autobiographical MSS, including writings about her initial conversations with RH. Archive material held by Joan Slater/Monica Still. (The initial research into this material was carried out by Monica Still and her partner Marya Burrell, now deceased.) Discussions and communications between Joan Slater and the author regarding Souline's relationship with RH took place on 17, 20, 21 February, 6, 14, 22 March and 3 April 1996.
8. Author's several conversations with Ariadne Nicolaeff, January 1996.
9. ES, autobiographical MSS. Slater/Still. Also, written material given by ES to Ariadne Nicolaeff. (Initial research carried out by Monica Still and her partner Marya Burrell, now deceased.)
10. Ibid.
11. Author's conversations with Ariadne Nicolaeff, Iris Furlong, Professor R. Smith, and others in Souline's circle. January, February, March 1996.
12. Author's conversations with Ariadne Nicolaeff, January 1996.
13. ES, op. cit.
14. UVT, small diary, 2 July 1934.
15. UVT, Rye and Covent Garden Day Book, 8 July 1934.
16. Ibid.

17. ES, op. cit.
18. Ibid.
19. Ibid.
20. Ibid.
21. Ibid.
22. Ibid.
23. Ibid.
24. RH to ES, from Viareggio, 5 February 1939.
25. ES, op. cit.
26. Ibid.
27. Ibid.
28. Ibid.
29. RH to ES, from Sirmione, 18 September 1934.
30. Ibid.
31. RH to ES, Letter no. 194, from Beauvallon, 7 June 1935.
32. RH to ES, 18 September 1934.
33. RH to ES, Letter no. 79, from Rye, 27 November 1934.
34. RH to ES, 24 July 1934.
35. RH to ES, 26 January 1939.
36. Manuscript of *Emblem Hurlstone*, written August 1934. Rome.
37. Ibid.
38. ES, op. cit.
39. Ibid.
40. Ibid.
41. *Life and Death*, pp. 115–16.
42. UVT, Rye and Covent Garden Day Book, 21 January 1935.
43. Richard Ormrod, *Una Troubridge*, pp. 217–18.
44. Michael Baker, *Our Three Selves*, pp. 297–8.
45. Author's interview with Monica Still, November 1995.
46. Author's conversations with Professor R. Smith, January 1996. He lodged with Evguenia Souline Makaroff from 1947 to 1950.
47. RH to ES, from Via dei Bardi, Florence, 3 March 1939.
48. UVT, Rye and Covent Garden Day Book, 12 July 1934.
49. UVT, small diary, 2, 5, 6 July; Day Book, 5, 6 July 1934.
50. UVT, Rye and Covent Garden Day Book, 10 July 1934.
51. Ibid., 5, 8 July 1934.
52. Ibid., 8 July 1934.
53. Ibid., 26 July 1934.
54. ES, op. cit.
55. UVT, Rye and Covent Garden Day Book, 14, 15 July 1934.
56. RH to ES, 17 July 1934.
57. ES, op. cit.
58. Ibid.
59. RH to ES, Letter no. 2, from Hotel des Thermes, 20 July 1934.
60. ES, op. cit.
61. RH to ES, Letter no. 3, from Pont Royal Hotel, Paris, 24 July 1934.
62. ES, op. cit. Slater/Still and A. Nicolaeff.
63. Ibid.
64. Ibid.
65. UVT, Diaries, 26 July 1934.
66. RH to ES, Letter no. 34, 6 September 1934.
67. RH to ES, 1, 6 September 1934.
68. ES, op. cit.
69. Ibid.

70. RH to ES, Letter no. 4, from Pont Royal Hotel, Paris, 27 July 1934.
71. Ibid.
72. RH to ES, Letter no. 40, from Sirmione, 12 September 1934.
73. RH to ES, Letter no. 115, from Rye, 30 December 1934.
74. Naomi Jacob, *Me and the Swans*, p. 121.
75. Ibid.

20: SAME HEART AND SEVERE DIFFERENCES

1. UVT, Engagement Diary and Rye and Covent Garden Day Book, 31 July, 1, 2, 3 August 1934.
2. *Life and Death*, p. 115.
3. RH to ES from Sirmione, 31 July 1934.
4. RH to ES, 1 August 1934.
5. *Adam's Breed*, p. 27.
6. RH to ES, 12 August 1934.
7. RH to ES, Letter no. 6, 31 July 1934 in answer to letter from ES, 28 July 1934.
8. RH to ES, 19 August 1934.
9. RH to ES, Letter no. 38, 11 September 1934.
10. RH to ES, 1 August 1934.
11. RH to ES, 7 August 1934.
12. RH to ES, 29 August 1934.
13. RH to ES, Letter no. 9, 4 August 1934.
14. ES, autobiographical essay. Slater/Still.
15. Ibid., drafts 1 and 2.
16. RH to ES, 13 August 1934.
17. RH to ES, from Rye, 28 December 1934.
18. UVT, Rye and Covent Garden Day Book, 19 January 1935.
19. Audrie Atcheson, unpublished memoir of her aunt Naomi Jacob and RH, lent to the author. Several conversations between Audrie Atcheson and the author.
20. Ibid.
21. Ibid.
22. Ibid.
23. Ibid.
24. Naomi Jacob, *Me in War Time*, Hutchinson, London, 1940, p. 131.
25. Naomi Jacob, *A Chronicle About Other People*, Hutchinson, London, 1933, p. 59.
26. RH to ES, 12 August 1934.
27. UVT, Diaries, 17 September 1934.
28. Ibid., 11 September 1934.
29. Ibid., 17 December 1934.
30. Ibid., 17 January 1935.
31. UVT, Day Book, December [undated] 1934.
32. News first received 16 March 1934. An Italian translation of *The Master of the House* was agreed on 30 October.
33. UVT, Rye and Covent Garden Daybook, 10, 11, 16 August 1934.
34. RH, *Emblem Hurlstone*, unpublished novel, 1934.
35. UVT, Diaries, 5 September 1934.
36. UVT, Rye and Covent Garden Day Book, 3 November 1934.
37. Audrie Atcheson, op. cit. Several conversations between Audrie Atcheson and the author.
38. ES, op. cit.
39. RH to ES, 29 August 1934.
40. RH to ES, Letter no. 149, from Talbot House, London, 12 April 1935.
41. Destruction of flat occurred 21 June 1936. See also UVT, Day Book, 22 June 1936.
42. RH to ES, 29 August 1934.

43. RH to ES, Letter no. 115, 30 December 1934.
44. RH to ES, Letter no. 194, from Beauvallon, 7 June 1935.
45. Author's interview with Ariadne Nicolaeff, 20 January 1996.
46. Ibid.
47. *Life and Death*, p. 116.
48. Author's interview with Ariadne Nicolaeff, 20 January 1996.
49. ES, op. cit.
50. Author's interview with Ariadne Nicolaeff, 20 January 1996, and later conversations. Similar views were expressed by Professor R. Smith and Iris Furlong in conversations with the author, January 1996.
51. UVT, Diaries, 19 December 1934 and 12 February 1935.
52. *Life and Death*, p. 116.
53. RH to ES, 1 December 1934.
54. RH to ES, 5, 10 December 1934.
55. RH to ES, Letter no. 156 from Forecastle, Rye, Easter Sunday 1935.
56. RH to ES, from Forecastle, Rye, 26 April 1935.
57. RH to ES, Letter no. 182, from Beauvallon, Ascension Day, 30 May 1935.
58. RH to ES, 28 October 1935.
59. RH, *The Sixth Beatitude*, 1959, p. 36.
60. Ibid., p. 37.
61. UVT, Diaries, 22–30 September 1934.
62. UVT, Rye and Covent Garden Day Book, 10 October 1934.
63. UVT to ES, 19 October 1934.
64. UVT, Day Book, 17 January 1935.
65. Ibid., 18 January 1935.
66. Ibid., 19 January 1935.
67. Ibid., 21 January 1935.
68. UVT, Rye and Covent Garden Day Book, 21 January 1935.
69. UVT, Diaries, 12 February 1935.
70. Ibid., 1 February 1935.
71. RH to ES, 4 December 1934.
72. ES, op. cit.
73. RH to ES, 13 August 1934.
74. Ibid.
75. *The Well of Loneliness*, 1982, p. 432.
76. UVT, Rye and Covent Garden Day Book, 13 October 1934.
77. RH to ES, 23 November 1934.
78. ES, op. cit.
79. UVT, Diaries, 8 February 1935.
80. ES, op. cit.
81. UVT, Rye and Covent Garden Day Book, 9 November 1935.
82. Ibid., 13 November 1935.
83. Una also noted that by June 1934 sales of *Miss Ogilvy* were 4,700.
84. RH to ES, Letter no. 111, 26 December 1934.
85. RH to ES, 17 October 1935.
86. UVT, Rye and Covent Garden Book, 8 February 1935.
87. ES, op. cit.
88. Ibid.

21: SICKNESS, DEATH AND BEYOND

1. In the University of Texas Research Library where the Book of Letters is housed, Pat Fox, the librarian who catalogued and filed them, told me: 'When I first read the Letters I felt like an intruder. They are so private, so raw.'

2. ES, autobiographical MSS. Slater/Still.

3. RH to ES, 23 July 1937.

4. ES, op. cit.

5. RH to ES, 24 July 1937.

6. *The Sixth Beatitude*, 1959, p. 59.

7. June 1937. Lease to run from August 1937.

8. RH to ES, 28 June 1938.

9. RH to ES, 23 July 1937.

10. ES, op. cit.

11. UVT, Day Book, 3 July 1937.

12. RH to ES, from Florence, 23 June 1938.

13. RH to ES, 16 July 1937.

14. RH to ES, 1 August 1937. I have omitted some items from the list.

15. RH to ES, 18 September 1938.

16. ES, op. cit.

17. RH to ES, from Florence, undated [winter 1938].

18. ES, op. cit.

19. RH to ES, 1 February 1939.

20. Ibid.

21. RH to ES, 16 July 1937.

22. RH to ES, 18 July 1937.

23. ES, op. cit.

24. RH to ES, 18 and 25 July 1937.

25. RH to ES, 19 July 1937, concerning Andrea's visit the previous day.

26. RH to ES, 25 July 1937.

27. Information from Neil Somerville, Senior Document Assistant, BBC Information and Archives. Correspondence with author, September 1996.

28. 'SHE'S on the AIR' by Georgian, in *Woman's Journal*, March 1943, copyright of the *Author/Speaker Newspaper*, BBC.

29. RH to ES, 25 July 1937.

30. RH to ES, 30 July 1937.

31. ES, op. cit.

32. Ibid.

33. RH to ES, 18 August 1937.

34. RH to ES, from Rye, 25 August 1937.

35. RH to ES, 5 February 1939.

36. 10 November 1937.

37. RH to ES, 5 January 1938, Souline's birthday. Lame dog letter accompanied by bouquet of flowers. Also undated February 1938. Texas.

38. UVT, Diaries, 13 November 1934.

39. ES, op. cit. Also information based on conversations with Ariadne Nicolaeff.

40. June 1938. ES, op. cit.

41. RH to ES, 16 June 1938.

42. RH to ES, 4 June 1938.

43. 13 June 1938.

44. RH to ES, 26 June 1938.

45. RH to ES, 4 and 16 June 1938.

46. RH to ES, 21 June 1938.

47. RH to ES, 29 June 1938.

48. *The Sixth Beatitude*, 1959, p. 76.

49. Ibid., p. 82.

50. RH to ES, from Rye, 12 August 1938.

51. RH to ES, 16 December 1938.

52. RH to ES, 16 June 1938 (and repeated many times).

53. RH to ES, 3 March 1939.
54. RH to ES, 16 December 1938.
55. RH to ES, 5 February 1939.
56. ES to RH, 7 June 1939, her only extant letter to RH. Texas.
57. Ibid.
58. UVT, Day Book, 4 March 1935.
59. RH to ES, 7 August 1938.
60. RH to ES, 10 September 1938.
61. RH to ES, 18 September 1938.
62. RH to ES, 13 September 1938.
63. RH to ES, 14 September 1938.
64. RH to ES, 23 September 1938.
65. RH to ES, from Viareggio, 9 February 1939.
66. ES, op. cit.
67. RH to ES, 16 September 1938.
68. RH to ES, 21 September 1938.
69. Ibid.
70. ES, op. cit.
71. RH to ES, 2 August 1938.
72. Naomi Jacob, *Me in War Time*, Hutchinson, London, 1940.
73. RH to ES, 22 March 1939.
74. Virginia Woolf to Ethel Smyth, 2 August 1930. Nigel Nicolson and Joanna Trautmann (eds.), *Letters*, vol. 4, no. 2215, p. 195.
75. RH to ES, 20 December 1942.
76. Ibid.
77. RH to ES, 3 March 1939.
78. Ibid.
79. Ibid.
80. RH to ES, 1 June 1939.
81. RH to ES, from Imperial Hotel, Lynton, 14 April 1940.
82. RH to ES, 25 April 1940.
83. Ibid.
84. RH to ES, 29 April 1940.
85. RH to ES, 22 August 1941.
86. Vet's message relayed in letter from RH to ES, 25 August 1941.
87. RH to ES, 22 August 1941.
88. RH to ES, from Francis Hotel, Bath, 26 August 1941.
89. Ibid.
90. RH to ES, 7 September 1941, in Una's handwriting.
91. RH to ES, 5 September 1941, in Una's handwriting.
92. RH to ES, 11 September 1941, in Una's handwriting.
93. RH to ES, 28 September 1941, in Una's handwriting.
94. Ibid.
95. RH to ES, 7 October 1941, in Una's handwriting.
96. RH to ES, 21 October 1941.
97. RH to ES, 7 November 1941.
98. RH to ES, from The Wayside, Lynton, 19 November 1941.
99. RH to ES, 26 November 1941.
100. RH to ES, 12 December 1941.
101. RH to ES, from Francis Hotel, Bath, 3 December 1941.
102. RH to ES, 16 November 1941.
103. RH to ES, 12 December 1941.
104. RH to ES, 26 December 1941.
105. Ibid.

106. RH to ES, 29 December 1941.

107. RH to ES, 7 March 1942.

108. ES, op. cit.

109. UVT to ES, 6 April 1942. Ottawa.

110. RH to ES, 12 August 1942.

111. RH to ES, 2 August 1942.

112. RH to ES, 25 November 1942.

113. Thomas Campbell (1777–1844), 'Lochiel's Warning'.

114. 'The Quest of the White Heather' in Marguerite Radclyffe-Hall, *A Sheaf of Verses*, 1985, pp. 18, 19, 20.

115. RH to ES, 24 December 1942.

116. RH to ES, 26 December 1942.

117. See Michael Baker, *Our Three Selves*, pp. 338–9.

118. UVT, Day Book, 1 September 1943. Account written up after the events.

119. *The Sixth Beatitude*, 1959, p. 16.

120. UVT, Day Book, 1 September 1943.

121. RH to ES, 23 June 1938.

122. RH to ES, 9 February 1939.

123. UVT, Day Book, 2 October 1943.

124. Ariadne Nicolaeff, 'The Love Letters of John Radclyffe Hall to Evguenia Souline', unpublished article.

125. *Life and Death*, p. 190.

126. UVT, Day Book, 6 October 1943.

127. Una believed that 'My Beloved went straight to God and saw the Beatific Vision.' UVT, Day Book, 7 October 1943.

128. 'Little Gidding' in T.S. Eliot, *Collected Poems 1909–1962*, Faber & Faber, 1963, p. 221.

22: AFTER WORDS

1. Naomi Jacob, *Me and the Swans*, p. 128.

2. ES, autobiographical MSS, first and second drafts.

3. *The Times*, Monday 11 October 1943.

4. *Daily Telegraph*, 11 October 1943.

5. Elizabeth Barrett Browning, 'Sonnets from the Portuguese'.

6. Notice of Requiem Mass in *The Times*, 18 October 1943.

7. UVT, Letters to John, 1944. Ottawa. Cited in Richard Ormrod, *Una Troubridge*, p. 287.

8. In the fifties Naomi Jacob held a similar position to that of the journalist and broadcaster Nancy Spain in media portrayals.

9. *Arena Three*, 3 (4), April/May 1965.

10. *Arena Three*, 4 (9), September 1967.

11. UVT, Letters to John, 7 September 1944.

12. Ormrod, op. cit., p. 291.

13. UVT to Naomi Jacob. 25 November 1961. Cited in Michael Baker, *Our Three Selves*.

14. Article by Andrea Troubridge, and editor's notes on contributor, in *The Writer*, vol. 12, no. 1, July 1953, pp. 32, 33.

15. *The Author/Speaker Newspaper*, written and edited by BBC staff, 22 January 1944.

16. Ormrod, op. cit., p. 315.

17. *The Writer*, op. cit., p. 33.

18. Jacqueline Hope-Nicholson, cited in Ormrod, op. cit., p. 292.

19. UVT, Letters to John. Cited in Ormrod, op. cit., p. 283.

20. UVT, Letters to John. Ibid., p. 274.

21. Author's interview with Ariadne Nicolaeff, January 1996, and subsequent correspondence.

22. Author's interview with Professor R. Smith, January 1996.

23. UVT, Letters to John. Cited in Ormrod, op. cit., p. 298.

24. ES to UVT, 6 October 1950. Rome.

25. UVT, Letters to John, 16 January 1944.

26. Ibid., 27 January 1944.

27. Ormrod, op. cit., pp. 280, 281.

28. Ariadne Nicolaeff, 'The Love Letters of John Radclyffe Hall to Evguenia Souline', unpublished article.

29. ES to Mr Wilenkin, from 227 Sussex Gardens, W2, 27 September and 5 November 1957. Iris Furlong Collection.

30. Ibid., 30 August 1957.

31. Ibid., 25 November 1957.

32. Ibid., 26 November 1957.

33. Ibid., 27 January 1958.

BIBLIOGRAPHY

The place of publication is London unless otherwise stated.

A. WORKS BY RADCLYFFE HALL

Published works

Poetry
'Twixt Earth and Stars, Bumpus, 1906.
A Sheaf of Verses, Bumpus, 1908; Gaby Goldscheider, Windsor, 1985.
Poems of the Past and Present, Chapman & Hall, 1910.
Songs of Three Counties and Other Poems, Chapman & Hall, 1913.
The Forgotten Island, Chapman & Hall, 1915.
Rhymes and Rhythms. Rime et Ritmi, Orsa maggiore, Milano, 1948.

Novels and Short Stories
The Forge, Arrowsmith, 1924.
The Unlit Lamp, Cassell, 1924; Virago, 1981.
A Saturday Life, Arrowsmith, 1925; Virago, 1987.
Adam's Breed, Cassell, 1926; Virago, 1985.
The Well of Loneliness, Jonathan Cape, 1928; Virago, 1982.
The Master of the House, Jonathan Cape, 1932; Falcon Press, 1952.
Miss Ogilvy Finds Herself, William Heinemann, 1934.
The Sixth Beatitude, William Heinemann, 1936; Hammond, Hammond, 1959.

Unpublished works

The following are to be found in the Ottawa and Rome Collections:
Michael West
'The Woman in a Crêpe Bonnet'
'Paul Collett'
'The Career of Mark Anthony Brakes'
'Malise'
The World
Emblem Hurlstone
Autobiographical sketches and essays

Books

Baker, Michael, *Our Three Selves: A Life of Radclyffe Hall*, Hamish Hamilton, 1985; GMP
  Publishers, 1985.
Brittain, Vera, *Radclyffe Hall: A Case of Obscenity?*, A.S. Barnes, New York, 1968.
Castle, Terry, *Noël Coward and Radclyffe Hall: Kindred Spirits*, Columbia University Press, New
  York, 1996.
Dickson, Lovat, *Radclyffe Hall at the Well of Loneliness: A Sapphic Chronicle*, Collins, 1975.
Franks, Claudia Stillman, *Beyond the Well of Loneliness: The Fiction of Radclyffe Hall*, Avebury
  Publishing Company, England, 1982.
Glasgow, Joanne, *Your John*, New York University Press, New York, 1997.
Ormrod, Richard, *Una Troubridge: The Friend of Radclyffe Hall*, Jonathan Cape, 1984.
O'Rourke, Rebecca, *Reflecting on The Well of Loneliness*, Routledge, London and New York,
  1989.
Troubridge, Una Lady, *The Life and Death of Radclyffe Hall*, Hammond, Hammond, 1961.

Archive Material

Harry Ransom Humanities Research Center, University of Texas, Austin.
Lovat Dickson Collection, National Archives of Canada, Ottawa.
Alessandro Rossi-Lemeni (Rome Collection).
Cara Lancaster Papers, London.
Iris Furlong Papers, London.
Ariadne Nicolaeff Papers, Suffolk.
Joan Slater/Monica Still (Research Material).
Audrie Atcheson Papers, Warwickshire.
Lesbian Herstory Educational Foundation, New York (Munson Letter).
Society for Psychical Research, London (Psychic Records).

Books

Abbott, Sidney, and Love, Barbara, *Sappho Was a Right-on Woman: a Liberated View of
  Lesbianism*, Stein & Day, New York, 1974.
Abel, Elizabeth (ed.), *Writing and Sexual Difference*, University of Chicago Press, Chicago, 1982.
Allen, Mary Sophia, *The Pioneer Policewoman*, Chatto & Windus, 1925.
Atkinson, Diane, *Suffragettes in the Purple, White and Green: London 1906–14*, Museum of
  London, 1992.
Barnes, Djuna, *Nightwood*, Faber, 1936; New Directions, New York, 1961.
——*Ladies Almanack* (1928), Dalkey Archive Press, Illinois, USA, 1992.
Beauman, Nicola, *A Very Great Profession: The Woman's Novel 1914–39*, Virago, 1995.
Bell, Anne Olivier (ed.), *The Diary of Virginia Woolf*, Volume III: *1925–1930*, The Hogarth
  Press, 1980.
Benstock, Shari, *Women of the Left Bank: Paris, 1900–1940*, Virago, 1987.
Berg, A. Scott, *Max Perkins: Editor of Genius*, Pocket Books, New York, 1975.
Berry, Paul and Bostridge, Mark, *Vera Brittain: A Life*, Chatto & Windus, 1995.
Blain, Virginia, Clements, Patricia and Grundy, Isobel (eds.), *The Feminist Companion to
  Literature in English: Women Writers from the Middle Ages to the Present*, Batsford, 1990.
Boll, T.E.M., *Miss May Sinclair, Novelist: A Biography and Critical Introduction*, Associated
  University Presses, New Jersey, USA, 1973.
Brittain, Vera, *Testament of Friendship*, Virago, 1980.
Brunt, R. and Coward, R. (eds.), *Feminism, Culture and Politics*, Lawrence & Wishart, 1982.

Caplan, Pat (ed.), *The Cultural Construction of Sexuality*, Routledge, London and New York, 1989.

Carpenter, Edward, *The Intermediate Sex*, George Allen & Unwin, 1908.

Chalon, Jean, *Portrait of a Seductress: The World of Natalie Barney*, trans. C. Barko, Crown, New York, 1979.

Cline, Sally, *Just Desserts: Women and Food*, André Deutsch, 1990.

——*Women, Celibacy and Passion*, André Deutsch, 1993.

——*Lifting the Taboo: Women, Death and Dying*, Little, Brown, 1995.

——and Spender, Dale, *Reflecting Men at Twice Their Natural Size*, André Deutsch, 1987.

Collis, Louise, *Impetuous Heart: The Story of Ethel Smyth*, William Kimber, 1984.

Collis, Rose, *Portraits to the Wall: Historic Lesbian Lives Unveiled*, Cassell, 1994.

Coveney, L., Jackson, M., Jeffreys, S., Kay, L. and Mahoney, P., *The Sexuality Papers: Male Sexuality and the Social Control of Women*, Hutchinson, London and Dover, New Hampshire, in association with the Explorations in Feminism Collective, 1984.

Cruikshank, Margaret, *Lesbian Studies: Present and Future*, Feminist Press, New York, 1982.

Dane, Clemence, *A Regiment of Women*, Virago, 1995.

de Lauretis, Teresa, *The Practice of Love: Lesbian Sexuality and Perverse Desire*, Indiana University Press, Bloomington and Indianopolis, 1994.

DeSalvo, Louise, *Virginia Woolf: The Impact of Childhood Sexual Abuse on her Life and Work*, Women's Press, 1989.

——and Leaska, Mitchell A. (eds.), *Letters of Vita to Virginia*, Hutchinson, 1985.

Donoghue, Emma, *Passions Between Women: British Lesbian Culture 1668–1801*, Scarlet Press, 1993.

Douglas-Home, Jessica, *Violet: The Life and Loves of Violet Gordon Woodhouse*, Harvill Press, 1996.

Duberman, Martin Bauml, Vicinus, Martha and Chauncey, George Jr (eds.), *Hidden from History: Reclaiming the Gay and Lesbian Past*, Penguin, Harmondsworth, 1991.

Dunn, Jane, *A Very Close Conspiracy: Vanessa Bell and Virginia Woolf*, Jonathan Cape, 1990.

Ellis, Havelock, *Psychology of Sex*, Long & Smith, New York, 1933; William Heinemann, 1944.

Ellmann, Richard, *Oscar Wilde*, Hamish Hamilton, 1987; Knopf, New York, 1988.

Ettore, E.M., *Lesbians, Women and Society*, Routledge & Kegan Paul, 1980.

Faderman, Lillian, *Surpassing the Love of Men: Romantic Friendship and Love Between Women from the Renaissance to the Present*, Junction Books, 1980.

——*Odd Girls and Twilight Lovers: A History of Lesbian Life in Twentieth-Century America*, Penguin, Harmondsworth, 1992.

Feminist Review (ed.), *Sexuality: A Reader*, Virago, 1987.

Field, Andrew, *The Life and Times of Djuna Barnes*, Putnam, New York, 1983.

Finlayson, Iain, *Writers in Romney Marsh*, Severn House, 1986.

Fitzgerald, Penelope, *Charlotte Mew and Her Friends*, Collins, 1984.

Foster, Jeannette Howard, *Sex Variant Women in Literature*, Naiad Press, Florida.

Foucault, Michel, *The History of Sexuality*, trans. Robert Hurley, Vintage, New York, 1978.

Freedman, Estelle B., Gelpi, Barbara C., Johnson, Susan L. and Weston, Kathleen M. (eds.), *The Lesbian Issue: Essays from Signs*, University of Chicago Press, Chicago, 1985.

Furbank, P.N., *E.M. Forster – A Life*, Oxford University Press, Oxford, 1979.

Gibbs, Liz (ed.), *Daring to Dissent: Lesbian Culture from Margin to Mainstream*, Cassell, 1994.

Gilbert, Sandra M. and Gubar, Susan, *No Man's Land: The Place of the Woman Writer in the Twentieth Century*, Volume 1: *The War of the Words*, Yale University Press, New Haven and London, 1988.

——*No Man's Land: The Place of the Woman Writer in the Twentieth Century*, Volume 2: *Sexchanges*, Yale University Press, New Haven and London, 1993.

Gill, Brendan, *Tallulah*, Holt, Rinehart & Winston, New York, 1972.

Glendinning, Victoria, *Vita: The Life of Vita Sackville-West*, Penguin, Harmondsworth, 1984.

Goldring, Douglas, *South Lodge: Reminiscences of Violet Hunt, Ford Madox Ford and the English Review Circle*, Constable, 1943.

——*Life Interests*, Macdonald, 1948.

Grier, Barbara, *The Lesbian in Literature*, Naiad Press, Florida.

Griffin, Gabriele, *Heavenly Love? Lesbian Images in Twentieth-Century Women's Writing*, Manchester University Press, Manchester and New York, 1994.

——(ed.), *Outwrite: Lesbianism and Popular Culture*, Pluto Press, London and Colorado, 1993.

Grosskurth, Phyllis, *Havelock Ellis: A Biography*, Allen Lane, 1980.

Hamer, Diane and Budge, Belinda (eds.), *The Good, the Bad and the Gorgeous: Popular Culture's Romance with Lesbianism*, Pandora, 1994.

Hamer, Emily, *Britannia's Glory: A History of Twentieth-Century Lesbians*, Cassell, 1996.

Hanscombe, Gillian and Smyers, Virginia L., *Writing for their Lives: The Modernist Women, 1910–1940*, Women's Press, 1987.

Hardwick, Joan, *An Immodest Violet: The Life of Violet Hunt*, André Deutsch, 1990.

Herman, Judith Lewis and Hirschman, Lisa, *Father-Daughter Incest*, Harvard University Press, Cambridge, Massachusetts, 1981.

Higgins, Patrick (ed.), *A Queer Reader*, Fourth Estate, 1994.

Hoagland, Sara Lucia, *Lesbian Ethics: Toward New Value*, Institute of Lesbian Studies, California, 1988.

——and Penelope, Julia (eds.), *For Lesbians Only: A Separatist Anthology*, Onlywomen Press, 1988.

Humm, Maggie, *The Dictionary of Feminist Theory*, Harvester Wheatsheaf, London and New York, 1989.

Hunt, Violet, *The Maiden's Progress: A Novel in Dialogue*, Osgoode, McIlvaine & Co., 1894.

——*Affairs of the Heart*, Freemantle, 1900.

——*The Celebrity at Home*, Chapman & Hall, 1904.

——*Sooner or Later: The Story of an Ingenious Ingenue*, Chapman & Hall, 1904.

——*The Workaday Woman*, T. Werner Laurie, 1906.

——*Tales of the Uneasy*, Heinemann, 1911.

——*The Desirable Alien*, Chatto & Windus, 1913.

——*The Celebrity's Daughter*, Stanley Paul, 1913.

——*The House of Many Mirrors*, Stanley Paul, 1915.

——*Their Lives*, Stanley Paul, 1916.

——*Their Hearts*, Stanley Paul, 1921.

——*More Tales of the Uneasy*, Heinemann, 1925.

——*The Flurried Years*, Hurst & Blackett, 1926.

Irwin, Margaret, *Still She Wished for Company*, Heinemann, 1924.

Isherwood, Christopher, *Goodbye to Berlin*, Penguin, Harmondsworth, 1939.

Jacob, Naomi, *Me and the Swans*, William Kimber, 1963.

——*The Heart of the House*, Book Club.

——*Second Harvest*, Hutchinson.

James, Henry, *The Bostonians*, Penguin, Harmondsworth, 1984.

Jay, Karla, *The Amazon and the Page: Natalie Clifford Barney and Renée Vivien*, Indiana University Press, Bloomington and Indianapolis, 1980.

——and Glasgow, Joanne (eds.), *Lesbian Texts and Contexts: Radical Revisions*, Onlywomen Press, 1992.

Jeffreys, Sheila, *The Spinster and her Enemies: Feminism and Sexuality 1880–1930*, Pandora Press, 1985.

——*Anticlimax: A Feminist Perspective on the Sexual Revolution*, Women's Press, 1990.

——*The Lesbian Heresy: A Feminist Perspective on the Lesbian Sexual Revolution*, Women's Press, 1994.

Judd, Alan, *Ford Madox Ford*, Collins, 1990.

Julian, Philippe and Phillips, John, *The Other Woman: The Life of Violet Trefusis*, Houghton Mifflin, Boston, 1976.

Kaye-Smith, Sheila, *Joanna Godden*, Virago, 1983.

——*All the Books of My Life*, Cassell, 1956.

Kenyon, Olga, *800 Years of Women's Letters*, Alan Sutton, Stroud, UK, 1995.

King, James, *Virginia Woolf*, Hamish Hamilton, 1994.

Klaich, Dolores, *Woman Plus Woman*, Naiad Press, USA, 1989.

Lauritsen, John and Thorstad, David, *The Early Homosexual Rights Movement (1864–1935)*, Times Change Press, New York.

Lawrence, Margaret, *The School of Feminity*, Frederick A. Stokes Company, New York, 1936.

Lee, Hermione, *Virginia Woolf*, Chatto & Windus, 1996.

Lehmann, Rosamond, *Dusty Answer*, Flamingo, 1996.

Linklater, Andro, *Compton Mackenzie: A Life*, Chatto & Windus, 1987.

Longford, Elizabeth, *A Pilgrimage of Passion: The Life of Wilfrid Scawen Blunt*, Weidenfeld & Nicolson, 1979.

Ludwig, Richard M. (ed.), *Letters of Ford Madox Ford*, Princeton University Press, New Jersey, 1965.

Mackenzie, Compton, *Extraordinary Women: Theme and Variations*, Martin Secker, 1928.

——*My Life and Times*, Chatto & Windus, 1965.

Mannin, Ethel, *Confessions and Impressions*, Hutchinson & Co., 1930.

——*Young in the Twenties: A Chapter of Autobiography*, Hutchinson & Co., 1971.

Mansfield, Katherine, *In a German Pension*, Penguin, Harmondsworth, 1964.

——*Bliss and Other Stories*, Penguin, Harmondsworth, 1964.

Marcus, Jane, *Virginia Woolf and the Languages of Patriarchy*, Indiana University Press, Bloomington and Indianapolis, 1987.

——(ed.), *New Feminist Essays on Virginia Woolf*, Macmillan, 1981.

——(ed.), *The Young Rebecca: Writings of Rebecca West 1911–17*, Virago, 1983.

Martin, Del and Lyon, Phyllis, *Lesbian/Woman*, Bantam Books, New York, 1972.

Melville, Joy, *Ellen and Edy*, Pandora, 1987.

Miles, Rosalind, *The Fiction of Sex: Themes and Functions of Sex Differences in the Modern Novel*, Vision Press, 1971.

Miller, Alice, *Thou Shalt Not Be Aware: Society's Betrayal of the Child*, Pluto Press, 1986.

Mizener, Arthur, *The Saddest Story: A Biography of Ford Madox Ford*, Bodley Head, 1971.

Mulford, Wendy, *This Narrow Place: Sylvia Townsend Warner and Valentine Ackland*, Pandora Press, 1988.

Myron, Nancy and Bunch, Charlotte (eds.), *Lesbianism and the Women's Movement*, Diana Press, Baltimore, 1975.

Nestle, Joan, *A Restricted Country: Essays and Short Stories*, Sheba Feminist Publishers, 1988.

——(ed.), *The Persistent Desire: A Femme–Butch Reader*, Alyson Publications, Boston, USA, 1992.

Nicolson, Nigel (ed.), *The Letters of Virginia Woolf*, Volume III: *A Change of Perspective, 1923–1928*, Hogarth Press, 1977.

——*The Letters of Virginia Woolf*, Volume IV: *A Reflection of the Other Person, 1929–1931*, Hogarth Press, 1978.

Ortner, Sherry B. and Whitehead, Harriet (eds.), *Sexual Meanings: The Cultural Construction of Gender and Sexuality*, Cambridge University Press, Cambridge, 1988.

Palmer, Paulina, *Contemporary Lesbian Writing: Dreams, Desire, Difference*, Open University Press, Buckingham, 1993.

Pankhurst, Sylvia, *The Suffragette Movement*, (1931), Virago, 1977.

Patmore, Derek (ed.), *My Friends When Young: The Memoirs of Brigit Patmore*, William Heinemann, 1968.

Penelope, Julia, *Call me Lesbian: Lesbian Lives, Lesbian Theory*, The Crossing Press, Freedom, USA, 1992.

Presence, Peter (ed.), *The Book of Key Facts*, Paddington Press, New York and London, 1978.

Raitt, Suzanne, *Vita and Virginia: The Work and Friendship of V. Sackville-West and Virginia Woolf*, Oxford University Press, Oxford, 1993.

Reynolds, Margaret (ed.), *The Penguin Book of Lesbian Short Stories*, Viking, 1993.

Rich, Adrienne, *Compulsory Heterosexuality and Lesbian Existence*, Onlywomen Press, 1981.

Rose, Phyllis, *Writing of Women: Essays in a Renaissance*, Wesleyan University Press, Connecticut, 1985.

——*A Woman of Letters: A Life of Virginia Woolf*, Pandora, 1986.

Rothblum, Esther D. and Brehony, Kathleen A. (eds.), *Boston Marriages: Romantic but Asexual Relationships among Contemporary Lesbians*, University of Massachusetts Press, Amherst, USA, 1993.

Rule, Jane, *Lesbian Images*, Peter Davies, 1976.

Rush, Florence, *The Best-Kept Secret: Sexual Abuse of Children*, McGraw-Hill, New York, 1980.

Russell, Diana E.H., *The Secret Trauma: Incest in the Lives of Girls and Women*, Basic Books, New York, 1986.

Sarah, Elizabeth (ed.), *Reassessments of 'First Wave' Feminism*, Pergamon Press, Oxford, 1983.

Schur, E.M., *Labelling Women Deviant: Gender, Stigma, and Social Control*, Random House, New York, 1984.

Scott, Bonnie Kime, *Refiguring Modernism*, Volume 1: *The Women of 1928*, Indiana University Press, Bloomington and Indianapolis, 1995.

——*Refiguring Modernism*, Volume 2: *Postmodern Feminist Readings of Woolf, West, and Barnes*, Indiana University Press, Bloomington and Indianaopolis, 1995.

——(ed.), *The Gender of Modernism*, Indiana University Press, Bloomington and Indianapolis, 1990.

Secrest, Meryle, *Between Me and Life: A Biography of Romaine Brooks*, Macdonald & Jane's, 1976.

Sinclair, May, *The Three Brontës*, Hutchinson & Co., 1911.

——*The Three Sisters*, Hutchinson, 1914; Macmillan, New York, 1914.

——*The Life and Death of Harriett Frean*, Virago, 1980.

——*Mary Olivier: A Life*, Virago, 1980.

Sladen, Douglas, *Twenty Years of My Life*, Constable, 1915.

Snitow, Ann, Stansell, Christine and Thompson, Sharon (eds.), *Desire: The Politics of Sexuality*, Virago, 1984.

Spencer, Colin, *Homosexuality: A History*, Fourth Estate, 1995.

St John, Christopher, *Ethel Smyth: A Biography*, Longmans, Green, 1959.

Strachey, Ray, *The Cause: A Short History of the Women's Movement in Great Britain*, Virago, 1979.

Sturtevant, Katherine, *Our Sisters' London: Feminist Walking Tours*, Chicago Review Press, Chicago, 1990.

Sullivan, Andrew, *Virtually Normal*, Picador, 1995.

Summers, Claude J. (ed.), *The Gay and Lesbian Literary Heritage: A Reader's Companion to the Writers and their Works, from Antiquity to the Present*, Henry Holt, New York, 1995.

Tsuzuki, Chushichi, *Edward Carpenter 1844–1929: Prophet of Human Fellowship*, Cambridge University Press, Cambridge, 1980.

Turnbull, Andrew, *Scott Fitzgerald: A Biography*, Bodley Head, 1962.

Vance, Carole S. (ed.), *Pleasure and Danger: Exploring Female Sexuality*, Routledge & Kegan Paul, Boston, USA, 1984.

von Arnim, Elizabeth, *Elizabeth and her German Garden*, Virago, 1995.

Warner, Sylvia Townsend, *Lolly Willowes*, Chatto & Windus, 1926.

Weeks, Jeffrey, *Coming Out: Homosexual Politics in Britain, from the Nineteenth Century to the Present*, Quartet Books, 1977.

——*Sexuality and its Discontents: Meanings, Myths and Modern Sexualities*, Routledge & Kegan Paul, 1989.

Weldon, Fay, *Rebecca West*, Penguin, Harmondsworth, 1985.

West, Rebecca, *The Meaning of Treason*, Reprint Society, 1952.

——*Rebecca West: A Celebration (selected from her writings by her publishers with her help)*, Penguin, Harmondsworth, 1979.

——*Harriet Hume: A London Fantasy*, Virago, 1980.

——*The Judge*, Virago, 1980.

Wickes, George, *Americans in Paris*, Doubleday, Garden City, USA, 1969.
——*The Amazon of Letters: The Life and Loves of Natalie Barney*, G.P. Putnam's Sons, New York, 1976.
Wolf, Naomi, *The Beauty Myth*, Vintage, 1991.
Wolfe, Susan J. and Penelope, Julia, *Sexual Practice/Textual Theory: Lesbian Cultural Criticism*, Blackwell, Cambridge, Massachusetts, and Oxford, 1993.
Woolf, Leonard (ed.), *A Writer's Diary, Being Extracts from the Diary of Virginia Woolf*, Hogarth Press, 1975; Triad, Panther, 1978.
Woolf, Virginia, *Orlando*, Panther, 1977.
——*A Room of One's Own*, Hogarth Press, 1929; Panther, 1977; Oxford University Press, Oxford, 1992.
Wylie, I.A.R., *Daughter of Brahma*, 1912.
——*Towards Morning*, 1918.
——*Home are the Hunted*, Cassell, 1959.
Zegger, Hrisey Dimitrakis, *May Sinclair*, Twayne Publishers, G.K. Hall & Co., Boston, 1976.

Articles, journals, magazines, pamphlets

DeSalvo, Louise A., 'Lighting the Cave: The Relationship between Vita Sackville-West and Virginia Woolf', *Signs: Journal of Women in Culture and Society*, 8:2, 195–214, Autumn 1982.
Feminist Review, 35, Summer 1990.
Feminist Studies (Lesbian Special Issue), 18:3, Spring 1992.
Gossip, A Journal of Lesbian Feminist Ethics, 1, 1986.
Gossip, A Journal of Lesbian Feminist Ethics, 2, 1986.
Gossip, A Journal of Lesbian Feminist Ethics, 5, 1987
Gossip, A Journal of Lesbian Feminist Ethics, 6, 1987.
Granta 41 (Biography), Autumn 1992.
Grindea, Miron, 'Natalie Clifford Barney: an Ornament of Parisian Literary Life' (obituary), *The Times*, 4 February 1972.
Hall, Marny, Kitzinger, Celia, Loulan, JoAnn and Perkins, Rachel, 'Lesbian Psychology, Lesbian Politics', *Feminism and Psychology* (SAGE, London, Newbury Park and New Delhi), 2:1, 1992.
Hecate: A Women's Interdisciplinary Journal, X:2, 1984.
Hunt, Violet, unpublished diaries, Cornell University, USA.
Ingram, Angela, '"Unutterable Putrefaction" and "Foul Stuff": Two "Obscene" Novels of the 1920s', *Women's Studies International Forum*, 9:4, 341–54, 1986.
Jay, Karla, 'The Disciples of the Tenth Muse: Natalie Clifford Barney and Renée Vivien', dissertation, University of New York, 1984.
Jones, Parry, 'Agnes Nicholls (Lady Harty), 1877–1959: An Appreciation', *Opera*, 10:11, November 1959.
Laver, James, 'Gabrielle Enthoven and the Enthoven Theatre Collection', in *Studies in English Theatre History. In Memory of Gabrielle Enthoven, O.B.E., First President of the Society for Theatre Research, 1948–1950*, printed for the Society of Theatre Research, London, 1952.
'Love Your Enemy, the Debate between Heterosexual Feminism and Political Lesbianism', collection of letters and papers, Onlywomen Press, April 1981.
Newton, Esther: 'The Mythic Mannish Lesbian: Radclyffe Hall and the New Woman', *Signs: Journal of Women in Culture and Society*, 9:4, 557–75, 1984.
Nixon, Elizabeth, 'Some Significant Women Novelists of the Twentieth Century', *The Englishwoman*, XXXVI, 137–51, 1917.
Rolley, Katrina, 'Cutting a Dash: The Dress of Radclyffe Hall and Una Troubridge', *Feminist Review* 35, Summer 1994.
Rothblum, Esther D., 'Transforming Lesbian Sexuality', unpublished article.
Schneider, M., 'Sappho was a Right-on Adolescent: Growing up Lesbian', *Journal of Homosexuality*, 17, 111–30, 1989.

Secor, Robert and Secor, Marie, 'Lives and Hearts in Pre-Raphaelite England: The Autobiographical Novels of Violet Hunt', *Pre-Raphaelite Review*, 59–70, May 1979.

——'The Return of the Good Soldier: Ford Madox Ford and Violet Hunt's 1917 Diary', *English Literary Studies*, 30, University of Victoria Press, 1983.

Silber, L., 'Negotiating Sexual Identity: Non-Lesbians in a Lesbian Feminist Community', research note, *Journal of Sex Research*, 17, 131–40, 1990.

Sinclair, May, 'The Novels of Violet Hunt', *English Review*, 118, February 1922.

Stanley, Liz, 'Romantic Friendship? Some Issues in Researching History and Biography', *Women's History Review*, 1:2, 1992.

Vetere, V.A., 'The Role of Friendship in the Development and Maintenance of Lesbian Love Relationships', *Journal of Homosexuality*, 8, 51–65, 1982.

Wekker, G., 'Mati-ism and Black Lesbianism: Two Idealtypical Expressions of Female Homosexuality in Black Communities of the Diaspora', *Journal of Homosexuality*, 24, 145–58, 1993.

Whitlock, Gillian, 'A Disgusting Book', *Hecate*, X:2, 8–37, 1984.

——'Everything Is Out Of Place: Radclyffe Hall and the Lesbian Literary Tradition', *Feminist Studies*, 13:3, Fall 1987.

'Working the Archive', *Auto/Biography*, Bulletin of the British Sociological Association Study Group on Auto/Biography, 2:2, 1993.

INDEX

The following abbreviations are used:

MVB   Mabel Veronica Batten
RH   Radclyffe Hall
ES   Evguenia Souline
UVT   Una Vincenzo Troubridge

Abercrombie, Lascelles 248, 255
Ackland, Valentine 214
Adam's Breed (RH) 200, 202, 203, 238; genesis of
   204–5; writing of (as *Food*) 204, 205, (as *Adam's
   Breed*) 208, 209; title changed 206; contract with
   Cassells 208; US contract with Doubleday Page
   208–9; published (March 1926) 211; reviews 211,
   219; published overseas 211–12; critical acclaim
   3, 14, 203, 211–12, 218–21, 230; sales 2, 211–12,
   219, 221, 230; submitted for Prix Femina 210,
   213, shortlisted for Prix Femina 214; wins Prix
   Femina 2, 218–19, 220, 222; wins James Tait
   Black Prize 2, 221; wins Eichelberger Gold
   Medal 221; Cape buys American rights 272;
   translations 272; possible stage version 306;
   Italian translation 335; mentioned in obituary 371
      research for 215; analysis of 215–18;
   characters: Gian-Luca 87, 205, 215–18; Teresa
   Boselli 132, 216, 349; Fabio Boselli 132, 215–16,
   349; Ugo Doria 189, 217
      see also themes
Adcock, St John 199, 220
After Many Days see Unlit Lamp, The
Agate, James 248, 255
Aiken, Clarissa 289
Aiken, Conrad 288, 289
Aladdin 63
Aldington, Richard 57
alienation *see* Radclyffe Hall; themes
Allen, Grant 176
Allen, Guy 187
Allen, Mary 'Robert' 54, 293–4, 334
ambulance units, all-women 74, 97, 163, 226, 263;
   Plate 11

American ancestry, RH's 15
Amor Dura (Vernon Lee) 64
Amyat, Katinka 21
Anderson, Margaret 109, 253, 254
Anderson, Sherwood 1, 271
animals, RH's love of *see* Radclyffe Hall
anti-Semitism 336–7, 359, 360–1
Arena Three 374
Arlen, Michael 178, 187, 188, 197
Arrowsmith (publishers) 185, 188, 199, 201, 272
art/artists 21, 48, 63, 259; Pre-Raphaelites 52;
   Sargent portrait of MVB 60–1, sold by RH 270;
   Buchel portrait of RH 137, 374; RH buys
   painting by Dorothy Burroughes-Burroughes
   186; painting of UVT by Romaine Brooks
   195–6; Buchel drawing of RH 239; in Rye 288;
   Tony Atwood's work 292; Dorothy Burroughes-
   Burroughes' work 300; Romaine Brooks gives
   RH two paintings 336; in RH's writings *see*
   themes; *see also* Troubridge, Una
Art, Royal College of 39, 113
Asquith family 117
Atcheson, Audrie (niece of Mickie Jacob) 328, 333,
   336
Atherton, Gertrude 248
Atwood, Clare 'Tony' 21, 291, 292, 300, 304, 305,
   306; *Plate 21*
Auckland Star 219–20
Austen, Jane 218
Austin, Harold 43, 68, 80, 92
Austin, Peggy (née Llewellyn) 43–4, 68, 80, 92, 94,
   140, 146, 152–3, 199, 209, 218–19; death 356
autobiographical essays, unpublished (RH) 4, 5;
   childhood 16, 19, 20, 28; versions of birth 16–17;
   naming 18; mother's cruelty 19; relationship with
   grandmother 21; early poetic talent 28; longing
   for ideal mother 163; about *Adam's Breed* 204–5

Babbit (Sinclair Lewis) 218
Baden-Powell, Robert 254

Baker, Dr Jo 306, 342
Baker, Michael 321
Baldwin, Oliver 252, 257
Baldwin, Stanley 110, 252, 266
Balfour, Arthur 143
Balfour, Gerald 144
Bankhead, Tallulah 177, 187, 269, 306
Barn Theatre, Smallhythe 291, 292, 303
Barnes, Djuna 2, 109, 177, 194, 213, 229, 230,
  231–2, 259, 274, 275; *Plate 18*
Barney, Natalie Clifford 2, 36,170,178, 187, 193,
  221, 229, 230–2, 234, 236, 273–4, 281, 334, 335,
  354; lesbianism 194, 275; literary salon 194–5,
  273; model for Valérie Seymour in *The Well* 195,
  226, 228; mentor to RH 195, 196, 239;
  introduces RH and UVT to Colette 213–14;
  death 374; *Plate 18*
Barrett, Rachel 54, 172, 173, 186, 187, 199, 202,
  205, 209, 275, 334, 342
Barry, Gerald 257
Barrymore, John 208
Batten, George marriage to MVB 61; relationship
  with MVB 62; attitude to RH as MVB's lover 65,
  66, 67, 71; last illness and death 68–9, 73; in
  seance 141
Batten, Mabel Veronica (Ladye) 3, 11, 26, 58, 268;
  appearance 60–1, 62; background 59–61; death
  of husband 69; illnesses 68, 80, 83, 89; increasing
  frailty 94; incapacity following car crash 97–8,
  125; 'immorality': affairs in India 61–2; alleged in
  Fox-Pitt slander case 164–7
    influence on RH's work: composes music for
  RH's poems 63, 86; acts as unofficial
  editor/publicist 63, 85, 88, 99, 102, 108;
  marriage to George Batten 61; musical gifts 58,
  61, 63; nicknames, love of 66; patriotism 68
    relationship with daughter Cara Harris 67, 69,
  81, 130; relationship with husband 62, 65–7, 68–9
    relationship with RH: first meeting 59–60, 62;
  becomes RH's lover 62–3; holidays with RH 63,
  66; gives RH name of John 11, 66; cultural
  explorations with RH 63–4; introduces RH to
  same-sex literature 64; redrafts will 70, 71;
  moves into 59 Cadogan Square with RH 69–72;
  introduces RH into her 'Circle' 73–6; shared
  interest in suffrage movement 80; move into
  White Cottage, Malvern 79–80; introduces RH
  to Catholicism 81–2; visit to Rome and audience
  with Pope Pius X 82–3; dedication of *Poems of
  the Past and Present* to MVB 86; beginning of
  deterioration in relationship 89; effect of RH's
  affair with Phoebe Hoare 90–6; Cadogan Square
  flat let, move to Malvern 96; car crash 97–8; RH
  starts relationship with UVT 108, 120, 121–4;
  White Cottage and Cadogan Square sold 121–2;
  move to Vernon Court Hotel 122; move to 22
  Cadogan Court 124; increasing frailty 125; final
  quarrel, illness and death 125
    post-death relationship: RH guilt 126, 129–30,
  132, 201; funeral and Requiem Mass 129–31;
  Cadogan Court flat as shrine to MVB 129;
  forgiveness through spiritualism 134, 140–2, 171;

mementos 134, 148; RH memories 181–2, 193,
  206, 275; dedication of *Unlit Lamp* 199; becomes
  less important 205; Mass in memory of MVB
  234; UVT reliance on MVB 290; UVT remorse
  345; RH buried in same vault 372
Baumgarten, Bernice 239
BBC: *Well of Loneliness* broadcast as Book at
  Bedtime 5; RH broadcast 213; employs ES 312,
  322, 366, 377; Andrea's career with 353, 375
Beach, Sylvia 253
Beauchamp, Lord 254
Beauman, Nicola 161
Beaverbrook, Lord 109
Begley, Revd Walter 16, 24
Belgrade *see* Serbia
Bell, Quentin 255
Bell, Vanessa 251, 255
Bennett, Arnold 30, 57, 64, 110, 188, 197; reviews
  Well of Loneliness 241; support for *Well of
  Loneliness* 248, 249, 250; declines to be witness at
  trial 255
Benson, E.F. (Dodo) 289, 306
Beresford, J.D. 182, 183, 184, 289
Berkeley Milne, Sir Archibald 117, 119
Bernhardt, Sarah 73, 110
Berry, Paul and Bostridge, Mark 264, 265
Between Me and Life (Meryle Secrest) 191
Beveridge, Sir William 254
Bigham, Mrs Trevor 90
Binyon, Laurence 248
biographers of RH 3, 4, 108, 204, 229, 357, 373;
  descriptions of ES by 314, 321
Birkett, Norman 260–1, 262, 265, 301
Birmingham, Bishop of 254
Birmingham Post 219
Biron, Sir Chartres 244, 258, 260, 261, 262–3,
  282–3
birth control 109, 177
bisexuality 35, 187
Bishop, Sarah *see* Diehl, Sarah
Bitter Sweet (Noël Coward) 269
'Blind Ploughman, The' (RH) *see Songs of Three
  Counties*
Bliss (Katherine Mansfield) 214
Bliss, Arthur 288
Bliss, Eileen 205, 209, 230
Blithe Spirit (Noël Coward) 269
Bloomsbury writers 249, 250, 255
'Blossoms, The' (RH short story) 212
Blunt, Wilfred 58, 61
Bodkin, Sir Archibald 260
Bohème, La 92
'Bonaparte' (RH short story) 99
Boni & Liveright (UVT's New York publishers) 234
Bookman Circle 218
Book of Letters (RH) 3, 342, 348–9, 377–8;
  comparison with RH's other writings 349; *see
  also* themes
Borgatti, Renate 193, 213
Boughton, George 51
Bournemouth 16, 17, 27, 134, 162, 215
Bourne, Mabel 267, 270, 290

Bowden, Fr Sebastien 82
Bowen, Stella 173–4
Box, Muriel 265
Braithwaite, Lillian 306
Brandt, Carl 213, 234, 235, 238–9, 240, 252
Brave New World (Aldous Huxley) 301
Bremer, Marie 63
Breslau (German ship) 118–19
Bridges, Robert 85
Brighton 93, 121, 153, 209, 232, 296, 306
Brittain, Shirley 264
Brittain, Vera 241–2, 248, 256, 264–5, 275; *Plate 24*
broadcasting: RH acquires first wireless 212; TV service begins 270; *see also* BBC
Bromfield, Louis 197
Brompton Oratory 81, 82
Brontë, Charlotte 101, 218
Brooks, John Ellingham 192
Brooks, Romaine 2, 36, 77, 178, 187, 190–4, 232; friendship with RH 191–4, 196, 273–4, 281, 335–6, 354; lesbianism 193–4, 275; model for Venetia Ford in *The Forge* 189, 191, 196; relationship with UVT 194, 195–6, 374; similarity of childhood to RH's 191–2, 230; *Plate 16*
Brown, Ivor 248
Browning, Elizabeth Barrett 53, 87, 94, 372
Browning, Robert 53, 86, 94, 185
Bryant, Louise 109
Bryant, William Cullen 41
Buchan, John 110–11, 248
Buchel, Charles: portrait of RH 137, 144, 239, 374
Budge *see* Burroughes-Burroughes, Dorothy
Bumpus (publishers) 47, 84, 146
Burne-Jones, Sir Edward 52, 110
Burra, Edward 288
Burroughes-Burroughes, Dorothy (Budge) 172, 186, 188, 189, 197, 199–200, 205–6, 241, 300
butch–femme roles 6, 67, 69, 140, 144; *see also* cross-dressing; lesbianism; Batten, Mabel: relationship with RH; Troubridge, Una: relationship with RH
Butt, Dame Clara 88, 192
Bystander 202

Calthrop, Gladys 306
Cameron, Julia 259
Campbell, Mrs Patrick 73
Cape, Jonathan: publishes *Well of Loneliness* 237–8, 239–40, 256, 269; told in advance about *Sunday Express* denunciation 243; submits *Well of Loneliness* to Home Secretary 246–7; stops UK printing of *Well of Loneliness*, arranges publication in Paris 247–8; takes over US rights of *Well of Loneliness* 252; summonsed to defend publication 253; trial 257, 258, 260, 262, 263, 265; sets up US company, buys US rights of *Adam's Breed*, publishes US edition of *Unlit Lamp* 272; lampooned in 'Sink of Solitude' 280; publishes *Master of the House* 301; releases rights in *Master of the House* 303
Cape & Harrison Smith Inc. 272, 296; publish

Master of the House in US 301; renamed Cape Ballou, bankruptcy 303
Capiello 191
'Career of Mark Anthony Brakes, The' (RH short story): writing of 99; praised by William Heinemann 102; *see also* themes
Carpenter, Edward 6, 227–8
Carpenter's Son, The (RH) (original title for *Master of the House*) *see Master of the House, The*
cars/motoring: MVB injured in car crash 97; RH's passion for cars 153; RH's Buick 178, 187; RH buys car for UVT 212
Carstairs, Jo 178
Caruth, Harry 45
Caruth, Jane *see* Randolph, Jane
Casati, Marchesa 193
Cassells (publishers) 185, 197, 198–9, 208–9, 211, 212, 234, 235
Casson, Lewis 220
Castle, Terry 269
Catholicism 2, 14, 28, 84, 121, 257; RH's conversion 81–3; Catholicism/lesbianism 84, 280; UVT's conversion 84; Catholicism/spiritualism 143; Christopher St John 291; Tony Atwood 292
Cavalcade (Noël Coward) 301–2
censorship 1, 5, 81; *see also* obscenity
Chains (RH) *see Forge, The*
Chaliapin, Boris 88
Chaplin, Olive 334
Chapman & Hall: publish RH's poems 86, 88; 198
Chappells: publish RH's song 'Cuckoo' 147
Cheadle, Dr 97, 98
Chéri (Colette) 213, 290
Chesterton, G.K. 212; *Plate 25*
Child, Dr Armando 368, 369
Chinoise Qui S'Emancipe, La (Charles Pettit, trans. UVT) 234
'Christopher Tennant' (RH short story) 146
Churchill, Dr Stella 257
Churchill, Winston 115, 117, 118
Clarendon, Emmie Lady (sister of MVB) 60, 61, 65, 106, 108, 120, 131, 132
Clarke, Dolly (Dorothy), née Diehl: affair with RH 46–7, 51, 107, 130; receives allowance from RH 47; marries Robert Coningsby Clarke 48; appearance 46, 52; friendship with RH 47, 56–7, 65, 69, 76, 77, 80, 120, 129; role in RH's affair with Phoebe Hoare 90, 92, 93, 94; fictionalized by RH 104; role in RH's relationship with UVT 123, 133, 134; death of husband 129; attends seances with RH 141; hears RH's psychical research paper 144; estrangement from RH 145
Clarke, Robert Coningsby (Bobby) 47, 52; marries Dolly Diehl 48; friendship with RH and MVB 65, 69, 76, 80; sets RH's poems to music 48, 86, 88; enlists in First World War 96, 97; killed in action 129
Clermont Tonnerre, Elizabeth (Lily) de Gramont, Duchess of 194, 195, 214, 273, 274, 275, 374
Clynes, J.R. 296
Cocteau, Jean 194

Colette 2, 194, 213–14, 221, 229, 234, 273, 281, 354, 373; works translated by UVT 118, 213, 290; *Plate 17*
Collins (publishers) 182, 183
communism 181
Conan Doyle, Arthur 254
concerts 61, 63, 75, 125, 195
Confessions (J.-J. Rousseau) 257
congenital inversion *see* essentialism
Connolly, Cyril 249
Conrad, Joseph 111, 287, 288
Constable, Rosalind 289
Constant Nymph, The (Margaret Kennedy) 255
Coppard, A.E. 202
Coster, Howard 300, 301
Country Life 246
court cases 1, 11, 97–8 (following car crash), 253–4, 259–66, 269–70
        court martial (Ernest Troubridge) 119
        see also Well of Loneliness; Fox-Pitt
Covici Friede (US publishers) 252, 271
Coward, Noël 252, 258, 295, 301–2; possible model for Jonathan Brockett in *Well of Loneliness* 269
Craig, Edith (Edy) 29; founds Pioneer Players 74; involvement in suffrage movement 75; friendship with RH/UVT 291, 292–3, 300, 306, 334; relationship with Christopher St John and Tony Atwood 291–2, 304–5; death 373; *Plate 21*
Crane, Cora 288
Crane, Stephen 287, 288
Crawfurd, Oswald 51, 53, 55
Crichton-Miller, Dr Hugh: consulted by UVT 116, 117, 118, 137, 138, 140, 145; consulted by Viola Woods 117; rents Cheltenham Terrace 148
cross-dressing 2, 22, 35, 76, 82, 112, 144, 193–4, 219, 294; *see also* Radclyffe Hall: appearance; Troubridge, Una: appearance
Crufts dog show 151, 187
Crystal Cup, The (Gertrude Atherton) 248
Cub, Cubby *see* Troubridge, Andrea
Cunard, Nancy 178
Cunninghame Graham, J.B. (Robert) 89, 218, 220
Cunninghams, The (RH unfinished novel): drafts 53; 102, 162, 186
Cure for Souls, A (May Sinclair) 186
Cust, Robert 248, 257

Daily Express 109, 242, 246, 249, 252
Daily Herald 245–6, 248, 252–3, 257, 258, 259
Daily Mail 149, 220, 276, 303, 356
Daily Mirror 103, 263
Daily Telegraph 88, 89, 149, 199, 242, 372
dance/dancing 63, 116, 163, 169–70, 177, 178, 179, 187, 193; *see also* Nijinsky, Vaslav
Dancers, The 187
Dane, Clemence 64, 147, 213, 229, 235, 277, 293; *Plate 10*
Dangerous Ages (Rose Macaulay) 214
D'Annunzio, Gabriele 74, 181, 191, 192, 195, 335, 336, 359
Darantière, Maurice 232
Dark Flower, The (John Galsworthy) 100

Datchet (Berkshire) 136–8, 201, 207, 208, 234, 277
Daughter of Brahma (Ida Wylie) 172
Davison, Emily 80
Dawson, Arnold, 245–6, 257
Dawson, Lord 365, 366
Dawson, Margaret Damer 293–4
Death in the Afternoon (Ernest Hemingway) 301
De Profundis (Oscar Wilde) 239
de la Roche, Mazo 323
de Quincey, Thomas 12
Diaghilev, Sergei 116
Diana of the Crossways (George Meredith) 176
Dickens, Charles 218
Dickie (friend of RH and UVT in Rye) 252, 294
Diehl, Aunt Lode *Plate 2*
Diehl, Dolly (Dorothy) *see* Clarke, Dolly
Diehl, Edwin (father of Marie Diehl Visetti) 15
Diehl, Mary Jane *see* Visetti, Marie Diehl
Diehl, Sarah Bishop (mother of Marie Diehl Visetti): relationship with RH 12, 15, 20, 21, 27, 65; commissions portrait of RH 21; religious influence on RH 28, 81; model for Puddle (*Well of Loneliness*) 29, 226; goes to live with RH 43; illness and death 68–9, legacy to Visettis 233; *Plate 1*
Dingwall, Dr E.J. 144
divorce law reform 84
Dodge, Mabel 109
dogs, dog-breeding 150, 187, 196; *see also* Radclyffe Hall: animals
Doolittle, Hilda (H.D.) 57, 229, 288
Dos Passos, John 271
Doubleday, Page & Co. 208, 212, 238, 239, 272
Doubleday, Russell 208
Douglas (photographer) 212
Douglas, James 243–4, 246, 260, 267, 278
Douglas, Norman 192
Douglas-Home, Jessica 98
Dreiser, Theodore 1, 271
Dresser, Marcia van 288
Drinkwater, John 248, 254
Dubliners, The (James Joyce) 253
Duckworth, Gerald 248
Dukes, Ashley 248
Du Maurier, Gerald 133, 146
Duncan, Isadora 195
Dusty Answer (Rosamond Lehmann) 64, 235, 248

Edward VII, King 59, 60, 68, 114, 193
Edwards, Powell 88
Egan, Beresford 278–80, 285
Egerton, George 176
Eichelberger Gold Medal 221
Einstein, Albert 109
Elder, Sir Duke 365
Elgar, Edward 125
Elgar, Lady 92
Eliot, George 218
Eliot, T.S. 57, 248, 288, 370
Elizabeth and Her German Garden (Elizabeth von Arnim) 189

Ellen Young (Gabrielle Enthoven) 74
Elliot, Enid 163
Ellis, Havelock 6, 35, 42, 84, 221, 227–8, 235, 294; writes 'opinion' for *Well of Loneliness* 237–8, 241, 242; refuses to testify at trial of *Well of Loneliness* 256; *Plate 19*
Elman, Mischa 61
Elsner, Anne 241, 267
Elwes, Gervase 63
Emblem Hurlstone (RH unfinished novel): drafts 4; character Felia based on ES 315, 320–1; writing of 335, 339, 348; as 'child' of RH and ES 339–40; *see also* themes
Enthoven, Gabrielle: friendship with RH and MVB 63, 80, 92, 122; appearance, background, theatrical achievements 73–4, 292; friendship with RH and UVT 153, 163, 177, 179, 187, 199, 201, 209, 221, 269, 275; quarrel with UVT 290; Director of Theatre Collection at V&A 200
Ernst, Morris 271
essentialism 2, 5, 35–6, 182, 183, 227, 235, 242, 274
Etheline 178, 187, 205, 230, 252, 281
Eton College 14
Evans, Caradoc 257
Evans, Charles 236
Evans, Edith 293
Evening Standard 241, 248
exiles *see* alienation
Extraordinary Women (Compton Mackenzie) 232, 236, 239, 240, 249, 253, 259, 278

Faber, Geoffrey 254
Faber, Gladys 328
Fabienne 201, 209, 230, 246, 252, 266, 275
Façade (Edith Sitwell) 188
Faderman, Lillian 42, 274
Fairbairns, Zoë 182
Fallen Angels (Noël Coward) 269
Fane, Violet 64
Farewell to Arms, A (Ernest Hemingway) 269
Farrar, Gwen 177, 187
Fascism 181, 336
Faulkner, Sir Keith 26
Faulkner, William 269
'Faun' *see* Nijinsky, Vaslav
Fauré, Gabriel 61, 73
Fawcett, Millicent Garrett 78
Feda (spirit-guide in seances) 141–2, 143
Felicia (niece of Naomi Jacob) 328, 333
Femina Books 265
feminism *see* sexual politics
Ferber, Edna 1, 271
Field, St John 167
Field, The 189
Finnegans Wake (James Joyce) 232
First World War *see* war
Fitzgerald, F. Scott 1, 169, 170, 187, 213, 271
Fitzgerald, Penelope 273 (n. 13)
Fitzgerald, Zelda 170, 187, 194
Flanner, Janet 2, 231, 232
Florence, Italy *see* Italy
Flower, Newman 197, 198, 206, 211, 220, 234, 235

Food see Adam's Breed
Ford, Ford Madox 56, 57, 78, 103, 146, 173–4, 269, 270, 287, 288
Forge, The (RH): writing of 184–5, 186; original title *Chains* 185; published by Arrowsmith (January 1924) 185; dedicated to UVT 185; success 3, 197, 201–2; reviews 188–9; Romaine Brooks' opinion 195–6; cheap second edition 102; reprinted 272
   analysis: autobiographical nature 185; costume ball 178; effects of childhood 14; lightheartedness of 169, 184, 185; love of oak 148; psychological delineation 188; restlessness 44; RH's self-appraisal in 48; themes 150; characters: Hilary Brent 13, 14, 19, 44, 48, 148, 149, 150, 185, 189–90; Susan Brent 13, 19, 44, 76, 149, 178, 185, 189–91, 202; Venetia Ford 6, 76, 189–91
   see also themes
Forgotten Island, The (RH) 98–9; dedicated to Violet Gordon Woodhouse 98; praised by Sir Arthur Quiller-Couch 99
Forster, E.M. 1, 2, 221, 248–51, 256
Fox-Pitt, St George Lane 62, 144; RH's slander action against 145, 164–8, 179, 209
Foyles luncheon 300
Frampton, Walter 260, 265
France: Bagnoles 197, 213, 281, 308, 316–19, 323; Beauvallon 281, 346; Paris 68, 69, 70, 192, 193, 194–5, 196–7, 213–14, 221, 227, 230–1, 268, 270, 272, 273–4, 281, 316, 323–6, 337–8, 346, 347, 355, 356
Franchetti, Mimi 193, 213, 232
Franck, César: *Panis Angelicus* 373
Françoise (Havelock Ellis's mistress) 256
Franks, Claudia Stillman 7
'Fräulein Schwartz' (RH short story) 7, 200–1, 205, 307
Freytag-Loringhoven, Elsa, Baroness von 109
Friede, Donald 252, 271, 272
'friend' as euphemism for lover 77, 165, 219, 373
friendship(s): in Rye 288–9, 305; *see also* women's friendships
Fry, Penrose 289, 294, 300, 306
Fry, Roger 251
Fulton, Eustace 260, 265
Furlong, Iris 378

Gallimard 272
Galsworthy, John 30, 100, 103, 173, 220, 255–6, 291
Galsworthy, Mrs John 221
Garnett, David 214
Garnett, Edward 237, 248, 256, 288
Garnett, Richard 100
Garvin, J.L. 180, 199, 209, 210, 240, 276, 373
Garvin, Viola *see* Taylor, Viola
Genée, Adeline 113, 121
General Strike, 1926 212; Women's Emergency Corps 294
Gerard, Teddie 177, 187, 200, 205, 269, 306
Gide, André 194
Gielgud, John 291, 293, 306

Gissing, George 176
Glasgow, Ellen 218, 271, 290
Glasgow, Joanne 35, 82, 83–4
Goeben (German battle cruiser) 118–19
Goldingham, Isobel 'Toto' 293, 294
Gollancz, Victor 248, 257
Good Soldier, The (Ford Madox Ford) 103, 174
Goossens, Eugene 187
Goossens, Boonie 187
Gordon, Taylor 220
Gorrell, Elizabeth 300
Gosse, Edmund 197
Goudeket, Maurice 213
Gourmont, Rémy de 194
Grainger, Percy 61
Grand Eunuque, Le (Charles Pettit, trans. UVT) 234
Grand, Sarah 176
Granville-Barker, Harley 248, 255
Great Waters (Vere Hutchinson) 188, 200
Green Hat, The (Michael Arlen) 178, 188; stage
  version 187
Growth of the Soil (Knut Hamsun) 218
Gruber, Dr R. 257
Gurney, Chatty *see* Troubridge, Chatty
Gurney, Violet Troubridge 109, 138
Guys and Dolls (Damon Runyan) 301

Hackett, Norah Desmond 74, 163
Haire, Dr Norman 257
Hales, Winifred *see* Reed, Winifred Hales
Hall, Dr John (ancestor of RH) 13
Hall, John Radcliffe (great-grandfather of RH) 12,
  13
Hall, Samuel (great-great-grandfather of RH) 12,
  13
Hamilton, Cicely 292
Hamlet 208
Hammond, Hammond (publishers) 5
Hamsun, Knut 218
Handcock, Robert French 112
Harcourt Brace (US publishers) 239, 308
Hardwick, Joan 56
Hardy, Thomas 57
Harris, Austin 65, 67, 80, 90, 92, 95, 132, 134
Harris, Cara: birth 61; relationship with MVB 60,
  67–8, 69, 81, 92, 93, 94, 95, 96; relationship with
  MVB and RH as couple 63, 65, 67–8, 80, 97,
  120; relationship with father 66; relationship
  with RH 67–8, 80, 99; friendship with Dolly
  Clarke 65, 145; gives birth to Karen 94; rift with
  RH 129–32, 134, 144–5, 153
Harris, Karen: birth 94; 132, 134
Harris, Pamela (Honey): as child 60, 66, 67, 68, 92,
  93, 94; attends MVB's Requiem 131; later
  relationship with RH 132, 134, 144; *Plate 6*
Harris, Peter 60, 67, 94, 132; *Plate 6*
Harry Ransom Research Center, University of
  Texas 378
Hart-Davis, Rupert 67
Harter, Ethel 94
Hartley, L.P. reviews *Well of Loneliness* 241
Harty, Hamilton 40

Hastie, Mr (solicitor) 25, 26, 138
Hastie & Co. 25, 138
Hatch, George Cliffe (father of MVB) 61
Hatch, Mary Cecilia (mother of MVB) 61
Hatch, Miss (sister of MVB) 131
H.D. *see* Doolittle, Hilda
Head, Dr Henry 251
Heap, Jane 109, 253, 254
Heath, Audrey (Robin): sets up A.M. Heath
  literary agency 183; meets RH and UVT 184;
  work as RH's literary agent 184–5, 186, 187, 188,
  201, 209–10, 212, 222, 234; negotiates contract
  for *Unlit Lamp* 198; friendship with RH and
  UVT 20, 267, 269, 272–3, 277, 278, 306, 373;
  US contract for *Adam's Breed* 208; introduces
  RH to US literary agent 213; negotiations with
  publishers over *Well of Loneliness* 235–40, 252;
  during *Well of Loneliness* trial 262; agent for
  UVT 276; accused of 'muddles' by RH 291;
  Plate 20
Heavenly Twins, The (Sarah Grand) 176
Heinemann (publishers) 184, 236, 237, 307, 341
Heinemann, William 102, 104, 147, 184
Hemingway, Ernest 1, 237, 269, 271, 301
Henderson, H.D., 248
Hennegan, Alison 203
Herbert, A.P., 248, 256
Hermes Press 278
heterosexuality 4, 5, 33–4, 35, 52, 56, 118, 331
Highgate Cemetery 131, 135, 201, 205, 372
Hill, Leopold 252, 253, 257, 260, 263
Hirschfeld, Magnus 6, 227
Hoare, Oliver 90, 91, 94–5, 96, 125
Hoare, Phoebe 88, 89, 90; affair with RH 91–5, 96,
  98, 105–6, 108, 122, 123, 125, 130, 268; UVT's
  description of RH/Phoebe Hoare relationship
  105–6; friendship with RH 120, 121, 152
Holme, Vera 'Jack' 292, 334; involvement in
  suffrage movement 293; *Plate 21*
Holroyd-Reece, Jeanne 273, 373
Holroyd-Reece, John 247, 248, 252, 258, 261, 262,
  273, 278, 373
Holtby, Winifred 241–2, 256, 264
Homburg, Germany 59, 61, 103
Home Office 247, 252, 256, 265, 294, 354, 360
homophobia 6, 71, 166–8, 229, 242–4, 245–7, 254,
  260–6, 271, 284, 294
homosexuality 2, 5, 7, 67, 70–1, 83, 162, 227–30,
  232, 237–8, 242, 246–7, 251, 254–5, 257, 273–4,
  280, 284; same-sex marriage 275; *see also*
  lesbianism
Honey (friend of RH and UVT) 163, 177, 179
Honeysuckle, The (Gabriele D'Annunzio; trans.
  Gabrielle Enthoven) 74
Hoover, Herbert 269
Hope, Adrian 111
Hope, Jacqueline 111, 114, 115, 134, 135, 297, 373;
  marriage to Hedley Nicholson 139
Hope, Laura Troubridge 109, 111, 114, 138, 139,
  142, 144
Hope-Nicholson, Jacqueline *see* Hope, Jacqueline
Hopkins, Gerard 220, 248, 261

horses, RH's love of *see* Radclyffe Hall
Houghton Mifflin (US publishers) 235, 238; rights in *Master of the House* 303
Housman, A.E. 88
Housman, Laurence 248, 257, 292
Howard, George Wren 237
Howard, Michael 258
Hudson, W.H. 287
Hume-Williams, Sir Ellis 164, 165–6, 167, 168
humour in RH's writings 146, 169, 184, 185, 189, 203
Hunt, Alfred and Margaret 52
Hunt, Holman 52
Hunt, Violet: affair with Ford Madox Ford 56, 78, 103, 173–4, 269, 287, 288; affair with RH 51–8, 77, 219; appearance 52; considers *Adam's Breed* for Prix Femina 210, 213; early love affairs 51; family background 52; friendship with RH 3, 103, 121, 133, 173, 174, 177, 179, 197, 199, 200, 209, 221; friendship with UVT 201; infected with syphilis 51, 57, 103, 174; involvement in sexual politics 54, 55, 78–9; literary mentor of RH 29, 89, 102–3, 108, 173, 188–9, 218–19, 220; literary salon 57, 103, 174; similarity to UVT 113; as writer 4, 48, 53, 57, 174–5; *Plate 9*
Hurst, Fannie 218
Hutchinson, A.S.M. 172
Hutchinson, Vere 4; friendship with RH 172, 173, 186, 188–9, 197, 209; serious illness 199–200, 205–6, 227, 241; death 300
Huxley, Aldous 188, 301
Huxley, Julian 248, 257, 261
hypnosis 13, 116, 117

Idylle Sapphique (Liane de Pougy) 229
If Winter Comes (A.S.M. Hutchinson) 172
In a German Pension (Katherine Mansfield) 200
Informer, The (Liam O'Flaherty) 214
Innes, James 74
Inskip, Sir Thomas 265
Intelligent Woman's Guide to Socialism and Capitalism (G.B. Shaw) 264
inversion, sexual 6; *see also* lesbianism, homosexuality, sexology
Irons, Evelyn 220, 276; affair with Vita Sackville-West 303–5; 'marriage' with Olive Rinder 303–4
Irving, Henry 291
Irwin, Margaret 197, 220
Isherwood, Christopher 200
Italy: Florence 53, 61, 94, 115, 140, 170, 181, 193, 347, 350, 352, 353, 355; Levanto 115, 154, 170, 181; Merano 342, 347; Sirmione 317, 320, 322, 327–37, 340, 346, 347; in *A Sheaf of Verses* (RH) 86

Jacks, L.B. 142
Jacob, Naomi (Mickie): background 333–5; involvement in sexual politics 54; war work 334; writings 334; frienship with RH 271, 322, 328, 337, 369; attracted to UVT 334; escapes from Italy 361; excluded by UVT after RH's death 371; reconciled to UVT 374; *Plate 22*

Jacob Usher (Naomi Jacob) 334
Jalna (Mazo de la Roche) 323
James, Henry 51, 57, 288
Jameson, Storm 4, 248, 256, 260, 270
James Tait Black Memorial Prize 2, 221
Jix *see* Joynson-Hicks, Sir William
Joanna Godden (Sheila Kaye-Smith) 172
John, Augustus 197; *Plate 25*
John Bull 253
John O'London's Weekly 197
Johnson, Rosamund 220
Joll, Dr Cecil 368
Joly, Dr 322
Jones, Elijah (great-grandfather of RH) 15, 44
Jones, Jane (great-grandmother of RH) 15, 44; *Plate 1*
Joyce, James 190, 194, 232, 253–4
Joynson-Hicks, Sir William (Jix) 247, 278–80

Kaye-Smith, Sheila 4; friendship with RH 172, 197, 209, 220, 252, 289, 294, 300, 306; on Prix Femina committee 213; support for *Well of Loneliness* 248, 256
Kennedy, Margaret 255
Kershaw, Wilette 277–8
Keynotes (George Egerton) 176
Kipling, Rudyard 110, 206, 288
Knopf, Alfred 238–40, 252
Knopf, Blanche 238, 239, 252
Knott, Miss (RH's governess) 26, 27
Koopman (painter) 60
Krafft-Ebing, Richard von 6, 35, 42, 227–8; in *Well of Loneliness* 228

Ladies Almanack (Djuna Barnes) 231–2
Ladies Whose Bright Eyes (Ford Madox Ford) 146, 174, 270
Lady Chatterley's Lover (D.H. Lawrence) 269–70
Lady into Fox (David Garnett) 214
Lady magazine 48, 89, 131, 199
Ladye *see* Batten, Mabel Veronica
Lady's Pictorial 246
Lafayette (photographer) 199
Lakin, Mrs Frances 97
Lakin, Francis 198
Lakmé 63
Lancashire Daily Post 219
Lancaster, Cara 66, 67 (n. 23), 76, 131–2
Lancet 13, 257
Lanteri, Edouard 113, 114
Laver, James 74
Lawrence, D.H. 57, 111, 253, 254, 269–70
Lawrence, Margaret 7, 81
Lawrence, T.E. 237
League of Nations 264
Lee, Hermione 251
Lee, Vernon 64
Lehmann, Liza 86, 88, 92
Lehmann, Rosamond 64, 229, 235, 248
Leonard, Gladys 134, 135, 137, 140–2, 198, 290; *Plate 12*
Leonard, Mrs Osborne *see* Leonard, Gladys

Lesbian Minorities Research Group 374
lesbianism 1, 2, 3, 5, 6, 7, 14, 33, 35–6, 39, 41–7,
   56, 57, 148, 166–8, 183, 193–4, 217–18, 219, 221,
   226–30, 237, 241, 246–7, 249–55, 257, 260–5,
   271, 273–5, 333, 339; born-lesbian *see*
   essentialism; and Catholicism 82–4, 280; closeted
   lesbians 284; in *A Room of One's Own* 282–3; in
   Extraordinary Women 236; in women's police
   294; lack of recognition for lesbian couples
   205–6; lesbian love 56, 331, 357–8; lesbian
   relationships 56, 71, 140, 193–4, 303–5; 'married
   lesbians' 70, 250, 303; self-chosen 2, 6, 14, 35,
   36, 182–3; in society 274–5; theories of 35–6,
   183, 193, 227–8; *see also* homosexuality;
   Radclyffe Hall (especially: lesbianism/sexual
   identity; lovers); sexologists; sexual politics;
   themes; women's friendships; *Well of Loneliness*
lesbian literature/writers 6, 57, 63, 64, 71, 83,
   182–3, 217–18, 221, 231–2, 235, 237, 244, 248,
   259, 266; *see also* Barnes, Djuna; Barney, Natalie;
   Dane, Clemence; Lehmann, Rosamond;
   Radclyffe Hall
Lewis, Sir George 138, 145, 164–5, 168
Lewis, Sinclair 169, 172, 218, 237, 271
Lewis, Wyndham 57
Life and Death of Harriett Frean, The (May
   Sinclair) 101
Life and Death of Radclyffe Hall, The
   see Troubridge, Una
Life and Letters 257
Lister, Anne 42
Little Review, The 253
Llewellyn, Colonel (father of Peggy) 43
Llewellyn, Maud (sister of Peggy) 43
Llewellyn, Peggy *see* Austin, Peggy
Lodge, Lady 134, 142, 144
Lodge, Sir Oliver: hospitality to RH and UVT 134,
   142; writes *Raymond* 140 (n. 23); recommends
   the medium Gladys Leonard to RH 140; support
   for RH (psychical research) 143, 144, (Fox-Pitt
   case) 145, 164
Lolly Willowes (Sylvia Townsend Warner) 214–15
Lovat Dickson, Rache 229, 234, 373, 375
'Lover of Things, The' (RH short story) 23, 33,
   198, 215, 307; *see also* themes
Lowell, Amy 235
Lowry, Malcolm 288, 289
Lowther, Barbara (Toupie): model for characters in
   RH's works 63, 74–5; background 74–5; war work
   74, 163, 173, 263, 334; friendship with RH and
   MVB 92, 122; teaches RH and UVT to drive 153;
   friendship with RH and UVT 153–4, 163, 177,
   178, 181, 187, 193, 196, 201, 209, 221, 230, 251,
   275; end of friendship with RH and UVT 276–7;
   Plate 11
Lowther, Claude 75, 92, 163
Loy, Mina 109, 232
Lucas, E.V. 197, 199
Lummox (Fannie Hurst) 218
Lynton, Devon 136, 147, 175, 206, 362–3, 364, 365,
   366, 368, 375
Lytton, Robert, Earl of 61

MacAlmon, Robert 232
Macaulay, Rose 1, 188, 214, 248, 255, 256
MacCarthy, Desmond 248, 257, 261
MacDonald, Ramsay 269
Macey, Winifred (née Randolph) 34, 44, 219,
   233
Macey's US promoters of *Extraordinary Women*
   278
Mackenzie, Compton 193, 197, 232, 236, 239, 249,
   253, 278, 285; *Plate 25*
Mackenzie, Dr Dan 154
McLean, Miss 150
McRobert, Captain 89
Mädchen in Uniform (film) 300
Maddison, Adela 73, 92, 93, 96, 99, 122
Main Street (Sinclair Lewis) 169, 172, 218
Maison de Claudine, La (Colette) 214
Makaroff, Vladimir 376, 378
'Malise' (RH short story) 226; lesbianism 33, 54;
   war work 74; feminism 97
Malta 114–15, 116, 117, 118
'Mandalay' (RH short story) 102
Manners, Lady Diana 178
Mannin, Ethel 84, 146, 169, 170 (n. 1)
Mansfield, Katherine 200, 214
'Mapp and Lucia' novels (E.F. Benson) 289
'March of the Women' (Ethel Smyth) 79
Marjoribanks, Mrs George (sister of MVB) 131
Markham, Violet 248, 256
Married Love (Marie Stopes) 177
Martindale, Elsie (wife of Ford Madox Ford) 103,
   288
Martisius, Dr 209
Mary Olivier: A Life (May Sinclair) 101, 147, 158,
   160–1
masculine dress-style *see* cross-dressing; RH
   appearance; UVT appearance
Massey-Brown literary agency 183
Massola, Cencio 115, 118, 153–4, 181
Massola, May 111, 115, 118, 153–4, 181, 297
Master of the House, The (RH) 7; writing of 18, 150,
   285; RH develops stigmata 295; as *The
   Carpenter's Son* 287, 288, 290, 295, 298;
   completed 299; title changed to *Master of the
   House* 299; genesis of 280; setting 281;
   spirituality in 202, 285, 302; research 281; Foyles
   luncheon 300; published UK and US 301;
   special edition 301; initial success 301; reviews
   302–3, 341
      characters: Christophe Bénédit 7, 281, 302,
      349, 352; lack of psychological delineation 301
   see also themes
Mata Hari 194
Maugham, W. Somerset 100, 192
Maupassant, Guy de 64, 229
Maurice (E.M. Forster) 248
May, Dr 171
Mayfield, Convent of the Holy Child 139, 154
Mayne, Ethel Colburn 174, 213
Melba, Dame Nellie 63
Melville, James B. 260, 261–2, 263, 265, 269
ménages à trois see triangular relationships

Mencken, H.L. 271
Merano Shoemaker, The (RH unfinished novel) 342, 348; possible portrayal of RH/ES relationship 377; destroyed by UVT 377
Meredith, George 176
mesmerism *see* hypnosis
metaphysical themes *see* spirituality
Metcalf, Herbert 260
Mew, Charlotte 273
Michael West (RH unfinished novel): drafts 4; writing of 100, 102
   characters: Michael West 19–20, 25, 27–8, 30, 32, 105, 161, 162; Mrs Billings 19, 32; Richard West 27, 30, Sarah West 19–20, 25, 30; Auntinot 27, 28, 30
   see also themes
Michaelis, Karen 272
Michel, Marguerite 117–18, 181
Middleton Murry, John 248, 256
Millay, Edna St Vincent 271
Milton, Ernest 353
Miners' Federation, South Wales 258
Miracle, The 81
Miriam (Naomi Jacob's lover) 334
misfits *see* alienation
Miss Ogilvy Finds Herself (RH collection of short stories) 3, 198, 306; connection with *The World* 200, 268–9; UK and US publication 307–8; poor reviews 308; sales 308, 335; French translation 345
'Miss Ogilvy Finds Herself' (RH short story) 226; lesbianism 6, 7, 54; feminism 97; Toupie Lowther as model for Miss Ogilvy 63, 198; importance of 212; setting for 212; *see also* themes
Mitchison, Naomi 256
'Modern Miss Thompson' (RH short story) 99
Modernism 2; *see also* Paris Modernist Group
money in RH's life: father's 15, 24; inheritance from grandfather 24, 36, 43; mother's divorce settlement 25; in relationships with MVB, UVT, ES 26; stepfather's irresponsibility over 27, 43, 80, 233; financial support for Jane Randolph 45, for Dolly Clarke 46, 47, for George Batten 67; in relationship with UVT 136; cuts off Dolly Clarke's allowance 145; financial drain of *Well of Loneliness* case 266–7, 269; improvement in finances 272, 273; losses on US stock market 307; UVT's inheritance 373
   see also Radclyffe Hall; Souline, Evguenia
Montesquiou, Robert de 196
Montmartre (Gabrielle Enthoven) 74
Moore, George 261
Morena *see* Woodhouse, Violet Gordon
Morning Post 131, 241
Morrell, Lady Ottoline 251
Morris, Margaret 187
mother–child relationships: RH's view of ideal mother 162–3; *see also* Radclyffe Hall; Souline, Evguenia; themes; Troubridge, Una; Visetti, Marie
Mount Music (Edith Somerville) 171

Mrs Neville Tyson: Two Sides of a Question (May Sinclair) 186
Mrs Warren's Profession (G.B. Shaw) 80, 292
Mulford, Wendy 214
Mundt, Martha 92, 96, 99
Munson, Gorham 245, 263–4, 266–7, 271–2, 275, 280
Munthe, Axel 192, 290, 353
Murat, Princess Violette 187
Murray, Gilbert 254
Murray, John 199
music: father's talent for 14; in childhood 27; own talent 28, 38; with Agnes Nicholls 37–8; poems set to music 1, 38, 47, 48, 86, 88–9; with MVB 61, 63; buys mandolin 69, 94; composes music for songs 146–7; listens to jazz 153; as solace 28, 163; with Ethel Smyth 171–2; *see also* concerts; opera
Music, Royal College of 26, 37
Musical Times 37
Mussolini, Benito 181

Nadine ('Whang'): attracted to UVT 334–5
Naked Man, The (Vere Hutchinson) 200
naming: in RH's family and childhood 11–12, 13, 18; Marie Visetti's own renaming 18; in RH's life and writings 5, 11–12, 57; RH adopts the name John 2, 11, 66; renaming of same-sex friendships 42; in RH's poetry 86; after MVB's death 131–2; by Ernest Troubridge 138; RH adopts Radclyffe Hall as writing name 185; nickname for UVT 120; nickname for ES 337; naming and misnaming after RH's death 372; *see also* themes
Nansen (passport) 343, 360
Nash, Paul 288
Nation and Athenaeum 241, 248, 250, 251
National Council of Labour Colleges' Students Association 270
National Union of Women's Suffrage Societies (NUWSS) 77–8
nature 1, 21, 101, 102, 160, 286–7, 330–1, 348–9; *see also* themes
Nevada, Mignon 89, 134, 146–7
Newton, Esther 193
Newton, Isobel 143–4, 145, 153, 166, 167, 179
New Statesman 249
'New Woman' 62, 109, 159, 175–6; *see also* sexual politics/feminism
New Yorker 231
New York Herald 131
New York Times 278
New York World 278
Nicholls, Agnes: relationship with RH 36–42, 51, 192, 373; UVT describes Agnes Nicholls' voice 37; marriage to Hamilton Harty 40, 48; Elgar concert 125
Nicholson, Hedley 139
Nicolaeff, Ariadne 311–12, 322, 339–40, 369, 378
Nicolsky, Lisa 324, 337, 356, 358
Nicolson, Harold 304
Nightwood (Djuna Barnes) 259

Nijinsky, Vaslav: sculpted as Debussy's 'Faun' by UVT 116, 119

Nikisch, Arthur 28

Nobel Prize 218

No Pleasant Memories (Romaine Brooks) 191

Northcliffe, Lord 254

Nottie *see* Knott, Miss

novellas, RH's 4

novels, RH's (including those unpublished/unfinished) 2, 3, 5, 6, 7, 11, 148, 149, 162, 163, 169, 214, 217–18, 266; *see also* individual works

Noyes, Alfred 211, 213, 220

obituaries of RH 371–2

Obscene Publications Act 1857 253, 255, 258, 262

obscenity 1, 81, 243, 247, 253–66, 271, 272; *see also* *Well of Loneliness*

Observer 180, 209, 211, 240, 276, 302

Octopi see Unlit Lamp, The

Odd Woman, The (George Gissing) 176

Of Human Bondage (W. Somerset Maugham) 100

O'Flaherty, Liam 214

O'Leary, Con 242, 257

opera and opera-going 63, 91, 92, 118, 374

Opera magazine 37

Orlando (Virginia Woolf) 229, 232, 251, 258–9, 282

Ormrod, Richard 90, 321

Orphan Island (Rose Macaulay) 188

Orpheus 63

Ould, Hermon 255–6

'Out of the Night' (RH short story) 99

outsiders *see* alienation

Paganini (Ernest Milton) 353

Paget, Violet *see* Lee, Vernon

Pall Mall Gazette 79, 88, 99

Pankhurst, Adele 78

Pankhurst, Christabel 78, 293

Pankhurst, Emmeline 75, 78, 79, 293

Pankhurst, Sylvia 78, 293, 333

Paris: Modernist Group 2, 192, 194–5, 213, 230–2, 273–4; *see also* France

Passage to India, A (E.M. Forster) 221

Patmore, Brigit 52

Patmore, Coventry 287

Pavlova, Anna 63

Pearsall-Smith, Logan 248

Pegasus Press 247, 248, 252, 253, 265, 272

Pelléas and Mélisande 73

PEN club 173, 188, 199, 200, 210, 213, 255–6, 265

Pensées d'une Amazone (Natalie Barney) 229

People, The 189, 245

Perkins, Maxwell 213

Perrin, Alice 213

Peter Ibbetson (G. Du Maurier) 133

Pettit, Charles 234

Phillpotts, Eden 248, 254

Pigott, Mrs 97, 98

Pilgrimage (Dorothy Richardson) 101

Pioneer Players 74, 80, 292

Pius X, Pope 82–3

Playfair, Sir Nigel 248

Plunkett, Eileen 163

Poems of the Past and Present (RH) 86–8; influence of R. and E.B. Browning on 53, 87; dedicated to MVB 86; lesbianism 86; press reviews 88–9; *see also* themes

poetry (RH's): RH as poet 3, 5, 11, 155; *Collected Poems* 146; early work 28, 38–9; 'Jericho' 146; later poems 349; love poetry 47; musical nature of 28, 38; poems of mourning 129; poems set to music 38, 47, 48, 63; 'Salvation' 225; songs: 'Cuckoo' 147, 155, 164; themes: 1–2, lesbian 6, 86, autobiographical 17; 'Waking' 133–4; war poems 146; writing encouraged by MVB 63, 85; *see also Forgotten Island, The, Poems of the Past and Present, Rhymes and Rhythms, Sheaf of Verses, A, Songs of Three Counties, 'Twixt Earth and Stars*

police 78; women's 293–4

Policewoman Review 294

Polignac, Princesse de *see* Singer, Winaretta

Poppy (friend of RH and UVT) 163, 177, 187, 209

Pougy, Liane de 194, 229

Pound, Ezra 57, 174, 194, 254, 272

Poynter, Sir Edward 60, 110

Prix Femina Vie Heureuse 2, 210, 213, 214, 218, 220–2, 282

prizes, literary 2, 203; *see also* Eichelberger Gold Medal, Prix Femina Vie Heureuse, James Tait Black Memorial Prize

Prothero, Chief Inspector John 258, 260

Proust, Marcel 190, 195

psychic research *see* Society for Psychical Research, spiritualism

psychological delineation 30, 57, 100, 101–2, 182, 188, 202, 259, 301; *see also* Hunt, Violet; Sinclair, May

psychological theories: *see* homosexuality, lesbianism, sexology, sexual abuse

Psychopathia Sexualis (Krafft-Ebing) 228

Publisher and Bookseller 48

publishers 1, 2, 5, 184–5, 232, 234–40, 246–7, 269

Punch 202

Purchase, Mr B. 265

Queen magazine 48, 199, 203

'Queen's Last Ride' (MVB) 61

Quelques Portraits-Sonnets de Femmes (Natalie Barney) 229

Quiller-Couch, Sir Arthur 89, 99

Quinn, John 254

racism 104–5

Radcliffe, Edward (ancestor of RH) 13

Radclyffe Hall
    admiration of achievement (of 'people who do things') 4, 75–6, 164, 194, 355–6
    alienation, feelings of 1, 7, 21, 70, 105, 159, 162, 184, 266, 268–70, 273, 308, 361
    animals, RH's love of 14, 21, 171, 172, 181, 206, 346; Joseph (hunter) 44, 69
    animals and birds kept by 26, 28, 69–70, 80,

Radclyffe Hall (*cont.*)
92, 93, 96, 125, 150–1, 181, 209, 212, 214, 276, 318, 362–3, Fido 363, *Plates 29, 30*; dog-breeding 150, 187, 219; riding and hunting 40, 43–4, 65, 69, 93, 94, 362

  anti-Semitism 336–7, 359, 360–1
  appearance: in childhood 12, 21, 22, 27; as adult 23, 44, 60, 109, 184, 193, 219, 239, 246, 259, 262; described by ES 317–18; hair 21–2, 27, 44, 76, 109, 148, 168, 184, 219, 316, 333; clothes 22, 60, 76, 122, 144, 151, 152, 166, 189, 193, 197, 221, 243, 269; lampooned in *Ladies Almanack* 232
  character (*see also* Souline: themes in relationship with RH): anger 164, 239, 247, 249, 256, 261, 263, 277–8, 301, 303, 348, 364; contradictions and ambivalence 2, 3, 5, 13–14, 22, 71, 76, 184, 301, 344; control, need for 20, 25–6, 34, 355; depression, mood-swings 21, 60, 110, 133, 149, 163, 184, 268–70, 273, 275–6, 281, 290, 296, 307–8, 348, 362; dilettantism 14, 23, 146, 186; fidelity/infidelity 2, 71, 82, 89, 93, 95, 103, 124–5, 129–30, 140, 145, 275–7, 328, 329–30, 337, 342, 344; money as liberating 38–9, 43; money as affection 36; money as means of control 25–6, 180, 234; orderliness 149–50, 152, 156, 311, 368; protectiveness 21, 45, 46, 123, 125, 140, 206; restlessness 24, 44, 68, 180, 207, 231, 346; shyness 2, 71, 76, 151, 197, 213, 220, 280–1; sense of humour 220, 318, 365 *see also* humour
    as crusader/martyr 239, 246, 258, 259, 261–4, 266
    conflict between art and life 190–1, 201, 202–3, 274
    hands, theme of, in life 20, 36, 45, 52, 60; ES's 319; *see also* themes
    health 3; childhood 20, 24, 26; 90; German measles 134; 136; 149; 154–5; exhaustion 178–9, 187, 206, 212, 220; eye problems 179, 305, 359, 362; eye operations 363–5; general 180, 270, 290; flu 210, 296; stigmata 295; painful leg 308; broken ankle 354–5; nervous collapse 355
    lesbianism/sexual identity 1, 2, 3, 14, 30–1, 34, 35, 37–42, 44–5, 46–7, 56, 57, 67, 148, 160, 162, 165, 168, 182–3, 190, 197, 296, 333; advocates same-sex marriage 274–5; public standing in lesbian society 339–40
    life and career: ancestry 12–16; birth 16–18; childhood 3, 5, 11, 18–22; portrait painted 21; relationship with father 12, 14, 16–18; father leaves home 18; last meeting with father 23; father's death 24; early relationship with mother 3, 16–22; relationship with grandmother 12, 21; childhood illnesses 3, 20, 24; travels with mother 24; parents' divorce 25; mother's remarriage 24; return to London 27; relationship with stepfather 26–7, 28; stepfather's sexual advances 30–1; musical talent 28; early writings 27, 28; education 29, 30; romantic friendship with Agnes Nicholls 37–41; inheritance from grandfather 24, 43; sets up house in Campden Hill Terrace, London and Highfield House, Malvern 43; visits USA 44–5; affair with Jane

Randolph 44–5; affair with Dolly Diehl 46–7; *'Twixt Earth and Stars* published 47; poems set to music 28, 47, 48; affair with Violet Hunt 51–8; meets May Sinclair 57; meets MVB 58, 59; cultural education by MVB 63; moves to Shelley Court, Tite Street 65; *A Sheaf of Verses* published 84; hunting accident 65; adopts the name John 66; relationship with George Batten 66–7; *Poems of Past and Present* published 86; buys 59 Cadogan Square as joint home with MVB 69; gives up hunting 69; interest in suffrage movement 77–80; sells Highfield House and buys White Cottage, Malvern 80; conversion to Roman Catholicism 81–3; visit to Rome 83; *Songs of Three Counties* published 88; affair with Phoebe Hoare 89–96; First World War activities 74; *The Forgotten Island* published 98; infatuation with Violet Gordon Woodhouse 98–9; early short stories and novels 99–102; meets UVT 90, 107–8; sells 59 Cadogan Square and White Cottage 121–2; moves into Vernon Court Hotel with MVB 122; moves to 22 Cadogan Court with MVB 124; MVB's death and its effect on RH 125–6, 129–33; stays with Dolly Clarke 129; turns to spiritualism 134; seances with Gladys Leonard 134, 141–2; moves to Grimston, Datchet with UVT 136; makes new will 136; moves to Swanmead, Datchet with UVT 137; conflict between Catholicism and spiritualism 142; gives paper for Society for Psychical Research 144–5; threatens Cara Harris with libel over SPR paper 145; slander action against Fox-Pitt 145; taught to drive by Toupie Lowther 153; cuts hair short 168; meets Ida Wylie 172; social life in 1920s 169–79, 187; holiday in Italy with UVT 180–2; finishes *Unlit Lamp* 182; acquires literary agent 184; publishes *The Forge* and *Unlit Lamp* 185; social/literary life in Paris (Djuna Barnes, Natalie Barney, Romaine Brooks, etc.) 194–5; 'lionized' in London 197, 199, 213; resigns from Council of Society for Psychical Research 198; publishes *A Saturday Life* 201; publishes *Adam's Breed* 211; meets Colette 213–14; awarded Prix Femina 218–20; James Tait Black Prize, Eichelberger Gold Medal 221; finishes *Well of Loneliness* 234; death of stepfather 240; *Well of Loneliness* published in UK by Cape 240; press controversy over *Well of Loneliness* 245–7; anger over poor reviews and tone of protest letter 249–50; reaction to customs seizure of *Well of Loneliness* 252–3; *Well of Loneliness* published in US by Covici Friede 252, 267; meets Noël Coward 252; prepares for *Well of Loneliness* trial 254–8; reactions to trial, verdict and failure of appeal 258, 259, 261–7; moves to Rye 267; reaction to success of US appeal 271–2; 'dryness' following *Well of Loneliness* trials 275–6; loss of friendships 276; distress over stage production of *Well of Loneliness*, alleged links with *Extraordinary Women*, lampoon by Beresford Egan 277–80; life in Rye 286–90; develops stigmata while writing *Master of the*

Radclyffe Hall (*cont.*)
  House 295; Foyles luncheon 300; UK and US publication of *Master of the House* 301; reaction to failure of *Master of the House* 303; UK and US publication of *Miss Ogilvy Finds Herself* 307–8; meets ES 308; RH–ES letters begin 323; meets D'Annunzio 336; abandons *Emblem Hurlstone* 340; *Sixth Beatitude* published 341; Peggy Austin's death 356; eye operations, general breakdown in health 362–70; rewrites will 369; death 370; funeral 372; Requiem Mass 373
  loneliness in childhood 12, 18, 27–8, 73
  lovers: *see* Batten, Mabel; Clarke, Dolly; Hoare, Phoebe; Hunt, Violet; Nicholls, Agnes; Randolph, Jane; Souline, Evguenia; Troubridge, Una; Woodhouse, Violet Gordon
  mother, relationship with, and its effects on RH's life and work 3, 16–22, 24–8, 52, 148, 149, 159, 162, 163, 184, 192; mother's rejection 17; mother's violence 19, 20, 25, 34, 36, 93, 191; need for mothering 36, 39–40, 68, 130, 192, 209, 297; resentment/concern re mother 208, 209, 232–4, 346; *see also* Visetti, Marie Diehl
  parenthood, desire for 139–40, 346, 352–3
  naming *see* separate entry
  oak, love of 148, 149, 150, 219
  parenting of Andrea 134, 135, 139, 154–5, 180–1, 192, 207–8, 375; deterioration in relationship 290, 295, 299–300; improvement in relationship 353
  political views: Conservative 2, 14, 71, 80, 181, 212, 266; pro-Fascist 181, 336; anti-Communist 181, 336; support for 'working people' 270; interest in world affairs 269, 289–90; horror at approaching war 359
  residences: Sunny Lawn, Bournemouth 16, 17; Addison Road, London 27; buys Campden Hill Terrace 43; buys Highfield, Malvern Wells 43; Albert Gate, Kensington 46; Shelley Court, Tite Street 65; buys 59 Cadogan Square 69; sells Highfield 80; buys White Cottage, Malvern 80; sells White Cottage and Cadogan Square 121–2; buys 22 Cadogan Court 124; Grimston, Datchet (rented by UVT) 136; rents Swanmead, Datchet 137; buys Chip Chase, Hadley Wood 137; sells Chip Chase 170–1; rents 7 Trevor Square, buys 10 Sterling Street 170; buys 37 Holland Street 201; sells Holland Street, moves to Rye (Mermaid Inn, Journey's End) 267; buys The Black Boy, Rye 285; buys Santa Maria, Rye as investment 289; buys 17 Talbot House, St Martin's Lane 306; sells The Black Boy, buys Journey's End (The Forecastle), Rye 307; decides to sell Talbot House flat 346; leases 18 Lungarno Acciaivoli, Florence 350; sells Forecastle 362
  sexual abuse: of RH 31–2, 34, 36, 54, 162; effect of 93, 105, 175
  sight/seeing 206, 359, 365; *see also* themes
  spelling 18, 30, 108, 378
  spirituality *see* separate entry
  themes in writings *see* themes
  as writer 5, 6, 7, 11, 148, 149, 164, 184–5, 186, 187–8, 192, 206, 234, 239, 355; critical acclaim 2, 88–9, 197, 199, 201–2, 203, 212–13, 218–21, 246, 272; critical failure 302–3, 308 *see also* reviews; fanmail 218, 252, 270; fear of plagiarism 291; literary standing 2, 5, 6, 11, 218, 221, Foyles luncheon 300, 301; press interviews 219–20, 246, 252–3; prose style 30, 203, 215–16; research methods 215, 227–8, 231, 281; speaking engagements 218, 220, 270–1; writing method/routine 34, 99, 100, 150, 152, 155–7, 158, 181–2, 205, 207, 209, 295, 307; *see also* individual works; Batten, Mabel Veronica; Souline, Evguenia; Troubridge, Una
  Plates 1, 2, 4, 5, 7, 15, 27, 29, 30
Radclyffe Hall: A Case of Obscenity (Vera Brittain) 264, 265
Radclyffe-Hall, Charles (grandfather of RH) 12, 13, 14, 15, 24, 43, 185
Radclyffe-Hall, Florence Maude (sister of RH) 18
Radclyffe-Hall, Marguerite *see* Radclyffe Hall
Radclyffe-Hall, Marie *see* Visetti, Marie Diehl
Radclyffe-Hall, Radclyffe 'Rat' (father of RH):
  family background 12–15; relationship with RH as child 12, 14, 16–18; education 14; musical ability 14; career as actor 15; love affairs 15; marriage to Mary Jane Diehl 15; appearance 16; love of diamonds 14, 16, 69; violence in marriage 16–18; deserts marriage 18; last meeting with RH 23; last illness and death 23–4; memorial 24; in RH's writings 24, 25, 39, 87
Railwaymen, National Union of 258
Rainbow, The (D.H. Lawrence) 111, 253, 269
Randolph, Jane 19, 34, 233, 373; affair with RH 44–5, 51, 107, 178; marriage to Harry Caruth 45, 48; friendship with RH 77, 152, 212–13; *Plate 2*
Randolph, Thomas and Decan (Jane's sons) 45; *Plate 2*
Randolph Winifred (Jane's daughter) *see* Macey, Winifred
Raymond (Oliver Lodge), 140 (n. 23), 142
Raymond, Ernest 197, 218
Reade, Emma Jones (great-aunt of RH) 15; *Plate 2*
Reade, James (cousin of RH) 15
'Recording Angel, The' (RH short story) 99
Red Cross 74, 366
Red-Haired Alibi (film) 302
Reed, Winifred Hales 18, 88, 150, 156, 297–9
Rees, Leonard 197, 199, 202, 220, 221, 240; death 302
Rees, Molly 197, 199, 220, 221
Regiment of Women, A (Clemence Dane) 64, 147
reincarnation 7, 85; *see also Saturday Life, A*
Reinhardt, Max 81
'Rest Cure – 1932, The' (RH short story) 7, 12, 198, 307; *see also* themes
reviews of RH's work 48, 88–9, 188–9, 199, 202, 208, 211, 219–20, 240–3, 302–3, 308, 341
Rhymes and Rhythms (RH) 13
Rich, Adrienne 183
Richardson, Lady Constance Stewart 63
Richardson, Dorothy 4, 101
Ricketts, Charles 257

Rinder, Olive 220, 303–5; 'marriage' to Evelyn Irons 303–4
Robeson, Paul 88
Romer, Dr Frank 98
Romney Marsh 58, 267, 269, 270, 286–7, 307
Room of One's Own, A (Virginia Woolf): connection with *Well of Loneliness* 282–4
Ross, Patience 267, 276, 291, 373
Ross, Violet 'Martin' 171
Rossetti, Dante Gabriel 52
Rossi-Lemeni, Dr Alessandro 21, 374
Rossi-Lemeni, Nicola 88, 374
Rostand, Maurice 354
Rota, Bertram 378
Rousseau, Jean-Jacques 257
Rowe, Nellie 153, 163, 177, 179
Royde-Smith, Naomi 248, 256, 270
Rubinstein, Harold 252, 254, 256, 258, 261, 297, 303, 369, 373, 375
Rubinstein, Ida 190
Rubinstein & Nash (solicitors) 260
Runyan, Damon 301
Ruskin, John 51, 52
Russell, Elizabeth (great-great-grandmother of RH) 13
Russell, Radcliffe (great-great-great-grandfather of RH) 13
Rye, Sussex 241, 252, 258, 267, 285, 286–90, 306, 307, 317, 344, 345, 346, 350, 354

Sachs, Dr Alfred 155, 165, 171, 178, 201
Sackville-West, Vita 1, 30, 69, 178, 218, 242, 273; support for *Well of Loneliness* 249–50, 255, 266; affair with Virginia Woolf 70, 255, 258, 259, 283–4; affairs 303–5; *Plate 23*
Sadler, Sir Michael 257
Sager, Mary Jane *see* Visetti, Marie Diehl
'Saint Ethelfrida' (RH short story) 212
St George's Convent, Harpenden 195, 207, 210
St John, Christopher: friendship with RH 54, 74, 291, 300, 306; founder of Pioneer Players 74; background 291–2, 334; love for Vita Sackville-West 304–5
St Leonard's Convent 154, 179–80
sales 1; *Adam's Breed* 2, 211–12, 219, 221, 230, 272; *Forge* 188, 197, 201–2, 272; *Master of the House* 301; *Miss Ogilvy Finds Herself* 308, 335; *Saturday Life* 201–2, 272, 296; *Sixth Beatitude* 341; *Unlit Lamp* 272, 296; *Well of Loneliness* 2, 241, 245, 247, 252, 267, 271, 272, 291
Salter, Helen 143, 145, 166, 167
'Salvation' (RH poem) 225
same-sex marriage 274–5
Sand, George 64, 75, 220
Sanger, Margaret: author of *Family Limitation* (birth control) 109; 177
Sanger, Mary Jane *see* Visetti, Marie Diehl
Sappho 64, 75, 86, 235, 236
Sargent, John Singer 61, 179, 270
Saturday Evening Post 342
Saturday Life, A (RH): success 3, 201–2; writing of 185, 186, 198–9; published April 1925 201;

dedicated to RH herself 201; reviews 202, 208; reprinted 272; US sales 296
    comedy 146, 203; psychological delineation 202; reincarnation 146, 202; characters: Liza Ferrari 40, 202; Elinar Jensen 39, 113, 114, 189, 202; Frances Reide 6, based on RH 201, 202–3; Sidonia Shore 28, 39–40, 113, 114, 146, 189, possessing some of UVT's traits 201, 202–3; Lady Shore 201; *see also* themes
Saturday Review 241, 257
Sawyer, Vaughan 257
Scaife, Roger 235, 238
Scales, Mrs (medium) 140
'The Scarecrow' (RH short story) 186
Schiff, Mrs Sidney 188
School for Scandal, The 15
Schreiner, Olive 176
Scribners 213
seances *see* spiritualism
Sea Wrack (Vere Hutchinson) 172
Secker, Martin 236, 239
Second World War *see* war
Secrest, Meryle 191
self-realization 40, 161, 203
Serbia 119, 121
servants 97, 136, 137, 150, 170, 207, 208, 212, 233, 267, 296
Seven Pillars of Wisdom, The (T.E. Lawrence) 237
sexology 6, 35–6, 42, 84, 193, 227–8, 275; *see also* Carpenter, Edward; Ellis, Havelock; Hirschfeld, Magnus; Krafft-Ebing, Richard von; Ulrichs, Karl
sexual politics/feminism 2, 3, 6, 35, 48, 53, 54, 109, 171, 228–9, 251, 259, 264, 282–4, 293–4; *see also* *The Forge*; lesbianism; *Saturday Life*; suffrage movement; *Unlit Lamp*; *Well of Loneliness*
Sexual Reform, World League for 275
sexuality *see* heterosexuality, homosexuality, lesbianism, sexologists
Shakespeare, Susannah 13
Shakespeare, William 13, 282
Shaw, George Bernard 80, 248, 252, 255, 264, 288, 292
Sheaf of Verses, A (RH) 55, 84–6; MVB's influence on 85
Shiletto, Violet 83
Shoemaker of Merano (RH) *see* Merano Shoemaker, The
short stories (RH's) 3, 5, 6, 99–100, 102, 146, 186, 201, 205, 212, 269; lesbianism 6, 11; Heinemann's response to 102; read by J.D. Beresford 182; encouraged to write by Newman Flower 198; in *Miss Ogilvy Finds Herself* 307; *see also* individual works; themes
Sidgwick, Eleanor 143–4, 145, 165, 167, 179
Sinclair, May: friendship with RH 3, 172, 174, 199, 205, 209; as writer 4, 48, 78, 101–2, 158, 182; influence on RH 29, 57, 100, 147, 158, 160–1, 173, 186, 220; involvement in sexual politics/suffrage movement 78–9; review of Violet Hunt's *Their Hearts* 175; on Prix

Sinclair, May (*cont.*)
  Femina committee 213; lack of support for *Well
    of Loneliness* 254; disapproval of lesbianism 273;
    Plate 8
Sinclair, Upton 1
Singer, Winaretta (Princesse de Polignac):
  friendship with MVB 64, 73, 122, 192; with
  MVB and RH 75, 92; with RH and UVT 187
'Sink of Solitude' (Beresford Egan) 278–80
Sitwell, Edith 188
Sitwell, Osbert 188
Sixth Beatitude, The 3, 217, 270, 286–7, 340–1; as
  'child' of RH and ES 340; published by
  Heinemann 1936 341; reviews, sales 341–2
    characters: Hannah Bullen 87, 102, 270, 341,
    350; *see also* themes
Sladen, Douglas 99
Slater, Joan 314
Smallhythe *see* Barn Theatre; Craig, Edy
Smith, Professor Robert (Bob) 322
Smyth, Ethel: friendship with RH 3, 64, 73, 75,
  218; achievements as composer 75; involvement
  in suffrage movement 75, 78–9; interest in
  divorce law reform 84; friendship with MVB 93;
  interest in spiritualism 171; feminism 171;
  friendship with Violet Hunt 173; friendship with
  UVT 171, 201; portrayed in *Extraordinary
  Women* 236; supports *Well of Loneliness* 248;
  friendship with Virginia Woolf 361; *Plate 26*
Society for Psychical Research (SPR) 62, 140; RH
  joins 143; RH's research paper for 144–5; 153,
  164–5, 167, 168; RH threatens resignation 179;
  RH resigns from Council 198; *see also*
  spiritualism
Solano, Solita 232
Somerville, Edith 79, 171
Songs of Three Counties (RH) 88–9; 'The Blind
  Ploughman': sung at Usher Hall 1, 88–9; 217;
  critical success 98; *see also* themes
Sooner or Later: The Story of an Ingenious Ingenue
  (Violet Hunt) 53
Souchon, Admiral (German naval commander) 118
Souline, Evguenia 3, 4, 11, 107, 108; background:
  family, education, nursing career 311, 313,
  315–16; experiences in Russian Revolution 311,
  313, 315–16; name 312; age 314
    character 311–14: insecurity 313, 332
    anti-Semitism 337
    appearance 319, 321–2
    command of English 319, 322
    health: tuberculosis 316, 321; operation on
      sinuses 346; final illness 378
    life after meeting RH: engaged as nurse for
      UVT 308; first meeting 316–18; early days
      318–19, 322–8; first letters 323–4; first kiss 326;
      nickname Royal Chink Pig 337; become lovers
      338; reactions 339; first visit to England/UVT's
      humiliation 344–5; UVT's help over visa for
      England, RH's financial help 343; travel *à trois*
      346–7; ambitions 350; refuses to spend winter in
      Florence *à trois* 350; meets Colette 354; obtains
      annual visa 354; new quarrels 354–5; separate

flats in Florence 355; fails Sorbonne entrance
  356; quarrels with UVT 355–6; RH threatens
  suicide 356–7; holiday in Malvern 357; change in
  sexual relationship 356–8; only surviving letter
  to RH 358; RH's new will puts UVT and ES on
  equal footing 360; unconditional visa obtained
  360; life *à trois* in Rye and Lynton, quarrels with
  UVT 362; concern for RH 363; excluded by
  UVT 363–5; typing course in Oxford 364–5; jobs
  with Red Cross, BBC, Foreign Office 366–7;
  gives RH white heather 367–8; RH's last letter
  367; constant visits 369; RH changes will
  369–70; last visit 370; personal epitaph 371;
  attends Requiem Mass 373; relationship with
  UVT after RH's death 375–8; work for BBC 375,
  377; marriage to Vladimir Makaroff 376; ES
  letters to RH destroyed by UVT 377
    themes in RH/ES relationship/letters:
      physical desire 311, 319, 326, 327–8, 338, 345,
      357; friendship 319; 'Same Heart' 314, 356, 369,
      378; ES as inspiration for RH 275, 340, 342;
      spiritual aspects 327, 331, 332, 358; RH
      protection/control 312, 322, 324–5, 331, 332,
      336, 349, 350–1, 355–7, 358–9, 363; RH
      guilt/responsibility re UVT 332, 344, 345;
      money/control 26, 331, 332, 349, 356, 360, 364,
      366–7; triangle with RH/UVT 95, 110, 266, 317,
      325, 332, 335, 344–7, 348, 350, 355–6, 362–70;
      jealousy 337, 358; ES desire for independence
      312–13, 332, 346–7, 349–50, 355–6, 358–9, 363,
      364, 366; innocence 312, 327–8; mother/child
      roles 352–3, 359–60, 363
    relationship with RH as writer: has read *Well
      of Loneliness* 326; 339; RH's works as their
      'children' 339–41, 352–3; work on Book of
      Letters 377–8
    Plate 28
Sound and the Fury, The (William Faulkner) 269
Spectator 289
Spencer, Constance 205
Spencer, Grace 218
spiritualism (RH's involvement in) 2, 192, 219, 269;
  psychical research 3, 13, 134, 137, 139, 152;
  seances 134, 135, 140–3, 290; conflict with
  Catholicism 143; gives research paper 144–5;
  effects on relationships: with Dolly Clarke and
  Cara Harris 145, with UVT 146; Fox-Pitt's
  allegations and subsequent slander case 164–8;
  resigns from Council of SPR 198
spirituality 2, 7, 16, 21, 28, 280–1, 290, 295;
  spiritual dimension in sexual relationships 33,
  70–1, 327; in RH's writings 81, 85, 88, 160–1,
  198, 201, 215–18, 302–3; *see also* themes
Spurgeon, Professor C. 213
Stein, Gertrude 194, 229
Stephen see Well of Loneliness, The
Stephen, Dr Karen 257
stereotypes 67, 109, 203, 294
Stern, G.B. 255, 273, 293
Stevenson, Sylvia 248
stigmata 295, 302
Still, Monica 321

Stitch, Wilhelmina 218, 220
Stopes, Marie 177
Story of an African Farm, The (Olive Schreiner) 176
Strachey, Lytton 248
Straus, Ralph 302
Streaks of Life (Ethel Smyth) 171
'stream of consciousness' technique 101
Studies in the Psychology of Sex (Havelock Ellis) 256
Studies of the Eighteenth Century in Italy (Vernon Lee) 64
suffrage movement 3, 54, 71, 75, 77–80, 170, 173, 292, 293–4, 333–4
Sullivan, Sir Arthur 12
Sumner, John 271
Sunday Chronicle 245
Sunday Express 242–4, 246
Sunday Herald 211
Sunday Times 188, 197, 199, 202, 211, 240, 241, 248, 302
Surplus (Sylvia Stevenson) 248
Susan (friend of RH and UVT) 177, 179, 252
Sussex Daily News 88
Swinburne, Algernon 85, 100
Swinnerton, Frank 254
syphilis 51, 57, 103, 174
Syrett, Netta 199, 273

Taggart, Miss 294
Tagore, Rabindranath 194
Tamarisk Town (Sheila Kaye-Smith) 289
Tarn, Pauline *see* Vivien, Renée
Tavistock Clinic 116
Taylor, Coleridge 86
Taylor, Harry (father of UVT) 110, 114, 115
Taylor, Henry (grandfather of UVT) 110
Taylor, Minna (mother of UVT) 116, 138, 144, 154, 180, 199, 209–11, 221, 222, 297, 306; family background 112; relationship with UVT as child 112; illnesses 153; death 373
Taylor, Viola (sister of UVT) 199, 209, 210–11, 221, 276, 297, 306, 353, 369, 373; close relationship with UVT 112, 114, 116; marriage to Maurice Woods 116; martial problems 117; marries J.L. Garvin 180
Tealdi family (Italian cousins of UVT) 107, 115, 117–18, 119
Tempest, Marie 187
Temple, Bill 136, 201, 208, 248
Temple, Ida 136, 139, 201, 208, 248; death 277
Temple of Dawn (Ida Wylie) 172
Temple, Shirley 302
Tenerife 63, 65, 68, 226
Terry, Ellen 291, 293, 305
Thackeray, William 218
theatre and theatre-going: Radclyffe Radclyffe-Hall as actor 15; RH with MVB 63, 95, 292; Pioneer Players 74, 80, 292; UVT sees Sarah Bernhardt 110; RH with UVT 153; 177, 187, 269; RH at first nights 197, 208, 219, 234, 258; Theatre Collection at V&A 200; John Barrymore as *Hamlet* 208; stage production of *Well of*

Loneliness 277–8; *Chéri* 290; mood in 1930s 301–2; Andrea's career 306, 353; *see also* Barn Theatre, Smallhythe
Their Hearts (Violet Hunt) 174
Their Lives (Violet Hunt) 174
themes (in RH writings):
    admiration of achievement: *The Forge* 76; *Unlit Lamp* 175–6
    alienation 1, 2, 7, 70, 105, 198, 266, 308; *Adam's Breed* 216–18; Book of Letters 349; 'The Career of Mark Anthony Brakes' 104–5; 132; 'Lover of Things' 7, 21; 'Malise' 216; 'Miss Ogilvy Finds Herself' 7, 216; 'The Rest Cure – 1932' 7, 198; *The Unlit Lamp* 159, 162, 184; 'Upon the Mountains' 201; *Well of Loneliness* 2, 6, 7, 216, 225, 227–8, 274; 'The Woman in a Crêpe Bonnet' 103; *The World* 200–1, 280
    art/artists: in RH's work 189–91; Book of Letters 349; *The Forge* 13, 76, 185, 189–91, 202; *Saturday Life* 28, 39, 113, 114, 146, 189, 202; *Unlit Lamp* 28, 189; 'Upon the Mountains' 189; *Well of Loneliness* 189, 259, 274
    chains 114, 266; *The Forge* 19; *Michael West* 19–20, 161: 'The Rest Cure – 1932' 12; *Sheaf of Verses* 85; *Unlit Lamp* 19, 161, 169, 185
    father–child relationship: 'Lover of Things' 23; *Michael West* 27, 30; *Well of Loneliness* 25
    fidelity/betrayal: Book of Letters 349; 'Woman in a Crêpe Bonnet' 103–4, 105
    governesses/mentors 52; *Saturday Life* 39, 113, 114; *Unlit Lamp* 29; *Well of Loneliness* 29
    hair: 'Miss Ogilvy Finds Herself' 22; *Unlit Lamp* 22, 175; *Well of Loneliness* 22
    hands: *Adam's Breed* 217; *Emblem Hurlstone* 32–3, 320–1; 'Career of Mark Anthony Brakes' 32; *Michael West* 32; *Well of Loneliness* 39; 'Woman in a Crêpe Bonnet' 32, 54
    lesbianism 6, 7, 33, 182–3; *The Forge* 6, 190; 'Malise' 33, 54; 'Miss Ogilvy Finds Herself' 6, 7, 54; *Poems of Past and Present* 86; *Saturday Life* 6, 39; '*Twixt Earth and Stars* 40; *Unlit Lamp* 2, 6, 139–40, 160–2, 182–3; *Well of Loneliness* 2, 5, 6, 39, 54, 66, 183, 226–30, 235, 274
    loneliness: *Michael West* 27–8
    male violence: 'Career of Mark Anthony Brakes' 32; 'Woman in a Crêpe Bonnet' 32, 54
    martyrdom: *Well of Loneliness* 228
    mother–child relationship: *Emblem Hurlstone* 32–3; 'Lover of Things' 21; *Michael West* 19–20, 25, 27, 30, 105, 162; *Saturday Life* 39, 203; *Unlit Lamp* 147, 158–63, 182; 'Woman in a Crêpe Bonnet' 103–4
    naming: 'Miss Ogilvy Finds Herself' 11; 'The Rest Cure – 1932' 12; *Well of Loneliness* 11
    nature 1, 101; *Adam's Breed* 215–16; Book of Letters 349; *Sixth Beatitude* 102, 270, 286–7, 341; *Unlit Lamp* 123, 160
    need for mothering: *The Forge* 149; *Saturday Life* 39–40
    service: *Adam's Breed* 204–5, 217; *Saturday Life* 202–3; *Sixth Beatitude* 217; *Unlit Lamp* 147, 158–61

themes (in RH writings) (*cont.*)

sight/seeing 186; *Adam's Breed* 217; *Poems of Past and Present* 87, 217; *Sixth Beatitude* 87, 217, 341, 359; *Songs of Three Counties* 88

spirituality 217–18; *Adam's Breed* 87, 202, 215–18, 302; Book of Letters 349; 'Lover of Things' 198, 215; *Master of the House* 202, 302–3; 'Miss Ogilvy Finds Herself' 198; 'The Rest Cure – 1932' 198; *Saturday Life* 146, 202, 215; *Songs of Three Counties* 88; 'Upon the Mountains' 198, 201; *Well of Loneliness* 225, 302; *The World* 198, 200, 215; *Unlit Lamp* 160–1, 217, 302

suffering: *Adam's Breed* 132; *Emblem Hurlstone* 17; *Master of the House* 302; 'Upon the Mountains' 201; *Well of Loneliness* 228, 302

tradition: *The Forge* 13

war work: 'Miss Ogilvy Finds Herself' 6, 74, 226; 'Malise' 74, 226; *Well of Loneliness* 74, 226, 263; *see also* lesbianism, sexual politics

Thesiger, Ernest 99–100, 178, 187, 220

Thirty-Nine Steps, The (John Buchan) 111

This Marriage (play) 187

This Side of Paradise (Scott Fitzgerald) 169

This Year of Grace (Noël Coward) 258

Thoreau, Henry 100

Thorndike, Sybil 220, 290

Three Sisters, The (May Sinclair) 101

Tilley, Vesta 63

Time and Tide 241

Times, The 79, 88, 158, 165, 211, 247, 303, 328, 346, 371–2

Times Literary Supplement 202, 241, 260, 303

Tizzard, Dr 363, 364–5

Toklas, Alice B. 194

'Tomlinson' (Rudyard Kipling): source of title for *Adam's Breed* 206

Torquay 13, 15, 25

Tortoiseshell Cat, The (Naomi Royde-Smith) 248

Tosca 91

Toupie *see* Lowther, Barbara

Towards Morning (Ida Wylie) 173

Townsend Warner, Sylvia 214–15

T.P.'s Weekly 242, 257

translations of RH's work 272, 296, 335, 345

Tree, Charles 88

Tree, Iris 144, 178

Tree, Viola 63

Trefusis, Violet 178, 273

Trelawny of the Wells 63

triangular relationships 214, 294; RH/MVB/Phoebe Hoare 90–6, 106; in *The Unlit Lamp* 95, 123–4, 161, 202; RH/MVB/UVT 90, 106, 120–6, 161, 'Our Three Selves' 142, 373; in *Saturday Life* 202; RH/UVT/Dolly Clarke 133; RH/UVT/Ernest Troubridge 135; in 'Upon the Mountains' 201; RH/UVT/ES 95, 110, 266, 317, 322, 325, 335, 344–7, 355–6; at Smallhythe 292, 304–5

Triple Fugue (Osbert Sitwell) 188

Troubridge, Andrea 90; birth 115; early childhood 117, 118, 119, 120, 121, 124, 133, 134;

tonsillectomy 135; mothering by UVT 133, 134, 135, 138–9, 154–5, 164, 179–80, 195, 207–8, 209, 210, 214, 234, 270, 281–2, 353, 375; parenting by RH 134, 135, 139, 154–5, 180–1, 192, 207–8, 375; deterioration in relationship 290, 295, 299–300; improvement in relationship 353; lives at Grimston, Datchet, with UVT and RH 136, 137; legal separation of parents 138; relationship with UVT 139, 154–5; sent to boarding school 139; lives at Chip Chase, Hadley Wood, with UVT and RH 148, 150; illnesses 154–5, 208, 209; visits to father 154, 164, 180, 201; in trouble at school 179–80; school prizes 180; left in England while UVT and RH in Italy 180–1; acting in play at new school 195; fourteenth birthday 200; Christmas with RH and UVT 201; with RH and UVT at Holland Street 207–8; Guide camp 208; in 'disgrace' 210; last visit to father 210; attends father's memorial service 211; passes Responsions for Oxford 240; Christmas 1928 with RH and UVT 267; mothered by Ida Temple 277; wins scholarship to Oxford 277; visits RH and UVT in Paris 281–2; starts at Oxford 282; Christmas in Rye 285; deterioration in relationship with RH and UVT 295, 297; leaves Oxford for the stage 299–300; theatrical career 306, 353; engagement and marriage to Toby Warren 306–7; birth of son 346; BBC career 353, 375; appearance 353; divorce 353; visits RH 369; attends Requiem Mass 373; remarries 374; death 375; *Plate 14*

Troubridge, 'Chatty' (daughter of Ernest) 115, 118, 211, 297

Troubridge, Ernest 90; marriage to UVT 115; nicknamed 'Zyp' by UVT 115; birth of Andrea 115; children from first marriage 115; background and naval career 114–15; stationed in Malta 116, 117, 118; infects UVT with venereal disease 118; 'disgrace' and court martial 118–19; acquittal 119; stationed in Serbia 119; escapes from Belgrade 121; returns to England 123; strained relationship with UVT 124–5, 133; attends Requiem Mass for MVB 131; posted to Greece 133; returns to England 135; *ménage à trois* with UVT and RH 135; returns to Greece 135–6; promoted to Admiral 1919 137; arrives in England 138; legal separation from UVT 138; receives KCMG 140; involvement in Fox-Pitt slander case 145, 164, 165, 168; retires 180; visits from Andrea 154, 180, 201, 210; death 210; funeral and memorial service 211; *Plate 14*

Troubridge, Laura *see* Hope, Laura

Troubridge, Mary (daughter of Ernest) 115, 211

Troubridge, Tom (son of Ernest) 115; responsible for UVT financial arrangements 210, 297; 211

Troubridge, Una Vincenzo 3

appearance: in childhood 112; as adult 219, 260, 333; clothes 115, 151, 167, 196; hair 120

artistic career 113; draws Sarah Bernhardt 110; early talent and scholarship to Royal College of Art 113; sculpts statuette of Adeline Genée 113; gives up art for marriage, later for RH 113;

Troubridge, Una Vincenzo (*cont.*)
  resumes painting, sculpting, singing 115, 116;
  begins etching 'The Wicked Voice', sculpts
  Nijinsky 116; bust of Nijinsky exhibited in
  Venice 119; starts statuette and draws profile of
  RH 121; designs book jackets 201, 234
    character: jealousy 4, 46, 129, 141, 299;
  lacking sense of humour 134; loyalty 294, 330,
  332; orderliness 110, 116, 311; patience 133, 341;
  persistence 110, 133, 348, 368; snobbery 108,
  111, 140; talent for friendship 77, 111; sexual
  identity 116–17, 118
    diaries and day books 4, 31, 84, 108; destroys
  1915–16 diaries 122; starts keeping day books 290
    health: enjoyment of illness 112, 115–16, 136,
  275, 306; ectopic pregnancy 115; venereal disease
  118, 171, cured 201; heart trouble 133, 134,
  346–7; gynaecological 154–5, 164, 275; flu 296;
  hysterectomy 305–6; enteritis and convalescence
  308, 318, 322
    life: birth and family background 107, 112;
  childhood illnesses 112; relationship with mother
  112; education 112–13; relationship with father
  114–15; father's death 114; friendship with
  Marguerite Michel 117–18; conversion to
  Catholicism 84, 118; marriage to Ernest
  Troubridge 115; gives birth to Andrea 115;
  relationship with stepchildren 115; life as naval
  wife 115–16; ill-health 115–16; hypnotherapy
  with Crichton-Miller 116–17; in Malta with
  husband 117; return to England 117; in Malta
  again 118; discovers husband has infected her
  with venereal disease 118; return to England 119;
  cuts hair short 120; moves to Royal Hospital
  Road, then to Vernon Court Hotel 123; moves to
  live with husband at Beaufort Gardens 124;
  moves back to Royal Hospital Road on husband's
  departure for Greece 133; moves to St Leonard's
  Terrace 133; leases Cheltenham Terrace 134;
  leases Grimston, Datchet 136; separation from
  husband 137, 138; acquires title of Lady 140;
  taught to drive by Toupie Lowther 153; tensions
  with husband over Andrea 164; on Committee of
  Cruft's 187; attracts Romaine Brooks 194;
  painted by Romaine Brooks 195–6; finds mother
  'tiresome' 209; financial situation on death of
  husband 210–11; attends husband's memorial
  service 211; mother tries to persuade her to
  remarry 211; own literary and artistic work 201,
  213–14, 234, 272, 275, 290; hysterectomy and
  convalescence 305–6; attraction for other women
  334–5; plans for own burial 373; meets Nicola
  Rossi-Lemeni 374; last years 374–5; will 374–5;
  writes RH biography 377; death 377
    linguistic skills 112, 118
    literary work 275; book reviews 201, 234;
  translations 118, 201, 234; of Colette 213–14;
  stage version of *Chéri* 290; French translations of
  Well of Loneliness 272, 290; RH biography 377
    mothering of Andrea 133, 134, 135, 138–9,
  154–5, 164, 179–80, 195, 207–8, 209, 210, 214,
  234, 270, 281–2, 353, 375; deterioration in

  relationship 290, 295, 297, 299–300; ignores 21st
  birthday 299; brief reconciliation 306; rift over
  Andrea's marriage 307; visits Andrea and baby
  346; provision in will 375
    naming 107, 120
    political views: pro-Fascist 181; Conservative
  212
    relationship with RH: first meeting 90; second
  meeting and start of relationship 106, 107–8,
  120–1; nicknamed Squiggie by RH 120; joins
  RH and MVB on holiday in Cornwall 121;
  makes love with RH for first time 122; destroys
  diaries for 1915–16 122; constant meetings with
  RH 123; moves into Vernon Court Hotel with
  RH and MVB 123; spends night at Maidenhead
  with RH 125; RH's withdrawal following MVB's
  death 129–32; 'triangle' with Dolly Clarke 133;
  reconciliation with RH 134; nurses RH through
  German measles 134; permission for burial in
  same vault as RH and MVB 135; sets up house
  with RH at Grimston, Datchet 136; 'marriage'
  and roles 137; arranges for Buchel portrait of RH
  137; psychical research with RH 140–6; live as
  couple at Chip Chase 148, 153; supports RH
  during Fox-Pitt slander case 167–8; holidays in
  Italy with RH 170, 180–1; separate bedrooms
  171; reading habits 188; enduring nature of
  relationship 193; seen as conventional couple
  198; share bedroom 201; voluntary work during
  General Strike 212; meet Colette 213–14;
  domestic routine 220; entertain literary
  establishment 220; Visettis' problems 233;
  portrayed in *Extraordinary Women* 236; loyalty
  during *Well of Loneliness* controversy 252, 257,
  258, 259, 260, 266, 267; cracks in relationship
  following *Well of Loneliness* 275–6; holiday in
  Beauvallon 281; RH buys The Black Boy, Rye,
  for UVT 285; social life in Rye 289–90; fifteenth
  Christmas together 294; relationship deteriorates
  295–6; drawn into tensions at Smallthyche 305;
  hysterectomy 306; arrival of ES 308; early
  reactions to ES 312–14, 322–3, 325; first
  reactions to RH's passion for ES 328–30; helps
  ES to get visa 343; problems of continuing
  triangle 347–59; control measures 363, 365; takes
  full possession 371; inheritance 373; mourning
  373–4; post-death letters 31, 377
    roles in RH/UVT relationship: RH's
  'husbandly' role 26, 137; UVT's supporting role
  108, 155, 209; dress-style as role signifier 144,
  152; UVT's 'mothering' of RH 155, 207, 209,
  212, 281, 288, 333; UVT has curls painted out
  on childhood portrait of RH 21
    UVT's role in relation to RH as writer 108,
  reads RH's work aloud 156–7; 'literary assistant'
  155; goes with RH to meet Audrey Heath 184;
  The Forge dedicated to UVT 185; suggests title
  for *Unlit Lamp* 185; UVT's support inadequate
  on its own 186; promotes RH's work 188; collects
  press cuttings 188; arranges publicity
  photograph 199; genesis of *Adam's Breed* 204;
  names *Adam's Breed* 206; records sales 212;